THE PORTABLE CERVANTES

The Viking Portable Library

Each Portable Library volume is made up of
representative works of a favorite modern or
classic author, or is a comprehensive anthology
on a special subject. The format is designed
for compactness and for pleasurable reading.
The books average about 700 pages in length.
Each is intended to fill a need not hitherto
met by any single book. Each is edited by
an authority distinguished in his field, who
adds a thoroughgoing introductory essay and
other helpful material. Most "Portables" are
available both in durable cloth and
in stiff paper covers.

THE PORTABLE

Cervantes

TRANSLATED AND EDITED,
WITH AN INTRODUCTION
AND NOTES, BY

SAMUEL PUTNAM

NEW YORK

THE VIKING PRESS

COPYRIGHT 1949, 1950, 1951 BY THE VIKING PRESS, INC.

PUBLISHED IN OCTOBER 1951

PUBLISHED ON THE SAME DAY IN THE DOMINION OF CANADA

BY THE MACMILLAN COMPANY OF CANADA LIMITED

LIBRARY OF CONGRESS CATALOG CARD NUMBER: 51-7568

TWENTY-SEVENTH PRINTING AUGUST 1969

PRINTED IN U.S.A. BY THE COLONIAL PRESS INC.

Contents

Introduction

*"Cervantes—a patient gentleman who wrote a book—
has been seated in the Elysian Fields for three centuries now,
where he casts melancholy glances about him as he waits
for a descendant to be born who shall be capable of understanding him."* JOSÉ ORTEGA Y GASSET

It was early in the year 1605 that the Madrid bookseller Francisco de Robles placed on sale a wretchedly
printed volume from the press of Juan de la Cuesta,
entitled *The Ingenious Gentleman Don Quixote de la
Mancha*. The author, Miguel de Cervantes Saavedra,
then in his fifty-eighth year, was all but unknown. His
brilliant contemporaries of Spain's Golden Age—Lope
de Vega and the many others—insofar as they were
aware of his existence, doubtless looked upon him as a
literary failure and a hack. Old and poverty-stricken,
with a maimed left hand and other wounds incurred
in the battle of Lepanto, he had been writing poems,
plays, and pastoral romances for a quarter of a century
with an equal lack of success. Back in 1595 he had
won a first prize, consisting of three silver spoons, in a
poetry contest (if that may be termed success), and
three years later his verses for the funeral of Philip II
had attracted some attention. So far as either recognition or achievement went, there was little more than
that.

Yet Cervantes had worked hard, desperately hard,
at the new trade he had chosen in his mid-thirties.
Spurred on by want and the burden of a large household, he had turned to the theater in the hope of
monetary gain, and in the 1580s, so it was said, had

1

written between twenty and thirty unactable plays in three years' time, though only two of these earlier pieces have come down to us. On one occasion we find him contracting with a theatrical manager for six comedies at fifty ducats (about thirty dollars) each. And it was, no doubt, the need of money that led him to undertake the composition of a tale destined to become one of the world's greatest fictional masterpieces.

Age without a substantial means of support has its terrors for any man, and Cervantes' life had been filled to overflowing with hardships and misfortunes. It was not alone in literature that he had failed. Despite his battle scars and his honorable record as a soldier, which included a period spent as a captive of the Moors in Tunis, he had been unable to obtain military preferment. Refused a coveted post in the Indies, he had been appointed a tax gatherer for the Crown, only to be thrown into prison for a shortage in his accounts—there was even an unfounded rumor to the effect that the first part of *Don Quixote* had been composed in a prison cell. In short, had his been a nature that was capable of knowing an ultimate despair, had it not been for that high courage and profound geniality that are so close to the heart of his genius, Cervantes might well have considered himself a failure in every worldly respect: as poet, dramatist, novelist, soldier, public official and, finally, as a husband and family man.

And now with the years his health was deteriorating, his eyes were dimming, his poverty was growing ever more oppressive, his responsibilities more onerous. What, then, could be more natural than that his thoughts should keep coming back to the idea of producing a popular work that might bring him in a little money while he labored at what he believed to be more important tasks from the aesthetic point of view, such as would give him a lasting fame? It was also natural that, in casting about for a theme, he thought of those romances of chivalry that had enjoyed so tremendous a vogue in the sixteenth century but were already beginning to fall into disrepute. Why not a humorous parody on these high-flown chronicles with their impossible adventures and knightly deeds of valor? The subject matter would be familiar while the treatment would be novel and mirth-provoking. An aging and threadbare but noble-minded country gentleman has read so many books of chivalry that he has gone strangely "mad" on this one subject alone, and he now resolves to turn knight-errant and sally forth in quest of adventure along the highways of the modern world. Here was a tale that offered unlimited possibilities, and one that was to grow with the telling.

There are, I know, those who will disagree with such a view of the genesis of *Don Quixote,* who would have it that Cervantes sat down and, from the start, carefully plotted out an involved masterpiece of baroque art. This is a question that will be discussed later on. Here, I may merely state my own humble opinion—that of one who has lived with Cervantes for a good many years and who has wrestled with the task of translating him—which is that the author's *original intention* was to write a book that would have a widely popular appeal. It was to be a book addressed not to the cultivated few of the Spanish Renaissance but rather to the innkeepers, page boys, students, soldiers, as well as the dukes and duchesses of the realm, that great newly literate audience that the printing press had brought into existence.

There has been a good deal of debate as to whether or not Cervantes was a "careless" writer—this, despite the rather numerous and glaring slips and inconsistencies that are to be discovered in his text; but one thing, as Professor Rudolph Schevill has pointed out, appears certain: he neither revised the manuscript nor read proofs on the *Don Quixote* but left it to the printer's far from tender mercies. The result of such negligence is to be viewed in the jumbled episode of the theft of Sancho's ass, in Part I, and in minor discrepancies throughout the work.

Such was the book that Francisco de Robles found on his hands. What did he think of it? We may ask ourselves: What would a present-day publisher think of an author nearing sixty whose reputation was still to be made? Would he be likely to expect either a masterpiece—say, the great American novel—or a best-seller? He certainly would not look for a story that would revolutionize the art of fiction and become one of the best-sellers of all time. And Robles apparently felt the same way about it, for he did not take the trouble to protect either his own or the author's rights beyond the confines of Castile. Then the miracle occurred. Pirated editions began to appear almost at once, and there were five printings within a year, including a second authorized one the rights for which, this time, were secured not only for Castile but for Aragón and Portugal as well. All these editions were exhausted in less than three years.

By 1610 the whole of Spain was laughing over the fantastic adventures of the windmill-tilting Don and the inimitable drolleries of Sancho Panza. The king on his balcony one day, so runs the anecdote, glanced down into the street and saw a student walking along, book in hand. The youth was slapping his forehead and roaring with merriment, which led His Majesty to remark: "I'll wager that young man is reading *Don Quixote*." About the only ones who did not join in the great popular chorus of appreciation were the intellectuals, Lope de Vega and his friends and the followers of Góngora, the *culto* poets; and it was with them that the making of literary reputations lay. No one, Lope declared, would be so foolish as to praise the book. He had been offended by the criticism of his own work which it contained, but other writers were similarly cold and silent toward it. The people, on the other hand, promptly took it to themselves and claimed it for their own; and it was not until a couple of centuries later that artists and thinkers began to discover its true aesthetic worth and philosophic depth of meaning. The legend of the slapstick *farceur* gave way to a Cervantes who now seems so big and many-sided as to elude all our attempts to comprehend him fully.

The author's fame, meanwhile, was spreading rapidly in other lands. In 1607, two years after the first publication of *Don Quixote,* an edition appeared at Brussels, and the following year Robles brought out a third printing, making seven in all. There was an Italian edition at Milan in 1610, and a second one at Brussels in 1611. Nine editions of Part I were published during Cervantes' lifetime, between 1605 and 1616, and a tenth came out at Barcelona the year after his death. Part II, published in 1615, fared equally well, with five editions inside of two years, all copies of which were gone by 1634. Meanwhile the translators were also busy, and within twenty years, by 1625, English, French, German, and Italian renderings were to be had. The first to appear was Shelton's version of Part I in 1612. This will serve to give an idea of the book's immediate and ever-growing popularity.

Today *Don Quixote* has been translated into more than a hundred languages, including such idioms as Hebrew, Arabic, Japanese, and Tibetan. In this respect it is exceeded only by the Bible—a fact which reminds one of Sainte-Beuve's description of it as "the Bible of humanity." "Of all the books in the world," says John Ormsby in his introduction to his translation of the *Don Quixote* (1885), "*Don Quixote* is the most catholic." The author himself was well aware of this universal appeal, and through the mouth of the bachelor Sansón Carrasco is to be heard boasting that "there soon will not be a nation that does not know it." Cervantes was gratified that old and young alike found enjoyment in its pages; and indeed, one may agree with Aubrey F. G. Bell that here is a book that every thinking man who lives out his years should read at least three times: in youth, in middle age, and in his declining days.

As for the effect that *Don Quixote* has had upon the art of the novel and upon writers in general, there is much to be said. But it is not my purpose to clutter this Introduction by quoting at length from the countless tributes—many of which would sound extravagant to anyone who does not know the work at first hand— that have been paid to Cervantes. It will be sufficient here to state that he has touched the finest creative minds in every major literature (our own Melville is a case in point), has exerted a determining influence on literary and philosophic trends (as in the case of German Romanticism), and has provided inspiration for more than one masterpiece (such as Dostoevski's *The Idiot*). Music and the plastic arts also have been affected by him. He has furnished themes for a small library of operas, ballets, and orchestral compositions, and famous artists, from Doré and Cruikshank to Salvador Dali, have done some of their best work in illustrating him.

In twentieth-century America, owing largely to the unattractive, when not spurious, English-language garb in which he has been presented, Cervantes has fallen into a sad neglect that for us is most unfortunate. We have heard a good deal in these recent, postwar years of the plight of our native fictional product. In this connection we might do worse than to recall the words of William Dean Howells, in speaking of *Don Quixote*: "I cannot help thinking that if we ever have a great American novel, it must be built upon such large and noble lines." Nor is the aesthetic interest the only one by any means. Cervantes has a life-view, a world-view, that we cannot afford to overlook in this troubled and bemuddled age. How alive he is may be seen when we turn to him with our deepest problems and our latest solutions. This has been superbly brought out by Aubrey Bell in his book-length essay. It was in 1930 that Joseph Wood Krutch took occasion to compare certain aspects of Cervantes' thinking with the philosophy of "As If." Listen closely, and you may hear—or fancy that you hear—the voice of the new Jean-Paul whose name is Sartre.

And yet we do not even know the exact date on which this man Miguel de Cervantes was born or where he was buried!

II

Despite all the labor that has been expended by modern scholars, Cervantes' life, like that of Shakespeare, remains shrouded for the most part in darkness, with only a formal document here and there to serve as a reliable guidepost; all the rest is patchwork and conjecture. His works, naturally, have a certain light to shed upon his career, but it is always difficult and somewhat perilous to undertake to separate the autobiographic strands. If we except Quevedo, Cervantes would seem to have been on terms of friendship with but few of the literary men of his day; as a result not many allusions to him are to be found in the writings of his contemporaries, and no attempt at a biography was made until more than a century after his death. For the facts, the probabilities, and the possibilities as established by trustworthy specialists, the reader can do no better than turn to the recent volume by Entwhistle or the earlier ones by Schevill and Fitzmaurice-Kelly.

As has been said, the day on which the author of *Don Quixote* was born remains unknown, but it may have been Michaelmas Day, September 29, 1547, since it was this saint whose name he bore. We do know that his birth occurred at Alcalá de Henares, a former university town and a printing center some twenty miles northeast of Madrid, and that he was christened there, in the Church of Santa Maria, on October 9. He came of an old family, from the mountainous region of northern Spain, that had seen better days; and it is possible that among his ancestors there had been more than one knight-errant. His father, Rodrigo de Cervantes, was an apothecary-surgeon and something of a wanderer and ne'er-do-well, though he passed for a gentleman. His grandfather, the advocate Juan de Cervantes, an individual of some prominence, had held important public posts, but Miguel's immediate family circle was disunited and harassed by debt and financial worries. Of his three brothers, one died in youth, another was killed in the wars. One of his sisters became the prioress of a convent, which appears to indicate that she was possessed of some intelligence and strength of character; the other two led lives that were, to say the least, unconventional.

For the first twenty-one years Cervantes' biography is a blank so far as documentary evidence of any kind is concerned. Regarding his adolescence there can be only surmises, but it is safe to assume that he was fond of reading and that he was drawn to poetry and the drama. It may be that his family moved from Alcalá to Madrid when he was about thirteen or fourteen (1560-61); and there are some who see the household as settled in Seville around 1564 and who believe that Miguel attended the Jesuit college there, a supposition that is unlikely in view of the comparatively slight knowledge of the classics that he reveals. There is nothing to show that he had a university education. It may be, however, that he left school to serve with the army in Flanders and then returned to complete his studies, for his soldiering began at an early age.

The first dependable date that we have, following his christening, is 1568, at which time he was a student in the City School of Madrid. By December of the following year he was in Rome as chamberlain to Cardinal Acquaviva. Some months before, in September 1569, a warrant had been issued in Madrid for one Miguel de Cervantes in connection with wounds that had been inflicted in a duel, and he may have fled the country on this account. From Italy he wrote home for a certificate of legitimacy setting forth that he was of "old Christian" stock with no Jewish blood in his veins, such an affidavit being necessary for one who wished to enter the armed forces. Having obtained it, Miguel left the cardinal's service and enlisted in the Spanish legion stationed in the Italian peninsula. In 1571 he took part in the campaign under John of Austria that culminated in the battle of Lepanto, on October 7.

In this famous naval encounter between Christian and Turk, Cervantes is said to have displayed an almost incredible degree of bravery and endurance. Lying ill with malarial fever, the story goes, he insisted that his comrades carry him on deck so that he could take part in the fight, and even after he had been severely wounded he fought on. Two of his wounds were in the chest; a third one was to deprive him of the use of his left hand for the rest of his life. For him this was a glorious day which he was never to forget, and in later years he could assert: "If it were possible now to work a miracle in my case, I still would rather have taken part in that prodigious battle than be today free of my wounds without having been there."

He continued his military career in the Tunis campaign in the fall of 1573, but by November of the following year his military service, in Italy, was at an end. That he had acquitted himself well is indicated by the letters of commendation to His Majesty that were given him by John of Austria himself and by the Duke of Sessa, the Spanish viceroy in Naples.

In September 1575 Miguel and his soldier brother Rodrigo embarked for Spain, but on the way they had the misfortune to be captured by Algerian pirates. As a captive Cervantes again exhibited remarkable courage and ingenuity and was the ringleader in a number of unsuccessful attempts at escape. Despite his rebellious spirit, he was treated rather well, it seems, by his Moorish master, who looked upon him as a person of some importance, worth a sizable ransom. After five years, his family and friends succeeded in raising a sum sufficient to procure his release, and by December 1580 he was back in Madrid. All this should be kept in mind as one reads the captive's tale in Part I. The episode may sound romantic in the extreme, but its basis is factual. Cervantes was writing of something that had happened to himself.

He was by now thirty-three years of age, and in May 1581 we find him in the service of the King as a messenger. He may have had another taste of battle in the campaign of the Azores, though there is no evidence to this effect. It is known that during these years following his captivity he became the father of a natural daughter, Isabel, whose mother, possibly, was an actress. For his career as an aspiring playwright had begun, and he was also trying his hand at fiction. His first published literary work was an Arcadian romance, the *Galatea*, which, like its author, saw the light at Alcalá, in 1585. This, it is to be remembered, was the age of Spenser and Sir Philip Sidney in England, but it was from such Hispanic writers as Montemayor, Gil Polo, and Montalvo that Cervantes drew his inspiration.

While the *Galatea* was on the press, Cervantes married, on December 12, 1584, a lady by the name of Catalina de Palacios Salazar y Vozmediano, daughter of a peasant of Esquivias who seems to have been a man of means. Doña Catalina, however, brought her husband but a negligible dowry, and from then on he was saddled with family cares. They had no children, but for a good part of his life Miguel was to have a houseful of womenfolk to support; besides his wife, his two sisters, his daughter Isabel, a niece, and a maidservant. The pair probably set up housekeeping at Esquivias and later moved to Seville. There, in 1587, he eked out a precarious livelihood by jobs of various sorts.

In 1588 he was appointed deputy purveyor to the fleet, his task being to requisition supplies for the Invincible Armada, preparations for which were under way at that time. The territory assigned him was Andalusia, and it was while roaming the countryside as a government commissary that he became familiar with the folk speech and folklore of that colorful province, an influence clearly to be discerned in *Don Quixote*.

His position was anything but a sinecure, and it was not long before he was in trouble. Having seized certain supplies belonging to the dean of the cathedral chapter at Seville, he was temporarily excommunicated; and on two, perhaps three, occasions—in 1592, 1597, and possibly again in 1602—he was thrown into jail because his accounts failed to balance.

For this the Andalusian peasants and not Cervantes were no doubt to blame. They must have made it hard for him, and his was the temperament of a poet, not that of an auditor. Schevill rightly sums the matter up when he says that these jail episodes are "insignificant and worthy of only the briefest consideration." One thing that Cervantes the writer acquired from his prison experiences was a firsthand knowledge of underworld types, of which he was to make good use in his plays and stories.

It was in May 1590 that, obviously desirous of bettering his condition, he applied to the King for a New World appointment, only to be told that he should "look for something nearer home." The poetry contest at Saragossa and the three silver spoons (1595) and Don Miguel's sonnet "At the Bier of King Philip II in Seville" (1598) have been referred to earlier in this Introduction. From November 1598, at which time he was in Seville, until 1603, when he was summoned to Valladolid in connection with money due the government, the records are silent as to Cervantes' whereabouts. He may have been living in retirement with his wife at Esquivias, or possibly at Valladolid; but in any event he must have been at work on Part I of the *Don Quixote,* which was off the press by the end of 1604.

The fame that this work brought its author even while he lived still does not enable us to penetrate to any extent the shadows that envelop the final decade of his life. His burdens, seemingly, were not appreciably lightened, and misfortunes continued to pursue him. About the time the book appeared upon the stalls, in 1605, he was involved in an investigation concerning the death of a nobleman who had been slain in a duel near the Cervantes' home; and from 1605 to 1608 he disappears from view completely. From 1608 until his death his chief residence was at Madrid, where he labored upon the two productions that represent the ripened fruit of his creative powers: Part II of the *Don Quixote* and the *Exemplary Novels,* as well as upon his plays, his long poem, the *Journey to Parnassus,* and (assuming it was written at this time) his *Persiles and Sigismunda.* Thus, between the ages of fifty-eight and sixty-nine, did Miguel de Cervantes enjoy a youth of the mind and spirit that any writer well might envy. It is one of the miracles of literary history.

It may seem strange to us that he delayed so long in providing a sequel to a work that had achieved so startling a success as the *Don Quixote.* It surely would not happen today: one cannot conceive a best-selling author waiting ten years to cash in on his gains. But Cervantes had other irons in the fire. For one thing, he clung to his ambition to become a dramatist, and a year before his death his *Eight Comedies and Eight Interludes,* which, he tells us significantly, had "never been performed," were given to the public by way of the printed page. And it is likely, too, that his shorter *novelas* (published under the title of *Novelas Ejemplares* in 1613) and his poetry (the *Viaje del Parnaso* appeared in 1614) took precedence with him over a tale that he was still inclined to look upon as something of a potboiler.

In any event, we are justified in believing that he worked on Part II by fits and starts. We have seen how careless he was with regard to revisions and the proof; and although he was in Madrid at the time this second part was on the press, he seems to have paid no attention to it, being more interested at that moment in his plays. On the other hand, even though he may have wearied of the theme upon occasion, and there is internal evidence that he did, there can be no doubt that he had come to realize the magnitude of his creation, a consciousness which was further heightened when, in 1614, there fell into his hands a "sequel" supposed to have been written by one Alonso Fernández de Avellaneda, "native of the town of Tordesillas."

The Avellaneda volume is one of the most disgraceful performances in all literature. Wholly lacking in originality and stylistic grace, it is an utter betrayal of a great work, filled with vulgarities and obscenities of which Cervantes never would have been guilty, while the characters of Don Quixote and Sancho are debased beyond recognition. In addition, it contains a vicious personal attack on the original author, in the course of which his crippled hand—to him a glorious symbol of Lepanto—his old age, and his poverty are held up to ridicule. Who the real perpetrator of this outrage was, and what his motives were, are questions that have not as yet been answered.

The "apocryphal *Don Quixote*" had a galvanizing effect on the creator of the real one. Cervantes had reached Chapter LIX of his second part when Avellaneda's book came into his possession. How he reacted to it may be seen from the later chapters that he wrote and from his angry but severely controlled Prologue. In a way, his embittered preoccupation with Avellaneda led him to distort the concluding portion of the narrative—and to kill off his hero once and for all to save him from being manhandled again.

The life of Miguel de Cervantes was a hard one, and his troubles were with him to the edge of the grave; nevertheless it would be a mistake to assume that his last years were spent in bitterness of spirit. His works, alone, would tell us that in spite of all disillusionments he had succeeded in preserving to the very end his profound humaneness and geniality; which must mean that, somewhere, there was an underlying faith to sustain him. He had had many buffetings, but there had also been flashes of splendor, and it is clear that he died with the conviction that his name would live. In his latter days he had two patrons, the Count of Lemos and the Archbishop of Toledo, but they did little to render his existence easier. Patrons were at best undependable, as he had found in the case of the Duke of Béjar, to whom he had dedicated Part I.

It was, rather, to the Church that he turned as the shadows fell and deepened. A couple of years before his death he joined the Tertiary Order of St. Francis, and it was the Franciscans who in 1616 carried him to his last, unknown resting place. Four days prior to his death, which occurred on April 23 of that year, he penned the Dedication to his *Persiles,* a touching farewell addressed to the Count of Lemos: "With one foot already in the stirrup, and with the agony of death upon me, great Lord, I write to you. Yesterday they gave me Extreme Unction. . . . The time is short, my pains are increasing, my hopes are diminishing; and yet, with it all, the desire I have to live keeps me alive." It is at once a cry for life and a courageous acceptance of the inevitable.

III

As a writer, Cervantes in the realm of prose must be considered as the culminating and finest product of the *siglo de oro,* the period that in Spain witnessed the brilliant flowering of the Renaissance impulse. If we are to understand the man and his age, we must remember that this was the Spain not only of Lope de Vega, Góngora, Alarcón, Tirso de Molina, and Hurtado de Mendoza, but also of St. Theresa, John of the Cross, and El Greco—yes, and of the Counter-Reformation and the Inquisition as well. Contemporaries of Shakespeare, Camões, Tasso, Montaigne, and Ronsard, the creator of the Ingenious Gentleman of La Mancha and his fellow writers belong to the later phase of the European renascence, such figures as Ariosto, Erasmus, and Sir Thomas More having disappeared from the scene in the course of the twenty years preceding Cervantes' birth, while Rabelais died when Cervantes was but six years old. Calderón and Velázquez were yet to come, but the high point was reached with Part II of *Don Quixote.*

There has been in the past a good deal of misunderstanding as to the character of the Spanish Renaissance. This has been due to the effort of partisan, prejudiced, and often inadequately equipped literary historians to make the facts of the case fit a preconceived theory. Catholic Spain, we are told, held out against the Renaissance and effectively blocked it, with the Inquisition as the savage watchdog that suppressed all intellectual life and creative activity. That is the way it must be if the theory is correct, and so that is the way it is; and such commentators will accordingly assure us that the era in question was a barren one, unworthy of serious notice, when a mere listing of names would show that this was the most fruitful period in the entire history of Spanish letters.

There were, it is true, profound differences between the Renaissance spirit as manifested in the Iberian peninsula and the forms it assumed in Italy, France, and other countries. Aubrey Bell sums the matter up nicely by observing that Spain, like England, was not overwhelmed by the Humanist tide. In a land where, as Salvador de Madariaga puts it, the illiterates "speak like Seneca and sing like Blake," the movement took on more of a deeply rooted popular and national character, and, like Sancho Panza himself, was at once less rationalistic and more realistic. What is to be seen here is a mingling of currents. The Italian Renaissance influence that came as a result of the southern wars found expression in the Arcadian theme and in the conceits of Góngora and his imitators; but alongside this more refined literature there existed another, that of the people, which is to be met with in the old *cancioneros,* or ballad collections, and in those romances of chivalry that, following the resurrection of *Amadis of Gaul* at the beginning of the sixteenth century, swept over the country like a deluge.

For the very reason that he is so thoroughly Spanish, Cervantes is not a "typical" Renaissance writer in the sense that Rabelais, for example, is—Rabelais who in his cloister had fought and won the battle of the forbidden Greek books. There rests upon Cervantes no burden of the New Learning; there will be found in his pages no wealth of classical allusions as in the *Gargantua and Pantagruel.* He was somewhat self-conscious in this regard, as is to be perceived from the Prologue to Part I of the *Don Quixote,* which may be taken as truth spoken in jest. A man of little formal schooling, he had but a slight acquaintance with the classics. Although he was not wholly untouched by Italy there are few traces of his experiences to be made out in his work, and such impressions as he does record seem superficial—a fact that may perhaps be explained by his confinement to camp and barracks. However, while his knowledge of the language was such as a soldier might pick up, he must have read Ariosto, Pulci, Boiardo, and other Italians whose influence to a greater or less extent is apparent in his work.

It is in his poems, by something of an effort which the reader cannot help feeling, that he comes nearest to the Renaissance-Humanist type. In his plays and *novelas,* though he is now and again seduced by the Arcadian motive, as in his *Galatea* and *Persiles,* his tendency always, at his best, is to depict the world about him and the flesh-and-blood characters he has known as soldier, captive, royal messenger, tax gatherer, hapless man of letters, and prison inmate. The rogue and the adventurer hold a special attraction for him (the germ of *Don Quixote* may be found in his "Rinconete and Cortadillo"), and in this he reveals an affinity with the picaresque novelists of his day, with writers like Quevedo and the author of *Lazarillo de Tormes.* In any case, it was the people, the common people of Spain, who inspired his most successful artistic creations. He can portray a peasant like Sancho Panza, Sancho's wife or daughter, to perfection; but when he undertakes to give us a duke or a duchess, he is far less convincing and the result is likely to be a puppet rather than a character.

That Cervantes was sharply aware of the two audiences, the cultured and the popular one, in the Spain of his day, is clear from his own remarks in *Don Quixote.* His appeal was sometimes to one, sometimes to the other, but most often to the latter; and it was to the wider audience that he addressed his major work. Indeed, it might be said that it was he who brought the Renaissance to his people, just as Rabelais, who is otherwise so different, did in France. He was steeped in their literature, their magnificent old ballads and those foolishly inflated tales of wandering knights and damsels in distress of which they were so inordinately fond. Most of these romances he would, like the village curate, have consigned to the flames, but for the ballads he had a high esteem, as representing the work of the people themselves. And when he came to write *Don Quixote*, it was popular sources that he drew upon; for the theme of madness or monomania induced by reading books of chivalry was not original with Cervantes but may be traced as far back as the fourteenth century, and as late as 1597 it forms the subject of an interlude that may have afforded the stimulus for the creation of the Knight of La Mancha.

At this point, in view of the encomiums that have been lavished upon it, one may ask what it is that gives *Don Quixote* its outstanding importance in the field of fiction. What is it that makes this story the first truly modern novel and one of the greatest—many have said, the greatest—of all time? This is a question to which any intelligent reader with a critical sense that is at all developed should be able to find the answer for himself. Let him try an experiment. After laying down his Cervantes, let him take up Boccaccio or any teller of tales from the Greeks down to the seventeenth century, and he will quickly become conscious of a significant difference. Let him look more closely, and he will discover where that difference lies: *in the delineation and growth of character and the dynamic psychological movement of the narrative.* A Boccaccio character, for instance, is a social type, belonging to a fixed category and thereby incapable of any kind of internal evolution; things happen *to* him but not *inside* him, and in the end, with all his seeming quirks which are in reality the product of circumstance, he remains the same person that he was in the beginning, with the same view of life and the world.

Such, for centuries, had been the form that fiction assumed in Western Europe. Starting in the Alexandrian age as a picture of manners, it had continued, down through the *Decameron,* the *Cent Nouvelles Nouvelles,* the *Heptameron,* and the *Gargantua and Pantagruel,* to be just that and nothing more. Cervantes' supreme merit lies in having broken the mold and introduced the element of dynamism. By so doing, as Krutch says, he discovered "the essential method of the modern novel." This represents a rupture with the prevailing fictional forms of his day, the Arcadian romance on the one hand and the romance of chivalry on the other. His principal characters are anything but black or white; they are complex human beings who constantly change, grow, expand. They think about life and its meaning, and their thinking does things to them.

Could this conceivably be said of any character in Boccaccio? Can it be said of Gargantua (who has to be purged with "Anticyrian hellebore" before he is transformed), or of Pantagruel, or Panurge, or Friar John? If one contrasts them with the "simple" Sancho Panza, not to speak of his master, who is still an enigma to the wise, one perceives what cardboard creatures they are, however diverting. Rabelais was a great Humanist, a great master of the comic, but he did not advance the art of fiction as Cervantes did.

In *Don Quixote* it is not only the characters that grow: we can see the author growing with them. This again is a trait of the significant, worth-while modern novelist, and one that had not appeared before. It may have been Cervantes' original intention to compose a tale "for the entertainment of the peoples," but before he had finished he found himself plumbing the depths of human existence, confronting the most profound of philosophic problems: that of appearance and reality, of being and non-being. Don Quixote and Sancho each represent one aspect of this problem, and the manner in which they are portrayed as complementing and reacting upon each other constitutes an artistic achievement of the first order. Each becomes more like the other, and the two may be looked upon as embodying the drama and the dialogue that is taking place in Cervantes' mind and soul; he learns from them, and as he learns, his stature as an artist increases.

It is with good reason, then, that Coleridge, Brandes, Yeats, and others have spoken of Cervantes in the same breath with the Shakespeare of Lear and Hamlet. Both men wrote out of stern necessity and the tensions of the spirit, and by the gift of genius were able to turn what might have been potboilers into great works of art. With Cervantes, this process of spiritual growth on the part of the author is reflected in the far greater depth and maturity of the second part of Don Quixote— though there are some, Thomas Mann among them, who still prefer Part I.

In recent years there has been a good deal of controversy as to whether or not Don Quixote is an "accidental" masterpiece. "The book grew without any definite plan," says Schevill; and with this a number of earlier highly respected Cervantes scholars would agree. "Never," Ormsby declares, "was a great work so neglected by its author." "The most careless great book in the world," is the judgment of W. P. Ker. In fact, from Diego Clemencín to Rodríguez Marín, we find those who would more or less assent to Benedetto Croce's assertion that "Cervantes was not fully aware of his own genius." The present trend, however, appears to be away from this view and toward a frequently exaggerated conception of the author's initial awareness. The textual discrepancies, we are assured, are not in reality slips of the pen but are due to a metaphysical disdain for the factual. All of which—if the academic specialists will pardon me for saying so—impresses me as being the result of overspecialization, with a tendency to erect a sort of esoteric Cervantes cult.

The man who wrote *Don Quixote* could not have been an unconscious artist, we will grant that, and there is ample evidence in the work itself to show that he was constantly thinking about the forms that he practiced: fiction, poetry, and the drama. Singleton has predicted that "the intellectual and artistic life of Cervantes will eventually be clearly shown to have been a slow, conscious, and completely coherent process" (Schevill phrased it: "he required years to be born"), and I am willing to accept the hypothesis; for a *Don Quixote* is not created out of the void, and this would explain the late ripening of so amazing a talent. The only thing is, I would put a question mark after the words "completely coherent" as being inapplicable, I suspect, to the development of any individual, and above all, to that of one so life-battered as we know Cervantes was.

But this does not mean that we must at the same time accept the statement that the author knew from the start he was creating a master work and had definitely plotted it out. Both the external and the internal evidence are against the supposition. After the opening chapters, which deal with the knight's first sally, there are signs of a distinct break, as if Cervantes had suddenly changed and broadened his plan; and throughout Part I, with its interpolated pastoral episodes and old-fashioned *novelas,* there is a certain unsureness, a groping between the old and hackneyed and the new and original—in a manner, a feeling of the public's pulse—that is wholly absent from Part II, a fact of which the author in his Prologue shows himself to be aware. This phenomenon of growth, the growth of the creator with his creation, is, when all is said, the most marvelous thing about the book.

An idolatrous attitude is of no service to any writer or any work. However great the critic's admiration and even reverence, it is not his business to endeavor to explain away every fault and shortcoming, every failure, and to insist that all the author wrote is perfect, the result of subtle or far-seeing design. Cervantes was a fine artist, there is no question as to that, though he did not prove it, did not develop fully, until he neared the seventh decade of his life; but he was also very human and he labored under tremendous odds. As a delineator of character he is thoroughly original and unrivaled when at his best, yet not all his characters come to life; as he goes upward in the social scale, treading less familiar ground, his portraits lose in depth, and his women on the whole (unless they are peasants, like Teresa and her daughter) are shadowy creatures as compared to the men; as for Dulcinea, who represents the only "heart interest" outside of the episodes in Part I, she is, of course, no more than a meaningful figment. And his art of character-drawing and storytelling breaks down completely when he tries to make convincing Fernando's sudden and utterly unrealistic change of heart toward Dorotea.

The basis of Cervantes' art is an essential realism based upon "verisimilitude and the imitation of nature." He himself tells us this in connection with his criticism of the romances of chivalry, in Part I, Chapter XLVII. The real is here to be understood as the true rather than as "fact," or the truth that our senses give us, and the artist's task is to see that "the impossible is made to appear possible" through being clothed in the familiar. In its complete fusion, at once homely and poetic, of fantasy and reality, *Don Quixote* is unique among works of literature. Its dominant quality is invention, the play of the creative imagination; and in achieving his effects, the author relies upon his graphic powers of description and his close-to-life, astonishingly modern-sounding dialogue, which, as Schevill notes, becomes a "process of self-revelation" on the part of the speaker. His scenes are really pictorial, and he is notably adept at describing the costume (especially feminine costume) and personal appearance of his characters. All this, the description and the dialogue, points to a keenly perceptive observation of daily life and a wide experience with his fellow men; Cervantes was in no sense an Ivory Tower writer.

One cannot speak of *Don Quixote* without mentioning Cervantes' humor, which is inseparably associated with his fantasy and which has caused him to be compared to Shakespeare, Sterne, and Swift among English writers. It is an expression of the Comic Spirit—"the richer laughter of heart and mind in one"—that Meredith fully appreciated. It is a humor that has nothing to do with the hearty, rumbling belly-laugh of a Rabelais, expressive of physical well-being and a joy in living and in new-found horizons such as characterized the earlier stages of the Renaissance. This is a metaphysical humor the essence of which lies in a startling juxtaposition of the incongruous; and it finds a perfect embodiment, not in the protagonist of the tale, who evokes tears more often than laughter, but in Sancho Panza, who has been termed "the most humorous creation in the whole range of fiction." Nor is there any dependence here upon the smutty jest or upon levity with regard to the Church and accepted institutions; instead, the author could boast that his was "the least harmful of any book that has been published up to now."

As a prose writer, master of a beautifully pure and limpid Castilian, Cervantes is the best that the Golden Age has to show, neither Lope nor Quevedo being comparable to him in this regard. His native style is admirably terse, vigorous, and direct, and reminds one somewhat of Swift's. He has his faults, to be sure, and there are occasional traces of "fine" writing, possibly due to the Góngora influence; but, on the whole, he is true to the apothegm that occurs twice in the *Don Quixote: "Toda afectación es mala"*—"All affectation is bad."

The discussion thus far has been confined almost exclusively to the *Don Quixote,* but we must not forget that other masterly work that Cervantes has left us, the *Exemplary Novels,* unfortunately little known to American readers though it has had a ponderable effect upon the literature of England and the Continent. There are two translations, one by N. Maccoll, the other by Walter K. Kelly, the former being by far the better of the two, but both have long been out of print and are difficult to procure. This is to be regretted; had they been accessible, these novels would surely have made themselves felt by writers and by students of the art of fiction generally. There are some who see in the *Novelas Ejemplares* Cervantes' most mature production from the point of view of a highly conscious and refined literary artistry.

It is Cervantes the fiction writer who is presented in the following pages. Like Fielding and Smollett, he was unsuccessful as a dramatist. It may be that he was too much the realist to adapt himself to the Spanish theater of his time—Lope de Vega, let us remember, was a very ordinary novelist. The best of Cervantes' dramatic work is contained in the *Entremeses*, or *Interludes*, recently rendered available in English in the distinguished translation of S. Griswold Morley. There would, accordingly, appear to be little reason for including any of the theatrical pieces in a volume of this sort; and the same is true of the poems, which were adequately translated by James Y. Gibson, in the 1880s. That the author of *Don Quixote* was at heart a poet few would deny, but he did not often succeed in achieving a formal expression in verse that was above the mediocre.

So much for the work. To undertake to trace its influence upon the principal cultures of the world would be a stupendous task, requiring volumes and the cooperation of many minds. A mere list of the more important of the world's writers who in one way or another have felt the breath of the Cervantine spirit must of necessity sound like a catalogue. In France, to mention but a few, we should encounter such names as Molière, Voltaire, Chateaubriand, Stendhal, Balzac, Flaubert, and Victor Hugo. In Germany, thanks in good part to Cervantes' translator, Ludwig Tieck, *Don Quixote* was caught up into the full tide of the Romantic movement, and Goethe, Jean Paul Richter, Schiller, Heine, Hofmannsthal, Hegel, Lessing, Humboldt, Schlegel, Novalis, Wieland, Grillparzer, Immermann, Herder, Klinger—all bear witness to his presence. And Dostoevski was not the only one in Russia; there were Pushkin, Turgenev, Gogol (*Dead Souls*, like *The Idiot*, drew inspiration from this source). It is not impossible that Shakespeare read Part I of *Don Quixote* in Shelton's translation, and Butler's *Hudibras* owes much to the Spanish masterpiece. Beaumont and Fletcher, espe-

cially, made use of the *Exemplary Novels*. Fielding
wrote his *Joseph Andrews* "in imitation of the manner
of Cervantes" and composed a comedy or ballad-opera
entitled *Don Quixote in England*. Sterne, Smollett,
Defoe, Richardson, Swift, Pope, Johnson, Addison,
Steele, Wordsworth, Scott, Byron, Lamb, Coleridge,
Meredith, Francis Thompson, Arthur Machen, and
Wyndham Lewis are among those who have enjoyed
and paid tribute to the Knight of La Mancha.

In America, although much remains to be done in
tracing it, the Cervantes influence is clearly seen to be
less than elsewhere. It shows unmistakably in Irving
and Melville and in Mark Twain's *Connecticut Yankee
in King Arthur's Court*. We have heard Howells'
opinion, we know that Hawthorne admired the *Exemplary Novels*, and Professor Harry Levin would find a
certain relation between the Quixotic spirit and the
flight of a Henry James or the mood of disillusionment of such contemporary novelists as Sinclair Lewis,
Ernest Hemingway, James T. Farrell, and others. He
also discovers "a striking resemblance to that expatriate
waste land which T. S. Eliot invokes." It is a long
way from La Mancha to Main Street and from Don
Quixote to Studs Lonigan, but there may be something
in it for all that.

IV

Any intelligent reader of *Don Quixote*, in the course
of the story or upon laying it down, must inevitably ask
himself: What was the author's intention in writing
the book—aside from that of earning a little much-
needed money? And this question will be followed by
another: What is the outlook upon the world, the life
view, that is here given body and substance?

Recalling all the "explanations" and "interpretations" that have been advanced by editors, commentators, scholars, and critics, one is inclined to accept Ortega y Gasset's picture of a tired Cervantes seated in the Elysian Fields and waiting—waiting for a comprehension which he hopes posterity may bestow. No other book, unless it is the Bible, ever came so near to meaning all things to all men. Children and the simple of heart still can revel in the pure entertainment it affords; and for long after the author's death, imperceptive adults who were far from simple continued to look upon it as a farcical work, the English "wits" being especially to blame here, though the French were not far behind them. When at last it came to be taken seriously, the hunt for meanings and hidden motives began, and the commentators were in their element. Attempts were even made to identify Don Quixote with Ignatius Loyola, the Emperor Charles V, and other real-life personages.

One of the most widespread misconceptions of the past was popularized by Byron, who asserted that Cervantes had "smiled Spain's chivalry away." It was such a view as this that led Ruskin, after having praised the novel highly ten years before, to turn against it and condemn it as a "deadly book," for the reason that "all true chivalry is thus by implication accused of madness and involved in shame." Had they given the matter a little thought, both critic and poet should have remembered that chivalry as a formalized institution died with the Middle Ages, while the knight-errant, in any case, was a romantic creation rather than a historic reality. What Cervantes was attacking, insofar as he was attacking anything, was not the chivalric principle, which the hero of Lepanto undoubtedly respected, but a false and aesthetically repugnant variety of tale that had grown up around the subject of knighthood; and here his aim was so effective that no further romance of this kind appeared after the publication of Part I. Richardson, in the following century, was to undertake much the same task when he sat down to write his *Pamela*.

In other words, Cevantes' purpose was not social but, as it took shape in his mind, aesthetic and philosophic in character. Notwithstanding the fact that he has given us what has rightly been termed "the great social novel of Spain at the beginning of the seventeenth century" as well as "the best essay ever written on the Spanish national character," he is in no wise a reformer. He may be capable of extracting a sublime humor from an attempt to turn back the clock of history, but he evidences no desire to turn it forward. In fact, such evidence as we have is on the other side. Old soldier that he was, he exhibits an intense and, I believe, wholly unfeigned loyalty to Church and King and the laws and institutions of his land; and more than one attitude that he reveals on the questions of his age—on the Inquisition and the expulsion of the Moors, toward the "founders of new sects and ways of life," on censorship and licensing, to mention but a few—would today earn him the epithet of reactionary from those who are ever ready with their labels.

After reading and rereading *Don Quixote* many times and studying every line and word, as a translator must, I remain unconvinced by Professor Castro's theory to the effect that Cervantes wrote with tongue in cheek and dissimulated his real views in order to evade the censures of the Holy Office. The argument is an ingenious one, based largely upon textual and linguistic interpretations, but it may be met with an equal degree of ingenuity, as Aubrey Bell and Father Rubio have shown. In the end, one who knows the author must rely upon his own feeling, in the absence of specific and dependable data; and for myself I can but think of Rabelais, in whom I also had a thorough immersion. Maître François familiarized me with the tongue-in-cheek attitude, and I can only say that I find nothing of the sort in Cervantes. Even Castro is compelled to admit that "beyond the shadow of a doubt, Cervantes was a good Catholic," though an audacious one like Erasmus and other Renaissance thinkers outside of Spain.

To accept such a view, however, one must either ignore the distinct character of the Spanish Renaissance or else assume that Cervantes was not representative of it. Casalduero speaks of "the Catholic Cervantes, a Catholic of his epoch, that is, of the Counter-Reformation," a description with which Helmut Hatzfeld would agree, and this seems to me a much more reasonable estimate. Cervantes' Catholicism, like that of the Spanish people, the Sanchos and their kind, was so deeply ingrained that he could afford now and then to smile— he never laughs boisterously—at the observances and ministers of religion but he is at bottom a fervent Catholic and essentially a Catholic writer. I cannot believe, as a number of authorities have held, that he was indifferent to theological and philosophical speculation; his theology, out of the Spain of St. Ignatius and St. Theresa and St. John of the Cross, is the bridge to a philosophy that becomes the major theme of his work, conferring upon it a special interest for the student of the novel.

The world of social relationships, for Cervantes as for Don Quixote, has always something of an air of unreality and illusion, or at most, of relativity, in confrontation with and in reference to the ideal and the absolute. If there are problems to be solved, the solution lies inside man, not in external circumstance; and he who starts out to set the world right is embarking upon a truly Quixotic enterprise. This is the other aspect of the Knight of La Mancha. He has commonly been regarded as a reactionary with an *idée fixe,* but he may quite as well be looked upon as "the prototype of the modern utopian who spends himself in the interest of the general good and makes himself guilty of many a particular evil, as Don Quixote does when he comes to the rescue of the farmer's lad, Andrés. This is that third type of comedy of which Auden speaks, "based on a sense that the relations of the individual and society to each other and of both to the true good contain insoluble contradictions which are not so much comic as ironic."

We are thus brought to the question of Don Quixote's "madness," on which the meaning of the book hinges. Though the psychiatrists occasionally have tried to claim him, it should no longer be necessary to point out that his is no ordinary case of insanity, mental derangement, or "abnormality" of any kind. Hence the old objection that it is cruel to laugh at the actions of the insane does not stand; and any adult who gets no more than this out of the story had best put it aside. In the admirable statement of Waldo Frank, "Don Quixote . . . is a man possessed: not a madman"; and there is all the difference in the world between the two. He is fully aware of the true character of his hallucinations; he knows, for example, that enchanters do not actually transform shapes but merely *appear* to do so; and with this realization, exit the madman, enter the poet-philosopher, intent upon defending the rights of the imagination—the poet in action. In this sense, one feels like exclaiming with Merimée: "Pity the man who has not had some of Don Quixote's ideas!" The Surrealists, if they would leave their Freudian baggage behind, might find something here (Dali caught the spirit), but it will be barren ground for the psychoanalyst as for the sociologist.

With the Cervantes of Part II we are in an intellectual, speculative-metaphysical stratosphere where "conditioning," whether social or psychological, will explain nothing, and the id and libido and economic determinism may as well be discarded. This is the realm into which a dazed Pontius Pilate once stumbled. What is truth? What is the truth behind the show of things? And in how far is a man justified in fashioning for himself a truer truth that may serve his soul's need— *Così è (se vi pare)—Right You Are, If You Think You Are*—the modern Pirandello theme? As Eric Bentley has pointed out, this is also the theme of Shaw and Chaplin, who, like Pirandello, must have been born "under the sign of Cervantes." In this respect, *Don Quixote* is the first work, the first *comedy*, of its kind, embodying a humor based upon the incongruous clash of reality and appearance and not to be dissociated from that "tragic sense of life" that haunts Unamuno.

Joseph Wood Krutch has observed that Cervantes is here stating "the chief intellectual problem of his age in a novel"; and one of the finest of American critics, Lionel Trilling, further notes that this problem, that of illusion and reality, is the novelist's supreme concern. I will act, says Don Quixote, *as if* the world were what I would have it be, *as if* the ideal were the real. He is under no delusion regarding his lady Dulcinea: "God knows whether or not there is a Dulcinea in this world . . . I contemplate her as she needs must be [*como conviene que sea*]." Can anyone today read this passage without a start, without thinking of Kierkegaard and Sartre and the Existentialists? In Cervantes' time it was Augustine and Plato. It was Plato and Augustine versus Aristotle; for what we have here is a manifestation, in Spanish Counter-Reformationist terms, of that late Renaissance revival of Platonism that had begun in the sixteenth century, with Marguerite of Navarre as its leading exponent in France.

It is, to repeat, this conflict of ideas that in Part II becomes the major theme and takes over the story— this, and not the attack on the books of chivalry, which persists as a fictional device, nothing more. And it is through the interplay, the constant spoken and unspoken dialogue between the knight and his squire, that the drama is realized. Sancho Panza is not a personification of common sense, as he is commonly supposed to be; he too has his "island," and his attitude toward the problem of reality is essentially the same as that of his master; he views the matter from a different angle, that is all. He is the man of the people who has been seduced into following the man of the study on a highly dangerous adventure, and one fares no better than the other.

What is the moral of the tale? Opinions differ, just as they do regarding the character of the hero and the nature of his madness. The knight's final overthrow is, assuredly, one of the saddest episodes ever contrived. Does it mean, as Thomas Mann sees it, no more than a "bitter and disillusioned submission to vulgar reality" such as constitutes "the essence of humor"? It is to be suspected that the author of *The Magic Mountain* is fashioning a Don Quixote in his own image; but isn't that what we all do? Aubrey Bell, on the other hand, discovers in the marvelous deathbed scene with which the book closes a spiritual victory in the form of a self-purification; and he would find the moral in the housekeeper's admonition: "Stay at home, attend to your affairs, go often to confession, be charitable to the poor. . . ."

This latter view, it should be stressed, does not of necessity imply an unquestioning acceptance of things as they are, the *status quo*, but has to do, rather, with the individual and his personal vision of his inner self in relation to a solid-seeming but insubstantial universe. I was recently reminded of the housekeeper's words when I read in Käthe Kollwitz's diary the following entry: ". . . I am not only allowed to finish my work, I am bidden to finish it. This, it seems to me, is the meaning of all the talk about civilization. It can exist only where each individual fills his own personal sphere of duty. If everybody recognizes and takes upon himself the duty to which he is called, genuine life will result. The civilization of an entire nation cannot be based on anything else."

It sounds like a homely, prosaic lesson, but a man may have to go through hell to learn it. If he is a thinking man, he may have to draw aside a curtain that had best be left undrawn, since the tragicomic spectacle revealed is one that can only lead to madness in the eyes of those who remain on the other side. It is with good reason that Melville puts Don Quixote alongside Hamlet and the Satan of *Paradise Lost*.

Yet, with it all, was there ever a more genial work? *Don Quixote* is at once the saddest and the most serene of masterpieces. In Part I, Chapter L, we are told of a certain knight-errant who dives to the bottom of a lake of pitch and there has a rewarding vision. Cervantes must have had a comparable experience upon the intellectual plane. That, it may be, is the meaning of his twilight smile—but one might as well attempt to wrest the secret of El Greco!

Suggested Readings in English

BIBLIOGRAPHY

Grismer, Raymond L. *Cervantes: A Bibliography. Books, Essays, Articles and Other Studies on the Life of Cervantes, His Works and His Imitators.* Vol. I, New York: H. W. Wilson Co., 1946; Vol. II, Minneapolis, Minn.: Burgess-Beckwith, 1962.

BIOGRAPHIES AND GENERAL STUDIES

Arbó, Sebastián J. C. *Cervantes: The Man and His Times.* New York: Vanguard Press, 1955.

Bell, Aubrey F. G. *Cervantes.* Norman, Okla., University of Oklahoma Press, 1947; London: Collier-Macmillan, 1961.

Brenan, Gerald. "Cervantes," *Horizon* (London), XVIII (June 1948), 25–46.

Entwistle, William J. *Cervantes.* Oxford: Clarendon Press, 1940.

Fitzmaurice-Kelly, James. *Miguel de Cervantes Saavedra.* London: Chapman & Hall, 1892.

―――. *Miguel de Cervantes Saavedra. A Memoir.* Oxford: Clarendon Press, 1913.

Flores, Angel, and Benardete, M. J. (eds.). *Cervantes Across the Centuries.* (Nineteen essays by specialists, among them R. Menéndez Pidal, "The Genesis of *Don Quixote*"; Helmut Hatzfeld on the style; Américo Castro on "Incarnation in *Don Quixote*.") New York: Dryden Press, 1947 (rep. New York: Gordian Press, 1969).

Frank, Bruno. *A Man Called Cervantes.* New York: The Viking Press, 1935.

Levin, Harry. "The Example of Cervantes," in Mark Schorer (ed.), *Society and Self in the Novel.* New York: Columbia University Press, 1956, pp. 3–25.

Lewis, D. B. Wyndham. *The Shadow of Cervantes.* London: Hollis & Carter, 1962; New York: Sheed & Ward, 1962.

Ryner, Han. *The Ingenious Hidalgo Miguel de Cervantes.* New York: Harcourt Brace, 1927.

35

Schevill, Rudolph. *Cervantes*. New York: Duffield, 1919 (rep. New York: Ungar, 1966).

Smith, Robinson. *The Life of Cervantes*. London: G. Routledge, 1914.

Tomás, Mariano. *The Life and Misadventures of Miguel de Cervantes*. Boston: Houghton Mifflin, 1934.

Watts, Henry E. *Miguel de Cervantes, His Life and Works*. London: A. & C. Bell, 1895.

Ybarra, Thomas R. *Cervantes*. New York: A. & C. Boni, 1931.

DON QUIXOTE: PROBLEMS AND PERSPECTIVES

Bell, Michael. "The Structure of *Don Quixote*," *Essays in Criticism*, XVIII (July 1968), 241–257.

Bishop, John Peale; Barzun, Jacques; and Van Doren, Mark; "Cervantes: Don Quixote," in Mark Van Doren (ed.), *The New Invitation to Learning*. New York: Random House, 1942.

Chambers, Leland H. "Structure and the Search for Truth in the *Quijote*," *Hispanic Review*, XXXV (1967), 309–326.

Cook, Albert S. "The Beginning of Fiction: Cervantes," in *The Meaning of Fiction*. Detroit: Wayne University Press, 1960, pp. 7–23.

Duffield, Alexander J. *Don Quixote, His Critics and Commentators*. London: C. K. Paul, 1881.

Flores, Angel, and Benardete, M. J. (eds.). *The Anatomy of Don Quixote*. Ithaca, N.Y.: The Dragon Press, 1932.

Goggio, Emilio. "The Dual Role of Dulcinea in Cervantes' *Don Quixote*," *Modern Language Quarterly*, XIII (1952), 285–291.

Guilbeau, John J. "Some Folk-Motifs in *Don Quixote*," in Waldo F. McNeir (ed.), *Studies in Comparative Literature*. Baton Rouge, La.: Louisiana State University, 1962.

Haley, George. "The Narrator in *Don Quixote*: Maese Pedro's Puppet Show," *Modern Language Notes*, LXXX, 145–165.

Honig, Edwin. "Reality and Realism in Cervantes and Lorca," *New Mexico Quarterly*, XXXIV (1964), 31–47.

Immerwahr, Raymond. "*Structural Symmetry in the Episodic Narratives of Don Quixote, Part I*," *Comparative Literature*, X (1958), 121–135.

Ker, W. P. "Don Quixote," in his *Collected Essays*. London: Macmillan, 1925, 2 vols., Vol. II, pp. 28–45.

Kirchner, Nora I. "Don Quijote de la Mancha: A Study in Classical Paranoia," *Annali Istituto Universitario Orientali, Napoli, Sezione Romanza*, IX (1967), 229–249.

Madariaga, Salvador de. *Don Quixote*. Oxford: Clarendon Press, 1935.

Mandel, Oscar. "The Function of the Norm in *Don Quixote*," *Modern Philology*, LV (1958), 154–163.

Mann, Thomas. "Ocean Crossing with Don Quixote," in his *Essays of Three Decades*. New York: Knopf, 1947; London: Secker & Warburg, 1947.

Mones, Sidney. "The Lion in the Cage: The Quixote of Reality," *Massachusetts Review*, I (1959), 156–175.

Murillo, Luis A. "Cervantic Irony in *Don Quixote*," in *Homenaje a Rodríguez-Moñino*. Madrid: Castalia, 1966, 2 vols., Vol. II, pp. 21–27.

Neugaard, Edward J. "The 'Curioso Impertinente' and Its Relationship to the *Quijote*," *Language Quarterly* (University of South Florida), IV, iii–iv (1966), 2–6.

Novitsky, Pavel I. *Cervantes and "Don Quixote."* New York: The Critics Group, 1936.

Oelschläger, Victor R. B. "Quixotessence," *Quaderni Ibero-Americani*, XXVII (1961), 143–157.

Predmore, Richard L. *The World of Don Quixote*. Cambridge, Mass.: Harvard University Press, 1967; London: Oxford University Press, 1968.

Riley, E. C. *Cervantes' Theory of the Novel*. Oxford: Clarendon Press, 1962.

Salingar, L. G. "Don Quixote as a Prose Epic," *Forum for Modern Language Studies* (University of St. Andrews, Scotland), II (1966), 53–68.

Spitzer, Leo. "On the Significance of *Don Quixote*," *Modern Language Notes*, LXXVII (1962), 113–129.

Suarez, Manuel F. *The Revelations of Don Quixote*. New York: Harbinger House, 1947.

Swanson, Roy A. "The Humor of *Don Quixote*," *Romanic Review*, LIV (1963), 161–170.

Turgenev, Ivan. "Hamlet and Don Quixote," in Angel Flores and M. J. Benardete (eds.), *The Anatomy of Don Quixote*. Ithaca, N.Y.: Dragon Press, 1932, pp. 98–120.

Turkevich, Ludmilla B. *Cervantes in Russia*. Princeton, N.J.: Princeton University Press, 1950.

Unamuno, Miguel de. *The Life of Don Quixote and Sancho according to Miguel de Cervantes*. New York: Knopf,

1927; Princeton, N.J.: Princeton University Press, 1968.

Van Doren, Mark. *Don Quixote's Profession.* New York: Columbia University Press, 1957.

Van Ghent, Dorothy. "Essays in Analysis—on *Don Quixote,*" in *The English Novel.* New York: Rinehart, 1953, pp. 9–19.

Van Maelsaeke, D. "The Paradox of Humor: A Comparative Study of *Don Quixote,*" *Theoria* (Natal, South Africa), XXVIII (1967), 24–42.

Wardropper, Bruce W. "The Pertinence of 'El Curioso Impertinente,'" *PMLA,* LXXII (1957), 587–600.

WORKS BY CERVANTES OTHER THAN "DON QUIXOTE"

Journey to Parnassus, tr. by James Y. Gibson. London: Kegan Paul, Trench & Co., 1883.

Numantia, tr. by James Y. Gibson. London: Kegan Paul, Trench & Co., 1885.

The Exemplary Novels, tr. by N. Maccoll. Glasgow: Gowans & Gray, 1902.

The Exemplary Novels, tr. by Walter K. Kelly. London: Bohn, 1846; New York: Bell & Sons, 1894.

Three Exemplary Novels, tr. by Samuel Putnam. New York: The Viking Press, 1950.

Six Exemplary Novels, tr. by Harriet de Onis. Great Neck, N.Y.: Barrons, 1960.

"The Power of the Blood," tr. by William M. Davis, in Angel Flores (ed.), *Spanish Stories.* New York: Bantam Books, 1960, pp. 65–89.

The Interludes of Cervantes, tr. by S. Griswold Morley. Princeton, N.J.: Princeton University Press, 1948.

"Pedro the Artful Dodger" and "The Jealous Old Man," tr. by Walter Starkie, in Walter Starkie (ed.), *Eight Spanish Plays of the Golden Age.* New York: Modern Library, 1964.

"The Faithful Dog," tr. by Angel Flores and Joseph Liss, *Poet Lore,* XLVI (Autumn 1940), 195–207.

"The Vigilant Sentinel," tr. by Angel Flores and Joseph Liss, in Angel Flores (ed.), *Spanish Drama.* New York: Bantam Books, 1962, pp. 19–31.

—ANGEL FLORES

THE INGENIOUS GENTLEMAN,
DON QUIXOTE DE LA MANCHA

"1 hope your Don Quixote *will not be too portable, i.e., that not too much of it will be cut." Such was the advice of a friend to the editor of the present volume. In the case of a work like this there is certainly cause for apprehension when a condensation of any sort is undertaken.* Don Quixote *is not only the first and greatest novel, it is also one of the longest ever written—half a million words or more. One hardly expects to find the same high level of creative achievement maintained throughout in a tale of that length; there are bound to be weaker and sometimes more or less irrelevant passages which it would seem might well be dispensed with; but when one gets down to the actual business of deciding what is to go and what is to be retained, one discovers that the problem is by no means an easy one.*

Take, for example, the interpolated novelas *in Part I. What is to be done with them? Cervantes has frequently been criticized in the past for having included them. He appears to have done so out of a lack of confidence in the new form, the new type of hero and story that he was inventing, feeling that the adventures of the knight and his squire would not in themselves be sufficient to sustain the interest. For this reason he deemed it best to introduce a few episodes of a more conventional kind, modeled after the Italian* novella *or the pastoral romance that was so popular at the time. His earliest readers, however, did not bear out the author's judgment; they wanted more of Don Quixote and Sancho and were willing to do without the novelettes, a lesson*

41

which Cervantes took to heart when he came to write
Part II (see Part II, Chapter III).

And yet if one looks closely one will perceive that
even in such passages as these something new has been
added. By way of illustration, the tale commonly known
in English as "The Curious Impertinent" may be regarded as a rather boring and distracting imitation of
the Italians that had better have been omitted since it
bears no relation to the plot of the novel as a whole; but
is this the truth?

The eighteenth-century German Romantics did not
feel that way about it; for them "El Curioso Impertinente" was a miniature Don Quixote, dealing with the
same metaphysical theme: the audacious attempt to
penetrate the wall of illusion (appearances) and bring
down to earth the heaven of the ideal, the ultimate real.
And there is the contemporary French Cervantist Jean
Cassou, who declares that this story "for narrative power
and psychological depth is one of the marvels of universal art" (see his paper, "An Introduction to Cervantes,"
in Cervantes Across the Centuries, pp. 3-31).

The fact of the matter is that, putting aside all metaphysical considerations and speaking only from the psychological point of view, this interlude strikes a modern
note that is not sounded by any of Cervantes' predeces-
sors in the field of fiction. Is an editor justified, then, in
leaving it out? I believe that he is, if he takes into account the taste in the matter that most readers have
manifested, especially those that prefer the broader,
rollicking humor of Part I to the more subtle and profound second part; they are likely to view the story as a
somewhat irritating intrusion that merely holds up the
action. Perhaps, after all, this is an item for the connois-
seur or the student who would plumb the depths of
Cervantes' mind and art.

In any event, this will serve to give an idea of the kind of problem with which the editor has had to deal. Not all are as difficult as the one just cited, but each calls for careful thought, and the Cervantes lover, steeped in Don Quixote, *will understandably be loath to see any portion of the book omitted.*

By way of contrast, take the romance in the latter chapters of Part I, which involves the two pairs of lovers. It is more than a little trite and bookish in flavor with complications that are finally resolved in a highly unconvincing deus ex machina *fashion. This entire episode could, I think, be dropped without loss if it were not so interwoven with the main plot. I have accordingly condensed it insofar as possible, keeping only so much of it as was necessary.*

The incident (also in Part I) of the shepherd who died of unrequited love may appear at first sight simply to be a working over of the Arcadian theme for the sake of relief as the author conceived it, but in the speech which the "cruel" maid delivers from the mountainside (Chapter XIV*) anyone familiar with the pastoral novel of the period will at once recognize a difference. Here again is the modern attitude, later to be expressed by Madame de La Fayette and later still by Ibsen, Shaw, and others: the right of woman to call her soul her own. For this reason I have retained Marcela's allocution as well as Antonio's ballad (Chapter* XI*), which occurs in the same episode and is one of the best examples of Cervantes' versification to be found in the* Don Quixote. *The rest of the passage has been summarized.*

The captive's story (Part I, Chapters XXXIX-XLI*) I have kept, but condensed, not only for its autobiographic interest but because it happens to be a good story—I can almost see Hollywood doing it—and affords an unusual picture of the life of the times. On the other hand,*

*I have had no scruple about deleting the goatherd's
meandering tale at the end of Part I.*

*It is when an editor bent upon condensation comes to
the magnificent second part that his troubles really begin.
Cervantes is now no longer feeling his way as he often
does in Part I. There is a great deal that he wants to
say, he knows what it is, and in spite of his apparent
discursiveness and divagations he hews to the line—at
least until Chapter LIX is reached, from which point on
he is distracted by thoughts of Avellaneda and the latter's spurious sequel. In the first fifty-eight chapters
there is scarcely an incident that may be said to be
irrelevant to the author's broad design, and selection
becomes an increasingly arduous and perilous task.*

*It is, nevertheless, one that must be accomplished
somehow; and I found that the best way to set
about it was to decide first of all upon those passages
that, for the sake of the major theme, must at all costs
be retained. The account of Sancho and his "government" is one of these, the visit to the Cave of Montesinos is another. Then there are such well-known and
delightful incidents as the conversation between Sancho
Panza and his wife Teresa with regard to their daughter's becoming a countess (Chapter V) and the "flight"
of Don Quixote and Sancho on the "winged" steed
Clavileño (Chapter XLI)—these, obviously, are not to be
sacrificed.*

*If anything in Part II is to be omitted or curtailed, it
would seem that it might be the account of the cruel
and foolish jokes that are played on Don Quixote by the
ducal pair who are his hosts; though even here one must
leave enough to show the author's intent. Some of the
adventures resembling those in Part I, such as that of
the Parliament of Death (Chapter XI) and the enchanted
bark (Chapter XXIX), are also less essential, but the en-*

counter with the lions (Chapter XVII) and the braying adventure (Chapter XXV) are quite too good to lose.

The expanded episode of Camacho's wedding (Chapters XIX-XXI) is another that to my way of thinking is of minor interest and importance. As for the meeting between the Knight of the Mournful Countenance and the Knight of the Green-colored Greatcoat (Chapters XVI-XVIII), it has a certain historical-sociological interest as depicting the good burgher, l'honnête homme, of the period in confrontation with the visionary idealist, but, again, it possibly is better left to the one who would delve more deeply into the meaning of the tale.

Meanwhile, in both parts of the book, some of the best things to be met with are those indescribably droll conversations between master and man on the subject of knighthood, and the inclusion of these chapters is, I assume, not open to question. In general, I have been at pains to preserve the views which Cervantes puts into the mouth of Don Quixote but which we may take to be his own, on poetry, the novel, the theater of his day, the life of a man of letters, the nature of human existence and what we call the real, and the destiny of man in a world of illusion.

What I have tried to do, in short, for readers of the Portable is to present not so much an "abridged" as an essential version of Don Quixote, one that aims at giving insofar as possible all that is best, most significant, and indispensable in this, one of the richest works in our entire cultural patrimony. An abridgment too often means a mutilation, and that was what I wished to avoid. Above all, I have sought to preserve the line of the story, which is a good deal more than plot and which runs all the way through it from beginning to end. If I have accomplished this objective, I shall feel that I have not wholly failed in my task.

The text here presented is taken from my version of the complete Don Quixote, *published by The Viking Press in 1949. It is based upon the first Spanish editions of 1605 (Part I) and 1615 (Part II), as reproduced in the* Obras Completas *of Cervantes edited by Rudolph Schevill and Adolfo Bonilla (Don Quixote de la Mancha, Tomos I-IV, Madrid, 1928-41). For the other editors, commentators, lexicographers, etc., whom I have consulted—special mention should be made of Francisco Rodríguez Marín—the interested student may be referred to the Introduction which I wrote for the full work, in which I set forth the considerations which led me to feel that a new rendering was needed and stated the principles by which I was governed in my attempt.*

As a translator I have endeavored always to steer a middle course between an affectedly archaic style and an offensively modern one, feeling as I did that either would be a betrayal of the author. I have done my best to follow Cervantes' precept, "Toda afectación es mala" —"All affectation is bad." It is chiefly in connection with the punctuation, paragraphing, dialogue transitions, and, to a degree, the sentence structure that I have taken certain liberties in consonance with the spirit of the text, which I deemed necessary in the interest of a higher fidelity to my author.

As to the notes, which appear at the end of this volume, they are not intended for scholars or special students but for the general reading public. For this reason they have been held down to a minimum, and I have tried to keep them as concise as possible. No attempt has been made to trace all the references and parallels to the literature of chivalry; instead, my concern has been with the aspects of daily life in Cervantes' time, with folk customs, traditions, proverbs, and the like.

For the benefit of those who may find them to be of help I have inserted subtitles of my own here and there to mark the broad divisions of the story. The chapter titles, in full or condensed, are Cervantes'. And for readers who may wish to refer to the complete text, in my own or some other translation or in the original Spanish, I have indicated the chapter numbers in connection with each passage. Where omissions have been made, this is also indicated and a summary of the omitted portions given.

PART ONE

Prologue

IDLING READER, you may believe me when I tell you that I should have liked this book, which is the child of my brain, to be the fairest, the sprightliest, and the cleverest that could be imagined; but I have not been able to contravene the law of nature which would have it that like begets like. And so, what was to be expected of a sterile and uncultivated wit such as that which I possess if not an offspring that was dried up, shriveled, and eccentric: a story filled with thoughts that never occurred to anyone else, of a sort that might be engendered in a prison where every annoyance has its home and every mournful sound its habitation? [1] Peace and tranquillity, the pleasures of the countryside, the serenity of the heavens, the murmur of fountains, and ease of mind can do much toward causing the most unproductive of muses to become fecund and bring forth progeny that will be the marvel and delight of mankind.

It sometimes happens that a father has an ugly son with no redeeming grace whatever, yet love will draw

48

a veil over the parental eyes which then behold only cleverness and beauty in place of defects, and in speaking to his friends he will make those defects out to be the signs of comeliness and intellect. I, however, who am but Don Quixote's stepfather, have no desire to go with the current of custom, nor would I, dearest reader, beseech you with tears in my eyes as others do to pardon or overlook the faults you discover in this book; you are neither relative nor friend but may call your soul your own and exercise your free judgment. You are in your own house where you are master as the king is of his taxes, for you are familiar with the saying, "Under my cloak I kill the king." [2] All of which exempts and frees you from any kind of respect or obligation; you may say of this story whatever you choose without fear of being slandered for an ill opinion any more than you will be rewarded for a good one.

I should like to bring you the tale unadulterated and unadorned, stripped of the usual prologue and the endless string of sonnets, epigrams, and eulogies such as are commonly found at the beginning of books. For I may tell you that, although I expended no little labor upon the work itself, I have found no task more difficult than the composition of this preface which you are now reading. Many times I took up my pen and many times I laid it down again, not knowing what to write. On one occasion when I was thus in suspense, paper before me, pen over my ear, elbow on the table, and chin in hand, a very clever friend of mine came in. Seeing me lost in thought, he inquired as to the reason, and I made no effort to conceal from him the fact that my mind was on the preface which I had to write for the story of Don Quixote, and that it was giving me so much trouble that I had about decided not to write any at all and to abandon entirely the idea of publishing the exploits of so noble a knight.

"How," I said to him, "can you expect me not to be concerned over what that venerable legislator, the Public, will say when it sees me, at my age, after all these years of silent slumber, coming out with a tale that is as dried as a rush, a stranger to invention, paltry in style, impoverished in content, and wholly lacking in learning and wisdom, without marginal citations or notes at the end of the book when other works of this sort, even though they be fabulous and profane, are so packed with maxims from Aristotle and Plato and the whole crowd of philosophers as to fill the reader with admiration and lead him to regard the author as a well read, learned, and eloquent individual? Not to speak of the citations from Holy Writ! You would think they were at the very least so many St. Thomases and other doctors of the Church; for they are so adroit at maintaining a solemn face that, having portrayed in one line a distracted lover, in the next they will give you a nice little Christian sermon that is a joy and a privilege to hear and read.

"All this my book will lack, for I have no citations for the margins, no notes for the end. To tell the truth, I do not even know who the authors are to whom I am indebted, and so am unable to follow the example of all the others by listing them alphabetically at the beginning, starting with Aristotle and closing with Xenophon, or, perhaps, with Zoilus or Zeuxis, notwithstanding the fact that the former was a snarling critic, the latter a painter. This work will also be found lacking in prefatory sonnets by dukes, marquises, counts, bishops, ladies, and poets of great renown; although if I were to ask two or three colleagues of mine, they would supply the deficiency by furnishing me with productions that could not be equaled by the authors of most repute in all Spain.

"In short, my friend," I went on, "I am resolved that Señor Don Quixote shall remain buried in the archives of La Mancha until Heaven shall provide him with someone to deck him out with all the ornaments that he lacks; for I find myself incapable of remedying the situation, being possessed of little learning or aptitude, and I am, moreover, extremely lazy when it comes to hunting up authors who will say for me what I am unable to say for myself. And if I am in a state of suspense and my thoughts are woolgathering, you will find a sufficient explanation in what I have just told you."

Hearing this, my friend struck his forehead with the palm of his hand and burst into a loud laugh.

"In the name of God, brother," he said, "you have just deprived me of an illusion. I have known you for a long time, and I have always taken you to be clever and prudent in all your actions; but I now perceive that you are as far from all that as Heaven from the earth. How is it that things of so little moment and so easily remedied can worry and perplex a mind as mature as yours and ordinarily so well adapted to break down and trample underfoot far greater obstacles? I give you my word, this does not come from any lack of cleverness on your part, but rather from excessive indolence and a lack of experience. Do you ask for proof of what I say? Then pay attention closely and in the blink of an eye you shall see how I am going to solve all your difficulties and supply all those things the want of which, so you tell me, is keeping you in suspense, as a result of which you hesitate to publish the history of that famous Don Quixote of yours, the light and mirror of all knight-errantry."

"Tell me, then," I replied, "how you propose to go about curing my diffidence and bringing clarity out of the chaos and confusion of my mind?"

"Take that first matter," he continued, "of the sonnets, epigrams, or eulogies, which should bear the names of grave and titled personages: you can remedy that by taking a little trouble and composing the pieces yourself, and afterward you can baptize them with any name you see fit, fathering them on Prester John of the Indies or the Emperor of Trebizond, for I have heard tell that they were famous poets; and supposing they were not and that a few pedants and bachelors of arts should go around muttering behind your back that it is not so, you should not give so much as a pair of maravedis for all their carping, since even though they make you out to be a liar, they are not going to cut off the hand that put these things on paper.

"As for marginal citations and authors in whom you may find maxims and sayings that you may put in your story, you have but to make use of those scraps of Latin that you know by heart or can look up without too much bother. Thus, when you come to treat of liberty and slavery, jot down:

Non bene pro toto libertas venditur auro.[3]

And then in the margin you will cite Horace or whoever it was that said it. If the subject is death, come up with:

Pallida mors aequo pulsat pede pauperum tabernas
Regumque turres.[4]

If it is friendship or the love that God commands us to show our enemies, then is the time to fall back on the Scriptures, which you can do by putting yourself out very little; you have but to quote the words of God himself:

Ego autem dico vobis: diligite inimicos vestros.[5]

If it is evil thoughts, lose no time in turning to the Gospels:

De corde exeunt cogitationes malae.[6]

If it is the instability of friends, here is Cato for you with a distich:

Donec eris felix multos numerabis amicos;
Tempora si fuerint nubila, solus eris.[7]

With these odds and ends of Latin and others of the same sort, you can cause yourself to be taken for a grammarian, although I must say that is no great honor or advantage these days.

"So far as notes at the end of the book are concerned, you may safely go about it in this manner: let us suppose that you mentioned some giant, Goliath let us say; with this one allusion which costs you little or nothing, you have a fine note which you may set down as follows: *The giant Golias or Goliath. This was a Philistine whom the shepherd David slew with a mighty cast from his slingshot in the valley of Terebinth,*[8] *according to what we read in the Book of Kings,* chapter so-and-so where you find it written.

"In addition to this, by way of showing that you are a learned humanist and a cosmographer, contrive to bring into your story the name of the River Tagus, and there you are with another great little note: *The River Tagus was so called after a king of Spain; it rises in such and such a place and empties into the ocean, washing the walls of the famous city of Lisbon; it is supposed to have golden sands,* etc. If it is robbers, I will let you have the story of Cacus,[9] which I know by heart. If it is loose women, there is the Bishop of Mondoñedo,[10] who will lend you Lamia, Laïs, and Flora, an allusion that will do you great credit. If the subject is cruelty, Ovid will supply you with Medea; or if it is enchantresses and witches, Homer has Calypso and Vergil Circe. If it is valorous captains, Julius Caesar will lend you himself, in his *Commentaries,* and Plutarch will furnish a thousand Alexanders. If it is loves, with the ounce or two of Tuscan that you know you may make the acquaintance of Leon the Hebrew,[11] who will satisfy you to your heart's content. And in case you do not care to go abroad, here in your own house you have Fonseca's *Of the Love of God,*[12] where you will encounter in condensed form all that the most imaginative person could wish upon this subject. The short of the matter is, you have but to allude to these names or touch upon those stories that I have mentioned and leave to me the business of the notes and citations; I will guarantee you enough to fill the margins and four whole sheets at the back.

"And now we come to the list of authors cited, such as other works contain but in which your own is lacking. Here again the remedy is an easy one; you have but to look up some book that has them all, from A to Z as you were saying, and transfer the entire list as it stands. What if the imposition is plain for all to see? You have little need to refer to them, and so it does not matter; and some may be so simple-minded as to believe that you have drawn upon them all in your simple unpretentious little story. If it serves no other purpose, this imposing list of authors will at least give your book an unlooked-for air of authority. What is more, no one is going to put himself to the trouble of verifying your references .o see whether or not you have followed all these authors, since it will not be worth his pains to do so.

"This is especially true in view of the fact that your book stands in no need of all these things whose absence you lament; for the entire work is an attack upon the books of chivalry of which Aristotle never dreamed, of which St. Basil has nothing to say, and of which Cicero had no knowledge; nor do the fine points of truth or the observations of astrology have anything to do with its fanciful absurdities; geometrical measurements, likewise, and rhetorical argumentations serve for nothing here; you have no sermon to preach to anyone by mingling the human with the divine, a kind of motley in which no Christian intellect should be willing to clothe itself.

"All that you have to do is to make proper use of imitation in what you write, and the more perfect the imitation the better will your writing be. Inasmuch as you have no other object in view than that of overthrowing the authority and prestige which books of chivalry enjoy in the world at large and among the vulgar, there is no reason why you should go begging maxims of the philosophers, counsels of Holy Writ, fables of the poets, orations of the rhetoricians, or miracles of the saints; see to it, rather, that your style flows along smoothly, pleasingly, and sonorously, and that your words are the proper ones, meaningful and well placed, expressive of your intention in setting them down and of what you wish to say, without any intricacy or obscurity.

"Let it be your aim that, by reading your story, the melancholy may be moved to laughter and the cheerful man made merrier still; let the simple not be bored, but may the clever admire your originality; let the grave ones not despise you, but let the prudent praise you. And keep in mind, above all, your purpose, which is that of undermining the ill-founded edifice that is constituted by those books of chivalry, so abhorred by many but admired by many more; if you succeed in attaining it, you will have accomplished no little."

Listening in profound silence to what my friend had to say, I was so impressed by his reasoning that, with no thought of questioning them, I decided to make use of his arguments in composing this prologue. Here, gentle reader, you will perceive my friend's cleverness, my own good fortune in coming upon such a counselor at a time when I needed him so badly, and the profit which you yourselves are to have in finding so sincere and straightforward an account of the famous Don Quixote de la Mancha, who is held by the inhabitants of the Campo de Montiel region[13] to have been the most chaste lover and the most valiant knight that had been seen in those parts for many a year. I have no desire to enlarge upon the service I am rendering you in bringing you the story of so notable and honored a gentleman; I merely would have you thank me for having made you acquainted with the famous Sancho Panza, his squire, in whom, to my mind, is to be found an epitome of all the squires and their drolleries scattered here and there throughout the pages of those vain and empty books of chivalry. And with this, may God give you health, and may He be not unmindful of me as well. VALE.

The Prologue is followed by a number of sets of burlesque verses, parodies on the poetical tributes to the author and his work, which commonly served to preface a book in Cervantes' time. With their involved humor and recondite allusions, these pieces are hardly to the taste of the modern reader.

Don Quixote's Background and First Sally

(CHAPTERS I-VI)

CHAPTER I. *Which treats of the station in life and the pursuits of the famous gentleman, Don Quixote de la Mancha.*

IN A VILLAGE [1] of La Mancha the name of which I have no desire to recall, there lived not so long ago one of those gentlemen who always have a lance in the rack, an ancient buckler, a skinny nag, and a greyhound for the chase. A stew with more beef than mutton in it, chopped meat for his evening meal, scraps for a Saturday, lentils on Friday, and a young pigeon as a special delicacy for Sunday, went to account for three-quarters of his income. The rest of it he laid out on a broadcloth greatcoat and velvet stockings for feast days, with slippers to match, while the other days of the week he cut a figure in a suit of the finest homespun. Living with him were a housekeeper in her forties, a niece who was not yet twenty, and a lad of the field and market place who saddled his horse for him and wielded the pruning knife.

This gentleman of ours was close on to fifty, of a robust constitution but with little flesh on his bones and a face that was lean and gaunt. He was noted for his early rising, being very fond of the hunt. They will try to tell you that his surname was Quijada or Quesada—there is some difference of opinion among those who have written on the subject—but according to the most likely conjectures we are to understand that it was really Quejana. But all this means very little so far as our story is concerned, providing that in the telling of it we do not depart one iota from the truth.

You may know, then, that the aforesaid gentleman, on those occasions when he was at leisure, which was most of the year around, was in the habit of reading books of chivalry with such pleasure and devotion as to lead him almost wholly to forget the life of a hunter and even the administration of his estate. So great was his curiosity and infatuation in this regard that he even sold many acres of tillable land in order to be able to buy and read the books that he loved, and he would carry home with him as many of them as he could obtain.

Of all those that he thus devoured none pleased him so well as the ones that had been composed by the famous Feliciano de Silva,[2] whose lucid prose style and involved conceits were as precious to him as pearls; especially when he came to read those tales of love and amorous challenges that are to be met with in many places, such a passage as the following, for example: "The reason of the unreason that afflicts my reason, in such a manner weakens my reason that I with reason lament me of your comeliness." And he was similarly affected when his eyes fell upon such lines as these: ". . . the high Heaven of your divinity divinely fortifies you with the stars and renders you deserving of that desert your greatness doth deserve."

The poor fellow used to lie awake nights in an effort to disentangle the meaning and make sense out of passages such as these, although Aristotle himself would not have been able to understand them, even if he had been resurrected for that sole purpose. He was not at ease in his mind over those wounds that Don Belianís[3] gave and received; for no matter how great the surgeons who treated him, the poor fellow must have been left with his face and his entire body covered with marks and scars. Nevertheless, he was grateful to the author for closing the book with the promise of an interminable adventure to come; many a time he was tempted to take up his pen and literally finish the tale as had been promised, and he undoubtedly would have done so, and would have succeeded at it very well, if his thoughts had not been constantly occupied with other things of greater moment.

He often talked it over with the village curate, who was a learned man, a graduate of Sigüenza,[4] and they would hold long discussions as to who had been the better knight, Palmerin of England or Amadis of Gaul; but Master Nicholas, the barber of the same village, was in the habit of saying that no one could come up to the Knight of Phoebus, and that if anyone *could* compare with him it was Don Galaor, brother of Amadis of Gaul, for Galaor was ready for anything—he was none of your finical knights, who went around whimpering as his brother did, and in point of valor he did not lag behind him.

In short, our gentleman became so immersed in his reading that he spent whole nights from sundown to sunup and his days from dawn to dusk in poring over his books, until, finally, from so little sleeping and so much reading, his brain dried up and he went completely out of his mind. He had filled his imagination with everything that he had read, with enchantments, knightly encounters, battles, challenges, wounds, with tales of love and its torments, and all sorts of impossible things, and as a result had come to believe that all these fictitious happenings were true; they were more real to him than anything else in the world. He would remark that the Cid Ruy Díaz had been a very good knight, but there was no comparison between him and the Knight of the Flaming Sword,[5] who with a single backward stroke had cut in half two fierce and monstrous giants. He preferred Bernardo del Carpio, who at Roncesvalles had slain Roland despite the charm the latter bore, availing himself of the stratagem which Hercules employed when he strangled Antaeus, the son of Earth, in his arms.

He had much good to say for Morgante who, though he belonged to the haughty, overbearing race of giants, was of an affable disposition and well brought up. But, above all, he cherished an admiration for Rinaldo of Montalbán,[6] especially as he beheld him sallying forth from his castle to rob all those that crossed his path, or when he thought of him overseas stealing the image of Mohammed which, so the story has it, was all of gold. And he would have liked very well to have had his fill of kicking that traitor Galalón,[7] a privilege for which he would have given his housekeeper with his niece thrown into the bargain.

At last, when his wits were gone beyond repair, he came to conceive the strangest idea that ever occurred to any madman in this world. It now appeared to him fitting and necessary, in order to win a greater amount of honor for himself and serve his country at the same time, to become a knight-errant and roam the world on horseback, in a suit of armor; he would go in quest of adventures, by way of putting into practice all that he had read in his books; he would right every manner of wrong, placing himself in situations of the greatest peril such as would redound to the eternal glory of his name. As a reward for his valor and the might of his arm, the poor fellow could already see himself crowned Emperor of Trebizond at the very least; and so, carried away by the strange pleasure that he found in such thoughts as these, he at once set about putting his plan into effect.

The first thing he did was to burnish up some old pieces of armor, left him by his great-grandfather, which for ages had lain in a corner, moldering and forgotten. He polished and adjusted them as best he could, and then he noticed that one very important thing was lacking: there was no closed helmet, but only a morion, or visorless headpiece, with turned up brim of the kind foot soldiers wore. His ingenuity, however, enabled him to remedy this, and he proceeded to fashion out of cardboard a kind of half-helmet, which, when attached to the morion, gave the appearance of a whole one. True, when he went to see if it was strong enough to withstand a good slashing blow, he was somewhat disappointed; for when he drew his sword and gave it a couple of thrusts, he succeeded only in undoing a whole week's labor. The ease with which he had hewed it to bits disturbed him no little, and he decided to make it over. This time he placed a few strips of iron on the inside, and then, convinced that it was strong enough, refrained from putting it to any further test; instead, he adopted it then and there as the finest helmet ever made.

After this, he went out to have a look at his nag; and although the animal had more *cuartos,* or cracks, in its hoof than there are quarters in a real,[8] and more blemishes than Gonela's[9] steed which *tantum pellis et ossa fuit,*[10] it nonetheless looked to its master like a far better horse than Alexander's Bucephalus or the Babieca of the Cid. He spent all of four days in trying to think up a name for his mount; for—so he told himself—seeing that it belonged to so famous and worthy a knight, there was no reason why it should not have a name of equal renown. The kind of name he wanted was one that would at once indicate what the nag had been before it came to belong to a knight-errant and what its present status was; for it stood to reason that, when the master's wordly condition changed, his horse also ought to have a famous, high-sounding appellation, one suited to the new order of things and the new profession that it was to follow.

After he in his memory and imagination had made up, struck out, and discarded many names, now adding to and now subtracting from the list, he finally hit upon "Rocinante," a name that impressed him as being sonorous and at the same time indicative of what the steed had been when it was but a hack,[11] whereas now it was nothing other than the first and foremost of all the hacks in the world.

Having found a name for his horse that pleased his fancy, he then desired to do as much for himself, and this required another week, and by the end of that period he had made up his mind that he was henceforth to be known as Don Quixote,[12] which, as has been stated, has led the authors of this veracious history to assume that his real name must undoubtedly have been Quijada, and not Quesada as others would have it. But remembering that the valiant Amadis was not content to call himself that and nothing more, but added the name of his kingdom and fatherland that he might make it famous also, and thus came to take the name Amadis of Gaul, so our good knight chose to add his place of origin and become "Don Quixote de la Mancha"; for by this means, as he saw it, he was making very plain his lineage and was conferring honor upon his country by taking its name as his own.

And so, having polished up his armor and made the morion over into a closed helmet, and having given himself and his horse a name, he naturally found but one thing lacking still: he must seek out a lady of whom he could become enamored; for a knight-errant without a ladylove was like a tree without leaves or fruit, a body without a soul.

"If," he said to himself, "as a punishment for my sins' or by a stroke of fortune I should come upon some giant hereabouts, a thing that very commonly happens to knights-errant, and if I should slay him in a hand-to-hand encounter or perhaps cut him in two, or, finally, if I should vanquish and subdue him, would it not be well to have someone to whom I may send him as a present, in order that he, if he is living, may come in, fall upon his knees in front of my sweet lady, and say in a humble and submissive tone of voice, 'I, lady, am the giant Caraculiambro, lord of the island Malindrania, who has been overcome in single combat by that knight who never can be praised enough, Don Quixote de la Mancha, the same who sent me to present myself before your Grace that your Highness may dispose of me as you see fit'?"

Oh, how our good knight reveled in this speech, and more than ever when he came to think of the name that he should give his lady! As the story goes, there was a very good-looking farm girl who lived near by, with whom he had once been smitten, although it is generally believed that she never knew or suspected it. Her name was Aldonza Lorenzo, and it seemed to him that she was the one upon whom he should bestow the title of mistress of his thoughts. For her he wished a name that should not be incongruous with his own and that would convey the suggestion of a princess or a great lady; and, accordingly, he resolved to call her "Dulcinea del Toboso," she being a native of that place. A musical name to his ears, out of the ordinary and significant, like the others he had chosen for himself and his appurtenances.

CHAPTER II. *Which treats of the first sally that the ingenious Don Quixote made from his native heath.*

HAVING, then, made all these preparations, he did not wish to lose any time in putting his plan into effect, for he could not but blame himself for what the world was losing by his delay, so many were the wrongs that were to be righted, the grievances to be redressed, the abuses to be done away with, and the duties to be performed. Accordingly, without informing anyone of his intention and without letting anyone see him, he set out one morning before daybreak on one of those very hot days in July. Donning all his armor, mounting Rocinante, adjusting his ill-contrived helmet, bracing his shield on his arm, and taking up his lance, he sallied forth by the back gate of his stable yard into the open countryside. It was with great contentment and joy that he saw how easily he had made a beginning toward the fulfillment of his desire.

No sooner was he out on the plain, however, than a terrible thought assailed him, one that all but caused him to abandon the enterprise he had undertaken. This occurred when he suddenly remembered that he had never formally been dubbed a knight, and so, in accordance with the law of knighthood, was not permitted to bear arms against one who had a right to that title. And even if he had been, as a novice knight he would have had to wear white armor,[1] without any device on his shield, until he should have earned one by his exploits. These thoughts led him to waver in his purpose, but, madness prevailing over reason, he resolved to have himself knighted by the first person he met, as many others had done if what he had read in those books that he had at home was true. And so far as white armor was concerned, he would scour his own the first chance that offered until it shone whiter than any ermine. With this he became more tranquil and continued on his way, letting his horse take whatever path it chose, for he believed that therein lay the very essence of adventures.

And so we find our newly fledged adventurer jogging along and talking to himself. "Undoubtedly," he is saying, "in the days to come, when the true history of my famous deeds is published, the learned chronicler who records them, when he comes to describe my first sally so early in the morning, will put down something like this: 'No sooner had the rubicund Apollo spread over the face of the broad and spacious earth the gilded filaments of his beauteous locks, and no sooner had the little singing birds of painted plumage greeted with their sweet and mellifluous harmony the coming of the Dawn, who, leaving the soft couch of her jealous spouse, now showed herself to mortals at all the doors and balconies of the horizon that bounds La Mancha—no sooner had this happened than the famous knight, Don Quixote de la Mancha, forsaking his own downy bed and mounting his famous steed, Rocinante, fared forth and began riding over the ancient and famous Campo de Montiel.' " [2]

And this was the truth, for he was indeed riding over that stretch of plain.

"O happy age and happy century," he went on, "in which my famous exploits shall be published, exploits worthy of being engraved in bronze, sculptured in marble, and depicted in paintings for the benefit of posterity. O wise magician, whoever you be, to whom shall fall the task of chronicling this extraordinary history of mine! I beg of you not to forget my good Rocinante, eternal companion of my wayfarings and my wanderings."

Then, as though he really had been in love: "O Princess Dulcinea, lady of this captive heart! Much wrong have you done me in thus sending me forth with your reproaches and sternly commanding me not to appear in your beauteous presence. O lady, deign to be mindful of this your subject who endures so many woes for the love of you."

And so he went on, stringing together absurdities, all of a kind that his books had taught him, imitating insofar as he was able the language of their authors. He rode slowly, and the sun came up so swiftly and with so much heat that it would have been sufficient to melt his brains if he had had any. He had been on the road almost the entire day without anything happening that is worthy of being set down here; and he was on the verge of despair, for he wished to meet someone at once with whom he might try the valor of his good right arm. Certain authors say that his first adventure was that of Puerto Lápice, while others state that it was that of the windmills;³ but in this particular instance I am in a position to affirm what I have read in the annals of La Mancha; and that is to the effect that he went all that day until nightfall, when he and his hack found themselves tired to death and famished. Gazing all around him to see if he could discover some castle or shepherd's hut where he might take shelter and attend to his pressing needs, he caught sight of an inn⁴ not far off the road along which they were traveling, and this to him was like a star guiding him not merely to the gates, but rather, let us say, to the palace of redemption. Quickening his pace, he came up to it just as night was falling.

By chance there stood in the doorway two lasses of

the sort known as "of the district"; they were on their way to Seville in the company of some mule drivers who were spending the night in the inn. Now, everything that this adventurer of ours thought, saw, or imagined seemed to him to be directly out of one of the storybooks he had read, and so, when he caught sight of the inn, it at once became a castle with its four turrets and its pinnacles of gleaming silver, not to speak of the drawbridge and moat and all the other things that are commonly supposed to go with a castle. As he rode up to it, he accordingly reined in Rocinante and sat there waiting for a dwarf to appear upon the battlements and blow his trumpet by way of announcing the arrival of a knight. The dwarf, however, was slow in coming, and as Rocinante was anxious to reach the stable, Don Quixote drew up to the door of the hostelry and surveyed the two merry maidens, who to him were a pair of beauteous damsels or gracious ladies taking their ease at the castle gate.

And then a swineherd came along, engaged in rounding up his drove of hogs—for, without any apology, that is what they were. He gave a blast on his horn to bring them together, and this at once became for Don Quixote just what he wished it to be: some dwarf who was heralding his coming; and so it was with a vast deal of satisfaction that he presented himself before the ladies in question, who, upon beholding a man in full armor like this, with lance and buckler, were filled with fright and made as if to flee indoors. Realizing that they were afraid, Don Quixote raised his pasteboard visor and revealed his withered, dust-covered face.

"Do not flee, your Ladyships," he said to them in a courteous manner and gentle voice. "You need not fear that any wrong will be done you, for it is not in accordance with the order of knighthood which I profess to wrong anyone, much less such highborn damsels as your appearance shows you to be."

The girls looked at him, endeavoring to scan his face, which was half hidden by his ill-made visor. Never having heard women of their profession called damsels before, they were unable to restrain their laughter, at which Don Quixote took offense.

"Modesty," he observed, "well becomes those with the dower of beauty, and, moreover, laughter that has not good cause is a very foolish thing. But I do not say this to be discourteous or to hurt your feelings; my only desire is to serve you."

The ladies did not understand what he was talking about, but felt more than ever like laughing at our knight's unprepossessing figure. This increased his annoyance, and there is no telling what would have happened if at that moment the innkeeper had not come out. He was very fat and very peaceably inclined; but upon sighting this grotesque personage clad in bits of armor that were quite as oddly matched as were his bridle, lance, buckler, and corselet, mine host was not at all indisposed to join the lasses in their merriment. He was suspicious, however, of all this paraphernalia and decided that it would be better to keep a civil tongue in his head.

"If, Sir Knight," he said, "your Grace desires a lodging, aside from a bed—for there is none to be had in this inn—you will find all else that you may want in great abundance."

When Don Quixote saw how humble the governor of the castle was—for he took the innkeeper and his inn to be no less than that—he replied, "For me, Sir Castellan, anything will do, since

> *Arms are my only ornament,*
> *My only rest the fight,* etc."

The landlord thought that the knight had called him a castellan because he took him for one of those worthies of Castile,[5] whereas the truth was, he was an Andalusian from the beach of Sanlúcar, no less a thief than Cacus himself, and as full of tricks as a student or a page boy.

"In that case," he said,

> *"Your bed will be the solid rock,*
> *Your sleep: to watch all night.*[6]

This being so, you may be assured of finding beneath this roof enough to keep you awake for a whole year, to say nothing of a single night."

With this, he went up to hold the stirrup for Don Quixote, who encountered much difficulty in dismounting, not having broken his fast all day long. The knight then directed his host to take good care of the steed, as it was the best piece of horseflesh in all the world. The innkeeper looked it over, and it did not impress him as being half as good as Don Quixote had said it was. Having stabled the animal, he came back to see what his guest would have and found the latter being relieved of his armor by the damsels, who by now had made their peace with the new arrival. They had already removed his breastplate and backpiece but had no idea how they were going to open his gorget or get his improvised helmet off. That piece of armor had been tied on with green ribbons which it would be necessary to cut, since the knots could not be undone, but he would not hear of this, and so spent all the rest of that night with his headpiece in place, which gave him the weirdest, most laughable appearance that could be imagined.

Don Quixote fancied that these wenches who were assisting him must surely be the chatelaine and other ladies of the castle, and so proceeded to address them very gracefully and with much wit:

> *"Never was knight so served*
> *By any noble dame*
> *As was Don Quixote*
> *When from his village he came,*
> *With damsels to wait on his every need*
> *While princesses cared for his hack . . .*[7]

"By hack," he explained, "is meant my steed Rocinante, for that is his name, and mine is Don Quixote de la Mancha. I had no intention of revealing my identity until my exploits done in your service should have made me known to you; but the necessity of adapting to present circumstances that old ballad of Lancelot has led to your becoming acquainted with it prematurely. However, the time will come when your Ladyships shall command and I will obey and with the valor of my good right arm show you how eager I am to serve you."

The young women were not used to listening to speeches like this and had not a word to say, but merely asked him if he desired to eat anything.

"I could eat a bite of something, yes," replied Don Quixote. "Indeed, I feel that a little food would go very nicely just now."

He thereupon learned that, since it was Friday, there was nothing to be had in all the inn except a few portions of codfish, which in Castile is called *abadejo,* in Andalusia *bacalao,* in some places *curadillo,* and elsewhere *truchuella* or small trout. Would his Grace, then, have some small trout, seeing that was all there was that they could offer him?

"If there are enough of them," said Don Quixote, "they will take the place of a trout, for it is all one to me whether I am given in change eight reales or one piece of eight. What is more, those small trout may be like veal, which is better than beef, or like kid, which is better than goat. But however that may be, bring them on at once, for the weight and burden of arms is not to be borne without inner sustenance."

Placing the table at the door of the hostelry, in the open air, they brought the guest a portion of badly soaked and worse cooked codfish and a piece of bread as black and moldy as the suit of armor that he wore. It was a mirth-provoking sight to see him eat, for he still had his helmet on with his visor fastened, which made it impossible for him to put anything into his mouth with his hands, and so it was necessary for one of the girls to feed him. As for giving him anything to drink, that would have been out of the question if the innkeeper had not hollowed out a reed, placing one end in Don Quixote's mouth while through the other end he poured the wine. All this the knight bore very patiently rather than have them cut the ribbons of his helmet.

At this point a gelder of pigs approached the inn, announcing his arrival with four or five blasts on his horn, all of which confirmed Don Quixote in the belief that this was indeed a famous castle, for what was this if not music that they were playing for him? The fish was trout, the bread was of the finest, the wenches were ladies, and the innkeeper was the castellan. He was convinced that he had been right in his resolve to sally forth and roam the world at large, but there was one thing that still distressed him greatly, and that was the fact that he had not as yet been dubbed a knight; as he saw it, he could not legitimately engage in any adventure until he had received the order of knighthood.

CHAPTER III. *Of the amusing manner in which Don Quixote had himself dubbed a knight.*

WEARIED of his thoughts, Don Quixote lost no time over the scanty repast which the inn afforded him. When he had finished, he summoned the landlord and, taking him out to the stable, closed the doors and fell on his knees in front of him.

"Never, valiant knight," he said, "shall I arise from here until you have courteously granted me the boon I seek, one which will redound to your praise and to the good of the human race."

Seeing his guest at his feet and hearing him utter such words as these, the innkeeper could only stare at him in bewilderment, not knowing what to say or do. It was in vain that he entreated him to rise, for Don Quixote refused to do so until his request had been granted.

"I expected nothing less of your great magnificence, my lord," the latter then continued, "and so I may tell you that the boon I asked and which you have so generously conceded me is that tomorrow morning you dub me a knight. Until that time, in the chapel of this your castle, I will watch over my armor, and when morning comes, as I have said, that which I so desire shall then be done, in order that I may lawfully go to the four corners of the earth in quest of adventures and to succor the needy, which is the chivalrous duty of all knights-errant such as I who long to engage in deeds of high emprise."

The innkeeper, as we have said, was a sharp fellow. He already had a suspicion that his guest was not quite right in the head, and he was now convinced of it as he listened to such remarks as these. However, just for the sport of it, he determined to humor him; and so he went on to assure Don Quixote that he was fully justified in his request and that such a desire and purpose was only natural on the part of so distinguished a knight as his gallant bearing plainly showed him to be.

He himself, the landlord added, when he was a young man, had followed the same honorable calling. He had gone through various parts of the world seeking adventures, among the places he had visited being the Percheles of Málaga, the Isles of Riarán, the District of Seville, the Little Market Place of Segovia, the Olivera of Valencia, the Rondilla of Granada, the beach of Sanlúcar, the Horse Fountain of Cordova, the Small Taverns of Toledo, and numerous other localities[1] where his nimble feet and light fingers had found much exercise. He had done many wrongs, cheated many widows, ruined many maidens, and swindled not a few minors until he had finally come to be known in almost all the courts and tribunals that are to be found in the whole of Spain.

At last he had retired to his castle here, where he lived upon his own income and the property of others; and here it was that he received all knights-errant of whatever quality and condition, simply out of the great affection that he bore them and that they might share with him their possessions in payment of his good will. Unfortunately, in this castle there was no chapel where Don Quixote might keep watch over his arms, for the old chapel had been torn down to make way for a new one; but in case of necessity, he felt quite sure that such a vigil could be maintained anywhere, and for the present occasion the courtyard of the castle would do; and then in the morning, please God, the requisite ceremony could be performed and his guest be duly dubbed a knight, as much a knight as anyone ever was.

He then inquired if Don Quixote had any money on his person, and the latter replied that he had not a cent, for in all the storybooks he had never read of knights-errant carrying any. But the innkeeper told him he was mistaken on this point: supposing the authors of those stories had not set down the fact in black and white, that was because they did not deem it necessary to speak of things as indispensable as money and a clean shirt, and one was not to assume for that reason that those knights-errant of whom the books were so full did not have any. He looked upon it as an absolute certainty that they all had well-stuffed purses, that they might be prepared for any emergency; and they also carried shirts and a little box of ointment for healing the wounds that they received.

For when they had been wounded in combat on the plains and in desert places, there was not always someone at hand to treat them, unless they had some skilled enchanter for a friend who then would succor them, bringing to them through the air, upon a cloud, some damsel or dwarf bearing a vial of water of such virtue that one had but to taste a drop of it and at once his wounds were healed and he was as sound as if he had never received any.

But even if this was not the case, knights in times past saw to it that their squires were well provided with money and other necessities, such as lint and ointment for healing purposes; and if they had no squires—which happened very rarely—they themselves carried these objects in a pair of saddlebags very cleverly attached to their horses' croups in such a manner as to be scarcely noticeable, as if they held something of greater importance than that, for among the knights-errant saddlebags as a rule were not favored. Accordingly, he would advise the novice before him, and inasmuch as the latter was soon to be his godson, he might even command him, that henceforth he should not go without money and a supply of those things that have been mentioned, as he would find that they came in useful at a time when he least expected it.

Don Quixote promised to follow his host's advice punctiliously; and so it was arranged that he should watch his armor in a large barnyard at one side of the inn. He gathered up all the pieces, placed them in a horse trough that stood near the well, and, bracing his shield on his arm, took up his lance and with stately demeanor began pacing up and down in front of the trough even as night was closing in.

The innkeeper informed his other guests of what was going on, of Don Quixote's vigil and his expectation of being dubbed a knight; and, marveling greatly at so extraordinary a variety of madness, they all went out to see for themselves and stood there watching from a distance. For a while the knight-to-be, with tranquil mien, would merely walk up and down; then, leaning on his lance, he would pause to survey his armor, gazing fixedly at it for a considerable length of time. As has been said, it was night now, but the brightness of the moon, which well might rival that of Him who lent it, was such that everything the novice knight did was plainly visible to all.

At this point one of the mule drivers who were stopping at the inn came out to water his drove, and in order to do this it was necessary to remove the armor from the trough.

As he saw the man approaching, Don Quixote cried out to him, "O bold knight, whoever you may be, who thus would dare to lay hands upon the accouterments of the most valiant man of arms that ever girded on a sword, look well what you do and desist if you do not wish to pay with your life for your insolence!"

The muleteer gave no heed to these words—it would have been better for his own sake had he done so—but, taking it up by the straps, tossed the armor some distance from him. When he beheld this, Don Quixote rolled his eyes heavenward and with his thoughts apparently upon his Dulcinea exclaimed, "Succor, O lady mine, this vassal heart in this my first encounter; let not your favor and protection fail me in the peril in which for the first time I now find myself."

With these and other similar words, he loosed his buckler, grasped his lance in both his hands, and let the mule driver have such a blow on the head that the man fell to the ground stunned; and had it been followed by another one, he would have had no need of a surgeon to treat him. Having done this, Don Quixote gathered up his armor and resumed his pacing up and down with the same calm manner as before. Not long afterward, without knowing what had happened—for the first muleteer was still lying there unconscious—another came out with the same intention of watering his mules, and he too was about to remove the armor from the trough when the knight, without saying a word or asking favor of anyone, once more adjusted his buckler and raised his lance, and if he did not break the second mule driver's head to bits, he made more than three pieces of it by dividing it into quarters. At the sound of the fracas everybody in the inn came running out, among them the innkeeper; whereupon Don Quixote again lifted his buckler and laid his hand on his sword.

"O lady of beauty," he said, "strength and vigor of this fainting heart of mine! Now is the time to turn the eyes of your greatness upon this captive knight of yours who must face so formidable an adventure."

By this time he had worked himself up to such a pitch of anger that if all the mule drivers in the world had attacked him he would not have taken one step backward. The comrades of the wounded men, seeing the plight those two were in, now began showering stones on Don Quixote, who shielded himself as best he could with his buckler, although he did not dare stir from the trough for fear of leaving his armor unprotected. The landlord, meanwhile, kept calling to them to stop, for he had told them that this was a madman who would be sure to go free even though he killed them all. The knight was shouting louder than ever, calling them knaves and traitors. As for the lord of the castle, who allowed knights-errant to be treated in this fashion, he was a lowborn villain, and if he, Don Quixote, had but received the order of knighthood, he would make him pay for his treachery.

"As for you others, vile and filthy rabble, I take no account of you; you may stone me or come forward and attack me all you like; you shall see what the reward of your folly and insolence will be."

He spoke so vigorously and was so undaunted in bearing as to strike terror in those who would assail him; and for this reason, and owing also to the persuasions of the innkeeper, they ceased stoning him. He then permitted them to carry away the wounded, and went back to watching his armor with the same tranquil, unconcerned air that he had previously displayed.

The landlord was none too well pleased with these mad pranks on the part of his guest and determined to confer upon him that accursed order of knighthood before something else happened. Going up to him, he begged Don Quixote's pardon for the insolence which, without his knowledge, had been shown the knight by those of low degree. They, however, had been well punished for their impudence. As he had said, there was no chapel in this castle, but for that which remained to be done there was no need of any. According to what he had read of the ceremonial of the order, there was nothing to this business of being dubbed a knight except a slap on the neck and one across the shoulder, and that could be performed in the middle of a field as well as anywhere else. All that was required was for the knight-to-be to keep watch over his armor for a couple of hours, and Don Quixote had been at it more than four. The latter believed all this and announced that he was ready to obey and get the matter over with as speedily as possible. Once dubbed a knight, if he were attacked one more time, he did not think that he would leave a single person in the castle alive, save such as he might command be spared, at the bidding of his host and out of respect to him.

Thus warned, and fearful that it might occur, the castellan brought out the book in which he had jotted down the hay and barley for which the mule drivers owed him, and, accompanied by a lad bearing the butt of a candle and the two aforesaid damsels, he came up to where Don Quixote stood and commanded him to kneel. Reading from the account book—as if he had been saying a prayer—he raised his hand and, with the knight's own sword, gave him a good thwack upon the neck and another lusty one upon the shoulder, muttering all the while between his teeth. He then directed one of the ladies to gird on Don Quixote's sword, which she did with much gravity and composure; for it was all they could do to keep from laughing at every point of the ceremony, but the thought of the knight's prowess which they had already witnessed was sufficient to restrain their mirth.

"May God give your Grace much good fortune," said the worthy lady as she attached the blade, "and prosper you in battle."

Don Quixote thereupon inquired her name, for he desired to know to whom it was he was indebted for the favor he had just received, that he might share with her some of the honor which his strong right arm was sure to bring him. She replied very humbly that her name was Tolosa and that she was the daughter of a shoemaker, a native of Toledo who lived in the stalls of Sancho Bienaya.[2] To this the knight replied that she would do him a very great favor if from then on she would call herself Doña Tolosa, and she promised to do so. The other girl then helped him on with his spurs, and practically the same conversation was repeated. When asked her name, she stated that it was La Molinera and added that she was the daughter of a respectable miller of Antequera. Don Quixote likewise requested her to assume the "don" and become Doña Molinera and offered to render her further services and favors.

These unheard-of ceremonies having been dispatched in great haste, Don Quixote could scarcely wait to be astride his horse and sally forth on his quest for adventures. Saddling and mounting Rocinante, he embraced his host, thanking him for the favor of having dubbed him a knight and saying such strange things that it would be quite impossible to record them here. The innkeeper, who was only too glad to be rid of him, answered with a speech that was no less flowery, though somewhat shorter, and he did not so much as ask him for the price of a lodging, so glad was he to see him go.

CHAPTER IV. *Of what happened to our knight when he sallied forth from the inn.*

DAY was dawning when Don Quixote left the inn, so well satisfied with himself, so gay, so exhilarated, that the very girths of his steed all but burst with joy. But remembering the advice which his host had given him concerning the stock of necessary provisions that he should carry with him, especially money and shirts, he decided to turn back home and supply himself with whatever he needed, and with a squire as well; he had in mind a farmer who was a neighbor of his, a poor man and the father of a family but very well suited to fulfill the duties of squire to a man of arms. With this thought in mind he guided Rocinante toward the village once more, and that animal, realizing that he was homeward bound, began stepping out at so lively a gait that it seemed as if his feet barely touched the ground.

The knight had not gone far when from a hedge on his right hand he heard the sound of faint moans as of someone in distress.

"Thanks be to Heaven," he at once exclaimed, "for the favor it has shown me by providing me so soon with an opportunity to fulfill the obligations that I owe to my profession, a chance to pluck the fruit of my worthy desires. Those, undoubtedly, are the cries of someone in distress, who stands in need of my favor and assistance."

Turning Rocinante's head, he rode back to the place from which the cries appeared to be coming. Entering the wood, he had gone but a few paces when he saw a mare attached to an oak, while bound to another tree was a lad of fifteen or thereabouts, naked from the waist up. It was he who was uttering the cries, and not without reason, for there in front of him was a lusty farmer with a girdle who was giving him many lashes, each one accompanied by a reproof and a command, "Hold your tongue and keep your eyes open"; and the lad was saying, "I won't do it again, sir; by God's Passion, I won't do it again. I promise you that after this I'll take better care of the flock."

When he saw what was going on, Don Quixote was very angry. "Discourteous knight," he said, "it ill becomes you to strike one who is powerless to defend himself. Mount your steed and take your lance in hand"—for there was a lance leaning against the oak to which the mare was tied—"and I will show you what a coward you are."

The farmer, seeing before him this figure all clad in armor and brandishing a lance, decided that he was as good as done for. "Sir Knight," he said, speaking very mildly, "this lad that I am punishing here is my servant; he tends a flock of sheep which I have in these parts and he is so careless that every day one of them shows up missing. And when I punish him for his carelessness or his roguery, he says it is just because I am a miser and do not want to pay him the wages that I owe him, but I swear to God and upon my soul that he lies."

"It is you who lie, base lout," said Don Quixote, "and in my presence; and by the sun that gives us light, I am minded to run you through with this lance. Pay him and say no more about it, or else, by the God who rules us, I will make an end of you and annihilate you here and now. Release him at once."

The farmer hung his head and without a word untied his servant. Don Quixote then asked the boy how much his master owed him. For nine months' work, the lad told him, at seven reales the month. The knight did a little reckoning and found that this came to sixty-three reales; whereupon he ordered the farmer to pay over the money immediately, as he valued his life. The cowardly bumpkin replied that, facing death as he was and by the oath that he had sworn—he had not sworn any oath as yet—it did not amount to as much as that; for there were three pairs of shoes which he had given the lad that were to be deducted and taken into account, and a real for two blood-lettings when his servant was ill.

"That," said Don Quixote, "is all very well; but let the shoes and the blood-lettings go for the undeserved lashes which you have given him; if he has worn out the leather of the shoes that you paid for, you have taken the hide off his body, and if the barber[1] let a little blood for him when he was sick, you have done the same when he was well; and so far as that goes, he owes you nothing."

"But the trouble is, Sir Knight, that I have no money with me. Come along home with me, Andrés, and I will pay you real for real."

"I go home with him!" cried the lad. "Never in the world! No, sir, I would not even think of it; for once he has me alone he'll flay me like a St. Bartholomew."

"He will do nothing of the sort," said Don Quixote. "It is sufficient for me to command, and he out of respect will obey. Since he has sworn to me by the order of knighthood which he has received, I shall let him go free and I will guarantee that you will be paid."

"But look, your Grace," the lad remonstrated, "my master is no knight; he has never received any order of knighthood whatsoever. He is Juan Haldudo, a rich man and a resident of Quintanar."

"That makes little difference," declared Don Quixote, "for there may well be knights among the Haldudos,[2] all the more so in view of the fact that every man is the son of his works."

"That is true enough," said Andrés, "but this master of mine—of what works is he the son, seeing that he refuses me the pay for my sweat and labor?"

"I do not refuse you, brother Andrés," said the farmer. "Do me the favor of coming with me, and I swear to you by all the orders of knighthood that there are in this world to pay you, as I have said, real for real, and perfumed [3] at that."

"You can dispense with the perfume," said Don Quixote; "just give him the reales and I shall be satisfied. And see to it that you keep your oath, or by the one that I myself have sworn I shall return to seek you out and chastise you, and I shall find you though you be as well hidden as a lizard. In case you would like to know who it is that is giving you this command in order that you may feel the more obliged to comply with it, I may tell you that I am the valorous Don Quixote de la Mancha, righter of wrongs and injustices; and so, God be with you, and do not fail to do as you have promised, under that penalty that I have pronounced."

As he said this, he put spurs to Rocinante and was off. The farmer watched him go, and when he saw that Don Quixote was out of the wood and out of sight, he turned to his servant, Andrés.

"Come here, my son," he said. "I want to pay you what I owe you as that righter of wrongs has commanded me."

"Take my word for it," replied Andrés, "your Grace would do well to observe the command of that good knight—may he live a thousand years; for as he is valorous and a righteous judge, if you don't pay me then, by Roque,[4] he will come back and do just what he said!"

"And I will give you my word as well," said the farmer; "but seeing that I am so fond of you, I wish to increase the debt, that I may owe you all the more." And with this he seized the lad's arm and bound him to the tree again and flogged him within an inch of his life. "There, Master Andrés, you may call on that righter of wrongs if you like and you will see whether or not he rights this one. I do not think I have quite finished with you yet, for I have a good mind to flay you alive as you feared."

Finally, however, he unbound him and told him he might go look for that judge of his to carry out the sentence that had been pronounced. Andrés left, rather down in the mouth, swearing that he would indeed go look for the brave Don Quixote de la Mancha; he would relate to him everything that had happened, point by point, and the farmer would have to pay for it seven times over. But for all that, he went away weeping, and his master stood laughing at him.

Such was the manner in which the valorous knight righted this particular wrong. Don Quixote was quite content with the way everything had turned out; it seemed to him that he had made a very fortunate and noble beginning with his deeds of chivalry, and he was very well satisfied with himself as he jogged along in the direction of his native village, talking to himself in a low voice all the while.

"Well may'st thou call thyself fortunate today, above all other women on earth, O fairest of the fair, Dulcinea del Toboso! Seeing that it has fallen to thy lot to hold subject and submissive to thine every wish and pleasure so valiant and renowned a knight as Don Quixote de la Mancha is and shall be, who, as everyone knows, yesterday received the order of knighthood and this day has righted the greatest wrong and grievance that injustice ever conceived or cruelty ever perpetrated, by snatching the lash from the hand of the merciless foe, man who was so unreasonably flogging that tender child."

At this point he came to a road that forked off in four directions, and at once he thought of those crossroads where knights-errant would pause to consider which path they should take. By way of imitating them, he halted there for a while; and when he had given the subject much thought, he slackened Rocinante's rein and let the hack follow its inclination. The animal's first impulse was to make straight for its own stable. After they had gone a couple of miles or so Don Quixote caught sight of what appeared to be a great throng of people, who, as was afterward learned, were certain merchants of Toledo on their way to purchase silk at Murcia. There were six of them altogether with their sunshades, accompanied by four attendants on horseback and three mule drivers on foot.

No sooner had he sighted them than Don Quixote imagined that he was on the brink of some fresh adventure. He was eager to imitate those passages at arms of which he had read in his books, and here, so it seemed to him, was one made to order. And so, with bold and knightly bearing, he settled himself firmly in the stirrups, couched his lance, covered himself with his shield, and took up a position in the middle of the road, where he paused to wait for those other knights-errant (for such he took them to be) to come up to him. When they were near enough to see and hear plainly, Don Quixote raised his voice and made a haughty gesture.

"Let everyone," he cried, "stand where he is, unless everyone will confess that there is not in all the world a more beauteous damsel than the Empress of La Mancha, the peerless Dulcinea del Toboso."

Upon hearing these words and beholding the weird figure who uttered them, the merchants stopped short. From the knight's appearance and his speech they knew at once that they had to deal with a madman; but they were curious to know what was meant by that confession that was demanded of them, and one of their number who was somewhat of a jester and a very clever fellow raised his voice.

"Sir Knight," he said, "we do not know who this beauteous lady is of whom you speak. Show her to us, and if she is as beautiful as you say, then we will right willingly and without any compulsion confess the truth as you have asked of us."

"If I were to show her to you," replied Don Quixote, "what merit would there be in your confessing a truth so self-evident? The important thing is for you, without seeing her, to believe, confess, affirm, swear, and defend that truth. Otherwise, monstrous and arrogant creatures that you are, you shall do battle with me. Come on, then, one by one, as the order of knighthood prescribes; or all of you together, if you will have it so, as is the sorry custom with those of your breed. Come on, and I will await you here, for I am confident that my cause is just."

"Sir Knight," responded the merchant, "I beg your Grace, in the name of all the princes here present, in order that we may not have upon our consciences the burden of confessing a thing which we have never seen nor heard, and one, moreover, so prejudicial to the empresses and queens of Alcarria and Estremadura,[5] that your Grace will show us some portrait of this lady, even though it be no larger than a grain of wheat, for by the thread one comes to the ball of yarn; and with this we shall remain satisfied and assured, and your Grace will likewise be content and satisfied. The truth is, I believe that we are already so much of your way of thinking that though it should show her to be blind of one eye and distilling vermilion and brimstone from the other, nevertheless, to please your Grace, we would say in her behalf all that you desire."

"She distills nothing of the sort, infamous rabble!" shouted Don Quixote, for his wrath was kindling now. "I tell you, she does not distill what you say at all, but amber and civet wrapped in cotton;[6] and she is neither one-eyed nor hunchbacked but straighter than a spindle that comes from Guadarrama.[7] You shall pay for the great blasphemy which you have uttered against such a beauty as is my lady!"

Saying this, he came on with lowered lance against the one who had spoken, charging with such wrath and fury that if fortune had not caused Rocinante to stumble and fall in mid-career, things would have gone badly with the merchant and he would have paid for his insolent gibe. As it was, Don Quixote went rolling over the plain for some little distance, and when he tried to get to his feet, found that he was unable to do so, being too encumbered with his lance, shield, spurs, helmet, and the weight of that ancient suit of armor.

"Do not flee, cowardly ones," he cried even as he struggled to rise. "Stay, cravens, for it is not my fault but that of my steed that I am stretched out here."

One of the muleteers, who must have been an ill-natured lad, upon hearing the poor fallen knight speak so arrogantly, could not refrain from giving him an answer in the ribs. Going up to him, he took the knight's lance and broke it into bits, and then with a companion proceeded to belabor him so mercilessly that in spite of his armor they milled him like a hopper of wheat. The merchants called to them not to lay on so hard, saying that was enough and they should desist, but the mule driver by this time had warmed up to the sport and would not stop until he had vented his wrath, and, snatching up the broken pieces of the lance, he began hurling them at the wretched victim as he lay there on the ground. And through all this tempest of sticks that rained upon him Don Quixote never once closed his mouth nor ceased threatening Heaven and earth and these ruffians, for such he took them to be, who were thus mishandling him.

Finally the lad grew tired, and the merchants went their way with a good story to tell about the poor fellow who had had such a cudgeling. Finding himself alone, the knight endeavored to see if he could rise; but if this was a feat that he could not accomplish when he was sound and whole, how was he to achieve it when he had been thrashed and pounded to a pulp? Yet nonetheless he considered himself fortunate; for as he saw it, misfortunes such as this were common to knights-errant, and he put all the blame upon his horse; and if he was unable to rise, that was because his body was so bruised and battered all over.

CHAPTER V. *In which is continued the narrative of the misfortune that befell our knight.*

SEEING, then, that he was indeed unable to stir, he decided to fall back upon a favorite remedy of his, which was to think of some passage or other in his books; and as it happened, the one that he in his madness now recalled was the story of Baldwin[1] and the Marquis of Mantua, when Carloto left the former wounded upon the mountainside, a tale that is known to children, not unknown to young men, celebrated and believed in by the old, and, for all of that, not any truer than the miracles of Mohammed. Moreover, it impressed him as being especially suited to the straits in which he found himself; and, accordingly, with a great show of feeling, he began rolling and tossing on the ground as he feebly gasped out the lines which the wounded knight of the wood is supposed to have uttered:

> *"Where art thou, lady mine,*
> *That thou dost not grieve for my woe?*
> *Either thou art disloyal,*
> *Or my grief thou dost not know."*

He went on reciting the old ballad until he came to the following verses:

> *"O noble Marquis of Mantua,*
> *My uncle and liege lord true!"*

He had reached this point when down the road came a farmer of the same village, a neighbor of his, who had been to the mill with a load of wheat. Seeing a man lying there stretched out like that, he went up to him and inquired who he was and what was the trouble that caused him to utter such mournful complaints. Thinking that this must undoubtedly be his uncle, the Marquis of Mantua, Don Quixote did not answer but went on with his recitation of the ballad, giving an account of the Marquis' misfortunes and the amours of his wife and the emperor's son, exactly as the ballad has it.

The farmer was astounded at hearing all these absurdities, and after removing the knight's visor which had been battered to pieces by the blows it had received, the good man bathed the victim's face, only to discover, once the dust was off, that he knew him very well.

"Señor Quijana," he said (for such must have been Don Quixote's real name when he was in his right senses and before he had given up the life of a quiet country gentleman to become a knight-errant), "who is responsible for your Grace's being in such a plight as this?"

But the knight merely went on with his ballad in response to all the questions asked of him. Perceiving that it was impossible to obtain any information from him, the farmer as best he could relieved him of his breastplate and backpiece to see if he had any wounds, but there was no blood and no mark of any sort. He then tried to lift him from the ground, and with a great deal of effort finally managed to get him astride the ass, which appeared to be the easier mount for him. Gathering up the armor, including even the splinters from the lance, he made a bundle and tied it on Rocinante's back, and, taking the horse by the reins and the ass by the halter, he started out for the village. He was worried in his mind at hearing all the foolish things that Don Quixote said, and that individual himself was far from being at ease. Unable by reason of his bruises and his soreness to sit upright on the donkey, our knight-errant kept sighing to Heaven, which led the farmer to ask him once more what it was that ailed him.

It must have been the devil himself who caused him to remember those tales that seemed to fit his own case; for at this point he forgot all about Baldwin and recalled Abindarráez,[2] and how the governor of Antequera, Rodrigo de Narváez, had taken him prisoner and carried him off captive to his castle. Accordingly, when the countryman turned to inquire how he was and what was troubling him, Don Quixote replied with the very same words and phrases that the captive Abindarráez used in answering Rodrigo, just as he had read in the story *Diana* of Jorge de Montemayor, where it is all written down, applying them very aptly to the present circumstances as the farmer went along cursing his luck for having to listen to such a lot of nonsense. Realizing that his neighbor was quite mad, he made haste to reach the village that he might not have to be annoyed any longer by Don Quixote's tiresome harangue.

"Señor Don Rodrigo de Narváez," the knight was saying, "I may inform your Grace that this beautiful Jarifa of whom I speak is not the lovely Dulcinea del Toboso, in whose behalf I have done, am doing, and shall do the most famous deeds of chivalry that ever have been or will be seen in all the world."

"But, sir," replied the farmer, "sinner that I am, cannot your Grace see that I am not Don Rodrigo de Narváez nor the Marquis of Mantua, but Pedro Alonso, your neighbor? And your Grace is neither Baldwin nor Abindarráez but a respectable gentleman by the name of Señor Quijana."

"I know who I am," said Don Quxiote, "and who I may be, if I choose: not only those I have mentioned but all the Twelve Peers of France and the Nine Worthies as well; for the exploits of all of them together, or separately, cannot compare with mine."

With such talk as this they reached their destination just as night was falling; but the farmer decided to wait until it was a little darker in order that the badly battered gentleman might not be seen arriving in such a condition and mounted on an ass. When he thought the proper time had come, they entered the village and proceeded to Don Quixote's house, where they found everything in confusion. The curate and the barber were there, for they were great friends of the knight, and the housekeeper was speaking to them.

"Señor Licentiate Pero Pérez," she was saying, for that was the manner in which she addressed the curate, "what does your Grace think could have happened to my master? Three days now, and not a word of him, nor the hack, nor the buckler, nor the lance, nor the suit of armor. Ah, poor me! I am as certain as I am that I was born to die that it is those cursed books of chivalry he is always reading that have turned his head; for now that I recall, I have often heard him muttering to himself that he must become a knight-errant and go through the world in search of adventures. May such books as those be consigned to Satan and Barabbas, for they have sent to perdition the finest mind in all La Mancha."

The niece was of the same opinion. "I may tell you, Señor Master Nicholas," she said, for that was the barber's name, "that many times my uncle would sit reading those impious tales of misadventure for two whole days and nights at a stretch; and when he was through, he would toss the book aside, lay his hand on his sword, and begin slashing at the walls. When he was completely exhausted, he would tell us that he had just killed four giants as big as castle towers, while the sweat that poured off him was blood from the wounds that he had received in battle. He would then drink a big jug of cold water, after which he would be very calm and peaceful, saying that the water was the most precious liquid which the wise Esquife, a great magician and his friend, had brought to him. But I blame myself for everything. I should have advised your Worships of my uncle's nonsensical actions so that you could have done something about it by burning those damnable books of his before things came to such a pass; for he has many that ought to be burned as if they were heretics."

"I agree with you," said the curate, "and before to-morrow's sun has set there shall be a public *auto de fe,* and those works shall be condemned to the flames that they may not lead some other who reads them to follow the example of my good friend."

Don Quixote and the farmer overheard all this, and it was then that the latter came to understand the nature of his neighbor's affliction.

"Open the door, your Worships," the good man cried. "Open for Sir Baldwin and the Marquis of Mantua, who comes badly wounded, and for Señor Abindarráez the Moor whom the valiant Rodrigo de Narváez, governor of Antequera, brings captive."

At the sound of his voice they all ran out, recognizing at once friend, master, and uncle, who as yet was unable to get down off the donkey's back. They all ran up to embrace him.

"Wait, all of you," said Don Quixote, "for I am sorely wounded through fault of my steed. Bear me to my couch and summon, if it be possible, the wise Urganda to treat and care for my wounds."

"There!" exclaimed the housekeeper. "Plague take it! Did not my heart tell me right as to which foot my master limped on? To bed with your Grace at once, and we will take care of you without sending for that Urganda of yours. A curse, I say, and a hundred other curses, on those books of chivalry that have brought your Grace to this."

And so they carried him off to bed, but when they went to look for his wounds, they found none at all. He told them it was all the result of a great fall he had taken with Rocinante, his horse, while engaged in combating ten giants, the hugest and most insolent that were ever heard of in all the world.

"Tut, tut," said the curate. "So there are giants in the

dance now, are there? Then, by the sign of the cross, I'll have them burned before nightfall tomorrow."

They had a thousand questions to put to Don Quixote, but his only answer was that they should give him something to eat and let him sleep, for that was the most important thing of all; so they humored him in this. The curate then interrogated the farmer at great length concerning the conversation he had had with his neighbor. The peasant told him everything, all the absurd things their friend had said when he found him lying there and afterward on the way home, all of which made the licentiate more anxious than ever to do what he did the following day, when he summoned Master Nicholas and went with him to Don Quixote's house.

CHAPTER VI. *Of the great and diverting scrutiny which the curate and the barber made in the library of our ingenious gentleman.*

AS Don Quixote was still sleeping, the curate asked the niece for the keys to the room where those books responsible for all the trouble were, and she gave them to him very willingly. They all went in, the housekeeper too, and found more than a hundred large-sized volumes very well bound and a number of smaller ones. No sooner had the housekeeper laid eyes on them than she left the room, returning shortly with a basin of holy water and a sprinkling-pot.

"Here, Señor Licentiate," she said, "take this and sprinkle well, that no enchanter of the many these books contain may remain here to cast a spell on us for wishing to banish them from the world."

The curate could not but laugh at her simplicity as

he directed the barber to hand him the volumes one by one so that he might see what their subject matter was, since it was possible that there were some there that did not deserve a punishment by fire.

"No," said the niece, "you must not pardon any of them, for they are all to blame. It would be better to toss them out the window into the courtyard, make a heap of them, and then set fire to it; or else you can take them out to the stable yard and make a bonfire there where the smoke will not annoy anyone."

The housekeeper said the same thing, both of them being very anxious to witness the death of these innocents, but the curate would not hear of this until he had read the titles. The first that Master Nicholas handed him was *The Four Books of Amadis of Gaul.*

"There seems to be some doubt about this one," he said, "for according to what I have heard, it was the first romance of chivalry to be printed in Spain and is the beginning and origin of all the others; but for that very reason I think that we should condemn it to the flames without any mercy whatsoever as the work that supplied the dogmas for so vile a sect."

"No, my dear sir," said the barber, "for I have heard that it is better than all the other books of this sort that have been composed, and inasmuch as it is unique of its kind, it ought to be pardoned."

"True enough," said the curate, "and for that reason we will spare its life for the present. Let us see the one next to it."

"It is the *Exploits of Esplandián,*[1] legitimate son of Amadis of Gaul."

"Well, I must say," the curate replied, "that the father's merits are not to be set down to the credit of his offspring. Take it, Mistress Housekeeper; open that window and throw it out into the stable yard; it will make a beginning for that bonfire of ours."

The housekeeper complied with a great deal of satisfaction, and the worthy Esplandián went flying out into the yard to wait as patiently as anyone could wish for the threatened conflagration.

"Let's have some more," said the curate.

"This one coming next," said the barber, "is *Amadis of Greece;*[2] in fact, all those on this side, so far as I can see, are of the same lineage—descendants of Amadis."

"Then out with them all," was the curate's verdict; "for in order to be able to burn Queen Pintiquinestra and the shepherd Darinel and his elegies and the author's diabolic and involved conceits, I would set fire, along with them, to the father that bore me if he were going around in the guise of a knight-errant."

"I agree with you on that," said the barber.

"And I also," put in the niece.

"Well, since that is the way it is," said the housekeeper, "to the stable yard with them."

They handed her a whole stack of them, and, to avoid the stair, she dumped them out the window into the yard below.

"What is that tub there?" inquired the curate.

"That," replied the barber, "is *Don Olivante de Laura.*"[3]

"The author of this book," observed the curate, "was the same one who composed the *Garden of Flowers,* and, in truth, there is no telling which of the two is the truer, or, to put it better, less filled with lies; I can only say that this one is going out into the yard as an arrogant braggart."

"The next," announced the barber, "is *Florismarte of Hircania.*"[4]

"So, Señor Florismarte is with us, is he? Then, upon

my word, he is due in the yard this minute, in spite of his strange birth and imaginary adventures, for the stiffness and dryness of his style deserve nothing better. Out with him, and with the other as well, Mistress Housekeeper."

"With great pleasure," she said, and she gleefully carried out the order that had been given her.

"This," said the barber, "is *Platir the Knight*." [5]

"A very old book," said the curate, "and I find nothing in it deserving of clemency. Let it accompany the others without appeal."

Once again sentence was carried out. They opened another volume and saw that its title was *The Knight of the Cross*.[6]

"Out of respect for a name so holy as the one this book bears, one might think that its ignorance should be pardoned; but you know the old saying, 'The devil takes refuge behind the cross,' so to the fire with it."

"And this," said the barber, taking up yet another, "is *The Mirror of Chivalry*." [7]

"Ah, your Grace, I know you," said the curate. "Here we have Sir Rinaldo of Montalbán with his friends and companions, bigger thieves than Cacus, all of them, and the Twelve Peers along with the veracious historian Turpin.[8] To tell you the truth, I am inclined to sentence them to no more than perpetual banishment, seeing that they have about them something of the inventiveness of Matteo Boiardo,[9] and it was out of them, also, that the Christian poet Ludovico Ariosto wove his tapestry—and by the way, if I find him here speaking any language other than his own, I will show him no respect, but if I meet with him in his own tongue, I will place him upon my head." [10]

"Yes," said the barber, "I have him at home in Italian, but I can't understand him."

"It is just as well that you cannot," said the curate. "And for this reason we might pardon the Captain[11] if he had not brought him to Spain and made him over into a Castilian, depriving him thereby of much of his native strength, as happens with all those who would render books of verse into another language; for however much care they may take, and however much cleverness they may display, they can never equal the original. I say, in short, that this work and all those on French themes ought to be thrown into, or deposited in, some dry well until we make up our minds just what should be done with them, with the exception of one *Bernardo del Carpio*,[12] which is going the rounds, and another called *Roncesvalles*;[13] for these books, if they fall into my hands, shall be transferred to those of the housekeeper at once, and from there they go into the fire without any reprieve whatever."

The barber thoroughly approved of everything, being convinced that the curate was so good a Christian and so honest a man that he would not for anything in the world utter an untruth. Opening another book, he saw that it was *Palmerin de Oliva*, and next to it was one entitled *Palmerin of England*.[14]

The curate took one look at them. "Let this olive," he said, "be sliced to bits and burned until not even the ashes are left; but let this palm of England be guarded and preserved as something unique, and let there be made for it another case such as Alexander found among the spoils of Darius and set aside for the safekeeping of the works of the poet Homer. This book, my good friend, is deserving of respect for two reasons: first, because it is very good; and second, because it is reputed to have been composed by a wise and witty king of Portugal. All the adventures at Miraguarda's castle are excellently contrived, and the dialogue is clear and polished, the character and condition of the one who is speaking being observed with much propriety and understanding. And so, saving your good pleasure, Master Nicholas, I say that this book and *Amadis of Gaul* should be spared the flames, but all the others without more ado about it should perish."

"No, my friend," replied the barber, "for this one that I hold here in my hand is the famous *Don Belianís.*" [15]

"Well," said the curate, "the second, third, and fourth parts need a little rhubarb to purge them of an excess of bile, and we shall have to relieve them of that Castle of Fame and other worse follies; but let them have the benefit of the overseas clause,[16] and, providing they mend their ways, they shall be shown justice and mercy. Meanwhile, friend, take them home with you and see to it that no one reads them."

"I shall be glad to do so," the barber assented. And not wishing to tire himself any further by reading these romances of knighthood, he told the housekeeper to take all the big ones and throw them into the yard. This was not said to one who was deaf or dull-witted, but to one who took more pleasure in such a bonfire than in the largest and finest tapestry that she could have woven. Snatching them up seven or eight at a time, she started flinging them out the window; but taking too big an armful, she let one of them fall at the barber's feet. Curious to see what it was, he bent over and picked it up. It was *The History of the Famous Knight, Tirant lo Blanch.*[17]

"Well, bless my soul!" cried the curate, "if that isn't *Tirant lo Blanch!* Let me have it, my friend, for I cannot but remember that I have found in it a treasure of contentment and a mine of recreation. Here we have Don Quirieleison de Montalbán, that valiant knight, and his brother, Tomás de Montalbán, and the knight Fonseca, along with the combat which brave Tirant waged with the mastiff, as well as the witty sayings of the damsel Placerdemivida and the amours and deceits of the Empress, who was enamored of Hipólito, her squire. Tell the truth, friend, and admit that in the matter of style this is the best book in the world. Here knights eat and sleep and die in their beds and make their wills before they die and do other things that are never heard of in books of this kind. But for all that, I am telling you that the one who needlessly composed so nonsensical a work deserves to be sent to the galleys for the rest of his life. Take it along home with you and read it and see if what I say is not so."

"That I will," said the barber, "but what are we going to do with these little ones that are left?"

"Those, I take it," replied the curate, "are not romances but poetry." Opening one of them, he saw that it was Jorge de Montemayor's *Diana,* and being under the impression that all the rest were of the same sort, he added, "These do not deserve to be burned like the others, for they are not harmful like the books of chivalry; they are works of imagination such as may be read without detriment."

"Ah, but Señor!" exclaimed the niece, "your Grace should send them to be burned along with the rest; for I shouldn't wonder at all if my uncle, after he has been cured of this chivalry sickness, reading one of these books, should take it into his head to become a shepherd and go wandering through the woods and meadows singing and piping, or, what is worse, become a poet, which they say is an incurable disease and one that is very catching."

"The young lady is right," said the curate. "It would be just as well to remove this stumbling block and temptation out of our friend's way. And so, to begin with Montemayor's *Diana*,[18] I am of the opinion that it should not be burned, but rather that we should take out of it everything that has to do with that enchantress Felicia and her charmed potion, together with nearly all the longer verse pieces, while we willingly leave it the prose and the honor of being first and best among books of its kind."

"This one coming up now," said the barber, "is *The Second Part of La Diana*, 'by the Salamancan'; and here is yet another bearing the same title, whose author is Gil Polo."

"As for the Salamancan's work," said the curate, "let it go to swell the number of the condemned out in the stable yard, but keep the Gil Polo as if it were from Apollo's own hand. Come, my friend, let us hurry, for it is growing late."

"This," said the barber as he opened another volume, "is *The Ten Books of the Fortunes of Love*, composed by Antonio de Lofraso, the Sardinian poet." [19]

"By the holy orders that I have received," the curate declared, "since Apollo was Apollo, since the Muses were Muses and poets were poets, so droll and absurd a book as this has not been written; in its own way it is unique among all those of its kind that have seen the light of day, and he who has not read it does not know what he has missed. Give it to me, my friend, for I am more pleased at having found it than if they had presented me with a cassock of Florentine cloth."

Saying this, he laid the book aside with great glee as the barber went on, "Those that we have here are *The Shepherd of Iberia*, *The Nymphs of Henares*, and *The Disenchantments of Jealousy*." [20]

"Well," said the curate, "there is nothing to do with those but to turn them over to the housekeeper's secular arm; and do not ask me why, or we shall never be finished."

"And this is *Filida's Shepherd*." [21]

"He is no shepherd but a polished courtier. Guard him as you would a precious jewel."

"And this big one that I am handing you now is called *Treasury of Various Poems*." [22]

"If there were not so many of them," remarked the curate, "they would be held in greater esteem. This is a book that must be weeded out and cleansed of certain trivialities among the many fine things that it contains. Keep it, for the reason that its author is my friend and out of respect for other more heroic and lofty works that he has produced."

"This," said the barber, "is the *Song Book* of López de Maldonado." [23]

"Another great friend of mine; and when he himself recites or, better, sings his verses, all who hear them are filled with admiration for the charm and sweetness of his voice. His eclogues are a bit too long; for that which is good never did exist in great abundance. Put it with the others that we have laid aside. But what is that one next to it?"

"*La Galatea* of Miguel de Cervantes," said the barber.

"Ah, that fellow Cervantes and I have been friends these many years, but, to my knowledge, he is better versed in misfortune than he is in verses. His book has a fairly good plot; it starts out well and ends up nowhere. We shall have to wait for the second part which he has promised us, and perhaps when it has been corrected somewhat it will find the favor that is now denied it. Meanwhile, keep it locked up in your house."

"That I will gladly do," replied the barber. "And here we have three more—I will hand them to you all together: the *Araucana* of Don Alonso de Ercilla; the

Austriada of Juan Rufo, magistrate of Cordova; and the *Monserrate* of Cristóbal de Virués, the poet of Valencia." [24]

"These three books," said the curate, "are the best that have been written in heroic verse in the Castilian tongue and may well compete with the most famous of Italy; keep them as the richest jewels of poetry that Spain has to show."

By this time his Reverence was too tired to look at any more books and accordingly decided that the rest should be burned without further inspection. The barber, however, had already opened one called *The Tears of Angélica*.[25]

"I should have wept myself," said the curate when he heard the title, "if I had sent that one to the flames; for its author was one of the most famous poets in the world, and not in Spain alone, and he was most happy in the translation that he made of certain of the fables of Ovid."

The Second Sally: Adventure of the Windmills, Encounter with the Biscayan

(CHAPTERS VII-X)

CHAPTER VII. *Of the second sally of our good knight, Don Quixote de la Mancha.*

AT THAT instant Don Quixote began shouting "Here! here! good knights, now is the time to show the strength of your mighty arms, for they of the court are gaining the better of the tourney!"

Called away by this noise and uproar, they went no further with the scrutinizing of those books that remained; and as a consequence it is believed that *La Carolea* and the *León of Spain*[1] went to the fire unseen and unheard, along with *The Deeds of the Emperor* as set down by Don Luis de Avila,[2] for these undoubtedly must have been among the works that were left, and possibly if the curate had seen them he would not have passed so severe a sentence upon them.

When they reached Don Quixote's side, he had already risen from his bed and was shouting and raving, laying about him on all sides with slashes and backstrokes, as wide awake as if he had never been asleep. Seizing him with their arms, they forced him into bed.

When he had quieted down a little he turned to the curate and said, "Most certainly, Señor Archbishop Turpin, it is a great disgrace for us who call ourselves the Twelve Peers so carelessly to allow the knights of the court to gain the victory in this tournament, seeing that previously we adventurers had carried off the prize for three days running."

"Be quiet, my friend," said the curate, "for, God willing, luck may change, and that which is lost today shall be won tomorrow. For the present, your Grace should look after your health, for you must be very tired, if not, perhaps, badly wounded."

"Wounded, no," said Don Quixote, "but bruised to a pulp, there is no doubt of that; for that bastard of a Don Orlando flayed me with the trunk of an oak, and all out of envy, because he knows that I am his only rival in feats of valor. But my name is not Rinaldo of Montalbán if on arising from this couch I do not make him pay for it in spite of all his enchantments. In the meantime, you may bring me something to eat, for I think that would do me more good than anything else. I will see to avenging myself in due course."

They did as he asked, brought him a bite of supper, and he once more fell asleep, while the others wondered at the strange madness that had laid hold of him. That night the housekeeper burned all the books there were in the stable yard and in all the house; and there must have been some that went up in smoke which should have been preserved in everlasting archives, if the one who did the scrutinizing had not been so indolent. Thus we see the truth of the old saying, to the effect that the innocent must sometimes pay for the sins of the guilty.

One of the things that the curate and the barber advised as a remedy for their friend's sickness was to wall up the room where the books had been, so that, when he arose, he would not find them missing—it might be that the cause being removed, the effect would cease—and they could tell him that a magician had made away with them, room and all. This they proceeded to do as quickly as possible. Two days later, when Don Quixote rose from his bed, the first thing he did was to go have a look at his library, and, not finding it where he had left it, he went from one part of the house to another searching for it. Going up to where the door had been, he ran his hands over the wall and rolled his eyes in every direction without saying a word; but after some little while he asked the housekeeper where his study was with all his books.

She had been well instructed in what to answer him. "Whatever study is your Grace talking about?" she said. "There is no study, and no books, in this house; the devil took them all away."

"No," said the niece, "it was not the devil but an enchanter who came upon a cloud one night, the day after

your Grace left here; dismounting from a serpent that
he rode, he entered your study, and I don't know what
all he did there, but after a bit he went flying off
through the roof, leaving the house full of smoke; and
when we went to see what he had done, there was no
study and not a book in sight. There is one thing,
though, that the housekeeper and I remember very
well: at the time that wicked old fellow left, he cried
out in a loud voice that it was all on account of a secret
enmity that he bore the owner of those books and that
study, and that was why he had done the mischief in
this house which we would discover. He also said that
he was called Muñatón the Magician."

"Frestón, he should have said," remarked Don
Quixote.

"I can't say as to that," replied the housekeeper,
"whether he was called Frestón or Fritón;³ all I know
is that his name ended in a *tón.*"

"So it does," said Don Quixote. "He is a wise enchanter, a great enemy of mine, who has a grudge
against me because he knows by his arts and learning
that in the course of time I am to fight in single combat
with a knight whom he favors, and that I am to be
the victor and he can do nothing to prevent it. For
this reason he seeks to cause me all the trouble that he
can, but I am warning him that it will be hard to gainsay
or shun that which Heaven has ordained."

"Who could doubt that it is so?" said the niece. "But
tell me, uncle, who is responsible for your being involved in these quarrels? Would it not be better to
remain peacefully here at home and not go roaming
through the world in search of better bread than is
made from wheat, without taking into consideration
that many who go for wool come back shorn?"

"My dear niece," replied Don Quixote, "how little

you understand of these matters! Before they shear me, I will have plucked and stripped the beards of any who dare to touch the tip of a single hair of mine."

The niece and the housekeeper did not care to answer him any further, for they saw that his wrath was rising.

After that he remained at home very tranquilly for a couple of weeks, without giving sign of any desire to repeat his former madness. During that time he had the most pleasant conversations with his two old friends, the curate and the barber, on the point he had raised to the effect that what the world needed most was knights-errant and a revival of chivalry. The curate would occasionally contradict him and again would give in, for it was only by means of this artifice that he could carry on a conversation with him at all.

In the meanwhile Don Quixote was bringing his powers of persuasion to bear upon a farmer who lived near by, a good man—if this title may be applied to one who is poor—but with very few wits in his head. The short of it is, by pleas and promises, he got the hapless rustic to agree to ride forth with him and serve him as his squire. Among other things, Don Quixote told him that he ought to be more than willing to go, because no telling what adventure might occur which would win them an island, and then he (the farmer) would be left to be the governor of it. As a result of these and other similar assurances, Sancho Panza forsook his wife and children and consented to take upon himself the duties of squire to his neighbor.

Next, Don Quixote set out to raise some money, and by selling this thing and pawning that and getting the worst of the bargain always, he finally scraped together a reasonable amount. He also asked a friend of his for the loan of a buckler and patched up his broken helmet

as well as he could. He advised his squire, Sancho, of
the day and hour when they were to take the road and
told him to see to laying in a supply of those things that
were most necessary, and, above all, not to forget the
saddlebags. Sancho replied that he would see to all
this and added that he was also thinking of taking along
with him a very good ass that he had, as he was not
much used to going on foot.

With regard to the ass, Don Quixote had to do a little
thinking, trying to recall if any knight-errant had ever
had a squire thus asininely mounted. He could not think
of any, but nevertheless he decided to take Sancho with
the intention of providing him with a nobler steed as
soon as occasion offered; he had but to appropriate the
horse of the first discourteous knight he met. Having
furnished himself with shirts and all the other things
that the innkeeper had recommended, he and Panza
rode forth one night unseen by anyone and without
taking leave of wife and children, housekeeper or
niece. They went so far that by the time morning came
they were safe from discovery had a hunt been started
for them.

Mounted on his ass, Sancho Panza rode along like a
patriarch, with saddlebags and flask, his mind set upon
becoming governor of that island that his master had
promised him. Don Quixote determined to take the
same route and road over the Campo de Montiel that
he had followed on his first journey; but he was not so
uncomfortable this time, for it was early morning and
the sun's rays fell upon them slantingly and accordingly
did not tire them too much.

"Look, Sir Knight-errant," said Sancho, "your Grace
should not forget that island you promised me; for no
matter how big it is, I'll be able to govern it right
enough."

"I would have you know, friend Sancho Panza," replied Don Quixote, "that among the knights-errant of old it was a very common custom to make their squires governors of the islands or the kingdoms that they won, and I am resolved that in my case so pleasing a usage shall not fall into desuetude. I even mean to go them one better; for they very often, perhaps most of the time, waited until their squires were old men who had had their fill of serving their masters during bad days and worse nights, whereupon they would give them the title of count, or marquis at most, of some valley or province more or less. But if you live and I live, it well may be that within a week I shall win some kingdom with others dependent upon it, and it will be the easiest thing in the world to crown you king of one of them. You need not marvel at this, for all sorts of unforeseen things happen to knights like me, and I may readily be able to give you even more than I have promised."

"In that case," said Sancho Panza, "if by one of those miracles of which your Grace was speaking I should become king, I would certainly send for Juana Gutiérrez, my old lady, to come and be my queen, and the young ones could be infantes."

"There is no doubt about it," Don Quixote assured him.

"Well, I doubt it," said Sancho, "for I think that even if God were to rain kingdoms upon the earth, no crown would sit well on the head of Mari Gutiérrez,[4] for I am telling you, sir, as a queen she is not worth two maravedis. She would do better as a countess, God help her."

"Leave everything to God, Sancho," said Don Quixote, "and he will give you whatever is most fitting; but I trust you will not be so pusillanimous as to be content with anything less than the title of viceroy."

"That I will not," said Sancho Panza, "especially seeing that I have in your Grace so illustrious a master who can give me all that is suitable to me and all that I can manage."

CHAPTER VIII. *Of the good fortune which the valorous Don Quixote had in the terrifying and never-before-imagined adventure of the windmills, along with other events that deserve to be suitably recorded.*

AT THIS point they caught sight of thirty or forty windmills which were standing on the plain there, and no sooner had Don Quixote laid eyes upon them than he turned to his squire and said, "Fortune is guiding our affairs better than we could have wished; for you see there before you, friend Sancho Panza, some thirty or more lawless giants with whom I mean to do battle. I shall deprive them of their lives, and with the spoils from this encounter we shall begin to enrich ourselves; for this is righteous warfare, and it is a great service to God to remove so accursed a breed from the face of the earth."

"What giants?" said Sancho Panza.

"Those that you see there," replied his master, "those with the long arms some of which are as much as two leagues in length."

"But look, your Grace, those are not giants but windmills, and what appear to be arms are their wings which, when whirled in the breeze, cause the millstone to go."

"It is plain to be seen," said Don Quixote, "that you have had little experience in this matter of adventures. If you are afraid, go off to one side and say your prayers while I am engaging them in fierce, unequal combat."

Saying this, he gave spurs to his steed Rocinante, without paying any heed to Sancho's warning that these were truly windmills and not giants that he was riding forth to attack. Nor even when he was close upon them did he perceive what they really were, but shouted at the top of his lungs, "Do not seek to flee, cowards and vile creatures that you are, for it is but a single knight with whom you have to deal!"

At that moment a little wind came up and the big wings began turning.

"Though you flourish as many arms as did the giant Briareus," said Don Quixote when he perceived this, "you still shall have to answer to me."

He thereupon commended himself with all his heart to his lady Dulcinea, beseeching her to succor him in this peril; and, being well covered with his shield and with his lance at rest, he bore down upon them at a full gallop and fell upon the first mill that stood in his way, giving a thrust at the wing, which was whirling at such a speed that his lance was broken into bits and both horse and horseman went rolling over the plain, very much battered indeed. Sancho upon his donkey came hurrying to his master's assistance as fast as he could, but when he reached the spot, the knight was unable to move, so great was the shock with which he and Rocinante had hit the ground.

"God help us!" exclaimed Sancho, "did I not tell your Grace to look well, that those were nothing but windmills, a fact which no one could fail to see unless he had other mills of the same sort in his head?"

"Be quiet, friend Sancho," said Don Quixote. "Such are the fortunes of war, which more than any other are subject to constant change. What is more, when I come to think of it, I am sure that this must be the work of that magician Frestón, the one who robbed me of my study and my books, and who has thus changed the giants into windmills in order to deprive me of the glory of overcoming them, so great is the enmity that he bears me; but in the end his evil arts shall not prevail against this trusty sword of mine."

"May God's will be done," was Sancho Panza's response. And with the aid of his squire the knight was once more mounted on Rocinante, who stood there with one shoulder half out of joint. And so, speaking of the adventure that had just befallen them, they continued along the Puerto Lápice highway; for there, Don Quixote said, they could not fail to find many and varied adventures, this being a much traveled thoroughfare. The only thing was, the knight was exceedingly downcast over the loss of his lance.

"I remember," he said to his squire, "having read of a Spanish knight by the name of Diego Pérez de Vargas, who, having broken his sword in battle, tore from an oak a heavy bough or branch and with it did such feats of valor that day, and pounded so many Moors, that he came to be known as Machuca,[1] and he and his descendants from that day forth have been called Vargas y Machuca. I tell you this because I too intend to provide myself with just such a bough as the one he wielded, and with it I propose to do such exploits that you shall deem yourself fortunate to have been found worthy to come with me and behold and witness things that are almost beyond belief."

"God's will be done," said Sancho. "I believe everything that your Grace says; but straighten yourself up in the saddle a little, for you seem to be slipping down on one side, owing, no doubt, to the shaking-up that you received in your fall."

"Ah, that is the truth," replied Don Quixote, "and if

I do not speak of my sufferings, it is for the reason that it is not permitted knights-errant to complain of any wound whatsoever, even though their bowels may be dropping out."

"If that is the way it is," said Sancho, "I have nothing more to say; but, God knows, it would suit me better if your Grace did complain when something hurts him. I can assure you that I mean to do so, over the least little thing that ails me—that is, unless the same rule applies to squires as well."

Don Quixote laughed long and heartily over Sancho's simplicity, telling him that he might complain as much as he liked and where and when he liked, whether he had good cause or not; for he had read nothing to the contrary in the ordinances of chivalry. Sancho then called his master's attention to the fact that it was time to eat. The knight replied that he himself had no need of food at the moment, but his squire might eat whenever he chose. Having been granted this permission, Sancho seated himself as best he could upon his beast, and, taking out from his saddlebags the provisions that he had stored there, he rode along leisurely behind his master, munching his victuals and taking a good, hearty swig now and then at the leather flask in a manner that might well have caused the biggest-bellied tavernkeeper of Málaga to envy him. Between draughts he gave not so much as a thought to any promise that his master might have made him, nor did he look upon it as any hardship, but rather as good sport, to go in quest of adventures however hazardous they might be.

The short of the matter is, they spent the night under some trees, from one of which Don Quixote tore off a withered bough to serve him as a lance, placing it in the lance head from which he had removed the broken one. He did not sleep all night long for thinking of his lady

Dulcinea; for this was in accordance with what he had read in his books, of men of arms in the forest or desert places who kept a wakeful vigil, sustained by the memory of their ladies fair. Not so with Sancho, whose stomach was full, and not with chicory water. He fell into a dreamless slumber, and had not his master called him, he would not have been awakened either by the rays of the sun in his face or by the many birds who greeted the coming of the new day with their merry song.

Upon arising, he had another go at the flask, finding it somewhat more flaccid than it had been the night before, a circumstance which grieved his heart, for he could not see that they were on the way to remedying the deficiency within any very short space of time. Don Quixote did not wish any breakfast; for, as has been said, he was in the habit of nourishing himself on savorous memories. They then set out once more along the road to Puerto Lápice, and around three in the afternoon they came in sight of the pass that bears that name.

"There," said Don Quixote as his eyes fell upon it, "we may plunge our arms up to the elbow in what are known as adventures. But I must warn you that even though you see me in the greatest peril in the world, you are not to lay hand upon your sword to defend me, unless it be that those who attack me are rabble and men of low degree, in which case you may very well come to my aid; but if they be gentlemen, it is in no wise permitted by the laws of chivalry that you should assist me until you yourself shall have been dubbed a knight."

"Most certainly, sir," replied Sancho, "your Grace shall be very well obeyed in this; all the more so for the reason that I myself am of a peaceful disposition and not fond of meddling in the quarrels and feuds of others. However, when it comes to protecting my own person, I shall not take account of those laws of which you speak, seeing that all laws, human and divine, permit each one to defend himself whenever he is attacked."

"I am willing to grant you that," assented Don Quixote, "but in this matter of defending me against gentlemen you must restrain your natural impulses."

"I promise you I shall do so," said Sancho. "I will observe this precept as I would the Sabbath day."

As they were conversing in this manner, there appeared in the road in front of them two friars of the Order of St. Benedict, mounted upon dromedaries—for the she-mules they rode were certainly no smaller than that. The friars wore travelers' spectacles and carried sunshades, and behind them came a coach accompanied by four or five men on horseback and a couple of muleteers on foot. In the coach, as was afterwards learned, was a lady of Biscay, on her way to Seville to bid farewell to her husband, who had been appointed to some high post in the Indies. The religious were not of her company although they were going by the same road.

The instant Don Quixote laid eyes upon them he turned to his squire. "Either I am mistaken or this is going to be the most famous adventure that ever was seen; for those black-clad figures that you behold must be, and without any doubt are, certain enchanters who are bearing with them a captive princess in that coach, and I must do all I can to right this wrong."

"It will be worse than the windmills," declared Sancho. "Look you, sir, those are Benedictine friars and the coach must be that of some travelers. Mark well what I say and what you do, lest the devil lead you astray."

"I have already told you, Sancho," replied Don Quixote, "that you know little where the subject of adventures is concerned. What I am saying to you is the truth, as you shall now see."

With this, he rode forward and took up a position in the middle of the road along which the friars were coming, and as soon as they appeared to be within earshot he cried out to them in a loud voice, "O devilish and monstrous beings, set free at once the highborn princesses whom you bear captive in that coach, or else prepare at once to meet your death as the just punishment of your evil deeds."

The friars drew rein and sat there in astonishment, marveling as much at Don Quixote's appearance as at the words he spoke. "Sir Knight," they answered him, "we are neither devilish nor monstrous but religious of the Order of St. Benedict who are merely going our way. We know nothing of those who are in that coach, nor of any captive princesses either."

"Soft words," said Don Quixote, "have no effect on me. I know you for what you are, lying rabble!" And without waiting for any further parley he gave spur to Rocinante and, with lowered lance, bore down upon the first friar with such fury and intrepidity that, had not the fellow tumbled from his mule of his own accord, he would have been hurled to the ground and either killed or badly wounded. The second religious, seeing how his companion had been treated, dug his legs into his she-mule's flanks and scurried away over the countryside faster than the wind.

Seeing the friar upon the ground, Sancho Panza slipped lightly from his mount and, falling upon him, began stripping him of his habit. The two mule drivers accompanying the religious thereupon came running up and asked Sancho why he was doing this. The latter replied that the friar's garments belonged to him as legitimate spoils of the battle that his master Don Quixote had just won. The muleteers, however, were lads with no sense of humor, nor did they know what all this talk of spoils and battles was about; but, perceiving that Don Quixote had ridden off to one side to converse with those inside the coach, they pounced upon Sancho, threw him to the ground, and proceeded to pull out the hair of his beard and kick him to a pulp, after which they went off and left him stretched out there, bereft at once of breath and sense.

Without losing any time, they then assisted the friar to remount. The good brother was trembling all over from fright, and there was not a speck of color in his face, but when he found himself in the saddle once more, he quickly spurred his beast to where his companion, at some little distance, sat watching and waiting to see what the result of the encounter would be. Having no curiosity as to the final outcome of the fray, the two of them now resumed their journey, making more signs of the cross than the devil would be able to carry upon his back.

Meanwhile Don Quixote, as we have said, was speaking to the lady in the coach.

"Your beauty, my lady, may now dispose of your person as best may please you, for the arrogance of your abductors lies upon the ground, overthrown by this good arm of mine; and in order that you may not pine to know the name of your liberator, I may inform you that I am Don Quixote de la Mancha, knight-errant and adventurer and captive of the peerless and beauteous Doña Dulcinea del Toboso. In payment of the favor which you have received from me, I ask nothing other than that you return to El Toboso and on my behalf pay your respects to this lady, telling her that it was I who set you free."

One of the squires accompanying those in the coach, a Biscayan, was listening to Don Quixote's words, and when he saw that the knight did not propose to let the coach proceed upon its way but was bent upon having it turn back to El Toboso, he promptly went up to him, seized his lance, and said to him in bad Castilian and worse Biscayan,[2] "Go, *caballero*, and bad luck go with you; for by the God that created me, if you do not let this coach pass, me kill you or me no Biscayan."

Don Quixote heard him attentively enough and answered him very mildly, "If you were a *caballero*, which you are not, I should already have chastised you, wretched creature, for your foolhardiness and your impudence."

"Me no *caballero?*" cried the Biscayan.[3] "Me swear to God, you lie like a Christian. If you will but lay aside your lance and unsheath your sword, you will soon see that you are carrying water to the cat![4] Biscayan on land, gentleman at sea, but a gentleman in spite of the devil, and you lie if you say otherwise."

" ' "You shall see as to that presently," said Agrajes,' " Don Quixote quoted.[5] He cast his lance to the earth, drew his sword, and, taking his buckler on his arm, attacked the Biscayan with intent to slay him. The latter, when he saw his adversary approaching, would have liked to dismount from his mule, for she was one of the worthless sort that are let for hire and he had no confidence in her; but there was no time for this, and so he had no choice but to draw his own sword in turn and make the best of it. However, he was near enough to the coach to be able to snatch a cushion from it to serve him as a shield; and then they fell upon each other as though they were mortal enemies. The rest of those present sought to make peace between them but did not succeed, for the Biscayan with his disjointed phrases kept muttering that if they did not let him finish the battle then he himself would have to kill his mistress and anyone else who tried to stop him.

The lady inside the carriage, amazed by it all and trembling at what she saw, directed her coachman to drive on a little way; and there from a distance she watched the deadly combat, in the course of which the Biscayan came down with a great blow on Don Quixote's shoulder, over the top of the latter's shield, and had not the knight been clad in armor, it would have split him to the waist.

Feeling the weight of this blow, Don Quixote cried out, "O lady of my soul, Dulcinea, flower of beauty, succor this your champion who out of gratitude for your many favors finds himself in so perilous a plight!" To utter these words, lay hold of his sword, cover himself with his buckler, and attack the Biscayan was but the work of a moment; for he was now resolved to risk everything upon a single stroke.

As he saw Don Quixote approaching with so dauntless a bearing, the Biscayan was well aware of his adversary's courage and forthwith determined to imitate the example thus set him. He kept himself protected with his cushion, but he was unable to get his she-mule to budge to one side or the other, for the beast, out of sheer exhaustion and being, moreover, unused to such childish play, was incapable of taking a single step. And so, then, as has been stated, Don Quixote was approaching the wary Biscayan, his sword raised on high and with the firm resolve of cleaving his enemy in two; and the Biscayan was awaiting the knight in the same posture, cushion in front of him and with uplifted sword.

All the bystanders were trembling with suspense at what would happen as a result of the terrible blows that were threatened, and the lady in the coach and her maids were making a thousand vows and offerings to all the images and shrines in Spain, praying that God would save them all and the lady's squire from this great peril that confronted them.

But the unfortunate part of the matter is that at this very point the author of the history breaks off and leaves the battle pending, excusing himself upon the ground that he has been unable to find anything else in writing concerning the exploits of Don Quixote beyond those already set forth. It is true, on the other hand, that the second author of this work could not bring himself to believe that so unusual a chronicle would have been consigned to oblivion, nor that the learned ones of La Mancha were possessed of so little curiosity as not to be able to discover in their archives or registry offices certain papers that have to do with this famous knight. Being convinced of this, he did not despair of coming upon the end of this pleasing story, and Heaven favoring him, he did find it, as shall be related in the second part.[6]

CHAPTER IX. *In which is concluded and brought to an end the stupendous battle between the gallant Biscayan and the valiant Knight of La Mancha.*

IN THE first part of the history we left the valorous Biscayan and the famous Don Quixote with swords unsheathed and raised aloft, about to let fall furious slashing blows which, had they been delivered fairly and squarely, would at the very least have split them in two and laid them wide open from top to bottom like a pomegranate; and it was at this doubtful point that the pleasing chronicle came to a halt and broke off, without the author's informing us as to where the rest of it might be found.

I was deeply grieved by such a circumstance, and the

pleasure I had had in reading so slight a portion was turned into annoyance as I thought of how difficult it would be to come upon the greater part which it seemed to me must still be missing. It appeared impossible and contrary to all good precedent that so worthy a knight should not have had some scribe to take upon himself the task of writing an account of these unheard-of exploits; for that was something that had happened to none of the knights-errant who, as the saying has it, had gone forth in quest of adventures, seeing that each of them had one or two chroniclers, as if ready at hand, who not only had set down their deeds, but had depicted their most trivial thoughts and amiable weaknesses, however well concealed they might be. The good knight of La Mancha surely could not have been so unfortunate as to have lacked what Platir and others like him had in abundance. And so I could not bring myself to believe that this gallant history could have remained thus lopped off and mutilated, and I could not but lay the blame upon the malignity of time, that devourer and consumer of all things, which must either have consumed it or kept it hidden.

On the other hand, I reflected that inasmuch as among the knight's books had been found such modern works as *The Disenchantments of Jealousy* and *The Nymphs and Shepherds of Henares,* his story likewise must be modern, and that even though it might not have been written down, it must remain in the memory of the good folk of his village and the surrounding ones. This thought left me somewhat confused and more than ever desirous of knowing the real and true story, the whole story, of the life and wondrous deeds of our famous Spaniard, Don Quixote, light and mirror of the chivalry of La Mancha, the first in our age and in these calamitous times to devote himself to the hardships and exercises of knight-errantry and to go about righting wrongs, succoring widows, and protecting damsels—damsels such as those who, mounted upon their palfreys and with riding-whip in hand, in full possession of their virginity, were in the habit of going from mountain to mountain and from valley to valley; for unless there were some villain, some rustic with an ax and hood, or some monstrous giant to force them, there were in times past maiden ladies who at the end of eighty years, during all which time they had not slept for a single day beneath a roof, would go to their graves as virginal as when their mothers had borne them.

If I speak of these things, it is for the reason that in this and in all other respects our gallant Quixote is deserving of constant memory and praise, and even I am not to be denied my share of it for my diligence and the labor to which I put myself in searching out the conclusion of this agreeable narrative; although if heaven, luck, and circumstance had not aided me, the world would have had to do without the pleasure and the pastime which anyone may enjoy who will read this work attentively for an hour or two. The manner in which it came about was as follows:

I was standing one day in the Alcaná, or market place, of Toledo when a lad came up to sell some old notebooks and other papers to a silk weaver who was there. As I am extremely fond of reading anything, even though it be but the scraps of paper in the streets, I followed my natural inclination and took one of the books, whereupon I at once perceived that it was written in characters which I recognized as Arabic. I recognized them, but reading them was another thing; and so I began looking around to see if there was any Spanish-speaking Moor near by who would be able to read them for me. It was not very hard to find such an interpreter, nor would it have been even if the tongue in question had been an older and a better one.[1] To make a long story short, chance brought a fellow my way; and when I told him what it was I wished and placed the book in his hands, he opened it in the middle and began reading and at once fell to laughing. When I asked him what the cause of his laughter was, he replied that it was a note which had been written in the margin.

I besought him to tell me the content of the note, and he, laughing still, went on, "As I told you, it is something in the margin here: 'This Dulcinea del Toboso, so often referred to, is said to have been the best hand at salting pigs of any woman in all La Mancha.'"

No sooner had I heard the name Dulcinea del Toboso than I was astonished and held in suspense, for at once the thought occurred to me that those notebooks must contain the history of Don Quixote. With this in mind I urged him to read me the title, and he proceeded to do so, turning the Arabic into Castilian upon the spot: *History of Don Quixote de la Mancha, Written by Cid Hamete Benengeli, Arabic Historian.* It was all I could do to conceal my satisfaction and, snatching them from the silk weaver, I bought from the lad all the papers and notebooks that he had for half a real; but if he had known or suspected how very much I wanted them, he might well have had more than six reales for them.

The Moor and I then betook ourselves to the cathedral cloister, where I requested him to translate for me into the Castilian tongue all the books that had to do with Don Quixote, adding nothing and subtracting nothing; and I offered him whatever payment he desired. He was content with two arrobas of raisins and two fanegas[2] of wheat and promised to translate them well and faithfully and with all dispatch. However, in order to facilitate matters, and also because I did not wish to let such a find as this out of my hands, I took the fellow home with me, where in a little more than a month and a half he translated the whole of the work just as you will find it set down here.

In the first of the books there was a very lifelike picture of the battle between Don Quixote and the Biscayan, the two being in precisely the same posture as described in the history, their swords upraised, the one covered by his buckler, the other with his cushion. As for the Biscayan's mule, you could see at the distance of a crossbow shot that it was one for hire. Beneath the Biscayan there was a rubric which read: "Don Sancho de Azpeitia," which must undoubtedly have been his name; while beneath the feet of Rocinante was another inscription: "Don Quixote." Rocinante was marvelously portrayed: so long and lank, so lean and flabby, so extremely consumptive-looking that one could well understand the justness and propriety with which the name of "hack" had been bestowed upon him.

Alongside Rocinante stood Sancho Panza, holding the halter of his ass, and below was the legend: "Sancho Zancas." The picture showed him with a big belly, a short body, and long shanks, and that must have been where he got the names of Panza y Zancas[3] by which he is a number of times called in the course of the history. There are other small details that might be mentioned, but they are of little importance and have nothing to do with the truth of the story—and no story is bad so long as it is true.

If there is any objection to be raised against the veracity of the present one, it can be only that the author was an Arab, and that nation is known for its lying propensities; but even though they be our enemies, it may readily be understood that they would more likely have detracted from, rather than added to, the chronicle. So it seems to me, at any rate; for whenever he might and should deploy the resources of his pen in praise of so worthy a knight, the author appears to take pains to pass over the matter in silence; all of which in my opinion is ill done and ill conceived, for it should be the duty of historians to be exact, truthful, and dispassionate, and neither interest nor fear nor rancor nor affection should swerve them from the path of truth, whose mother is history, rival of time, depository of deeds, witness of the past, exemplar and adviser to the present, and the future's counselor. In this work, I am sure, will be found all that could be desired in the way of pleasant reading; and if it is lacking in any way, I maintain that this is the fault of that hound of an author rather than of the subject.

But to come to the point, the second part, according to the translation, began as follows:

As the two valorous and enraged combatants stood there, swords upraised and poised on high, it seemed from their bold mien as if they must surely be threatening heaven, earth, and hell itself. The first to let fall a blow was the choleric Biscayan, and he came down with such force and fury that, had not his sword been deflected in mid-air, that single stroke would have sufficed to put an end to this fearful combat and to all our knight's adventures at the same time; but fortune, which was reserving him for greater things, turned aside his adversary's blade in such a manner that, even though it fell upon his left shoulder, it did him no other damage than to strip him completely of his armor on that side, carrying with it a good part of his helmet along with half an ear, the headpiece clattering to the ground with a dreadful din, leaving its wearer in a sorry state.

Heaven help me! Who could properly describe the rage that now entered the heart of our hero of La

Mancha as he saw himself treated in this fashion? It may merely be said that he once more reared himself in the stirrups, laid hold of his sword with both hands, and dealt the Biscayan such a blow, over the cushion and upon the head, that, even so good a defense proving useless, it was as if a mountain had fallen upon his enemy. The latter now began bleeding through the mouth, nose, and ears; he seemed about to fall from his mule, and would have fallen, no doubt, if he had not grasped the beast about the neck, but at that moment his feet slipped from the stirrups and his arms let go, and the mule, frightened by the terrible blow, began running across the plain, hurling its rider to the earth with a few quick plunges.

Don Quixote stood watching all this very calmly. When he saw his enemy fall, he leaped from his horse, ran over very nimbly, and thrust the point of his sword into the Biscayan's eyes, calling upon him at the same time to surrender or otherwise he would cut off his head. The Biscayan was so bewildered that he was unable to utter a single word in reply, and things would have gone badly with him, so blind was Don Quixote in his rage, if the ladies of the coach, who up to then had watched the struggle in dismay, had not come up to him at this point and begged him with many blandishments to do them the very great favor of sparing their squire's life.

To which Don Quixote replied with much haughtiness and dignity, "Most certainly, lovely ladies, I shall be very happy to do that which you ask of me, but upon one condition and understanding, and that is that this knight promise me that he will go to El Toboso and present himself in my behalf before Doña Dulcinea, in order that she may do with him as she may see fit."

Trembling and disconsolate, the ladies did not pause

to discuss Don Quixote's request, but without so much
as inquiring who Dulcinea might be they promised him
that the squire would fulfill that which was commanded
of him.

"Very well, then, trusting in your word, I will do him
no further harm, even though he has well deserved it."

CHAPTER X. *Of the pleasing conversation that took
place between Don Quixote and Sancho Panza, his
squire.*

BY THIS time Sancho Panza had got to his feet, somewhat the worse for wear as the result of the treatment he had received from the friars' lads. He had been
watching the battle attentively and praying God in his
heart to give the victory to his master, Don Quixote, in
order that he, Sancho, might gain some island where he
could go to be governor as had been promised him.
Seeing now that the combat was over and the knight
was returning to mount Rocinante once more, he went
up to hold the stirrup for him; but first he fell on his
knees in front of him and, taking his hand, kissed it and
said, "May your Grace be pleased, Señor Don Quixote,
to grant me the governorship of that island which you
have won in this deadly affray; for however large it may
be, I feel that I am indeed capable of governing it as
well as any man in this world has ever done."

To which Don Quixote replied, "Be advised, brother
Sancho, that this adventure and other similar ones have
nothing to do with islands; they are affairs of the crossroads in which one gains nothing more than a broken
head or an ear the less. Be patient, for there will be
others which will not only make you a governor, but
more than that."

Sancho thanked him very much and, kissing his hand again and the skirt of his cuirass, he assisted him up on Rocinante's back, after which the squire bestraddled his own mount and started jogging along behind his master, who was now going at a good clip. Without pausing for any further converse with those in the coach, the knight made for a near-by wood, with Sancho following as fast as his beast could trot; but Rocinante was making such speed that the ass and its rider were left behind, and it was necessary to call out to Don Quixote to pull up and wait for them. He did so, reining in Rocinante until the weary Sancho had drawn abreast of him.

"It strikes me, sir," said the squire as he reached his master's side, "that it would be better for us to take refuge in some church; for in view of the way you have treated that one with whom you were fighting, it would be small wonder if they did not lay the matter before the Holy Brotherhood [1] and have us arrested; and faith, if they do that, we shall have to sweat a-plenty before we come out of jail."

"Be quiet," said Don Quixote. "And where have you ever seen, or read of, a knight being brought to justice no matter how many homicides he might have committed?"

"I know nothing about omecils," [2] replied Sancho, "nor ever in my life did I bear one to anybody; all I know is that the Holy Brotherhood has something to say about those who go around fighting on the highway, and I want nothing of it."

"Do not let it worry you," said Don Quixote, "for I will rescue you from the hands of the Chaldeans, not to speak of the Brotherhood. But answer me upon your life: have you ever seen a more valorous knight than I on all the known face of the earth? Have you ever read in the histories of any other who had more mettle in the attack, more perseverance in sustaining it, more dexterity in wounding his enemy, or more skill in overthrowing him?"

"The truth is," said Sancho, "I have never read any history whatsoever, for I do not know how to read or write; but what I would wager is that in all the days of my life I have never served a more courageous master than your Grace; I only hope your courage is not paid for in the place that I have mentioned. What I would suggest is that your Grace allow me to do something for that ear, for there is much blood coming from it, and I have here in my saddlebags some lint and a little white ointment."

"We could well dispense with all that," said Don Quixote, "if only I had remembered to bring along a vial of Fierabras's balm, a single drop of which saves time and medicines."

"What vial and what balm is that?" inquired Sancho Panza.

"It is a balm the receipt for which I know by heart; with it one need have no fear of death nor think of dying from any wound. I shall make some of it and give it to you; and thereafter, whenever in any attle you see my body cut in two—as very often happens—all that is necessary is for you to take the part that lies on the ground, before the blood has congealed, and fit it very neatly and with great nicety upon the other part that remains in the saddle, taking care to adjust it evenly and exactly. Then you will give me but a couple of swallows of the balm of which I have told you, and you will see me sounder than an apple in no time at all."

"If that is so," said Panza, "I herewith renounce the

governorship of the island you promised me and ask
nothing other in payment of my many and faithful
services than that your Grace give me the receipt for
this wonderful potion, for I am sure that it would be
worth more than two reales the ounce anywhere, and
that is all I need for a life of ease and honor. But may I
be so bold as to ask how much it costs to make it?"

"For less than three reales you can make something
like six quarts," Don Quixote told him.

"Sinner that I am!" exclaimed Sancho. "Then why
does your Grace not make some at once and teach me
also?"

"Hush, my friend," said the knight, "I mean to teach
you greater secrets than that and do you greater favors;
but, for the present, let us look after this ear of mine,
for it is hurting me more than I like."

Sancho thereupon took the lint and the ointment from
his saddlebags; but when Don Quixote caught a glimpse
of his helmet, he almost went out of his mind and, laying his hand upon his sword and lifting his eyes heavenward, he cried, "I make a vow to the Creator of all
things and to the four holy Gospels in all their fullness
of meaning that I will lead from now on the life that
the great Marquis of Mantua did after he had sworn
to avenge the death of his nephew Baldwin: not to eat
bread off a tablecloth, not to embrace his wife, and
other things which, although I am unable to recall them,
we will look upon as understood—all this until I shall
have wreaked an utter vengeance upon the one who
has perpetrated such an outrage upon me."

"But let me remind your Grace," said Sancho when
he heard these words, "that if the knight fulfills that
which was commanded of him, by going to present
himself before my lady Dulcinea del Toboso, then he
will have paid his debt to you and merits no further

punishment at your hands, unless it be for some fresh offense."

"You have spoken very well and to the point," said Don Quixote, "and so I annul the vow I have just made insofar as it has to do with any further vengeance, but I make it and confirm it anew so far as leading the life of which I have spoken is concerned, until such time as I shall have obtained by force of arms from some other knight another headpiece as good as this. And do not think, Sancho, that I am making smoke out of straw; there is one whom I well may imitate in this matter, for the same thing happened in all literalness in the case of Mambrino's helmet which cost Sacripante so dear." [3]

"I wish," said Sancho, "that your Grace would send all such oaths to the devil, for they are very bad for the health and harmful for the conscience as well. Tell me, please: supposing that for many days to come we meet no man wearing a helmet, then what are we to do? Must you still keep your vow in spite of all the inconveniences and discomforts, such as sleeping with your clothes on, not sleeping in any town, and a thousand other penances contained in the oath of that old madman of a Marquis of Mantua, an oath which you would now revive? Mark you, sir, along all these roads you meet no men of arms but only muleteers and carters, who not only do not wear helmets but quite likely have never heard tell of them in all their livelong days."

"In that you are wrong," said Don Quixote, "for we shall not be at these crossroads for the space of two hours before we shall see more men of arms than came to Albraca to win the fair Angélica."

"Very well, then," said Sancho, "so be it, and pray God that all turns out for the best so that I may at last win that island that is costing me so dearly, and then let me die."

"I have already told you, Sancho, that you are to give no thought to that; should the island fail, there is the kingdom of Denmark or that of Sobradisa,[4] which would fit you like a ring on your finger, and you ought, moreover, to be happy to be on *terra firma*.[5] But let us leave all this for some other time, while you look and see if you have something in those saddlebags for us to eat, after which we will go in search of some castle where we may lodge for the night and prepare that balm of which I was telling you, for I swear to God that my ear is paining me greatly."

"I have here an onion, a little cheese, and a few crusts of bread," said Sancho, "but they are not victuals fit for a valiant knight like your Grace."

"How little you know about it!" replied Don Quixote. "I would inform you, Sancho, that it is a point of honor with knights-errant to go for a month at a time without eating, and when they do eat, it is whatever may be at hand. You would certainly know that if you had read the histories as I have. There are many of them, and in none have I found any mention of knights eating unless it was by chance or at some sumptuous banquet that was tendered them; on other days they fasted. And even though it is well understood that, being men like us, they could not go without food entirely, any more than they could fail to satisfy the other necessities of nature, nevertheless, since they spent the greater part of their lives in forests and desert places without any cook to prepare their meals, their diet ordinarily consisted of rustic viands such as those that you now offer me. And so, Sancho my friend, do not be grieved at that which pleases me, nor seek to make the world over, nor to unhinge the institution of knight-errantry."

"Pardon me, your Grace," said Sancho, "but seeing that, as I have told you, I do not know how to read or write, I am consequently not familiar with the rules of the knightly calling. Hereafter, I will stuff my saddle-bags with all manner of dried fruit for your Grace, but inasmuch as I am not a knight, I shall lay in for myself a stock of fowls and other more substantial fare."

"I am not saying, Sancho, that it is incumbent upon knights-errant to eat only those fruits of which you speak; what I am saying is that their ordinary suste-nance should consist of fruit and a few herbs such as are to be found in the fields and with which they are well acquainted, as am I myself."

"It is a good thing," said Sancho, "to know those herbs, for, so far as I can see, we are going to have need of that knowledge one of these days."

With this, he brought out the articles he had men-tioned, and the two of them ate in peace, and most companionably. Being desirous, however, of seeking a lodging for the night, they did not tarry long over their humble and unsavory repast. They then mounted and made what haste they could that they might arrive at a shelter before nightfall; but the sun failed them, and with it went the hope of attaining their wish. As the day ended they found themselves beside some goatherds' huts, and they accordingly decided to spend the night there. Sancho was as much disappointed at their not having reached a town as his master was content with sleeping under the open sky; for it seemed to Don Quixote that every time this happened it merely pro-vided him with yet another opportunity to establish his claim to the title of knight-errant.

A Pastoral Interlude

(CHAPTERS XI-XIV)

Don Quixote and Sancho are received very hospitably by the goatherds and share their hosts' humble evening meal. The herders are puzzled by the talk of chivalry between the knight and his squire; and then, at the end of the repast—

FROM CHAPTER XI: *Of what happened to Don Quixote in the company of certain goatherds.*

AFTER Don Quixote had well satisfied his stomach, he took up a handful of acorns and, gazing at them attentively, fell into a soliloquy.

"Happy the age and happy those centuries to which the ancients gave the name of golden, and not because gold, which is so esteemed in this iron age of ours, was then to be had without toil, but because those who lived in that time did not know the meaning of the words 'thine' and 'mine.' In that blessed era all things were held in common, and to gain his daily sustenance no labor was required of any man save to reach forth his hand and take it from the sturdy oaks that stood liberally inviting him with their sweet and seasoned fruit. The clear-running fountains and rivers in magnificent abundance offered him palatable and transparent water for his thirst; while in the clefts of the rocks and the hollows of the trees the wise and busy honey-makers set up their republic so that any hand whatever might avail itself, fully and freely, of the fertile harvest which their fragrant toil had produced. The vigorous cork trees of their own free will and grace, without the asking, shed their broad, light bark with which men began to cover their dwellings, erected upon rude stakes merely as a protection against the inclemency of the heavens.

"All then was peace, all was concord and friendship; the crooked plowshare had not as yet grievously laid open and pried into the merciful bowels of our first mother, who without any forcing on man's part yielded her spacious fertile bosom on every hand for the satisfaction, sustenance, and delight of her first sons. Then it was that lovely and unspoiled young shepherdesses, with locks that were sometimes braided, sometimes flowing, went roaming from valley to valley and hillock to hillock with no more garments than were needed to cover decently that which modesty requires and always has required should remain covered. Nor were their adornments such as those in use today—of Tyrian purple and silk worked up in tortured patterns; a few green leaves of burdock or of ivy, and they were as splendidly and as becomingly clad as our ladies of the court with all the rare and exotic tricks of fashion that idle curiosity has taught them.

"Thoughts of love, also, in those days were set forth as simply as the simple hearts that conceived them, without any roundabout and artificial play of words by way of ornament. Fraud, deceit, and malice had not yet come to mingle with truth and plain-speaking. Justice kept its own domain, where favor and self-interest dared not trespass, dared not impair her rights, becloud, and persecute her as they now do. There was no such thing then as arbitrary judgments, for the reason that there was no one to judge or be judged. Maidens in all their modesty, as I have said, went where they would and unattended; whereas in this hateful age of ours none is safe, even though she go to hide and shut herself up in some new labyrinth like that of Crete; for in spite of all her seclusion, through chinks and crevices or borne upon the air, the amorous plague with all its cursed importunities will find her out and lead her to her ruin.

"It was for the safety of such as these, as time went on and depravity increased, that the order of knights-errant was instituted, for the protection of damsels, the aid of widows and orphans, and the succoring of the needy. It is to this order that I belong, my brothers, and I thank you for the welcome and the kindly treatment that you have accorded to me and my squire. By natural law, all living men are obliged to show favor to knights-errant, yet without being aware of this you have received and entertained me; and so it is with all possible good will that I acknowledge your own good will to me."

This long harangue on the part of our knight—it might very well have been dispensed with—was all due to the acorns they had given him, which had brought back to memory the age of gold; whereupon the whim had seized him to indulge in this futile harangue with the goatherds as his auditors. They listened in open-mouthed wonderment, saying not a word, and Sancho himself kept quiet and went on munching acorns, taking occasion very frequently to pay a visit to the second wine bag, which they had suspended from a cork tree to keep it cool.[1]

The goatherds then introduce a young shepherd who, to the strains of a lute, sings a love ballad for the entertainment of the guests.

THE BALLAD THAT ANTONIO SANG

I know well that thou dost love me,
My Olalla, even though
Eyes of thine have never spoken—
Love's mute tongues—to tell me so.

Since I know thou knowest my passion,
Of thy love I am more sure:
No love ever was unhappy
When it was both frank and pure.

True it is, Olalla, sometimes
Thou a heart of bronze hast shown,
And it seemed to me that bosom,
White and fair, was made of stone.

Yet in spite of all repulses
And a chastity so cold,
It appeared that I Hope's garment
By the hem did clutch and hold.

For my faith I ever cherished;
It would rise to meet the bait;
Spurned, it never did diminish;
Favored, it preferred to wait.

Love, they say, hath gentle manners:
Thus it is it shows its face;
Then may I take hope, Olalla,
Trust to win a longed for grace.

If devotion hath the power
Hearts to move and make them kind,
Let the loyalty I've shown thee
Plead my cause, be kept in mind.

For if thou didst note my costume,
More than once thou must have seen,
Worn upon a simple Monday

Sunday's garb so bright and clean.
        Love and brightness go together.
Dost thou ask the reason why
I thus deck myself on Monday?
It is but to catch thine eye.

        I say nothing of the dances
I have danced for thy sweet sake;
Nor the serenades I've sung thee
Till the first cock did awake.

        Nor will I repeat my praises
Of that beauty all can see;
True my words but oft unwelcome—
Certain lasses hated me.

        One girl there is, I well remember—
She's Teresa on the hill—
Said, "You think you love an angel,
But she is a monkey still.

        "Thanks to all her many trinkets
And her artificial hair
And her many aids to beauty,
Love's own self she would ensnare."

        She was lying, I was angry,
And her cousin, very bold,
Challenged me upon my honor;
What ensued need not be told.

        Highflown words do not become me;
I'm a plain and simple man.
Pure the love that I would offer,
Serving thee as best I can.

        Silken are the bonds of marriage,
When two hearts do intertwine;
Mother Church the yoke will fasten;
Bow your neck and I'll bow mine.

        Or if not, my word I'll give thee,
From these mountains I'll come down—

Saint most holy be my witness—
Wearing a Capuchin gown.[2]

A lad from the village now arrives with news that the student Grisóstomo has died of love for the beautiful shepherdess Marcela. The daughter of a wealthy peasant, Marcela upon the death of her parents had become the ward of her uncle, the village priest. He kept her closely confined, but word of her beauty spread and she had many suitors. She disdained them all, however, and, bent upon remaining fancy free and living her own life, suddenly astonished every one by donning the garb of a shepherdess and taking up her abode in the fields. Many of her suitors, Grisóstomo and his friend Ambrosio among them, thereupon followed her example by becoming shepherds, each hoping that in this manner he might be able to win her. Their hopes proved vain, for she was as obdurate as ever in her attitude toward love. And now Grisóstomo has succumbed and in accordance with his own request is to be "buried in the field, as if he were a Moor," at the foot of a cliff near a spring where he had seen Marcela for the first time. The funeral ceremony is to be a most unusual one, and people from far and wide are coming to witness it. The goatherds are attending in a body, and Don Quixote decides that he too will go. On the way he falls in with a company of gentlemen on horseback and one of them engages him in conversation. After Grisóstomo's death and Marcela's "cruelty" have been duly discussed, the talk turns to the subject of knighthood.

FROM CHAPTER XIII: *In which is brought to a close the story of the shepherdess Marcela, along with other events.*

"I THINK so too," agreed Vivaldo. "I should be willing to delay our journey not one day, but four, for the sake of seeing it."

Don Quixote then asked them what it was they had heard of Marcela and Grisóstomo. The traveler replied that on that very morning they had fallen in with those shepherds and, seeing them so mournfully trigged out, had asked them what the occasion for it was. One of the fellows had then told them of the beauty and strange demeanor of a shepherdess by the name of Marcela, her many suitors, and the death of this Grisóstomo, to whose funeral they were bound. He related, in short, the entire story as Don Quixote had heard it from Pedro.

Changing the subject, the gentleman called Vivaldo inquired of Don Quixote what it was that led him to go armed in that manner in a land that was so peaceful.

"The calling that I profess," replied Don Quixote, "does not permit me to do otherwise. An easy pace, pleasure, and repose—those things were invented for delicate courtiers; but toil, anxiety, and arms—they are for those whom the world knows as knights-errant, of whom I, though unworthy, am the very least."

No sooner had they heard this than all of them immediately took him for a madman. By way of assuring himself further and seeing what kind of madness it was of which Don Quixote was possessed, Vivaldo now asked him what was meant by the term knights-errant.

"Have not your Worships read the annals and the

histories of England that treat of the famous exploits of King Arthur, who in our Castilian balladry is always called King Artús? According to a very old tradition that is common throughout the entire realm of Great Britain, this king did not die, but by an act of enchantment was changed into a raven; and in due course of time he is to return and reign once more, recovering his kingdom and his scepter; for which reason, from that day to this, no Englishman is known to have killed one of those birds. It was, moreover, in the time of that good king that the famous order of the Knights of the Round Table was instituted; and as for the love of Sir Lancelot of the Lake and Queen Guinevere, everything took place exactly as the story has it, their confidante and go-between being the honored matron Quintañona;[1] whence comes that charming ballad that is such a favorite with us Spaniards:

> *Never was there a knight*
> *So served by maid and dame*
> *As the one they call Sir Lancelot*
> *When from Britain he came—*[2]

to carry on the gentle, pleasing course of his loves and noble deeds.

"From that time forth, the order of chivalry was passed on and propagated from one individual to another until it had spread through many and various parts of the world. Among those famed for their exploits was the valiant Amadis of Gaul, with all his sons and grandsons to the fifth generation; and there was also the brave Felixmarte of Hircania,[3] and the never sufficiently praised Tirant lo Blanch; and in view of the fact that he lived in our own day, almost, we came near to seeing, hearing, and conversing with that other courageous knight, Don Belianís of Greece.

"And that, gentlemen, is what it means to be a knight-errant, and what I have been telling you of is the order of chivalry which such a knight professes, an order to which, as I have already informed you, I, although a sinner, have the honor of belonging; for I have made the same profession as have those other knights. That is why it is you find me in these wild and lonely places, riding in quest of adventure, being resolved to offer my arm and my person in the most dangerous undertaking fate may have in store for me, that I may be of aid to the weak and needy."

Listening to this speech, the travelers had some while since come to the conclusion that Don Quixote was out of his mind, and were likewise able to perceive the peculiar nature of his madness, and they wondered at it quite as much as did all those who encountered it for the first time. Being endowed with a ready wit and a merry disposition and thinking to pass the time until they reached the end of the short journey which, so he was told, awaited them before they should arrive at the mountain where the burial was to take place, Vivaldo decided to give him a further opportunity of displaying his absurdities.

"It strikes me, Sir Knight-errant," he said, "that your Grace has espoused one of the most austere professions to be found anywhere on earth—even more austere, if I am not mistaken, than that of the Carthusian monks."

"Theirs may be as austere as ours," Don Quixote replied, "but that it is as necessary I am very much inclined to doubt. For if the truth be told, the soldier who carries out his captain's order does no less than the captain who gives the order. By that I mean to say that the religious, in all peace and tranquility, pray to Heaven for earth's good, but we soldiers and knights put their prayers into execution by defending with the might of our good right arms and at the edge of the sword those things for which they pray; and we do this not under cover of a roof but under the open sky, beneath the insufferable rays of the summer sun and the biting cold of winter. Thus we become the ministers of God on earth, and our arms the means by which He executes His decrees. And just as war and all the things that have to do with it are impossible without toil, sweat, and anxiety, it follows that those who have taken upon themselves such a profession must unquestionably labor harder than do those who in peace and tranquility and at their ease pray God to favor the ones who can do little in their own behalf.

"I do not mean to say—I should not think of saying— that the state of knight-errant is as holy as that of the cloistered monk; I merely would imply, from what I myself endure, that ours is beyond a doubt the more laborious and arduous calling, more beset by hunger and thirst, more wretched, ragged, and ridden with lice. It is an absolute certainty that the knights-errant of old experienced much misfortune in the course of their lives; and if some by their might and valor came to be emperors, you may take my word for it, it cost them dearly in blood and sweat, and if those who rose to such a rank had lacked enchanters and magicians to aid them, they surely would have been cheated of their desires, deceived in their hopes and expectations."

"I agree with you on that," said the traveler, "but there is one thing among others that gives me a very bad impression of the knights-errant, and that is the fact that when they are about to enter upon some great and perilous adventure in which they are in danger of losing their lives, they never at that moment think of commending themselves to God as every good Christian is obliged to do under similar circumstances, but, rather, commend themselves to their ladies with as much fervor and devotion as if their mistresses were God himself; all of which to me smacks somewhat of paganism."

"Sir," Don Quixote answered him, "it could not by any means be otherwise; the knight-errant who did not do so would fall into disgrace, for it is the usage and custom of chivalry that the knight, before engaging in some great feat of arms, shall behold his lady in front of him and shall turn his eyes toward her, gently and lovingly, as if beseeching her favor and protection in the hazardous encounter that awaits him, and even though no one hears him, he is obliged to utter certain words between his teeth, commending himself to her with all his heart; and of this we have numerous examples in the histories. Nor is it to be assumed that he does not commend himself to God also, but the time and place for that is in the course of the undertaking."

"All the same," said the traveler, "I am not wholly clear in this matter; for I have often read of two knights-errant exchanging words until, one word leading to another, their wrath is kindled; whereupon, turning their steeds and taking a good run up the field, they whirl about and bear down upon each other at full speed, commending themselves to their ladies in the midst of it all. What commonly happens then is that one of the two topples from his horse's flanks and is run through and through with the other's lance; and his adversary would also fall to the ground if he did not cling to his horse's mane. What I do not understand is how the dead man would have had time to commend himself to God in the course of this accelerated combat. It would be better if the words he wasted in calling upon his lady as he ran toward the other knight had been spent in paying the debt that he owed as a Christian. Moreover, it is my personal opinion that not all knights-errant have ladies to whom to commend themselves, for not all of them are in love."

"That," said Don Quixote, "is impossible. I assert there can be no knight-errant without a lady; for it is as natural and proper for them to be in love as it is for the heavens to have stars, and I am quite sure that no one ever read a story in which a loveless man of arms was to be met with, for the simple reason that such a one would not be looked upon as a legitimate knight but as a bastard one who had entered the fortress of chivalry not by the main gate, but over the walls, like a robber and a thief."

"Nevertheless," said the traveler, "if my memory serves me right, I have read that Don Galaor, brother of the valorous Amadis of Gaul, never had a special lady to whom he prayed, yet he was not held in any the less esteem for that but was a very brave and famous knight."

Once again, our Don Quixote had an answer. "Sir, one swallow does not make a summer. And in any event, I happen to know that this knight was secretly very much in love. As for his habit of paying court to all the ladies that caught his fancy, that was a natural propensity on his part and one that he was unable to resist. There was, however, one particular lady whom he had made the mistress of his will and to whom he did commend himself very frequently and privately; for he prided himself upon being a reticent knight."

"Well, then," said the traveler, "if it is essential that every knight-errant be in love, it is to be presumed that your Grace is also, since you are of the profession. And unless it be that you pride yourself upon your reticence as much as did Don Galaor, then I truly, on my own behalf and in the name of all this company, beseech your Grace to tell us your lady's name, the name of the country where she resides, what her rank is, and something of the beauty of her person, that she may esteem herself fortunate in having all the world know that she is loved and served by such a knight as your Grace appears to me to be."

At this, Don Quixote heaved a deep sigh. "I cannot say," he began, "as to whether or not my sweet enemy would be pleased that all the world should know I serve her. I can only tell you, in response to the question which you have so politely put to me, that her name is Dulcinea, her place of residence El Toboso, a village of La Mancha. As to her rank, she should be at the very least a princess, seeing that she is my lady and my queen. Her beauty is superhuman, for in it are realized all the impossible and chimerical attributes that poets are accustomed to give their fair ones. Her locks are golden, her brow the Elysian Fields, her eyebrows rainbows, her eyes suns, her cheeks roses, her lips coral, her teeth pearls, her neck alabaster, her bosom marble, her hands ivory, her complexion snow-white. As for those parts which modesty keeps covered from the human sight, it is my opinion that, discreetly considered, they are only to be extolled and not compared to any other."

"We should like," said Vivaldo, "to know something as well of her lineage, her race and ancestry."

"She is not," said Don Quixote, "of the ancient Roman Curtii, Caii, or Scipios, nor of the modern Colonnas and Orsini, nor of the Moncadas and Requesenses of Catalonia, nor is she of the Rebellas and Villanovas of Valencia, or the Palafoxes, Nuzas, Rocabertis, Corellas, Lunas, Alagones, Urreas, or Gurreas of Aragon, the Cerdas, Manriques, Mendozas, or Guzmanes of Castile, the Alencastros, Pallas, or Menezes of Portugal; but she is of the Tobosos of La Mancha, and although the line is a modern one, it well may give rise to the most illustrious families of the centuries to come. And let none dispute this with me, unless it be under the conditions which Zerbino has set forth in the inscription beneath Orlando's arms:

> *These let none move*
> *Who dares not with Orlando his valor prove."* [4]

"Although my own line," replied the traveler, "is that of the Gachupins[5] of Laredo, I should not venture to compare it with the Tobosos of La Mancha, in view of the fact that, to tell you the truth, I have never heard the name before."

"How does it come that you have never heard it!" exclaimed Don Quixote.

The others were listening most attentively to the conversation of these two, and even the goatherds and shepherds were by now aware that our knight of La Mancha was more than a little insane. Sancho Panza alone thought that all his master said was the truth, for he was well acquainted with him, having known him since birth. The only doubt in his mind had to do with the beauteous Dulcinea del Toboso, for he knew of no such princess and the name was strange to his ears, although he lived not far from that place.

There follows an account of the strange burial, in the course of which Vivaldo reads one of Grisóstomo's despairing poems.

FROM CHAPTER XIV: *In which are . . . other unlooked-for happenings.*

HE WAS about to read another of the papers he had saved from the fire when he was stopped by a marvelous vision—for such it appeared—that suddenly met his sight; for there atop the rock beside which the grave was being hollowed out stood the shepherdess Marcela herself, more beautiful even than she was reputed to be. Those who up to then had never seen her looked on in silent admiration, while those who were accustomed to beholding her were held in as great a suspense as the ones who were gazing upon her for the first time.

No sooner had Ambrosio glimpsed her than, with a show of indignation, he called out to her, "So, fierce basilisk of these mountains, have you perchance come to see if in your presence blood will flow from the wounds of this poor wretch whom you by your cruelty have deprived of life? Have you come to gloat over your inhuman exploits, or would you from that height look down like another pitiless Nero upon your Rome in flames and ashes? Or perhaps you would arrogantly tread under foot this poor corpse, as an ungrateful daughter did that of her father Tarquinius? Tell us quickly why you have come and what it is that you want most; for I know that Grisóstomo's thoughts never failed to obey you in life, and though he is dead now, I will see that all those who call themselves his friends obey you likewise."

"I do not come, O Ambrosio, for any of the reasons that you have mentioned," replied Marcela. "I come to defend myself and to demonstrate how unreasonable all those persons are who blame me for their sufferings and for Grisóstomo's death. I therefore ask all present to hear me attentively. It will not take long and I shall not have to spend many words in persuading those of you who are sensible that I speak the truth.

"Heaven made me beautiful, you say, so beautiful that you are compelled to love me whether you will or no; and in return for the love that you show me, you would have it that I am obliged to love you in return. I know, with that natural understanding that God has given me, that everything beautiful is lovable; but I cannot see that it follows that the object that is loved for its beauty must love the one who loves it. Let us suppose that the lover of the beautiful were ugly and, being ugly, deserved to be shunned; it would then be highly absurd for him to say, 'I love you because you are beautiful; you must love me because I am ugly.'

"But assuming that two individuals are equally beautiful, it does not mean that their desires are the same; for not all beauty inspires love, but may sometimes merely delight the eye and leave the will intact. If it were otherwise, no one would know what he wanted, but all would wander vaguely and aimlessly with nothing upon which to settle their affections; for the number of beautiful objects being infinite, desires similarly would be boundless. I have heard it said that true love knows no division and must be voluntary and not forced. This being so, as I believe it is, then why would you compel me to surrender my will for no other reason than that you say you love me? But tell me: supposing that Heaven which made me beautiful had made me ugly instead, should I have any right to complain because you did not love me? You must remember, moreover, that I did not choose this beauty that is mine; such as it is, Heaven gave it to me of its grace, without any choice or asking on my part. As the viper is not to be blamed for the deadly poison that it bears, since that is a gift of nature, so I do not deserve to be reprehended for my comeliness of form.

"Beauty in a modest woman is like a distant fire or a sharp-edged sword: the one does not burn, the other does not cut, those who do not come near it. Honor and virtue are the adornments of the soul, without which the body is not beautiful though it may appear to be. If modesty is one of the virtues that most adorn and beautify body and soul, why should she who is loved for her beauty part with that virtue merely to satisfy the whim of one who solely for his own pleasure strives with all his force and energy to cause her to lose it? I was born a free being, and in order to live freely I chose the solitude of the fields; these mountain trees are my company, the clear-running waters in these brooks are my mirror, and to the trees and waters I communicate my thoughts and lend them of my beauty.

"In short, I am that distant fire, that sharp-edged sword, that does not burn or cut. Those who have been enamored by the sight of me I have disillusioned with my words; and if desire is sustained by hope, I gave none to Grisóstomo or any other, and of none of them can it be said that I killed them with my cruelty, for it was rather their own obstinacy that was to blame. And if you reproach me with the fact that his intentions were honorable and that I ought for that reason to have complied with them, I will tell you that when, on this very spot where his grave is now being dug, he revealed them to me, I replied that it was my own intention to live in perpetual solitude and that only the earth should enjoy the fruit of my retirement and the spoils of my beauty; and if he with all this plain-speaking was still stubbornly bent upon hoping against hope and sailing against the wind, is it to be wondered at if he drowned in the gulf of his own folly?

"Had I led him on, it would have been falsely; had I gratified his passion, it would have been against my own best judgment and intentions; but, though I had disillusioned him, he persisted, and though I did not hate him, he was driven to despair. Ask yourselves, then, if it is reasonable to blame me for his woes! Let him who has been truly deceived complain; let him despair who has been cheated of his promised hopes; if I have enticed any, let him speak up; if I have accepted the attentions of any, let him boast of it; but let not him to whom I have promised nothing, whom I have neither enticed nor accepted, apply to me such terms as cruel and homicidal. It has not as yet been Heaven's will to destine me to love any man, and there is no use expecting me to love of my own free choice.

"Let what I am saying now apply to each and every one of those who would have me for their own, and let it be understood from now on that if any die on account of me, he is not to be regarded as an unfortunate victim of jealousy, since she that cares for none can give to none the occasion for being jealous; nor is my plain-speaking to be taken as disdain. He who calls me a wild beast and a basilisk, let him leave me alone as something that is evil and harmful; let him who calls me ungrateful cease to wait upon me; let him who finds me strange shun my acquaintance; if I am cruel, do not run after me; in which case this wild beast, this basilisk, this strange, cruel, ungrateful creature will not run after them, seek them out, wait upon them, nor endeavor to know them in any way.

"The thing that killed Grisóstomo was his impatience and the impetuosity of his desire; so why blame my modest conduct and retiring life? If I choose to preserve my purity here in the company of the trees, how can he complain of my unwillingness to lose it who would have me keep it with other men? I, as you know, have a worldly fortune of my own and do not covet that of others. My life is a free one, and I do not wish to be subject to another in any way. I neither love nor hate anyone; I do not repel this one and allure that one; I do not play fast and loose with any. The modest conversation of these village lasses and the care of my goats is sufficient to occupy me. Those mountains there represent the bounds of my desire, and should my wishes go beyond them, it is but to contemplate the beauty of the heavens, that pathway by which the soul travels to its first dwelling place."

Saying this and without waiting for any reply, she turned her back and entered the thickest part of a near-by wood, leaving all present lost in admiration of her wit as well as her beauty. A few—those who had felt the powerful dart of her glances and bore the wounds inflicted by her lovely eyes—were of a mind to follow her, taking no heed of the plainly worded warning they had just had from her lips; whereupon Don Quixote, seeing this and thinking to himself that here was an opportunity to display his chivalry by succoring a damsel in distress, laid his hand upon the hilt of his sword and cried out, loudly and distinctly, "Let no person of whatever state or condition he may be dare to follow the beauteous Marcela under pain of incurring my furious wrath. She has shown with clear and sufficient reasons that little or no blame for Grisóstomo's death is to be attached to her; she has likewise shown how far she is from acceding to the desires of any of her suitors, and it is accordingly only just that in place of being hounded and persecuted she should be honored and esteemed by all good people in this world as the only woman in it who lives with such modesty and good intentions."

After the burial Don Quixote declines the invitation of Vivaldo and his companions to accompany them to Seville, saying he must first rid the mountains of the robbers and bandits with which they were said to be infested. The travelers accordingly take leave of him.

More Adventures along the Way

(CHAPTERS XV-XXII)

CHAPTER XV. *In which is related the unfortunate adventure that befell Don Quixote when he encountered certain wicked Yanguesans.*

THE learned Cid Benengeli tells us that, upon taking leave of their hosts and all those who had attended the shepherd Grisóstomo's funeral, Don Quixote and his squire entered the same wood into which they had seen the shepherdess Marcela disappear, and that, having journeyed in the forest for more than two hours, looking for her everywhere without being able to discover her, they finally came to a meadow covered with fresh young grass, alongside the cool and placid waters of a mountain stream which irresistibly invited them to pause there during the noontide heat, for the sun was now beating down upon them. The two of them accordingly dismounted and, turning Rocinante and the ass out to feed upon the plentiful pasturage, proceeded to investigate the contents of the saddlebags, after which, without further ceremony, master and man sat down together very peaceably and sociably to eat what they had found there.

Now, Sancho had not taken the trouble to put fetters on Rocinante, knowing the hack to be so tame and so little inclined to lust that, he felt certain, all the mares in the Cordovan meadowlands would not be able to tempt him to an indiscretion. But fate and the devil—

who is not always sleeping—had ordained that a herd of Galician ponies belonging to some carters of Yanguas[1] should be feeding in this same valley; for it was the custom of these men to stop for their siesta in some place where grass and water were to be had for their teams, and as it happened, the spot the Yanguesans had chosen on this occasion was not far from where Don Quixote was.

Then it was that Rocinante suddenly felt the desire to have a little sport with the ladies. The moment he scented them, he abandoned his customary gait and staid behavior and, without asking his master's leave, trotted briskly over to them to acquaint them with his needs. They, however, preferred to go on eating, or so it seemed, for they received him with their hoofs and teeth, to such good effect that they broke his girth and left him naked and without a saddle. But the worst of it was when the carters, seeing the violence that he was offering their mares, came running up with poles and so belabored him that they left him lying there badly battered on the ground.

At this point Don Quixote and Sancho, who had witnessed the drubbing that Rocinante received, also ran up, panting. It was the master who spoke first.

"So far as I can see, friend Sancho," he said, "those are not knights but low fellows of ignoble birth; and so you may very well aid me in wreaking a deserved vengeance upon them for the wrong they have done to Rocinante in front of our very eyes."

"What the devil kind of vengeance are we going to take," asked Sancho, "seeing there are more than twenty of them and not more than two of us, or maybe only one and a half?"

"I," replied Don Quixote, "am worth a hundred." Without saying anything more, he drew his sword and fell upon the Yanguesans, and, moved and incited by his master's example, Sancho Panza did the same.

At the first slashing blow he dealt, the knight laid open the leather jacket that the man wore along with a good part of one shoulder. Seeing themselves assaulted like this by two lone individuals while they were so many in number, the Yanguesans again ran up with their poles and, surrounding their assailants, began flaying them with great ardor and vehemence. The truth is that the second blow sufficed to lay Sancho low, and the same thing happened with Don Quixote, all his dexterity and high courage availing him not at all. As luck would have it, he fell at Rocinante's feet, for the animal had not yet been able to rise; all of which goes to show what damage poles can do when furiously wielded by angry rustics. When the Yanguesans saw what mischief they had wrought, they lost no time in loading their teams and were soon off down the road, leaving the two adventurers in a sorry plight and a worse mood.

The first to recover his senses was Sancho Panza. Finding himself beside his master, he called out to him in a weak and piteous voice, "Señor Don Quixote! Ah, Señor Don Quixote!"

"What do you want, brother Sancho?" said the knight in the same feeble, suffering tone that the squire had used.

"I'd like, if possible," said Sancho, "for your Grace to give me a couple of draughts of that ugly Bras,[2] if you happen to have any of it at hand. Perhaps it would be as good for broken bones as it is for wounds."

"If I only did have some of it, wretch that I am," said Don Quixote, "what more could we ask for? But I swear to you, Sancho Panza, on the word of a knight-errant, that before two days have passed, unless fortune should rule otherwise, I shall have it in my possession, or else my hands will have failed me."

"But how many days do you think it will be, your Grace, before we are able to move our feet?" Sancho wanted to know.

"For my part," said his well-cudgeled master, "I must confess that I cannot answer that question. I hold myself to blame for everything. I had no business putting hand to sword against men who had not been dubbed knights and so were not my equals. Because I thus violated the laws of knighthood, the God of battles has permitted this punishment to be inflicted upon me. For which reason, Sancho, you should pay attention to what I am about to say to you, for it may have much to do with the safety of both of us. Hereafter, when you see a rabble of this sort committing some offense against us, do not wait for me to draw my sword, for I shall not do so under any circumstances, but, rather, draw your own and chastise them to your heart's content. If any knights come to their aid and defense, I will protect you by attacking them with all my might; and you already know by a thousand proofs and experiences the valor of this, my strong right arm."

For the poor gentleman was still feeling puffed up as a result of his victory over the valiant Biscayan. His advice, however, did not strike Sancho as being so good that he could let it pass without an answer.

"Sir," he said, "I am a peaceful man, calm and quiet, and I can put up with any insult because I have a wife and young ones to support and bring up; and so let me advise your Grace, since it is not for me to lay down the law, that under no consideration will I draw my sword, either against rustic or against knight, but from now on, as God is my witness, I hereby pardon all wrongs that have been done or may be done to me by any person high or low, rich or poor, gentleman or commoner, without excepting any rank or walk in life whatsoever."

"I wish," said his master, "that I had a little breath so that I could speak to you without so much effort; I wish the pain in this rib would subside somewhat so that I might be able, Sancho, to show you how wrong you are. Come now, you sinner, supposing that the wind of fortune, which up to now has been so contrary a one, should veer in our favor, filling the sails of our desire so that we should certainly and without anything to hinder us be able to put into port at one of those islands that I have promised you, what would happen to you if, winning the victory, I were to make you the ruler of it? You will have rendered that impossible by not being a knight nor caring to become one, and by having no intention of avenging the insults offered you or defending your seignorial rights.

"For you must know that in newly conquered kingdoms and provinces the minds of the inhabitants are never tranquil, nor do they like their new lords so well that there is not to be feared some fresh move on their part to alter the existing state of affairs and, as the saying goes, see what their luck will bring. And so it is necessary that the new ruler possess the ability to govern and the valor to attack or defend himself as the case may be."

"Well, in the present case," said Sancho, "I can only wish I had that ability and that valor of which your Grace speaks; but I swear to you on the word of a poor man that I need a poultice more than I do an argument. If your Grace will try to rise, we will help Rocinante up, although he does not deserve it, seeing that he is the principal cause of this thrashing we have received. I never would have thought it of him; I always took him to be as chaste and peaceful as I am. Oh, well, they say it takes a lot of time to get to know a person and nothing in this life is certain. Who would have thought that those mighty slashes your Grace gave that poor knight-errant would be followed posthaste by such a tempest of blows as they let fall upon our shoulders?"

"Your shoulders, at any rate," observed Don Quixote, "ought to be used to such squalls as that, but mine, accustomed to fine cambric and Dutch linen, naturally feel more acutely the pain of this misfortune that has befallen us. And if I did not imagine—why do I say imagine?—if I did not know for a certainty that all these discomforts are the inevitable accompaniment of the profession of arms, I should straightway lay me down and die of pure vexation."

"Sir," replied the squire, "seeing that these mishaps are what one reaps when one is a knight, I wish your Grace would tell me if they happen very often or only at certain times; for it seems to me that after two such harvests, there will not be much left of us for the third, unless God in His infinite mercy sees fit to succor us."

"Be assured, friend Sancho," said Don Quixote, "that the life of knights-errant is subject to a thousand perils and misadventures. At the same time, it is within the power of those same knights to become at almost any moment kings and emperors, as experience has shown in the case of many different ones whose histories I know well. If this pain of mine permitted me, I could tell you right now of some who merely by the might of their arm have risen to the highest stations such as I have mentioned; yet these very ones, both before and after, endured various troubles and calamities.

"There was the valorous Amadis of Gaul, who fell into the power of his mortal enemy, Arcalaus the enchanter, who, after he had taken him prisoner and had bound him to a pillar in the courtyard, is known for a fact to have given him more than two hundred lashes with his horse's reins. And there is a certain author of no little repute, though his name is not widely known, who tells us how the Knight of the Sun, in a certain castle, was caught in a trapdoor that opened beneath his feet; on falling through the trap, he found himself in a deep underground pit, bound hand and foot, and they gave him one of those so-called clysters of sand and snow-water that all but finished him. Indeed, if in this great peril a magician who was a great friend of his had not come to his aid, it would have gone very badly with the poor knight.

"And so I well may suffer in the company of such worthy ones; for the indignities that they endured are worse than those that we have had to suffer. I would inform you, Sancho, that those wounds that are inflicted by any instruments that chance to be in the assailant's hand do not constitute an affront, as is expressly laid down in the dueling code. Thus, if the shoemaker strike another with the last that he holds, although it is really of wood, it cannot for that reason be said that the one attacked with it has been cudgeled. I tell you this in order that you may not think that, because we have been beaten to a pulp in this combat, an affront has thereby been offered us; for the arms that those men bore and with which they pommeled us were nothing other than stakes, and none of them, so far as I can recall, carried a rapier, sword, or dagger."

"They did not give me time to see what they carried," said Sancho, "for I had no sooner laid hands on my blade than they made the sign of the cross over my shoulder with their clubs, taking away the sight of my eyes and the strength of my feet, after which they went off and left me lying here where I am now, and I am not taking the trouble to think whether or not those blows they gave me with their poles were an affront; all I can think of is the pain they have caused me, which is as deeply imprinted on my memory as it is on my shoulders."

"But with all that, brother Panza," said Don Quixote, "I must remind you that there is no memory to which time does not put an end and no pain that death does not abolish."

"Well," said Panza, "what greater misfortune could there be than that of having to wait on time and death? If this trouble of ours were one of those that are cured with a couple of poultices, it would not be so bad. But I am beginning to think that all the plasters in a hospital will not be enough to put us in shape again."

"Leave all that," said Don Quixote, "and draw strength from weakness as I propose to do. Come, let us see how Rocinante is; for, it appears to me, the poor beast has had the worst of this mishap."

"I am not surprised at that," said Sancho, "in view of the fact that he is a knight-errant also. What does astonish me is that my donkey should have gone free and without costs while we have come off without our ribs." [3]

"Fortune," said Don Quixote, "always leaves a door open in adversity as a means of remedying it. What I would say is, this little beast may take the place of Rocinante now by carrying me to some castle where I may be healed of my wounds. And I may add that I do not look upon it as a disgrace to go mounted like that, for I recall having read that good old Silenus, the tutor and instructor of the merry god of laughter, when he entered the city of the hundred gates,[4] was pleased to do so mounted upon a very handsome ass."

"That may very well be," said Sancho, "but there is a big difference between going mounted and being slung across the animal's flanks like a bag of refuse."

"Wounds received in battle," replied Don Quixote, "confer honor, they do not take it away; and so, friend Sancho, say no more, but, as I have already told you, lift me up the best you can and place me on the ass in any fashion that pleases you, and we will then be on our way before night descends upon us here in this wilderness."

"But I thought I heard your Grace say," remarked Panza, "that it is very fitting for knights-errant to sleep out in the cold wastes and desert places the better part of the year, and that they esteem it a great good fortune to be able to do so."

"That," said Don Quixote, "is when they have no choice in the matter or when they are in love; and, it is true, there have been knights who for two years' time have remained upon a rock, in sun and shade and through all the inclemencies of the heavens, without their ladies knowing anything about it. One of these was Amadis, who, under the name of Beltenebros, took up his lodging on the rock known as Peña Pobre, remaining there either eight years or eight months, I am not quite certain as to the exact length of time; what matters is that he was there doing penance for some slight offense that he had given to his lady Oriana. But let us quit this talk, Sancho, and make haste before something happens to the ass as it did to Rocinante."

"There will be the devil to pay in that case," said Sancho; and venting himself of thirty "Ohs" and "Ahs" and sixty sighs and a hundred-twenty imprecations of various sorts, with curses for the one who had got him into this, he arose, pausing halfway like a Turkish bow bent in the middle, without the power to straighten

himself. It was with the greatest difficulty that he succeeded in saddling his ass, which, making use of the
unwonted freedom it had enjoyed that day, had wandered off some little distance. He then managed to get
Rocinante on his feet, and if that animal had possessed
the power to complain, you may be sure that he would
have been an equal for Sancho and his master.

The end of the matter was, Sancho seated Don
Quixote upon the donkey, tying Rocinante on behind,
and then started off leading the ass by the halter, proceeding more or less in the direction in which he thought
the main highway ought to be; and as chance was now
guiding their affairs from good to better, he had gone
but a short league when there before them was the
road—not only the road but an inn, which greatly to
Sancho's disgust and his master's delight had, of course,
to be a castle. The squire stubbornly insisted that it was
not a castle but a hostelry, while his master maintained
the contrary. The argument lasted so long that they
had reached the inn before it was ended, and with
the point still unsettled, Sancho entered the gateway,
followed by his cavalcade.

CHAPTER XVI. *Of what happened to the ingenious
gentleman in the inn which he imagined was a
castle.*

UPON seeing Don Quixote thus slung across the ass,
the innkeeper inquired of Sancho what was wrong.
The squire replied that it was nothing; his master had
fallen from a cliff and bruised a few ribs, that was all.
Now, the innkeeper had a wife who was not the kind
one would expect to find among women of her calling,
for she was naturally of a charitable disposition and

inclined to sympathize with those of her neighbors who were in trouble. She accordingly came running up to take care of her injured guest and called upon her daughter, who was young and very good-looking, to lend her a helping hand.

Serving in the inn, also, was a lass from Asturia, broad-faced, flat-headed, and with a snub nose; she was blind in one eye and could not see very well out of the other. To be sure, her bodily graces made up for her other defects: she measured not more than seven palms from head to foot, and, being slightly hunchbacked, she had to keep looking at the ground a good deal more than she liked. This gentle creature in turn aided the daughter of the house, and the two made up a very uncomfortable bed for Don Quixote in an attic which gave every evidence of having formerly been a hay-loft and which held another lodger, a mule driver, whose bed stood a little beyond the one they had prepared for our friend.

The muleteer's couch was composed of the pack-saddles and blankets from his beasts, but it was a better one for all of that. The other consisted merely of four smooth planks laid upon two trestles of uneven height, and had a mattress so thin that it looked more like a counterpane, with lumps which, had they not been seen through the rents to be of wool, might from the feel of them have been taken for pebbles. To cover him, the knight had a pair of sheets made of the kind of leather they use on bucklers and a quilt whose threads anyone who chose might have counted without missing a single one.

On this wretched pallet Don Quixote stretched himself out, and then the innkeeper's wife and daughter proceeded to cover him from top to toe with plasters while Maritornes (for that was the Asturian girl's name) held the light. As she applied the poultices, the mistress of the house remarked that he was so black-and-blue in spots that his bruises looked more like the marks of blows than like those caused by a fall.

"They were not blows," said Sancho, adding that the rock had many sharp points and jutting edges and each one had left its imprint. "If your Ladyship," he went on, "can manage to save a little of that tow, it will come in handy, for my loins also hurt me a little."

"So, then," replied the innkeeper's wife, "you must have fallen too."

"I did not fall," said Sancho Panza, "but the shock I had at seeing my master take such a tumble makes my body ache as if I had received a thousand whacks."

"That may very well be," said the daughter, "for I have often dreamed that I was falling from a tower and yet I never reached the ground, and when I awoke from my dream I would feel as bruised and broken as if I had really fallen."

"The point is, lady," Sancho explained, "that I was not dreaming at all, but was more wide awake than I am at this minute, and yet I find myself with scarcely less bruises than my master, Don Quixote."

"What did you say the gentleman's name was?" asked Maritornes, the Asturian.

"Don Quixote de la Mancha," replied Sancho, "and he is a knightly adventurer and one of the best and bravest that the world has seen for a long time."

"What is a knightly adventurer?" the girl wished to know.

"Are you so unused to the ways of the world that you don't know that?" he said. "Then let me inform you, my sister, that it is something that can be summed up in two or three words: well thrashed and an emperor; today, he is the most wretched and needy creature that there is, and tomorrow he will have the crowns of two or three kingdoms to give to his squire."

"If that is so," said the innkeeper's wife, "how does it come that you, being this worthy gentleman's squire, have not so much as an earldom, to judge by appearances?"

"It is early yet," was Sancho's answer. "We have been looking for adventures for only a month now, and so far have not fallen in with what could rightly be called one. Sometimes you look for one thing and you find another. The truth is, once my master Don Quixote is healed of this wound or fall, providing I am none the worse for it all, I would not exchange my expectations for the best title in all Spain."

The knight had been following this conversation very closely; and at this point, raising himself up in the bed as well as he was able, he took the landlady's hand and said to her, "Believe me, beautiful lady, you well may call yourself fortunate for having given a lodging in this your castle to my person. If I myself do not tell you of my merits, it is for the reason that, as the saying goes, self-praise is degrading; but my squire can inform you as to who I am. I will only say that I have written down in my memory for all eternity the service which you have rendered me, that I may give you thanks as long as life endures. And I would to high Heaven that love did not hold me so captive and subject to its laws, and to the eyes of that beauteous but ungrateful one whose name I mutter between my teeth;[1] for then the orbs of this lovely damsel here would surely be the mistress of my liberty."

The landlady, her daughter, and the worthy Maritornes were very much bewildered by these remarks of the knight-errant; they understood about as much of them as if he had been speaking Greek, although they were able to make out that he was offering them flattery and compliments. Being wholly unused to such language, they could but stare at him in amazement, for he seemed to them a different kind of man from any they had known. And so, thanking him in their own idiom, which was that of a wayside tavern, they left him, while Maritornes looked after Sancho, who had no less need of attention than did his master.

The mule driver had arranged with the Asturian to have a little sport with her that night, and she had given him her word that, as soon as the guests were quiet and her master and mistress asleep, she would come to him and let him have his way. It was commonly said of the good lass that she never made such a promise without keeping it, even though it was in a forest and without witnesses, for she prided herself greatly upon being a lady and did not look upon it as any disgrace to be a servant in an inn, for, as she was in the habit of saying, it was misfortunes and ill luck that had brought her to such a state.

Don Quixote's hard, narrow, cramped, makeshift bed stood in the middle of this starry stable[2] and was the first that one encountered upon entering the room. Next to it was that of his squire, Sancho, which consisted solely of a cattail mat and a blanket that looked as if it was of shorn canvas rather than of wool. And beyond these two was that of the mule driver, made up, as has been said, of packsaddles and all the trappings of his two best mules, although he had twelve of them altogether, sleek, fat, and in fine condition; for he was one of the richest carters of Arévalo, according to the author of this history who knew him well and makes special mention of him—some say they were related in one way or another. In any event, Cid Hamete Benengeli was a historian who was at great

pains to ascertain the truth and very accurate in everything, as is evident from the fact that he did not see fit
to pass over in silence those details that have been
mentioned, however trifling and insignificant they may
appear to be.

All of which might serve as an example to those grave
chroniclers who give us such brief and succinct accounts
that we barely get a taste, the gist of the matter being
left in their inkwells out of carelessness, malice, or ignorance. Blessings on the author of the *Tablante de
Ricamonte*[3] and the one who wrote that other work in
which are related the deeds of Count Tomillas[4]—with
what exactitude they describe everything!

But to go on with our story, the mule driver, after he
had looked in on his beasts and had given them their
second feeding, came back and stretched out on his
packsaddles to await that model of conscientiousness,
Maritornes. Sancho, having been duly poulticed, had
also lain down and was doing his best to sleep, but the
pain in his ribs would not let him. As for Don Quixote,
he was suffering so much that he kept his eyes open like
a rabbit. The inn was silent now, and there was no
light other than from a lantern which hung in the
middle of the gateway.

This uncanny silence, and our knight's constant habit
of thinking of incidents described at every turn in those
books that had been the cause of all his troubles, now
led him to conceive as weird a delusion as could well
be imagined. He fancied that he had reached a famous
castle—for, as has been said, every inn where he
stopped was a castle to him—and that the daughter of
the lord (innkeeper) who dwelt there, having been
won over by his gentle bearing, had fallen in love with
him and had promised him that she would come that
night, without her parents' knowledge, to lie beside

him for a while. And taking this chimerical fancy which
he had woven out of his imagination to be an established fact, he then began to be grieved at the thought
that his virtue was thus being endangered, and firmly
resolved not be false to his lady Dulcinea del Toboso,
even though Queen Guinevere with her waiting-
woman Quintañona should present themselves in person before him.

As he lay there, his mind filled with such nonsense as
his, the hour that had been fixed for the Asturian's
visit came, and an unlucky one it proved to be for Don
Quixote. Clad in her nightgown and barefoot, her
hair done up in a fustian net, Maritornes with silent,
cautious steps stole into the room where the three were
lodged, in search of the muleteer. She had no sooner
crossed the threshold, however, than the knight became aware of her presence; and, sitting up in bed
despite his poultices and the pain from his ribs, he held
out his arms as if to receive the beautiful maiden. The
latter, all doubled up and saying nothing, was groping
her way to her lover's cot when she encountered Don
Quixote. Seizing her firmly by the wrists, he drew her
to him, without her daring to utter a sound.

Forcing her to sit down upon the bed, he began
fingering her nightgown, and although it was of sackcloth, it impressed him as being of the finest and flim-
siest silken gauze. On her wrists she wore some glass
beads, but to him they gave off the gleam of oriental
pearls. Her hair, which resembled a horse's mane rather
than anything else, he decided was like filaments of the
brightest gold of Araby whose splendor darkened even
that of the sun. Her breath without a doubt smelled of
yesterday's stale salad, but for Don Quixote it was a
sweet and aromatic odor that came from her mouth.

The short of it is, he pictured her in his imagination

as having the same appearance and manners as those other princesses whom he had read about in his books, who, overcome by love and similarly bedecked, came to visit their badly wounded knights. So great was the poor gentleman's blindness that neither his sense of touch nor the girl's breath nor anything else about her could disillusion him, although they were enough to cause anyone to vomit who did not happen to be a mule driver. To him it seemed that it was the goddess of beauty herself whom he held in his arms.

Clasping her tightly, he went on to speak to her in a low and amorous tone of voice. "Would that I were in a position, O beauteous and highborn lady, to be able to repay the favor that you have accorded me by thus affording me the sight of your great loveliness; but Fortune, which never tires of persecuting those who are worthy, has willed to place me in this bed where I lie so bruised and broken that, even though my desire were to satisfy yours, such a thing would be impossible. And added to this impossibility is another, greater one: my word and promise given to the peerless Dulcinea del Toboso, the one and only lady of my most secret thoughts. If this did not stand in the way, I should not be so insensible a knight as to let slip the fortunate opportunity which you out of your great goodness of heart have placed in my way."

Maritornes was extremely vexed and all a-sweat at finding herself held fast in Don Quixote's embrace, and without paying any heed to what he was saying she struggled silently to break away. Meanwhile, the mule driver, whose evil desires had kept him awake, had been aware of his wench's presence ever since she entered the door and had been listening attentively to everything that Don Quixote said. Jealous because the Asturian lass, as he thought, had broken her word and deserted him for another, he came up to the knight's cot and, without being able to make head or tail of all this talk, stood there waiting to see what the outcome would be.

When he saw that the girl was doing her best to free herself and Don Quixote was trying to hold her, he decided that the joke had gone far enough; raising his fist high above his head, he came down with so fearful a blow on the gaunt jaws of the enamored knight as to fill the poor man's mouth with blood. Not satisfied with this, the mule driver jumped on his ribs and at a pace somewhat faster than a trot gave them a thorough going-over from one end to the other. The bed, which was rather weak and not very firm on its foundations, was unable to support the muleteer's added weight and sank to the floor with a loud crash. This awoke the innkeeper, who imagined that Maritornes must be involved in some brawl, since he had called twice to her and had received no answer. Suspicious of what was going on, he arose, lighted a lamp, and made his way to the place from which the sound of the scuffle appeared to be coming. Frightened out of her wits when she heard her master, for she knew what a terrible temper he had, the girl took refuge beside Sancho Panza, who was still sleeping, and huddled herself there like a ball of yarn.

"Where are you, whore?" cried the landlord as he came in; "for I am certain that this is all your doing."

At that moment Sancho awoke and, feeling a bulky object almost on top of him and thinking it must be a nightmare, began throwing his fists about on one side and the other, giving Maritornes no telling how many punches. Feeling the pain, the wench cast all modesty aside and let him have so many blows in return that he very soon emerged from his sleepy state. When he saw himself being treated like this by an unknown assailant, he rose the best way he could and grappled with her, and there then began between the two of them the prettiest and most stubbornly fought skirmish that ever you saw.

When the muleteer perceived by the light of the lamp what was happening to his lady, he left Don Quixote and went to her assistance. The innkeeper also came over to her, but with different intentions, for he meant to punish the girl, thinking that, undoubtedly, she was the cause of all the disturbance that prevailed. And so, then, as the saying goes, it was "the cat to the rat, the rat to the rope, the rope to the stick." [5] There was the mule driver pounding Sancho, Sancho and the wench flaying each other, and the landlord drubbing the girl; and they all laid on most vigorously, without allowing themselves a moment's rest. The best part of it was, the lamp went out, leaving them in darkness, whereupon there ensued a general and merciless melee, until there was not a hand's breadth left on any of their bodies that was not sore and aching.

As chance would have it, there was lodged at the inn that night a patrolman of the old Holy Brotherhood of Toledo, who, hearing all this uproar and the sounds of a struggle, at once snatched up his staff of office and the tin box containing his warrants and went groping his way through the darkness to the room above, as he cried, "Hold, in the name of the law! Hold, in the name of the Holy Brotherhood!" The first one whom he encountered was the well-pommeled Don Quixote, who lay flat on his back and senseless on his broken-down bed. Grasping the knight's beard, the officer cried, "I charge you to aid the law!" But when he perceived that the one whom he thus held did not budge nor stir, he concluded that the man must be dead and the others in the room his murderers. Acting upon this suspicion, he called out in a booming voice, "Close the gateway of the inn! See that no one leaves, for someone here has killed a man!"

This cry startled them all, and each one left off his pommeling at the point where he was. The innkeeper then retired to his room, the mule driver to his pack-saddles, and the wench to her stall, the poor unfortunate Don Quixote and Sancho being the only ones that could not move. The officer now let go of our friend's beard and left the room to go look for a light, that he might arrest the offenders. He did not find any, however, for the innkeeper had taken care to put out the lantern when he retired to his room, and the representative of the Holy Brotherhood was accordingly compelled to have recourse to the hearth, where with a great deal of time and trouble he finally succeeded in lighting another lamp.

CHAPTER XVII. *Wherein is continued the account of the innumerable troubles that the brave Don Quixote and his good squire Sancho Panza endured in the inn, which, to his sorrow, the knight took to be a castle.*

HAVING by this time recovered from his swoon, Don Quixote called to his squire in the same tone of voice that he had used the day before as they lay stretched out in the "vale of stakes." [1] "Sancho, my friend, are you asleep? Are you asleep, friend Sancho?"

"How do you expect me to sleep, curses on it?" replied the squire, who was filled with bitterness and sorrow. "I think all the devils in Hell must have been after me tonight."

"You are undoubtedly right about that," said his master; "for either I know little about it or this castle is an enchanted one. I may as well tell you—but first you must swear that you will keep it a secret until after I am dead."

"I swear," said Sancho.

"I ask that," Don Quixote went on, "because I hate taking away anyone's good name."

"I told you," Sancho repeated, "that I will say nothing about it until your Grace has reached the end of his days; and please God I may be able to reveal it tomorrow."

"Do I treat you so harshly, Sancho, that you wish to see me die so soon?"

"It is not for that reason," said Sancho. "It is just that I am opposed to keeping things too long—I don't like them to spoil on my hands."

"Be that as it may," said Don Quixote, "I am willing to trust your friendship and your courtesy. And so I may tell you that one of the weirdest adventures happened to me that I could possibly describe. To make a long story short, you must know that, a short while ago, the daughter of the lord of this castle came to me. She is the most genteel and lovely damsel to be found in many a land. How can I describe to you the grace of her person, her sprightly wit, or all those other hidden charms which, in order to keep faith with my lady Dulcinea, I must leave untouched and pass over in silence? I can only say that Heaven was envious of this gift that fortune had placed in my hands—or it may be (and this is more likely) that this castle, as I have remarked to you, is enchanted; at any rate, just as I was engaged with her in most sweet and amorous parley, without my seeing him or knowing whence he came, a monstrous giant seized me by the arm and gave me such a blow on the jaw that my mouth was bathed in blood; and after that he flayed me in such a manner that I am even worse off today than yesterday, when those carters on account of Rocinante's excesses did us that wrong with which you are acquainted. I therefore can only conjecture that the treasure of this damsel's beauty must be in the keeping of some enchanted Moor, and that it is not for me."

"Not for me either," said Sancho; "for more than four hundred Moors have been mauling me and have made such a job of it that the thrashing those fellows gave me with their poles was but cakes and gingerbread by comparison. But tell me, sir, what name do you give to this fine and rare adventure which has left us where we are now? Your Grace, it is true, did not have quite so bad a time of it, with that incomparable beauty in your arms that you have been telling me about; but what was there in it for me except the worst beating that I hope to receive in all my born days? Pity me and the mother that bore me, for I am not a knight-errant nor ever expect to be, yet I always get the worst of whatever's coming!"

"So, you were beaten too, were you?" said Don Quixote.

"Did not I tell you I was, curses on it?" said Sancho.

"Well, do not let it worry you, my friend," said the knight; "for I will now make some of that precious balm and we shall both of us be healed in the blink of an eye."

The officer of the Brotherhood had lighted his lamp by this time and now came in to have a look at the one he thought was dead. The moment Sancho caught sight of him, in his nightgown, with a lamp in his hand, a towel around his head, and an evil-looking face, the squire turned to his master and said, "Could this be the enchanted Moor coming back to give us some more punishment, if there is any left in the inkwell?"

"No," replied Don Quixote, "it cannot be; for those who are under a spell do not let themselves be seen by anyone."

"If they do not let themselves be seen," remarked Sancho, "they certainly make themselves felt; if you do not believe it, let my ribs speak for me."

"Mine," said Don Quixote, "could tell the same story; but that is not a sufficient reason for believing that he whom we see here is the enchanted Moor."

Upon seeing them talking together so calmly, the officer did not know what to make of it, although the knight, true enough, was still flat on his back and unable to move, on account of his plasters and because he was still so stiff and sore.

"Well," said the officer coming up to him, "and how goes it, my good man?"

"If I were you," said Don Quixote, "I would speak a little more politely. Is it the custom in this country to address knights-errant in such a fashion, you dunce?"

Unable to bear being treated so ill by one whose appearance was so unimpressive, the patrolman raised his lamp with all the oil that was in it and let him have it over the head, a good stiff blow at that; after which, in the darkness, he slipped out of the room.

"Undoubtedly, sir," said Sancho, "that must be the enchanted Moor. He must be keeping the treasure for others, seeing all that he gives us is punches with his fist and blows with the lamp."

"Yes," said Don Quixote, "that is it; but no notice is to be taken of such things where enchantments are concerned, nor should one be angry or annoyed by them. Since these are invisible and fanciful beings, we should find no one on whom to take revenge even if we were

to go looking for him. Arise, Sancho, if you can, summon the governor of this fortress, and tell him to let
me have a little oil, wine, salt, and rosemary that I may
make that health-giving balm. I think that truly I have
need of it now, for there is much blood coming from the
wound which that phantom gave me."

His bones aching all over, Sancho got to his feet and
went out into the darkness to look for the landlord. On
the way he met the officer, who was listening to find
out what happened to his enemy.

"Sir," said the squire, "whoever you may be, kindly
do us the favor of giving us a little rosemary, oil, salt,
and wine, for they are needed to heal one of the most
gallant knights-errant that ever walked the earth; he lies
now in that bed, badly wounded at the hands of the
enchanted Moor who is lodged in this inn."

Hearing this, the officer thought the man must be out
of his senses, but inasmuch as day was already dawning, he threw open the inn door and told the proprietor
what it was that Sancho required. The innkeeper provided all the things mentioned, and Sancho then took
them to Don Quixote, who was lying there with his
hands to his head, complaining of the pain from the
blow that had been dealt him with the lamp, although
the fact of the matter was that it had done him no more
harm than to raise a couple of rather large bumps,
while what he fancied to be blood was in reality nothing other than sweat, due to the anxiety he felt over
the tempest that had but recently subsided.

Taking the ingredients, he now made a compound
of them, mixing them all together and boiling them for
some little while until he thought they were properly
steeped. He then asked for a small vial into which he
might pour the liquid, but as there was none to be had,
he resolved to make use of an oil flask made of tinplate

which the innkeeper presented to him free of charge. Above this flask he muttered more than eighty Our Fathers and as many Hail Marys and other prayers, each word being accompanied by the sign of the cross in way of benediction. All of which was witnessed by Sancho, the landlord, and the officer of the Holy Brotherhood. As for the carter, he had quietly gone out to look after his mules.

Having done this, the knight wished to try out the virtues of this precious balm, as he fancied it to be, and so he drank what remained in the pot, amounting to nearly half a quart. No sooner had he swallowed it than he at once began to vomit and kept it up until there was absolutely nothing left in his stomach; and with all his anxiety and the agitation of vomiting, a most copious sweat broke out upon him, whereupon he asked them to throw some covering over him and leave him alone. They did so, and he slept for more than three hours, at the end of which time he awoke, feeling greatly relieved in body and especially in his much battered bones. This led him to believe that he had been cured and that he had indeed discovered Fierabras's balm; from now on he would be able to face with no fear whatsoever any kind of destruction, battle, or combat, no matter how perilous the undertaking.

Marveling at the change for the better that had been wrought in his master, Sancho Panza asked that what remained in the pot, which was no small quantity, be given to him. Don Quixote consented; and, taking the kettle in both hands, with good faith and right good will, the squire gulped down only a trifle less than his master had taken. Now, Sancho's stomach was not so delicate as the knight's, for he did not vomit at first but suffered such cramps and nausea, perspired so freely, and felt so faint, that he thought surely his last hour had come; and, finding himself in such misery and affliction, he cursed the balm and the thief who had given it to him.

"It is my opinion, Sancho," said Don Quixote, "that all this comes of your not having been dubbed a knight, for which reason this liquor is not suited to you."

"If your Grace knew that all the time," replied his squire, "then, curse me and all my kin, why did you let me taste it?"

At this point the beverage took effect and poor Sancho began to discharge at both ends and with such force that neither the cattail mat on which he had dropped down nor the coarse linen coverlet that had been tossed over him was of much use afterward. The sweat poured off him in such abundance, accompanied by such spasms and convulsions, that not only he but all who saw him thought that he was dying. This untoward squall kept up for nearly two hours, and when it was over he was not left in better condition as his master had been, but was so tired and weak that he was not able to stand.

But Don Quixote, who, as has been said, felt greatly relieved and quite himself again, was all for setting out at once in search of adventures; for, as he saw it, every moment that he tarried he was cheating the world and the needy ones in it of his favor and assistance—especially in view of the sense of security and confidence which the possession of his balm now afforded him. Accordingly, impelled by this desire, he himself saddled Rocinante and the ass and then aided his squire to clothe himself and straddle his beast, after which the knight mounted his steed and prepared to ride away. As he passed a corner of the inn, he seized a pike that was standing there to serve him as a lance.

All the guests in the hostelry, more than twenty per-

sons, stood around watching, among them the innkeeper's daughter, and the knight in turn could not keep
his eyes off the lass; every so often he would heave a
sigh which it seemed must come from the depths of his
entrails, but the others thought it must be from the pain
in his ribs—at least, those who had seen him covered
with plasters as he had been the night before were of
this opinion.

As the two rode up to the gateway of the inn, Don
Quixote called to his host and said to him, gravely and
calmly, "Many and great are the favors, Sir Governor,
which I have received in this your castle, and I shall
be under obligations to you all the days of my life. If
I can repay you by avenging the wrong done you by
some haughty foe, you know that my profession is
none other than that of helping those who cannot help
themselves, avenging those who have been wronged,
and chastising traitors. Search well your memory, and if
you find anything of this sort with which to entrust me,
you have but to speak, and I promise you by the order
of chivalry which I have received to see that you are
given satisfaction and are paid in accordance with your
wishes."

The innkeeper's manner was equally tranquil as he
replied, "Sir Knight, I have no need of your favor nor
that you should avenge me of any wrong; for I can take
such vengeance as I see fit when the need arises. The
only thing needed in this case is for your Grace to pay
me what you owe me for last night, including straw
and barley for the two animals, your supper, and beds."

"Then this is an inn, is it?" said Don Quixote.

"And a very respectable one," replied the innkeeper.

"In that case I have been laboring under a mistake
all this time," said the knight; "for the truth is, I thought
it was a castle, and not a bad one at that. However, see-

ing it is not a castle but an inn, the only thing for you to do is to overlook the payment, since I cannot contravene the rule of knights-errant, none of whom, I am sure— at least, up to now, I have read nothing to the contrary —ever paid for his lodging or anything else when he stopped at an inn; for any hospitality that is offered to knights is only their just due, in return for all the hardships they suffer as they go in quest of adventures day and night, in summer and in winter, on horseback and on foot, enduring hunger and thirst and heat and cold, being subject to all the inclemencies of Heaven and all the discomforts of earth."

"I have little to do with all that," said the landlord. "Pay me what you owe me and let us hear no more of these accounts of chivalry. The only accounts that interest me are those that are due me."

"You are but a stupid, evil-minded tavernkeeper," was Don Quixote's answer; and, putting spurs to Rocinante and bringing his lance into position, he sallied out of the inn with no one to stop him. Without looking back to see if his squire was following him, he rode along for some distance. The innkeeper, meanwhile, seeing him leave like this without settling his account, straightway made for Sancho Panza, who said that since his master would not pay, neither would he, for being squire to a knight-errant as he was, he came under the same rule with regard to inns and taverns.

The landlord grew very indignant at this and began to threaten him, telling him that if he did not pay he would regret it. But Sancho replied that, by the law of knighthood which his master had received, he would not part with a single coronado,[2] even though it cost him his life; for if the worthy and ancient custom of knights-errant was to be violated, it would not be by him, nor would the squires of those knights who were

yet to come into the world have any cause to complain
of him or to reproach him for breaking so just a code.

As poor Sancho's ill luck would have it, stopping at
the inn that day were four wool carders of Segovia,[3]
three needlemakers from the vicinity of the Horse
Fountain of Cordova,[4] and a couple of lads from the
Fair of Seville,[5] merry fellows all of them, well intentioned, mischievous, and playful. They now, as if
moved and instigated by one and the same impulse,
came up to Sancho and pulled him off his donkey, and
then one of them entered the inn to get the blanket off
the host's bed. Throwing Sancho into it, they glanced
up and saw that the roof was a little too low for the
work in hand; so they went out into the stable yard,
which was bounded only by the sky above. Placing the
squire in the middle of the blanket, they began tossing
him up and down, having as much sport with him as
one does with a dog at Shrovetide.

The cries of the poor wretch in the blanket were
so loud that they reached his master's ears. Reining
in his steed to listen attentively, Don Quixote at first
thought that it must be some new adventure that
awaited him, until he came to distinguish clearly the
voice of his squire. Turning about then, he returned to
the inn at a painful gallop and, finding it closed, started
circling the hostelry to see if he could find an entrance
of some sort. The moment he reached the walls of the
stable yard, which were not very high, he saw the
scurvy trick that was being played on Sancho. He saw
the latter going up and down in the air with such grace
and dexterity that, had the knight's mounting wrath
permitted him to do so, it is my opinion that he would
have laughed at the sight.

He then endeavored to climb down from his horse
onto the wall, but he was so stiff and sore that he was

unable to dismount; whereupon, from his seat in the saddle he began hurling so many insults and maledictions at those who were doing the tossing that it would be quite impossible to set them all down here. The men in the yard, however, did not for this reason leave off their laughing sport, nor did the flying Sancho cease his lamentations, mingled now with threats and now with entreaties, all of which were of no avail until his tormentors saw fit to stop from pure exhaustion. After that, they brought his ass and set him upon it, bundling him in his greatcoat. Seeing him so done in, Maritornes felt sorry for him and, in order to refresh him, brought him a jug of water which she got from the well that it might be cooler. Taking the jug and raising it to his mouth, Sancho paused at sound of his master's words.

"Sancho, my son, do not drink that water. Do not drink it, my son, for it will kill you. Do you not see? I have here the most blessed balm"—and he showed him the vial containing the beverage—"of which you have but to imbibe two drops and you shall be healed without a doubt."

At this, Sancho rolled his eyes and cried out in a voice that was even louder than his master's, "Can it be your Grace has forgotten that I am not a knight, or do you want me to vomit up what guts I have left from last night? Keep your liquor and to the devil with it; just leave me alone, that's all."

Even as he finished saying this he started to take a drink; but perceiving at the first swallow that it was only water, he stopped and asked Maritornes to bring him some wine instead. She complied right willingly, paying for it out of her own money; for it is said of her that, although she occupied so lowly a station in life, there was something about her that remotely resembled a Christian woman. When he had drunk his fill, Sancho dug his heels into his ass's flanks, and the gate of the inn having been thrown wide open for him, he rode away quite well satisfied with himself because he had not had to pay anything, even though it had been at the expense of those usual bondsmen, his shoulders.

The truth is, the innkeeper had kept his saddlebags, but Sancho was so excited when he left that he did not notice they were gone. Once the two unwelcome guests were safely outside, the landlord was all for barring the gate; but the blanket-tossers would not hear of this, for they were fellows to whom it would not have made a penny's worth of difference if Don Quixote had really been one of the Knights of the Round Table.

CHAPTER XVIII. *In which is set forth the conversation that Sancho Panza had with his master, Don Quixote, along with other adventures deserving of record.*

B Y THE time Sancho reached his master, he was so exhausted and felt so faint that he was not even able any longer to urge on his beast.

"Well, Sancho," said Don Quixote when he saw him, "I am now convinced that yonder castle or inn is without a doubt enchanted; for what sort of creatures could they be who had such atrocious sport with you if not phantoms from another world? The thing that confirms me in this belief is the fact that, when I was alongside the stable-yard wall, witnessing the acts of that sad tragedy, it was not possible for me to climb it or even so much as get down off Rocinante, and that shows they must have cast a spell on me. But I swear to you, by the sword of a knight, that if I had been able to dismount and come over that wall, I should have wreaked such vengeance in your behalf that those villainous knaves would never have forgotten their little jest; and I should have done this even though it be against the laws of knighthood; for as I have told you many times, it is not permitted that a knight raise his hand against one who is not of his calling, save it be in defense of his own life and person in a case of great and urgent necessity."

"I would have avenged myself, if I had been able," said Sancho, "whether I had been dubbed a knight or not; although it is my opinion that those who had such sport with me were not phantoms or human beings under a spell as your Grace says, but flesh-and-blood men like us. They all had names, for I heard them calling one another by them as they were tossing me. There was one who was called Pedro Martínez, and another Tenorio Hernández, and the innkeeper's name was Juan Palomeque the Left-Handed. And so, Señor, your not being able to leap over the stable-yard wall or even get down off your horse was due to something other than enchantments. What I make out of it all is that these adventures that we go looking for will end by bringing us so many misadventures that we shan't know which is our right foot. The best and most sensible thing to do, in my judgment, would be for us to return home, now that it is harvest time, and stop running about from Ceca to Mecca[1] and from pail to bucket, as the saying goes."

"How little you know, Sancho, about the matter of chivalry!" Don Quixote replied. "Hush, and have patience; the day shall come when you will see with your own eyes how honorable a calling it is that we follow. For tell me, if you will: what greater pleasure or satisfaction is to be had in this world than that of winning

a battle and triumphing over one's enemy? None, undoubtedly none."

"That may be," said Sancho; "I cannot say as to
that; but one thing I know is that since we have been
knights-errant, or since your Grace has been one, for I
am not to be counted among that honored number, we
have not won a single battle, unless it was with the
Biscayan, and even there your Grace came out with
half an ear and half a helmet the less. Since then, all
that we have had has been poundings, punches, and
more poundings; and over and above that, I got the
blanketing at the hands of certain persons who were
under a spell, and so I do not know what that pleasure
of conquering an enemy, of which your Grace speaks, is
like."

"That," said Don Quixote, "is the thing that vexes me,
and I can understand that it should vex you as well,
Sancho. But from this time forth I shall endeavor to
have at hand some sword made by so masterful an art
that anyone who carries it with him cannot suffer any
manner of enchantment. It may even be that fortune
will procure for me the blade of Amadis,[2] the one he
bore when he was called the Knight of the Flaming
Sword. It was one of the best that ever a knight had
in this world, for in addition to the aforesaid virtue
which it possessed, it cut like a razor, and there was no
suit of armor, however strong or enchanted it might be,
that could withstand it."

"It would be just my luck," said Sancho, "that if your
Grace did find a sword like that, it would be of use
only to those who had been dubbed knights; as for the
squires, they are out of luck."

"Never fear, Sancho," said his master, "Heaven will
do better by you than that."

As they went along conversing in this manner, Don

Quixote caught sight down the road of a large cloud of dust that was drawing nearer.

"This, O Sancho," he said, turning to his squire, "is the day when you shall see the boon that fate has in store for me; this, I repeat, is the day when, as well as on any other, shall be displayed the valor of my good right arm. On this day I shall perform deeds that will be written down in the book of fame for all centuries to come. Do you see that dust cloud rising there, Sancho? That is the dust stirred up by a vast army marching in this direction and composed of many nations."

"At that rate," said Sancho, "there must be two of them, for there is another one just like it on the other side."

Don Quixote turned to look and saw that this was so. He was overjoyed by the thought that these were indeed two armies about to meet and clash in the middle of the broad plain; for at every hour and every moment his imagination was filled with battles, enchantments, nonsensical adventures, tales of love, amorous challenges, and the like, such as he had read of in the books of chivalry, and every word he uttered, every thought that crossed his mind, every act he performed, had to do with such things as these. The dust clouds he had sighted were raised by two large droves of sheep coming along the road in opposite directions, which by reason of the dust were not visible until they were close at hand, but Don Quixote insisted so earnestly that they were armies that Sancho came to believe it.

"Sir," he said, "what are we to do?"

"What are we to do?" echoed his master. "Favor and aid the weak and needy. I would inform you, Sancho, that the one coming toward us is led and commanded by the great emperor Alifanfarón, lord of the great isle of

Trapobana. This other one at my back is that of his enemy, the king of the Garamantas, Pentapolín of the Rolled-up Sleeve, for he always goes into battle with his right arm bare." [3]

"But why are they such enemies?" Sancho asked.

"Because," said Don Quixote, "this Alifanfarón is a terrible pagan and in love with Pentapolín's daughter, who is a very beautiful and gracious lady and a Christian, for which reason her father does not wish to give her to the pagan king unless the latter first abjures the law of the false prophet, Mohammed, and adopts the faith that is Pentapolín's own."

"Then, by my beard," said Sancho, "if Pentapolín isn't right, and I am going to aid him all I can."

"In that," said Don Quixote, "you will only be doing your duty; for to engage in battles of this sort you need not have been dubbed a knight."

"I can understand that," said Sancho, "but where are we going to put this ass so that we will be certain of finding him after the fray is over? As for going into battle on such a mount, I do not think that has been done up to now."

"That is true enough," said Don Quixote. "What you had best do with him is to turn him loose and run the risk of losing him; for after we emerge the victors we shall have so many horses that even Rocinante will be in danger of being exchanged for another. But listen closely to what I am about to tell you, for I wish to give you an account of the principal knights that are accompanying these two armies; and in order that you may be the better able to see and take note of them, let us retire to that hillock over there which will afford us a very good view."

They then stationed themselves upon a slight elevation from which they would have been able to see very

well the two droves of sheep that Don Quixote took
to be armies if it had not been for the blinding clouds
of dust. In spite of this, however, the worthy gentleman contrived to behold in his imagination what he did
not see and what did not exist in reality.

Raising his voice, he went on to explain, "That
knight in the gilded armor that you see there, bearing
upon his shield a crowned lion crouched at the feet of
a damsel, is the valiant Laurcalco, lord of the Silver
Bridge; the other with the golden flowers on his armor,
and on his shield three crowns argent on an azure
field, is the dread Micocolembo, grand duke of Quirocia.
And that one on Micocolembo's right hand, with the
limbs of a giant, is the ever undaunted Brandabarbarán
de Boliche, lord of the three Arabias. He goes armored
in a serpent's skin and has for shield a door which, so
report has it, is one of those from the temple that
Samson pulled down, that time when he avenged himself on his enemies with his own death.

"But turn your eyes in this direction, and you will
behold at the head of the other army the ever victorious, never vanquished Timonel de Carcajona, prince of
New Biscay, who comes with quartered arms—azure,
vert, argent, and or—and who has upon his shield a
cat or on a field tawny, with the inscription *Miau*, which
is the beginning of his lady's name; for she, so it is said,
is the peerless Miulina, daughter of Alfeñiquén, duke
of Algarve. And that one over there, who weights down
and presses the loins of that powerful charger, in a suit
of snow-white armor with a white shield that bears no
device whatever—he is a novice knight of the French
nation, called Pierres Papin, lord of the baronies of
Utrique. As for him you see digging his iron spurs into
the flanks of that fleet-footed zebra courser and whose
arms are vairs azure, he is the mighty duke of Nervia.

Espartafilardo of the Wood, who has for device upon his shield an asparagus plant with a motto in Castilian that says *'Rastrea mi suerte.'* " [4]

In this manner he went on naming any number of imaginary knights on either side, describing on the spur of the moment their arms, colors, devices, and mottoes; for he was completely carried away by his imagination and by this unheard-of madness that had laid hold of him.

Without pausing, he went on, "This squadron in front of us is composed of men of various nations. There are those who drink the sweet waters of the famous Xanthus; woodsmen who tread the Massilian plain; those that sift the fine gold nuggets of Arabia Felix; those that are so fortunate as to dwell on the banks of the clear-running Thermodon, famed for their coolness; those who in many and diverse ways drain the golden Pactolus; Numidians, whose word is never to be trusted; Persians, with their famous bows and arrows; Medes and Parthians, who fight as they flee; Scythians, as cruel as they are fair of skin; Ethiopians, with their pierced lips; and an infinite number of other nationalities whose visages I see and recognize although I cannot recall their names.

"In this other squadron come those that drink from the crystal currents of the olive-bearing Betis;[5] those that smooth and polish their faces with the liquid of the ever rich and gilded Tagus; those that enjoy the beneficial waters of the divine Genil;[6] those that roam the Tartessian[7] plains with their abundant pasturage; those that disport themselves in the Elysian meadows of Jerez;[8] the men of La Mancha, rich and crowned with golden ears of corn; others clad in iron garments, ancient relics of the Gothic race; those that bathe in the Pisuerga,[9] noted for the mildness of its current; those that feed their herds in the widespreading pasture lands along the banks of the winding Guadiana, celebrated for its underground course;[10] those that shiver from the cold of the wooded Pyrenees or dwell amid the white peaks of the lofty Apennines—in short, all those whom Europe holds within its girth."

So help me God! How many provinces, how many nations did he not mention by name, giving to each one with marvelous readiness its proper attributes; for he was wholly absorbed and filled to the brim with what he had read in those lying books of his! Sancho Panza hung on his words, saying nothing, merely turning his head from time to time to have a look at those knights and giants that his master was pointing out to him; but he was unable to discover any of them.

"Sir," he said, "may I go to the devil if I see a single man, giant, or knight of all those that your Grace is talking about. Who knows? Maybe it is another spell, like last night."

"How can you say that?" replied Don Quixote. "Can you not hear the neighing of the horses, the sound of trumpets, the roll of drums?"

"I hear nothing," said Sancho, "except the bleating of sheep."

And this, of course, was the truth; for the flocks were drawing near.

"The trouble is, Sancho," said Don Quixote, "you are so afraid that you cannot see or hear properly; for one of the effects of fear is to disturb the senses and cause things to appear other than what they are. If you are so craven as all that, go off to one side and leave me alone, and I without your help will assure the victory to that side to which I lend my aid."

Saying this, he put spurs to Rocinante and, with his

lance at rest, darted down the hillside like a flash of
lightning.

As he did so, Sancho called after him, "Come back,
your Grace, Señor Don Quixote; I vow to God those
are sheep that you are charging. Come back! O
wretched father that bore me! What madness is this?
Look you, there are no giants, nor knights, nor cats,
nor shields either quartered or whole, nor vairs azure
or bedeviled. What is this you are doing, O sinner that
I am in God's sight?"

But all this did not cause Don Quixote to turn back.
Instead, he rode on, crying out at the top of his voice,
"Ho, knights, those of you who follow and fight under
the banners of the valiant Pentapolín of the Rolled-up
Sleeve; follow me, all of you, and you shall see how
easily I give you revenge on your enemy, Alifanfarón of
Trapobana."

With these words he charged into the middle of the
flock of sheep and began spearing at them with as much
courage and boldness as if they had been his mortal
enemies. The shepherds and herdsmen who were with
the animals called to him to stop; but seeing it was no
use, they unloosed their slings and saluted his ears with
stones as big as your fist.

Don Quixote paid no attention to the missiles and,
dashing about here and there, kept crying, "Where are
you, haughty Alifanfarón? Come out to me; for here
is a solitary knight who desires in single combat to test
your strength and deprive you of your life, as a punishment for that which you have done to the valorous
Pentapolín Garamanta."

At that instant a pebble[11] from the brook struck him
in the side and buried a couple of ribs in his body.
Believing himself dead or badly wounded, and remem-

bering his potion, he took out his vial, placed it to his mouth, and began to swallow the balm; but before he had had what he thought was enough, there came another almond,[12] which struck him in the hand, crushing the tin vial and carrying away with it a couple of grinders from his mouth, as well as badly mashing two of his fingers. As a result of these blows the poor knight tumbled from his horse. Believing that they had killed him, the shepherds hastily collected their flock and, picking up the dead beasts, of which there were more than seven, they went off down the road without more ado.

Sancho all this time was standing on the slope observing the insane things that his master was doing; and as he plucked savagely at his beard he cursed the hour and minute when luck had brought them together. But when he saw him lying there on the ground and perceived that the shepherds were gone, he went down the hill and came up to him, finding him in very bad shape though not unconscious.

"Didn't I tell you, Señor Don Quixote," he said, "that you should come back, that those were not armies you were charging but flocks of sheep?"

"This," said Don Quixote, "is the work of that thieving magician, my enemy, who thus counterfeits things and causes them to disappear. You must know, Sancho, that it is very easy for them to make us assume any appearance that they choose; and so it is that malign one who persecutes me, envious of the glory he saw me about to achieve in this battle, changed the squadrons of the foe into flocks of sheep. If you do not believe me, I beseech you on my life to do one thing for me, that you may be undeceived and discover for yourself that what I say is true. Mount your ass and follow them quietly, and when you have gone a short way from here, you will see them become their former selves once more; they will no longer be sheep but men exactly as I described them to you in the first place. But do not go now, for I need your kind assistance; come over here and have a look and tell me how many grinders are missing, for it feels as if I did not have a single one left."

Sancho went over and almost put his eyes into his master's mouth. Now, as it happened, this was the moment when the balm in Don Quixote's stomach began to work, and he promptly discharged its entire contents with more force than a musket straight into the beard of his good-hearted squire.

"Holy Mary!" exclaimed Sancho, "and what is this that has happened now? This sinner must surely be mortally wounded, for he is vomiting blood from his mouth."

When he investigated a little more closely, however, he discovered from the color, taste, and smell that this was not blood but balm from the vial from which he had seen his master drinking; and so great was the disgust he felt that, his stomach turning over, he now vomited up his insides all over Don Quixote, and both of them were in a fine state indeed. Sancho then made for his saddlebags to get something with which to wipe the vomit off them, and when he found the bags were missing, it was more than he could do to contain himself. Cursing himself anew, he made up his mind that he would leave the knight and return home, even though he did lose what was coming to him for his services, along with all hope of becoming governor of that promised island.

Don Quixote then rose and, with his left hand to his mouth to keep his teeth from popping out, grasped Rocinante's reins in the other hand—for the animal had not stirred from his side, so loyal and well trained was he—and went over to where the squire was bending above his donkey with his hand to his cheek like one lost in thought.

Seeing him so downcast, his master said to him, "Bear in mind, Sancho, that one man is worth no more than another unless he does more. All these squalls that we have met with are merely a sign that the weather is going to clear and everything will turn out for the best; for it is impossible that either good or evil should be lasting; and from this it follows that, the evil having lasted so long, the good must be near at hand. And so you should not grieve for the misfortunes that have befallen me, since you have had no part in them."

"How is that?" replied Sancho. "I suppose the one they tossed in a blanket yesterday was somebody else than my father's son? And my saddlebags, which are gone now, did they belong to some other person?"

"You mean to say your saddlebags are missing, Sancho?"

"Yes," replied the squire, "that they are."

"Well, in that case, we shan't have anything to eat today," said Don Quixote.

"Not unless these meadows have some of those herbs which your Grace was saying he knows so well, with which unfortunate knights-errant like your Grace are in the habit of supplying their needs."

"So far as that goes," said his master, "right now I would rather have a quarter of a loaf or a loaf of bread and a couple of pilchards' heads than all the herbs that Dioscorides describes, even with Doctor Laguna's commentary.[13] But, nevertheless, Sancho, mount your ass and follow me; for inasmuch as God is the provider of all things, He will not fail us, especially seeing that we are so active in His service; for gnats never lack the air, grubs the earth, nor polliwogs the water; and He is so merciful that He causes His sun to shine on the good and the bad and the rain to fall on the just and the unjust."

"It strikes me," said Sancho, "that your Grace is better fitted to be a preacher than a knight-errant."

"Knights-errant," was Don Quixote's rejoinder, "have always known, and have to know, everything; for they might be called upon to deliver a sermon or make a speech in the middle of the open country, just as if they were graduates of the University of Paris; from which it may be deduced that the lance never yet blunted the pen nor the pen the lance."

"That may all very well be as your Grace says," replied Sancho, "but let us leave here at once and go look for a lodging for tonight; and God grant it may be someplace where there are no blankets or blanket-tossers, nor phantoms nor enchanted Moors, for if I come upon any of those, I'll have nothing whatever to do with them." 14

"Pray God, then, my son," said Don Quixote, "and lead the way where you will; for this time I will leave the lodging to your choice. But, first, put your finger in my mouth and feel how many teeth and grinders are missing on this right side of my upper jaw, for that is where the pain is."

Sancho did as he was told. "How many grinders did your Grace have on this side?"

"Four besides the double tooth and all of them whole and healthy."

"Mind what you are saying, your Grace," Sancho warned.

"I am telling you: four, if not five," said Don Quixote;

"for in all my life I have never had a tooth or grinder pulled, nor has any fallen out or been destroyed by decay or abscess."

"Well, in this lower jaw," Sancho went on, "your Grace has not more than two grinders and a half left; and in the upper jaw, there is not even a half, there is none at all—it is all as smooth as the palm of your hand."

"How unfortunate I am!" cried Don Quixote as he heard this sad news from his squire. "I would rather they had robbed me of an arm so long as it was not my sword arm. For I must tell you, Sancho, that a mouth without grinders is like a mill without a millstone, and a tooth is more to be prized than a diamond. But to all this we are subject, those of us who follow the arduous profession of knighthood. So mount, my friend, and lead on, and I will follow at whatever pace you will."

Sancho obeyed, heading in the direction in which he thought they might be able to find a lodging without leaving the highway, which at this point was a much-traveled stretch of road. They went along slowly, for Don Quixote's jaws were hurting him so much that he could think of nothing else and was in no mood to make haste. Perceiving this, Sancho sought to divert him and to take his mind off his troubles by small talk of one kind or another; and some of the things he said to him are set forth in the chapter that follows.

CHAPTER XIX. *Of the shrewd things that Sancho Panza said to his master and the adventure that happened to him in connection with a dead body, along with other famous events.*

"IT SEEMS to me, sir, that all these misadventures that have happened to us of late are without any doubt a punishment for the sin your Grace committed against the order of knighthood by failing to keep the vow that you made not to eat bread off a tablecloth, or embrace the queen, and all the rest of it; your Grace swore not to do any of these things until you had taken a helmet from that Moor Malandrino[1] or whatever his name is, I don't rightly remember."

"There is much in what you say, Sancho," replied Don Quixote, "but to tell you the truth, I had forgotten about it; and you may be sure that it was because you had failed to remind me in time that the business of the blanket occurred. But I will see to making amends for it all; for in knighthood there are ways of adjusting everything."

"Why," said Sancho, "did I take some kind of oath, then?"

"It makes no difference whether you did or not," said Don Quixote. "It appears to me that you are not wholly clear of complicity in this matter, and so it will not be a bad thing to provide ourselves with a remedy."

"In that case," said his squire, "will your Grace please be sure not to forget the remedy as you did the vow? For who knows, the phantoms may take it into their heads to have sport with me again, and with your Grace as well, if they see you so stubborn."

While they were engaged in this and similar talk,

night descended upon them as they were going along the highway, before they had as yet found a lodging; and what made matters worse, they were very hungry, for with their saddlebags they had lost their entire pantry and store of provisions. And on top of all their misfortunes, they now had an experience which, if it was not a real adventure, certainly had all the earmarks of one. Although it was already quite dark, they continued on their way, for Sancho was sure that, since this was a main highway, they would have to go but a league or two before they came upon some kind of inn. And as they were riding along through the darkness like that, the squire hungry and the master with a great desire to eat, they suddenly saw coming toward them a great number of lights which looked exactly like moving stars. Sancho was stunned by the sight, while Don Quixote did not feel altogether easy about it, and the one pulled on the halter of his ass, the other on his horse's reins. They sat there watching closely, trying to make out what these lights could be, which were all the time coming nearer—and the nearer they came, the bigger they seemed. Sancho was shaking like someone who had had a dose of mercury, and his master's hair was standing on end. Then Don Quioxte managed to pluck up a little courage.

"There can be no doubt, Sancho," he said, "that this is going to be a very great and perilous adventure in which it will be necessary for me to display all my strength and valor."

"Poor me!" said his squire. "If by any chance this is to be another adventure with phantoms, where am I going to find the ribs to bear it?"

"Phantoms or not," said the knight, "I will not permit them to touch the nap of your garments. If they had sport with you last time, it was only because I was unable to get over the stable-yard wall; but here we are in the open where I can wield my sword as I like."

"And what if they enchant and benumb you as they did before, what difference will it make whether or not you are in the open?"

"Nonetheless," replied Don Quixote, "I beg of you, Sancho, to keep up your courage; for experience will teach you what mine is."

"Very well, I will keep it up, God willing," was Sancho's answer.

Retiring then to one side of the road, the two of them continued watching attentively to see what those moving lights could be; and it was not long before they caught sight of a large number of white-shirted figures,[2] a vision so frightening that Sancho lost what courage he had. His teeth began chattering like those of a person who has the quartan fever, and they chattered more than ever as the apparition came near enough to be distinguishable; for there were some twenty of those shirted figures, all mounted on horseback and with lighted torches in their hands, and behind them came a litter covered with mourning, followed by six other riders all in black down to the feet of their mules, for it was obvious from their leisurely gait that these animals were not horses. As the cavalcade approached, it could be seen that the shirted ones were muttering something to themselves in a low and mournful tone of voice.

This weird vision, at such an hour and in so out-of-the-way a place, was sufficient to strike terror to Sancho's heart, and his master would have felt the same way had he been anyone else than Don Quixote. As it was, the former had by now reached the end of his strength, but not so the latter, whose vivid imagination was already at work and who saw here another adven-

ture out of his storybooks. The litter had to be a bier,
bearing some knight either dead or badly wounded, and
it was for him, Don Quixote, and him alone, to exact
vengeance; and so, without another word, he rested his
lance, settled himself well in the saddle, and, with highborn mettle and intrepid bearing, took up his stand in
the middle of the road along which the shirted figures
had to pass.

When they were close upon him, he raised his voice
and cried, "Halt, knight, or whoever you may be, and
give an account of yourself; tell me whence you come
and whither you are bound, and who it is that you bring
with you on that bier; for to all appearances either you
have done some wrong or some wrong has been done to
you, and it is fitting and necessary that I should know of
it, either to punish you for your evil deeds or to avenge
you for the misdoings of another."

At this point, one of the figures spoke up. "We are in
a hurry," he said, "and the inn is far, and we cannot
stop to give you the information that you seek." And, so
saying, he spurred his mule forward.

Don Quixote was greatly put out at such a reply and,
seizing the mule by the bridle, he repeated, "Halt, I
say, and show a little better breeding by giving me an
answer to my questions. Otherwise, you shall all do
battle with me."

Now, the mule as it happened was a little shy, and
when Don Quixote laid hold of the bridle, it reared on
its hind legs and threw its master to the ground. A
lad who was on foot, upon seeing the shirted one fall,
began reviling the knight; but our friend's wrath was
up, and without further delay he brought his lance into
position and bore down upon one of those who were
clad in mourning, wounding him badly and tumbling
him from his mount. Then he turned upon the others,

and it was something to see the dexterity with which he attacked and routed them. It seemed as if at that moment Rocinante had sprouted wings, so proud-stepping and light-footed did he show himself to be.

All these shirt-wearers were timid folk, without arms, and so, naturally enough, they speedily quit the fray and started running across the fields, still bearing their lighted torches in their hands, which gave them the appearance of masked figures darting here and there on some night when a fiesta or other celebration is being held. Those who wore the mourning, on the other hand, wrapped and swathed in their skirts and gowns, were unable to move; and, accordingly, with no risk to himself, Don Quixote smote them all and drove them off against their will; for they thought that this surely was no man but a devil straight out of Hell who had come to rob them of the body that they carried on the litter.

Sancho watched it all, greatly admiring his master's ardor. "No doubt about it," he told himself, "he is as brave and powerful as he says he is."

There was a flaming torch that had been stuck in the ground near the first one who had fallen from his mule; and by its light Don Quixote could be seen coming up to the fellow, sticking the point of his lance in his face, and calling upon him to surrender as he valued his life.

"I am prisoner enough as it is," the man said; "for my leg is broken and I cannot stir. I beg your Grace, if you are a Christian knight, not to slay me; if you were to do so, you would be committing a great sacrilege, for I am a licentiate and have already taken my first orders."

"Well," said Don Quixote, "what in the devil brings you here if you are a churchman?"

"What, sir?" said the man on the ground. "My bad luck, that's all."

"Still worse luck awaits you," said Don Quixote, "if

you do not answer to my satisfaction all those questions that I put to you in the first place."

"Your Grace shall be easily satisfied as to all that," replied the licentiate. "To begin with, I may tell your Grace that, although I said I was a licentiate, I am really but a bachelor, and my name is Alonso López, a native of Alcobendas. I come from the city of Baeza with eleven other priests, the ones that are carrying the torches. We are on our way to the city of Segovia, accompanying the corpse that is in that litter, the body of a gentleman who died in Baeza, where he was first interred; and now we are taking his bones to their last resting place in Segovia, where he was born."

"And who killed him?" demanded Don Quixote.

"God," said the bachelor, "by means of a pestilential fever that took him off."

"In that way," said the knight, "Our Lord has absolved me of the trouble of avenging him, as I should have had to do had he met his death at the hands of another; but He who slew him having slain him, there is nothing to do but be silent and shrug one's shoulders, and I should do the same if it were I whom He was slaying. I would have your reverence know that I am a knight of La Mancha, Don Quixote by name, and it is my calling and profession to go through the world righting wrongs and redressing injuries."

"I do not know what you mean by righting wrongs, seeing that you found me quite all right and left me very wrong indeed, with a broken leg which will not be right[3] again as long as I live; and if you have redressed any injury in my case, it has been done in such a way as to leave me injured forever. It was a great misadventure for me to fall in with you who go hunting adventures."

"Everything," replied Don Quixote, "does not occur

in the same manner. The big mistake you made, Sir Bachelor Alonso López, was in coming as you did, by night, dressed in those surplices, bearing lighted torches and praying, all of which gave the appearance of something evil and of the other world. I accordingly could not fail to fulfill my obligation by attacking you, and I would have done so even though I knew for a certainty that you were devils out of Hell; for such I took you to be all the time."

"Since that is the way fate has willed it," said the bachelor, "I beseech your Grace, Sir Knight-errant—whose errantry has done me so bad a turn—I beseech you to help me up from under this mule, for one of my legs is caught between the stirrup and the saddle."

"Why," exclaimed Don Quixote, "I might have talked on until tomorrow! How long were you going to wait to tell me of your distress?"

He then called to Sancho to come, but the squire did not see fit to do so, being engaged at that moment in robbing a sumpter mule of the larder which these gentlemen were carrying with them and which was well stocked with things to eat. Having made a sack of his greatcoat, he dumped into it all that it would hold and threw it across his ass's back; and then, and only then, did he answer his master's call to come and help get the bachelor out from under the mule. Setting the fellow on his beast once more, they gave him his torch, and Don Quixote told him to follow in the track of his companions and beg their pardon on his behalf for the wrong which he had not been able to avoid doing them.

"And if," said Sancho, "those gentlemen wish to know who the valiant one was who did this to them, your Grace may inform them that he is the famous Don Quixote de la Mancha, otherwise known as the Knight of the Mournful Countenance."

At this the knight inquired of his squire what had led him to call him by such a title at that particular moment.

"I can tell you," said Sancho. "I was looking at you for a time by the light of the torch that poor fellow carried; and truly, your Grace now has the worst-looking countenance that I have ever seen, whether due to exhaustion from this combat or the lack of teeth and grinders, I cannot say."

"It is not that," said Don Quixote; "it is simply that the sage who is to write the history of my exploits must have thought that it would be a good thing for me to take another appellation as all knights of the past have done. Thus one was called the Knight of the Flaming Sword; another the Knight of the Unicorn; one the Knight of Damsels, and one the Knight of the Phoenix; another the Knight of the Griffin; and still another the Knight of Death: and by these names and insignia were they known all the world over. And so, I tell you, it must have been that sage of whom I was speaking who put it into your mind and on your tongue to dub me the Knight of the Mournful Countenance. This title I mean to adopt as my own from now on; and in order that it may better fit me, I propose, as soon as opportunity offers, to have painted on my shield a very sad-looking face."

"There is no necessity of wasting time and money on having a face made for you," said Sancho. "All that your Grace has to do is to uncover your own to those who look at you, and without need of any image or shield they will call you that. This is the truth I speak; for I assure your Grace—not meaning any harm—that hunger and the lack of grinders have given you so ill a countenance that you can very well do without the painted one."

Don Quixote laughed heartily at Sancho's wit, but still he could not give up the idea of calling himself by that name and having a suitable device painted on his buckler or shield just as he had conceived it.

At this point the bachelor prepared to take his departure.[4] "I neglected to warn your Grace," he said, "that you are hereby excommunicated for having laid violent hands on a holy thing: *Iuxta illud, si quis, suadente diabolo,* etc." [5]

"I do not understand that Latin of yours," said Don Quixote, "but I am quite sure that I did not lay my hands on anything; I laid on with this lance. What is more, I did not realize that I was insulting priests or sacred things of the Church, which I respect and revere as the good Catholic and loyal Christian that I am; I thought, rather, that it was phantoms and monsters from the other world that I was attacking. But, even so, I cannot but recall what happened to Cid Ruy Díaz when he broke the chair of the royal ambassador in the presence of his Holiness the Pope, that day when the worthy Rodrigo de Vivar showed himself to be a brave and honored knight." [6]

Having listened to this speech, the bachelor went his way without saying a word in reply.

Don Quixote then wanted to see whether it really was bones they had in that litter or not; but Sancho would not consent.

"Sir," he said, "your Grace has concluded this adventure in the safest manner of any yet. But those fellows whom you overcame and routed may come to realize that it was, after all, only one individual who conquered them; and being thoroughly ashamed of themselves, they may pluck up courage and return to look for us, in which case they could give us plenty of trouble. The ass is ready, the mountains near by, and we are hungry;

there is nothing for us to do but to retire as decently as may be, and as the saying goes, 'To the grave with the dead and the living to the bread.' " [7]

Urging his ass forward, he begged his master to follow him, and the latter, deciding that his squire was right, made no reply but fell in behind. After going a short distance they found themselves between two small mountains, in a broad and hidden valley. Here they dismounted, and Sancho relieved the donkey of its burden; after which, stretched upon the green grass and with hunger as a sauce, they breakfasted, lunched, dined, and supped at one and the same time, satisfying their stomachs with more than one cold cut which the gentlemen of the clergy attending the deceased—who seldom stint themselves in this regard—had brought along in their well-stocked larder upon the back of their sumpter mule.

But they still had one misfortune to endure, which for Sancho was the worst of all: they had no wine, nor even water, to drink, and so were harassed by thirst. Whereupon, noting the green young grass of the meadow round about, he conceived an idea which will be set forth in the following chapter.

CHAPTER XX. *Of an adventure such as never was seen or heard of, which was completed by the valorous Don Quixote de la Mancha with less perii than any famous knight in all the world ever incurred in a similar undertaking.*

"IT IS not possible, sir," said Sancho, "that this grass should not betoken the presence near by of some spring or brook that provides it with moisture; and so, it would be a good thing if we were to go a little farther.

for I am sure we should be able to find someplace where we might quench this terrible thirst that is consuming us and that, undoubtedly, is more painful to bear than hunger."

This impressed Don Quixote as being good advice; and after they had placed upon the ass what was left of their dinner, he took Rocinante's rein and Sancho took the halter of his beast and they started feeling their way up the meadow, for the night was so dark that they were unable to see anything at all. They had not gone two hundred paces when they heard a roaring sound, which appeared to be that of water falling from great, high cliffs. This cheered them enormously; but as they paused to determine the direction from which it came, another and terrible din fell upon their ears, watering down the satisfaction they had felt at the thought of finding water,[1] especially for Sancho, who was by nature timid and lacking in spirit. What they heard, I am telling you, was the sound of measured blows, together with the rattling of iron chains, accompanied by so furious a thunder of waters as to strike terror in any other heart than that of Don Quixote.

It was night, as has been stated, and they now chanced to reach a cluster of tall trees, whose leaves, stirred by the mild wind that was blowing, rustled with a soft and gentle murmur. The solitude, the place, the darkness, the din of the water, the rustling of the leaves —all this was frightful, horror-inspiring, especially when they found that the blows did not cease, nor did the wind fall asleep or morning come; and added to it all was the fact that they had no idea where they were. Don Quixote, however, with his own intrepid heart to keep him company, leaped upon Rocinante's back and, bracing his buckler on his arm, brought his lance into play.

"Sancho, my friend," he said, "you may know that I was born, by Heaven's will, in this age of iron, to revive what is known as the Golden Age. I am he for whom are reserved the perils, the great exploits, the valiant deeds. I am—I say again—he who is to revive the Knights of the Round Table, the Twelve Peers of France, and the Nine Worthies. I am he who is to cast into oblivion the Platirs, the Tablantes, the Olivantes, and the Tirants, the Knights of the Sun and the Belianises, together with the entire throng of famous knights-errant of times past, by performing in this age in which I live such great and wonderful feats of arms as shall darken the brightest of their achievements. Note well, my rightful and my loyal squire, the shades of night that lie about us; this uncanny silence; the low and indistinct rustling of those trees; the frightful sound made by that water that we came to seek, which appears to be falling precipitously from the tall mountains of the moon; those unceasing blows that grieve and wound our ears; all of which things together, and each one singly, are sufficient to strike fear, dread, and terror in the breast of Mars himself, not to speak of him who is not accustomed to such happenings and adventures.

"Well, all these things that I have been describing are for me but the incentives and awakeners of my courage, causing the heart within my bosom to burst with the desire of entering upon this adventure, however difficult it may be. And so, tighten Rocinante's girth a bit if you will, and God be with you. Wait for me here three days, no longer. If at the end of that time I have not returned, you may go back to our village; and then, as a special favor to me, you will go to El Toboso, where you will tell that incomparable lady, my Dulcinea, how her captive knight died, undertak-

ing things that would render him worthy of being
called hers."

Hearing his master speak these words, Sancho began
weeping as if his heart would break. "Sir," he said, "I
do not know why your Grace is so bent upon this fearful undertaking. It is night now, no one can see us,
and we can easily turn about and take ourselves out of
danger's path, even though we do not drink for the
next three days. Since there is none here to see us, the
fewer will there be to call us cowards. What's more,
I have often heard the curate of our village say in his
sermons—your Grace knows him very well—that whoever goes looking for danger will perish by it. It is not
good to tempt God by entering upon some monstrous
undertaking from which you can escape only by a
miracle, and Heaven has performed enough of them for
your Grace by saving you from being tossed in a
blanket as I was and by bringing you out the victor,
safe and free, over all those enemies who were accompanying that corpse.

"And if all this does not suffice to move or soften that
hard heart of yours, let it be moved by the thought, the
certain knowledge, that no sooner will you have left
this spot than I out of fear will yield my soul to any that
cares to take it. I have left my native land, my wife
and young ones, to come and serve your Grace, believing that by so doing I would better my lot, not make
it worse; but as avarice always bursts the bag,[2] so has
it torn my hopes to shreds. Just when they are brightest
and I seem nearest to obtaining that wretched island,
that cursed island, which your Grace so many times
has promised me, I perceive that, in place of fulfilling
that hope, you are about to go away and leave me in
a place like this, so far from any human beings.

"In God's name, sir, do me not this wrong. If your Grace will not wholly desist from this enterprise, at least put it off until morning; for according to that knowledge of the heavens that I acquired as a shepherd, it should not be as much as three hours from now until dawn, seeing that the mouth of the Horn is directly overhead and midnight is in line with the left arm." [3]

"How, Sancho," said Don Quixote, "can you see that line or where the mouth of the Horn or your own head is, when it is so dark and there is not a star in the sky?"

"That," replied Sancho, "is because fear has many eyes and can see things under the earth and much more in the heavens above; and anyway, it stands to reason that daybreak cannot be far off."

"Far off or near," said his master, "it shall not be said of me, either now or at any other time, that tears and entreaties kept me from fulfilling my duties as a knight; and so, Sancho, I beg you to be quiet; for God, who has put it into my heart to undertake this dread adventure such as never before was heard of—God will see to my well-being and will comfort you in your sorrow. The thing for you to do is to tighten Rocinante's girth and remain here, and I shall return soon, either living or dead."

Perceiving his master's firm resolve, and seeing of how little avail were his own tears, advice, and entreaties, Sancho determined to have resort to his ingenuity in compelling him, if he could, to wait until daylight. Accordingly, when he went to tighten Rocinante's girth, he very deftly and without being observed slipped the halter of his ass over the hack's two front feet so that when Don Quixote started to ride away, he found that his steed was unable to move except by little hops and jumps.

"Ah, sir," Sancho said to his master when he saw that his trick had worked, "Heaven itself, moved by my tears and supplications, has ordained that Rocinante should not stir; and if you stubbornly insist upon spurring and whipping him, you will merely be angering fortune and, so to speak, kicking against the prick."

Don Quixote was truly in despair now; for the more he dug his legs into his horse's flanks the less inclined that animal was to budge; and without noticing that the hack's feet had been bound, the knight decided there was nothing for him to do but be calm and wait until daylight should come or Rocinante should see fit to move; for he was convinced that all this came of something other than his squire's cleverness.

"Since Rocinante will not go," he said, "I am content, Sancho, to wait until dawn shall smile, even though I myself may weep that she is so long in coming."

"There is no occasion for weeping," replied Sancho, "for I will entertain your Grace by telling stories from now until daybreak, unless you care to dismount and lie down to sleep for a little while upon this green grass, as knights-errant are accustomed to do, so that you may be rested when day comes and fit to undertake this unlikely adventure that awaits you."

"Why," said Don Quixote, "do you call upon me to dismount or to sleep? Am I, perchance, one of those knights who take their repose amid dangers? Sleep, then, if you will, for you were born to sleep, or do whatever you like, and I shall do that which best befits my knightly character."

"Sir," said Sancho, "let not your Grace be angry, for I did not mean it in that way."

Coming up to his master, then, he laid both hands on the saddletree in such a manner that he stood embracing Don Quixote's left leg; and he did not stir an inch from there, so great was his fear of those blows which were still to be heard in regular cadence. Don Quixote then remarked that his squire might tell him a story by way of amusing him as he had promised; to which Sancho replied that he would be glad to do so if the fear which that sound inspired in him would only let him.

"But, in spite of all that," he said, "I will try to tell you a story which, if it does not escape me in the telling, and nobody stops me, is one of the best there is; and pay attention, your Grace, for I am about to begin.[4] Let bygones be bygones; and may the good come to all and the evil to him who goes to look for it. For your Grace must know that when the ancients began their fables the beginning was by no means left to the choice of the one who told the tale; instead, they always began with a maxim from Cato Zonzorino,[5] the Roman, who uttered the words that I have quoted, '. . . and the evil to him who goes to look for it,' a saying that fits like the ring on your finger, signifying that your Grace should remain here and not go hunting trouble anywhere else, and that we should return by another road since there is no one to compel us to keep following this one where there are so many frightful things to startle us."

"Go on with your story, Sancho," said Don Quixote, "and as for the road that we are to follow, leave that to me."

"I will tell you, then," continued Sancho, "that in a village of Estremadura there lived a certain goat shepherd—I mean, one who tended goats—and this shepherd or goatherd of my story was named Lope Ruiz;

and this Lope Ruiz was in love with a shepherd lass whose name was Torralba, which shepherd lass called Torralba was the daughter of a wealthy cattle-raiser, and this wealthy cattle-raiser—"

"If that is the way you are going to tell your story, Sancho, saying everything over twice, you will not be finished in a couple of days. Tell it in a straightforward manner, like a man of good sense, or otherwise do not tell it at all."

"In my country," said Sancho, "they tell all fables just the way I am telling this one, and I cannot tell it any other way, nor is it right for your Grace to ask me to adopt new customs."

"As you like, then," said Don Quixote, "and since fate has willed that I must listen, proceed with it."

"And so, then, my dear master, as I was saying, this shepherd was in love with Torralba, the shepherd lass, who was sturdy of figure, wild in her ways, and somewhat mannish—I can see yet those little mustaches of hers."

"You knew her, then?" asked Don Quixote.

"I did not know her, but the one who told me the story described her for me so truly and faithfully that, when I go to tell it to another, I could swear and affirm that I have seen her with my own eyes. And so, as days and days went by, the devil, who never sleeps but sweeps everything up into his pile, saw to it that the shepherd's love for the shepherd lass turned into hatred and ill will. The reason for this, according to the gossiping tongues, was that she had given him certain grounds for jealousy, which crossed the line and reached forbidden territory. And as a result of all this, the shepherd hated her from then on, so much, that in order not to have to see her again, he made up his mind to leave his native land and go where his eyes would never behold her. Finding herself thus spurned, La Torralba, who had never loved him before, became enamored of him."

"That is the way with women," said Don Quixote; "they spurn those that care for them and love those that hate them. But go on, Sancho."

"The shepherd then proceeded to do as he had resolved; and, getting together his goats, he set out through the countryside of Estremadura on his way to the kingdom of Portugal. Learning of this, La Torralba set out after him, following him, barefoot, from afar, a shepherd's staff in her hand and a knapsack around her neck, in which, so it is said, she carried a broken mirror, a piece of a comb, and some kind of paint or other for her face; but whatever it was she carried, I am not going to take the trouble to find out. I will merely tell you that the shepherd with his flock had by this time crossed the Guadiana River, which in that season was swollen and almost out of its banks; and at the point where he was, there was neither boat nor bark to be had, nor anyone to ferry him and his goats to the other side; all of which grieved him sorely, for he could now see La Torralba close on his heels and knew that she would be bound to annoy him greatly with her tears and pleas.

"As he was looking about, he saw a fisherman alongside a boat so small that it would hold only one person and a goat, but, nevertheless, he spoke to the man, who agreed to take the shepherd and his flock of three hundred to the opposite bank. The fisherman would climb into the boat and row one of the animals across and then return for another, and he kept this up, rowing across with a goat and coming back, rowing across and coming back— Your Grace must be sure to keep count of the goats that the fisherman rowed across the stream, for if a single one of them escapes your memory, the story is ended and it will not be possible to tell another word of it.

"I will go on, then, and tell you that the landing place on the other side was full of mud and slippery, and it took the fisherman a good while to make the trip each time; but in spite of that, he came back for another goat, and another, and another—"

"Just say he rowed them all across," said Don Quixote; "you need not be coming and going in that manner, or it will take you a year to get them all on the other side."

"How many have gone across up to now?" Sancho demanded.

"How the devil should I know?" replied Don Quixote.

"There, what did I tell you? You should have kept better count. Well, then, by God, the story's ended, for there is no going on with it."

"How can that be?" said the knight. "Is it so essential to know the exact number of goats that if I lose count of one of them you cannot tell the rest of the tale?"

"No, sir, I cannot by any means," said Sancho; "for when I asked your Grace to tell me how many goats had been rowed across and you replied that you did not know, at the very instant everything that I was about to say slipped my memory; and you may take my word for it, it was very good and you would have liked it."

"So," said Don Quixote, "the story is ended, is it?"

"As much ended as my own mother is," Sancho replied.

"Well, then," said Don Quixote, "I can assure you that you have told me one of the most novel fables, stories, or histories that anyone in the world could possibly conceive. And I may add that such a way of telling and ending it has never been nor will be heard of in the course of a lifetime; although I expected nothing else from one with a wit like yours. However, I do not marvel at it, for it is possible that those ceaseless blows we hear have disturbed your understanding."

"Anything may be," said Sancho; "but in the matter of my story, I know that there is nothing more to be told, for it ends where you begin to lose count of the number of goats that have crossed."

"Let it end where it will, and well and good. But come, let us see if Rocinante can carry me now." With this, he applied the spurs once more, and the hack once again gave a start, but without budging from the spot, so well was he shackled.

At this juncture, whether it was the cool of the morning which was coming on, or something laxative he had eaten at supper, or—which is most likely—merely a necessity of nature, Sancho felt the will and desire to do that which no one else could do for him;[6] but so great was the fear that had lodged in his heart that he did not dare stir by so much as the tip of a fingernail from his master's side. It was, however, out of the question not to satisfy the need he felt; and what he did, accordingly, in order to have a little peace, was to remove his right hand which held the back of the saddle, and with this hand he very adroitly and without making any noise unloosed the slip-knot which alone sustained his breeches, thus letting them drop to the ground, where they lay like fetters about his feet; after which, he lifted his shirt and bared his behind, no small one by any means.

Having done this—and he thought it was all he needed to do in order to be rid of his agonizing cramps —he encountered another difficulty: how was he to vent himself without making some noise or sound? Gritting his teeth and huddling his shoulders, he held his breath as best he could; but despite all these precautions, the poor fellow ended by emitting a little sound quite different from the one that had filled him with such fear.

"What noise was that, Sancho?" said Don Quixote.

"I do not know, sir," he replied. "It must be something new; for adventures and misadventures never come singly."

He then tried his luck again and succeeded so well that, without any more noise or disturbance than the last time, he found himself free of the load that had given him so much discomfort. But Don Quixote's sense of smell was quite as keen as his sense of hearing, and Sancho was so close upon him that the fumes rose in almost a direct line, and so it is not surprising if some of them reached the knight's nostrils, whereupon he came to the aid of his nose by compressing it between two fingers.

"It strikes me, Sancho," he said in a somewhat snuffling tone of voice, "that you are very much frightened."

"That I am," replied his squire, "but how does your Grace happen to notice it, now more than ever?"

"Because you smell now more than ever, and it is not of ambergris."

"That may well be," said Sancho, "but I am not to blame; it is rather your Grace, for keeping me up at such hours and putting me through such unaccustomed paces."

"Retire, if you will, three or four paces from here, my friend," said Don Quixote, without taking his fingers from his nose; "and from now on, see to it that you take better care of your person and show more respect for mine. It is my familiarity with you that has bred this contempt."

"I'll wager," said Sancho, "your Grace thinks I have done something with my person that I ought not to have done."

"It only makes it worse to stir it, friend Sancho," Don Quixote answered him.

In talk such as this master and man spent the rest of the night; and when Sancho saw that morning was near he very cautiously removed the fetters from Rocinante and tied up his breeches. Finding himself free, although he was by no means a mettlesome animal, the hack appeared to be in high spirits and began pawing the earth, since—begging his pardon—he was not capable of leaping and prancing. When he beheld his steed in motion, Don Quixote took it for a good sign, a sign that he should begin that dread adventure.

It was light now and things could be clearly seen, and he discovered that they were in a grove of chestnut trees that cast a very deep shade. He was aware, also, that the sound of blows continued, although he could see no cause for it; and so, without any further delay, he dug his spurs into Rocinante and, turning to Sancho to bid him good-by, commanded him to wait three days at the most, as he had told him before. If at the end of that time he had not returned, his squire would know for a certainty that it had pleased God to have him end his life's span in this perilous undertaking.

Once again he reminded Sancho of the mission which the latter was to fulfill by bearing a message on his master's behalf to the lady Dulcinea. As to pay for his services, Sancho was not to let that worry him, as the knight before leaving home had made out his will in which his squire would find himself recompensed in full for all the wages due him in accordance with the time he had served. If, on the other hand, God should bring him, Don Quixote, safe, sound, and unscathed out of this peril, then his faithful servitor might be more than certain of obtaining that promised island. At hearing these sad words from his good master, Sancho again fell to weeping and resolved not to leave him until the final outcome and end of the business.

These tears and this noble resolve on the part of Sancho Panza are duly recorded by the author of the history, who must have been well bred and at the very least an old Christian.[7] Such a display of sentiment somewhat softened his master's heart. Not that Don Quixote showed any weakness, however; on the contrary, hiding his feelings as well as he could, he rode away in the direction from which the noise of water and the sound of blows appeared to be coming, with Sancho following on foot, leading his ass by the halter as usual, for that beast was his constant companion in good fortune or adversity.

When they had gone quite a way through the dense shade of the chestnut trees, they came out upon a little meadow at the foot of some tall cliffs over which poured a huge stream of water. Down below were a number of rude huts which looked more like ruins than houses, and it was from here that the hammering noise which never ceased was coming. Rocinante was frightened by the din of the waters and the sound of the blows, but Don Quixote quieted him and gradually made his way to where the huts stood, commending himself with all his heart to his lady and begging her favor in this dread enterprise; and as he went, he likewise commended himself to God, praying that He would not forget him. Sancho, meanwhile, never left his master's side but kept stretching his neck as far as he could between Rocinante's legs to see if the thing that had caused him so much fear and suspense was at last visible.

They had gone perhaps a hundred yards farther when, upon turning a corner, they discovered the obvious, unmistakable cause of that horrendous and, for them, terror-inspiring noise that all night long had so bewildered and alarmed them. And that cause was—if, O reader! you will not be too disappointed and disgusted —six fulling hammers which with their alternating strokes produced the clangor that resembled the sound of blows.

When Don Quixote saw what it was, he was speechless and remained as if paralyzed from head to foot. Gazing at him, Sancho saw that his head was on his bosom, as if he were abashed. The knight then glanced at his squire and perceived that his cheeks were puffed with laughter as if about to explode, and in spite of the melancholy that possessed him he in turn could not help laughing at the sight. Thus encouraged, Sancho gave in to his mirth and laughed so hard that he had to hold his sides to keep from bursting. He would stop for a while and then begin all over again, any number of times, laughing as hard as he had at first.

Don Quixote was furious at this, especially when he heard his squire saying, as if to mock him, " 'Sancho, my friend, you may know that I was born by Heaven's will, in this our age of iron, to revive what is known as the Golden Age. I am he for whom are reserved the perils, the great exploits, the valiant deeds . . .' " And he went on repeating all the other things that Don Quixote had said the first time they heard those frightening blows.

At seeing himself thus made sport of, the knight was so exceedingly wroth that he raised his lance and let Sancho have a couple of whacks, which, had they been received upon the head instead of across the shoulders, would have freed Don Quixote from the necessity of paying his wages, unless it had been to his heirs. The jest was becoming serious, and Sancho was afraid things might go further. He was very humble now.

"Calm yourself, your Grace," he said. "In God's name, I was only joking."

"Well, you may be joking, but I am not," said Don Quixote. "Come over here, my merry gentleman, I want to ask you a question. Supposing that, in place of fulling hammers, this had really been another dangerous adventure, did not I display the requisite courage for undertaking and carrying it through? Am I obliged, being a gentleman as I am, to recognize and distinguish sounds and know whether they come from fulling hammers or not? Especially when I may never before have laid eyes on such things, as happens to be the case, whereas you, rude bumpkin that you are, were born and brought up among them. But turn these six hammers into six giants and beard me with them one by one, or with all of them together, and if I do not cause them all to turn up their toes, then you may make as much sport of me as you like."

"I shall do so no more, sir," replied Sancho, "for I admit that I carried the joke a little too far. But tell me, your Grace, now that there is peace between us— and may God in the future bring you out of all adventures as safe and sound as He has brought you out of this one—tell me if it was not truly a laughing matter, and a good story as well, that great fright of ours? For I, at least, was afraid, although I am well aware that your Grace does not know what fear is."

"I do not deny," said Don Quixote, "that what happened to us has its comical aspects; but it is best not to tell the story, for not everyone is wise enough to see the point of the thing."

"Well, at any rate," said Sancho, "your Grace saw

the point when you pointed your lance at my head—
but it fell on my shoulders, thank God, and thanks also
to my quickness in dodging it. But never mind, it will
all come out in the wash;[8] and I have heard it said,
'He loves you well who makes you weep.' It is the custom of great lords, after they have scolded a servant,
to give him a pair of breeches; although I am sure
I do not know what they would give him after a good
clubbing, unless they happened to be knights-errant,
and then perhaps they would give him a few islands or
some kingdoms on *terra firma*." [9]

"The dice may so fall," replied Don Quixote, "that
everything you say will come true. But let us overlook
the past; for you are shrewd enough to know that the
first instinctive movements a man makes are not within
his control. Be advised of one thing for the future,
however: you are to abstain and refrain from conversing with me so much; for in all the books of chivalry
that I have read, and they are infinite in number, I
have never heard of any squire talking so much to his
master as you do to me. The truth is, I look upon it as
a great fault, on your part and on mine: on your part
because it shows that you have little respect for me;
and on mine because I do not make myself more respected.

"There was, for example, Gandalín, squire to Amadis
of Gaul, who was count of Firm Island. I have read of
him that he never spoke to his master save with cap in
hand, with lowered head and body bent double *more
turquesco*.[10] Then, what shall we say of Gasabal, squire
to Don Galaor, who was so very silent that, by way of
indicating how excellent a thing such taciturnity on his
part was, the author of that history, which is as volu-
minous as it is veracious, sees fit to mention his name
only once?

"From all this that I have told you, Sancho, you are to infer that it is necessary that there be a difference between master and man, lord and servant, a knight and his squire. And so, from now on, we must treat each other with more respect and less bantering; for in whatever way I may become annoyed with you, it will be bad for the pitcher.[11] The favors and benefits that I have promised you will all come in due time; and if they should not, your wages at least are safe as I have told you."

"That is all well and good," said Sancho, "but what I should like to know of your Grace is, if by any chance the time for the granting of favors does not come and it is necessary to think of the wages, how much did the squire of a knight-errant earn in those times, and was it reckoned by months, or by days as in the case of bricklayers?"

"I do not think," said Don Quixote, "that the squires of old received wages, but only favors; and if I have provided a wage for you, in the sealed will which I have left at home, it was in view of what might happen; as yet I do not know how chivalry will work out in these calamitous times in which we live, and I do not wish my soul in the other world to have to suffer on account of trifles; for I may tell you, Sancho, that there is no calling anywhere more dangerous than that of adventurer."

"That is the truth," said Sancho, "seeing that the mere sound of fulling hammers can disturb and agitate the heart of so valiant a knightly adventurer as is your Grace. But you may be sure that from now on I will not open my mouth to make light of what concerns your Grace, but will speak only to honor you as my liege lord and master."

"By so doing," replied Don Quixote, "you will live long upon the face of the earth; for after parents, masters are to be respected as if they were the ones that bore us."

CHAPTER XXI. *Which treats of the high and richly rewarded adventure of Mambrino's helmet, together with other things that happened to our invincible knight.*

AT THIS point it began to rain a little, and Sancho suggested that they enter the fulling mill; but Don Quixote had conceived such a dislike for the place by reason of the offensive joke[1] associated with it that he would not hear of their setting foot inside it; and so, turning to the right, they came out into another road like the one they had traveled the day before.

They had not gone far before Don Quixote sighted a man on horseback wearing something on his head that gleamed like gold, and no sooner had he laid eyes upon him than he said to his squire, "It is my opinion, Sancho, that there is no proverb that is not true; for they are all drawn from experience itself, mother of all the sciences, and especially that saying that runs, 'Where one door closes another opens.' By this I mean to say that if, last night, fortune closed the door on what we were seeking by deceiving us with those fulling hammers, she is now opening another upon a better and more assured adventure, and if I do not embark upon that undertaking the fault will be mine, and I shall not be able to blame it upon those hammers or the darkness of night. I tell you this for the reason that, if I am not mistaken, there comes toward us now one who wears upon his head that helmet of Mambrino concerning which, as you know, I have taken a vow."

"But, your Grace," said Sancho, "mark well what I

say and even better what you do; for I should not like
to have any more fulling hammers fulling and finishing
us off and cudgeling our brains."

"To the devil with the fellow!" exclaimed Don
Quixote. "What has the helmet to do with fulling mills?"

"I know nothing about that," replied Sancho, "but
upon my word, if I were free to talk as I used to, I
could give you such reasons that your Grace would see
he was mistaken in what he just said."

"How could I be mistaken in what I said, you un-
believing traitor? Tell me, do you not see that knight
coming toward us, mounted on a dappled gray steed
and with a golden helmet on his head?"

"What I see and perceive," said Sancho, "is a man
upon an ass, a gray ass like mine, with something or
other on his head that shines."

"Well," said Don Quixote, "that is Mambrino's helmet. Go off to one side and let me meet him singlehanded; and you shall see me end this adventure without wasting a word in parley, and when it is ended, the
helmet which I have so greatly desired shall be mine."

"I will take care to go to one side, right enough,"
said Sancho; "but—I say again—I only pray God that
it may turn out to be marjoram and not fulling hammers." [2]

"I have told you, brother," said Don Quixote, "not
to think of mentioning those hammers to me again; and
if you do, I vow—I need say no more—that I will full
your very soul."

Sancho was silent, for he was afraid that his master
would carry out this vow which he had hurled at him
like a bowling ball.

The truth concerning that helmet and the horse and
horseman that Don Quixote had sighted was this: in
these parts there were two villages, one so small that

it had neither apothecary nor barber, whereas the other had both; and as a consequence, the barber of the larger village served the smaller one, in which, as it happened, there was a sick man who had need of a blood-letting and another individual who needed to have his beard trimmed; and so the barber was on his way now, carrying with him a brass basin, and as it had started to rain and he did not wish to have his hat spoiled (it was probably a new one), he had placed the basin on his head, and since it was very clean it could be seen glittering half a league away. He was riding on an ass, a gray one as Sancho had remarked, and it was all this that had given Don Quixote the impression of a knight, a dappled steed, and a helmet of gold, for he readily fitted all the things that he saw to his own mad, ill-errant[3] thoughts of chivalry.

As he saw the poor fellow whom he took to be a knight approaching, without pausing for any exchange of words he bore down upon him with lowered lance at the best speed that Rocinante could make, with intent to run him through with his pike. As he drew near, without abating his fury in the least, he cried out, "Defend yourself, vile wretch, or else render to me of your own free will that which is so justly my due!"

The barber who, without any thought or fear of what was about to happen, had seen this apparition descending upon him, now had no other recourse by way of protecting himself from the lance blow than to slide down off his ass's back, and he had no more than touched the earth when he was up and running away across the fields faster than the wind, leaving his basin behind him upon the ground. Don Quixote was content with this, observing that the heathenish fellow had been wise in imitating the beaver, which, when it finds itself hard pressed by the hunters, bites and tears off [4] with its teeth that for which it knows it is being pursued. He commanded Sancho to pick up the helmet for him.

"By God," said the squire, taking it in his hands, "if it isn't a very good basin and worth a piece of eight if it's worth a maravedi."

With this, he handed it to his master, and Don Quixote at once placed it on his head, turning it round and round in search of the visor.

"Undoubtedly," he said when he failed to find one, "the pagan to whose measure this helmet was originally made must have had a very large head. The regrettable part of it is, half of it is missing."

Upon hearing the basin called a helmet, Sancho could not help laughing, but mindful of his master's ire, he stopped short.

"What are you laughing at, Sancho?" said Don Quixote.

"I was just thinking what a big pate that pagan had who owned it, for this helmet looks exactly like a barber's basin."

"Do you know what I think, Sancho? I think that this famous piece of that enchanted helmet must by some strange accident have fallen into the hands of someone who did not know, and was incapable of estimating, its worth, and who, seeing that it was of the purest gold and not realizing what he was doing, must have melted down the other half for what he could get for it, while from the remaining portion he fashioned what appears, as you have said, to be a barber's basin. But be that as it may; I recognize its value, and the transformation that it has undergone makes no difference to me; the first village that we come to where there is a blacksmith, I will have it repaired in such a manner that the helmet which the god of smithies made and forged for the god of battles shall not surpass or even come up to it. In the meanwhile, I will wear it the best way I can, for something is better than nothing at all, especially seeing that it will serve quite well to protect me from stones."

"That is," said Sancho, "providing it is not a stone from a slingshot of the kind they let you have in the battle of the two armies, that time they made the sign of the cross on your Grace's grinders and broke the vial which held that blessed potion that made me vomit up my guts."

"I am not greatly grieved over having lost it," said Don Quixote, "for as you know, Sancho, I have the receipt in my memory."

"So have I," replied Sancho, "but if I ever in all my life make it or try it again, may this be my last hour on earth. What is more, I do not expect to have any occasion to use it, for I mean to see to it with all my five senses that I neither wound anybody nor am wounded by anyone else. As to being tossed in a blanket, I say nothing about that. Troubles of that kind are hard to foresee, and if they come, there is nothing to do but shrug your shoulders, hold your breath, shut your eyes, and let yourself go where luck and the blanket take you."

"You are a bad Christian, Sancho," said his master when he heard this, "for you never forget an injury that once has been done you. You should know that it is characteristic of noble and generous hearts to pay no attention to trifles. You have no lame leg, no fractured rib, no broken head to show for it; so why can you not forget that bit of buffoonery? For when you look at it closely, that is all it was: a jest and a little pastime; for had I not regarded it in that light, I should have returned and, in avenging you, should have wrought more damage than those Greeks did who stole Helen of Troy—who, you may be sure, if she had lived in these times or my Dulcinea had lived in those, would not have been so famed for her beauty as she now is." With this, he breathed a sigh and wafted it heavenward.

"Let it pass for a jest," said Sancho, "seeing that it cannot be avenged in earnest; but I know what jest and earnest mean, and I further know that this joke will never slip from my memory any more than it will from my shoulders. But leaving all that aside, tell me, your Grace, what are we to do with this dappled gray steed that looks like a gray-colored ass, which that fellow Martino[5] whom your Grace just routed has left here? For judging by the way he took to his heels, I don't think he ever means to come back for it; and by my beard, but the gray is a good one!"

"It is not my custom," said Don Quixote, "to despoil those whom I conquer, nor is it in accordance with the usages of knighthood to deprive one's enemy of his steed and leave him to go away on foot, unless it be that the victor has lost his own mount in the fray, in which case it is permitted to take that of the vanquished as something that has been won in lawful warfare. And so, Sancho, leave this horse, or ass, or whatever you choose to call him; for as soon as its master sees that we are gone, he will come back for it."

"God knows I'd like to take it," said Sancho, "or at least exchange it for this one of mine, which does not strike me as being a very good one. Surely the laws of knighthood must be pretty strict if they cannot be stretched far enough to permit you to exchange one ass for another. Could I not at least exchange trappings?"

"I am none too certain as to that," replied Don Quixote; "but being in doubt and until I am better informed, I should say that you might exchange them in case of extreme necessity."

"The necessity," said Sancho, "is so extreme that I

could not need them more if they were for my own person."

Having been granted permission to do so, he now effected the *mutatio capparum*,[6] trigging his own beast out in great style, in such a manner as to alter its appearance most advantageously. This being done, they made their lunch on what was left over from the spoils of the sumpter mule, drinking water from the brook where the fulling hammers were but without turning their heads to look at them, for they still could not forget the fright which those distasteful objects had given them.

At length, all anger and melancholy gone, they mounted again and without taking any definite direction, as was the custom of knights-errant, they let Rocinante follow his own will, his master's inclinations and those of the ass falling in behind; for the ass followed wherever the hack led, very sociably and affectionately. Proceeding in this manner, they came back to the highway and continued riding along, leaving everything to chance and with no plan whatsoever.

Finally Sancho spoke up and addressed the knight. "Sir," he said, "would your Grace grant me permission to have a word with you? Ever since you gave me that order to be silent, a number of things in my stomach have gone to rot, and I have one now on the tip of my tongue that I do not want to see wasted."

"Say what you have to say," said Don Quixote, "and be brief about it, for there is no pleasure in listening to long speeches."

"Very well, sir," replied Sancho. "I just wanted to tell you that for some days now I have been thinking how little gain or profit there is in your Grace's going in search of adventures in these wasteland and crossroad places; for even if you come out the victor in the most dangerous of them, there is no one to witness them or know about them, and as a result, nothing will ever be heard of them, which is contrary to what your Grace had in mind and what they deserve. And, accordingly, it seems to me that it would be better—saving, always, your Grace's better judgment—for us to go serve some emperor or other great prince who has some war on his hands and in whose service your Grace would have an opportunity to display the valor of your person, the great feats of which you are capable, and your superior understanding. For when the lord we served beheld all this, being obliged to reward each according to his merits, he could not fail to have your Grace's exploits set down in writing, that they might never be forgotten. Of my own I say nothing, for they do not go beyond the bounds of what is becoming in a squire; although I may say this much: that if it were the custom of knighthood to record squirely achievements, I do not think mine would be left out."

"There is something in what you say, Sancho," replied Don Quixote; "but before we come to that, it is necessary for a knight to roam the world in quest of adventures and, so to speak, serve a period of probation, in order that, having brought a number of those adventures to a successful conclusion, he may win such name and fame as will render him well known for his accomplishments by the time he arrives at the court of some great monarch. He must be so well known that, when he enters the gate of the city, all the young lads will follow and surround him, shouting, 'There goes the Knight of the Sun,' or of the Serpent, or whatever insignia it was under which he performed his feats of valor. 'He,' they will say, 'is the one who overcame singlehanded the giant Brocabruno of the Mighty Strength; he it was who freed the Mameluke of Persia of the spell under which he had been for nearly nine hundred years.'

"Thus from mouth to mouth his fame will spread, until at last, aroused by the tumult of the lads and the throng that will have gathered, the king of that realm will appear at the windows of his royal palace, and as soon as he sees the knight, recognizing him by his armor or by the device on his shield, he will be certain to cry, 'What, ho! Up, all ye knights that be in my court and go forth to receive the flower of chivalry who cometh hither.' At this command, they will all come out, and the monarch himself, descending the stair halfway, will welcome the new arrival, giving him a warm embrace and a kiss on the cheek, after which he will conduct him to the apartment of my lady the queen, and in her company the knight will be presented to her daughter, who will be one of the most beautiful and faultless damsels to be met with anywhere in the known world. And then it will come to pass that she will rest her eyes on the knight and he will rest his on her, and each will appear to the other as something that is nearer divine than human; and, without knowing how or why it comes about, they will find themselves caught and entangled in love's inextricable net, with a deep pain in their hearts at not being able to put into words their longings and desires.

"After that, they undoubtedly will take him to some room in the palace that is richly fitted out, and there, having relieved him of his armor, they will bring him a sumptuous scarlet cloak to wear; and if he presented a handsome appearance in his suit of armor, he will be even handsomer in a doublet. When night comes, he will sup with the king, queen, and infanta, and he will never take his eyes off the princess but will steal glances at her without the others seeing him, and she with equal cunning will do the same, for, as I have said, she is a very circumspect young lady. And then, when the tables have been cleared, through the door of the great hall there will at once enter a small and ugly dwarf, followed by a beautiful duenna between two giants, who comes to propose a certain adventure conceived by a wise man of very long ago; and whoever carries it through is to be looked upon as the best knight in the world.

"The king will thereupon command all those present to undertake the adventure, and none will bring it to an end and conclusion except the knight who is their guest. This will greatly add to his fame, and the infanta will be very happy and feel well recompensed for having placed her affections upon so exalted a personage. But the best part of it is, this king or prince or whoever he may be is engaged in a bitter war with another monarch who is quite as powerful as he; and the stranger knight—after a few days spent at court—will then beg his royal host's permission to go serve him in the said war. His Majesty will grant this request with right good grace, and the knight will courteously kiss the king's hand in return for the favor shown him.

"That night, he will take leave of his lady the infanta through the grating of her chamber overlooking the garden where he has already conversed with her many times, the go-between and confidante in the affair being a maid-in-waiting whom the princess greatly trusts. He will sigh and she will swoon, and the damsel will bring water to revive her. He will be very much distressed at this, for morning is near, and for the sake of his lady's honor he would not have them discovered. Finally the infanta will come to herself and will hold out her white hands through the bars to her knight, who will kiss them thousands upon thousands of times, bathing them with his tears.

"It will be arranged between them how they are to keep each other informed as to the good or ill that befalls them, and the princess will entreat him not to remain away any longer than need be. He will give her this promise, with many oaths to bind it, and then he will kiss her hands once more and depart, so deeply moved that he is on the verge of dying. Going to his apartment, he will cast himself down upon his bed, but will be unable to sleep from the pain of parting. In the morning, very early, he will go to bid adieu to the king, queen, and infanta; but after he has paid his respects to the royal pair, he is informed that the princess is indisposed and cannot receive any visitors. The knight will think that she too must be suffering at prospect of their separation, his heart will be transfixed, and it will be all he can do to hide his feelings.

"But the damsel who is the go-between will be there; she will take note of everything and will go to report it all to her mistress, who will receive her with tears. The princess will then tell her maid-in-waiting that one of the things that cause her most sorrow is the fact that she does not know who her knight is, or whether he is of royal lineage or not. The damsel will assure her that so much courtesy, gentleness of bearing, and valor could be displayed only by a grave and royal personage, and with such words as these she will endeavor to assuage her mistress's grief. The princess will then seek to compose herself so as not to make a bad impression upon her parents, and after a couple of days she will appear in public once more.

"Meanwhile, the knight has left for the wars; he conquers the king's enemy, takes many cities, is victorious in many battles, returns to court, meets his lady in the accustomed place, and they agree that he is to ask her father for her hand in payment of his services. The king is unwilling to grant this request, for he does not know who the knight is; but, nevertheless, whether she is carried off or however it happens, she becomes his bride, and her father in the end comes to look upon it as a piece of great good fortune, for he has learned that the knight is the son of the valiant king of some realm or other which I do not think you will find on the map. The king then dies, the infanta inherits the throne, and, in a couple of words, the knight becomes king.[7]

"And here is where the bestowal of favors comes in, as he rewards his squire and all those who have assisted him in rising to so exalted a state. He marries the squire to one of the infanta's damsels, undoubtedly the one who was the go-between in his courting of the princess, and who is the daughter of a very great duke."

"That's what I want, and no mistake about it," said Sancho. "That is what I'm waiting for. All of this, word for word, is bound to happen to your Grace now that you bear the title Knight of the Mournful Countenance."

"Do not doubt it, Sancho," Don Quixote assured him; "for in this very manner and by these very steps of which I have told you, many come, and have come, to be kings and emperors. It only remains to find out what king of the Christians or the pagans is at war and has a beautiful daughter. But there will be time to think of all that; for, as I have said, one must achieve fame else-where before repairing to court. There is one other thing: supposing that I find a king with a war and with a beautiful daughter, and supposing that I have won an incredible amount of fame throughout the universe, I do not know how I am going to make myself out to be of royal line or even second cousin to an emperor; for the king will not wish to give me his daughter's hand unless he is first thoroughly satisfied on this point, however much my deeds may merit the honor; and for this reason I fear losing that which my good right arm has so well earned for me. It is true that I am a gentleman property-holder with a country house and estate, and am entitled to an income of five hundred sueldos;[8] and it may further be that the learned scribe who writes my history will so clear up my relationships and ancestry that I shall be found to be the descendant, fifth or sixth in line, of some king.

"For I would have you know, Sancho," he went on, "that there are in this world two kinds of ancestral lines. In the one case, there are those who trace their descent from princes and monarchs whom time has little by little reduced until they come to end in a point like a pyramid upside down; and in the other case, there are those who spring from the lower classes and who go upward, one step after another, until they come to be great lords; the difference being that the former were what they no longer are, while the latter are what they formerly were not. And I may be one of those who, after it has been ascertained that they are of great and famous origin, are accepted for what they are, and the king, my father-in-law, in that case will be content; but should he not be, the infanta will love me so much that, in spite of her father's wishes and even though she definitely knows me to be a water carrier's son, she still will insist upon my being received as a gentleman and her consort. And if everything else fails, then it will come to my abducting and carrying her off wherever I see fit; for time or death must eventually put an end to her parents' wrath."

"It comes to something else as well," said Sancho.

"For I am reminded here of what certain wicked ones say: 'Never beg as a favor what you can take by force'; although they might better say: 'An escape from the slaughter is worth more than good men's prayers.' I tell you this because if the king, your Grace's father-in-law, will not condescend to give you my lady the infanta, then, as your Grace says, there is nothing for it but to abduct and carry her off. But the trouble is that until you make your peace and come into the tranquil enjoyment of your kingdom, your poor squire can whistle for his favors—that is, unless the damsel who was the go-between and who is to be his wife accompanies the princess and shares her ill fortune with her until Heaven ordains otherwise; for I take it that his master will give her to him at once as his lawful spouse."

"No one can deny him that," said Don Quixote.

"Well, then," replied Sancho, "if that is so, we have nothing to do but to commend ourselves to God and let fortune take whatever course it will."

"May God fulfill my desires and your needs, Sancho," said Don Quixote; "and let him be vile who looks upon himself as such." [9]

"In God's name, so let him be," said Sancho. "I am an old Christian, and that in itself is enough to make me a count."

"Enough and more than enough for you," said Don Quixote; "and even if you were not, it would make no difference; for once I am king, I can very well make a noble of you without any purchase price or service on your part; and in making you a count, I make a gentleman of you at the same time, and then let them say what they will, upon my word they will have to call you 'my lordship' whether they like it or not."

"And I would lend dignity to the tittle!" [10] said Sancho.

"*Title*, you mean to say, not *tittle*," his master corrected him.

"So be it," said Sancho. "I'd know how to behave myself properly; for there was a time in my life when I was the beadle of a confraternity, and the beadle's gown sat so well upon me that everybody said I ought to be the steward. So what will it be when I put a ducal robe on my back or dress myself out in gold and pearls like one of those foreign counts? I think, myself, that folks will be coming to see me for a hundred leagues around."

"You will cut a fine figure," said Don Quixote, "but it will be necessary for you to shave your beard quite often, for it is so thick and unkempt that unless you use the razor on it every other day at the least, people will be able to see what you are at the distance of a musket shot."

"What more have I to do," said Sancho, "than to hire a barber and keep him in the house? If necessary, I can even have him walk behind me like a nobleman's equerry."

"How do you know," asked Don Quixote, "that noblemen have equerries walking behind them?"

"I will tell you about that," Sancho replied. "Years ago I spent a month near the court, and there I saw a very small gentleman who, they told me, was a very great lord.[11] He was out for a stroll, and there was a man on horseback following him at every turn he took just as if he had been his tail. I asked why it was this man did not join the other one but always rode along behind him, and they replied that he was an equerry and that such was the custom of the nobility. I have known it ever since then, for I have never forgotten it."

"You are right," said Don Quixote, "and you may take your barber with you in the same manner; for all customs did not come into use, nor were they invented, at one and the same time; and so you may be the first count to be followed by his barber, for shaving the beard is a more intimate matter than saddling a horse."

"Just leave the barber to me," said Sancho, "while your Grace sees to becoming a king and making a count of me."

"So shall it be," said Don Quixote; and, raising his eyes, he saw something that will be related in the following chapter.

CHAPTER XXII. *Of how Don Quixote freed many unfortunate ones who, much against their will, were being taken where they did not wish to go.*

C ID HAMETE BENENGELI, the Arabic and Manchegan[1] author, in the course of this most grave, high-sounding, minute, delightful, and imaginative history, informs us that, following the remarks that were exchanged between Don Quixote de la Mancha and Sancho Panza, his squire, as related at the end of Chapter XXI, the knight looked up and saw coming toward them down the road which they were following a dozen or so men on foot, strung together by their necks like beads on an iron chain and all of them wearing handcuffs. They were accompanied by two men on horseback and two on foot, the former carrying wheel-lock muskets while the other two were armed with swords and javelins.

"That," said Sancho as soon as he saw them, "is a chain of galley slaves, people on their way to the galleys where by order of the king they are forced to labor."

"What do you mean by 'forced'?" asked Don Quixote.

"Is it possible that the king uses force on anyone?"

"I did not say that," replied Sancho. "What I did say was that these are folks who have been condemned for their crimes to forced labor in the galleys for his Majesty the King."

"The short of it is," said the knight, "whichever way you put it, these people are being taken there by force and not of their own free will."

"That is the way it is," said Sancho.

"Well, in that case," said his master, "now is the time for me to fulfill the duties of my calling, which is to right wrongs and come to the aid of the wretched."

"But take note, your Grace," said Sancho, "that justice, that is to say, the king himself, is not using any force upon, or doing any wrong to, people like these, but is merely punishing them for the crimes they have committed."

The chain of galley slaves had come up to them by this time, whereupon Don Quixote very courteously requested the guards to inform him of the reason or reasons why they were conducting these people in such a manner as this. One of the men on horseback then replied that the men were prisoners who had been condemned by his Majesty to serve in the galleys, whither they were bound, and that was all there was to be said about it and all that he, Don Quixote, need know.

"Nevertheless," said the latter, "I should like to inquire of each one of them, individually, the cause of his misfortune." And he went on speaking so very politely in an effort to persuade them to tell him what he wanted to know that the other mounted guard finally said, "Although we have here the record and certificate of sentence of each one of these wretches, we have not the time to get them out and read them to you; and so your Grace may come over and ask the prisoners themselves, and they will tell you if they choose, and you may be sure that they will, for these fellows take a delight in their knavish exploits and in boasting of them afterward."

With this permission, even though he would have done so if it had not been granted him, Don Quixote went up to the chain of prisoners and asked the first whom he encountered what sins had brought him to so sorry a plight. The man replied that it was for being a lover that he found himself in that line.

"For that and nothing more?" said Don Quixote. "And do they, then, send lovers to the galleys? If so, I should have been rowing there long ago."

"But it was not the kind of love that your Grace has in mind," the prisoner went on. "I loved a wash basket full of white linen so well and hugged it so tightly that, if they had not taken it away from me by force, I would never of my own choice have let go of it to this very minute. I was caught in the act, there was no need to torture me, the case was soon disposed of, and they supplied me with a hundred lashes across the shoulders and, in addition, a three-year stretch[2] in the *gurapas,* and that's all there is to tell."

"What are *gurapas?*" asked Don Quixote.

"*Gurapas* are the galleys," replied the prisoner. He was a lad of around twenty-four and stated that he was a native of Piedrahita.

The knight then put the same question to a second man, who appeared to be very downcast and melancholy and did not have a word to say. The first man answered for him.

"This one, sir," he said, "is going as a canary—I mean, as a musician and singer."

"How is that?" Don Quixote wanted to know. "Do musicians and singers go to the galleys too?"

"Yes, sir; and there is nothing worse than singing when you're in trouble."

"On the contrary," said Don Quixote, "I have heard it said that he who sings frightens away his sorrows."

"It is just the opposite," said the prisoner; "for he who sings once weeps all his life long."

"I do not understand," said the knight.

One of the guards then explained. "Sir Knight, with this *non sancta* tribe, to sing when you're in trouble means to confess under torture. This sinner was put to the torture and confessed his crime, which was that of being a *cuatrero,* or cattle thief, and as a result of his confession he was condemned to six years in the galleys in addition to two hundred lashes which he took on his shoulders; and so it is he is always downcast and moody, for the other thieves, those back where he came from and the ones here, mistreat, snub, ridicule, and despise him for having confessed and for not having had the courage to deny his guilt. They are in the habit of saying that the word *no* has the same number of letters as the word *sí,* and that a culprit is in luck when his life or death depends on his own tongue and not that of witnesses or upon evidence; and, in my opinion, they are not very far wrong."

"And I," said Don Quixote, "feel the same way about it." He then went on to a third prisoner and repeated his question.

The fellow answered at once, quite unconcernedly. "I'm going to my ladies, the *gurapas,* for five years, for the lack of five ducats."

"I would gladly give twenty," said Don Quixote, "to get you out of this."

"That," said the prisoner, "reminds me of the man in the middle of the ocean who has money and is dying of hunger because there is no place to buy what he needs.

I say this for the reason that if I had had, at the right time, those twenty ducats your Grace is now offering me, I'd have greased the notary's quill and freshened up the attorney's wit with them, and I'd now be living in the middle of Zocodover Square in Toledo instead of being here on this highway coupled like a greyhound. But God is great; patience, and that's enough of it."

Don Quixote went on to a fourth prisoner, a venerable-looking old fellow with a white beard that fell over his bosom. When asked how he came to be there, this one began weeping and made no reply, but a fifth comrade spoke up in his behalf.

"This worthy man," he said, "is on his way to the galleys after having made the usual rounds clad in a robe of state and on horseback." [3]

"That means, I take it," said Sancho, "that he has been put to shame in public."

"That is it," said the prisoner, "and the offense for which he is being punished is that of having been an ear broker, or, better, a body broker. By that I mean to say, in short, that the gentleman is a pimp, and besides, he has his points as a sorcerer."

"If that point had not been thrown in," said Don Quixote, "he would not deserve, for merely being a pimp, to have to row in the galleys, but rather should be the general and give orders there. For the office of pimp is not an indifferent one; it is a function to be performed by persons of discretion and is most necessary in a well-ordered state; it is a profession that should be followed only by the wellborn, and there should, moreover, be a supervisor or examiner as in the case of other offices, and the number of practitioners should be fixed by law as is done with brokers on the exchange. In that way many evils would be averted that arise when this office is filled and this calling practiced by stupid folk and those with little sense, such as silly women and pages or mountebanks with few years and less experience to their credit, who, on the most pressing occasions, when it is necessary to use one's wits, let the crumbs freeze between their hand and their mouth[4] and do not know which is their right hand and which is the left.

"I would go on and give reasons why it is fitting to choose carefully those who are to fulfill so necessary a state function, but this is not the place for it. One of these days I will speak of the matter to someone who is able to do something about it. I will say here only that the pain I felt at seeing those white hairs and this venerable countenance in such a plight, and all for his having been a pimp, has been offset for me by the additional information you have given me, to the effect that he is a sorcerer as well; for I am convinced that there are no sorcerers in the world who can move and compel the will, as some simple-minded persons think, but that our will is free and no herb or charm can force it. All that certain foolish women and cunning tricksters do is to compound a few mixtures and poisons with which they deprive men of their senses while pretending that they have the power to make them loved,[5] although, as I have just said, one cannot affect another's will in that manner."

"That is so," said the worthy old man; "but the truth is, sir, I am not guilty on the sorcery charge. As for being a pimp, that is something I cannot deny. I never thought there was any harm in it, however, my only desire being that everyone should enjoy himself and live in peace and quiet, without any quarrels or troubles. But these good intentions on my part cannot prevent me from going where I do not want to go, to a place from which I do not expect to return; for my years are heavy upon me and an affection of the urine that I have will not give me a moment's rest."

With this, he began weeping once more, and Sancho was so touched by it that he took a four-real piece from his bosom and gave it to him as an act of charity.

Don Quixote then went on and asked another what his offense was. The fellow answered him, not with less, but with much more, briskness than the preceding one had shown.

"I am here," he said, "for the reason that I carried a joke too far with a couple of cousins-german of mine and a couple of others who were not mine, and I ended by jesting with all of them to such an extent that the devil [6] himself would never be able to straighten out the relationship. They proved everything on me, there was no one to show me favor, I had no money, I came near swinging for it, they sentenced me to the galleys for six years, and I accepted the sentence as the punishment that was due me. I am young yet, and if I live long enough, everything will come out all right. If, Sir Knight, your Grace has anything with which to aid these poor creatures that you see before you, God will reward you in Heaven, and we here on earth will make it a point to ask God in our prayers to grant you long life and good health, as long and as good as your amiable presence deserves."

This man was dressed as a student, and one of the guards told Don Quixote that he was a great talker and a very fine Latinist.

Back of these came a man around thirty years of age and of very good appearance, except that when he looked at you his eyes were seen to be a little crossed. He was shackled in a different manner from the others, for he dragged behind him a chain so huge that it was wrapped all round his body, with two rings at the throat, one of which was attached to the chain while the other was fastened to what is known as a keep-friend or friend's foot, from which two irons hung down to his waist, ending in handcuffs secured by a heavy padlock in such a manner that he could neither raise his hands to his mouth nor lower his head to reach his hands.

When Don Quixote asked why this man was so much more heavily chained than the others, the guard replied that it was because he had more crimes against him than all the others put together, and he was so bold and cunning that, even though they had him chained like this, they were by no means sure of him but feared that he might escape from them.

"What crimes could he have committed," asked the knight, "if he has merited a punishment no greater than that of being sent to the galleys?"

"He is being sent there for ten years," replied the guard, "and that is equivalent to civil death. I need tell you no more than that this good man is the famous Ginés de Pasamonte, otherwise known as Ginesillo de Parapilla."

"Señor Commissary," spoke up the prisoner at this point, "go easy there and let us not be so free with names and surnames. My just name is Ginés and not Ginesillo; and Pasamonte, not Parapilla as you make it out to be, is my family name. Let each one mind his own affairs and he will have his hands full."

"Speak a little more respectfully, you big thief, you," said the commissary, "unless you want me to make you be quiet in a way you won't like."

"Man goes as God pleases, that is plain to be seen," replied the galley slave, "but someday someone will know whether my name is Ginesillo de Parapilla or not."

"But, you liar, isn't that what they call you?"

"Yes," said Ginés, "they do call me that; but I'll put a stop to it, or else I'll skin their you-know-what. And you, sir, if you have anything to give us, give it and may God go with you, for I am tired of all this prying into other people's lives. If you want to know anything about my life, know that I am Ginés de Pasamonte whose life story has been written down by these fingers that you see here."

"He speaks the truth," said the commissary, "for he has himself written his story, as big as you please, and has left the book in the prison, having pawned it for two hundred reales."

"And I mean to redeem it," said Ginés, "even if it costs me two hundred ducats."

"Is it as good as that?" inquired Don Quixote.

"It is so good," replied Ginés, "that it will cast into the shade *Lazarillo de Tormes*⁷ and all others of that sort that have been or will be written. What I would tell you is that it deals with facts, and facts so interesting and amusing that no lies could equal them."

"And what is the title of the book?" asked Don Quixote.

"The Life of Ginés de Pasamonte."

"Is it finished?"

"How could it be finished," said Ginés, "when my life is not finished as yet? What I have written thus far is an account of what happened to me from the time I was born up to the last time that they sent me to the galleys."

"Then you have been there before?"

"In the service of God and the king I was there four years, and I know what the biscuit and the cowhide are like. I don't mind going very much, for there I will have a chance to finish my book. I still have many things to say, and in the Spanish galleys I shall have all the leisure that I need, though I don't need much, since I know by heart what it is I want to write."

"You seem to be a clever fellow," said Don Quixote.

"And an unfortunate one," said Ginés; "for misfortunes always pursue men of genius."

"They pursue rogues," said the commissary.

"I have told you to go easy, Señor Commissary," said Pasamonte, "for their Lordships did not give you that staff in order that you might mistreat us poor devils with it, but they intended that you should guide and conduct us in accordance with his Majesty's command. Otherwise, by the life of— But enough. It may be that someday the stains made in the inn will come out in the wash. Meanwhile, let everyone hold his tongue, behave well, and speak better, and let us be on our way. We've had enough of this foolishness."

At this point the commissary raised his staff as if to let Pasamonte have it in answer to his threats, but Don Quixote placed himself between them and begged the officer not to abuse the man; for it was not to be wondered at if one who had his hands so bound should be a trifle free with his tongue. With this, he turned and addressed them all.

"From all that you have told me, my dearest brothers," he said, "one thing stands out clearly for me, and that is the fact that, even though it is a punishment for offenses which you have committed, the penalty you are about to pay is not greatly to your liking and you are going to the galleys very much against your own will and desire. It may be that the lack of spirit which one of you displayed under torture, the lack of money on the part of another, the lack of influential friends, or, finally, warped judgment on the part of the magistrate, was the thing that led to your downfall;

and, as a result, justice was not done you. All of which presents itself to my mind in such a fashion that I am at this moment engaged in trying to persuade and even force myself to show you what the purpose was for which Heaven sent me into this world, why it was it led me to adopt the calling of knighthood which I profess and take the knightly vow to favor the needy and aid those who are oppressed by the powerful.

"However, knowing as I do that it is not the part of prudence to do by foul means what can be accomplished by fair ones, I propose to ask these gentlemen, your guards, and the commissary to be so good as to unshackle you and permit you to go in peace. There will be no dearth of others to serve his Majesty under more propitious circumstances; and it does not appear to me to be just to make slaves of those whom God created as free men. What is more, gentlemen of the guard, these poor fellows have committed no offense against you. Up there, each of us will have to answer for his own sins; for God in Heaven will not fail to punish the evil and reward the good; and it is not good for self-respecting men to be executioners of their fellow-men in something that does not concern them. And so, I ask this of you, gently and quietly, in order that, if you comply with my request, I shall have reason to thank you; and if you do not do so of your own accord, then this lance and this sword and the valor of my arm shall compel you to do it by force."

"A fine lot of foolishness!" exclaimed the commissary. "So he comes out at last with this nonsense! He would have us let the prisoners of the king go free, as if we had any authority to do so or he any right to command it! Be on your way, sir, at once; straighten that basin that you have on your head, and do not go looking for three feet on a cat." [8]

"You," replied Don Quixote, "are the cat and the rat and the rascal!" And, saying this, he charged the commissary so quickly that the latter had no chance to defend himself but fell to the ground badly wounded by the lance blow. The other guards were astounded by this unexpected occurrence; but, recovering their self-possession, those on horseback drew their swords,[9] those on foot leveled their javelins, and all bore down on Don Quixote, who stood waiting for them very calmly. Things undoubtedly would have gone badly for him if the galley slaves, seeing an opportunity to gain their freedom, had not succeeded in breaking the chain that linked them together. Such was the confusion that the guards, now running to fall upon the prisoners and now attacking Don Quixote, who in turn was attacking them, accomplished nothing that was of any use.

Sancho for his part aided Ginés de Pasamonte to free himself, and that individual was the first to drop his chains and leap out onto the field, where, attacking the fallen commissary, he took away that officer's sword and musket; and as he stood there, aiming first at one and then at another, though without firing, the plain was soon cleared of guards, for they had taken to their heels, fleeing at once Pasamonte's weapon and the stones which the galley slaves, freed now, were hurling at them. Sancho, meanwhile, was very much disturbed over this unfortunate event, as he felt sure that the fugitives would report the matter to the Holy Brotherhood, which, to the ringing of the alarm bell, would come out to search for the guilty parties. He said as much to his master, telling him that they should leave at once and go into hiding in the near-by mountains.

"That is all very well," said Don Quixote, "but I know

what had best be done now." He then summoned all the prisoners, who, running riot, had by this time despoiled the commissary of everything that he had, down to his skin, and as they gathered around to hear what he had to say, he addressed them as follows:

"It is fitting that those who are wellborn should give thanks for the benefits they have received, and one of the sins with which God is most offended is that of ingratitude. I say this, gentlemen, for the reason that you have seen and had manifest proof of what you owe to me; and now that you are free of the yoke which I have removed from about your necks, it is my will and desire that you should set out and proceed to the city of El Toboso and there present yourselves before the lady Dulcinea del Toboso and say to her that her champion, the Knight of the Mournful Countenance, has sent you; and then you will relate to her, point by point, the whole of this famous adventure which has won you your longed-for freedom. Having done that, you may go where you like, and may good luck go with you."

To this Ginés de Pasamonte replied in behalf of all of them, "It is absolutely impossible, your Grace, our liberator, for us to do what you have commanded. We cannot go down the highway all together but must separate and go singly, each in his own direction, endeavoring to hide ourselves in the bowels of the earth in order not to be found by the Holy Brotherhood, which undoubtedly will come out to search for us. What your Grace can do, and it is right that you should do so, is to change this service and toll that you require of us in connection with the lady Dulcinea del Toboso into a certain number of Credos and Hail Marys which we will say for your Grace's intention, as this is something that can be accomplished by day

or night, fleeing or resting, in peace or in war. To imagine, on the other hand, that we are going to return to
the fleshpots of Egypt, by which I mean, take up our
chains again by setting out along the highway for El
Toboso, is to believe that it is night now instead of ten
o'clock in the morning and is to ask of us something that
is the same as asking pears of the elm tree."

"Then by all that's holy!" exclaimed Don Quixote,
whose wrath was now aroused, "you, Don Son of a
Whore, Don Ginesillo de Parapilla, or whatever your
name is, you shall go alone, your tail between your
legs and the whole chain on your back."

Pasamonte, who was by no means a long-suffering
individual, was by this time convinced that Don Quixote
was not quite right in the head, seeing that he had been
guilty of such a folly as that of desiring to free them;
and so, when he heard himself insulted in this manner,
he merely gave the wink to his companions and, going
off to one side, began raining so many stones upon
the knight that the latter was wholly unable to protect
himself with his buckler, while poor Rocinante paid no
more attention to the spur than if he had been made of
brass. As for Sancho, he took refuge behind his donkey
as a protection against the cloud and shower of rocks
that was falling on both of them, but Don Quixote was
not able to shield himself so well, and there is no
telling how many struck his body, with such force as to
unhorse and bring him to the ground.

No sooner had he fallen than the student was upon
him. Seizing the basin from the knight's head, he struck
him three or four blows with it across the shoulders
and banged it against the ground an equal number of
times until it was fairly shattered to bits. They then
stripped Don Quixote of the doublet which he wore
over his armor, and would have taken his hose as well,

if his greaves had not prevented them from doing so, and made off with Sancho's greatcoat, leaving him naked; after which, dividing the rest of the battle spoils amongst themselves, each of them went his own way, being a good deal more concerned with eluding the dreaded Holy Brotherhood than they were with burdening themselves with a chain or going to present themselves before the lady Dulcinea del Toboso.

They were left alone now—the ass and Rocinante, Sancho and Don Quixote: the ass, crestfallen and pensive, wagging its ears now and then, being under the impression that the hurricane of stones that had raged about them was not yet over; Rocinante, stretched alongside his master, for the hack also had been felled by a stone; Sancho, naked and fearful of the Holy Brotherhood; and Don Quixote, making wry faces at seeing himself so mishandled by those to whom he had done so much good.

Don Quixote's Penance and Sancho's Embassy to Dulcinea

(CHAPTERS XXIII-XXIX)

Following the escapade of the galley slaves, Sancho insists that his master take refuge in the nearby mountains, the Sierra Morena, by way of avoiding the officers of the Holy Brotherhood. Don Quixote, on chivalric principle, is loath to do this at first, but his squire ends by convincing him that discretion is the better part of knightly valor.

FROM CHAPTER XXIII: *Of what happened to the famous Don Quixote in the Sierra Morena, which is one of the rarest adventures related in this true history.*

BY THE TIME darkness fell they had reached the heart of the highlands, where Sancho thought it would be a good thing for them to spend the night and a few days as well, at least as long as their supplies held out. And so they came to a halt in a dense cork-tree grove between two cliffs; and it was then that fate took a hand, fate which, according to those who are not enlightened by the true gospel, directs everything. Fate now directed and arranged things after its own fashion by ordaining that Ginés de Pasamonte, the famous rogue and thief who had been freed from his chains by Don Quixote's mad but kindly whim, should come their way again. Dreading the Holy Brotherhood, which he had good reason to fear, Pasamonte, also, had decided to hide out in these mountains, and fate and his fear brought him to the very same part of the highlands where the knight and Sancho Panza were.

Arriving while it was light enough to recognize them, he let them fall asleep; for as evildoers are always ungrateful, necessity prompting them to misdeeds and with present advantage outweighing future gains, Ginés, who was neither grateful nor well intentioned, had made up his mind to steal Sancho Panza's ass, not caring to bother with Rocinante since the hack could neither be pawned nor sold with profit. Accordingly, while Sancho slept, he drove the beast off, and by the time daylight came was too far away to be found.

The dawn brought cheer to the earth but sadness to

the heart of Sancho Panza, who, when he discovered that his gray ass was missing, began weeping so plaintively that Don Quixote was awakened by the sound.

"O son of my loins, born in my very house," he heard his squire exclaiming. "My children's playmate, joy of my wife, envy of my neighbors, solace in my cares, and, finally, half-supporter of my person, since the twenty-six maravedis that you earned each day met half of my expenses!"

Hearing the weeping and learning the cause, the knight did what he could to console Sancho. Begging him to be patient, he promised to give him a letter directing that three out of five ass-colts that he had at home be turned over to his squire to make up for the loss. Sancho was consoled by this and, drying his tears and repressing his sobs, thanked his master for this favor.[1]

As Don Quixote and Sancho resume their wanderings next day they come upon an old valise lying in their path. It is half rotted, and upon inspection is found to contain, in addition to a quantity of fine linen, a small heap of gold coins and a richly bound memorandum book. It is this last item that interests the knight, who tells his squire to keep the money for himself. Sancho is duly grateful and stores away the coins and linen in the provision bag.

The first thing that claims Don Quixote's attention when he opens the memorandum book is a lovelorn sonnet. Next comes the draft of a despairing note addressed by someone to a lady who apparently has wronged him. The knight's curiosity, needless to say, is excited by this. As they proceed on their way they catch sight of a half-naked figure on the top of a small mountain nearby. It is that of a man with a thick black beard, long tangled hair, and a few ragged remnants of cloth-

ing on his limbs. He is leaping from cliff to cliff and from one tuft of underbrush to another, and it at once occurs to Don Quixote that this must be the owner of the valise and they should go look for him.

Sancho is not at all eager to do this; for, his master tells him, if they find the man the money will have to be returned. Don Quixote insists, however, and they set out. As they round a side of the mountain they discover a mule, saddled and bridled, lying dead in a brook and half devoured by dogs and jackals. As they stand surveying the animal they hear a whistle and descry, up above them, a flock of goats and an aged goatherd, who calls down to inquire what they are doing there. They invite him to descend and he does so. In response to a question from Don Quixote he tells them the story as he knows it of the strange figure they have glimpsed.

The youth—for he was no more than that—had put in an appearance at a neighboring sheepfold some six months previously, mounted upon a mule and carrying a valise. He had asked to be shown the most rugged and inaccessible part of the highlands, and the shepherds had pointed it out to him, warning him that if he entered he would not be able to find his way back. Nevertheless he had turned and straightway made for the region indicated. The shepherds had heard no more of him until a few days ago, when he had suddenly assaulted one of their number and stolen their provisions of bread and cheese. A couple of days later they had met him and he had appeared courteous and contrite and had informed them that the reason for his going clothed in rags was that he was engaged in doing penance for his sins.

But even as he talked the young man fell into a fit of madness and violently attacked one of the bystanders, crying out curses all the while upon one Fernando, who

seemingly had done him a grievous wrong, after which
he ran off and hid himself once more. These fits, it appeared, came upon him at intervals; at other times he
was gentle and well-mannered. As a result, the shepherds
had made up their minds to have him taken to a town
not far distant to see if there was any cure for him and
to try to find out if he had any relatives whom they
might notify.

At this point the youth of whom they are speaking
emerges from a ravine and comes up to them. Don Quixote dismounts, goes over and embraces him, and begs him
to reveal the cause of his sorrow. The stranger replies
that if they will give him some food, he will comply
with their request on condition that they promise not
to interrupt him. The food is provided and he begins
his tale.

His name, it appears, is Cardenio and he is in love
with Luscinda, a childhood sweetheart. Just as his
courtship was progressing fairly well, he had been sent
to serve in the palace of a certain duke, where he had
struck up a close friendship with the duke's second son,
Fernando. The latter was bent upon seducing the
daughter of a wealthy peasant under a false promise to
marry her, and when efforts to dissuade him failed,
Cardenio had felt that he was in duty bound to inform
his patron as to how matters stood. Fernando had then
suggested that they pay a visit to Cardenio's home,
which they did.

Fernando's excuse had been that he wished to be
cured of his attachment, but what he really sought was
to avoid keeping a marriage promise he had already
given. Seeing Luscinda, he had at once fallen in love
with her, and Cardenio's jealousy had been aroused by
his friend's actions.

As he tells his story the stranger chances to refer to

the Amadis of Gaul, *and this promptly sets Don Quix-*
ote off on his favorite subject, chivalry. Cardenio is of-
fended by the interruption, makes a slighting remark
about one of Don Quixote's heroines, the knight calls
him a villain and a liar, and the mad lover thereupon
lets fly a stone which brings the gentleman of La
Mancha to the ground. Sancho tries to interfere but is
knocked down and trampled, and the goatherd meets
the same fate. Having beaten and mauled them all,
their assailant returns to his hiding-place, his story
uncompleted.

Sancho then becomes involved in an argument with
the goatherd over the question of who is to blame, and
this leads to fisticuffs and beard pulling until Don Quix-
ote parts them. (Conclusion of Chapter xxiv.*)*

FROM CHAPTER XXV: *Which treats of the strange*
things that happened to the valiant Knight of La
Mancha in the Sierra Morena and of his imitation
of Beltenebros's penance.

"SIR," said Sancho, "is it a good rule of chivalry for
us to be wandering lost in these mountains, without road or path, in search of a madman who, when we
find him, may undertake to finish what he has begun—
and I do not mean his story but your Grace's head and my
ribs, by smashing them altogether this time?"

"I tell you once again, Sancho, be quiet; for I will
inform you that it is not so much the desire to find a
madman that leads me to traverse these regions as it is
the hope of accomplishing here an exploit that will win
for me perpetual renown and fame throughout the
whole of the known world, one that will place the seal

on all that there is that can make a knight-errant famous and perfect."

"And is it a very dangerous exploit, that one?" Sancho
Panza asked.

"No," replied the Knight of the Mournful Countenance, "it is not—not if the dice fall right for us; but
everything will depend on your diligence."

"On my diligence?" said Sancho.

"Yes," said Don Quixote, "for if you return quickly from
where I mean to send you, my labors will soon be at an
end and my fame will begin to spread. And in order not
to keep you any longer in suspense with regard to the
meaning of my words, I want you to know, Sancho,
that the famous Amadis of Gaul was one of the most
perfect of knights-errant. But I am not correct in saying that he was 'one of the'; he was the sole and only
one, the very first, the lord of all those in the world in
his time. A plague on Don Belianís and all the others
who claimed to equal him in anything, for they are
wrong, I swear they are! When a painter wishes to become famous, he strives to imitate the works of the most
distinctive practitioners of his art; and the same rule
holds for all the other arts and crafts that serve as the
ornament of states and nations.

"Thus, he who would achieve a reputation for prudence and long-suffering must and does follow in the
footsteps of Ulysses; for in describing his character and
the hardships that he endured Homer gives us a lively
picture of the virtues mentioned. Similarly, Vergil, in
the person of Aeneas, portrays for us a dutiful son and
the sagacity of a brave and intelligent leader. And these
personages, be it noted, are not depicted or revealed
to us as they were but as they ought to have been, that
they may remain as an example of those qualities for

future generations. In this same way, Amadis was the north star, the morning star, the sun of all valiant and enamored knights, and all those of us who fight beneath the banner of love and chivalry should imitate him. This being true, and true it is, I am of the opinion, Sancho my friend, that the knight-errant who most closely models himself upon Amadis will come the nearest to attaining the perfection of chivalry.

"One of the occasions upon which that knight most clearly displayed his prudence, true worth, valor, endurance, firmness of will, and loving devotion was when, having been rejected by the lady Oriana, he retired to do penance on Poor Rock,[1] having changed his name to Beltenebros,[2] one that was certainly significant and suited to the life he had voluntarily chosen. Accordingly, seeing that it is easier for me to imitate him in this than by cleaving giants, beheading serpents, slaying dragons, routing armies, sinking fleets, and undoing enchanters' spells, and seeing, also, that this place where we are is better adapted to such a purpose as the one I have in mind, I feel that I should not let slip the opportunity that now so conveniently offers me its forelock."

"To get down to the purpose," said Sancho, "what is it that your Grace proposes to do in this lonely spot?"

"Have I not told you," replied Don Quixote, "that I mean to imitate Amadis by playing the part of a desperate and raving madman, thus imitating Orlando at the same time, on that occasion when he discovered in a fountain the signs that Angélica the Beautiful had committed a villainy with Medoro, which so grieved him that he went mad, tore up trees, muddied the waters of clear-running springs, slew shepherds, destroyed herds, set fire to huts, tore down houses, dragged mares along after him, and did a hundred thousand other outrageous things that are worthy of eternal renown and record? I grant you, I am not thinking of imitating point by point Roland, or Orlando, or Rotolando—for he went by all three names—in every mad thing that he did, said, and thought; what I shall give, rather, is a rough sketch, containing what appear to me to be the essentials; or it may be I shall content myself with merely imitating Amadis, whose madness did not prompt him to do any damage of that sort but who confined himself to tears and sighs and yet gained as much fame as the best of them."

"It strikes me," said Sancho, "that those knights who did all that had provocation and some cause for such foolish penances, but what reason has your Grace for going mad, what damsel has rejected you, or what signs have you found that lead you to think the lady Dulcinea del Toboso has been up to some foolishness with a Moor or Christian?"

"That," said Don Quixote, "is the point of the thing; that is the beautiful part of it. What thanks does a knight-errant deserve for going mad when he has good cause? The thing is to go out of my head without any occasion for it, thus letting my lady see, if I do this for her in the dry, what I would do in the wet. Moreover, I have occasion enough in the long absence I have endured from the side of her who shall ever be my lady, Dulcinea del Toboso; for you have heard that shepherd Ambrosio saying, 'He who is absent, suffers and fears all evils.' And so, Sancho my friend, do not waste time in advising me to forego so rare, so felicitous, and so unheard of an imitation as this. Mad I am and mad I must be until you return with a letter which I mean to send by you to my lady Dulcinea. If that answer be such as my devotion merits, there will be an end to my madness and my penance; but if the contrary is the case, I shall truly go mad and, being mad, suffer no more. Thus, whatever the manner in which she responds, I shall emerge from the painful struggle in which you leave me, either by enjoying as a sane man the good news you bring me, or, as one who is insane, by ceasing to feel the pain of the bad news.

"But tell me, Sancho, were you careful to preserve Mambrino's helmet? For I saw you pick it up from the ground when that wretch tried to smash it to bits but could not, from which you may see how finely tempered it is."

"God alive, Sir Knight of the Mournful Countenance," said Sancho, "I cannot bear in patience some of the things that your Grace says! Listening to you, I come to think that all you have told me about deeds of chivalry and winning kingdoms and empires and bestowing islands and other favors and dignities is but wind and lies, all buggery or humbuggery, or whatever you choose to call it. For when anyone hears your Grace saying that a barber's basin is Mambrino's helmet, and after four days you still insist that it is, what is he to think except that such a one is out of his mind? I have the basin in my bag, all crushed and dented. I'm taking it home to have it mended so that I can trim my beard into it, if God is only good enough to let me see my wife and children again someday."

"Look, Sancho," said Don Quixote, "by that same God I swear that you have less sense than any squire in the world ever had. How is it possible for you to have accompanied me all this time without coming to perceive that all the things that have to do with knights-errant appear to be mad, foolish, and chimerical, everything being done by contraries? Not that they are so in reality; it is simply that there are always a lot of enchanters going about among us, changing things and

giving them a deceitful appearance, directing them as
suits their fancy, depending upon whether they wish to
favor or destroy us. So, this that appears to you as a
barber's basin is for me Mambrino's helmet, and something else again to another person.

"It was a rare bit of foresight on the part of the
magician who is on my side to have what really is the
helmet appear to all others as a mere basin; for if it
were known that it is of so great a worth, everyone
would pursue me and endeavor to deprive me of it. On
the other hand, thinking that it is no more than what
it seems, they do not care to have it, as was shown when
that fellow tried to smash it and went off and left it
lying on the ground. Believe me, if he had known what
it was, he never would have done that. Take good care
of it, then, my friend, for I do not need it at present.
Indeed, it is my intention to lay aside all this armor and
remain naked as when I was born—that is to say, if I
decide to take Orlando rather than Amadis as a model
in doing my penance."

Conversing in this manner, they reached the foot of a
tall mountain, which, standing alone amid a number of
surrounding peaks, had almost the appearance of a
rock that had been carved out of them. Alongside it
flowed a gentle brook, while all about was a meadow
so green and luxuriant that it was a delight for the eyes
to behold. There were many forest trees and a number
of plants and flowers to add to the quiet charm of the
scene. And such was the spot which the Knight of the
Mournful Countenance was to choose for his penance.

The moment he caught sight of it he cried out in a
loud voice, as if he really had lost his senses, "This is the
place, O ye heavens! which I select and designate; it is
here that I will weep for that misfortune that ye yourselves have brought upon me. This is the place where

the fluid from my orbs shall increase the waters of this little brook while my deep and constant sighs shall keep in incessant motion the leaves of these mountain trees, as a sign and testimony of the pain my tortured heart is suffering. O ye rustic deities, whoever ye may be, who make your abode in this uninhabitable place, hear the complaints of this unfortunate lover who, suffering from long absence and a jealous imagination, has come here to voice his laments amid these rugged surroundings and to bemoan the harshness of that fair but thankless creature who is the end and sum of all that humankind may know in the way of beauty!

"And O ye nymphs and dryads too, who are accustomed to dwell in groves and thickets—may the light-footed and lascivious satyrs, who cherish for you an unrequited love, never disturb your sweet repose, but may you join me in weeping for my sorrows, or at least not tire of hearing them! And thou, O Dulcinea del Toboso, day of my night, glory of my sufferings, guide of my every path, star of my fortunes, may Heaven grant thee all thou seekest, and wilt thou look upon the place and state to which absence from thee has brought me and be moved to repay with kindness the debt that is due to my fidelity! Ye trees also, ye solitary trees that from this day forth are to be the companions of my solitude, give me a sign by the gentle murmuring of your leaves that my presence is not displeasing to you! And, finally, thou, my faithful squire, my congenial comrade in prosperity and adversity, remember well what thou seest me do here that thou mayest relate and recite it afterward to the one who is the sole cause of it all."

With these words he dismounted from Rocinante and in a moment had removed saddle and bridle, after which he gave the hack a slap on the rump.

"Freedom," said the knight, "he now gives thee who himself is left without it, O steed as unexcelled in deeds as thou art unfortunate in thy fate! Go where thou wilt, and bear with thee inscribed upon thy forehead this legend: that neither Astolfo's Hippogriff nor the renowned Frontino that cost Bardamante so dear[3] could equal thee in fleetness of foot."

As he saw his master do this, Sancho said, "Good luck to him who has saved us the trouble now of stripping the ass;[4] for upon my word, if the gray had been here, he too would have had a slap on the rump and a few words of praise. I'd never consent to it, however, for there would be no occasion, since there was nothing of the despairing lover about him any more than there was about his master, which I happened to be so long as God willed it. The truth of the matter is, Sir Knight of the Mournful Countenance, if you mean what you say about my departure and your fit of madness, then you'd better saddle Rocinante again so that he can take the gray's place, as that will save me time coming and going. If I go on foot, I cannot tell how long I'll be, for, the short of it is, I'm a very poor walker."

"You may do as you like, Sancho," said Don Quixote. "It is not a bad suggestion that you have made. You will set out three days from now. In the meantime, I want you to see all that I do for her sake and make note of all I say in order that you may be able to tell her of it."

"What more is there for me to see," said Sancho, "than what I've seen already?"

"You do not know what you are talking about," said Don Quixote. "I have yet to rend my garments, scatter my armor about, knock my head against those rocks, and other things of that sort, all of which you must witness."

"For the love of God!" exclaimed Sancho. "I hope your Grace has a care how you go about that head-knocking, for you may come up against such a rock or in such a way that with the very first knock you will put an end to this whole business of your penance. If your Grace feels that it is absolutely necessary to do this, and that you cannot go through with your undertaking without doing it, then it seems to me that, since it is all a matter of pretending and in the nature of a joke, you ought to be satisfied with bumping your head in water or something soft like cotton, and just leave the rest to me; I will tell my lady that your Grace did it against a piece of jutting rock hard as a diamond."

"I thank you for your good intentions, Sancho," said Don Quixote, "but you must know that the things I do are not done in jest but very much in earnest. Otherwise, I should be violating the rules of knighthood, which command that we shall tell no lie whatsoever under pain of suffering the penalty that is meted out for apostasy; and to do one thing in place of another is the same as lying. My head-knockings, therefore, have to be real ones, solid and substantial, with nothing sophistical or imaginary about them. And it will be necessary for you to leave me a little lint to dress my wounds, since fortune would have it that we should be without that balm that we lost."

"It was worse losing the ass," said Sancho, "for with it we lost the lint and all.[5] And I would ask your Grace not to remind me again of that accursed potion; the very mention of it turns my soul, not to speak of my stomach. I also beg of you to regard those three days that you gave me for witnessing your deeds of madness as being past; for, so far as I am concerned, that is the truth; I have seen and judged everything and will tell my lady marvels. Write the letter, then, at once and send me on my way, as I have a great desire to return and rescue your Grace from this purgatory in which I leave you."

"Purgatory you call it, Sancho?" said Don Quixote. "Better say Hell, or even worse, if there is anything worse than that."

"He who is in Hell," said Sancho, "has no retention,[6] so I've heard it said."

"I do not understand what you mean by *retention*," said Don Quixote.

"*Retention*," said Sancho, "means that he who is in Hell never can, and never will, get out. But it will be just the opposite with your Grace, or else my legs will fail me—that is, if I have spurs to put a little life into Rocinante. Just set me down once in El Toboso and in my lady Dulcinea's presence, and I will tell her such things about your Grace's foolishness and madness (it is all one), and all the things you are doing and have done, that, even though I find her harder than a cork tree, I will make her softer than a glove. And then when I have her gentle, honeyed answer, I will come flying back through the air like a witch and snatch your Grace out of this purgatory which seems to you to be a Hell but is not, seeing there is hope of your getting out of it; for as I have just said, those in Hell do not come out, and I do not think your Grace will contradict me on that."

"You speak the truth," said the Knight of the Mournful Countenance, "but how are we going to write the letter?"

"And the order for the ass-colts too," added Sancho.

"All that will be inserted," said Don Quixote, "and since we have no paper, it would be well for us to write it as the ancients did, on the leaves of trees or a

few wax tablets; although it would be about as hard
to find anything like that now as it would be to procure
paper. It would be a good idea, an excellent idea, for
me to write it in Cardenio's memorandum book, and
then you will take care to have it transcribed on paper,
in a fair hand, in the first village where you find a
schoolmaster, or, failing that, some sacristan; but do not
give it to any notary to be copied, for they write a legal
hand that Satan himself would not be able to make
out."

"But what is to be done about the signature?" asked
Sancho.

"The letters of Amadis were never signed," Don
Quixote assured him.

"That is all very well," said the squire, "but that order
you are to give me has to be signed, and if it is copied
over, they will say the signature is false and I'll not get
the ass-colts."

"The order, duly signed, will be in that same little
book, and when my niece sees it, she will not give you
any trouble about carrying out my instructions. As
for the love letter, you will have them put as the signature: 'Yours until death, the Knight of the Mournful
Countenance.' It will make little difference if it is in
some other person's handwriting, for, as I recall, Dulcinea does not know how to read or write, nor has
she ever in all her life seen a letter of mine or anything
else that I wrote; for our love has always been platonic
and has never gone beyond a modest glance. Even that
happened but rarely, since in the course of the dozen
years that I have loved her—more than the light of
these eyes which the earth will one day devour—I
can truthfully swear that I have not seen her four
times, and even then, it may be, she did not once perceive that I was looking at her, such is the seclusion

and retirement in which her father, Lorenzo Corchuelo,
and her mother, Aldonza Nogales, have reared her."

"Aha!" said Sancho, "so the lady Dulcinea del Toboso
is Lorenzo Corchuelo's daughter, otherwise known as
Aldonza Lorenzo?"

"That is the one," said Don Quixote, "and she deserves to be mistress of the entire universe."

"I know her well," Sancho went on, "and I may tell
you that she can toss a bar as well as the lustiest lad in
all the village. Long live the Giver of all good things,
but she's a sturdy wench, fit as a fiddle and right in
the middle of everything that's doing. She can take
care of any knight-errant or about to err that has her
for a mistress! Son of a whore, what strength she has
and what a voice! They tell me that one day she went
up into the village belfry to call some lads who were
out in the field that belongs to her father, and although
they were more than half a league away, they heard her
as plainly as if they had been standing at the foot of the
tower. And the best of it is, there's nothing prudish
about her; she's very friendly with everybody and always laughing and joking. And so, I say to you now, Sir
Knight of the Mournful Countenance, that you not
only may and ought to play mad for her sake, but
you have good reason to despair and go off and hang
yourself, and anyone who hears of it will say you did
exactly the right thing, even though the devil takes
you.

"I'd like to be on my way just to have a look at her
again, for it's been a long time since I saw her, and
the sun and air do a lot to the complexion of a woman
who's all the time working in the field. I must confess
the truth, Señor Don Quixote, that up to now I have
been laboring under a great mistake; for I thought,
right enough, that the lady Dulcinea must be some

princess with whom your Grace was smitten, or at least some personage that merited the rich presents which your Grace sent her, such as the Biscayan and the galley slaves, and many others as well, no doubt, for your Grace must have won many victories before I became your squire. But, come to think of it, what is there about Mistress Aldonza Lorenzo—I mean, Mistress Dulcinea del Toboso—that those conquered ones whom your Grace sends to her should bend the knee before her? For at the moment they arrived she may very well have been dressing flax or thrashing in the granary, and they would run away when they saw her and she'd be annoyed by the present."

"Sancho," said Don Quixote, "I have told you many times before that you are much too talkative; and although your wit is very dull, your tongue is all too sharp at times. In order that you may see how foolish you are and how sensible I am, I would have you listen to a brief story which I am about to relate to you. Once upon a time there was a beautiful widow, young, rich, unattached, and, above all, free and easy in her ways, who fell in love with a youthful cropped-headed lay brother[7] of large and sturdy build. When his superior heard of this, he took occasion to speak to the widow one day, giving her a word of brotherly reproof. 'I am astonished, Madam,' he said, 'and not without a good cause, that a woman of your standing, so beautiful and so rich as your Grace is, should be in love with a fellow so coarse, so low, so stupid as is So-and-So, in view of the fact that there are in this institution so many masters, graduates, and theologians from whom your Grace might have her pick as from among so many pears, saying, "This one I like, this one I do not care for."' She, however, answered him with much grace and sprightliness, 'You are mistaken, your Reverence, and very old-fashioned in your ideas, if you think that I have made a bad choice by taking So-and-So, stupid as he may appear to be, since so far as what I want him for is concerned, he knows as much and even more philosophy than Aristotle himself.'

"Similarly, Sancho, as regards my need of Dulcinea del Toboso, she is worth as much to me as any highborn princess on this earth. Not all the poets who praised their ladies under names of their own choosing actually had such mistresses. Do you think that the Amarillises, the Phyllises, the Sylvias, the Dianas, the Galateas, the Filidas, and all the others of whom the books, ballads, barbershops, and theaters are full were in reality flesh-and-blood women who belonged to those that hymned their praises? Certainly not; most of the writers merely invented these creatures to provide them with a subject for their verses in order that they might be taken for lovelorn swains and respected as individuals capable of an amorous passion. And so it is enough for me to think and believe that the good Aldonza Lorenzo is beautiful and modest. So far as her lineage is concerned, that is a matter of small importance; no one is going to look into it by way of conferring on her any robes of nobility, and, as for me, she is the most highborn princess in the world.

"For you should know, Sancho, if you do not know already, that the two things that more than any others incite to love are great beauty and a good name, and these two things are to be found to a consummate degree in Dulcinea; for in beauty none can vie with her, and in good name few can come up to her. But to bring all this to a conclusion: I am content to imagine that what I say is so and that she is neither more nor less than I picture her and would have her be, in comeliness and in high estate. Neither Helen nor Lucretia nor

any of the other women of bygone ages, Greek, Latin,
or barbarian, can hold a candle to her. And let anyone
say what he likes; if for this I am reprehended by the
ignorant, I shall not be blamed by men of discernment."

"I agree with all that your Grace says," replied
Sancho. "It is true that I am an ass—although I don't
know how that word ass happened to slip out, since you
do not speak of the rope in the house of a gallows bird.
But let us have that letter, and then, God be with you,
I am off."

Don Quixote thereupon took out the memorandum
book and, going off to one side, proceeded to compose
the letter with great deliberation. When he had finished
he called Sancho, telling him to listen while he read
it to him and to memorize it, in case the original
should be lost along the way, as he had reason to fear
from the ill luck that seemed to pursue him.

"Just write it two or three times in that book, your
Grace," Sancho said, "and then give it to me; for it is
nonsense to think I am going to learn it by heart when
my memory is so bad that I often forget my own name.
But go ahead and read it to me; I'll enjoy hearing it
very much, for it ought to be as smooth as if it were all
set down in print."

"Listen, then," said Don Quixote. "This is what it
says:

DON QUIXOTE'S LETTER
TO DULCINEA DEL TOBOSO

SOVEREIGN AND HIGHBORN LADY:

*He who is pricked by absence and wounded to the
heart, O sweetest Dulcinea del Toboso, wishes thee
the health that is not his. If thy beauty despise me, if
thy great worth be not for me, if my lot be thy disdain,*

even though I am sufficiently inured to suffering I
hardly shall sustain this affliction which, in addition
to being grievous, is lasting in the extreme. My good
squire Sancho will tell thee, O beauteous ingrate, my
beloved enemy! of the state in which I now find myself
on account of thee. Shouldst thou care to succor me, I
am thine; if not, do as thou seest fit, for by putting an
end to my life I shall pay the price exacted by thy
cruelty and mine own desire.

Thine until death.

THE KNIGHT OF THE MOURNFUL COUNTENANCE"

"By the life of my father," exclaimed Sancho when
he had heard the letter, "that is the most high-flown
thing I ever listened to. Why, damn me, how your
Grace does manage to say everything here just the way
it should be said, and how well you work that Knight
of the Mournful Countenance into the signature! To
tell the truth, your Grace is the very devil himself, and
there's nothing you don't know."

"In the profession that I follow," replied Don Quixote, "one needs to know everything."

"And now," said Sancho, "if your Grace will put the
order for the three ass-colts on this other page and sign
it very clearly so that they will recognize your signature when they see it—"

"With pleasure," said Don Quixote. Having written
the order, he read it aloud:

"Upon presentation of this first order for ass-colts,
mistress my niece, you will turn over to Sancho Panza,
my squire, three of the five that I left at home and in
your Grace's charge. The said three ass-colts to be
delivered in return for three others here received on ac-
count; upon presentation of this order and his receipt
they are to be duly turned over to him as specified.

"*Done in the heart of the Sierra Morena on the twenty-second day of August of this present year.*"

"That is very good," said Sancho, "and now sign it, your Grace."

"It is not necessary to sign it," said Don Quixote. "All I need do is to add my flourish, which is the same as a signature and will suffice for three, and even three hundred, asses."

"I will trust your Grace," said the squire. "And now, let me go saddle Rocinante, and do you be ready to give me your blessing, for I am thinking of leaving at once without waiting to witness the foolish things that your Grace has to do; but I will tell her that I saw you do so many of them that she will not want to hear any more."

"There is one thing at least that I should like to ask of you, Sancho," the knight said, "and if I do ask this, it is because it is necessary. I should like you to see me stripped and performing a couple of dozen acts of madness, which I can get through with in less than half an hour; for having seen them with your own eyes, you can safely swear to the other things that you may care to add, and I assure you I mean to do more than you will be able to relate."

"For the love of God, my master," Sancho replied, "let me not see your Grace stripped, for I'd feel so sorry that I'd never stop weeping, and I wept so much for the gray last night that I have no more tears left to shed. If your Grace wants me to witness some of your insane actions, please perform them with your clothes on and be brief about it and to the point. So far as I am concerned, all this is unnecessary; for as I have told you, it would save time if I were to leave now and I'd be back all the sooner with the news that your Grace desires and deserves. For if it is not such as you desire, let the lady Dulcinea be prepared; if she does not give me a reasonable answer, I solemnly swear I'll have one out of her stomach with kicks and cuffs. Why should a knight-errant as famous as is your Grace have to go mad without rhyme or reason for a— Her ladyship had better not force me to say it, or by God I'll speak out and lay them out by the dozen even though there's no buyer. I am pretty good at that sort of thing. She doesn't know me very well, or, faith, if she did, we'd have no trouble in coming to an understanding."

"And faith, Sancho," said Don Quixote, "you appear to me to be no sounder in mind than I am."

"I'm not as crazy as you are," said Sancho; "I've more of a temper, that's all. But leaving all this aside, what is your Grace going to eat until I return? Are you going out, as Cardenio did, and take it away from the shepherds?"

"Do not let that trouble you," said the knight, "for even if I had other food, I should eat nothing but the herbs and fruits with which this meadow and these trees shall provide me. The fine point of my undertaking lies in not eating and in putting up with other hardships of the same sort."

"And, by God," said Sancho, "there's another thing. Do you know what I am afraid of, your Grace? I'm afraid I'll not be able to find my way back to this place once I leave it, it's so out of the way."

"Get your bearings well," said Don Quixote, "and I will try not to stray far from this vicinity. I will also make it a point to go up on those high cliffs to see if I can catch a glimpse of you on your way back. But in order not to miss me and lose yourself, the best thing would be to cut a few branches of the broom plant that is so abundant around here and scatter them along the way at intervals until you come out onto the plain;

these will serve you as signs and landmarks, like the clues in Perseus's labyrinth,[8] and will help you to find me when you return."

"I will do that," said Sancho, and cutting a few of the brooms, he asked his master's benediction; after which, each of them shedding not a few tears, he took his departure. Mounting Rocinante—Don Quixote had charged him to take as good care of the steed as he would of his own person—he set out in the direction of the lowlands, scattering the branches at intervals as he had been advised to do. And so he went his way, although the knight still insisted that he wait and watch him perform at least a couple of mad acts. He had not gone a hundred paces when he turned and looked back.

"You know," he said, "I believe your Grace was right. In order to be able to swear without a weight on my conscience, I really ought to see you do at least one mad thing, although your remaining here is mad enough in itself."

"Did I not tell you that?" said Don Quixote. "Wait, Sancho, and you will see me do them before you can say a Credo!"

With this, he hastily slipped off his breeches and, naked from the waist down, leaped into the air a couple of times, falling heels over head and revealing things that caused Sancho to give Rocinante the rein, that he might not have to see them again. The squire was satisfied now; he could swear that his master was quite mad. And so we shall leave him to pursue his journey until his return, which was not to be long delayed.

Left alone upon the mountain, Don Quixote deliberates as to whether he should follow the example of Orlando Furioso by going mad or imitate Amadis of Gaul, who confined his penance to tears and prayers.

He decides upon the latter course, and, "tearing a large strip from the tail of his shirt, which hung down over his buttocks, he made eleven knots in it, one bigger than the others, and this it was that served him as a rosary as long as he was there." He also carves inscriptions on the bark of trees and writes verses in the sand, sighing all the while and calling on the fauns and satyrs of the wood. Herbs serve him for nourishment, and he grows leaner and more gaunt than ever.

As for Sancho, having reached the highway, he sets out at once for El Toboso and on the second day arrives at the inn where the blanketing occurred. As he approaches the hostelry two men come out. They prove to be the curate and the barber from the village who have come to look for Don Quixote and bring him home. They recognize Sancho at once and insist that he tell them where his master is. He is reluctant to do this, but by means of threats they prevail upon him to talk.

Sancho then describes Don Quixote's penance and informs them of the letter which the knight has written to his lady love. When they ask to see it, Sancho discovers to his consternation that he has lost the memorandum book (as a matter of fact, he has forgotten to bring it with him and his master still has it). The pair from the village comfort him, and the curate promises that he himself will make a fair copy as soon as occasion offers, if Sancho will dictate the contents. This the squire does in amusing fashion.

Having thought the matter over, the curate and the barber proceed to form a plan for luring Don Quixote back home. One of them will disguise himself as a damsel in distress while the other will act as her squire, and together they will go to the knight and beg him to accompany this "maiden" and right the wrong that has been done her (Chapter XXVI).

They borrow a dress from the landlady of the inn, and the barber, who is to be the squire, makes a beard out of a reddish-gray oxtail into which the innkeeper is in the habit of sticking his comb. Thus disguised, they start for the mountains with Sancho as their guide; they have not gone far when the curate, who feels that feminine attire is not suited to his calling, has the barber change costumes with him.

As they near the place where Sancho had left his master they alter their plan somewhat and decide that the squire shall first go find Don Quixote and tell him that Dulcinea has replied by word of mouth, saying her lover is to come to her at once. This they hope may in itself be sufficient to induce the knight to leave.

Taking their ease in the shade as they wait for the outcome of Sancho's mission, the curate and the barber are surprised to hear someone singing in an excellent voice. Upon investigation they find that it is Cardenio, whom they recognize from Sancho's description. Cardenio is in his right mind at the moment, and when the curate endeavors to persuade him to give up the life he is leading, he answers very courteously and requests them to hear his story before they judge him. This they readily agree to do. After repeating what he has already told Don Quixote, the young man continues the account of his romance from the point where he had found a letter from Luscinda in a copy of the Amadis of Gaul which he had lent her—the reference that had provoked the interruption and quarrel.

This note was one encouraging him to ask for her hand in marriage. Full of hesitancy, he had taken Don

Fernando into his confidence and the latter had promised to help him; instead of which, in order to get his rival out of the way, Fernando had sent him back to the ducal palace with a message for the elder brother. Here by a ruse Cardenio had been detained for a week or so, until finally a letter which Luscinda had sent him by stealth reached his hands with the information that Fernando had betrayed his trust and she was to be married to him, against her will, within the next couple of days.

Cardenio galloped home as fast as he could, but he found Luscinda in bridal dress, ready for her wedding to Fernando. She showed him a dagger, which she had concealed on her person, and announced her intention of killing herself rather than go through with the ceremony. Cardenio adjured her to remain firm, adding that he too would be there to defend her honor with his sword if necessary. But when the time came for Luscinda to say "I do," her courage failed her and she uttered the words expected of her in a weak, faint-hearted voice.

Cardenio, who was hidden behind the draperies, was dumfounded by this. He saw Luscinda fall back in a swoon, saw her mother open the bride's bodice and discover there a note which Don Fernando promptly read with a grim look on his face. Convinced that his loved one had played him false and maddened by it all, the unhappy suitor had then saddled a mule and fled to the highlands, where, at the end of their journey, his mount had dropped dead of weariness and hunger.

Such is the story that Cardenio tells. He goes on to describe his recurring fits of madness and his present mode of life, with a hollow cork tree for shelter and *such food as the shepherds may provide (Chapter xxvii).*

As Cardenio finishes his narrative they suddenly hear a voice from somewhere nearby, uttering a mournful lament, and they have gone but a few paces when they catch sight of a young shepherd lad (as it seems) seated upon the bank of a rivulet, bathing his feet. Those feet, which are unusually white and beautiful, appeared to belie his garb; and as he removes his cap a mass of long blond hair falls down, revealing the fact that it is not a boy but a young girl that they see before them. When they go forward to speak to her, she starts to flee but the sharp-edged stones are too much for her and she sinks to the ground. The curate reassures her and prevails upon her to stay, whereupon she feels impelled to relate to them the misfortune that has befallen her.

The gently reared daughter of a wealthy peasant family, she is the one who was seduced by Don Fernando. She gives a lengthy description of the manner in which she was betrayed and tells how, after Fernando had broken his promise and refused to marry her, she had fled her parents' home in the company of a young male servant. Arriving at the town where Luscinda lived, Dorotea—for that is her name—learned of the marriage that had taken place and the note that was found in the bride's bodice in which Luscinda stated that she could not marry Fernando for the reason that she belonged to Cardenio, and accordingly intended to take her life immediately following the ceremony. When he heard this, Fernando had fallen upon the girl and would have stabbed her to death if her parents and others had not restrained him. He had left the city at once, and Cardenio and Luscinda also had disappeared.

Dorotea's parents in the meantime had sent out a description of their daughter and her escort, and as she listened to this from the mouth of the town crier the young woman was deeply ashamed of the disgrace she had incurred and resolved to flee to the mountains. There fresh troubles awaited her. In order to repel her escort's advances she had been forced to push him over the edge of a cliff. After that, a herdsman had taken her on as a servant, but when he discovered that she was a girl, he in turn had become importunate and she had once more run away and hidden herself (Chapter XXVIII).

When she had finished, Cardenio reveals his own identity, pledging his honor as a gentleman that he will do all he can to avenge her wrongs. The curate begs them to accompany him to his village where they can make suitable plans, and they accept his invitation. He goes on to tell them of Don Quixote's strange madness.

At this moment a shout is heard and Sancho returns. His master, he reports, is determined not to leave until he has performed such exploits as will render him deserving of his lady's grace. The company hold a consultation as to what is to be done, and the curate discloses to Cardenio and Dorotea the scheme which he and the barber have concocted by way of rescuing the unfortunate gentleman. Dorotea suggests that she could play the damsel much better than the barber, and this is agreed upon, Sancho being told that she is the Princess Micomicona who has journeyed "all the way from Guinea" to seek out Don Quixote and implore him to redress the wrong that has been done her by a certain wicked giant.

And so, seated upon the curate's mule and accompanied by the barber with his false oxtail beard, Doro-

tea, who now has donned the rich feminine attire that she carried with her, goes to meet the knight of La Mancha. As soon as she sees him she rides up, dismounts from her "palfrey," and, casting herself at his feet, begs him to succor her. He urges her to rise, but she refuses until he shall have promised to grant the boon she seeks. He gives his knightly word, and is told that he must accompany her to the place to which she will conduct him. Meanwhile he is not to undertake any other adventures.

They lose no time in setting out—Don Quixote, Dorotea, and the barber-squire, followed by Sancho on foot. The curate and Cardenio are watching from behind a thicket, uncertain as to how they are to contrive to join the others. The priest solves the problem by taking out a pair of scissors and trimming Cardenio's beard, after which he gives the youth his drab-colored cape and black coat to serve as a further disguise while he himself remains in breeches and doublet.

Meeting the party at the highway, the curate accounts for his presence there by giving Don Quixote a story of having been on his way to Seville in the company of the barber when the pair were set upon by thieves—"certain galley slaves," as he puts it, who had been freed by some villainous madman or other (for Sancho has told his townsmen of the incident). The knight is greatly embarrassed and becomes violently angry when his squire speaks up to inform the company at large who it was that gave the rogues their freedom.

An amusing incident occurs when the barber, having yielded his saddle to the curate, goes to mount the crupper of his mule. The animal gives a couple of kicks and the barber's beard falls off, which comes

*near to disclosing his identity. The curate runs over
and sticks the beard on again, mumbling a few words
which, he says, are a psalm "appropriate to the sticking on of beards." Don Quixote is impressed and makes
the curate promise to teach him the psalm.*

*They then proceed on their way, supposedly to the
"great kingdom of Micomicon," though they are in
reality bound for Don Quixote's native village (Chapter
XXIX).*

The Return to the Village

(CHAPTERS XXX-LII)

*As they ride along Don Quixote urges the "Princess
Micomicona" to tell him of her misfortunes, and she
obliges, making up a fantastic tale on the spur of the
moment. When she falters or becomes confused, she is
prompted by the curate, and they all admire her cleverness and ready wit. Don Quixote and Sancho believe
her story, and the latter is greatly put out when his
master declares that, after he has rescued the princess,
he cannot marry her, for he is loyal to his lady Dulcinea. They have a quarrel over this and the squire is
severely chastised, with Dorotea intervening to allay
the knight's wrath. Then something happens that
brings joy to Sancho's heart. (The passage that follows
does not occur in the first edition but is found in the
second one of 1605.)*

FROM CHAPTER XXX: *Which treats of . . . matters very pleasant and amusing.*

A S THEY were proceeding in this manner, they saw coming down the road toward them a man mounted upon an ass, who, as he drew near, appeared to them to be a gypsy. But Sancho Panza, whose heart and soul were stirred every time he caught sight of a donkey, had no sooner laid eyes on the fellow than he recognized him as Ginés de Pasamonte, and in this case the gypsy served as the thread that led him to the yarn-ball of his stolen gray, for it was indeed the gray upon which Pasamonte was riding. That worthy, in order to dispose of the ass and avoid being identified, had got himself up in gypsy costume, for he knew how to speak their language and many others as if they had been his native tongue.

As soon as Sancho had seen and recognized him, he called out at the top of his voice, "Hey, Ginesillo, you thief! Release my jewel, my treasure, my life, the beast on which I take my rest. Flee, you whoring knave; begone, you robber, and leave me that which is not yours!"

All these words and insults were quite unnecessary, for at the first sound of Sancho's voice Ginés had leaped down and, trotting, or, better, running, away, had soon left them all behind. Sancho then went up to the gray and threw his arms around it.

"How have you been, old friend," he said, "joy of my life, apple of my eye?" With this, he kissed and caressed it as if it had been a person, the ass standing quietly all the while, submitting without a word to this show of affection. The others now came up and congratulated

him on the recovery of the beast, especially Don Quixote, who assured him that he would not for this reason
annul the order for the three ass-colts, for which Sancho
thanked him very much.

*A little later, as the others are engaged in conversa-
tion, Don Quixote asks Sancho to give him an account
of Dulcinea.*

While this conversation was in progress, Don Quixote was saying to Sancho, "Friend Sancho, let us make
up our quarrel. And now, laying aside all rancor and
irritation, tell me how and when it was you found
Dulcinea. What was she doing? What did you say to
her and what did she reply? What was the expression
on her face when she read my letter? Who copied it out
for you? Tell me all this and everything else that seems
to you worth knowing or asking about or concerning
which I might be curious, neither adding anything nor
telling me anything that is not true merely to please
me; and be sure that you do not shorten the story and
thereby deprive me of any of it."

"Sir," replied Sancho, "if I am to tell the truth, the
letter was not copied for me by anyone, for I did not
have it with me."

"That is true enough," said Don Quixote, "for a
couple of days after you had left I found the memorandum book in which I had written it out and was very
much grieved about it, not knowing what you would
do when you found you did not have it, though I felt
sure you would return for it."

"That is what I'd have done," said Sancho, "if I
hadn't learned it by heart while your Grace was reading
it to me, so that I was able to recite it to a sacristan who
copied it all down for me, point by point. And he said

that in the course of his life he had read many a letter of excommunication but never a pretty one like that."

"And do you still remember it, Sancho?" Don Quixote asked.

"No, sir, I do not; for as soon as I had said it over to him, seeing that I had no further need of remembering it, I proceeded to forget it. If there is anything I do recall, it is that business about the sufferable—I mean, sovereign—lady, and the ending, 'Yours until death, the Knight of the Mournful Countenance.' And between those two I put in 'my soul,' 'my life,' and 'light of my eyes,' more than three hundred times."

CHAPTER XXXI. *Of the delectable conversation that took place between Don Quixote and Sancho Panza, his squire, together with other events.*

"ALL this does not displease me," said Don Quixote. "You may continue. What was my beauteous queen engaged in doing when you arrived? Surely you must have found her stringing pearls or embroidering some device in gold thread for this her captive knight."

"No," replied Sancho, "I did not. I found her winnowing two fanegas[1] of wheat in the stable yard of her house."

"If that is so," said Don Quixote, "then you may be sure that those grains of wheat were so many pearls when her fingers touched them. And did you observe, my friend, if the wheat was fine and white or of the ordinary spring-sown variety?"

"It was neither," Sancho informed him; "it was the reddish kind."

"Then I assure you," the knight insisted, "that without a doubt, when winnowed by her hands, it made the finest of white bread. But go on. When you gave her my letter, did she kiss it? Did she place it on her head [2] or accord it any ceremony such as it deserved? If not, what was it that she did?"

"When I went to give it to her," said Sancho, "she was busy swinging the sieve, with a good part of the wheat in it, from side to side. 'Lay it on that sack,' she said to me. 'I'll not have time to read it until I have finished sifting all that there is here.'"

"Discreet lady!" said Don Quixote. "That was in order that she might take her time in reading it and revel in it. Continue, Sancho. While she was thus occupied, what words passed between you? Did she ask after me? And what did you say in reply? Come, tell me all and do not leave the smallest part of it in the inkwell."

"She asked me nothing," said Sancho, "but I told her how your Grace, in her service, was doing penance naked from the waist up, living in these mountains like a wild animal, sleeping on the ground, without eating bread off a tablecloth or combing your beard, and weeping and cursing over your unhappy fate."

"That was wrong to say that I was cursing my unhappy fate; the truth is, I bless it and shall do so all the days of my life, for having rendered me worthy of loving so highborn a lady as Dulcinea del Toboso."

"She is so high," said Sancho, "that she tops me by more than a hand's breadth."

"How do you come to know that, Sancho? Did you measure with her?"

"I measured in this way. When I went to help her lift a sack of wheat onto a mule's back, we stood so close alongside each other that I could see she was the taller by more than a good-sized palm."

"That may be true," said Don Quixote, "though her height is accompanied and set off by a thousand million spiritual graces! You will not deny one thing, Sancho: that when you come near her you are conscious of a Sabaean odor, an aromatic fragrance, an indescribable and pleasing something for which I can find no name? What I mean is, an exhalation or emanation, as if one were in the shop of some exquisite glovemaker."

"All I can tell you," said Sancho, "is that I did notice a sort of mannish smell about her—it must have been because she was working so hard and all in a sweat."

"No," said Don Quixote, "it could not have been that. You must have been suffering from a cold in the head, or else it was yourself that you were smelling; for I well know what the fragrance of that rose among thorns is like—that lily of the field, that bit of diluted amber."

"You may be right," said Sancho, "for very often that same smell comes from me that I then thought was coming from her Grace, the lady Dulcinea. There's nothing surprising in that, for one devil's like another, you know."

"Very well, then," continued Don Quixote, "she has finished sifting her wheat and sent it to the mill. What did she do when she read the letter?"

"She did not read it; for, as I have told you, she does not know how to read or write. Instead, she tore it up into small pieces, saying she did not want anyone else to see it and have her private affairs known in the village. It was enough what I had told her about the love your Grace has for her and the extraordinary penance you are doing for her sake. Finally, she said to tell your Grace that she kissed your hands and that she would rather see you than write to you. And she further begged and commanded you, upon receipt of this

message, to leave off your foolishness, come out of these
·woods, and set out at once for El Toboso before something worse happened to you, for she was very anxious
for a sight of your Grace. She had a good laugh when
I told her that your Grace was known as the Knight of
the Mournful Countenance. I asked her if the Biscayan
that we met a long while ago had been there, and she
told me that he had been and that he was a very fine
man. I also asked after the galley slaves, but she said
she had seen nothing of any of them as yet."

"All goes very well up to now," said Don Quixote.
"But tell me, what jewel was it that she gave you when
you took your leave, in return for the news of me that
you had brought her? For it is the usage and ancient
custom among knights- and ladies-errant to present to
the squires, damsels, or dwarfs who bring them word
of their mistresses or their champions some costly gem
as a guerdon and token of appreciation of the message
they have received."

"That may all be true," said Sancho, "and I think
it is a very good custom myself; but that must have been
in times past, for nowadays all that they commonly give
you is little bread and cheese, which is what I had
from my lady Dulcinea. She handed it to me over the
wall of the stable yard as I was leaving, and that it
might be still more of a token, it was cheese made
from sheep's milk."

"She is extremely generous," observed Don Quixote,
"and if she did not give you a golden jewel, it was undoubtedly because she did not have one at hand, for
sleeves are good after Easter.[3] I shall see her and everything will be taken care of. But do you know what
astonishes me, Sancho? I think you must have gone and
returned through the air, for it has taken you less than
three days to make the journey from here to El Toboso

and back, a distance of more than thirty leagues. Which leads me to think that the wise necromancer who watches over my affairs and is a friend of mine—for there must be someone of that sort or else I should not be a real knight-errant—I think he must have aided you without your knowing it. For there are cases in which one of those magicians will snatch up a knight-errant as he lies sleeping in his bed and, without his knowing how or in what manner it was done, the next morning that knight will find himself thousands of leagues away from where he was the evening before.

"If it were not for this, knights-errant would not be able to succor one another when in peril as they are in the habit of doing all the time. For it may happen that one of them is fighting in the mountains of Armenia with some dragon or other fierce monster or with another knight, and he is having the worst of the battle and is at the point of death when suddenly, just as he least expects it, there appears over his head upon a cloud or a chariot of fire another knight, a friend of his, who a short while before was in England and who has now come to aid him and save him from death; and that same evening he is back at his lodgings having a pleasant dinner, although from one place to the other is a distance of two or three thousand leagues. All this is done through the wisdom and ingenuity of those skilled enchanters who watch over valiant knights. And so, friend Sancho, it is not hard for me to believe that you have gone from here to El Toboso and back in so short a space of time, for, as I have said, some wise magician must have carried you through the air without your knowing it."

"That may be," said Sancho, "for 'pon my word, if Rocinante didn't go as if he had been a gypsy's donkey with quicksilver in his ears!" [4]

"Quicksilver indeed!" exclaimed Don Quixote; "and a legion of devils besides, for they are folk who can travel and cause others to travel without growing weary, whenever the fancy takes them. But, putting all this aside, what do you think I should do now about going to see my lady as she has commanded? On the one hand, I am obligated to obey her command, and on the other, this is rendered impossible by the promise I have given to the princess who accompanies us, and the law of knighthood requires that I should keep my word before satisfying my own inclinations. I am wearied and harassed with longing to see my lady, yet my pledged word and the glory to be won in this undertaking calls to me and spurs me on.

"What I plan to do, accordingly, is to go with all haste to where this giant is, and then, after I have cut off his head and restored the princess to the peaceful possession of her throne, I shall return at once to see the light that illuminates my senses, giving her such excuses for my delay that she will come to be glad of it, inasmuch as it all redounds to her greater fame and glory. All that I have ever achieved or shall achieve by force of arms in this life is due to the favor she bestows upon me and the fact that I am hers."

"Ah," cried Sancho, "what a sad muddle your Grace's brains are in! For tell me, sir, do you mean to go all that way for nothing and let slip the chance of making so rich and important a match as this, where the bride's dowry is a kingdom? A kingdom which in all truth, I have heard them say, is more than twenty thousand leagues around, which abounds in all the things that are necessary to support human life, and which, in short, is greater than Portugal and Castile combined. For the love of God, do not talk like that, but be ashamed of what you have just said. Pardon me and

take my advice, which is that you get married in the
first village where you find a curate; or, for that matter, here is our own licentiate, who would do a first-
rate job. Believe me, I am old enough to be giving
advice, and this that I now give you is very pat; for a
small bird in the hand is worth more than a vulture on
the wing,[5] and he who has the good and chooses the
bad, let the good that he longs for not come to him." [6]

"See here, Sancho," said Don Quixote, "if the reason
for your advising me to marry is that you wish me,
when I have slain the giant, to become a king at once
so that I shall be in a position to grant you the favors
I have promised, I may inform you that without marrying I can very easily gratify your desires; for before
going into battle I shall lay down the condition that, in
case I come out victorious, whether I marry or not,
they are to give me a part of the kingdom which I may
bestow upon whomsoever I see fit, and to whom should
I give it if not to you?"

"That is fair enough," said Sancho, "but let your
Grace see to it that my part is on the seacoast, so that,
if I don't like the life there, I can take ship with my
Negro vassals and do with them what I have said.
Meanwhile, your Grace should not be seeing my lady
Dulcinea just now, but should rather go and kill the
giant and have done with this business; for, by God,
it strikes me there's great honor and profit in it."

"You are quite right about that, Sancho, and I shall
take your advice so far as going with the princess before
I see Dulcinea is concerned. And I would impress upon
you that you are to say nothing to anyone, including
those who come with us, regarding the subject that we
have just been discussing; for Dulcinea is of so retiring
a disposition that she would not have her thoughts
known, and it is not for me or any other to reveal them."

"Well, then," said Sancho, "how comes it that your Grace sends all those whom you conquer by the might of your arm to present themselves before my lady Dulcinea, this being as good as a signature to the effect that you are lovers? And since those that go there have to kneel before her and say that they come from your Grace to yield obedience to her, how can the thoughts of the two of you be kept hidden?"

"Oh, what a simple-minded fool you are!" exclaimed Don Quixote. "Can you not see that all this redounds to her greater praise? For you must know that in accordance with our rules of chivalry it is a great honor for a lady to have many knights-errant who serve her and whose thoughts never go beyond rendering her homage for her own sake, with no expectation of any reward for their many and praiseworthy endeavors other than that of being accepted as her champions."

"That," observed Sancho, "is the kind of love I have heard the preacher say we ought to give to Our Lord, for Himself alone, without being moved by any hope of eternal glory or fear of Hell; but, for my part, I prefer to love and serve Him for what He can do for me."

"May the devil take the bumpkin!" cried Don Quixote. "What a wit you show at times; one would think you had been a student."

"But, on my word," said Sancho, "I cannot even read."

At this point Master Nicholas called out to them to wait a while as the others wished to pause at a little roadside spring for a drink. Don Quixote accordingly came to a halt, and Sancho was by no means displeased with this, for he was tired by now of telling so many lies and was afraid that his master would catch him up, the truth being that, while he knew that Dulcinea was a peasant girl of El Toboso, he had never in his life laid eyes upon her.

Cardenio in the meantime had put on the clothes that Dorotea had worn when they found her. Though they were none too good, they were much better than the ones he took off. They then dismounted beside the spring, and with the food that the curate had procured at the inn, while it was not much, they all contrived to satisfy their hunger. As they were engaged in their repast, a lad came along the highway and, after studying them all attentively, ran over to Don Quixote and clasped him around the legs, weeping copiously.

"Ah sir! Do you not know me, your Grace? Look at me well, for I am the lad Andrés that your Grace freed from the oak tree to which he was bound."

The knight then recognized him and, taking him by the hand, he turned to the others and said, "In order that your Worships may see how important it is to have knights-errant in the world to right the wrongs and injuries done by the insolent and evil beings who inhabit it, you may know that some while ago, as I was passing through a wood, I heard certain pitiful cries and moans as from one who was afflicted and in distress. I then, as was my duty, went to the place from which the cries appeared to come, and there I found, bound to an oak tree, this lad who now stands before you. I am heartily glad that he is with us now, for he will be my witness that I do not lie in anything I say. He was, as I said, bound to that tree while a peasant, who, I later learned, was his master, lashed him unmercifully with the reins of his mare. The moment I saw this, I asked the man what was the reason for the flogging, and the lout replied that he was whipping the boy because he was his servant and had been guilty of certain acts of carelessness that indicated he was a thief rather than a dunce. At this, however, the lad spoke up and said, 'Sir, he is whipping me because I asked for my wages and for no other reason.' The master then made some excuses or other which, if I heard them, I did not accept as valid.

"The short of it was, I compelled the peasant to release the boy and made him promise to take him home and pay him every real of what he owed him, and perfumed into the bargain.[7] Is not that all true, Andrés, my son? Did you not note how imperiously I commanded him to do that and with what humility he promised to carry out all my orders and instructions? Speak up and tell these ladies and gentlemen, clearly and in a straightforward manner, just what happened; for I would have them see and be convinced that I was right when I said that it is very useful to have knights-errant going up and down the highroads."

"All that your Grace has said is very true," the lad replied, "but the end of the matter was quite different from what you think."

"What do you mean by saying that it was quite different?" Don Quixote demanded. "Did not the peasant pay you?"

"He not only did not pay me," said the boy, "but the moment your Grace had left the wood and we were alone, he tied me to that same tree again and gave me so many fresh lashes that I was like St. Bartholomew when they had done flaying him. And at each stroke he made some jest or gibe about how he had fooled you, so funny that I would have laughed myself if the pain had not been so great. In short, he mishandled me to such an extent that I have been in a hospital up to now with the cuts that wicked lout gave me. For all of which your Grace is to blame. If you had gone your way and had not come where you were not called nor meddled in the affairs of others, my master would have been satisfied with giving me one or two dozen lashes and then would have untied me and paid me what he owed me. But your Grace roused his anger by insulting him so unreasonably and calling him all those names, and since he could not avenge himself on you, the moment we were alone the storm burst on me, and, as a result, I do not think I shall ever be a man again as long as I live."

"My mistake," said Don Quixote, "was in going off and leaving you like that. I should not have left until I had seen you paid; for I ought to have known from long experience that there is no peasant who keeps his word if he finds that it is not in his interest to do so. But you remember, Andrés, I swore that if he did not pay you I would come looking for him, and would find him even though he were hidden in the belly of the whale."

"That you did," said Andrés, "but it was of no use."

"Well, we will see now whether it is of use or not," said Don Quixote. And, saying this, he hastily arose and ordered Sancho to put the bridle on Rocinante, for the hack had been grazing while they were eating. Dorotea then asked him what he proposed to do, and he replied that he meant to go look for the peasant and chastise him for his behavior, and he also intended to make him pay Andrés to the last maravedi, notwithstanding and in spite of all the clodhoppers in the world. She thereupon reminded him that in accordance with his promise he could not embark upon any enterprise until he had finished the undertaking with which she had charged him. After all, she added, he knew this better than anyone else and should restrain the fury in his bosom until he had returned from her realm.

"That is true," Don Quixote agreed. "As you say, lady, Andrés will have to be patient until I come back; but I hereby swear and promise him anew that I will not desist until I have avenged him and seen him paid."

"I do not believe in those oaths," said Andrés. "What I need now is enough to take me to Seville; I would rather have that than all the vengeance in the world. So, if you have here anything to eat that I can take with me, let me have it; and God be with your Grace and all knights-errant, and may they be as errant with themselves as they have been with me."

Sancho then produced a bit of bread and cheese and gave it to the lad.

"Take it, brother Andrés," he said, "for we all have a share in your troubles."

"Why, what share is yours?" Andrés asked.

"This portion of bread and cheese. God knows whether I am going to need it or not, for I may tell you, my friend, that the squires of knights-errant are greatly subject to hunger and misfortune and other things that are better felt than put into words."

Andrés accepted the food and, seeing that no one offered him anything else, lowered his head and, as the saying goes, took the road in hand. But, before leaving, he turned to Don Quixote.

"For the love of God, Sir Knight-errant," he said, "if ever again you meet me, even though they are hacking me to bits, do not aid or succor me but let me bear it, for no misfortune could be so great as that which comes of being helped by you. May God curse you and all the knights-errant that were ever born into this world!"

Don Quixote was about to arise and follow him, but the lad started running so swiftly that no one thought of trying to overtake him. The knight was exceedingly crestfallen over the story Andrés had told, and the others had to do their best to keep from laughing so as not to discomfit him entirely.

The next day the party arrives at the inn where Don Quixote and Sancho Panza had so unpleasant an experience upon a former occasion. Sancho is very much afraid of the place, but there is nothing for him to do but go along with the others. His master, on the other hand, maintains a dignified, condescending attitude and expresses the hope that he will have a better bed than the one given him the last time. The landlady assures him that he will have the best, if he pays better than he did before. He promises to do so, and they give him a comfortable pallet in the same "starry" garret. Being exceedingly weary and shaken, in mind and body, he goes to bed at once.

No sooner has the knight left the room than the landlady seizes the barber's oxtail beard with the demand that he return it. They engage in a tug-of-war over it, and the curate advises his friend to give it up. They agree upon what they will tell Don Quixote when he recognizes the barber. They will say that, after being robbed by the galley slaves, he had fled to this inn for protection; and they will explain the disappearance of the princess's squire by adding that he has been sent ahead to let her subjects know that she is on her way with one who will liberate them.

The curate directs the landlord and his wife to lay out a meal; and as they all sit at table—the entire company with the exception of Don Quixote, and the landlord and his household as well—the talk turns first on Don Quixote's strange madness and then on the subject of romances of chivalry. They all express their opinions, and the landlord goes to his room and comes back with an old valise containing a number of books and manuscripts. The books are of the kind found in the knight's library. When the curate voices his disapproval of them, the innkeeper stoutly defends them.

Catching sight of a bundle of papers in the valise, the curate asks permission to look at them. He finds this is a manuscript entitled "Story of the One Who Was Too Curious for His Own Good" ("El Curioso Impertinente"), and the landlord explains that the valise had been left behind by an absent-minded guest. When the priest offers to read the story aloud, they all gladly consent (Chapter XXXII).

The "One Who Was Too Curious" takes up two long chapters and part of a third (XXXIII-XXXV) but the substance of it may be given rather briefly.

Anselmo and Lotario were two young men of Florence whose friendship was proverbial. When Anselmo came to marry, he used Lotario as his intermediary in obtaining the hand of the beauteous Camila, and after the wedding Lotario remained an intimate of the household. He himself did not deem this wise, but Anselmo had insisted. All went well for a while, and the wedded pair were very happy, until one day a terrible doubt entered the husband's soul.

He knew that his wife was virtuous, but then, he reflected, her virtue had never been put to the test; and what, after all, was it worth until it had been "proved . . . in the same manner that fire brings out the purity of gold"? He accordingly made the shocking suggestion —it was deeply shocking to Lotario—that his friend play the part of tempter. Lotario at first refused, and there was a prolonged argument between them, but he finally yielded, greatly against his will, when Anselmo threatened to appeal to someone else to enact the role.

In the beginning Lotario thought to deceive his friend

by maintaining a perfectly correct manner toward Camila while reporting to her husband that he had made advances to her and had been repulsed. Anselmo, however, spied upon them and discovered the deception. He was angry and reproached Lotario, whereupon the latter promised that from that time forth he would play the part in earnest. In order to give Lotario ample opportunity, Anselmo left the city for a couple of weeks, and then it was Lotario really fell in love with Camila.

Before long he was making open love to her, and she, nonplused by his changed behavior and not knowing what to do, sat down and wrote her husband a letter urging him to return at once. But Anselmo, pleased that Lotario had begun the undertaking, continued to stay away, with the result that his wife finally lost the virtue he so highly prized and had insisted on putting to the test.

When he eventually did return, Anselmo failed to perceive that anything was amiss. Lotario advised him to let matters rest, but Anselmo wished the experiment to be carried a little further. Camila, meanwhile, had become the victim of her maid Leonela, who, aware of what was happening, now held the upper hand over her mistress. Leonela herself was carrying on an amour with a young man of the town, whom she was in the habit of introducing into the house at night; and when one evening Lotario glimpsed the youth, muffled in his cloak and stealing away, he at once leaped to the conclusion that Camila was as unfaithful to him as she had been to Anselmo.

This led him to plot a mad revenge. Seeking out his friend, he told him that Camila was on the point of yielding at last and that he had arranged a meeting with her in a certain room of the house; if Anselmo desired to see for himself, he should hide there and the *proof would be his. But almost immediately Lotario's conscience began to hurt him. He might, he reflected, have taken a revenge that was less cruel and dishonorable. He went to Camila, to make a clean breast of it all, but before he had a chance to do this he was informed by her of Leonela's conduct, how the maid was in the habit of keeping her gallant in the house until daybreak. He realized at once what a terrible mistake he had made and was more conscience-stricken than ever.*

Camila was very angry when she learned of her lover's rashness and upbraided him bitterly for his lack of trust in her. She was gravely alarmed by the situation but at once began laying her own feminine plans. Lotario was to see that Anselmo was hidden in the room the next day, and he was to come when she sent for him and reply to anything she said to him exactly as he would have done if he had not known her husband was listening.

This plan was carried out. Anselmo, in hiding, heard a dialogue between mistress and maid the purpose of which was to give the impression that Camila, feeling that her virtue had been hopelessly compromised, was bent upon killing herself, and Leonela was seeking to dissuade her. Finally, with the promise that she would not lay hands upon herself until she first had slain the one who by his mere proposal had so dishonored her, she directed the girl to bring Lotario to her.

A bit of melodrama was then acted out, with Lotario playing the role of seducer and Camila that of his unwilling victim. As a climax she fell upon him in a realistic attempt to stab him and, failing in this, inflicted a slight wound upon herself and dropped in a faint. Lotario was loud in his laments and informed Leonela that he was going away "where no one would ever see him again." As Camila regained consciousness there followed another conversation between the two women, the subject being how they might conceal the wound and what they should tell Anselmo.

Convinced that the wound was a slight one, the husband was elated by all this and warm in his praise of Lotario's efforts. It was he himself who brought his betrayer back to the house for a reconciliation, and for a number of months the situation continued as it had been before.

At this point in the story the curate is interrupted.

CHAPTER XXXV. *In which the "Story of the One Who Was Too Curious for His Own Good" is brought to a close, and in which is related the fierce and monstrous battle that Don Quixote waged with certain skins of red wine.*

THE reading of the story was nearly completed when from the garret where Don Quixote was taking his repose Sancho Panza burst forth in great excitement, shouting, "Come quick, sirs, and help my master, for he is in the thick of the most stubborn and fiercest battle that ever my eyes beheld! By the living God but he gave that giant who is the enemy of my lady, the Princess Micomicona, such a slash that he cut his head off all the way around as if it had been a turnip!"

"What are you talking about, brother?" asked the curate as he paused in his reading. "Have you gone out of your head, Sancho? How in the devil could what you say be true when the giant is two thousand leagues from here?"

At this point there came a loud noise from the upper room and Don Quixote could be heard crying, "Hold, robber, scoundrel, knave! I have you now, and your scimitar will not avail you!" And then it sounded as if he were giving great slashes at the wall.

"Don't stop to listen," said Sancho, "but go on in and stop the fight or else help my master; although, come to think of it, that will not be necessary, for there is no doubt whatever that the giant is already dead by this time and is now giving an account to God of his past life and evil ways. I myself saw the blood running all over the floor and his head cut off and lying to one side, and it was big as a wineskin."

"May they slay me!" cried the innkeeper at this point. "I'll bet Don Quixote or Don Devil has been slashing at one of those skins full of red wine that are at the head of his bed, and it must have been the wine spilling over the floor that looked like blood to this good man."

He then made his way to the garret, followed by all the rest of them, and there they found Don Quixote in the strangest costume imaginable. He was clad in his shirt, which was not long enough in front to cover his thighs completely and was about six fingers shorter behind. His legs were very long, lean, and hairy and anything but clean. On his head he had a little greasy red cap that belonged to the innkeeper, and around his left arm he had rolled a red blanket—an object against which Sancho, for reasons of his own, had a special grudge—while in his right hand he held an unsheathed sword with which he was laying about him in every direction, and all the time he kept talking to himself as if he were really fighting with some giant. The best part of it was that he had his eyes shut, for he was still asleep and dreaming that he was doing battle with the giant, the adventure which he was about to undertake having so worked upon his imagination that he fancied in his dream that he had already reached the kingdom of Micomicon and was engaged in a struggle with his enemy.

Under this illusion he had given the skins so many thrusts, believing them to be the giant, that the entire room was filled with wine.[1] Seeing what his guest had done, the landlord was so angry that he fell upon Don Quixote with clenched fists and began pommeling him so hard that if Cardenio and the curate had not pulled him off, he would soon have concluded the war with the giant. But in spite of it all they did not succeed in awakening the poor gentleman until the barber had brought a large pot of cold water from the well and they had dashed its contents over the knight, who then regained consciousness but not sufficiently to be able to realize what had happened.

Seeing how scantily and thinly he was clad, Dorotea would not come in to witness the encounter between her champion and his adversary; and Sancho, meanwhile, was looking all over the floor for the giant's head, which he was unable to find.

"I knew all along," he said, "that everything about this house was under a spell. The other time, in this very room where I am now, they gave me any number of cuffs and blows without my knowing from where they came, for I was never able to see anyone doing it; and now I can't find that head though I saw it chopped off with my own eyes, with the blood spurting from his body as from a fountain."

"What blood and what fountain, enemy of God and his saints?" cried the innkeeper. "Can't you see, you brigand, that the blood and fountain you are talking about are nothing other than these skins that have been punctured and the red wine from them that is flowing all over the room—and I only wish I saw the soul of him who pierced them swimming in Hell!"

"I know nothing about that," said Sancho. "All I know is that, if I don't find that head, it will be my bad luck to see my earldom melting away like salt in water."

For Sancho awake was worse than his master asleep, such had been the effect of the promises Don Quixote had made him. The innkeeper was in despair at seeing this lack of concern on the part of the squire and the deviltry wrought by the knight, and he swore that it was not going to be like the last time, when they had left without paying. This time the privileges of knighthood would not let either one or the other of them off, but they would have to reimburse him even for the cost of the plugs to patch up the punctured skins. The curate all this while was holding Don Quixote's hands, and the knight, thinking that the exploit had been accomplished and that he was now in the presence of the Princess Micomicona, dropped to his knees in front of the priest.

"O exalted and famous lady," he said, "your Highness from this day forth may live assured against any harm this lowborn creature could have done you; and I too am now free of the promise I gave you, since with the help of Almighty God and the favor of her in whom I live and breathe, I have so thoroughly fulfilled it."

"There!" exclaimed Sancho upon hearing this, "what did I tell you? You see I was not drunk after all. Just look how my master has salted down that giant! You can depend on the bulls,[2] and my earldom is certain."

Who would not have laughed at hearing the nonsense the two of them talked, master and man? And laugh they all did with the exception of mine host, who was roundly cursing himself. At last, however, with no little effort, the barber, Cardenio, and the curate managed to get Don Quixote back into bed, and he at once fell asleep with every appearance of being utterly exhausted. Leaving him there, they then went down to the gateway of the inn to console Sancho Panza for not having found the giant's head; but they had a good deal more on their hands when it came to placating the landlord, who was in a rage over the sudden death of his wineskins. The landlady, for her part, was screaming and carrying on at a great rate.

"It was an evil moment and an unlucky hour," she shouted, "when that knight-errant entered my house. I had never laid eyes on him before, but he cost me dearly. The last time it was the price of a lodging, a dinner, a bed, and straw and barley, for himself, his squire, a hack, and an ass. He said he was a knightly adventurer—may God give him and all the adventurers in this world nothing but misadventures!—and for that reason was obliged to pay nothing, since that was the way it was written down in the tariff code of knight-errantry. And now, on account of him, this other gentleman comes along and carries off my tail and gives it back to me with more than two cuartillos'[3] worth of damage done to it, all stripped of its hair and of no further use for my husband's purpose. And as the finishing touch to everything, he punctures my wineskins and spills my wine—if I could only see his blood spilled instead! But let him not think he'll be able to do the same thing this time! By my father's bones and my mother's ghost, he's going to pay me every cuarto[4] that he owes me or my name is not what it is and I am not my parents' daughter!"

The innkeeper's wife had all this and many other things to say, for she was very angry indeed, and her slavey, the worthy Maritornes, joined in the scolding.

The daughter, however, was silent and merely smiled quietly to herself from time to time. The curate finally settled matters by promising to make good the loss to the best of his ability. He agreed to pay them for the wineskins and the wine and especially for the damage done to that tail of which they were forever talking. Dorotea, meanwhile, was comforting Sancho Panza by telling him that, the moment it was definitely established that his master had cut off the giant's head and she had come into peaceful possession of her kingdom, she would bestow upon him the finest earldom that it contained. Sancho felt better upon hearing this and assured the princess that he had seen the giant's head, adding by way of further identification that the monster had a beard that came all the way down to his waist, and if he was not to be seen at the moment, it was for the reason that everything that happened in that house was directed by an enchanter, as he himself had found to be the case the other time that he had stopped there. Dorotea said that she believed this to be true, but that he should not let it worry him, as things would come out all right in the end and he would have whatever he wished.

When they had all quieted down, the curate suggested that they finish reading the story, for there was still a little of it left. Cardenio, Dorotea, and the others thereupon begged him to continue, and by reason of the pleasure that he as well as they derived from it, he went on with the tale, as follows:

The curate then goes on to read the rest of the story: Following the mock-drama, Camila pretended to be cool toward Lotario, and the latter begged his friend's permission not to come to the house any more since his visits obviously were an annoyance to her. Anselmo, however, would not hear of this, being assured now of his wife's fidelity.

Things went along like this for some time, until Anselmo, in turn, discovered Leonela's lover in the act of leaving. His suspicions aroused by this, he threatened to kill the girl unless she told him the truth. She insisted that the man was her husband, but, being very much frightened, promised Anselmo that if he spared her, she would tell him "things that are more important than you can imagine." She begged him to give her until the next morning, as she was too excited to think at the moment. He agreed and locked her in her room.

He then went to his wife and informed her of what had occurred and Leonela's promised revelations. Camila, needless to say, was terrified. Getting together her jewels and money, she stole out that night and hastened to Lotario to implore his protection. Himself uncertain what to do, he took her to a convent of which his sister was the prioress, and that same night he too left the city, saying nothing to anyone.

When dawn came, Anselmo found that his wife, Leonela, and Lotario were all missing. At his wits' end, he resolved to go to the home of a friend in the country. On the way he learned from a passing traveler that the entire town was talking of the affair. Arriving at his friend's house, he asked permission to retire at once and further requested them to provide him with writing materials and bar the door. As the hours went by and he failed to call out, his host investigated and found him lying sprawled across the writing-table. He was dead. An unfinished note declared: ". . . a foolish and ill-advised curiosity has robbed me of my life." The note also expressed forgiveness of Camila, inasmuch as she "was under no obligation to perform miracles and I had no right to ask them of her. . . . I was the creator of my own dishonor. . . ."

As for Lotario, he went to the wars and was slain in battle, and Camila upon the news of his death took the veil and died a short while afterward. (Conclusion of Chapter xxxv.)

Just as the reading ends the landlord announces that a party of travelers is approaching the inn; it consists of four armed men wearing black masks, a white-clad woman, and two foot servants. Dorotea promptly covers her face and Cardenio retires into the room where Don Quixote is. The travelers enter without removing their masks, and the lady gives evidence of being faint and ill. Curious to know what the explanation is, the curate goes out to question the grooms. They tell him they are certain that the lady is being taken somewhere against her will, probably to a convent.

Dorotea, meanwhile, has gone up to speak to her. The sound of the woman's voice as she answers reaches Cardenio and he gives a startled cry. The lady, not seeing who had cried out, is about to go into the other room but is prevented from doing so by the gentleman who seems to be in charge. As he holds her firmly with both hands his mask falls off, and it is Dorotea's turn to cry out; she falls back, fainting in the arms of the barber, for she has recognized Don Fernando.

The curate goes over to remove Dorotea's veil and throw water in her face by way of reviving her, and Fernando turns pale as he sees before him the woman he has betrayed. Upon hearing Dorotea's scream Cardenio comes running out, for he and Luscinda (the masked lady) have recognized each other by their voices. He beholds Fernando with Luscinda in his arms, *and they all stand gazing at one another in amazement. Luscinda is the first to speak, declaring that Cardenio is her true husband. She implores Fernando to kill her so that Cardenio may see she has kept faith with him to the end.*

Dorotea has recovered from her swoon by now, and, throwing herself at Fernando's feet, she beseeches him to have pity on her, since "I am your wife, whether you like it or not." She sobs so passionately that they all burst into sympathetic tears, and in the end Fernando relents. "You have conquered, O beauteous Dorotea," he says, and releases Luscinda.

Forgetting all about decorum, Luscinda flings her arms around Cardenio's neck and presses her cheek to his. At this, Fernando changes color and lays a hand on his sword as if to intervene, but Dorotea restrains him, and the curate, the barber, and his own traveling companions also take a hand and reason with him. Once again he yields, lifts Dorotea to her feet, and embraces her. There is another display of tears and a general reconciliation.

Fernando then relates how he had found out where Luscinda was and had gone to the convent and taken her away by force. All she has done ever since, he states, is to weep and sigh without uttering a single word.

If the others weep out of sympathy with the lovers, Sancho's tears are due to a different cause. He is in despair at seeing the Princess Micomicona transformed into plain Dorotea, but when Don Quixote hears of it, he attributes it all to the work of enchanters.

In the meantime the curate tells the newcomers of the knight's madness and the stratagem employed to get him off Poor Rock. He remarks that they will have to evolve another plan now, but Dorotea assures him this will not be necessary, as she is quite willing to continue in her former role. Don Quixote comes out and there is an amusing dialogue between him and the "princess," in which she succeeds in removing all doubts from his mind. He is furious with Sancho and calls him "the greatest little rascal in all Spain."

At this moment a traveler enters the courtyard of the inn. His garb and accouterments indicate that he is a Christian who has been in the land of the Moors. He is accompanied by a woman dressed in the Moorish fashion and mounted upon a donkey. He asks for a lodging but is told there is none to be had. He appears greatly put out at this. Dorotea and Luscinda suggest that the woman lodge with them, and their offer is accepted by the man, who informs them that his companion understands little Spanish, being a Moor who has been converted to Christianity but not yet baptized.

Night is coming on, and Don Fernando's companions order the landlord to prepare a supper. At the table Don Quixote monopolizes the conversation with a long harangue on the theme of the knight's calling as compared with that of the man of letters. Then, at Fernando's request, the man, who turns out to be an escaped captive of the Moors, tells them the story of his life. It is a long one, extending over three chapters of Part I (Chapters XXXIX-XLI.)

The captive first gives an account of his early upbringing, tells how he chose the profession of arms, took ship for Italy, and there joined the Duke of Alva for the war in Flanders. After serving in three campaigns he returned to Italy to take part in the war against the Turks under John of Austria. In a naval engagement he was captured by the enemy commanded by El Uchali, King of Algiers, and taken to Constantinople, where he became a galley slave. Later he was taken to Algiers and imprisoned there.

Overlooking the prison yard was the home of a wealthy Moor, whose daughter began communicating with the captives below by means of a reed which she let down from her window. Having taken a fancy to the captain (the one who is telling the tale), she lowered to him a large quantity of gold crowns and a note written in Arabic. In order to have the message translated the captain was compelled to take into his confidence a certain renegade Christian in the service of the Moors.

From the note he learned that the writer had been converted to Christianity by a captive slave girl, now dead, who had advised her to make her way to the land of the Christians. She had selected the captain for the reason that he was the only one among the prisoners who appeared to be a gentleman, and she expressed a willingness to marry him if he could arrange for their escape. They were all delighted at this and, joined by the renegade, immediately started laying plans for flight.

The renegade made some inquiries and reported that the house adjoining the prison yard belonged to an enormously wealthy Moor, one Hadji Morato by name, whose daughter and only heir, Zoraida, was said to be the most beautiful woman in all Barbary, her hand in marriage having been sought by many of the viceroys. She had refused all suitors up to that time and was known to have had a female slave, now dead, who was a Christian. This bore out the statements made in the note, so they decided to wait for Zoraida to devise a way of escape for them.

Shortly afterward they received another note, saying

that she would be at her father's summer place near the sea. They were to procure a boat with the money she gave them and take her away from there by night. They accordingly gave the renegade fifteen hundred crowns with which to buy the boat, while the captain and his three companions set about making arrangements to effect their ransom with a portion of the funds Zoraida had given them.

Within a fortnight, under pretense of plying a coast-wise trade, the renegade had obtained a boat capable of carrying some thirty persons and employed some Moorish oarsmen, and he formed the habit of casting anchor near Hadji Morato's summer place in order to familiarize himself with the lay of the land. To the captain fell the task of providing a sufficient number of Christian oarsmen, who were directed to station themselves in the vicinity of the Moor's garden on the following Friday.

The plan thus formed was carried out, both Zoraida and her father being carried off in the middle of the night. It was necessary to take Hadji Morato with them because he had been awakened and had started to give the alarm. The father was carried on board bound and gagged. The daughter was grieved by this but they assured her there was no choice in the matter.

Later, at sea, when he learned the details of the escape and his daughter's part in it, and was informed that she had become a Christian, the old man leaped overboard and was hauled out nearly drowned and un-conscious. Compelled by a change of wind to put in to shore at a deserted point, the fugitives then unbound Hadji Morato and the other Moors and gave them their liberty, the father at once pleading with the girl and heaping curses upon her as he saw her borne away.

314   DON QUIXOTE

They had not gone far when a French pirate craft stood across their course and halted them with a couple of cannon shots, which brought down their mast and riddled their hull. Inasmuch as they were sinking, there was nothing to do but surrender. The pirates were content with stripping them of their valuables, not molesting Zoraida; then, being by that time in sight of the Spanish coast, put them in a small boat and set them adrift.

In a short while they were safely ashore and, after a minor adventure or two, were picked up by the coast guard and conducted to the nearest city. There the captain had purchased the ass for Zoraida to ride and had started for his father's home. It was his intention to have her baptized as soon as possible and then take her for his wife. (Conclusion of Chapter XLI.)

All the listeners are warm in their approval of it and offer to aid the captain in any way they can.

At this point a coach accompanied by a number of horsemen draws up at the inn, and one of these attendants announces that "room must be found at once for his Lordship the Judge." The landlady replies that accommodations will be arranged, and his Lordship then descends from his coach, leading by the hand his daughter, a beautiful young girl about sixteen years of age. The other guests come out to greet the new arrivals, and the moment the captain lays eyes on the judge he realizes that this is his own brother.

Uncertain of the reception that may be accorded him in his present straitened circumstances, the captain confides his doubts to the curate, and the latter, at the supper table, by way of testing the affection of the brother who has achieved such worldly success, repeats with

*certain variations the story that has just been narrated,
dwelling on the extreme want in which the captive and
the lovely Moor now find themselves; he does not indicate that they are present in the room.*

*The judge listens most attentively and is deeply
moved. He expresses the ardent wish that, before going
to assume the post in the Indies to which he has been
appointed, he might have word of his brother; he also
voices his gratitude for Zoraida's part in the escape and
adds that he would like to witness the wedding. Hearing this, the curate brings forward the captain and his
bride-to-be and there is another affecting scene. It is
decided that the pair are to accompany the judge to
Seville. From there they will send word to the captain's
father so that he may attend the baptism and the
wedding.*

*After this, they all retire for the night, with the
exception of Don Quixote, who goes outside to stand
sentinel. Shortly before daybreak the women, who are
lodged together, are awakened by the sound of an excellent male voice raised in a song. It is at first taken
to be that of a mule driver, since it comes from the
direction of the stables, but as soon as Doña Clara, the
judge's daughter, hears it she knows that the supposed
muleteer is a youth of gentle birth who is very much in
love with her, as she is with him; he has been following
her about in that disguise, and now is serenading her
with a love ballad of his own composition.*

*The girl feels that the young man is too far above
her in station for thought of marriage, and she is very
unhappy about it. Dorotea, of whom she makes a confidante, tries to comfort her and urges her to wait until
morning, when "everything will be all right or I shall
be greatly disappointed" (Chapter* XLIII*).*

FROM CHAPTER XLIII: *In which is related . . . other strange events that took place at the Inn.*

WITH this they settled down for what remained of the night, and all the inn was wrapped in silence, the only ones not asleep being the innkeeper's daughter and Maritornes the slavey, who, familiar with Don Quixote's whimsies and knowing that he was outside clad in his armor and on horseback, standing guard, decided to play some kind of practical joke on him, or at least to have a little amusement by listening to his nonsense. Now, as it happened, there was not a window in the house that looked out over the fields, but only an opening in a straw-loft through which they used to throw out the straw. At this opening the two demidamsels now stationed themselves. They could see Don Quixote in the saddle and leaning on his pike as he every now and then heaved such deep and mournful sighs that it seemed each one would tear his heart out; and they could also hear him talking to himself in a gentle, soft, and loving tone of voice.

"O my lady Dulcinea del Toboso," he was saying, "supreme model and ultimate goal of all beauty and discretion, treasury of grace, depository of virtue; in short, the ideal of all that is worth while, honorable, and delectable in this world! And what would thy Grace be doing now? Art thou perchance thinking of thy captive knight who, merely to serve thee and carry out thy wishes, hath seen fit to expose himself to all these perils? Give me some word of her, O luminary of the three faces! [1] It may be that out of envy of her face thou lookest upon her even now as she paces some gallery of her sumptuous palace, or as, leaning from a balcony, she considers how, without detriment to her modesty and exalted rank, she may assuage the torment that this grieving heart of mine endures for her sake. Does she think of the glory that should compensate me for my sufferings, the repose that should be mine after all my exertions, or, in brief, what life should be bestowed upon this my death, what reward I should have for my services?

"And thou, O Sun, who must even now be harnessing thy steeds that dawn may soon come and thou mayest emerge to behold my mistress, I beg thee when thou dost see her to greet her for me. But have a care that, when thou dost see and greet her, thou dost not kiss her face; for I shall be more jealous of thee than wast thou of that swift-footed and ungrateful one[2] that caused thee so to run and sweat over the plains of Thessaly and the banks of the Peneus—I do not rightly recall just where it was that thou didst run in thine amorous and jealous rage on that occasion."

Don Quixote had gone as far as this with his lugubrious monologue when the innkeeper's daughter began signaling to him.[3] "Good Sir," she called to him softly, "come over here, if your Grace is pleased to do so."

At this signal and the sound of her voice, Don Quixote raised his head, and by the light of the moon, which was then shining in all its brightness, he perceived that someone was summoning him from the opening in the loft, which to him appeared to be a window—a window with a gilded grating of the kind that a magnificent castle ought to have, for such he took the inn to be. And then, instantly, it occurred to his insane imagination that, as on a previous occasion, the daughter of the lord of this castle, overcome with love of him, was seeking to make a conquest. With this thought in mind and desiring not to be discourteous or unfeeling, he turned Rocinante and rode up to the opening where the two lasses were.

"It is a pity, lovely lady," he said as soon as he caught sight of them, "that thou shouldst have let thy affections roam where they can never be requited in a manner that befits thy great worth and high estate; but for this thou shouldst not blame this wretched knight-errant, for love hath rendered it impossible for him to yield his will to any other than her whom, the moment he beheld her, he made the absolute mistress of his heart. Forgive me, then, good lady, and withdraw into thy chamber, and do not display thy feeling for me any further, that I may not once more have to show myself ungrateful. If there is any other way, outside of love itself, in which I may gratify that love thou hast for me, thou hast but to ask it and I swear to thee by that sweet and absent enemy of mine that I will incontinently do thy bidding, even though the boon thou seekest be a lock of Medusa's serpent hair or the rays of the sun itself stoppered in a vial."

"My mistress has need of nothing of that sort," said Maritornes at this point.

"Then, discreet matron," replied Don Quixote, "what is it that she needs?"

"Merely one of your shapely hands," said Maritornes, "that she may vent upon it the consuming passion that has brought her to this loophole, at so great a risk to her honor that, if her father were to hear of it, the least slice of her that he would take would be her ear."

"I should like to see him do that!" said the knight. "Let him beware if he does not want to meet the most disastrous end of any father in this world for having laid hands upon the delicate members of his lovesick daughter."

Having no doubt that Don Quixote would offer his

hand as she had asked of him, Maritornes at once began thinking what she would do now; and, climbing down from the opening, she went out to the stable and took the halter of Sancho Panza's ass, returning with it quickly just as the knight was getting to his feet on Rocinante's saddle in order to be able to reach the gilded window-rail where, so he imagined, the broken-hearted damsel was.

"Lady," he was saying, "take this hand, or better, this avenger of the world's evildoers. The hand of no other woman has ever touched it, not even that of her who holds entire possession of my body. I extend it to thee, not that thou shouldst kiss it, but that thou mayest study the contexture of the sinews, the network of the muscles, the breadth and spaciousness of the veins, from which thou canst deduce how great must be the might of the arm that supports such a hand."

"That we shall soon see," said Maritornes. And, making a slip-knot in the halter, she put it over his wrist; then, getting down from the opening, she tied the other end to the bolt on the door of the loft.

"But it seems to me," said Don Quixote, as he felt the rope grating on his wrist, "that thy Grace is scraping rather than caressing my hand. Do not treat it so harshly, for it is not to blame for my unresponsive will. It is not right that thou shouldst wreak all thy vengeance upon so small a part, for remember that one who loves well should not avenge herself in a manner so ill."

But there was no one to hear these words; for as soon as Maritornes had attached the halter, she and the other girl left, fit to burst with laughing, and they left Don Quixote tied in such a way that it was impossible for him to free himself. As has been said, he was standing on Rocinante's back and his entire arm was through the opening while his wrist was fastened to the bolt on the door; and he was very much afraid that if Roci-nante should swerve to one side or the other, he would remain hanging there. For this reason, he dared not make the slightest movement, although Rocinante stood so quietly and patiently that he might have been expected not to stir for a century to come.

Finally, seeing that he was caught in this manner and the ladies had departed, the knight began imagining that all this was a kind of enchantment, like the last time when, in this very castle, that enchanted Moor of a carter had given him such a mauling. He now cursed himself for his lack of judgment and sound sense in having ventured to set foot there a second time after having fared so badly before; for it was generally accepted by knights-errant that, when they had essayed an adventure and had not succeeded in it, this meant that it was not for them but for others, and there was no necessity of trying again. Meanwhile, he kept pulling on his arm to see if he could loosen it, but it was well tied and all his efforts were in vain. It is true, he pulled very gently, lest Rocinante should move; but, in any event, he was unable to seat himself in the saddle, and there was nothing for it but to remain standing or wrench his hand off.

Then it was that he longed for the sword of Amadis, against which no enchantment whatever could prevail. Then it was that he cursed his ill fortune, exaggerating the loss which the world would suffer while he was held there under a spell, for he had no doubt that this was the case. Then he remembered once again his beloved Dulcinea del Toboso, and then too it was that he called for his good squire, Sancho Panza, who, lying stretched out on the packsaddle of his ass and dead to the world, was unmindful even of the mother who bore him. Then it was that he called upon the wise

Lirgandeo and Alquife[4] to aid him, beseeching also his good friend Urganda[5] to succor him. And then, at last, morning found him so despairing and bewildered that he brayed like a bull; for he had no hope that with the coming of day his sufferings would be ended; rather, he believed that, as a result of the magician's spell, they would be eternal. This belief was strengthened in him when he observed that Rocinante never so much as stirred. And so he was convinced that he and his steed would have to remain there in that condition, without eating, drinking, or sleeping, until the evil influence of the stars had waned or until another, more skillful enchanter came to disenchant him.

In this, however, he was greatly deceived; for it was no sooner daylight than four fully accoutered horsemen, their firelocks across their saddlebows, drew up at the inn. Finding the gateway closed, they pounded lustily upon it; and when he saw and heard this, even in his present position, Don Quixote did not fail to play the sentinel.

"Knights," he said to them, "or squires, or whoever you may be, you have no right to knock at the gates of this castle; for you should know that at such an hour those inside are asleep, or are not in the habit of throwing open the fortress until the sun is fully up. Withdraw, then, and wait for day, and we shall then see whether or not it is fitting that they open for you."

"What the devil kind of fortress or castle is this," asked one of them, "that we are obliged to stand on such ceremony? If you are the innkeeper, have them open the gate for us. We are travelers who desire no more than to give some barley to our horses and go on, for we are in a hurry."

"Do I impress you, gentlemen, as having the appearance of an innkeeper?" was Don Quixote's answer.

"I do not know what appearance you have," replied the man. "But I know that you are talking nonsense when you refer to this inn as a castle."

"A castle it is," Don Quixote insisted, "and one of the best in all this province. And there are those within who have held a scepter in their hands and have worn a crown upon their heads."

"It would have been better the other way around," said the traveler: "the scepter on the head and the crown in the hand; but it may be there is some company of actors inside, for they very often have those crowns and scepters that you are talking about, and I cannot believe that in a small tavern like this, where you cannot hear a sound, any persons would be lodged who are entitled to them in real life."

"You know little of the ways of the world," replied Don Quixote, "seeing that you are ignorant of the things that happen in connection with knight-errantry."

The companions of the one who asked the questions were by this time tired of the conversation between him and the knight, and they again began pounding so furiously that the innkeeper and all the others awoke and the landlord arose to inquire who was knocking. At that moment one of the horsemen's mounts came up to smell Rocinante as the hack, sad and melancholy, with his ears drooping, stood there motionless, supporting his well-stretched master's weight; and being, when all is said, only flesh and blood though he appeared to be of wood, Rocinante could not but weaken and in turn smell the one that had come to court him. In doing this, he moved ever so little, and at once Don Quixote's feet slipped from the saddle and he would have fallen to the ground if his arm had not been held fast, a circumstance which caused him so much pain that he thought his wrist would be cut off or his arm torn from his body. For he was left hanging so near the ground that he could touch the earth with the tips of his toes, which was all the worse for him since, being conscious of how little he lacked of being able to plant his feet firmly, he wore himself out by stretching himself as far as he could in an attempt to accomplish this. He was like those who, suffering the strappado and placed in the position of touch-without-touching, merely add to their pain by the effort they make to stretch their bodies, in the vain hope that with a little more straining they will be able to find solid footing.

CHAPTER XLIV. *In which are continued the unheard-of adventures at the inn.*

DON QUIXOTE by now was bawling so loudly that the landlord, very much alarmed, ran out and threw open the gate to see what the matter was, while those outside were equally curious. Maritornes also had been awakened by the shouts, and, suspecting what the cause of it all was, she hastened to the straw-loft without anyone's seeing her and unfastened the halter by which Don Quixote was supported, whereupon he at once dropped to the ground as the innkeeper and the travelers looked on. Coming up to him, they asked why he was shouting in that manner; but he without saying a word removed the rope from his wrist, rose to his feet, mounted Rocinante, braced his buckler on his arm, fixed his lance, and, retiring down the field for some little distance, came back at a half-gallop.

"If there be anyone," he cried, "who says that I deserved to have this spell put upon me, providing the

Princess Micomicona grant me permission to do so, I hereby give him the lie; I defy him and challenge him to single combat."

The new arrivals were amazed by Don Quixote's words, but the landlord explained matters to them by telling them who the knight was, adding that they were to pay no attention to him as he was out of his mind.

The horsemen then make inquiries of the landlord concerning a youth of about fifteen dressed like a muleteer, and he replies that he has not noticed among his guests anyone answering that description. They, however, have observed the judge's coach and are not satisfied with this answer but insist on making a thorough search of the premises.

When he perceived that none of the four travelers was paying the slightest attention to him nor would answer his challenge, Don Quixote was ready to die with rage and spite; and had he found by the ordinances of chivalry that a knight-errant could lawfully assume and undertake any other enterprise than the one for which he had given his word of honor, until his pledge had been fulfilled, he would have attacked them all and compelled them to answer him whether they wished to or not. As it was, he felt that he could not do this until he should have restored Micomicona's kingdom to her. In the meanwhile, he must keep silent, remain quietly where he was, and wait to see what the result of the horsemen's search would be.

Meanwhile the horsemen have found the youth, Don Luis, and inform him that he must come with them; for they are his father's servants who have been sent to look for him. He refuses and an argument ensues,

*with the men threatening to take him by force while he
defies them to do so. The other guests come out and
take a lively interest in the affair. Cardenio attempts
to intervene. His Lordship, recognizing his neighbor's
son, takes Don Luis aside for a talk, requesting the
four servants to be calm as all will be settled properly.
He begins questioning the lad.*

While these and other questions were being asked
and answered, a loud shouting was heard at the gateway of the inn. What had happened was this: two
guests who had been lodged there that night, observing
that everyone was occupied with questioning the four
travelers, had attempted to leave without paying what
they owed; but the innkeeper, who was more attentive
to his own business than to that of others, had waylaid
them as they went out the gate and was demanding that
they pay the score. His language to them was such
that they were led to reply to him with their fists, and
they were laying it on so heavily that the poor landlord
had to cry out for help. His wife and daughter looked
about for someone to aid him, but the only person
whose attention was not taken up was Don Quixote; so
the innkeeper's daughter addressed herself to him.

"Sir Knight," she said, "by the power that God has
reposed in you, I beg you to succor my poor father.
There are two wicked men out there who are beating
him to a pulp."

"Lovely damsel," was the knight's measured and
phlegmatic response, "your request is at this moment
out of place, for I am prevented from entering upon
any other adventure until I shall have fulfilled my word
and brought to a conclusion the one upon which I am at
present embarked. What I may do, however, in order
to serve you is this: run and tell your father to sustain

this combat as best he may and in no wise to allow himself to be vanquished while I go beg permission of the Princess Micomicona to succor him in his distress. If she but grant me that permission, you may rest assured that I will rescue him."

"Sinner that I am!" exclaimed Maritornes when she heard this, "before your Grace obtains the permission you speak of, my master will be in the other world."

"I beg you, lady," replied Don Quixote, "to give me leave to obtain it. Once I have the princess's consent, it will make little difference if your father is in the other world, for I will have him out of it in spite of all that the world in question can do; or, at the least, I will take such vengeance on those who have sent him there that you will be more than moderately satisfied."

Saying no more, he went over and dropped to his knees in front of Dorotea, imploring her in the language of knight-errantry that her Highness be pleased to grant him permission to aid and succor the castellan of that castle, who was in grave peril. The princess gave her consent readily enough, and he then, bracing his buckler and grasping his sword, ran out to the gate of the inn, where the two guests were still mistreating the landlord. But as he came up, he stopped short as if perplexed, although Maritornes and the landlady kept urging him to help their master and husband, asking him why he hesitated.

"If I hesitate," said Don Quixote, "it is for the reason that it is not permitted me to lay hand to sword against those of the rank of squire; but go call my own squire, Sancho, for me, for it appertains to him to undertake this defense and vengeance."

All this took place at the gateway of the inn, where many most effective blows and punches were being exchanged to the great detriment of the landlord as the wrath of Maritornes and of the landlady and her daughter increased; for they were now in despair over Don Quixote's cowardice and the beating that was being administered to their master, husband, and father.

But let us leave him there; for there will surely be someone to succor him; or, if not, let him bear it and hold his peace who is rash enough to attempt more than his strength will warrant.

In response to the judge's questioning the lad confesses that he is in love with Doña Clara and would make her his wife. His Lordship, agreeably surprised by all this, advises him to arrange with the servants not to take him back that day, in order that there may be time to consider what is best for all concerned. He urges him, meanwhile, to be of good cheer. Don Luis bursts into tears and kisses the judge's hands.

By this time the two guests out at the gate had made their peace with the innkeeper and, owing to Don Quixote's mild and persuasive reasoning rather than to any threats on his part, they had paid all that was asked of them. As for Don Luis' servants, they were waiting for him to finish his conversation with the judge and make up his mind what he was going to do, when at that moment—so the devil, who never sleeps, would have it—the very same barber from whom Don Quixote had taken Mambrino's helmet and Sancho the trappings for his ass, came up to the inn. The said barber, as he was leading his beast out to the stable, chanced to catch sight of Sancho Panza, who was engaged in tinkering with his packsaddle, and the instant that he saw him he recognized him.

"Hah! Sir Thief," he cried, "I have you now! Give me back my basin and my packsaddle and all the other things you stole from me."

Sancho, being unexpectedly assailed in this manner and hearing himself called such names, with one hand laid hold of the packsaddle and with the other dealt the barber such a blow that he drenched his teeth in blood. The barber, however, did not for this reason let go his prize in the form of the packsaddle, but began shouting so loud that everybody in the place came running out to see what was the cause of all the uproar and the fighting.

"Here, in the name of the king's justice!" he screamed. "Not satisfied with taking my property, he wants to kill me, this robber, this highway bandit!"

"You lie," said Sancho. "I am not a bandit. My master Don Quixote won those spoils in honorable warfare."

The knight was standing by while this was going on and was greatly pleased to see how well his squire could both defend himself and take the offensive. From that time forth, he was to look upon him as a man of mettle, and he resolved in his heart that upon the first occasion that offered he would have him dubbed a knight, for he felt sure that the order of knighthood might worthily be bestowed upon him. The barber, meanwhile, was running on.

"Gentlemen," he was saying, "this packsaddle is mine, as surely as I owe it to God to die someday. I know it as well as if I had given birth to it. And there is my donkey in the stable; he will not let me lie. If you don't believe me, try it on him, and if it doesn't fit him perfectly, then I'm a rogue. What is more, the same day that he took the packsaddle he also robbed me of a brass basin which I had not yet broken in and which was worth all of a crown."

At this point Don Quixote, unable to contain himself any longer, stepped between the two and parted them, and then, picking up the packsaddle, he placed it upon the ground where all could see it that it might lie there until the truth was established.

"In order," he said, "that your Worships may behold plainly and clearly the error into which this worthy squire has fallen, you have but to observe that he calls a basin that which was, is, and shall be Mambrino's helmet, a trophy won by me in honorable warfare and of which I took lawful and rightful possession! As for the packsaddle, I have nothing to do with that. All I can say is that my squire, Sancho, begged permission of me to strip the mount belonging to this conquered coward of its trappings. To this I consented, and he did so. As to how those trappings came to be converted into a packsaddle, I can give no explanation other than the usual one: namely, that such transformations frequently occur in connection with the practice of chivalry. And by way of confirming all this, run, Sancho my lad, and bring me that helmet which this good man says is a basin."

"Good Lord!" exclaimed Sancho, "if that is all the proof we have that what your Grace says is true, then that basin is just as much Malino's[1] helmet as this good man's trappings are a packsaddle."

"Do what I command you," said Don Quixote; "for surely everything in this castle cannot be controlled by enchantments."

Sancho went for the basin and returned with it, and as soon as Don Quixote saw it he took it up in his hands.

"Your Worships," he said, "can see what cheek this squire has to say that this is a basin and not the helmet of which I have told you. I swear by the calling of knighthood which I follow that this is the same one I took from him and that I have neither added anything to nor subtracted anything from it."

"There can be no doubt of that," remarked Sancho at this point; "for from the time my master won it until the present he has fought but one battle in it, and that was when he freed those poor unfortunate ones that were going along in chains; and if it had not been for this basin-helmet, it would have gone hard with him that time, for there were certainly enough stones thrown."

CHAPTER XLV. *In which the dispute over Mambrino's helmet and the packsaddle is finally settled, with other events that in all truth occurred.*

"WELL, gentlemen," said the barber, "and what do your Worships think of that which these fine fellows have to say, who still insist that this is not a basin but a helmet?"

"And if anyone states the contrary," maintained Don Quixote, "I will have him know that he lies, if he be a knight, and if he be a squire, that he lies a thousand times."

Our own barber, who had witnessed all this and who was well acquainted with Don Quixote's fancies, now decided to fall in with them and carry the joke a little further so that they might all have a good laugh.

"Master barber," he said, addressing the other one, "or whoever you may be, I may inform you that I also am of your profession and have held a license for more than twenty years, being quite familiar with each and every tool that a barber uses. And in my youth I was a soldier for some little while, and I likewise know what a helmet is, and a morion, and a closed helmet, along with other things having to do with a soldier's life. And I can tell you—standing always to be corrected by those of better judgment—that the piece we have before us here, which that worthy gentleman holds in his hands, is as far from being a barber's basin as white is from black or truth from falsehood; and I further assert that it is a helmet, though not a whole one."

"No, certainly not," agreed Don Quixote, "for half of it is missing, that is to say, the beaver."

"That is right," said the curate, who had already divined the intentions of his friend the barber.

Cardenio and Don Fernando and his companions confirmed this; and even the judge, had he not been so preoccupied with Don Luis' affair, would have helped carry on the jest, but, as it was, the weighty matters that he had on his mind prevented him from giving his attention to such trifles.

"God help me!" cried the barber of whom they were making sport. "Is it possible that so many worthy folk can say that this is not a basin but a helmet? It is enough to astonish an entire university, however learned it may be. But enough; if this basin is a helmet, then this saddlebag must be a horse's trappings, as this gentleman has just stated."

"It looks to me like a saddlebag," Don Quixote admitted, "but as I have said, it is something that does not concern me."

"As to whether it be a saddlebag or a horse's trappings," said the curate, "Don Quixote has but to give us his opinion, for in matters pertaining to chivalry, I and all these gentlemen bow to him."

"In God's name, my good folk," said Don Quixote, "so many strange things have happened in this castle on the two occasions that I have tarried here that I should not venture to give a positive reply to a question regarding anything that is in it, for it is my belief that all that takes place within its confines is the result of magic. The first time that I was here, there was an enchanted Moor who gave me a great deal of trouble, while Sancho did not make out any too well with some of his followers. And then, last night, I was strung up by this arm for nearly two hours without knowing how or why I came to be in such straits. And so, in a matter as far from clear as the present one, if I were to undertake to give an opinion, I should run the risk of rendering a rash decision. As to the charge that this is a basin and not a helmet, I have already answered that, but when it comes to declaring whether that is a saddlebag or a horse's trappings, I shall not venture to make any definite statement but shall leave it to your Worships' own good judgment. It may be that, inasmuch as you have not been dubbed knights as I have been, your Worships will not be subject to the enchantments of this place and, accordingly, your judgment being unimpaired, will be able to form an impression of things in this castle as they really and truly are and not as they appear to me to be."

"There is no doubt," said Don Fernando in reply to this, "that Don Quixote has put the case very well and that the decision rests with us; and in order that we may proceed upon firm ground, I will take the secret votes of these gentlemen and will announce the result plainly and fully."

To those acquainted with Don Quixote's mad whims, all this was very amusing indeed, but to the rest it seemed utter nonsense. This was especially true of Don Luis' four servants, and of their master as well, so far as that was concerned; besides whom there were three other travelers who had just arrived at the inn and who had the appearance of being patrolmen of the Holy Brotherhood, as in fact they were. The one, however, who was the most desperately bewildered of all was the barber, whose basin, there in front of his eyes, had turned into Mambrino's helmet, and whose packsaddle, also, he had not the slightest doubt, was due to turn into the rich caparison of a steed. The others, meanwhile, were laughing heartily as Don Fernando went around collecting the votes, whispering in the ear of each and asking him to give his private opinion as to whether the treasure over which there was so much dispute was a packsaddle or equine trappings.

Having obtained the votes of all those who knew Don Quixote, he turned to the barber and said, "The truth of the matter is, my good man, I am tired of gathering all these opinions; for there is not a one to whom I have put the question who has not assured me that it is non-sense to say that this is the packsaddle of an ass, when it is plain to be seen that it is the caparison of a horse and of a thoroughbred horse at that. And so there is nothing for you to do but yield, since in spite of you and your ass it is in fact a horse's trappings, and you have presented and proved your case very badly."

"May I forfeit my interest in Heaven!" [1] cried the poor barber, "if your Worships are not all mistaken. As my soul must appear before God, so does this appear to me to be a saddlebag; but 'laws go—' [2] I say no more; and I am not drunk, for I am fasting this morning—unless it be from sin."

These stupid remarks on the part of the barber aroused no less laughter than did Don Quixote's foolish talk; and it was now the knight's turn.

"There is nothing more to be done here," he announced, "except for each to take that which is his, and may St. Peter bless him to whom God has given it."

One of Don Luis' servants was the next to speak. "Unless this is a deliberate joke," he said, "I cannot believe that men of such good sense as all of those present are, or appear to be, would be so bold as to state and maintain that this is not a basin nor that a packsaddle; but inasmuch as I perceive that they do state and maintain it, I cannot but believe that there is some mystery behind their insistence upon something that is so contrary to what truth and experience teaches. For I swear"—and swear he did, a good round oath—"that all the people now living in the world will never convince me that this is not a barber's basin, and that, the packsaddle of an ass."

"It might be a she-ass," remarked the curate.

"It's all the same," said the servant. "That's not the point. The point is whether this is or, as your Graces say, is not a packsaddle."

Hearing this, one of the troopers who had come in and had been listening to the argument cried out angrily, "That is as much a packsaddle as my father is my father, and he who says anything else must be drunk."

"You lie like a peasant knave!" replied Don Quixote. And, raising his pike, which he never let out of his hands, he aimed such a blow at the trooper's head that if the officer had not dodged, it would have left him stretched out on the ground. The pike as it struck the ground was shattered to bits; whereupon the other officers, seeing their companion asaulted in this manner, cried out for help in the name of the Holy Brotherhood. The innkeeper, who was one of the band, at once ran to get his staff of office and his sword and, returning, took his place alongside his comrades. Don Luis' servants surrounded their master that he might not escape amid the excitement; and the barber, perceiving that the household was turned upside down, once more seized his packsaddle as Sancho did the same.

Drawing his sword, Don Quixote attacked the officers, while Don Luis cried to his servants to release him and go to the aid of the knight and of Cardenio and Don Fernando, both of whom were lending their support. The curate shouted, the landlady screamed, her daughter wailed, Maritornes wept, Dorotea was dumfounded, Luscinda terrified, and Doña Clara ready to faint. The barber cudgeled Sancho, and Sancho mauled the barber. Don Luis, when one of his servants seized his arm to keep him from running away, gave the fellow a punch that bloodied his mouth, and the judge came to the lad's defense. Don Fernando had a trooper down and was kicking him vigorously, and the innkeeper was again raising his voice to call for help for the Holy Brotherhood. In short, the entire hostelry was filled with shouts, cries, screams, with tumult, terror, and confusion, with sword slashes, fisticuffs, cudgelings, kickings, bloodshed, and mishaps of every sort. And in the midst of all this hubbub and labyrinthine chaos, Don Quixote came to imagine that he had been plunged headlong into the discord of Agramante's camp.[3]

"Hold, all of you!" he suddenly cried in a voice that rocked the inn like thunder. "Sheathe your swords, be calm, and hear me as you value your lives!"

At this mighty sound they all stopped short.

"Did I not tell you, gentlemen," he went on, "that this castle was enchanted and that it must be inhabited by some legion of devils? In confirmation of which, I would have you note how the strife that marked the camp of Agramante has been transferred and repeated here in front of your very eyes. Look you how here they fight for the sword, there for the horse, over there for the eagle, and there for the helmet. We are all engaged in fighting one another without knowing why. Come, then, your Lordship the judge and your Reverence the curate; let one of you take the part of King Agramante and the other that of King Sobrino, and make peace between us. For it is a very great shame for so many persons of high rank as are gathered here to be killing one another over causes so trifling."

The officers of the Brotherhood, who did not understand what Don Quixote was talking about, but who did know that they were being mishandled by Don Fernando, Cardenio, and their companions, were of no mind to calm themselves. The barber, however, was; for in the course of the fray both his beard and his packsaddle had suffered considerably. As for Sancho, he obeyed, as a good servant does, his master's slightest command, while Don Luis' four men likewise were quiet, seeing how little they had gained by not being so. The innkeeper alone was insisting that he had to punish the insolence of that madman who was all the time throwing his place into an uproar. But at last the tumult died down, the packsaddle remained a caparison and the basin a helmet until the Day of Judgment, and the inn was still a castle in Don Quixote's imagination.

As order is finally restored and all become friends once more, Don Luis' servants take him aside for a talk. The judge does the same with Fernando, Cardenio, and the curate, repeating to them what the lad has told him and asking their advice as to what should be done. It is decided that Don Fernando is to reveal his identity and rank to the servants and offer to take the young man with him to the home of Fernando's brother, a marquis, until an understanding can be reached with the youth's father.

Accordingly, when the four of them learned who Don Fernando was and saw how their master felt about it, they decided that three of their number should go back to inform the lad's father of how matters stood, while the fourth should remain to wait upon Don Luis, with the understanding that he was not to leave him until they returned or until it was known what the father's orders were.

In this manner, then, through the prestige of Agramante and the wisdom of King Sobrino, all the fighting at cross-purposes was finally quelled; but with this, the enemy of peace and concord, seeing himself thus despised and made sport of, and perceiving how little he had gained by setting them all against one another, resolved to try his hand once again by stirring up more strife and tumult.

As it happened, the officers of the Brotherhood had quieted down upon learning the rank of those with whom they were fighting and had been glad enough to retire from the fray, since it seemed to them that, whatever the outcome, they were bound to get the worst of it. One of them, however, the one who had been beaten and trampled by Don Fernando, chanced to remember that among the warrants he carried for the arrest of certain offenders was a writ for Don Quixote, whom the Holy Brotherhood had been instructed to apprehend on the charge of having freed the galley slaves, just as Sancho had rightly feared. An idea having come to him now, he wished to satisfy himself as to whether the knight answered the description that he had of him; and, taking a parchment out of his bosom, he found the document he was looking for and then began reading it slowly (for he was not a good reader), glancing up at every word to see if Don Quixote's features corresponded with those set down in the writ. Deciding that this was undoubtedly his man, he then took the parchment in his left hand and with his right seized Don Quixote by the collar so forcefully that he nearly choked him.

"Help for the Holy Brotherhood!" he cried in a loud voice. "And in order that you may see that I ask it in earnest, you have but to read this warrant where it is set forth that this highwayman is to be arrested."

The curate took the warrant and saw that what the officer said was true and that the description did indeed fit Don Quixote. But the knight, finding himself thus manhandled by this knavish boor, grew exceedingly angry and, with every bone in his body creaking, he seized the officer's throat with all the strength he could muster and would have choked the life out of him if the other troopers had not come to their comrade's rescue. The landlord, who was bound to render help to other members of the fraternity, now came running up, while his wife, believing her husband was again about to become involved in a fight, raised her voice and began screaming, in which she was at once joined by Maritornes and her daughter as all three of them called on Heaven and the others present to lend their aid.

"Good Lord!" cried Sancho, when he saw what was happening, "it is true what my master says about this castle being enchanted, for it is impossible to live an hour in peace here."

Don Fernando then separated the patrolman and Don Quixote, each of them being glad enough to have the other's firm grip released, on his jacket collar in the one case and on his throat in the other instance. The officers did not, however, for this reason give up their demand for the knight's arrest but insisted that the others help bind and deliver him into the hands of the law and thereby render a service to their king and to the Holy Brotherhood, in whose name they once more sought aid and assistance in effecting the capture of this highway bandit.

Don Quixote smiled as he heard these words. When he spoke, it was very calmly. "Come, now," he said, "you vile and lowborn wretches, do you call him a highwayman who gives freedom to those in chains, succors those who are in distress, lifts up the fallen, and brings aid to the needy? Ah, infamous rabble, by reason of your low and filthy minds you do not deserve that Heaven should reveal to you the true worth of knight-errantry and your own sin and ignorance when you fail to reverence the shadow, not to speak of the presence, of any knight-errant whatsoever! Come, come, you are a band of robbers, not of officers, footpads of the highway with the license of the Holy Brotherhood. Tell me, who was the ignorant one who signed that warrant for the arrest of such a knight as I am? Who is so ignorant as not to know that knights-errant are beyond all jurisdiction, their only law their swords, while their charter is their mettle and their will is their decrees?

"Who, I ask it again, is the stupid one who does not know that there are no letters-patent of nobility that confer such privileges and exemptions as those that a knight-errant acquires the day he is dubbed a knight and devotes himself to the rigorous duties of his calling? When did such a knight ever pay poll-tax, excise, queen's pattens, king's levies, toll, or ferry? What tailor ever took payment for the clothes he made for him? What castellan who received him in his castle ever made him pay his score? What king would not seat him at his board? What damsel but did love him, being ready to yield herself wholly to his will and pleasure? And, finally, what knight-errant was there ever, or ever will be in this world, without the mettle to deal single-handed four hundred sturdy blows to any four hundred officers of the Holy Brotherhood that come his way?"

CHAPTER XLVI. *Wherein is concluded the notable adventure of the troopers, together with an account of the great ferocity of our good knight, Don Quixote.*

EVEN as Don Quixote spoke, the curate was endeavoring to convince the officers that the knight was not in his right mind, as they should be able to see from what he said and did, and that, accordingly, they ought to let the matter drop, since even though they did arrest him and take him away, they would only have to turn him loose again as being a madman. To which the one who held the warrant replied that it was not for him to judge Don Quixote's sanity but rather to carry out the orders of his superior, adding that once he had made the arrest, they might let him go three hundred times over if they chose.

"Nevertheless," said the curate, "for this once you are not going to take him, nor will he permit himself to be taken unless I miss my guess."

The short of it is, the curate was so very persuasive, and Don Quixote so very mad in his actions, that the troopers would have been even madder than he was had they not recognized his want of wit. And so they thought it best to allow themselves to be pacified and even to act as peacemakers between the barber and Sancho Panza, who were still engaged in a heated quarrel. As the representatives of the law they proceeded to arbitrate the dispute and did it in such a manner that both parties were, if not wholly, at least somewhat satisfied; for they exchanged the packsaddles but not the girths nor the headstalls. As for Mambrino's helmet, the curate quietly, and without Don Quixote's knowledge, gave the barber eight reales for it, obtaining from him a receipt with the understanding that he was to make no more mistaken demands, for the present or for all time to come, Amen.

The landlord, noticing the gift that the curate made to the barber, now demands that Don Quixote pay for a night's lodging and also for the wineskins and the wine that was spilled. The curate soothes him and Don Fernando generously settles for everything.

Don Quixote then decides that the time has come to start on the expedition to Micomicon and indulges in a flowery exchange of speeches with Dorotea to this effect. But just as he is ordering Sancho to saddle Rocinante and the "queen's" palfrey and harness the ass, the squire blurts out a story about having seen Dorotea "rubbing noses with a certain one who is here, every time you turn your head, and behind every door"; for he has come upon her and Fernando in the act of kissing, and he is afraid the latter will "gather the fruit of our labor."

This provokes an outburst of rage on Don Quixote's part, directed at Sancho, whom he accuses of being a "villainous, ignorant, foul-mouthed, loose-tongued backbiter and slanderer." Dorotea, however, appeases the knight by explaining that, as he well knows, "everything in this castle happens by way of enchantment . . . and Sancho must have been led by diabolic means to see that which he says he beheld and which is so great an offense to my honor." As for Sancho, he is will-

ing to accept the enchantment theory except where his blanketing is concerned; that, he insists, was very, very real.

Two days had now gone by since all this illustrious company was gathered in the inn, and it seemed to them all that it was high time to be on their way. It was accordingly agreed that, without putting Dorotea and Don Fernando to the trouble of accompanying Don Quixote to his native village, under pretext of liberating the Queen Micomicona, the curate and the barber instead should take the knight with them as they had suggested, and once they had got him safely home, they would see what could be done about curing his madness. With this object in view, they proceeded to arrange with an ox-cart driver who chanced to be passing that way to bear their friend off in the following manner: first, they constructed a kind of cage with wooden bars, capable of holding him comfortably; after which, Don Fernando and his companions, along with Don Luis' servants, the troopers, and the landlord, all of them acting under the curate's direction, covered their faces and disguised themselves in one fashion or another so that Don Quixote would not recognize them as his acquaintances of the inn.

Having done this, they very quietly entered the room where he lay sleeping and resting from his recent frays, wholly unsuspecting of anything of this sort. Going up to him, they seized him firmly and bound him hand and foot, so that when he awoke with a start, he was unable to move or do anything except marvel at finding himself surrounded by so many strange faces. As a result, his disordered mind at once began to fancy that all these figures were phantoms of that enchanted castle and that he himself, without a doubt, was under a magic spell, seeing that he could not move nor defend himself. All of which was just as the curate, the originator of this scheme, had planned it.

Sancho alone of all those present was at once in his right mind and proper character, and while he was near to being as mad as his master, he did not fail to recognize these disguised figures; but he did not dare open his mouth until he saw what the outcome of this assault and capture would be. As for Don Quixote, he said not a word, for he too was waiting to see what was going to happen to him further. What happened was: they took him to the cage and shut him in it, nailing the bars so firmly that they could not easily be broken down.

As they lifted him on their shoulders and bore him from the room, there was heard an awe-inspiring voice —as much so as the barber (not he of the packsaddle but the other one) could make it.

"O Knight of the Mournful Countenance, be not grieved by the prison in which thou goest, for it is a fitting thing in order that thou mayest the sooner bring to a conclusion the adventure to which thy great courage hath impelled thee. That shall be when the raging Manchegan lion[1] and the white Tobosan dove shall have been made one, after they shall have bowed their proud necks to the gentle yoke of matrimony. And from this mating, of a kind that never was before, shall come forth into the light of this world brave whelps which shall emulate the ravening claws of their valiant sire. And this shall be ere the pursuer of the fleeing nymph in his swift and natural course shall twice have visited the luminous signs.

"And thou, O noblest and most obedient squire that ever girded on a sword, wore a beard on his face, or had a nose to smell with! be thou not dismayed nor unhappy at thus beholding the flower of knight-errantry borne

away in front of your very eyes; for soon, if it be pleasing to Him who fashioned this world, thou shalt see thyself raised to so sublime a height that thou shalt not
know thyself, nor shalt thou be defrauded of all the
promises which thy good master hath made thee. And
be assured on the part of the wise Mentironiana[2] that
thou shalt be paid thy wages, as thou shalt see in due
course. Do thou, then, continue to follow in the footsteps of this valiant and enchanted knight; for it behooves thee to go whither both of you are bound. It is
not permitted me to say more; and so, may God be with
thee, for I now return to the place that I well know."

As he concluded this prophecy, the barber raised and
lowered his voice with so intense an emotional effect
that even those who knew it to be a jest almost believed
that it was the truth they heard. Don Quixote was
greatly consoled by these predictions, for he at once
grasped their purport, to the effect that he was to be
united in holy and lawful bonds of matrimony with his
beloved Dulcinea del Toboso, from whose fortunate
loins should come forth whelps that were his sons, to
the perpetual glory of La Mancha. Thoroughly imbued
with this belief, he heaved a deep sigh and, lifting up
his voice, he spoke as follows:

"O thou, whoever thou art, who hast prophesied all
these blessings for me! I implore thee on my behalf to
ask the wise enchanter who hath these things in his
charge not to allow me to perish in this captivity in
which they now bear me away before I shall have seen
fulfilled all the joyful and incomparable promises that
have just been made me. Let this be granted me and I
shall glory in the sufferings of my prison house, my
chains will be light indeed, and this bed upon which
they lay me will be, not a hard-fought battlefield, but a
soft and happy nuptial couch. As for the consolation

that has been offered to Sancho Panza, my squire, I can only say that I rely upon his goodness and integrity, trusting him never to leave me in good fortune or in bad. And if by his or my own ill luck I should not be able to give him the island or some equivalent fief as I have promised, at least his wages shall not be forfeited; for in my will, which is already drawn up, I have declared that which is to be his, not in proportion to his many and faithful services, but in accordance with my means."

At this Sancho bowed most respectfully and kissed both his master's hands, it being impossible for him to kiss but one of them as they were tied together. Then those phantom figures put the cage upon their shoulders and carried it out and placed it on the ox-cart.

CHAPTER XLVII. *Of the strange manner in which a spell was laid on Don Quixote de la Mancha, together with other remarkable occurrences.*

WHEN Don Quixote found himself caged in this manner and placed upon the cart, he spoke as follows:

"Many very grave histories have I read of knights-errant, but never have I read, seen, or heard of enchanted knights being borne away in this fashion and at the slow pace that these lazy animals seem likely to provide; for it is the custom to spirit them through the air, with marvelous speed, wrapped in some dark, dense cloud or upon a chariot of fire or some hippogriff or other similar beast. But that they should now be taking me upon an ox-cart, Heaven help me, that is something I cannot understand! [1] However, it may be that chivalry and the art of magic in this our time must follow another path than the one it did in days gone by. And it may also be that, inasmuch as I am a new knight in this world, the first to revive the forgotten calling of knightly adventurers, they may likewise have invented other means of enchantment and other ways of carrying off the enchanted. What do you think of it, Sancho, my son?"

"I don't know what I think," replied Sancho, "not being as well read as is your Grace in the writings of errantry. But for all of that, I'd venture to swear and affirm that those apparitions are not altogether Catholic."

"Catholic? My father!" said Don Quixote. "How can they be Catholic if they are all demons who have assumed fantastic shapes in order to do this thing and put me in this condition? If you would ascertain the truth, you have but to touch and feel them and you will perceive that they have none but an airy body and consist only of appearances."

"By God, sir," Sancho answered him, "I've already touched them, and that devil you see bustling along there is as plump as can be and it's real flesh that's on him; and there is something else about him that is very different from what I have heard tell of demons, for they say that they all stink of sulphur and other evil smells, but you can scent the amber on this one half a league away."

He was speaking of Don Fernando, who as a gentleman must of necessity give off the odor that Sancho had mentioned.

"You need not marvel at that, friend Sancho," said Don Quixote; "for I would have you know that the devils are very wise, and while they bear odors with them, they themselves smell of nothing, since, being spirits, they can emit no scent whatsoever, or if they do smell, it is not of anything pleasant but rather something evil and fetid. The reason for this is that, wherever they may be, they bring with them Hell itself and can receive no manner of comfort in their torments; and inasmuch as a pleasing fragrance is something that gives delight and happiness, it is obviously impossible for them to be possessed of such a thing. Accordingly, if this devil appears to you to smell of amber, either you are mistaken or he is trying to deceive you so that you will not take him to be a devil."

As this conversation occurred between master and man, Don Fernando and Cardenio began to fear that Sancho would discover the entire plot, for he had already gone a long way toward doing so. They therefore decided to hasten their departure and, calling the landlord to one side, they directed him to saddle Rocinante and put the packsaddle on Sancho's ass, which he did very quickly. The curate, meanwhile, had arranged with the troopers to accompany them as far as the village, promising to pay them so much a day. Cardenio then hung the buckler on one side of the saddletree and the basin on the other and made signs to Sancho to mount his ass and take Rocinante's rein, while the two troopers[2] with their muskets were placed one on either side of the cart. Before that vehicle could get under way, however, the landlady, her daughter, and Maritornes came running out to say good-by to Don Quixote, shedding feigned tears of sorrow over his plight.

"Do not weep, my good ladies," he now said to them, "for all these misfortunes are such as go with the calling that I profess; indeed, if they did not befall me, I should not look upon myself as a famous knight-errant. Such things never happen to knights of little name and reputation for the reason that no one in the world gives them a thought. With the valiant ones it is otherwise, for many princes and many other knights envy them their virtue and their valor and are bent upon destroying the worthy by foul means. But in spite of all this, virtue is omnipotent and, notwithstanding all the necromancy that Zoroaster, first inventor of the art, ever knew, will emerge triumphant from every peril and bestow light on the world as does the sun in the heavens. Forgive me, fair ladies, if, without meaning to do so, I have given you any offense, for I would not willingly and knowingly offend anyone. Pray, then, to God to rescue me from this captivity in which some enchanter of evil intent has placed me; and when I am free, I will by no means forget the favors which you in this castle have shown me, but will acknowledge, requite, and reward them as they deserve."

As the "ladies of the castle" are conversing with Don Quixote, the others take leave of one another. The innkeeper comes up and hands the curate some papers which he says he found in the lining of the trunk or valise where the "Story of the One Who Was Too Curious for His Own Good" had been discovered. He tells the curate to keep them, as he himself does not know how to read. Among the manuscripts is "The Story of Rinconete and Cortadillo."

The party then gets under way. First comes the cart, driven by its owner. The two officers of the Holy Brotherhood march along at the side, and Sancho Panza follows on his ass, leading Rocinante, while the curate and the barber, seated on their mules and still wearing their masks, bring up the rear. Don Quixote sits in the cage with his hands bound and his feet stretched out; he leans patiently back against the bars and is as silent as a stone statue.

The procession has not gone far when it is over-

taken by a group of riders who prove to be a canon of Toledo and his attendants. His curiosity aroused by the sight before him, the canon inquires of the troopers what the meaning of it all is. Don Quixote answers him in the jargon of chivalry that he customarily speaks, asserting that he is being carried away "as a result of the envy and deceit of wicked magicians," and the curate bears him out in this, whereupon the churchman is more puzzled than ever.

When the canon heard both the prisoner and the one who walked free beside him speak in this manner, he was ready to cross himself from astonishment and could not believe his own ears, while all his companions were equally amazed. Then it was that Sancho Panza, who had drawn near to listen to their talk, put the finishing touch on it all.

"Well, sirs," he said, "whether or not you like what I am going to say, the fact is that my master, Don Quixote, is no more enchanted than my mother, for he has all his senses about him and eats and drinks and attends to his necessities like the rest of us, just as he did yesterday before they put him in this cage. This being so, how would you have me believe that he is enchanted? For I have heard many people say that those that are under a magic spell neither eat nor sleep nor speak, whereas my master, if you do not take him in hand, will do more talking than thirty lawyers."

Turning, then, to look the curate in the face, he went on, "Ah, Señor Curate! Señor Curate! So, your Grace thought I didn't know you and that I would not guess what the purpose of these new enchantments is? Well, then, I can tell you that I recognize you no matter how much you cover your face and that I know what you are up to no matter how cleverly and deceitfully you attempt to hide it. In short, where envy reigns virtue cannot live, nor generosity where there is miserliness. Devil take it all, if it wasn't for your Reverence, my master would be getting married to the Princess Micomicona right now and I would be a count at the very least, since I could expect no less from my kind-hearted master, him of the Mournful Countenance, after all that I have done for him. But now I see that it is true what they say hereabouts, that fortune's wheel turns faster than that of a mill, and those that yesterday were up on top today are down on the ground.

"It grieves me to think about my wife and children, who rightly expect to see their father and husband returning home and coming through the door as governor or viceroy of some island or kingdom, and instead they will see him coming in as a stable boy. All this that I am saying to you, Señor Curate, is by way of urging your Paternity to have a conscience and not treat my master so badly as you are doing; for look well to it that God in the other life does not ask you to account for holding Señor Don Quixote a prisoner like this, and hold you responsible for all the good my master might have done and the aid he might have given others during all this time."

"Trim those lamps for me!" [3] cried the barber at this point. "So you, Sancho, are of the same confraternity as your master, are you? Good lord, but I'm beginning to think you ought to be in the cage there with him, for you're as much bewitched as he is when it comes to the subject of chivalry! It was an evil day for you when your brains became impregnated with all those promises that he made you and you got that island into your head that you've so set your heart on."

"I'm not pregnant by anybody," declared Sancho, "nor am I the man to let myself be put in that condition by any king that ever lived. I may be poor, but I'm an old Christian and I don't owe anyone anything. If I want islands, there are others who want worse things. Each one is the son of his own works, and being a man I may come to be pope, not to speak of being governor of an island; for my master may win so many that there will not be people enough to give them to. Sir Barber, you had better watch what you say, for sharing isn't everything and there is some difference between Peter and Peter. I say this because we all know one another and it won't do to throw false dice with me. And as for my master's being enchanted, God knows the truth, so leave it as it is, for it is better not to stir it."

The barber did not care to answer Sancho for fear that the latter in his simple-mindedness would reveal what he and the curate were trying so hard to conceal.

The curate and the canon ride ahead together, and their talk turns to the romances of chivalry. The canon, after denouncing them as ridiculous, false, and "harmful to the well-being of the state," goes on to discuss what works of fiction should be.

"For in works of fiction there should be a mating between the plot and the reader's intelligence. They should be so written that the impossible is made to appear possible, things hard to believe being smoothed over and the mind held in suspense in such a manner as to create surprise and astonishment while at the same time they divert and entertain so that admiration and pleasure go hand in hand. But these are things which he cannot accomplish who flees verisimilitude and the imitation of nature, qualities that go to constitute perfection in the art of writing.

"Never," concluded the canon, "have I seen any book

of chivalry that held the body of a story completely
with all its members so that the middle was consistent
with the beginning and the end with the beginning and
the middle. Rather, they are made up of so many dis-
parate members that it would seem the author's intention was to create a chimera or a monster rather than
a well-proportioned figure. In addition to all this, they
are crude in style, unconvincing in the exploits that they
relate, lascivious in the love affairs that they portray, uncouth in their efforts at courtliness, prolix in their description of battles, absurd in their dialogue, nonsensical
in their accounts of journeyings, and, finally, destitute
of anything that resembles art; for which reason it is
they deserve to be banished from the Christian state as
not being of public utility."

*This discussion continues to the end of the chapter
(Chapter XLVII) and into the next.*

CHAPTER XLVIII. *In which the canon continues his
discourse on the subject of books of chivalry, with
other matters worthy of his intelligence.*

"IT IS as your Grace has said, Señor Canon," remarked the curate, "and for that reason they are all
the more deserving of reprehension who up to now have
composed such books without giving any thought to
good taste or the rules of art by which they might have
been guided, and thereby have rendered themselves as
famous in prose as the two princes of Greek and Latin
poetry are in verse."

"However that may be," replied the canon, "I myself
was once tempted to write a book of chivalry, observing
all the points that I have mentioned; and if I am to

confess the truth, I have more than a hundred sheets
already written. By way of putting them to the test and
seeing if they were as good as I thought they were, I
have submitted them to certain individuals who are
passionately fond of this type of reading. Some of these
persons were wise and learned, while others were ignorant, being concerned solely with the pleasure they
derive from listening to nonsense, but all of them were
warmly appreciative of my effort. I did not go on, however, for it seemed to me, on the one hand, that I was
engaged in doing something that was foreign to my
profession, and, on the other hand, the foolish impressed
me as being more numerous than the wise; and while
the praise of the discerning few offsets the scorn of the
unknowing many, I still did not care to subject myself
to the confused judgment of that vapid public to which
the reading of such works is for the most part confined.

"But what did most to stay my hand and even caused
me to give up all thought of finishing what I had begun
was an argument that I put to myself, drawn from the
comedies that are now being performed. It ran as follows: All of these pieces, or the greater part of them at
any rate, whether purely fictitious or historical in character, are obviously nonsensical, without head or tail,
yet the public takes pleasure in witnessing them and
regards them as worthy productions, though they are
far from good. And the authors who compose them and
the actors who perform them tell us that plays have to
be of this sort, since the public wants precisely that
kind of thing and nothing else, whereas those pieces
that have a plot and develop the story in an artistic
fashion will appeal only to a handful of intelligent persons who are able to understand them, while all the
others will fail to perceive the art that is in them. This
being so, they—the authors and actors—prefer to gain

their bread with the many rather than subsist on the good opinion of the few. In which case, my book, after I should have scorched my eyebrows in an attempt to observe the precepts I have mentioned, would meet with the same fate as other works of merit, and I should end up by being the tailor of El Campillo.[1]

"Although I have a number of times endeavored to persuade the actors that they are wrong in the view they hold, and that they would attract more people and win more fame for themselves by producing comedies that follow the rules of art than they do by performing in these silly ones, they are so firmly set in their opinion that no amount of reasoning or evidence will convince them that they are wrong. I remember saying to one of the stubborn fellows once upon a time: 'Do you not recall that, only a few years ago, there were three tragedies put upon the boards here in Spain, written by a famous poet of this realm, which were so pleasing as to arouse the admiration and hold the interest of all who heard them, the simple as well as the wise, the general public as well as the select few, and which brought in more money to the performers—these three alone— than thirty of the best that up to then had been produced?'

"'You mean, of course,' the author replied, 'the *Isabella*, the *Phyllis*, and the *Alexandra?*'[2]

"'Yes,' I said, 'those are the ones of which I am speaking, and see if they do not well observe the rules of art, and if, superior creations that they are, they are not still pleasing to everyone. The fault therefore lies not with the public that asks for silly pieces, but with those who do not know how to put on anything else. The *Ingratitude Avenged* was not nonsense; neither was the *Numantia*, nor *The Merchant Lover*, and certainly not *The Fair and Favoring Enemy;*[3] and the same might be said of others composed by intelligent poets, to their own fame and renown and the profit of those who put on the plays.'

"I had other things to say along the same line, which left him, I thought, a bit embarrassed but by no means sufficiently convinced to give up his erroneous opinion."

"Señor Canon," said the curate, "by touching upon this subject you have awakened an old grudge of mine against the comedies of today, one that is equal to that which I hold against books of chivalry. For, according to Tully, a comedy should be a mirror of human life, an example of manners, and an image of the truth;[4] yet those that we see now are mirrors of nonsense, examples of foolishness, and images of lasciviousness. In connection with the subject of which we are speaking, what could be more absurd than for a character to appear as an infant in Act I, Scene 1, and in the following scene step out as a full-bearded man? What more out of place than to depict for us an old man parading his valor, a youth who plays the cringing coward, an eloquent lackey, a page wise in giving counsel, a king turned porter, or a princess serving as a kitchen wench?

"And what shall I say of the attention that is paid to the element of time in connection with the action that is represented? I may merely tell you that I have witnessed a comedy in which the first act takes place in Europe, the second in Asia, and the third in Africa— and if there had been a fourth act, the scene would have been laid in America and thus they would have encompassed the four quarters of the globe. If fidelity to life be the principal object which a comedy should have in view, how is it possible for the most mediocre intelligence to find any satisfaction in one where the action is supposed to take place in the time of King Pepin or Charlemagne, yet which has for its leading character the

Emperor Heraclius entering Jerusalem with the Holy
Cross and recovering the Holy Sepulcher like Godefroi
de Bouillon, when there is a vast stretch of time between the two monarchs? Or in one which, essentially
fictitious, makes a pretense at historical accuracy by
mingling odds and ends of various events that happened
to different persons at different times, and this with no
attempt at verisimilitude but with obvious errors that
are utterly inexcusable? And the sad part of it is, there
are ignorant ones who say that this is the perfect thing
and all the rest is affectation.

"And then, coming to religious dramas, what do we
find? How many false miracles do their authors invent,
how many apocryphal and erroneous incidents, with
the wonders worked by one saint attributed to another!
And even in those comedies that deal with human
themes they dare to introduce miracles without rhyme
or reason, merely because they think that such a scenic
effect,[5] as they term it, will fit in well and serve to
attract the ignorant, who will come to see the play and
marvel at it. All of which is prejudicial to the truth,
tending to corrupt history and cast opprobrium upon the
Spanish genius; for those foreigners[6] that scrupulously
observe the rules of comedy are led to look upon us as
unschooled barbarians by reason of the absurdity and
nonsense to be found in the productions of our theater.

"Nor is it a sufficient excuse for all this to say that
the principal object which well-ordered states have in
view in permitting the public performance of comedies
is to provide the community with a little harmless recreation now and then and thus divert those evil impulses
that idleness is wont to breed. It may be said that this
end is attained by any comedy, good or bad, and that
there is no necessity of laying down laws to govern the
composition and performance of such pieces, since, as

I have said, the same object is achieved by any kind of play. To this I would reply that it is, beyond any comparison, better achieved by good plays than by the other kind.

"For when he has witnessed a comedy that is well and artfully constructed, the spectator will come out laughing at its humor, enlightened by the truths it contained, marveling at the various incidents, rendered wiser by the arguments, made more wary by the snares he has seen depicted, and more prudent by the examples afforded him; he will leave the theater hating vice and in love with virtue; such are the effects that a good comedy has upon the mind of the listener, however boorish and dull-witted he may be. Nothing, in short, is more impossible than that the play that contains all these qualities should fail to provide more entertainment, satisfaction, and pleasure than the one lacking in them, as is the case with the majority of those that are at present to be viewed.

"It is not the dramatic poets who are to blame for this state of affairs; for many of them are fully conscious of their faults and know very well what ought to be done. But inasmuch as comedies have become salable commodities, the poets in question will tell us, and in this they are right, that their plays will not be bought unless they are after the accepted pattern, and, accordingly, the author seeks to adapt himself to what the actor who is to pay him for his work requires of him. That this is so may be seen from the countless number of comedies composed by one of the most fertile minds[7] in this realm, plays so full of brilliancy and grace, marked by such polished versification, admirable dialogue, and profound wisdom, and, finally, so full of eloquence and so elevated in style, that his fame has gone out to all the world; and yet, owing to the necessity he has been under of having to adapt them to the taste of the players, not all his productions have attained that degree of perfection that is to be desired.

"Still others compose their pieces without giving a thought to what they are doing; and, as a result, after the performance, the actors have to take to their heels and flee for fear of being punished, as they oftentimes have been, for having put something on the stage that was offensive to a certain monarch or that cast aspersions on some noble house. But all these improprieties would cease, and with them many others that I do not mention, if there were at court some wise and intelligent person to examine all the comedies before they are put on,[8] not only those that are to be performed in the capital but those that are to be produced in other parts of Spain as well, and without the approval, seal, and signature of that individual no local officer of the crown should permit any comedy to be staged. Under such a system, the performers would be at pains to forward their plays to the capital for inspection and then would be able to act in them with safety, while the authors, knowing that their works would have to pass a rigorous and intelligent censorship and being fearful of offending, would devote more care and attention to them, and as a consequence would produce good comedies, thus achieving in a felicitous manner the objectives for which they strive: the entertainment of the people and, at the same time, the furthering of the reputation of Spanish dramatists and of the interest and security of the performers, the necessity of punishing the latter having been removed."

At this point, having reached a suitable place, they halt for their noontide rest and begin their preparations for a repast.

While this was going on, Sancho decided to take advantage of the opportunity to speak to his master without the constant presence of the curate and the barber, whom he looked upon with suspicion.

"Master," he said, going up to the cage, "I want to get a load off my conscience by telling you what goes on in connection with your enchantment. The truth of the matter is that those two with their faces covered are the curate of our village and the barber, and it is my belief that they have plotted to carry you off like this out of pure spite, because your Grace is so far ahead of them in famous deeds. If this is so, then it follows that you are not under a spell at all but have been hoodwinked and made a fool of. Just to prove this, I'd like to ask you one thing, and if you answer me as I think you will have to, then you'll be able to lay your hand on what's wrong and will see that you are not enchanted but simply out of your head."

"Ask me whatever you like, Sancho my son," replied Don Quixote, "and I will give you an answer that will satisfy you on every point. As to what you say about those who accompany us being the curate and the barber, our fellow townsmen whom we know very well, that is who they may appear to you to be, but you are not by any manner of means to believe that that is what they really and truly are. What you are rather to understand is that if they have, as you say, this appearance in your eyes, it must be for the reason that those who have put this spell upon me have seen fit to assume that form and likeness; for it is easy enough for enchanters to take whatever form they like, and so they must have assumed the appearance of our friends expressly for the purpose of leading you to think what you do, thus involving you in a labyrinth of fancies from which you would not succeed in extricating yourself even though you had the cord of Theseus.

"They also doubtless had another purpose, that of causing me to waver in my mind, so that I should not be able to form a conjecture as to the source of this wrong that is done me. For, if on the one hand you tell me it is the barber and the curate of our village who accompany us, and on the other hand I find myself shut up in a cage, knowing full well that no human but only a superhuman power could have put me behind these bars, what would you have me say to you or what would you have me think except that my enchantment, in view of the manner in which it has been accomplished, is like none that I have ever read about in all the histories that treat of knights-errant who have been laid under a spell? And so you may set your mind at rest as to the suspicions that you have voiced, for those two are no more what you say they are than I am a Turk. But you said that you had something to ask me; speak, then, and I will answer you, though you keep on asking until tomorrow morning."

"May Our Lady help me!" cried Sancho in a loud voice. "Is it possible your Grace is so thick-headed and so lacking in brains that you cannot see that I am telling you the simple truth when I say that malice has more to do than magic with your being in this plight? But since that is the way matters stand, I'd like to prove to you beyond a doubt that there is no magic about it. And now, tell me, as you would have God rescue you from this torment, and as you hope to find yourself in the arms of my lady Dulcinea when you least expect it—"

"Stop conjuring me," said Don Quixote, "and ask what you like. I have already told you that I will answer you point by point."

"What I ask is this," Sancho went on, "and what I

would have you tell me, without adding anything to it or leaving anything out, but in all truthfulness, as you would expect it to be told, and as it is told, by all those who like your Grace follow the calling of arms, under the title of knights-errant—"

"I have said that I will tell you no lies," replied Don Quixote. "Go ahead and finish your question; for in truth you weary me, Sancho, with all these solemn oaths, adjurations, and precautions."

"I am sure," said Sancho, "that my master is kind-hearted and truthful; and so, because it has a bearing on what we are talking about, I would ask your Grace, speaking with all due respect, if by any chance, since you have been in that cage and, as it seems to you, under a spell, you have felt the need of doing a major or a minor,[9] as the saying goes."

"I do not understand what you mean by 'doing a major or a minor,' Sancho. Speak more plainly if you wish me to give you a direct answer."

"Is it possible that your Grace doesn't know what 'a major or a minor' is? Why, lads in school are weaned on it. What I mean to say is, have you felt like doing that which can't be put off?"

"Ah, I understand you, Sancho! Yes, many times; and for that matter, right now. Get me out of this, or all will not be as clean here as it ought to be!"

Don Quixote having confessed that he must attend to the needs of nature, Sancho catches him up and they continue their conversation.

CHAPTER XLIX. *Of the shrewd conversation that Sancho Panza had with his master, Don Quixote.*

"HA!" cried Sancho, "I have you there! That is what I wanted with all my life and soul to know! Come now, sir, can you deny the common saying around here when a person is out of sorts: 'I don't know what's the matter with So-and-So; he neither eats nor drinks nor sleeps nor gives you a sensible answer to any question that you ask him; he must be bewitched?' From which we are to gather that while those that do not do any of these things or attend to those duties of nature that I have mentioned are under a spell, the ones like your Grace, on the other hand, who feel a desire to do them, who eat and drink what is set before them and answer all questions, are not enchanted."

"You speak the truth, Sancho," replied Don Quixote, "but as I have told you before there are many ways of being enchanted, and it may be that the fashion has changed with the course of time and that today those who are in such a plight do everything that I do, although formerly such was not the case. So, there is no use arguing against custom or drawing inferences as you are doing. I know for a certainty that I am the victim of an enchanter, and that is all I need to know to set my conscience at rest, for it would hurt me sorely if I thought that, without being enchanted, I had slothfully and like a coward permitted myself to be put into this cage, thus cheating the wretched and the needy who at this very moment may be in great distress for want of my aid and protection."

"But for all of that," said Sancho, "I still insist it would be better, in order to satisfy yourself completely,

if your Grace would try to get out of that jail. I promise
to do everything I can to help you out of it and see if
you can mount Rocinante once more, for he looks so
sad and melancholy, I think he must be enchanted too.
When you've done that, you can try your luck at seeking
more adventures, and if they don't turn out well, there
will be plenty of time for us to come back to the jail;
in which case I promise you, as the law says a good and
faithful squire should do, that I will shut myself up
with your Grace, if by any chance your Grace should
be so unlucky or I so foolish as not to be able to go
through with what I've told you."

"I am willing to do anything you say, brother Sancho," Don Quixote assured him; "and when you find an
opportunity to set me free, I will obey you in everything; but you will see, Sancho, that you are wrong in
your explanation of my misfortune."

*Sancho now begs the curate to permit his master to
leave the cage for a little while, "since otherwise it
would not remain as clean as decency required in the
case of such a knight." The curate agrees on condition
that Don Quixote give his word of honor not to try
to escape, which the latter does. When he has performed his "duty," the prisoner returns and there ensues
a long argument between him and the churchman on
the subject of knight-errantry. This takes up the balance
of the chapter (the title of which is somewhat mis-
leading).*

CHAPTER L. *Of the weighty argument that took place between Don Quixote and the canon.*

"THAT," replied Don Quixote, "is a fine thing to say! Do you mean to tell me that those books that have been printed with a royal license and with the approval of the ones to whom they have been submitted and which are read with general enjoyment and praised by young and old alike, by rich and poor, the learned and the ignorant, the gentry and the plain people—in brief, by all sort of persons of every condition and walk in life—do you mean to tell me that they are but lies? Do they not have every appearance of being true? Do they not tell us who the father, mother, relatives of these knights were, the name of the country from which they came, their age, the feats they performed, point by point and day by day, and the places where all these events occurred? Your Grace had best be silent and not utter such a blasphemy; for let me give you a bit of advice, which is something that, as a sensible man, I ought to do: if you do not believe me, read them for yourself and you will see what pleasure you will derive from them.

"Tell me: could there be anything more fascinating than to see before us, right here and now, so to speak, a lake of bubbling pitch, with a host of snakes, serpents, lizards, and all sorts of fierce and terrifying animals swimming about in it, while from the middle of it there comes as mournful a voice as ever was heard, saying, 'Thou, O knight, whoever thou mayest be, who standest gazing upon this dreadful lake, if thou wouldst attain the boon that lieth covered beneath these dark waters, show then thy valor and thy stout heart by leaping into the midst of this black and burning liquid; for if thou dost not, thou shalt not be held worthy of looking upon the mighty marvels locked and contained in the seven castles of the seven fays that are situated beneath its ebony expanse.' And no sooner does the knight hear that awful voice than, without taking any further thought or pausing to consider the peril involved, he plunges into that seething lagoon, burdened with the full weight of his armor and commending his soul to God and Our Lady.

"And then, not knowing where he is or what the outcome is to be, he suddenly finds himself amidst flowering meadows to which the Elysian fields cannot compare."

Don Quixote then describes the splendors of the place and the romantic adventures that befall the knight who plunged into the pitch. "What," he concludes, "could be more charming than this?"

He then continues with the virtues that knight-errantry has bestowed on him and expresses the desire to become an emperor in order to "make manifest the virtues of my heart by doing good to my friends and especially to this poor fellow, Sancho Panza, my squire, who is the best little man in the world"; and he adds, "I should like to reward him by conferring on him an earldom. The only thing is I do not know if he has the ability to govern it."

These last words were no sooner out of his mouth than Sancho broke in upon his master. "Just you see to it that I get that earldom, Señor Don Quixote," he said, "the one you promised me and which I have been waiting for all this time, and I give you my word that I'll be able to govern it all right; and if I should fail, i've heard them say that there are men in this world who rent such estates from their lords, giving them so much a year, while they themselves take over the government, in which case all the lord has to do is to stretch out his legs and enjoy his income without worrying about anything else. That's what I'll do. I'll not haggle over a penny here and a penny there. I'll get rid of all the bother and live like a duke on what's coming to me."

"What you are speaking of, brother Sancho," said the canon, "is the matter of revenues; but the lord of a great estate also has to administer justice, and it is this that calls for ability and sound judgment and, above all, a right intention on his part in ascertaining the truth; for if this be lacking in the beginning, the middle and the end will always be wrong, whence it is that God is inclined to favor the simple when their hearts are in the right place and to frustrate the clever designs of the wicked."

"I don't understand those philosophies," replied Sancho. "All I know is that once I have that earldom, I'll be able to rule it; for I have a soul like anybody else and a body like the rest of them, and I'll be as much a king in my state as the others are in theirs. And when I'm king, I'll do as I please, and doing as I please, I'll be satisfied; and when you're satisfied, there's nothing more to be desired, so bring it on. God be with you and we shall see, as one blind man said to another."

"That is not a bad philosophy, as you call it, Sancho," observed the canon, "but there still remains much to be said on this subject of earldoms."

"I do not know what more there is to be said," Don Quixote answered him. "I am guided simply by the example of the great Amadis of Gaul, who made his squire count of Firm Island; and so, I, without any conscientious scruples, may make a count of Sancho Panza, who is one of the best squires that a knight-errant ever had."

In pursuit of one of his flock a goatherd bursts in upon the company and they invite him to share their meal. When they express surprise at the manner in which he addresses the female goat—as if it were a woman—he volunteers to tell them a story, which provides the author with an excuse for another pastoral episode. Once again it is a tale of heartbroken suitors turned shepherds. In this case the names of the lovelorn swains are Eugenio (the narrator) and Anselmo, and the object of their passion is one Leandra, daughter of a wealthy farmer, noted for her great beauty. She has been enticed into an elopement with a swaggering soldier returned from the wars and, upon being abandoned by him, though a virgin still, has been shut up in a convent. The youths are now roaming the woods and meadows, singing her praises and lamenting her fickleness. This accounts for Eugenio's manner of addressing the goat—"as she is a female, I have little respect for her, even though she is the best of my flock" (Chapter LI).

As the goatherd finishes his story, Don Quixote offers to aid him in his usual knightly fashion (Chapter LII). The man in astonishment remarks to the curate that "this worthy gentleman must have a number of rooms to let inside his head"; whereupon Don Quixote becomes furious and the two engage in a lively tussle while the others roar with glee. Just at that moment, with the hapless knight pinned beneath his adversary, the sound of a trumpet is heard.

To Don Quixote this can mean but one thing—an-

other "adventure"—and he asks the goatherd to call a truce. As he rises to his feet he beholds a procession of white-clad penitents carrying an image of the Virgin on a litter, but he takes them to be some lovely lady and her abductors. He commands them to set their victim free, and when they greet him with a laugh he draws his sword and falls upon the litter. He is then felled by a mighty blow from a club wielded by one of the litter bearers. This ends the fray, as Sancho throws himself across his master's body and begins weeping and wailing. The curate from the village and a curate who is accompanying the penitents contrive to straighten matters out.

FROM CHAPTER LII: . . . *The rare adventure of the penitents, which the knight by the sweat of his brow brought to a happy conclusion.*

THE first curate then gave the second a very brief account of who Don Quixote was, whereupon all the penitents came up to see if the poor knight was dead. And as they did so, they heard Sancho Panza speaking with tears in his eyes.

"O flower of chivalry," he was saying, "the course of whose well-spent years has been brought to an end by a single blow of a club! O honor of your line, honor and glory of all La Mancha and of all the world, which, with you absent from it, will be full of evildoers who will not fear being punished for their deeds! O master more generous than all the Alexanders, who after only eight months of service presented me with the best island that the sea washes and surrounds! Humble with the proud, haughty with the humble, brave in facing dangers, long-suffering under outrages, in love without reason, imitator of the good, scourge of the wicked, enemy of the mean—in a word, a knight-errant, which is all there is to say."

At the sound of Sancho's cries and moans, Don Quixote revived, and the first thing he said was, "He who lives apart from thee, O fairest Dulcinea, is subject to greater woes than those I now endure. Friend Sancho, help me onto that enchanted cart, as I am in no condition to sit in Rocinante's saddle with this shoulder of mine knocked to pieces the way it is."

"That I will gladly do, my master," replied Sancho, "and we will go back to my village in the company of these gentlemen who are concerned for your welfare, and there we will arrange for another sally and one, let us hope, that will bring us more profit and fame than this one has."

"Well spoken, Sancho," said Don Quixote, "for it will be an act of great prudence to wait until the present evil influence of the stars has passed."

The canon, the curate, and the barber all assured him that he would be wise in doing this; and so, much amused by Sancho Panza's simplicity, they placed Don Quixote upon the cart as before, while the procession of penitents re-formed and continued on its way. The goatherd took leave of all of them, and the curate paid the troopers what was coming to them, since they did not wish to go any farther. The canon requested the priest to inform him of the outcome of Don Quixote's madness, as to whether it yielded to treatment or not; and with this he begged permission to resume his journey. In short, the party broke up and separated, leaving only the curate and the barber, Don Quixote and Panza, and the good Rocinante, who looked upon everything that he had seen with the same resignation as his master. Yoking his oxen, the carter made the knight comfortable upon a bale of hay, and then at his customary slow pace proceeded to follow the road that the curate directed him to take. At the end of six days they reached Don Quixote's village, making their entrance at noon of a Sunday, when the square was filled with a crowd of people through which the cart had to pass.

They all came running to see who it was, and when they recognized their townsman, they were vastly astonished. One lad sped to bring the news to the knight's housekeeper and his niece, telling them that their master had returned lean and jaundiced and lying stretched out upon a bale of hay on an ox-cart. It was pitiful to hear the good ladies' screams, to behold the way in which they beat their breasts, and listen to the curses which they once more heaped upon those damnable books of chivalry, and this demonstration increased as they saw Don Quixote coming through the doorway.

At news of the knight's return, Sancho Panza's wife had hurried to the scene, for she had some while since learned that her husband had accompanied him as his squire; and now, as soon as she laid eyes upon her man, the first question she asked was if all was well with the ass, to which Sancho replied that the beast was better off than his master.

"Thank God," she exclaimed, "for all his blessings! But tell me now, my dear, what have you brought me from all your squirings? A new cloak to wear? Or shoes for the young ones?"

"I've brought you nothing of the sort, good wife," said Sancho, "but other things of greater value and importance."

"I'm glad to hear that," she replied. "Show me those

things of greater value and importance, my dear. I'd like a sight of them just to cheer this heart of mine which has been so sad and unhappy all the centuries that you've been gone."

"I will show them to you at home, wife," said Sancho. "For the present be satisfied that if, God willing, we set out on another journey in search of adventures, you will see me in no time a count or the governor of an island, and not one of those around here, but the best that is to be had."

"I hope to Heaven it's true, my husband, for we certainly need it. But tell me, what is all this about islands? I don't understand."

"Honey," replied Sancho, "is not for the mouth of an ass. You will find out in good time, woman; and you're going to be surprised to hear yourself called 'my Ladyship' by all your vassals."

"What's this you are saying, Sancho, about ladyships, islands, and vassals?" Juana Panza insisted on knowing —for such was the name of Sancho's wife, although they were not blood relatives, it being the custom in La Mancha for wives to take their husband's surnames.

"Do not be in such a hurry to know all this, Juana," he said. "It is enough that I am telling you the truth. Sew up your mouth, then; for all I will say, in passing, is that there is nothing in the world that is more pleasant than being a respected man, squire to a knight-errant who goes in search of adventures. It is true that most of the adventures you meet with do not come out the way you'd like them to, for ninety-nine out of a hundred will prove to be all twisted and crosswise. I know that from experience, for I've come out of some of them blanketed and out of others beaten to a pulp. But, all the same, it's a fine thing to go along waiting for what will happen next, crossing mountains, making your way through woods, climbing over cliffs, visiting castles, and putting up at inns free of charge, and the devil take the maravedi that is to pay."

Such was the conversation that took place between Sancho Panza and Juana Panza, his wife, as Don Quixote's housekeeper and niece were taking him in, stripping him, and stretching him out on his old-time bed. He gazed at them blankly, being unable to make out where he was. The curate charged the niece to take great care to see that her uncle was comfortable and to keep close watch over him so that he would not slip away from them another time. He then told them of what it had been necessary to do in order to get him home, at which they once more screamed to Heaven and began cursing the books of chivalry all over again, praying God to plunge the authors of such lying nonsense into the center of the bottomless pit. In short, they scarcely knew what to do, for they were very much afraid that their master and uncle would give them the slip once more, the moment he was a little better, and it turned out just the way they feared it might.

But the author of this history, although he has made a most thorough and diligent search, has been unable to come upon any account—at least any based on authentic sources—of the deeds performed by Don Quixote on his third sally. There is only the tradition, handed down in La Mancha, to the effect that in the course of this third expedition he went to Saragossa, where he was present at some famous tourneys that were held in that city and where he met with adventures such as befitted his valor and sound judgment.

Part I ends with a set of mock sonnets and epitaphs supposed to have been found "in the crumbling foun-

dations of a very old hermitage that was being rebuilt. *
(This was a variety of sportive mystification popular in
the Renaissance; Rabelais, for example, employs it.)

END OF PART I

PART TWO

Prefixed to Part II are the usual Certificate of Price, Certificate of Errata, Approbations, and Royal Privilege. Then comes a Prologue, followed by a Dedication addressed to the Count of Lemos.

The Prologue is a furious document, inspired by Avellaneda's spurious sequel to Part I and the highly personal insults he had heaped on the author of the true Don Quixote. Inasmuch as it is wholly taken up with Cervantes' angry reply, its interest is chiefly biographical and it has, accordingly, been omitted here.

Preparations for the Third Sally

(CHAPTERS I-VII)

CHAPTER I. *Of the conversation which the curate and the barber had with Don Quixote concerning his malady.*

IN THE second part of this history, dealing with Don Quixote's third sally, Cid Hamete Benengeli tells us that the curate and the barber went nearly a month without seeing their friend, in order not to remind him of what had happened. But they did not for this reason leave off visiting the niece and housekeeper, whom they urged to treat the knight with the greatest of care by seeing to it that he had comforting things to eat and

such as would be good for his heart and for his brain
as well, the latter being to all appearances the seat of
his trouble and the cause of all his misfortunes. The
women replied that this was what they were doing, and
would continue to do, with a right good will and most
attentively; for they had noticed that the master of the
house at moments seemed to be in full possession of his
senses.

The curate and the barber were well pleased at hearing this, and concluded that they had done the wise
thing in having Don Quixote borne away in an ox-cart,
as has been related in the last chapter of the First Part
of this great and painstaking chronicle. They accordingly
determined to visit him and see for themselves what
improvement he had made, although they believed it to
be all but impossible that he could be any better. They
agreed that they would not bring up any subject that
had to do with knight-errantry, as they did not wish to
run the risk of reopening a wound that was still so sore.

When the pair came to pay their visit, they found
their host seated upon the bed, clad in a green baize
waistcoat and a red Toledo cap, and looking as withered
and dried up as an Egyptian mummy. He received them
very well and, when they made inquiries regarding his
health, discussed with them this and other matters
of a personal nature most sensibly and in words that
were very well chosen. In the course of their conversation they came to touch upon what is known as state-
craft and forms of government, correcting this abuse,
condemning that one, reforming one custom and banishing another, with each of the three setting himself up
as a new lawgiver, a modern Lycurgus or newly fledged
Solon. In this manner they proceeded to remodel the
State, as if they had placed it in a forge and had drawn
out something quite different from what they had put

in. And all the while Don Quixote displayed such good sound sense in connection with whatever topic was broached as to lead the two examiners to feel that he must undoubtedly be fully recovered and in his right mind.

The niece and housekeeper were present at this conversation and could not thank God enough when they saw how clear-headed their master apparently was. It was then that the curate changed his mind about not bringing up anything that had to do with chivalry; for he wished to make the test complete and assure himself as to whether the knight's recovery was real or not. And so, speaking of one thing and another, he came to relate various items of news that had just been received from the capital, including a report to the effect that it was looked upon as a certainty that the Turk was bearing down with a powerful fleet, although nothing was known of his plans as yet, nor where so great a storm as this would break, but as a result all Christendom was stirred by that feeling of dread that almost every year summons us to take up arms, and his Majesty had seen to fortifying the coasts of Naples and Sicily and the island of Malta.

"His Majesty," remarked Don Quixote, "has acted like a most prudent warrior in providing for the safety of his dominions while there is yet time, in order that the enemy may not take him unawares; but if he were to follow my advice, I should counsel him to adopt a measure which I am sure is far from his thoughts at the present moment."

"Poor Don Quixote," said the curate to himself when he heard this, "may God help you; for it looks to me as if you have fallen from the high cliff of madness into the abyss of simple-mindedness."

The same thought had occurred to the barber, who

now asked the knight what this measure was that in his opinion should be adopted, adding that perhaps it was one that would have to be added to the long list of impertinent suggestions of the kind commonly offered to princes.

"My suggestion, Master Shaver," replied Don Quixote, "is not an impertinent one but is very much to the point."

"That is not what I meant," said the barber, "but experience has shown that all or most of the expedients that are proposed to his Majesty are either impossible or nonsensical, or else would be detrimental to king and kingdom."

"But mine," Don Quixote insisted, "is not impossible nor is it nonsensical, but rather is the easiest, the most reasonable, the readiest, and most expeditious scheme that anyone could devise."

"It takes your Grace a long time to tell it," observed the curate.

"I do not care to tell it to you here and now," said the knight, "and, the first thing tomorrow morning, have it reach the ears of my lords, the councilors, so that some other person may carry off the reward and win the thanks that are rightly due me."

"For my part," the barber assured him, "I give you my word, here and before God, that I will say nothing of what your Grace may tell me, to king, rook, or earthly man.[1] That, by the way, is an oath I picked up from the ballad about the curate[2] who, in the prelude, tells the king of the thief who had robbed him of a hundred doblas[3] and his fast-pacing mule."

"I know nothing about such stories," said Don Quixote, "but I do know that the oath is a good one by reason of the faith that I have in this worthy man, our master barber."

"And even if he were not what you take him to be," the curate went on, "I would go bond and put in an appearance for him, to the effect that in this case he will be as silent as a mute, under pain of any sentence that might be pronounced upon him."

"And who will go your Grace's bond?" Don Quixote asked the priest.

"My profession," was the curate's reply, "which consists in keeping secrets."

"Then, damn it, sir!" exclaimed the knight, "what more need his Majesty do than command by public proclamation that all the knights-errant at present wandering over Spain shall assemble in the capital on a given day? Even if no more than half a dozen came, there well might be one among them who alone would be able to overthrow the Turk's mighty power. Pay attention, your Worships, and listen closely to what I am about to say. Is it by any chance an unheard-of thing for a single knight-errant to rout an army of two hundred thousand men, as if they all had but one throat or were made of sugar paste? Tell me, how many stories do we have that are filled with such marvels? If only, alas for me (I do not care to speak for any other), the famous Don Belianís were alive today, or any of the countless other descendants of Amadis of Gaul! Let one of these but confront the Turk, and my word, they would have the best of him. But God will look after his people and will provide someone who, if not so brave as the knights of old, will not be inferior to them in the matter of courage. God knows what I mean. I need say no more."

"Oh, dear," wailed the niece at this point, "may they slay me if my master doesn't want to go back to being a knight-errant!"

"A knight-errant I shall live and die," said Don Quixote, "and let the Turk come or go as he will, with all the strength he can muster. Again I say to you, God understands."

The barber now spoke up. "I beg your Worships to grant me permission to relate to you briefly something that happened in Seville. It is a story that is made for the present occasion, which is why I should like to tell it."

Don Quixote gave his consent, and the curate and the others prepared to lend him their attention.

"In the madhouse of Seville," he began, "was a certain individual who had been placed there by his relatives, as being out of his mind. He was a graduate of Osuna, in canon law; but it was the opinion of most people that even if he had been of Salamanca, he would have been mad all the same. After a few years of seclusion, this man took it into his head that he had been wholly cured, and, being so convinced, he wrote to the archbishop, begging that prelate, earnestly and in well-chosen words, to have him released from the misery in which he was living, since he had now recovered his lost reason, even though his family, which was enjoying his share of the estate, insisted upon keeping him there; for contrary to the truth of the matter, they would make him out to be a madman until his dying day.

"Impressed by the many well and sensibly written letters he had received from the man, the archbishop sent one of his chaplains to find out from the superintendent of the madhouse if what the licentiate had written was true or not. The chaplain was further directed to converse with the patient and if he found him to be sane, he was to take him out and set him at liberty. Following these instructions, he was informed by the superintendent that the man was as mad as ever, and that while he very frequently spoke like a person

of great intelligence, he would suddenly burst out with
so many absurdities that they more than made up, in
quantity and in quality, for all the sensible things he
had previously said, as was readily to be seen by talking with him. This the chaplain resolved to do, and,
sitting down with the patient, he carried on a conversation with him for more than an hour, during all of which
time the madman did not make one incoherent or foolish
remark but appeared to be so rational in everything he
said that his visitor was compelled to believe him sane.

"Among other things, the man stated that the superintendent had it in for him, being motivated by a desire not to lose the gifts that the relatives made him for
saying that his ward was still insane with lucid intervals.
The greatest misfortune that he had to contend with, the
poor fellow added, was his large estate, since it was for
the purpose of enjoying his wealth that his enemies
belied and cast doubts upon the grace which Our Lord
had shown him by turning him from a beast into a
man once more. In short, he spoke in such a way as to
make the superintendent's conduct seem highly suspicious, while his relatives were made out to be covetous and heartless creatures; all of which was uttered
with such a show of reason that the chaplain made up
his mind to take the man with him that the archbishop
might see him and come at the truth of this business.

"With this worthy intention, he asked the superintendent to send for the clothes which the licentiate had
worn when he entered the place, whereupon that official
once more begged him to look well to what he was
doing, as there was not the slightest doubt that the
patient was still mad; but all these cautions and warn-
ings were lost upon the chaplain, who was bent upon
having the man released. Seeing that it was the arch-

bishop's orders, the superintendent complied, and they then brought the licentiate his clothes, which were new and very presentable. When the latter saw himself dressed like one in his right senses and rid of his madman's garments, he begged the chaplain to be so kind as to permit him to take leave of his fellow patients. The chaplain consented, remarking that he would like to go along and see the others who were confined in the institution. They accordingly went upstairs, accompanied by some of those who were present, and came to a cell where one who was raving mad was lodged, though at that moment he was calm and quiet.

" 'Brother,' the licientiate said to him, 'think if there is anything that I can do for you. I am going home, God in His infinite goodness and mercy, and through no merit of my own, having seen fit to restore my reason to me. I am now cured and sane, since where the power of God is concerned, nothing is impossible. You must have a great hope and confidence in Him, who, just as He has restored me to my former state, will do the same for you if you trust in Him. I will make it a point to send you some good things to eat, and be sure that you do eat them; for as one who has gone through it, I may tell you that in my opinion all our madness comes from having our stomachs empty and our brains full of air. Pluck up your courage, then. Despondency in misfortune only impairs the health and brings death all the sooner.'

"Everything the licentiate said was heard by another madman in a cell across the way, and, rising from an old mat where he had been lying stark naked, this man now cried out in a loud voice, demanding to know who it was that was going away cured and sane.

" 'It is I, brother,' the licentiate replied. 'I am leaving you. There is no longer any need of my remaining here, thanks be to Heaven for having shown me this mercy.'

" 'Mind what you are saying, licentiate,' the other warned him, 'and do not let the devil deceive you. You had best not stir a foot but stay where you are and save yourself the trouble of coming back.'

" 'I know that I am all right,' was the reply, 'and that it will not be necessary for me to do the stations again.' [4]

" 'You are all right, are you?' said the madman across the way. 'We shall see as to that. May God go with you; but I swear to you, in the name of Jupiter whose majesty I represent on earth, that for this one sin which Seville today is committing by releasing you from this place as if you were cured, I shall have to inflict such a punishment upon it as will be remembered throughout all the ages to come. Amen. Do you not know, miserable little licentiate, that I can do this, seeing that, as I have said, I am Jupiter the Thunderer and hold in my hands the fiery bolts with which I am accustomed to threaten the world and by means of which I can destroy it? There is, however, only one way in which I wish to punish this ignorant town, and that is by not raining upon it or anywhere in the entire district and vicinity for three whole years, beginning with the day and moment when this threat is made. You free, cured, in your right senses, and I a madman, sickly minded and confined? I would no more think of sending rain than I would of hanging myself.'

"The bystanders all listened attentively to the madman's words and cries. Then our licentiate turned to the chaplain and seized his hands. 'Do not be disturbed, your Grace,' he pleaded, 'and pay no attention to what this fellow says. If he is Jupiter and will not rain, then I who am Neptune, father and god of the waters, will do so any time that I feel like it or whenever it may be necessary.'

" 'For all of that, Sir Neptune,' the chaplain answered him, 'it would be as well not to annoy Sir Jupiter. Stay here, your Grace, and another day, when we have more time and it is more convenient, we will return for you.'

"The superintendent and the others laughed at this, and the chaplain was greatly embarrassed. They then undressed the licentiate, and he remained where he was, and that is the end of the story."

"If that is the tale, Master Barber," said Don Quixote, "what did you mean by saying that it was made for the present occasion, for which reason you could not refrain from telling it? Ah, Master Shaver, Master Shaver, how blind is he who cannot see through a sieve! Is your Grace not aware that comparisons of mind with mind, valor with valor, beauty with beauty, birth with birth, are invariably odious and ill received? I, Master Barber, am not Neptune, god of the waters, nor would I have anyone take me for a wise man when I am not wise. My sole endeavor is to bring the world to realize the mistake it is making in failing to revive that happiest of times when the order of knight-errantry was in the field. But this degenerate age of ours does not deserve to enjoy so great a blessing as that which former ages knew, when wandering men of arms took upon themselves the defense of realms, the protection of damsels, the succor of orphans, the punishment of the proud, and the rewarding of the humble.

"The knights of the present time, for the most part, are accompanied by the rustling of damasks, brocades, and other rich stuffs that they wear, rather than by the rattling of coats of mail. There is none that sleeps in the field, exposed to the inclemency of the heavens and fully armed from head to foot. There is none who, as

they say, snatches forty winks without taking foot from
stirrup, merely leaning on his lance. There is none who,
sallying forth from a wood, will go up onto yonder
mountain, and from there come down to tread the barren and deserted shore beside a sea that is almost always
angry and tempest-tossed; or who, finding upon the
beach a small craft, without oars, sail, mast, or rigging
of any kind, will leap into it with intrepid heart and
entrust himself to the implacable waves of the stormy
deep, waves that now mount heavenward and now
drag him down into the abyss. Such a one, breasting
the irresistible tempest, may find himself more than
three thousand miles from the place where he embarked; in which case, bounding ashore upon the soil of
a remote and unknown land, he will meet with such
adventures as are worthy of being recorded, not upon
parchment, but in bronze.

"Today, sloth triumphs over diligence, idleness and
ease over exertion, vice over virtue, arrogance over
valor, and theory over practice of the warrior's art. Tell
me, if you will, who was more virtuous or more valiant
than the famous Amadis of Gaul? Who more prudent
than Palmerin of England? Who more gracious and
reasonable than Tirant lo Blanch? Who was more the
courtier than Lisuarte of Greece? Who was more slashed
or slashing than Don Belianís? Who more intrepid
than Perión of Gaul? Or who more forward in facing
danger than Felixmarte of Hircania? Who was more
sincere than Esplandián? More daring than Don Cir-
ongilio of Thrace? Who was braver than Rodamonte?
Wiser than King Sobrino? Bolder than Rinaldo? More
invincible than Orlando? Who was more gallant and
courteous than Ruggiero, from whom the present dukes
of Ferrara are descended, according to Turpin in his
Cosmography? [5]

"All these and many others whom I could mention, Señor Curate, were knights-errant, the light and glory of chivalry. It is these, or such as these, that I would have carry out my plan, in which case his majesty would be well served and would save himself much expense, while the Turk would be left tearing out his beard. For this reason, I do not propose to remain at home,[6] even though the chaplain does not take me out; and if Jupiter, as the barber has said, does not choose to rain, then I am here to do so whenever it pleases me. I say this in order that Master Basin may know that I understand him."

"Really, Señor Don Quixote," said the barber, "I did not mean it in that way. So help me God, my intentions were of the best, and your Grace ought not to take offense."

"Whether I take offense or not," replied Don Quixote, "is for me to decide."

With this, the curate took a hand in the conversation. "I have hardly said a word up to now, but there is one little doubt that gnaws and pecks at my conscience and that comes from what Don Quixote has just told us."

"You may go as far as you like, Señor Curate," said Don Quixote. "Feel perfectly free to state your doubt, for it is not pleasant to have something on one's conscience."

"Well, then, with your permission," the curate continued, "I will say that my doubt arises from the fact that I am unable to persuade myself by any manner of means that all the many knights-errant your Grace has mentioned were in reality flesh-and-blood beings who actually lived in this world. I rather fancy that it is all fiction, fables, and lies, a lot of dreams related by men just awakened from sleep, or, better, still half asleep."

"That," declared Don Quixote, "is another error into which many have fallen who do not believe that such knights ever existed; and I many times, with various persons and on various occasions, have endeavored to bring this all too common mistake to the light of truth. Sometimes I have not succeeded in my purpose, but other times, sustained upon the shoulders of the truth, I have been more fortunate. For the truth is so clear that I can almost assure you that I saw with my own eyes Amadis of Gaul. He was a tall man, of fair complexion and with a beard which, though black, was quite handsome. His countenance was half mild, half stern; his words were few, but he was slow to anger and quick to lay aside his wrath. And just as I have depicted Amadis for you, so I might go on, I think, to portray and describe[7] all the other knights-errant in all the storybooks of the world. For I feel sure that they were what the histories make them out to have been, and from the exploits that they performed and the kind of men they were it would be possible, with the aid of a little sound philosophy, to reconstruct their features, their complexions, and their stature."

"How big, Señor Don Quixote, was the giant Morgante as your Grace conceives him?" the barber asked.

"On this subject of giants," replied the knight, "opinions differ as to whether or not there ever were any in this world: but the Holy Scriptures, which do not depart from the truth by one iota, show us plainly that giants did exist, when they tell us the story of that big Philistine of a Goliath, who was seven cubits and a half in height, which is a very great size.[8] Moreover, in the island of Sicily they have found thigh and shoulder bones so large that they must have belonged to giants as tall as towers.[9] It is a matter of simple geometry. But for all of this, I should not be able to state with any certainty what Morgante's size was, although I imagine that he was not exceedingly tall, since I find in that history[10] where special mention is made of his exploits that he very frequently slept under a roof, and inasmuch as he found houses that were large enough to accommodate him, he could not have been too big after all."

"I agree with you," said the curate. And merely for the pleasure of listening to such utter nonsense, he went on to ask Don Quixote what he thought the countenances of Rinaldo of Montalbán, Don Orlando, and the other Twelve Peers of France must have been like, seeing that they were all knights-errant.

"Concerning Rinaldo," Don Quixote answered him, "I would venture to say that he had a broad face, a ruddy complexion, and twinkling, rather prominent eyes, and that he was punctilious, extremely choleric, and a friend of robbers and those beyond the pale of the law. As to Roldán, or Rotolando, or Orlando—for the histories give him all these names—I am of the opinion, indeed I would assert, that he was of medium stature, broad-shouldered, somewhat bowlegged, red-bearded, with a hairy body and a threatening expression, a man of few words, but very courteous and well bred."

"If Orlando," observed the curate, "had no more of a gentlemanly appearance than that, I do not wonder that the lady Angélica the Fair should have disdained him or that she should have left him for that downy-faced young Moor who was so gay, so sprightly, and so witty. It seems to me she did wisely in preferring the softness of Medoro[11] to Orlando's ruggedness."

"That Angélica," replied the knight, "was a giddy damsel, flighty and capricious, and filled the world with her whims as much as with the fame of her beauty.

She spurned a thousand gentlemen of wit and valor and was satisfied with a smooth-faced pageling with no other wealth or claim to fame than his reputation for gratitude, due to the affection that he showed his friend. The great poet who sang of her beauty, the famous Ariosto, either did not dare or did not wish to relate what happened to this lady following her disgraceful surrender, but her adventures could not have been any too edifying, and it is with these lines that the bard takes his leave of her:

> *How she received the scepter of Cathay,*
> *Another with better plectrum will sing someday.*[12]

There can be no doubt that this was a kind of prophecy; for poets are also called *vates*, which means 'diviners.' The truth of this is plainly to be seen in the fact that a famous Andalusian poet wept for her and sang of her tears, while another famous and exceptional one of Castile hymned her beauty." [13]

"But tell me, Señor Don Quixote," said the barber, "among all the poets who have praised her, has there been none to compose a satire on this Lady Angélica?"

"I can well believe," replied Don Quixote, "that if Sacripante or Orlando had been poets, they would have given the damsel a dressing-down; for when poets have been scorned and rejected by their ladies, whether the ladies in question be real or imaginary[14]—in short, when they have been spurned by those whom they have chosen to be the mistresses of their affection—it is natural for them to seek to avenge themselves by means of satires and libels, although, to be sure, this is something that is unworthy of generous hearts; but up to now I have not come upon any defamatory verses[15] directed at the Lady Angélica, who set the world on end."

"That is very strange," said the curate.

At that moment they heard the housekeeper and the niece, who had left the room a while ago, shouting at someone in the courtyard, and they all ran out to see what the uproar was about.

CHAPTER II. *Which treats of the notable quarrel that Sancho Panza had with Don Quixote's niece and housekeeper, along with other droll happenings.*

THE history tells us that the cries that Don Quixote, the curate, and the barber heard came from the niece and the housekeeper. They were shouting at Sancho Panza, who was struggling to get in to see the knight, while they were doing their best to keep him out.

"What is this vagabond doing here? Home with you, brother; for you and no one else are the one who puts these foolish notions into my master's head; it is you who lure him away to go wandering over the countryside."

"You devil's housekeeper, you!" exclaimed Sancho. "The one who has foolish notions put in his head and is lured away is I and not your master. He has taken me all over this world; and you do not know the half of it. It was through a trick that he persuaded me to leave home, by promising me an island which I am still waiting to see."

"May you choke on your cursed islands, Sancho, you wretch!" the niece replied. "What are islands anyway? Are they something to eat, glutton that you are?"

"No," replied Sancho, "they are not something to eat, but something to govern and rule over and better than four cities or four judgeships at court."

"Well, in spite of all that," said the housekeeper, "you are not coming in here, you bag of mischief. Go govern that weedpatch of yours and let us hear no more talk of islands[1] or drylands or what have you."

The curate and the barber greatly enjoyed listening to the conversation of these three; but Don Quixote, fearing that Sancho would talk too much, blurt out a lot of mischievous nonsense, and touch upon certain subjects that would not redound to his master's credit, now called his squire over to him and at the same time ordered the other two to hold their tongues and let the unwelcome visitor come in. Sancho entered the house as the curate and the barber took their leave. They were in despair over Don Quixote's state of mind, for they could not help perceiving how firmly fixed his hallucinations were and how imbued he was with those foolish ideas of his about knight-errantry.

"You will see, my friend," remarked the curate, "our gentleman will be off again one of these days when we least expect it."

"I have not the slightest doubt of that," replied the barber. "But I do not wonder so much at the knight's madness as I do at the simple-mindedness of his squire, who believes so firmly in that island that no matter what you did to disillusion him, you would never be able to get it out of his head. Such at least is my opinion."

"God help them," said the curate, "and let us keep a close watch to see what comes of all this falderal about knight and squire. It would seem they had both been turned out from the same mold and that the madness of the master without the foolishness of the man would not be worth a penny."

"You are right," agreed the barber, "and I would give a good deal to know what the two of them are talking about at this moment."

"I feel certain," replied the curate, "that the niece or the housekeeper will tell us all about it afterward, for it is not like them to fail to listen."

In the meanwhile Don Quixote had shut himself up in his room with Sancho.

"It grieves me very much, Sancho," he began as soon as they were alone, "to hear you saying that it was I who took you away from your cottage. You know very well that I did not remain in my own house. We sallied forth and rode away together, and together we wandered here and there. We shared the same fortune and the same fate, and if they blanketed you once, they flayed me a hundred times; that is the only advantage that I have over you."

"That is as it should be," Sancho told him, "for, according to what your Grace says, misfortunes are better suited to knights-errant than to their squires."

"That is where you are wrong, Sancho," replied the knight, "in accordance with the proverb 'Quando caput dolet,' etc."

"I understand no other language than my own," said Sancho.

"I mean," said Don Quixote, "that when the head suffers, all the other members suffer also. Being your master and lord, I am your head, and you, being my servant, are a part of me; and so it is that the evil which affects me must likewise affect you and your pain must be my own."

"It may be so," Sancho answered, "but I know that when they were blanketing me, as a member, my head was on the other side of the wall, watching me fly through the air, without feeling any pain whatever. And it does seem to me that if the members are obliged to suffer with the head, the head ought to suffer with them."

"Do you mean to stand there and tell me, Sancho, that I felt nothing when they were tossing you in the blanket? You must not say or think such a thing as that, for I felt more pain in my mind than you did in your body. However, let us put all this to one side; for there will be time enough later for us to consider this point and reach a conclusion. Rather, Sancho my friend, tell me, what are they saying about me here in the village? What opinion do the people have of me, and what do the gentry think, the *hidalgos* and the *caballeros*? [2] What do they say of my valor, of my exploits, of my courtesy? What kind of talk is there about my having undertaken to restore to the world the forgotten order of chivalry? In brief, Sancho, I would have you tell me everything that you have heard on this subject; and this you are to do without adding to the good or keeping back any of the bad; for it is fittng that loyal vassals should tell the truth to their lords, just as it is, without magnifying it out of adulation or diminishing it out of a feeling of false respect. I may tell you, Sancho, that if the naked truth could only reach the ears of princes, stripped of the garments of flattery, the times would be quite different from what they are and other eras would be known as the age of iron, not ours, which indeed I hold to be a golden epoch among those of the modern world. Give heed to this advice, Sancho, in order that you may be able to answer my questions intelligently and faithfully and tell me what you know to be the truth about these things."

"That I will do right willingly, my master," Sancho

replied, "on condition that your Grace will not be angry
at what I tell you, seeing that you would have me give
it to you stark naked, without putting any other clothes
on it than those in which it came to me."

"Of course I shall not be angry," said Don Quixote.
"You may speak freely, Sancho, without any beating
around the bush."

"Well, in the first place, the common people look
upon your Grace as an utter madman and me as no less
a fool. The *hidalgos* are saying that, not content with
being a gentleman, you have had to put a 'Don'[3] in
front of your name and at a bound have made yourself
into a *caballero*, with four vinestocks, a couple of acres[4]
of land, and one tatter in front and another behind.
The *caballeros*, on the other hand, do not relish having
the *hidalgos* set up in opposition to them, especially
those gentlemen who perform the duties of a squire by
polishing their own shoes and darning their black stockings with green silk."

"That," said the knight, "has nothing to do with me,
since I always go well dressed and never in patches.
Ragged I well may be, but rather from the wear and
tear of armor than of time."[5]

"So far as your Grace's valor is concerned," Sancho
went on, "your courtesy, exploits, and undertaking,
there are different opinions. Some say: 'Crazy but amusing'; others: 'Brave but unfortunate'; others still:
'Courteous but meddlesome'; and they go on clacking
their tongues about this thing and that until there is not
a whole bone left in your Grace's body or in mine."

"Look you, Sancho," replied his master, "wherever
virtue exists in an outstanding degree, it is always persecuted. Few or none of the famous men of the past
have escaped without being slandered by the malicious.

Julius Caesar, a most courageous, wise, and valiant captain, was charged with ambition and with being none too clean either in his dress or in his morals. Alexander, whose deeds won him the title of Great, was reported to be somewhat of a drunkard. Hercules—he of the many labors—if we are to believe what they say of him, was lascivious and inclined to effeminacy. Of Don Galaor, brother of Amadis of Gaul, it was whispered about that he was far too quarrelsome, while Amadis himself was called a whiner. So you see, Sancho, when good men have been traduced in this fashion, what they say about me may be overlooked, if it is no more than what you have told me."

"Body of my father!" exclaimed Sancho, "but there's the rub."

"What?" Don Quixote asked. "Is there more then?"

"That there is," said Sancho. "The tail is yet to be skinned.[6] All so far has been tarts and fancy cakes;[7] but if your Grace really wants to know what they are saying, I can bring you here at once one who will tell you everything, without leaving out the least particle of it. Bartolomé Carrasco's son came home last night. He has been studying at Salamanca and has just been made a bachelor. When I went to welcome him, he told me that the story of your Grace has already been put into a book called *The Ingenious Gentleman, Don Quixote de la Mancha*. And he says they mention me in it, under my own name, Sancho Panza, and the lady Dulcinea del Toboso as well, along with things that happened to us when we were alone together. I had to cross myself, for I could not help wondering how the one who wrote all those things down could have come to know about them."

"I can assure you, Sancho," said Don Quixote, "that the author of our history must be some wise enchanter;

for nothing that they choose to write about is hidden from those who practice that art."

"What do you mean by saying he was an enchanter?" Sancho asked. "Why, the bachelor Sansón Carrasco—which is the name of the man I was telling you of—says that the one who wrote the story is called Cid Hamete Berenjena."

"That," said Don Quixote, "is a Moorish name."

"It may be," replied Sancho; "for I have generally heard it said that the Moors are great lovers of egg-plant." [8]

"You must have made some mistake," said the knight, "regarding the surname of this Cid, a title which in Arabic means 'Señor.'"

"Maybe I did," replied Sancho; "but if your Grace would like me to bring the man here, I will go for him in a jiffy."

"It would give me much pleasure, my friend," said Don Quixote, "for I am astonished by what you have told me and shall not eat a mouthful that sets well on my stomach until I have learned all about it."

"Very well, then," said Sancho, "I will go fetch him." And, leaving his master, he went out to look for the bachelor. He returned with him a short while later, and the three of them then had a most amusing conversation.

CHAPTER III. *Of the laughable conversation that took place between Don Quixote, Sancho Panza, and the bachelor Sansón Carrasco.*

DON QUIXOTE remained in a thoughtful mood as he waited for the Bachelor Carrasco, from whom he hoped to hear the news as to how he had been put into a book, as Sancho had said. He could not bring

himself to believe that any such history existed, since
the blood of the enemies he had slain was not yet dry
on the blade of his sword; and here they were trying
to tell him that his high deeds of chivalry were already
circulating in printed form. But, for that matter, he
imagined that some sage, either friend or enemy, must
have seen to the printing of them through the art of
magic. If the chronicler was a friend, he must have
undertaken the task in order to magnify and exalt Don
Quixote's exploits above the most notable ones achieved
by knights-errant of old. If an enemy, his purpose
would have been to make them out as nothing at all,
by debasing them below the meanest acts ever recorded
of any mean squire. The only thing was, the knight
reflected, the exploits of squires never were set down
in writing. If it was true that such a history existed, being about a knight-errant, then it must be eloquent and
lofty in tone, a splendid and distinguished piece of work
and veracious in its details.

This consoled him somewhat, although he was a bit
put out at the thought that the author was a Moor, if
the appellation "Cid" was to be taken as an indication,
and from the Moors you could never hope for any
word of truth, seeing that they are all of them cheats,
forgers, and schemers. He feared lest his love should
not have been treated with becoming modesty but
rather in a way that would reflect upon the virtue of his
Lady Dulcinea del Toboso. He hoped that his fidelity
had been made clear, and the respect he had always
shown her, and that something had been said as to
how he had spurned queens, empresses, and damsels of
every rank while keeping a rein upon those impulses
that are natural to a man. He was still wrapped up in
these and many other similar thoughts when Sancho
returned with Carrasco.

Don Quixote received the bachelor very amiably. The latter, although his name was Sansón, or Samson, was not very big so far as bodily size went, but he was a great joker, with a sallow complexion and a ready wit. He was going on twenty-four and had a round face, a snub nose, and a large mouth, all of which showed him to be of a mischievous disposition and fond of jests and witticisms. This became apparent when, as soon as he saw Don Quixote, he fell upon his knees and addressed the knight as follows:

"O mighty Don Quixote de la Mancha, give me your hands; for by the habit of St. Peter[1] that I wear— though I have received but the first four orders—your Grace is one of the most famous knights-errant that ever have been or ever will be anywhere on this earth. Blessings upon Cid Hamete Benengeli who wrote down the history of your great achievements, and upon that curious-minded one who was at pains to have it translated from the Arabic into our Castilian vulgate for the universal entertainment of the people."

Don Quixote bade him rise. "Is it true, then," he asked, "that there is a book about me and that it was some Moorish sage who composed it?"

"By way of showing you how true it is," replied Sansón, "I may tell you that it is my belief that there are in existence today more than twelve thousand copies of that history. If you do not believe me, you have but to make inquiries in Portugal, Barcelona, and Valencia, where editions have been brought out, and there is even a report to the effect that one edition was printed at Antwerp.[2] In short, I feel certain that there will soon not be a nation that does not know it or a language into which it has not been translated."

"One of the things," remarked Don Quixote, "that should give most satisfaction to a virtuous and eminent man is to see his good name spread abroad during his own lifetime, by means of the printing press, through translations into the languages of the various peoples. I have said 'good name,' for if he has any other kind, his fate is worse than death."

"If it is a matter of good name and good reputation," said the bachelor, "your Grace bears off the palm from all the knights-errant in the world; for the Moor in his tongue and the Christian in his have most vividly depicted your Grace's gallantry, your courage in facing dangers, your patience in adversity and suffering, whether the suffering be due to wounds or to misfortunes of another sort, and your virtue and continence in love, in connection with that platonic relationship that exists between your Grace and my lady Doña Dulcinea del Toboso."

At this point Sancho spoke up. "Never in my life," he said, "have I heard my lady Dulcinea called 'Doña,' but only 'la Señora Dulcinea del Toboso'; so on that point, already, the history is wrong."

"That is not important," said Carrasco.

"No, certainly not," Don Quixote agreed. "But tell me, Señor Bachelor, what adventures of mine as set down in this book have made the deepest impression?"

"As to that," the bachelor answered, "opinions differ, for it is a matter of individual taste. There are some who are very fond of the adventure of the windmills—those windmills which to your Grace appeared to be so many Briareuses and giants. Others like the episode at the fulling mill. One relishes the story of the two armies which took on the appearance of droves of sheep, while another fancies the tale of the dead man whom they were taking to Segovia for burial. One will assert that the freeing of the galley slaves is the best of all, and yet another will maintain that nothing can come up to the Benedictine giants and the encounter with the valiant Biscayan."

Again Sancho interrupted him. "Tell me, Señor Bachelor," he said, "does the book say anything about the adventure with the Yanguesans, that time our good Rocinante took it into his head to go looking for tidbits in the sea?"

"The sage," replied Sansón, "has left nothing in the inkwell. He has told everything and to the point, even to the capers which the worthy Sancho cut as they tossed him in the blanket."

"I cut no capers in the blanket," objected Sancho, "but I did in the air, and more than I liked."

"I imagine," said Don Quixote, "that there is no history in the world, dealing with humankind, that does not have its ups and downs, and this is particularly true of those that have to do with deeds of chivalry, for they can never be filled with happy incidents alone."

"Nevertheless," the bachelor went on, "there are some who have read the book who say that they would have been glad if the authors had forgotten a few of the innumerable cudgelings[3] which Señor Don Quixote received in the course of his various encounters."

"But that is where the truth of the story comes in," Sancho protested.

"For all of that," observed Don Quixote, "they might well have said nothing about them; for there is no need of recording those events that do not alter the veracity of the chronicle, when they tend only to lessen the reader's respect for the hero. You may be sure that Aeneas was not as pious as Vergil would have us believe, nor was Ulysses as wise as Homer depicts him."

"That is true enough," replied Sansón, "but it is one

thing to write as a poet and another as a historian. The former may narrate or sing of things not as they were but as they should have been; the latter must describe them not as they should have been but as they were, without adding to or detracting from the truth in any degree whatsoever."

"Well," said Sancho, "if this Moorish gentleman is bent upon telling the truth, I have no doubt that among my master's thrashings my own will be found; for they never took the measure of his Grace's shoulders without measuring my whole body. But I don't wonder at that; for as my master himself says, when there's an ache in the head the members have to share it."

"You are a sly fox, Sancho," said Don Quixote. "My word, but you can remember things well enough when you choose to do so!"

"Even if I wanted to forget the whacks they gave me," Sancho answered him, "the welts on my ribs wouldn't let me, for they are still fresh."

"Be quiet, Sancho," his master admonished him, "and do not interrupt the bachelor. I beg him to go on and tell me what is said of me in this book."

"And what it says about me, too," put in Sancho, "for I have heard that I am one of the main presonages in it—"

"*Personages*, not *presonages*, Sancho my friend," said Sansón.

"So we have another one who catches you up on everything you say," was Sancho's retort. "If we go on at this rate, we'll never be through in a lifetime."

"May God put a curse on *my* life," the bachelor told him, "if you are not the second most important person in the story; and there are some who would rather listen to you talk than to anyone else in the book. It is true, there are those who say that you are too gullible in believing it to be the truth that you could become the governor of that island that was offered you by Señor Don Quixote, here present."

"There is still sun on the top of the wall," [4] said Don Quixote, "and when Sancho is a little older, with the experience that the years bring, he will be wiser and better fitted to be a governor that he is at the present time."

"By God, master," said Sancho, "the island that I couldn't govern right now I'd never be able to govern if I lived to be as old as Methuselah. The trouble is, I don't know where that island we are talking about is located; it is not due to any lack of noddle on my part."

"Leave it to God, Sancho," was Don Quixote's advice, "and everything will come out all right, perhaps even better than you think; for not a leaf on the tree stirs except by His will."

"Yes," said Sansón, "if it be God's will, Sancho will not lack a thousand islands to govern, not to speak of one island alone."

"I have seen governors around here," said Sancho, "that are not to be compared to the sole of my shoe, and yet they call them 'your Lordship' and serve them on silver plate."

"Those are not the same kind of governors," Sansón informed him. "Their task is a good deal easier. The ones that govern islands must at least know grammar."

"I could make out well enough with the *gram*," replied Sancho, "but with the *mar*[5] I want nothing to do, for I don't understand it at all. But leaving this business of the governorship in God's hands—for He will send me wherever I can best serve Him—I will tell you, Señor Bachelor Sansón Carrasco, that I am very much pleased that the author of the history should have spoken of me in such a way as does not offend me;

for, upon the word of a faithful squire, if he had said anything about me that was not becoming to an old Christian, the deaf would have heard of it."

"That would be to work miracles," said Sansón.

"Miracles or no miracles," was the answer, "let everyone take care as to what he says or writes about people and not be setting down the first thing that pops into his head."

"One of the faults to be found with the book," continued the bachelor, "is that the author has inserted in it a story entitled *The One Who Was Too Curious for His Own Good.* It is not that the story in itself is a bad one or badly written; it is simply that it is out of place there, having nothing to do with the story of his Grace, Señor Don Quixote."

"I will bet you," said Sancho, "that the son of a dog has mixed the cabbages with the baskets." [6]

"And I will say right now," declared Don Quixote, "that the author of this book was not a sage but some ignorant prattler who at haphazard and without any method set about the writing of it, being content to let things turn out as they might. In the same manner, Orbaneja,[7] the painter of Ubeda, when asked what he was painting would reply, 'Whatever it turns out to be.' Sometimes it would be a cock, in which case he would have to write alongside it, in Gothic letters, 'This is a cock.' And so it must be with my story, which will need a commentary to make it understandable."

"No," replied Sansón, "that it will not; for it is so clearly written that none can fail to understand it. Little children leaf through it, young people read it, adults appreciate it, and the aged sing its praises. In short, it is so thumbed and read and so well known to persons of every walk in life that no sooner do folks see some skinny nag than they at once cry, 'There goes Rocinante!' Those that like it best of all are the pages; for there is no lord's antechamber where a *Don Quixote* is not to be found. If one lays it down, another will pick it up; one will pounce upon it, and another will beg for it. It affords the pleasantest and least harmful reading of any book that has been published up to now. In the whole of it there is not to be found an indecent word or a thought that is other than Catholic." [8]

"To write in any other manner," observed Don Quixote, "would be to write lies and not the truth. Those historians who make use of falsehoods ought to be burned like the makers of counterfeit money. I do not know what could have led the author to introduce stories and episodes that are foreign to the subject matter when he had so much to write about in describing my adventures. He must, undoubtedly, have been inspired by the old saying, 'With straw or with hay . . .' [9] For, in truth, all he had to do was to record my thoughts, my sighs, my tears, my lofty purposes, and my undertakings, and he would have had a volume bigger than, or at least as big as, that which the works of El Tostado[10] would make. To sum the matter up, Señor Bachelor, it is my opinion that, in composing histories or books of any sort, a great deal of judgment and ripe understanding is called for. To say and write witty and amusing things is the mark of great genius. The cleverest character in a comedy is the clown, since he who would make himself out to be a simpleton cannot be one. History is a near-sacred thing, for it must be true, and where the truth is, there is God. And yet there are those who compose books and toss them out into the world as if they were no more than fritters."

"There is no book so bad," opined the bachelor, "that there is not some good in it." [11]

"Doubtless that is so," replied Don Quixote, "but it

very often happens that those who have won in advance a great and well-deserved reputation for their writings, lose it in whole or in part when they give their works to the printer."

"The reason for it," said Sansón, "is that, printed works being read at leisure, their faults are the more readily apparent, and the greater the reputation of the author the more closely are they scrutinized. Men famous for their genius, great poets, illustrious historians, are almost always envied by those who take a special delight in criticizing the writings of others without having produced anything of their own."

"That is not to be wondered at," said Don Quixote, "for there are many theologians who are not good enough for the pulpit but who are very good indeed when it comes to detecting the faults or excesses of those who preach."

"All of this is very true, Señor Don Quixote," replied Carrasco, "but, all the same, I could wish that these self-appointed censors were a bit more forbearing and less hypercritical; I wish they would pay a little less attention to the spots on the bright sun of the work that occasions their fault-finding. For if *aliquando bonus dormitat Homerus,*[12] let them consider how much of his time he spent awake, shedding the light of his genius with a minimum of shade. It well may be that what to them seems a flaw is but one of those moles which sometimes add to the beauty of a face. In any event, I insist that he who has a book printed runs a very great risk, inasmuch as it is an utter impossibility to write it in such a manner that it will please all who read it."

"This book about me must have pleased very few," remarked Don Quixote.

"Quite the contrary," said Sansón, "for just as *stul-*

torum infinitus est numerus,[13] so the number of those who have enjoyed this history is likewise infinite. Some, to be sure, have complained of the author's forgetfulness, seeing that he neglected to make it plain who the thief was who stole Sancho's gray; for it is not stated there, but merely implied, that the ass was stolen; and, a little further on, we find Sancho mounted on the same beast, although it has not made its reappearance in the story. They also say that the author forgot to tell us what Sancho did with those hundred crowns that he found in the valise on the Sierra Morena, as nothing more is said of them and there are many who would like to know how he disposed of the money or how he spent it. This is one of the serious omissions to be found in the work."

To this Sancho replied, "I, Señor Sansón, do not feel like giving any account or accounting just now; for I feel a little weak in my stomach, and if I don't do something about it by taking a few swigs of the old stuff, I'll be sitting on St. Lucy's thorn.[14] I have some of it at home, and my old woman is waiting for me. After I've had my dinner, I'll come back and answer any questions your Grace or anybody else wants to ask me, whether it's about the loss of the ass or the spending of the hundred crowns."

And without waiting for a reply or saying another word, he went on home. Don Quixote urged the bachelor to stay and take potluck with him,[15] and Sansón accepted the invitation and remained. In addition to the knight's ordinary fare, they had a couple of pigeons, and at table their talk was of chivalry and feats of arms. Carrasco was careful to humor his host, and when the meal was over they took their siesta. Then Sancho returned and their previous conversation was resumed.

CHAPTER IV. *Wherein Sancho Panza answers the bachelor's questions and removes his doubts, together with other events that are worthy of being known and set down.*

RETURNING to Don Quixote's house, Sancho began where they had left off.

"Señor Sansón has said that he would like to know who it was that stole my ass and how and when it was done. In answer to that, I can tell him that it was the same night that we went up onto the Sierra Morena, to get away from the Holy Brotherhood. It was after the adventure of the galley slaves and that of the dead man that they were taking to Segovia. My master and I had gone into a thicket; and there, with him leaning on his lance and me seated on my gray and the both of us bruised and tired from the scuffles we had been through, we dozed off and slept as if we had had four feather beds beneath us. As for me, I was so dead to the world that whoever it was that came along was able to put four stakes under the four sides of my packsaddle and leave me sitting astraddle of it while he took my gray out from under me without my knowing anything about it."

"That," said Sansón, "is an easy thing to do and has been done before. It happened to Sacripante when, at the siege of Albraca, the famous thief known as Brunello,[1] employing the same device, took the horse out from between the knight's legs."

"Well," Sancho went on, "morning came, and when I went to stretch myself the stakes gave way and I took a mighty tumble. I looked around for the ass and could not see it, and then the tears came to my eyes and

I set up such a howling that if the author of the book
did not put it in, then he left out something very good.
After I don't know how many days, going along with
her Ladyship, the Princess Micomicona, I caught sight
of Ginés de Pasamonte coming down the road dressed
like a gypsy and mounted on my beast—he was that big
rogue and trickster that my master and I freed from the
galley slaves' chain."

"That is not where the error lies," replied Sansón,
"but rather in the fact that before the ass turns up again
the author has Sancho riding on it."

"I don't know what answer to give you," said Sancho,
"except that the one who wrote the story must have
made a mistake, or else it must be due to carelessness on
the part of the printer."

"No doubt that is it," said Sansón, "but what became
of the hundred crowns? Did they vanish into thin air?"

"I spent them on myself and on my wife and young
ones, and that is why it is she puts up with my wanderings along the highways and byways in the service of
my master Don Quixote; for if after all that time I
had come home without my gray or a penny to my
name, I would have had one devil of a welcome. If
there is anything else you would like to know about me,
here I am, ready to answer in person to the king himself,
and it is nobody's business whether I took it or did not
take it, whether I spent it or didn't spend it. If all the
whacks they gave me on those journeys had to be paid
for in money, even if they valued them only at four
maravedis apiece, another hundred crowns would not
be enough to pay for the half of them. Let every man
look after himself and not be trying to make out that
white is black and black is white; for each one is as God
made him, and a good deal worse a lot of times."

"I shall make it a point," said Carrasco, "to remind

the author that if he has another edition printed, he is by no means to forget what the good Sancho has told us, which I am sure will greatly improve the book." [2]

"Are there any other corrections to be made in this work?" Don Quixote inquired.

"There probably are," the bachelor replied, "but the ones we have mentioned are the most important."

"And does the author by any chance promise a second part?"

"Yes, he does," said Sansón, "but he states that he has not yet come upon it, nor does he know in whose possession it is, and accordingly there is a doubt as to whether it will appear or not. Indeed, there is some question as to whether a second part is desirable. There are those who say, 'Sequels are never good,' while others assert, 'Enough has been written already about Don Quixote.' But certain ones who are more jovially inclined and not of so morose a disposition will tell you, 'Let us have more of these Quixotic adventures; let Don Quixote lay on and Sancho talk, and, come what may, we shall be satisfied.' "

"And how does the author feel about it?"

"If he finds the history he is looking for so diligently," said Sansón, "he will send it to the printer at once, being more interested in the profit that may come to him from it than in any praise it may earn him."

Sancho now put in his word. "So, he is interested in money, is he? Then it will be a wonder if he doesn't botch the job, for it will be nothing but hurry, hurry, hurry, as at the tailors on Easter Eve, and work done in haste is never done as it should be. Let that Moorish gentleman, or whoever he is, pay attention, and my master and I will supply him with enough stuff,[3] ready at hand, in the way of adventures and other happenings, to make not only one second part but a hundred of them. The good man thinks, no doubt, that we are asleep here in the straw, but let him hold up our hoofs to be shod and he will see which foot is the lame one. All I have to say is that if my master would take my advice, we would be in the field this minute, avenging outrages and righting wrongs as is the use and custom of good knights-errant."

No sooner had Sancho said this than they heard the whinnying of Rocinante, which Don Quixote took to be a very good omen; and he resolved then and there that they would sally forth again within the next three or four days. Announcing his intention to Carrasco, he asked the bachelor to advise him as to what direction he should take; whereupon Sansón replied that in his opinion the knight ought to head for the kingdom of Aragon and the city of Saragossa, as they were to have some ceremonious joustings there very shortly, in honor of the feast of St. George,[4] in which tournament Don Quixote might win a renown above that of all the knights of Aragon, who in turn would be sure to vanquish all others in the world. Sansón went on to praise his host's highly praiseworthy and valiant undertaking, but warned him to be a little more careful in confronting dangers, since his life was not his own but belonged to all those who had need of his succor and protection in the misfortunes that befell them.

"That is what I don't like about it, Señor Sansón," said Sancho. "My master will attack a hundred armed men just like a greedy boy falling on a half-dozen melons. Body of the world,[5] Señor Bachelor, but there is a time to attack and a time to retreat! Everything is not 'Santiago, and close in upon them, Spain!'[6] For I have heard it said—and I think my master himself was the one who said it—that true bravery lies somewhere in between being a coward and being foolhardy; and, for this reason, I would not have him run away when there is not good reason for it, nor have him attack when the odds are all against him. But, above everything else, I want to warn him that if he is going to take me with him, it will have to be on condition that he does all the fighting, it being understood that all I am to do is to look after his person and see to keeping him clean and comfortable. When it comes to that, I will be at his beck and call; but to look for me to lay hand to sword, even against the most rascally villains of hatchet and hood, is a waste of thinking.

"I do not expect, Señor Sansón," he continued, "to win fame as a fighting man, but only as the best and most loyal squire that ever served a knight-errant; and if my master Don Quixote, as a reward for my many faithful services, see fit to give me some island of all those that his Grace says are to be had, I will accept it as a great favor; but if he does not give it to me, well, I was born like everyone else, and a man should depend on no one but God, and what is more, my bread will taste as good, and it may be even better, without a governorship than if I was a governor. How do I know that in connection with governments the devil has not prepared some trap for me where I may stumble and fall and knock my grinders out? Sancho was born and Sancho expects to die; but, for all of that, if without much risk or trouble on my part Heaven should provide me with an island, fair and square, I am not such a fool as to refuse it. For they also have a saying, 'When they offer you a heifer, come running with a halter,' and, 'When good luck comes along, open the door and let it in.'" [7]

"Spoken like a professor, brother Sancho," said Carrasco. "Put your trust in God and in Señor Don Quixote.

and your master will see to it that you are provided with a kingdom and no mere island."

"More or less, it is all the same to me," replied Sancho. "I may tell you, Señor Carrasco, that my master would not be tossing that kingdom he is going to give me into a sack that was full of holes. I have taken my own pulse, and I find that I am man enough to rule over realms and govern islands, and I have already told him as much any number of times."

"But see here, Sancho," said the bachelor, "manners change when honors come,[8] and it may be that when you get to be governor you will not know the mother who bore you."

"That may be true of those that were born in the mallows,[9] but not of one like me with the fat of an old Christian four fingers deep on his soul. Do I look to you like the kind of man who would be ungrateful to anyone?"

"God's will be done," said Don Quixote. "We can tell better when the governorship comes, and it seems to me I can see it already."

Having said this, he turned to the bachelor and inquired if that gentleman was a poet. If so, would he do him the favor of composing some farewell verses for my lady Dulcinea del Toboso, each line to begin with a letter of her name, so that when the poem was complete those letters would spell out the name. Carrasco replied that, although he was not one of the famous poets of Spain—of whom, he said, there were but three and a half altogether[10]—he would not fail to do as Don Quixote had requested, although he found the task rather difficult, seeing that there were seventeen letters to be accounted for; if he made four stanzas of four lines each, there would be one letter left over, while if he employed one of those five-line stanzas known as *décimas* or *redondillas*,[11] he would be three letters short. Nevertheless, he would try, some way or other, to drop a letter in order that he might get the name Dulcinea del Toboso into a set of four-line stanzas.

"You must manage it somehow," said Don Quixote; "for if the name is not plainly to be made out, no woman would believe that the verses were written expressly for her."

This point having been settled, it was decided that the knight's departure should be one week from that day. The bachelor was charged to keep it secret, especially from the curate and Master Nicholas, and from the niece and housekeeper as well, in order that they might not prevent the carrying out of this commendable and valorous undertaking. Carrasco gave his promise and took his leave, and as he did so he urged Don Quixote to keep him informed, whenever the opportunity presented itself, of any good or ill fortune that might come to master and man. Thus they parted, and Sancho went away to make the necessary preparations for the expedition.

CHAPTER V. *Of the shrewd and droll remarks that passed between Sancho Panza and his wife, Teresa Panza, with other matters of a pleasant nature that deserve to be recorded.*

AS HE comes to set down this fifth chapter of our history, the translator desires to make it plain that he looks upon it as apocryphal, since in it Sancho Panza speaks in a manner that does not appear to go with his limited intelligence and indulges in such subtle observations that it is quite impossible to conceive of his saying the things attributed to him. However, the translator in question did not wish to leave his task unfinished; and the narrative is accordingly herewith resumed.

As Sancho approached his house, he was feeling so happy and so gay that his wife could tell it at the distance of a crossbow shot.

"What do you bring with you, friend Sancho," she asked, "that makes you so merry?"

"Wife," he replied, "if it was God's will, I'd be glad not to be as happy as I am."

"I don't understand you, husband," said she. "I don't know what you mean by wishing you were not as happy as you are. I may be a fool, but I fail to see how you can find pleasure in not having it."

"Look here, Teresa," said Sancho, "I am happy because I have made up my mind to go back to serving my master Don Quixote, who wants to go out a third time in search of adventures, and I mean to go with him. It is necessity that leads me to do this, and then, too, I like to think that I may be able to come upon another hundred crowns to take the place of those we've spent, although, naturally, it makes me sad to have to leave you and the young ones. If God would only let me eat my bread at home, dryshod, without dragging me through the byways and crossroads—and it would not cost Him anything, all He has to do is will it—it goes without saying that my happiness would be more solid and lasting than it is, whereas now it is mixed up with my sorrow at leaving you. That is what I meant when I said that I'd be glad if, God willing, I was not so happy."

"Listen to me, Sancho," his wife replied. "Ever since you joined up with a knight-errant, you've been talking in such a roundabout way that there's no understanding you."

"It is enough, wife, if God understands me; for He understands everything, and that is good enough for me. And I want to warn you, sister, that you are to keep an eye on the gray these next few days so that he will be in condition to take up arms. Give him double rations, and look after the packsaddle and the other harness, for it's not to a wedding that we're bound; we're out to roam the world and play give and take with giants, dragons, and other monsters. We'll be hearing hissings and roarings and bellowings and howlings. But all that would be lavender if we didn't have to count upon meeting with Yanguesans and enchanted Moors."

"I know well, my husband," said Teresa, "that the squires of knights-errant have to earn the bread they eat, and so I will keep on praying to Our Lord to get you out of all this hard luck."

"I can tell you one thing, wife," said Sancho, "that if I did not expect to see myself the governor of an island before long, I would die right here and now."

"No, not that, my husband," Teresa protested. "Let the hen live even though she may have the pip,[1] and in the same way you should go on living and to the devil with all the governorships in the world. Without a governorship you came out of your mother's belly, without a governorship you've lived up to now, and without a governorship you will go, or they will carry you, to your grave when God so wills. There are plenty of folk in this world who manage to get along without being governors, yet they do not for that reason give up but are still numbered among the living. The best sauce in the world is hunger, and since this is something they never lack, the poor always have an appetite. But look, Sancho, if by any chance you do fall in with a governorship, don't forget me and your children. Remember that little Sancho is already turned fifteen, and it is only right that he should go to school, if his uncle, the abbot, means to have him trained for the Church. Remember, too, that your daughter, Mari-Sancha, would not drop dead if we married her off; for I have my suspicions that she is as anxious for a husband as you are to be a governor, and, when all is said and done, a daughter badly married is better than one well kept outside of marriage."

"I promise you, wife," replied Sancho, "that if God only sees to it that I get hold of any kind of an island at all, I will get Mari-Sancha a husband so high up in the world that no one will be able to come near her without calling her 'my ladyship.'"

"No, Sancho," said his wife. "Marry her to someone who is her equal; that's the best way. If you take her out of wooden shoes and put her into pattens, if you take her out of gray flannel petticoat and put her into silken hoop skirts, if you stop saying 'thou' to her and change her from 'Marica' into 'Doña So-and-So' and 'my lady,' then the poor girl will not know where she is and every step she takes she will be making a thousand blunders and showing the thread of the coarse home-spun stuff she's made of."

"Be quiet, foolish woman," said Sancho. "All she will need is two or three years to get used to it, and, after that, dignity and fine manners will fit her like a glove; and if not, what does it matter? Let her be 'your Lady-ship' and come what may."

"Better keep to your own station, Sancho," Teresa admonished him, "and not be trying to lift yourself up to a higher one. Remember the old saying, 'Wipe the nose of your neighbor's son and take him into your house.' [2] It would be a fine thing, wouldn't it, to have our Maria married to some great count or high and mighty gentleman who every time he happened to feel like it would call her an upstart, a clodhopper's daughter, a country wench who ought to be at the spinning wheel. No, as I live, my husband, it was not for this that I brought up my daughter! You bring home the money, Sancho, and leave the marrying of her to me. There is Lope Tocho, Juan Tocho's boy. He's a strong, healthy lad and we know him well, and I can see he rather likes our lass. He's our kind, and she'll be making no mistake in marrying him. That way, we'll be able to keep an eye on her, and we'll all be together, parents and children, grandchildren, sons-in-law and daughters-in-law, and peace and God's blessing will be upon us. So don't go marrying her off in those courts and grand palaces where she will be a stranger to others and to herself."

"Why, you stupid creature!" exclaimed Sancho. "You wife of Barabbas! [3] What do you mean by trying to keep me from marrying my daughter to someone who will give me grandchildren that will be called 'your Lordship' and 'your Ladyship'? Look, Teresa, I have always heard the old folks say that the one that doesn't know how to make the most of luck when it comes his way has no business complaining if it passes him by. And now that luck is knocking at our door, we don't want to shut it out. Let us go with the favoring breeze that fills our sail." (It was this way of speaking, and what Sancho has to say a little further on, that led the translator of the history to remark that he looked upon this chapter as apocryphal.)

"Can't you see, you ninny," Sancho went on, "what a fine thing it will be for me to fall into some nice governorship or other that will help us get our feet out of the mud? Just let me find the husband I choose for Mari-Sancha, and you'll see how they'll be calling you 'Doña Teresa Panza,' and you will sit in church on a rug and cushions and fancy drapes in spite of the highborn ladies of the village. But no, you'd better stay the way you are, neither bigger nor smaller, like a figure on a tapestry, and we'll say no more about it. Little Sancha is going to be a countess, no matter what you think." [4]

"Husband," said Teresa, "are you sure you know what you are talking about? For I am very much afraid that if my daughter becomes a countess it will be her ruination. You can do what you like, you can make a duchess or a princess of her, but I want to tell you it will be without my will or consent. I always did believe in equality, brother, and I can't bear to see people put on airs without any reason for it. Teresa was the name they gave me when I was baptized, without any tags, or strings, or trimmings; there were no 'Dons' or 'Doñas' in my family. My father's name was Cascajo. As your wife, I am now called Teresa Panza, though by rights I should be known as Teresa Cascajo. But kings go where the laws would have them go,[5] and the name I have is good enough for me without their putting a 'Doña' on top of it and making it so heavy I can't carry it. I don't want to give people a chance to talk when they see me dressed like a countess or a governor's wife and have them saying, 'Just see the airs that hog-feeder puts on, will you? Only yesterday she was spinning flax and went to mass with the tail of her petticoat over her head in place of a mantle, and today she goes in hoops, with her brooches and her nose in the air, as if we didn't know her!'

"If God lets keep my six or seven senses, or whatever number it is that I have, I don't propose to give them a chance to see me in such a predicament. You, brother, go ahead and govern your island and strut all you like, but I tell you in the name of my sainted mother that neither my daughter nor I is going to stir one step from our village. The respectable woman has a broken leg and stays at home,[6] and to be busy at something is a

feast day for the maid that is virtuous. Go, then, to look
for adventures with that Don Quixote of yours, and
leave us to our misadventures; for God will make things
better for us if we deserve it. I'm sure I don't know,"
she added, "who made him a 'Don,' for neither his father
nor his grandfather was one before him."

"I do declare," said Sancho, "you must have a devil in
you. God help you, wife, but what a lot of things you
have strung together so that there's no making head nor
tail of any of them! What do the name Cascajo and
brooches and proverbs and haughty airs have to do with
what I'm saying? Look here, you foolish, ignorant
woman—for I have a right to call you that, seeing you
won't listen to reason but run away from good fortune.
If I had said that my daughter was to throw herself
from a tower or go wandering about the world as the
Infanta Doña Uracca[7] threatened to do, you would be
right in not agreeing with me; but when I want to put
a 'Doña' or a 'ladyship' on her back and in the blink of
an eye take her out of the stubble and seat her on a dais
under a canopy or on a divan with more velvet cushions[8]
than the Almohades of Morocco had Moors in their
family tree, why won't you give your consent and let
me have it my way?"

"Do you want to know why, husband?" Teresa asked
him. "It's on account of the proverb that says, 'He who
covers you discovers you.' To the poor, people give only
a passing glance, but the rich man holds their gaze; and
if he was poor once upon a time, then it is that the whispering and the evil gossip and the spitework begin, for
the slanderers in these streets are as thick as a swarm
of bees."

"Pay attention, Teresa," said Sancho, "and listen to
what I am about to tell you. It may be that you have
never heard it in all the days of your life. I am not speak-

ing for myself but am giving you the opinions of the reverend father who preached in this village during Lent, the last time. If I remember rightly, he said that all present things which our eyes behold make much more of an impression on us and remain better fixed in our memories than things that are past." (These remarks of Sancho's are another reason for the translator's saying what he did about the apocryphal character of this chapter, since they are beyond the mental capacity of the squire.) "Hence it is that when we see some person richly dressed and making a fine appearance, accompanied by a retinue of servants, we feel compelled to respect him, even though our memory at the moment may remind us of some lowly condition in which we had previously seen him. That condition, whether due to poverty or humble birth, being a thing of the past, does not exist, since the only thing that is real to us is what we have before our eyes. And—these were the padre's very words—if the one fortune has thus raised up out of the depths to the height of prosperity is well bred, generous, and courteous toward all and does not seek to vie with those that come of an old and noble line, then you may depend upon it, Teresa, there will be no one to remember what he was, but instead they will respect him for what he is, unless it be the envious, for no good fortune is safe against them."

"I do not understand you, husband," replied Teresa. "Do as you like and don't be addling my brains with your flowery speeches. If you have revolved to do what you say—"

"You mean *resolved*, wife, not *revolved*."

"Don't dispute my word," said Teresa. "I talk the way God would have me talk without beating around the bush. What I say is, if you are determined to be a governor, take your son Sancho with you so that you can teach him how to govern also; for it is a good thing for sons to learn and follow their father's trade."

"As soon as I have a government," said Sancho, "I will send for him posthaste. I will send you some money too; for there are always plenty of people to lend it to governors that do not have it. And I want you to dress him up in such a way as to hide what he is and make him look like what he is not."

"You send the money," Teresa replied, "and I'll see to that." 9

"So, then, it's understood, is it, that our daughter is to be a countess?"

"The day that I see her a countess," was Teresa's answer, "I'll feel that I am laying her in her grave. But I tell you again: do as you like; for we women are born with the obligation of obeying our husbands, however stupid they may be."

Saying this, she began weeping in earnest, as though she already saw her Sanchica dead and buried. Sancho consoled her by assuring her that, while he might have to make his daughter a countess, he would put off doing so as long as he could. Thus ended the conversation, and Sancho went back to see Don Quixote to make arrangements for their departure.

CHAPTER VI. *Of what took place between Don Quixote and his niece and housekeeper, which is one of the most important chapters in the entire history.*

WHILE Sancho Panza and his wife, Teresa Cascajo, were engaged in the irrelevant conversation that has just been reported, Don Quixote's niece and housekeeper were by no means idle, for they could tell by any number of signs that their uncle and master was about to slip away a third time and return to what they looked upon as being his ill-errant conception of knighthood. They accordingly strove in every way possible to get so evil a thought out of his mind, but all this was like preaching in the desert or hammering cold iron.

"In truth, my master," the housekeeper said to him in the course of their many talks on the subject, "if you do not make up your mind to stay quietly at home and stop wandering over mountains and valleys like a lost soul, seeking what I am told are called adventures but which I call misfortunes, there will be nothing for me to do but raise my voice to God and the king, as loud as I can, so that they may do something about it."

"My good woman," replied Don Quixote, "what answer God will make to your complaints, or his Majesty either, for that matter, I am sure I do not know. But I do know that if I were king, I would not trouble to reply to all the innumerable and foolish petitions presented to me every day. One of the greatest of the many trials kings have to endure is that of being obliged to listen to everybody and give everyone some kind of answer, and I do not care to add my troubles to the burden that his Majesty has to bear."

"Tell us one thing," said the housekeeper, "are there no knights at his Majesty's court?"

"There are, and many of them; and it is right and proper that there should be, to set off the greatness of princes and show forth the majesty of royal power."

"Well, then," persisted the housekeeper, "could not your Grace be one of those who, without stirring a foot, serve their lord and king at court?"

"Look, my friend," said Don Quixote, "not all knights can be courtiers, nor can all courtiers be, nor should they be, knights-errant. There have to be all kinds in this world, and even though we may all be knights, there is a great deal of difference between us. For the courtiers, without leaving their rooms or the threshold of the court, may travel all over the earth merely by looking at a map; it does not cost them anything and they do not suffer heat or cold, hunger or thirst. But those of us who are real knights-errant, we take the measure of the entire globe with our feet, beneath the sun of day and in the cold of night, out in the open and exposed to all the inclemencies of the weather. We know our enemies not from pictures but as they really are, and we attack them on every occasion and under no matter what conditions of combat. We pay no attention to the childish rules that are supposed to govern knightly duels; we are not concerned as to whether one has a longer lance or sword than the other or may carry upon him holy relics or some secret contrivance; we do not worry about the proper placing of the combatants with regard to the sun[1] nor any of the other ceremonious usages of this sort that commonly prevail in man-to-man encounters, with which you are unfamiliar but which I know well.

"And let me tell you something else. The good knight-errant, even though he may behold ten giants with heads that not merely touch but rise above the clouds; and even though each of these giants may have two tallest towers for legs while his arms resemble the masts of huge and powerful ships; even though each may have eyes that are like great mill wheels and that glow more brightly than any glass furnace—in spite of all this, he is not to be in the least frightened but with highborn mien and intrepid heart is to give them battle and if possible vanquish and destroy them in a moment's time. And this, though they bear armor made of the shells of a certain fish that are said to be harder than diamonds, and in place of swords carry keen-edged blades of Da-

mascus steel or clubs studded with spikes of the same
material such as I have more than once seen. I tell you
all this, my good woman, in order that you may perceive
what a difference there is between knights; and it would
be well if there were no prince who did not more esteem
this second, or, rather, first, variety of knight-errant.
For the history books tell us that some of the latter have
been the salvation not of one kingdom alone but of
many."

"Ah, sir!" cried the niece at this point, "your Grace
must remember that all this you are saying about knights-
errant is a fable and a lie. And as for those history books,
if they are not to be burned, they ought all to wear the
sambenito[2] or some other sign to show how infamous
they are and how they corrupt good manners."

"By the God who sustains me!" exclaimed Don Quixote, "if you were not my flesh-and-blood niece, being
the daughter of my own sister, I would so punish you
for the blasphemy you have uttered that all the world
would hear about it. How comes it that a lass who barely
knows how to handle a dozen lace bobbins should set
her tongue to wagging and presume to criticize these
knightly histories? What would my lord Amadis say if he
could hear such a thing? To be sure, he would pardon
you, since he was the most humble and courteous knight
of his age, and was, moreover, a great protector of damsels. But there are others who might have heard you,
and in that case it would not have gone so well with
you. For they were not all courteous and circumspect;
some of them were the most unmannerly of rascals.

"By no means all of those that call themselves knights,
or gentlemen, are what they pretend to be. Some are of
pure gold, others are a base alloy. They all look the part,
but not all can stand the touchstone of truth. Some there
are of low degree who split themselves trying to appear

gentlemanly. On the other hand, there are those of high station who, one would wager, are dying to be mistaken for their inferiors. The former pull themselves up through ambition or by reason of their merits, while the latter debase themselves by slothfulness or vice. And a good deal of wisdom is required to distinguish beween these two kinds of gentlemen who are alike in name but whose conduct is so different."

"So help me God, uncle," said the niece, "your Grace knows so much that in a pinch you could get right up in the pulpit or go out and start preaching in the streets. And yet, to think that you could be so blind and foolish as to try to make out that you are a hero when you are really an old man, that you are strong when you are sick, that you are able to straighten out the wrongs of the world when you yourself are bent with age, and, above all, that you are a knight; for, while the real gentry[3] may become knights, the poor never can."

"There is much in what you say, my niece," replied Don Quixote. "I could tell you things having to do with family trees that would astonish you; but since I do not wish to mix the human with the divine, I shall not mention them. You see, my friends—and pay attention to what I say—so far as family is concerned, all the people in this world may be divided into four classes: those who from humble beginnings have grown and expanded until they have attained a pinnacle of greatness; those who were great to begin with and who have since consistently maintained their original state; those who have arrived at a pyramidal point, having progressively diminished and consumed the greatness that was theirs at the start until, like the point of the pyramid with respect to its base or foundation, they have come to be nothing at all; and, finally, there is the vast majority who had neither a good start nor a subsequent history that was

in any way out of the ordinary and who accordingly will
have a nameless end, like the ordinary plebeian stock.

"Of the first group, who rose from humble origins to
a greatness which they continue to maintain, the House
of Ottoman may serve as an example; for it was founded
by a lowly shepherd and later attained the heights which
we now see it occupying. Of the second class, those who
have maintained their original greatness without adding
to or detracting from it, I may cite the case of many
princes who have been content to remain peacefully
within the confines of their kingdoms. As for those that
began great only to taper away in a point, there are
thousands of examples. For all the Pharaohs and Ptol-
emies of Egypt, the Caesars of Rome, and the countless
drove (if I may employ that word) of princes, monarchs,
and lords, of Medes, Persians, Greeks, and barbarians—
all these royal and noble lines have ended in the point
of nothingness, both they and their founders, and today
it would be impossible to find a single one of their descendants, or if one did come upon any of them, they
would be in some low and humble station. Of the plebeians I have nothing to say, except that they serve to
increase the number of the living without any other
claim to fame, since they have achieved no form of greatness that entitles them to praise.

"My reason for telling you all this, my innocent ones,
is that you may see how much confusion exists with
regard to the subject of family descent. They alone impress us as being great and illustrious that show themselves to be virtuous, rich, and generous. I say this for
the reason that the great man who was also vicious
would be no more than an outstanding example of vice,
and the rich man who was not generous would be but
a miserly beggar. What brings happiness to the pos-
sessor of wealth is not the having but the spending of it,

and by that I mean, spending it well and not simply to gratify his own whims. The gentleman who is poor, however, has no other means of proving that he is a gentleman than by following the path of virtue, by being affable, well bred, courteous and polite, and prompt to do favors for others; he will not be proud and haughty or a backbiter, and, above all, he will be charitable. With the two maravedis that he gives with a cheerful heart to the poor he will show himself to be as generous as the one who distributes alms to the ringing of a bell, and no one who sees him adorned with the virtues that I have mentioned, even though he may not know him, will fail to regard him as coming of good stock. It would be a wonder if it were not so, for praise has ever been the reward of virtue, and those who are virtuous are bound to be commended.

"There are two paths, my daughters, by which men may succeed in becoming rich and honored. One is that of letters, the other that of arms. For my part, I am more inclined to the latter than to the former. Indeed, so strong is my inclination that it would seem that I must have been born under the influence of the planet Mars. And so I am practically compelled to follow that path, and I shall keep to it in spite of all the world. It is useless for you to wear yourselves out trying to persuade me not to do what Heaven wills, fate ordains, reason asks, and, above all, my own will desires. Knowing as I do all the innumerable hardships that go with knight-errantry, I also know the infinite number of good things that are to be attained by it. I am aware that the path of virtue is a straight and narrow one, while that of vice is a broad and spacious highway. I realize that the ends and goals are different in the two cases, the highroad of vice leading to death, while virtue's narrow, thorny trail conducts us to life, and not a life that has a mortal close, but life everlasting. As our great Castilian poet has put it:

This is the rugged path, the toilsome way
That leads to immortality's fair heights,
Which none e'er reach who from that path do stray."[4]

"Oh, dear me!" said the niece, "my master is a poet, too. He knows everything and can do everything. I'll bet that if he chose to turn mason he could build a house as easily as he could a birdcage."

"I can tell you one thing, niece," replied Don Quixote, "that if my mind were not so wholly occupied with thoughts of chivalry, there is nothing that I could not do, no trinket that I could not turn out with my own hands, especially birdcages and toothpicks."

At that moment there was a knock at the door, and when they asked who was there, Sancho replied that it was he. No sooner did the housekeeper hear this than she ran and hid herself, so great was her abhorrence of the squire. The niece opened the door and Don Quixote came forward to meet the visitor with open arms, after which the two of them shut themselves up in the knight's room where they had another conversation that was in no way surpassed by their previous one.

CHAPTER VII. *Of what passed between Don Quixote and his squire, with other very famous incidents.*

SEEING her master and Sancho Panza closeted together, the housekeeper at once suspected what they were up to. Feeling certain that as a result of their consultation they would resolve to sally forth a third time, she snatched up her mantle and, full of anxiety and

deeply distressed, went out to look for the bachelor
Sansón Carrasco; for it seemed to her that, being a well-
spoken young man and a new acquaintance of Don
Quixote's, he might be able to persuade the knight to
give up so insane an undertaking. She found the bachelor walking up and down the patio of his house, and the
moment she caught sight of him she ran up to him and
fell on her knees in front of him, sweating all over and
giving every evidence of affliction. Carrasco was surprised to see her so upset and grief-stricken.

"What is the meaning of this, Mistress Housekeeper?"
he asked. "What has happened to cause you to appear
so heartbroken?"

"It is nothing, Señor Sansón," she replied, "except that
my master is breaking out again, there's no doubt of
that."

"Breaking out where, Señora? Has he burst any part
of his body?"

"No," said she, "it's through the door of his madness
that he's bursting. I mean to say, my dear Señor Bachelor, that he wants to leave home again, which will be the
third time, to go roaming the world and looking for what
he calls ventures,[1] though for the life of me I can't see
why he gives them that name. The first time he came
home to us slung over the back of an ass and nearly
clubbed to death. The second time it was in an oxcart,
locked in a cage, where he said he had been put through
some magic spell or other, and such a sorry-looking sight
he was that the mother who bore him would not have
recognized him. He was lean and yellow and his eyes
were deep-sunken in his head, and in order to bring him
around again to something of his old self I had to use
more than six hundred eggs, as God knows, and all the
world and my hens as well, for they wouldn't let me lie."

"I can well believe," the bachelor assured her, "that

those hens of yours are so good, so fat, and so well brought up that they would not say one thing in place of another even if they burst. In short, Mistress Housekeeper, nothing has happened except what you fear that Señor Don Quixote may do?"

"Nothing else," she said.

"Well, then," he told her, "don't worry, but go on home and prepare me a warm breakfast, and on the way you might repeat St. Apollonia's prayer, if you happen to know it. I will be with you shortly, and you shall see miracles."

"Ah, poor me!" said the housekeeper, "so it's St. Apollonia's prayer that I should be saying, is it? That would be all right if my master had the toothache,[2] but his trouble is not in his teeth but in his brains."

"I know what I am talking about, Mistress Housekeeper; so run along and do not dispute my word, for, as you know, I am a bachelor of Salamanca and that means the best there is." [3]

With this, the housekeeper returned home and Carrasco went to hunt up the curate and make certain arrangements with him which will be duly narrated when the time comes.

When they were shut up together, Don Quixote and Sancho had a conversation which the historian has very minutely and truthfully reported.

"Sir," began Sancho, "I have reduced my wife to let me go with your Grace wherever you choose to take me."

"*Induced,* you mean to say, Sancho, not *reduced.*"

"Once or twice before, if I remember rightly," said Sancho, "I have begged your Grace not to correct my words so long as you understand what I mean by them. When you don't understand, all you have to do is to say, 'Sancho, I don't know what the devil you mean';

and then, if I don't make myself plain, you can go ahead and correct me all you want to. You know how focile I am."

"I fail to understand you right now, Sancho," said Don Quixote, "for I'm sure I don't know what you mean when you say, 'I am so *focile.*'"

"So *focile,*" replied Sancho, "means, 'I am so much that way.'"

"I understand you less than ever," said his master.

"Well, if you can't make it out," answered the squire, "I don't know what to say to you. That's the best I can do, so help me God."

"Ah! I get it. What you mean to say is that you are so *docile,* easygoing, and tractable that you will accept whatever I say to you and follow my teachings."

"I will bet you," said Sancho, "that you understood what I meant all the time and just wanted to mix me up so that you could hear me make a lot more blunders."

"You may be right," replied Don Quixote, "but tell me, exactly what was it that Teresa said?"

"She said that I should get everything down in black and white with your Grace, to let papers talk and beards be still,[4] since he who binds does not wrangle,[5] and one 'take' is worth a couple of 'I'll give you's.'[6] And I can tell you that a woman's advice is of little worth and he who won't take it is a fool."[7]

"And so say I," observed Don Quixote. "Go on, friend Sancho, you are in rare form today."[8]

"The fact of the matter is, as your Grace well knows," continued Sancho, "we are all of us subject to death, we are here today and gone tomorrow, and the lamb goes as soon as the sheep,[9] and no one can promise himself more hours of life in this world than God may see fit to give him, for death is deaf, and when it comes to knock at the door of our life it is always in a hurry, and neither prayers nor force nor scepters nor miters can hold it back, all of which is a matter of common talk and knowledge and we hear it from the pulpit right along."

"That is all very true," said Don Quixote, "but I can't see what you are getting at."

"What I am getting at," replied Sancho, "is that your Grace ought to give me a fixed wage to be paid to me every month during the time that I am in your service, out of your estate. I don't like to depend on favors that come late or never and may not be what you expect— God help me where those that I am expecting are concerned. The short of it is, I'd like to know what I am earning, however much or little it may be; for a hen will set on one egg, and many littles make a much, and so long as something's gained nothing's lost. If it should turn out to be true—which I neither believe nor expect —that your Grace is going to give me that island you promised me, I am not so ungrateful nor would I go so far as to say that you shouldn't take what the income from the island amounts to out of my wages on a *pro cata* basis."

"Friend Sancho," remarked Don Quixote, "a cat may sometimes be as good as a rat."

"I get you," was Sancho's answer. "I'll bet you that what I should have said was *pro rata* and not *pro cata,* but it makes no difference, since your Grace understood me anyway."

"I understand you so well," said Don Quixote, "that I can read you like a book. I know what the bull's-eye is you're shooting at with all those proverbs of yours. Look, Sancho, I should be glad to give you a fixed wage if I could find in the histories of knights-errant any instance that would afford me the slightest hint as to what their squires used to receive by the month or by the year. I have read all or most of those histories, and

I cannot recall any knight who paid his squire such a wage. Rather, they all served for the favors that came to them; and when they least expected it, if things had gone well with their masters, they would find themselves rewarded with an island or something else that amounted to the same thing, or at the least they would have a title and a seigniory.

"If for the sake of these hopes and inducements, Sancho," the knight went on, "you choose to return to my service, well and good; but you are wasting your time if you think that I am going to violate and unhinge the ancient customs of chivalry. And so, my good Sancho, go back home and tell your Teresa how I feel about it, and if she and you are willing to depend upon my favors, *bene quidem*, and if not, we will be as good friends as we were before; for if there is no lack of food in the pigeon house, it will not lack pigeons. And remember, my son, a good hope is better than a bad holding,[10] and a good complaint better than bad pay.[11] If I speak in this manner, Sancho, it is to show you that I, too, can scatter proverbs like showers. In conclusion, I would say to you that if you do not choose to come with me on these terms and take the same chance that I do, may God keep you and make you a saint, for I shall not fail to find other squires who will be more obedient, more diligent, and not so stupid or so talkative as you."

When Sancho saw how firmly resolved his master was on this point, the heavens darkened over for him and the wings of his heart drooped; for he had felt certain that Don Quixote would not go without him for anything in the world. He was very much astonished and was still lost in thought when Sansón Carrasco, accompanied by the housekeeper and the niece,[12] entered

the room; for the womenfolk wished to hear the arguments which the bachelor would employ in persuading
their master not to go back to seeking adventures. Sansón, that famous wag, now came forward and embraced
Don Quixote as he had done on the previous occasion,
and, raising his voice, he addressed him as follows:

"O flower of knight-errantry, O shining light of the
profession of arms, O honor and mirror of the Spanish
nation! May it please Almighty God in His infinite
power that the person or persons who would prevent or
impede your third sally never find their way out of the
labyrinth of their schemings nor ever succeed in accomplishing what they most desire."

Turning then to the housekeeper, he went on, "Mistress Housekeeper, you may just as well leave off saying
St. Apollonia's prayer; for I now realize that it has been
definitely determined by the spheres that Don Quixote
shall carry out his new and lofty undertakings, and I
should be laying a great burden upon my conscience if
I did not urge and entreat this knight to keep his good
right arm and valiant spirit curbed and confined no
longer, since by his tarrying here he is cheating the
wronged of their rights, orphans of his protection, damsels of the honor he might save for them, widows of the
favors he might bestow upon them, and wives of the
support with which he might provide them, along with
other things of the sort that have to do with, appertain
to, and are the proper appurtenances of, the order of
knight-errantry. Come, then, my dear Señor Don Quixote, so handsome and so brave, let it be today rather
than tomorrow that your Grace and Highness takes
the road, and if anything be lacking for the carrying
out of your plan, here am I to supply the need. My person and my fortune are at your disposal, and, if needs

be, I will even serve your Magnificence as squire. Indeed, I should count myself most fortunate in being
allowed to do so."

At this point Don Quixote spoke up. "Did not I tell
you, Sancho," he said, "that I would have no trouble
in finding squires? Look who is now offering to serve me.
None other than the distinguished bachelor, Sansón
Carrasco, the darling and perpetual delight of the Salamancan schools. He is sound in body, agile-limbed, and
discreet, and can stand heat as well as cold, hunger as
well as thirst. In brief, he has all the qualifications that
are required of a squire to a knight-errant. But Heaven
forbid that, to gratify my own inclinations, I should
shatter this pillar of letters and vase of learning and cut
down this towering palm of the fine and liberal arts. Let
this new Samson remain in his own country, bringing
honor to it and at the same time to the gray hairs of his
aged parents. As for me, I shall make out with any
squire that comes along, seeing that Sancho does not
deign to come with me."

"I do deign to come," Sancho protested. He was
deeply moved and his eyes were filled with tears. "It
shall not be said of me, my master," he went on, "that
'once the bread is eaten, the company breaks up.' I do
not come of ungrateful stock; for all the world, and especially my village, knows who the Panzas were, and
I am descended from them. What's more, I know from
the many kind things you have done and the kind words
you have spoken how much your Grace desires to show
me favor. If I seem to have haggled a bit over my
wages, that was to please my wife. When she undertakes to get you to do something, there's no mallet that
drives in the hoops of a cask the way she drives you
until you've done it. But, after all, a man has to be a
man and a woman a woman; and, seeing that I'm a

man wherever I am, which there's no denying, I mean to be one in my own house as well, whatever anybody says. So, then, there is nothing more to be done except for your Grace to draw up your will, with a codicil that can't be provoked, and we will set out at once. That way, Señor Sansón will not have to suffer any more, for he says his conscience is nagging at him to persuade your Grace to sally out into the world a third time. And I offer to serve your Grace faithfully and loyally, as well as and better than all the squires that have served knights-errant in times past or present."

The bachelor was amazed at Sancho Panza's way of talking; for, although he had read the First Part of the history, he never would have believed that the squire was as droll as he was depicted there. But as he now heard him speaking of a will and codicil that could not be *provoked* (in place of *revoked*), he was convinced of the truth of it all and came to the conclusion that this was one of the greatest simpletons of the age. Never before in the world, he told himself, had the like been seen of such a pair of madmen as this master and his servant.

In the end, Don Quixote and Sancho embraced and were friends once more; and with the advice and approval of the great Carrasco, who for the present was their oracle, they set the date for their departure at three days from then, which would give them time enough to make the necessary preparations and look for a closed helmet, as Don Quixote insisted that he must by all means have one to take with him. Sansón offered to see to this, saying a friend of his had such a piece and would not refuse it to him, although, to be sure, it was not bright and clean as polished steel ought to be but was covered with rust and mildew.

The curses which the two women, the housekeeper

and the niece, heaped upon the bachelor's head were innumerable. They tore their hair, clawed their faces, and, like the hired mourners of old, set up such a wailing over their master's departure that one would have thought it was his death they were lamenting. In thus persuading the knight to sally forth again, Sansón had a plan in mind which the history relates further on. All that he did was on the advice of the curate and the barber, with whom he had previously discussed the matter.

The short of it is, in the course of those three days Don Quixote and Sancho provided themselves with what they thought was necessary, and, the squire having pacified his wife and the knight having calmed his niece and housekeeper, the two of them set out at nightfall for El Toboso, without being seen by anyone except the bachelor, who expressed a desire to accompany them for a distance of half a league from the village. Don Quixote was mounted upon his good Rocinante and Sancho upon his ancient gray, his saddlebags stuffed with certain victuals and his pocket with money which his master had given him for whatever might come up. Sansón gave the knight a farewell embrace, urging him to send back word of the good or ill fortune that the pair met with, in order that he, Carrasco, as the laws of friendship demanded, might rejoice over the former or grieve over the latter. Don Quixote promised that he would do so, and the bachelor thereupon returned to the village while the other two took the highway for the great city of El Toboso.

The "Enchantment" of Dulcinea

(CHAPTERS VIII-X)

CHAPTER VIII. *Wherein is related what happened to Don Quixote as he went to see his lady, Dulcinea del Toboso.*

"BLESSED be the mighty Allah!" exclaims Hamete Benengeli at the beginning of this eighth chapter; and he repeats it three times: "Blessed be Allah!" He goes on to tell us that the reason for the benediction is his thankfulness at seeing Don Quixote and Sancho together once more, and he wishes the readers of this pleasant chronicle to feel that the exploits and the drolleries of the knight and his squire really start at this point. Let them forget, he says, the chivalrous deeds which the Ingenious Gentleman has performed in the past and fix their eyes, rather, on those that are to come and that have their beginning here and now on the El Toboso highway just as the others began on the plains of Montiel. It surely is not much to ask in return for all he promises, and so he continues as follows:

No sooner had Sansón left Don Quixote and Sancho alone than Rocinante began neighing and the gray started sighing, which both knight and squire took to be a very good sign and most fortunate omen, even though, if the truth must be told, the sighings and brayings of the ass exceeded the whinnyings of the hack, which led Sancho to infer that his own good fortune was destined to surpass and overtop that of his master, in making which assumption it may be that he was relying upon some system of judicial astrology with which he chanced to be familiar, though the history is silent on this point. All that is known is that, when he stumbled or fell, he was heard to say that he wished he had not come out of the house, since nothing was to be had from it but a torn shoe or a set of broken ribs, and in this, fool that he was, he was not far wrong.

"Friend Sancho," remarked Don Quixote, "night is descending upon us and it is becoming so dark that we shall not be able to reach El Toboso while it is yet daylight; but I am determined to go there before embarking upon another adventure, for there it is that I shall receive the blessing and kind consent of my peerless Dulcinea, with whose favor I feel assured of bringing to a happy conclusion every dangerous undertaking, since nothing in this life inspires more valor in knights-errant than the knowledge that they are favored by their ladies."

"I can believe that," replied Sancho, "but if I am not mistaken, your Grace may have a hard time seeing or talking to her, at least in any place where she could give you her blessing, unless she was to toss it over the wall of the stable yard where I saw her the last time, when I took her the letter with the news about the mad and foolish things your Grace was doing in the heart of the Sierra Morena."

"And did you fancy that was a stable-yard wall," said Don Quixote, "where or at which you beheld that grace and beauty that never can be praised enough? It must have been in the gallery, corridor, or portico, or whatever you call it, of some rich and royal palace."

"That may all be true," said Sancho, "but it looked like a wall to me, if my memory serves me right."

"Nevertheless, Sancho, we are going there," Don Quixote insisted; "for so long as I see her, it is all the same to me whether it be over a wall, at a window, or through the chinks in a door or the railing of a garden. Let but one ray of the sun of her beauty fall upon these eyes and it shall illuminate my understanding and fortify my heart to such a degree that I shall be matchless and without an equal in wisdom and in valor."

"To tell you the truth," said Sancho, "when I saw the lady Dulcinea del Toboso's sun, it was not bright enough to shed rays of any kind. This must have been due to the fact that, as I told you, she was winnowing wheat at the time, and this raised a lot of dust which came before her face like a cloud and darkened it."

"What!" cried Don Quixote, "do you still persist, Sancho, in saying, thinking, and believing that my lady Dulcinea was winnowing wheat, when you know that this is a task and occupation that is at variance with everything that persons of high distinction do and are supposed to do, seeing that they are constituted and reserved for other employments and avocations such as make manifest their rank at the distance of a bowshot? I can see, O Sancho, that you have forgotten those verses[1] of our poet in which he describes for us the labors performed, up there in their crystal dwellings, by the four nymphs that rose from their beloved Tagus and set themselves down in a verdant meadow to embroider those rich tapestries, of which the bard tells us, that were all worked and woven of gold and silk and pearls.

"My lady, when you saw her, must have been busied at a similar task. The only thing is that some evil enchanter must be envious of me, since all things that give me pleasure he at once changes into shapes that are not their own. This leads me to fear that the history of my exploits, which they tell me has been printed, may be the work of some magician who is my enemy, in which case he would have set down one thing in place of another and, mingling a thousand lies with a little truth, would doubtless have amused himself by relating many things that have nothing to do with the true sequence of events. O envy, thou root of endless evils, thou cankerworm of the virtues! All the other vices, Sancho, have in them some element of pleasure, but envy brings with it only vexation, bitterness, and rage."

"That is what I say too," replied Sancho, "and I think that in this legend or history of our deeds which the bachelor Carrasco says he has seen, my honor must have been knocked around and dragged up and down in the mud;[2] they must have swept the streets with it. And yet, I give you my word as an honest man, I have never spoken ill of any enchanter, nor do I have so many worldly goods that anybody would envy me. It is true, I am somewhat sly, and I have certain marks of the rogue, but it is all covered over with the great cloak of my simplicity, which is always natural and never artificial; and if I had no other virtue than that of believing, as I always have believed, firmly and truly in God and in all that the holy Roman Catholic Church holds and believes, as well as that of being, as I am, a mortal enemy of the Jews, the historians ought to have mercy on me and treat me well in their writings. But let them say what they will, naked was I born and naked I find myself, and so I neither lose nor gain; and although I see myself being put into a book and going through the world from hand to hand, I still don't care a fig; let them say anything about me that they like."

"That reminds me, Sancho," said Don Quixote, "of what happened to a famous poet of these days who, having composed a malicious satire against all the court ladies,[3] failed to mention in it a particular lady as to whose standing there was some question. When she saw that she was not on the list with the others, she com-

plained to the poet, demanding to know what he had
seen in her that had caused him to leave her out. She
further insisted that he add a sequel to his satire and
put her in it, or, otherwise, let him beware of the consequences. The poet did so, making her out to be the
kind of woman of whom duennas do not speak, and she
was satisfied with the fame he bestowed upon her even
though it was infamy. Then there is the story they tell
of the shepherd who set fire and burned down the
famous temple of Diana, accounted one of the seven
wonders of the world, simply in order that his name
might be remembered for centuries to come. And although it was commanded that no one should mention
his name either by word of mouth or in writing, so that
his ambition might not be fulfilled, it is nevertheless
known that he was called Erostratus.

"Much the same thing happened in the case of the
great emperor, Charles V, and a certain gentleman in
Rome. The emperor was desirous of seeing the famous
temple of the Rotunda, which in antiquity was known
as the temple of all the gods and today is more appro-
priately named All Saints'.[4] Of all the pagan edifices in
Rome, this is the one that comes nearest to being preserved in its entirety, and it constitutes a fitting tribute
to the grandeur and magnificence of those who built it.
It is constructed in the shape of a half-orange and is
very large and well lighted, the only illumination being
afforded by a window, or, better, a rounded skylight at
the top, and it was from this point of vantage that the
emperor surveyed the building. At his side was a
Roman gentleman who explained to him all the beauties
and fine points of the huge and intricate structure with
its memorable architecture.

"As they made their way down from the skylight, the
gentleman turned to the emperor and said, 'A thousand

times, your Sacred Majesty, I had a desire to throw my arms about your Majesty and cast myself down from that dome in order that my fame might be eternal in this world.'

" 'I thank you,' the emperor replied, 'for not having yielded to so wicked an impulse. From now on, I shall see to it that you have no further opportunity to put your loyalty to the test. I accordingly command you not to speak to me or enter my presence again.' And with these words he made him a handsome gift.

"What I mean to say, Sancho, is that the desire of achieving fame is a powerful incentive. What do you think it was that threw Horatius down from the bridge, clad in full armor, into the depths of the Tiber? What was it burned Mutius's arm and hand? What was it that impelled Curtius to hurl himself into the deep and flaming abyss that yawned in the middle of the city of Rome? What was it led Julius Caesar to cross the Rubicon in spite of all the auguries which had warned against it? To come down to more modern times, what was it, in the New World, that scuttled and beached the ships and cut off those valiant Spaniards led by the most courtier-like Cortés? [5] All these and other great deeds of various sorts are, were, and shall continue to be a manifestation of the mortal desire for fame as a reward for notable achievements that confer upon man a portion of immortality. We Christians, Catholics, and knights-errant, on the other hand, are more concerned with the glory that, in ages to come, shall be eternal in the ethereal and celestial regions than we are with the vanity of that fame that is to be won in this present and finite time; for however long such fame may endure, it needs must finally end with the world itself, the close of which has been foreordained.

"And so, Sancho, our deeds should not exceed those

limits set by the Christian religion which we profess. In
confronting giants, it is the sin of pride that we slay,
even as we combat envy with generosity and goodness
of heart; anger, with equanimity and a calm bearing;
gluttony and an overfondness for sleep, by eating little
when we do eat and by keeping long vigils; lust and
lewdness, with the loyalty that we show to those whom
we have made the mistresses of our affections; and sloth,
by going everywhere in the world in search of opportunities that may and do make of us famous knights as
well as better Christians.[6] You behold here, Sancho, the
means by which one may attain the highest praise that
the right sort of fame brings with it."

"I have understood very well," Sancho told him, "all
that your Grace has said up to now; but still there is one
doubtful point I happened to think of that I wish your
Grace would dissolve for me."

"*Solve* is what you mean to say, Sancho," replied Don
Quixote. "Speak out, and I will answer you as best I
can."

"Tell me, then, sir," Sancho went on, "those Julys[7] or
Augusts, and all those knights you mentioned that were
always up and doing, seeing that they are dead, where
are they now?"

"The heathen ones," said Don Quixote, "are undoubtedly in Hell; the Christians, if they were good
Christians, are either in purgatory or in Heaven."

"That is all very well," said Sancho, "but what I want
to know is this: do the tombs where the bodies of those
great lords are preserved have silver lamps in front of
them, and are the walls of their chapels decorated with
crutches, shrouds, locks of hair, legs, and eyes made of
wax? Or, if not, what kind of decorations do they have?"

"The pagan sepulchers," Don Quixote answered him,
"were for the most part sumptuous temples. Julius

Caesar's ashes, for example, were placed upon a stone pyramid of enormous size which in the Rome of today is known as St. Peter's Needle. The Emperor Hadrian's burial place was a castle as big as a good-sized town and was called the Moles Adriani, which at the present time is St. Angelo's Castle. The Queen Artemisia buried her husband in a tomb that was reckoned one of the seven wonders of the world. But none of the many pagan tombs was adorned with shrouds or offerings and tokens such as you commonly see where saints are buried."

"I am coming to that," said Sancho. "And now, tell me, which is the greater thing, to bring a dead man to life or to kill a giant?"

"The answer to that question is easy," replied Don Quixote. "To bring the dead to life, of course."

"Ah," said Sancho, "that is where I have you. Then the fame of those who resurrect the dead, who give sight to the blind, who heal cripples and bring health to the sick, and who have burning lamps in front of their tombs while their chapels are filled with kneeling worshipers who have come to adore their relics—will not their fame, both in this world and in the world to come, be a better one than that which all the heathen emperors and knights-errant that ever were have left or shall ever leave behind them?"

"I am willing to grant you that also," Don Quixote admitted.

"Well, then," continued Sancho, "seeing that this fame, these favors, these privileges, or whatever you call them, belong to the bodies and relics of the saints, who, with the approval and permission of our Holy Mother Church, have lamps, candles, shrouds, crutches, paintings, locks of hair, eyes, legs, and what not, to spread their Christian fame and make the worshipers more devout; and seeing that kings are in the habit of taking the bodies of saints, or saints' relics, upon their backs, while they kiss the bits of bone and use them to decorate and enrich their chapels and their favorite altars—"

"What are you getting at, Sancho, with all this you are saying?" Don Quixote asked.

"What I mean," said Sancho, "is that we ought to become saints, and that way we'd have the fame we are after all the sooner. You may know, sir, that yesterday or day before yesterday—in a manner of speaking, for it was only a short while ago—they canonized or beatified two little barefoot friars,[8] and it is now considered a great piece of luck to be able to kiss and touch the iron chains with which they girt and tormented their bodies. Those chains, so it is said, are more venerated than is Orlando's sword in the armory of our lord the king, God save him. And so, my dear sir, it is better to be a humble little barefoot friar, whatever the order he belongs to, than a brave knight-errant. With God, a couple of dozen penances will get you more than two thousand lance thrusts, whether they be given to giants, dragons, or other monsters."

"I agree with all that," said Don Quixote, "but we cannot all be friars, and there are many paths by which God takes His own to Heaven. Chivalry is a religion in itself, and there are sainted knights in glory."

"Yes," said Sancho, "but I have heard that there are more friars in Heaven than there are knights-errant."

"That," Don Quixote explained, "is for the reason that the number of religious is greater than the number of knights."

"There are many errant ones," observed Sancho.

"Many," his master assented, "but few that deserve the name of knight."

. In talk of this kind they spent that night and the following day, without anything happening to them worthy of note, at which Don Quixote was not a little put out. On the day after that, at sunset, they sighted the great city of El Toboso. The knight was elated, but Sancho was downcast, for he did not know where Dulcinea lived nor had he ever in his life laid eyes upon her any more than his master had. As a result, each of them was uneasy in his mind, the one being anxious to behold her while the other was worried because he had not already seen her. Sancho could not imagine what he was going to do when his master should send him into the town; but Don Quixote finally decided that they would wait until nightfall to make their entrance, and in the meanwhile they tarried amid some oak trees that grew round about. When the time came, they made their way into the streets of El Toboso, where the things that happened to them were really something.[9]

CHAPTER IX. *A chapter in which is related what will be found set forth in it.*

It was midnight on the hour,[1]

a little more or less, when Don Quixote and Sancho left the wood [2] and entered the city of El Toboso. The town was wrapped in a peaceful silence, for all the good people were asleep, or were stretching a leg,[3] as the saying goes. The night was not wholly dark, though Sancho wished it had been, as that might have provided an excuse for his inability to find his way. Nothing was to be heard anywhere but the barking of dogs, which deafened Don Quixote's ears and troubled his squire's heart. Now and then an ass would bray, pigs would grunt, a cat would miaul, and these various noises grew in volume with the silence. All of which the lovelorn knight took to be an ill omen, but he nonetheless adhered to his purpose.

"Sancho, my son," he cried, "lead the way to Dulcinea's palace; it may be that we shall find her awake."

"Body of the sun!" cried Sancho, "to what palace should I lead you? When I saw her Highness, she was in a very small house."

"Then," replied Don Quixote, "she must merely have retired to some small apartment of her castle, to amuse herself in solitude with her damsels, as is the custom of highborn ladies and princesses."

"Sir," said Sancho, "seeing that, in spite of anything I say, your Grace will have it that my lady Dulcinea's house is a castle, are we likely at this hour to find the gate open? And would it be right for us to go knocking at the gate in order to arouse them so that they can let us in, thus creating an uproar and disturbing everybody? Do you think, by any chance, that we are going to the house where our concubines live, as those who keep such women do, who come and call out and go in at any time, however late it may be?"

"First of all," said Don Quixote, "let us find out where the palace is, and then, Sancho, I will tell you what we should do. Look you, either my eyes deceive me or that huge dark bulk that we see yonder must be it."

"Then lead the way, your Grace, for it may be you are right. But, though I see it with my eyes and touch it with my hands, I will believe it is a palace just as soon as I would that it is now day."

Don Quixote accordingly led on, and when they had gone some two hundred paces they came up to the dark object and saw that it was a great tower, and then they realized that this was not a palace but the principal church of the town. "It's the church we've lighted on," the knight remarked to Sancho.

"So I see," replied the squire, "and please God we don't light upon our graves as well. It's not a good sign to be wandering in cemeteries at this hour of the night; and what's more, I told your Grace, if I remember rightly, that this lady's house would be up a blind alley."

"May God curse you, you fool!" cried his master, "and when did you ever hear of castles and royal palaces being built in blind alleys?"

"Sir," was Sancho's answer, "every land has its own customs, and it may be that the custom here in El Toboso is to put up their palaces and other great buildings in alleyways. And so I beg your Grace to let me look through these streets and lanes, and in some nook or corner I may come upon this palace, though I'd like to see it eaten by dogs right now for leading us on such a wild goose chase."

"I wish, Sancho," said Don Quixote, "that you would show some respect in speaking of those things that pertain to my lady. Let us keep the feast and be merry and not throw the rope after the bucket." [4]

"I will control myself," said Sancho, "but how can I be patient when your Grace expects me, though I only saw our mistress's house once, to remember it always, and to find her in the middle of the night when your Grace, who must have seen her thousands of times, is unable to do so?"

"Sancho," said Don Quixote, "you will drive me to despair. Look, you heretic, have I not told you any number of times that I have never in all the days of my life laid eyes upon the peerless Dulcinea, that I have never crossed the threshold of her palace but am enamored of her only by hearsay, as she is famous far and wide for her beauty and her wit?"

"I hear you say it now," replied Sancho, "and I may tell you that if your Grace has never seen her, neither have I."

"But that cannot be," said Don Quixote, "or at any rate you have told me that you saw her winnowing wheat, that time you brought me back the answer to the letter that I sent to her by you."

"Pay no attention to that, sir, for I would have you know that it was also by hearsay that I saw her and brought her answer to you. I could no more tell you who the lady Dulcinea is than I could strike the sky with my fist."

"Sancho, Sancho," said Don Quixote, "there is a time for jesting and a time when jests are out of place. The fact that I tell you I have never seen nor spoken to the lady of my heart is no reason why you should say the same thing when you know it is not true."

As they were engaged in this conversation, they saw a man coming toward them with a team of mules hitched to a plow, which made a loud noise as it scraped along the ground. They assumed that he must be some farmer up before daybreak and on his way to the field, and this proved to be the case. The farmer was singing the ballad that runs:

The day of Roncesvalles was a dismal day for you,
Ye men of France . . .[5]

"May they slay me, Sancho," said Don Quixote when he heard it, "if anything good is going to come of this night. Do you hear what that rustic is singing?"

"Yes, I hear it," replied Sancho, "but what has the

pursuit of Roncesvalles to do with the business that we have in hand? It would be all the same if it was the ballad of Calainos." [6]

At this point the farmer came up to them, and Don Quixote proceeded to question him. "Can you tell me, my good friend," he asked, "and may God prosper you, where in this vicinity is the palace of the peerless princess Doña Dulcinea del Toboso?"

"Señor," the lad answered, "I am a stranger here. I have been in this town only a few days, in the service of a rich farmer whose fields I plow. In that house across the way the curate and the sacristan live, and either one of them can tell your Grace what you wish to know about this princess, for they have a list of all the good folk of El Toboso. But, for my part, I never saw any princess whatever anywhere in the entire city. There are many ladies of high rank, it is true, and each may be a princess in her own house."

"Then the one that I am inquiring about must be among them, my friend," said Don Quixote.

"It may be so," replied the lad, "and God be with you, for there comes the dawn." And, lashing his mules, he did not wait to be questioned any further.

Seeing the unhappy state of mind his master was in, Sancho now spoke to him. "Sir," he said, "it will soon be daylight, and it will not do for the sun to find us here in the street. It would be better for us to go outside the town and for your Grace to hide yourself in some near-by forest. I will then come back and look in every corner for my lady's house, castle, or palace. It will be too bad if I do not find it, and when I do I will speak to her Grace and tell her how your Worship is waiting for her to arrange for you to come and see her without damage to her honor and good name."

"Sancho," said Don Quixote, "you have uttered a

thousand sentences within the compass of a few words. I thank you for the advice you have given me and I accept it with right good grace. Come, my son, let us go look for a place where I may hide; after which, as you say, you will come back to look for and to see and talk with my lady, from whose discretion and courtesy I expect favors that will be more than miraculous."

Sancho was in furious haste to get his master out of the town so that the knight would not discover the lie that had been told him regarding Dulcinea's answer which his squire had brought back to the Sierra Morena. They set out at once, and at a distance of two miles from the city they found a forest or wood where Don Quixote might hide himself while Sancho returned to talk to Dulcinea in the course of which embassy things happened to the messenger that call for fresh attention and belief.

CHAPTER X. *Wherein is related the ingenuity that Sancho displayed by laying a spell upon the lady Dulcinea, with other events as outlandish as they are true.*

WHEN the author of this great history comes to relate the events set forth in the present chapter, he remarks that he would prefer to pass over them in silence, as he fears that he will not be believed. For Don Quixote's madness here reaches a point beyond which the imagination cannot go, and even exceeds that point by a couple of bowshots. Nevertheless, in spite of such fear and misgiving, the historian has written down the events in question just as they happened, without adding to the chronicle in any way or holding back one particle of the truth, being in the end wholly

unconcerned with the objections that might be raised by
those who would make him out to be a liar. And in
doing so he was right; for while the truth may run
thin, it never breaks, and always rises above falsehood
as oil does above water.[1]

The history, then, goes on to state that, after he had
hidden himself in the wood, forest, or oak grove near
El Toboso, Don Quixote ordered Sancho to return to the
city and not to appear in his master's presence again until
he should first have spoken in person to the lady Dulcinea and begged her to be pleased to grant her captive
knight a glimpse of her, that she might bestow her
blessing upon him, which would enable him to hope
for a most fortunate conclusion to all his difficult enter-
prises and undertakings. Taking upon himself this task
that had been assigned him, the squire promised to
bring back as fair a reply as he had on the previous
occasion.

"Go, my son," Don Quixote said to him, "and do not
let yourself be dazed by the light from that sun of
beauty that you go to seek. Ah, happy are you above
all the squires in the world! Be sure to remember, and
do not let it slip your mind, just how she receives you.
Note whether she changes color while you are giving
her my message and if she is restless and perturbed
upon hearing my name. It may be that you will find her
seated in sumptuous and royal state, in which case she
will perhaps fall back upon a cushion; or if she be standing, see if she rests first upon one foot and then upon
the other. Observe if she repeats two or three times the
answer she gives you and if her mood varies from mildness to austerity, from the harsh to the amorous. She
may raise a hand to her hair to smooth it back, though
it be not disordered.

"In short, my son, note her every action and move-ment. If you report to me faithfully all these things, I shall be able to make out the hidden secret of her heart and discover how she feels with regard to my love; for I may tell you, Sancho, if you do not know it already, that among lovers exterior signs of this sort are the most re-liable couriers that there are, bringing news of what goes on inside the heart. Go, then, my friend and may a better fortune than mine be your guide. May you be more successful than I dare hope in this fearful and bitter solitude in which you leave me."

"I go," said Sancho, "and I will return shortly. In the meantime, my master, cheer up that little heart of yours; for right now you must have one no bigger than a hazel-nut. Remember what they say, that a stout heart breaks bad luck, and where there is no bacon there are no pegs.[2] And they also say that when you least expect it the hare leaps out. I tell you this for the reason that, if we did not find my lady's palace or castle last night, now that it is day I expect to come upon it when I'm not looking for it; and once I've found it, leave it to me to deal with her."

"I must say, Sancho," replied Don Quixote, "that your proverbs always come in very pat no matter what it is we are talking about. May God give me luck and grant me that which I desire."

With this, Sancho turned his back on his master and, lashing his donkey, rode off, leaving the knight seated in the saddle, his feet in the stirrups, and leaning on his lance. We, too, shall leave Don Quixote there, full of sad and troubled thoughts, as we accompany his squire, who was quite as pensive and troubled as he. As soon as he was out of the wood, Sancho turned his head and looked back, and, perceiving that he was by this time out of sight, he dismounted from his ass and sat down at the foot of a tree, where he began talking to himself, as follows:

"Look here, brother Sancho, supposing that you tell us where your Grace is going. Is it to hunt for some ass that has strayed? No, certainly not. Then, what *are* you hunting for? I am going to hunt for a princess, nothing more or less than that, and in her I am to find the sun of beauty and all the heavens combined. And where do you think you are going to find all this, Sancho? Where? In the great city of El Toboso. Well and good; and who sent you to look for her? The famous knight, Don Quixote de la Mancha, who rights wrongs and gives food to the thirsty and drink to the hungry. That is all very well; but do you know where her house is, Sancho? My master says it will be some royal palace or proud castle. And have you ever laid eyes upon her by any chance? Neither I nor my master has ever seen her. And supposing the people of El Toboso knew that you were here luring their princesses and disturbing their ladies, don't you think it would be only right and proper if they came and clubbed your ribs without leaving a whole bone in your body? And, to tell the truth, they would be right, if you did not take into account that I am sent here under orders and that

> *A messenger you are, my friend,*
> *No blame belongs to you.*[3]

But don't put your trust in that, Sancho, for the Manchegan folks are as hot-tempered as they are honest and will not put up with anything from anybody. God help you if they get wind of you, for it will mean bad luck. Out with you, villian! Let the bolt fall![4] Am I to go looking for a cat with three feet just to please another?[5] Hunting for Dulcinea in El Toboso is like trying to find Marica in Rávena or a bachelor in Salamanca.[6] It was the devil, it was the devil himself and nobody else, that got me into this."

Such was Sancho's soliloquy. It had led him to no conclusion thus far, and so he continued:

"Well, there is a remedy for everything except death, beneath whose yoke we all have to pass, however heavy it may weigh upon us, when life draws to a close. I have seen by a thousand signs that this master of mine is a madman who ought to be in a cell, yet I am not behind him in that respect, seeing that I am foolish enough to follow and serve him. That is certainly the case if there's any truth in the old saying, 'Tell me what company you keep and I'll tell you who you are,' or that other one, 'Not with whom you are bred but with whom you are fed.'[7] And seeing that he is a madman, and that he is there can be no doubt—so mad that he takes one thing for another, white for black and black for white, like the time when he insisted the windmills were giants and the monks' mules were dromedaries, and the flocks of sheep were enemy armies, and other things of the same sort—seeing that this is so, it will not be hard to make him believe that the first farm girl I fall in with around here is the lady Dulcinea. If he doesn't believe it, I'll swear to it; and if he swears that it isn't so, I'll swear right back at him; and if he insists, I'll insist more than he does, so that, come what may, I'll always have my quoit on the peg. If I keep it up like that, I'll bring him around to the point where he won't be sending me on any more such errands as this, when he sees how little comes of it. Or maybe, and I imagine that this will more likely be the case, he will think that one of those wicked enchanters, who, he says, have it in for him has changed her form just to spite and harm him."

These reflections greatly calmed Sancho Panza's mind and led him to look upon his business as already accomplished. He accordingly remained where he was until the afternoon, in order that Don Quixote might think he had had time to go to El Toboso and return. Everything went off so well with him that when he arose to mount his gray again, he saw coming toward him from the direction of the city three peasant lasses astride three asscolts or fillies—the author is not specific on this point, but it seems more likely that they were she-asses, on which village girls commonly ride. However, it is of no great importance and there is no reason why we should stop to verify so trifling a detail.

The short of the matter is, as soon as Sancho saw the lasses he hastened to where Don Quixote was, only to find the knight sighing and uttering a thousand amorous laments.

"What is it, Sancho, my friend? Am I to be able to mark this day with a white stone or a black one?"

"It would be better," replied Sancho, "if your Grace marked it with red ocher like the lists on the professors' chairs,[8] so that all could see it very plainly."

"That means, I take it," said Don Quixote, "that you bring good news."

"Good news it is," replied Sancho. "All your Grace has to do is to put spur to Rocinante and ride out into the open, and there you will see the lady Dulcinea del Toboso in person, who with two of her damsels has come to pay her respects to your Grace."

"Good Lord, Sancho my friend, what is this you are telling me? Take care that you do not deceive me or try to relieve with false joy my very real sadness."

"And what would I get by deceiving your Grace," Sancho wanted to know, "when you will soon enough discover for yourself whether I am speaking the truth or not? Come quickly, sir, and you will see the princess, our mistress, clad and adorned as befits one of her quality. She and her damsels are all one blaze of gold, pearls, diamonds, rubies, and brocade cloth with more than ten borders.[9] Their hair falling loose over their shoulders are so many sunbeams playing with the wind. And, what is more, they come mounted upon three piebald cackneys,[10] the finest you ever saw."

"*Hackneys*, you mean to say, Sancho."

"*Hackneys* or *cackneys*, it makes very little difference," replied Sancho. "No matter what their mounts, they are the finest ladies you could wish for, especially the Princess Dulcinea, my lady, who stuns your senses."

"Come, Sancho, my son," said Don Quixote, "let us go. As a reward for the news you bring me, as good as it is unexpected, I promise you the best spoils that I win in my first adventure; and in case this is not enough to satisfy you, I will send you the colts which my three mares will give me this year—as you know, they are now out on the village common and are about to foal."

"I will take the colts," said Sancho, "for the spoils from that first adventure are rather uncertain."

At this point they emerged from the wood close to where the three village lasses were. Gazing up and down the highway that led to El Toboso, Don Quixote was completely bewildered, since all he could see was these country maidens. He then asked Sancho if the princess and her damsels had left the city or were, perhaps, waiting there.

"What do you mean?" said Sancho. "Are your Grace's eyes in the back of your head that you cannot see that those are the ones coming there, as bright and shining as the sun itself at midday?"

"I see nothing," declared Don Quixote, "except three farm girls on three jackasses."

"Then God deliver me from the devil!" exclaimed Sancho. "Is it possible that those three hackneys, or whatever you call them, white as the driven snow, look like jackasses to your Grace? By the living God, I would tear out this beard of mine if that were true!"

"But I tell you, friend Sancho, it is as true that those are jackasses, or she-asses, as it is that I am Don Quixote and you Sancho Panza. At least, that is the way they look to me."

"Be quiet, sir," Sancho admonished him, "you must not say such a thing as that. Open those eyes of yours and come do reverence to the lady of your affections, for she draws near."

Saying this, he rode on to meet the village maids and, slipping down off his donkey, seized one of their beasts' by the halter and fell on his knees in front of its rider.

"O queen and princess and duchess of beauty," he said, "may your Highness and Majesty be pleased to receive and show favor to your captive knight, who stands there as if turned to marble, overwhelmed and breathless at finding himself in your magnificent presence. I am Sancho Panza, his squire, and he is the world-weary knight Don Quixote, otherwise known as the Knight of the Mournful Countenance."

By this time Don Quixote was down on his knees beside Sancho. His eyes were fairly starting from their sockets and there was a deeply troubled look in them as he stared up at the one whom Sancho had called queen and lady; all that he could see in her was a village wench, and not a very pretty one at that, for she was round-faced and snub-nosed. He was astounded and perplexed and did not dare open his mouth. The girls were also very much astonished to behold these two men, so different in appearance, kneeling in front of one of them so that she could not pass. It was this one who most ungraciously broke the silence.

"Get out of my way," she said peevishly, "and let me pass. And bad luck go with you. For we are in a hurry."

"O princess and universal lady of El Toboso!" cried Sancho. "How can your magnanimous heart fail to melt as you behold kneeling before your sublimated presence the one who is the very pillar and support of knight-errantry?"

Hearing this, one of the others spoke up. "Whoa, there, she-ass of my father!" she said. "Wait until I curry you down.[11] Just look at the small-fry gentry, will you, who've come to make sport of us country girls! Just as if we couldn't give them tit for tat. Be on your way and get out of ours, if you know what's good for you."

"Arise, Sancho," said Don Quixote, "for I perceive that fortune has not had her fill of evil done to me but has taken possession of all the roads by which some happiness may come to what little soul is left within me. And thou, who art all that could be desired, the sum of human gentleness and sole remedy for this afflicted heart that doth adore thee! The malign enchanter who doth persecute me hath placed clouds and cataracts upon my eyes, and for them and them alone hath transformed thy peerless beauty into the face of a lowly peasant maid; and I can only hope that he has not likewise changed my face into that of some monster by way of rendering it abhorrent in thy sight. But for all of that, hesitate not to gaze upon me tenderly and lovingly, beholding in this act of submission as I kneel before thee a tribute to thy metamorphosed beauty from this humbly worshiping heart of mine."

"Just listen to him run on, will you? My grandmother!"

cried the lass. "Enough of such gibberish. We'll thank
you to let us go our way."

Sancho fell back and let her pass, being very thankful
to get out of it so easily.

No sooner did she find herself free than the girl who
was supposed to have Dulcinea's face began spurring
her "cackney" with a spike on the end of a long stick
that she carried with her, whereupon the beast set off
at top speed across the meadow. Feeling the prick, which
appeared to annoy it more than was ordinarily the case,
the ass started cutting such capers that the lady Dulcinea
was thrown to the ground. When he saw this, Don Quixote hastened to lift her up while Sancho busied himself
with tightening the girths and adjusting the packsaddle
which had slipped down under the animal's belly. This
having been accomplished, Don Quixote was about to
take his enchanted lady in his arms to place her upon the
she-ass when the girl saved him the trouble by jump-
ing up from the ground, stepping back a few paces,
and taking a run for it. Placing both hands upon the
crupper of the ass, she landed more lightly than a falcon upon the packsaddle and remained sitting there
astride it like a man.

"In the name of Roque!" [12] exclaimed Sancho, "our
lady is like a lanner, only lighter, and can teach the cleverest Cordovan or Mexican how to mount. She cleared
the back of the saddle in one jump, and without any
spurs she makes her hackney run like a zebra, and her
damsels are not far behind, for they all of them go like
the wind."

This was the truth. Seeing Dulcinea in the saddle, the
other two prodded their beasts and followed her on the
run, without so much as turning their heads to look back
for a distance of half a league. Don Quixote stood gazing

after them, and when they were no longer visible he turned to Sancho and spoke.

"Sancho," he said, "you can see now, can you not, how the enchanters hate me? And just see how far they carry their malice and the grudge they bear me, since they would deprive me of the happiness I might derive from a sight of my mistress. The truth of the matter is, I was born to be an example of misfortune and to be the target and mark at which the arrows of ill luck are aimed and directed. I would further call your attention, Sancho, to the fact that, not content with merely transforming my Dulcinea, they must change her into a figure as low and repulsive as that village girl, robbing her at the same time of that which is so characteristic of highborn ladies, namely, their pleasing scent, which comes from always being among amber and flowers. For I would have you know, Sancho, that when Dulcinea leaped upon her hackney as you call it (though I must say, it seemed to me more like a she-ass), the odor that she gave off was one of raw garlic that made my head swim and poisoned my heart."

"O you scum!" cried Sancho. "O wretched and evil-minded enchanters! If I could but see you strung up by the gills like sardines on a reed! Great is your wisdom, great is your power, and greater yet the harm you do! Was it not enough, O villainous ones, to have changed the pearls of my lady's eyes into cork galls[13] and her hair of purest gold into the bristles of red ox's tail? No, you had to change all of her features from good to ill, and even alter her smell, since had you not done so we might have discovered what lay concealed beneath that ugly bark. And yet, to tell the truth, I never noticed her ugliness but only her beauty, which was set off to perfection by a mole that she had on her right lip—it resembled a mustache, being surrounded by seven or eight red hairs of more than a palm in length."

"As a rule," observed Don Quixote, "moles on the face correspond to those on the body, and Dulcinea must accordingly have one of the same sort on the flat of her thigh, on the same side as the other. But hairs of the length you mentioned are very long for moles."

"Well, all I can tell you," answered Sancho, "is that there they were as big as life."

"I believe you, friend," said Don Quixote, "for everything pertaining to Dulcinea is by nature perfect and well finished, and so, if she had a hundred moles of the kind you have described, upon her they would not be moles but resplendent moons and stars. But tell me one thing, Sancho: that thing that looked to me like a packsaddle which you were adjusting, was it a flat saddle or a sidesaddle?"

"It was neither one nor the other," replied Sancho, "but a *jineta*,[14] with a field-covering so rich that it must have been worth half a kingdom."

"Oh, if I could but have seen all that, Sancho! I tell you again, and I will tell you a thousand times, that I am the most unfortunate of men."

It was all that the rogue of a Sancho could do to keep from laughing as he listened to this foolish talk on the part of his master, who had been so ingeniously deceived. Finally, after much other talk had passed between them, they mounted their beasts once more and took the road for Saragossa, hoping to arrive there in time for a certain important feast that is celebrated in that illustrious city every year. Before they reached their destination, however, many strange and noteworthy things were to happen to them that deserve to be set down and read, as will be seen further on.

To the Road Again

(CHAPTERS XI-XXIX)

CHAPTER XI. *Of the strange adventure that befell the valiant Don Quixote in connection with the cart or wagon of the Parliament of Death.*

CONTINUING on his way, Don Quixote was deeply dejected as he thought of the cruel joke which the enchanters had played upon him by transforming his lady Dulcinea into the ugly form of the village girl, nor could he imagine any means of restoring her to her original shape. He was so absorbed in these reflections that, without noticing it, he let go Rocinante's rein, and that animal, taking advantage of the freedom granted him, now paused at every step to feed upon the abundant green grass that covered the plain. It was Sancho who awakened the knight from his daydreams.

"Sir," he said, "sorrows are made not for beasts but for men, but if men feel them too much they become beasts. Your Grace ought to pull yourself together and pick up Rocinante's rein; you ought to wake up and cheer up and show that gallant spirit that knights-errant are supposed to have. What the devil is this, anyway? What kind of weakness is it? Are we here or in France? Let Satan carry off all the Dulcineas in the world; the welfare of a single knight means more than all the spells and transformations on this earth."

"Hush, Sancho," replied Don Quixote, in not too wan a voice, "hush, I say, and do not be uttering blasphemies against that enchanted lady, seeing that I alone am to blame for her misfortunes, which are due to the envy that the wicked ones bear me."

"That is what I say," agreed Sancho. "Who saw her once and saw her now, his heart would surely weep, I vow."

"You, Sancho, may well say that," was Don Quixote's response, "for you beheld her in all the fullness of her beauty; the spell did not go so far as to disturb *your* sight or conceal her loveliness from you; it was solely against me and these eyes of mine that the force of its venom was directed. And yet, Sancho, there is one thing that occurs to me. It would seem that you have not well described her; for, unless my memory serves me wrong, you said that she had eyes like pearls, and eyes of that sort are more characteristic of the sea bream than they are of a lady. Dulcinea's eyes must be green emeralds, large and luscious, with two rainbows for brows. Take those pearls from her eyes and bestow them upon her teeth, for undoubtedly, Sancho, you must have mistaken the former for the latter."

"That may be," said Sancho, "for her beauty disturbed me as much as her ugliness did your Grace. But let us leave it to God, for he knows all that is to happen in this vale of tears, in this evil world of ours, where you scarcely find anything that does not have in it some mixture of wickedness, deceit, and villainy. But there is one thing, my master, that worries me most of all: what is your Grace going to do when you have overcome some giant or knight and wish to send him to present himself before the beautiful Dulcinea? Where is that poor giant or wretched knight going to find her? I can see them now, wandering like a lot of nitwits through the streets of El Toboso looking for my lady. Even if they were to meet her in the middle of the street, they wouldn't know her from my father."

"It may be, Sancho," said Don Quixote, "that the spell will not prevent them from recognizing her as it does me. But we shall see as to that after we shall have dispatched one or two of them to seek her out; for I shall command them to return and give me an account of what happened."

"I must say," replied Sancho, "that your Grace has spoken very much to the point, and by this means we shall be able to find out what we wish to know. And since it is only to your Grace that her beauty is hidden, the misfortune is more yours than hers. So long as the lady Dulcinea has health and happiness, we will make the best of it and go on seeking adventures, leaving it to time to work a cure, for he is the best doctor for this and other greater ills."

At this point Don Quixote and Sancho encounter a cart filled with a company of strolling players in costume; the driver is garbed as a demon, while another actor represents Death with a human countenance; among the other figures are an angel with wings, an emperor wearing a gold crown, a Cupid complete with bow, quiver, arrows, and a bandage over his eyes, a knight in full armor, etc. Don Quixote stops the cart and demands an explanation. He is informed that the players are on their way to a nearby village to put on a piece called "The Parliament of Death" as part of the Corpus Christi celebration.

Satisfied with this answer, Don Quixote is about to permit the Thespians to proceed when one of the mummers, in a costume with bells and brandishing three cow's bladders on the end of a stick, so frightens Rocinante that the hack runs away and throws his rider violently to the ground. Sancho at once dismounts and runs to his master's assistance, whereupon the clown leaps upon the gray and begins beating it with the blad-ders, causing that animal also to take flight across the countryside. The actor then takes a fall off the donkey in imitation of Don Quixote, and the animal wanders back.

The knight insists upon exacting vengeance for the affront, though Sancho does his best to dissuade him. Perceiving his intentions, the players arm themselves with pebbles and line up for the attack. As Don Quixote pauses to consider what it would be best to do under the circumstances, Sancho reminds him that there is not a single knight-errant in the lot and that, accordingly, one who has been dubbed a knight cannot do battle with them. Such reasoning proves effective, and the "Parliament of Death" continues on its way as the knight and his squire ride off in the opposite direction, in search of further and "more legitimate" adventures.

(*This brief episode, reminiscent of some of the more farcical passages in Part I, takes up the balance of Chapter* xi.)

The following evening Don Quixote and Sancho retire to a grove with the object of spending the night there, and as they share their supper, master and man discuss the encounter with the actors. The knight takes this opportunity to hold forth on the theme of life viewed as a comedy in which death in the end disrobes the players and renders them all equal in the grave. Then they fall asleep, but the knight is awakened shortly afterward when two horsemen ride up and dismount.

The newcomers are to all appearances another knight and his squire—a lovelorn knight who at once begins uttering a poetic lament to his lady love, one Casildea

*de Vandalia, in terms similar to those that Don Quix-
ote employs in his apostrophes to Dulcinea. This lady
according to her lover, excels all others, including "all
those of La Mancha," a statement which Don Quixote,
making his presence known, promptly challenges. The
two of them strike up a conversation regarding their
amorous woes, while Sancho and the other squire go
off to have a talk of their own (Chapter* XII).

*The dialogue between the two squires is an amusing
one, the subject being the arduous life that is led by
those who serve knights-errant. The second squire
produces a jug of wine, and this loosens their tongues
still more, until finally they succumb to sleep (Chapter*
XIII).

In Chapter XIV *the author returns to Don Quixote and
his newfound companion. The Knight of the Wood is
boasting of his exploits and claims, among his other
achievements, to have met and overcome Don Quixote
de la Mancha and to have won from him an admission
that Casildea is more beautiful than Dulcinea. Don
Quixote, his ire aroused at this, reveals his identity and
challenges the other to combat. The Knight of the Wood
accepts, on one condition, that the conquered shall
submit to the will of the victor and do whatever is
commanded of him. Don Quixote agrees, and they arrange to fight at dawn.*

FROM CHAPTER XIV: *Wherein is continued the
adventure of the Knight of the Wood.*

WITH this, they went off to where their squires
were, only to find them snoring away as hard
as when sleep had first overtaken them. Awakening the

pair, they ordered them to look to the horses; for as soon as the sun was up the two knights meant to stage an arduous and bloody singlehanded combat. At this news Sancho was astonished and terrified, since, as a result of what the other squire had told him of the Knight of the Wood's prowess, he was led to fear for his master's safety. Nevertheless, he and his friend now went to seek the mounts without saying a word, and they found the animals all together, for by this time the two horses and the ass had smelled one another out. On the way the Squire of the Wood turned to Sancho and addressed him as follows:

"I must inform you, brother, that it is the custom of the fighters of Andalusia, when they are godfathers in any combat, not to remain idly by, with folded hands, while their godsons fight it out. I tell you this by way of warning you that while our masters are settling matters, we, too, shall have to come to blows and hack each other to bits."

"That custom, Sir Squire," replied Sancho, "may be all very well among the fighters and ruffians that you mention, but with the squires of knights-errant it is not to be thought of. At least, I have never heard my master speak of any such custom, and he knows all the laws of chivalry by heart. But granting that it is true and that there is a law which states in so many words that squires must fight while their masters do, I have no intention of obeying it but rather will pay whatever penalty is laid on peaceable-minded ones like myself, for I am sure it cannot be more than a couple of pounds of wax,[1] and that would be less expensive than the lint which it would take to heal my head—I can already see it split in two. What's more, it's out of the question for me to fight since I have no sword nor did I ever in my life carry one."

"That," said the one of the Wood, "is something that is easily remedied. I have here two linen bags of the same size. You take one and I'll take the other and we will fight that way, on equal terms."

"So be it, by all means," said Sancho, "for that will simply knock the dust out of us without wounding us."

"But that's not the way it's to be," said the other squire. "Inside the bags, to keep the wind from blowing them away, we will put a half-dozen nice smooth pebbles of the same weight, and so we'll be able to give each other a good pounding without doing ourselves any real harm or damage."

"Body of my father!" cried Sancho, "just look, will you, at the marten and sable and wads of carded cotton that he's stuffing into those bags so that we won't get our heads cracked or our bones crushed to a pulp. But I am telling you, *Señor mio,* that even though you fill them with silken pellets, I don't mean to fight. Let our masters fight and make the best of it, but as for us, let us drink and live; for time will see to ending our lives without any help on our part by way of bringing them to a close before they have reached their proper season and fall from ripeness."

"Nevertheless," replied the Squire of the Wood, "fight we must, if only for half an hour."

"No," Sancho insisted, "that I will not do. I will not be so impolite or so ungrateful as to pick any quarrel however slight with one whose food and drink I've shared. And, moreover, who in the devil could bring himself to fight in cold blood, when he's not angry or vexed in any way?"

"I can take care of that, right enough," said the one of the Wood. "Before we begin, I will come up to your Grace as nicely as you please and give you three or four punches that will stretch you out at my feet; and that will surely be enough to awaken your anger, even though it's sleeping sounder than a dormouse."

"And I," said Sancho, "have another idea that's every bit as good as yours. I will take a big club, and before your Grace has had a chance to awaken my anger I will put yours to sleep with such mighty whacks that if it wakes at all it will be in the other world; for it is known there that I am not the man to let my face be mussed by anyone, and let each look out for the arrow.[2] But the best thing to do would be to leave each one's anger to its slumbers, for no one knows the heart of any other, he who comes for wool may go back shorn,[3] and God bless peace and curse all strife. If a hunted cat when surrounded and cornered turns into a lion,[4] God knows what I who am a man might not become. And so from this time forth I am warning you, Sir Squire, that all the harm and damage that may result from our quarrel will be upon your head."

"Very well," the one of the Wood replied, "God will send the dawn and we shall make out somehow."

At that moment gay-colored birds of all sorts began warbling in the trees and with their merry and varied songs appeared to be greeting and welcoming the fresh-dawning day, which already at the gates and on the balconies of the east was revealing its beautiful face as it shook out from its hair an infinite number of liquid pearls. Bathed in this gentle moisture, the grass seemed to shed a pearly spray, the willows distilled a savory manna, the fountains laughed, the brooks murmured, the woods were glad, and the meadows put on their finest raiment. The first thing that Sancho Panza beheld, as soon as it was light enough to tell one object from another, was the Squire of the Wood's nose, which was so big as to cast into the shade all the rest of his body. In addition to being of enormous size, it is said to have been hooked in the middle and all covered with warts of a mulberry hue, like eggplant; it hung down for a couple of inches below his mouth, and the size, color, warts, and shape of this organ gave his face so ugly an appearance that Sancho began trembling hand and foot like a child with convulsions and made up his mind then and there that he would take a couple of hundred punches before he would let his anger be awakened to the point where he would fight with this monster.

Don Quixote in the meanwhile was surveying his opponent, who had already adjusted and closed his helmet so that it was impossible to make out what he looked like. It was apparent, however, that he was not very tall and was stockily built. Over his armor he wore a coat of some kind or other made of what appeared to be the finest cloth of gold, all bespangled with glittering mirrors that resembled little moons and that gave him a most gallant and festive air, while above his helmet were a large number of waving plumes, green, white, and yellow in color. His lance, which was leaning against a tree, was very long and stout and had a steel point of more than a palm in length. Don Quixote took all this in, and from what he observed concluded that his opponent must be of tremendous strength, but he was not for this reason filled with fear as Sancho Panza was. Rather, he proceeded to address the Knight of the Mirrors, quite boldly and in a highbred manner.

"Sir Knight," he said, "if in your eagerness to fight you have not lost your courtesy, I would beg you to be so good as to raise your visor a little in order that I may see if your face is as handsome as your trappings."

"Whether you come out of this emprise the victor or the vanquished, Sir Knight," he of the Mirrors replied, "there will be ample time and opportunity for you to have a sight of me. If I do not now gratify your desire,

it is because it seems to me that I should be doing a
very great wrong to the beauteous Casildea de Vandalia
by wasting the time it would take me to raise my visor
before having forced you to confess that I am right in
my contention, with which you are well acquainted."

"Well, then," said Don Quixote, "while we are mounting our steeds you might at least inform me if I am
that knight of La Mancha whom you say you conquered."

"To that our answer," [5] said he of the Mirrors, "is that
you are as like the knight I overcame as one egg is like
another; but since you assert that you are persecuted by
enchanters, I should not venture to state positively that
you are the one in question."

"All of which," said Don Quixote, "is sufficient to
convince me that you are laboring under a misapprehension; but in order to relieve you of it once and for
all, let them bring our steeds, and in less time than you
would spend in lifting your visor, if God, my lady, and
my arm give me strength, I will see your face and you
shall see that I am not the vanquished knight you take
me to be."

With this, they cut short their conversation and
mounted, and, turning Rocinante around, Don Quixote
began measuring off the proper length of field for a
run against his opponent as he of the Mirrors did the
same. But the Knight of La Mancha had not gone
twenty paces when he heard his adversary calling to
him, whereupon each of them turned halfway and he
of the Mirrors spoke.

"I must remind you, Sir Knight," he said, "of the condition under which we fight, which is that the vanquished, as I have said before, shall place himself
wholly at the disposition of the victor."

"I am aware of that," replied Don Quixote, "not forgetting the provision that the behest laid upon the vanquished shall not exceed the bounds of chivalry."

"Agreed," said the Knight of the Mirrors.

At that moment Don Quixote caught sight of the other squire's weird nose and was as greatly astonished by it as Sancho had been. Indeed, he took the fellow for some monster, or some new kind of human being wholly unlike those that people this world. As he saw his master riding away down the field preparatory to the tilt, Sancho was alarmed; for he did not like to be left alone with the big-nosed individual, fearing that one powerful swipe of that protuberance against his own nose would end the battle so far as he was concerned and he would be lying stretched out on the ground, from fear if not from the force of the blow.

He accordingly ran after the knight, clinging to one of Rocinante's stirrup straps, and when he thought it was time for Don Quixote to whirl about and bear down upon his opponent, he called to him and said, "Señor mio, I beg your Grace, before you turn for the charge, to help me up into that cork tree yonder where I can watch the encounter which your Grace is going to have with this knight better than I can from the ground and in a way that is much more to my liking."

"I rather think, Sancho," said Don Quixote, "that what you wish to do is to mount a platform where you can see the bulls without any danger to yourself."

"The truth of the matter is," Sancho admitted, "the monstrous nose on that squire has given me such a fright that I don't dare stay near him."

"It is indeed of such a sort," his master assured him, "that if I were not the person I am, I myself should be frightened. And so, come, I will help you up."

While Don Quixote tarried to see Sancho ensconced in the cork tree, the Knight of the Mirrors measured as much ground as seemed to him necessary and then, assuming that his adversary had done the same, without waiting for sound of trumpet or any other signal, he wheeled his horse, which was no swifter nor any more impressive-looking than Rocinante, and bore down upon his enemy at a mild trot; but when he saw that the Manchegan was busy helping his squire, he reined in his mount and came to a stop midway in his course, for which his horse was extremely grateful, being no longer able to stir a single step. To Don Quixote, on the other hand, it seemed as if his enemy was flying, and digging his spurs with all his might into Rocinante's lean flanks he caused that animal to run a bit for the first and only time, according to the history, for on all other occasions a simple trot had represented his utmost speed. And so it was that, with an unheard-of fury, the Knight of the Mournful Countenance came down upon the Knight of the Mirrors as the latter sat there sinking his spurs all the way up to the buttons[6] without being able to persuade his horse to budge a single inch from the spot where he had come to a sudden standstill.

It was at this fortunate moment, while his adversary was in such a predicament, that Don Quixote fell upon him, quite unmindful of the fact that the other knight was having trouble with his mount and either was unable or did not have time to put his lance at rest. The upshot of it was, he encountered him with such force that, much against his will, the Knight of the Mirrors went rolling over his horse's flanks and tumbled to the ground, where as a result of his terrific fall he lay as if dead, without moving hand or foot.

No sooner did Sancho perceive what had happened than he slipped down from the cork tree and ran up as fast as he could to where his master was. Dismounting from Rocinante, Don Quixote now stood over the

Knight of the Mirrors, and undoing the helmet straps to see if the man was dead, or to give him air in case he was alive, he beheld—who can say what he beheld without creating astonishment, wonder, and amazement in those who hear the tale? The history tells us that it was the very countenance, form, aspect, physiognomy, effigy, and image of the bachelor Sansón Carrasco!

"Come, Sancho," he cried in a loud voice, "and see what is to be seen but is not to be believed. Hasten, my son, and learn what magic can do and how great is the power of wizards and enchanters."

Sancho came, and the moment his eyes fell on the bachelor Carrasco's face he began crossing and blessing himself a countless number of times. Meanwhile, the overthrown knight gave no signs of life.

"If you ask me, master," said Sancho, "I would say that the best thing for your Grace to do is to run his sword down the mouth of this one who appears to be the bachelor Carrasco; maybe by so doing you would be killing one of your enemies, the enchanters."

"That is not a bad idea," replied Don Quixote, "for the fewer enemies the better." And, drawing his sword, he was about to act upon Sancho's advice and counsel when the Knight of the Mirrors' squire came up to them, now minus the nose which had made him so ugly.

"Look well what you are doing, Don Quixote!" he cried. "The one who lies there at your feet is your Grace's friend, the bachelor Sansón Carrasco, and I am his squire."

"And where is your nose?" inquired Sancho, who was surprised to see him without that deformity.

"Here in my pocket," was the reply. And, thrusting his hand into his coat, he drew out a nose of varnished pasteboard of the make that has been described. Study-

ing him more and more closely, Sancho finally ex,
claimed, in a voice that was filled with amazement,
"Holy Mary preserve me! And is this not my neighbor
and crony, Tomé Cecial?"

"That is who I am!" replied the de-nosed squire,
"your good friend Tomé Cecial, Sancho Panza. I will
tell you presently of the means and snares and falsehoods that brought me here. But, for the present, I beg
and entreat your master not to lay hands on, mistreat,
wound, or slay the Knight of the Mirrors whom he now
has at his feet; for without any doubt it is the rash
and ill-advised bachelor Sansón Carrasco, our fellow vil-
lager." 7

The Knight of the Mirrors now recovered consciousness, and, seeing this, Don Quixote at once placed the
naked point of his sword above the face of the vanquished one.

"Dead you are, knight," he said, "unless you confess
that the peerless Dulcinea del Toboso is more beautiful
than your Casildea de Vandalia. And what is more, you
will have to promise that, should you survive this encounter and the fall you have had, you will go to the
city of El Toboso and present yourself to her in my
behalf, that she may do with you as she may see fit.
And in case she leaves you free to follow your own will,
you are to return to seek me out—the trail of my exploits will serve as a guide to bring you wherever I
may be—and tell me all that has taken place between
you and her. These conditions are in conformity with
those that we arranged before our combat and they do
not go beyond the bounds of knight-errantry."

"I confess," said the fallen knight, "that the tattered
and filthy shoe of the lady Dulcinea del Toboso is of
greater worth than the badly combed if clean beard of
Casildea, and I promise to go to her presence and return

to yours and to give you a complete and detailed ac·
count concerning anything you may wish to know."

"Another thing," added Don Quixote, "that you will
have to confess and believe is that the knight you conquered was not and could not have been Don Quixote
de la Mancha, but was some other that resembled him,
just as I am convinced that you, though you appear to
be the bachelor Sansón Carrasco, are another person in
his form and likeness who has been put here by my
enemies to induce me to restrain and moderate the impetuosity of my wrath and make a gentle use of my
glorious victory."

"I confess, think, and feel as you feel, think, and
believe," replied the lamed knight. "Permit me to rise,
I beg of you, if the jolt I received in my fall will let me
do so, for I am in very bad shape."

Don Quixote and Tomé Cecial the squire now helped
him to his feet. As for Sancho, he could not take his
eyes off Tomé but kept asking him one question after
another, and although the answers he received afforded
clear enough proof that the man was really his fellow
townsman, the fear that had been aroused in him by his
master's words—about the enchanters' having transformed the Knight of the Mirrors into the bachelor
Sansón Carrasco—prevented him from believing the
truth that was apparent to his eyes. The short of it is,
both master and servant were left with this delusion as
the other ill-errant knight and his squire, in no pleasant
state of mind, took their departure with the object of
looking for some village where they might be able to
apply poultices and splints to the bachelor's battered
ribs.

Don Quixote and Sancho then resumed their journey
along the road to Saragossa, and here for the time being
the history leaves them in order to give an account of

who the Knight of the Mirrors and his long-nosed squire really were.

It appears (Chapter xv) that the Knight of the Mirrors incident was the result of a scheme on the part of the bachelor Sansón Carrasco, to which the curate and the barber had agreed. In accordance with this plan, since it was impossible to prevent Don Quixote from leaving, Sansón was to take the road as a knight-errant, pick a quarrel and do battle with him. They felt sure that it would be easy for the bachelor to overcome him; moreover, he would first have entered into a pact to the effect that the vanquished should do the bidding of the victor. The behest in this case was to be that the fallen one return to his native village and not leave it for the space of two years, in the course of which time they hoped Don Quixote would forget his fancies; in any case, it would give them the opportunity to seek a cure for his madness.

With this purpose in view, Sansón had taken Sancho's friend, Tomé Cecial (" a merry but featherbrained chap"), as his squire, and the latter had put on a mask to disguise his nose so that his crony would not recognize him. The adventure, however, had not turned out as they had expected, and the bachelor had come near to forfeiting his life. Tomé is now disgusted with the undertaking, and after they have reached a village and found a bonesetter to take care of Sansón's injuries, the two part company, the "squire" returning home while the bachelor, who is by now thoroughly angry, begins planning how he may obtain his revenge.

In the meantime (Chapter xvi) Don Quixote and Sancho continue on their way, with the knight in high spirits over the glorious victory he has just achieved. There follows a conversation between master and man

*regarding the identity of the Knight of the Mirrors, for
Sancho is unable to rid himself of the idea that the pair
were in reality his well-known fellow townsmen, but
Don Quixote meets this with his usual argument about
magicians, enchantments, transformations, and the like.*

*While they are engaged in this discussion they are
overtaken by a well-mounted gentleman in a green-colored greatcoat. From the elegance of his costume and
the trappings of his steed it is plain to be seen that he
is a man of means. Don Quixote suggests that they ride
along together, and the stranger graciously consents to
do so. The gentleman is at once struck by his companion's strange appearance, and, noticing this, Don Quixote introduces himself as the Knight of the Mournful
Countenance and launches forth on one of his harangues
on the subject of chivalry. The newcomer is convinced
that he has to do with some sort of crackbrain.*

*Nevertheless, when pressed to reveal his own identity,
the Knight of the Green-colored Greatcoat very courteously complies by giving a fairly detailed account of
the life he leads, that of an honest burgher (l'honnête
homme) of his day. The following passage may accordingly be looked upon as having a certain social significance. (What we have here is the incorrigible dreamer,
the visionary or "madman," in confrontation with the
solid citizen.)*

FROM CHAPTER XVI: *Of what happened to Don
Quixote upon his meeting with a prudent gentleman of La Mancha.*

"I, SIR KNIGHT of the Mournful Countenance," replied the one in the green-colored greatcoat, "am a
gentleman, and a native of the village where, please God,

we are going to dine today. I am more than moderately rich, and my name is Don Diego de Miranda. I spend my life with my wife and children and with my friends. My occupations are hunting and fishing, though I keep neither falcon nor hounds but only a tame partridge[1] and a bold ferret or two. I am the owner of about six dozen books, some of them in Spanish, others in Latin, including both histories and devotional works. As for books of chivalry, they have not as yet crossed the threshold of my door. My own preference is for profane rather than devotional writings, such as afford an innocent amusement, charming us by their style and arousing and holding our interest by their inventiveness, although I must say there are very few of that sort to be found in Spain.

"Sometimes," the man in green continued, "I dine with my friends and neighbors, and I often invite them to my house. My meals are wholesome and well prepared and there is always plenty to eat. I do not care for gossip, nor will I permit it in my presence. I am not lynx-eyed and do not pry into the lives and doings of others. I hear mass every day and share my substance with the poor, but make no parade of my good works lest hypocrisy and vainglory, those enemies that so imperceptibly take possession of the most modest heart, should find their way into mine. I try to make peace between those who are at strife. I am the devoted servant of Our Lady, and my trust is in the infinite mercy of God Our Saviour."

Sancho had listened most attentively to the gentleman's account of his mode of life, and inasmuch as it seemed to him that this was a good and holy way to live and that the one who followed such a pattern ought to be able to work miracles, he now jumped down from his gray's back and, running over to seize the stranger's right stir-

rup, began kissing the feet of the man in green with a
show of devotion that bordered on tears.

"Why are you doing that, brother?" the gentleman
asked him. "What is the meaning of these kisses?"

"Let me kiss your feet," Sancho insisted, "for if I am
not mistaken, your Grace is the first saint riding *jineta*
fashion² that I have seen in all the days of my life."

"I am not a saint," the gentleman assured him, "but
a great sinner. It is you, brother, who are the saint; for
you must be a good man, judging by the simplicity of
heart that you show."

Sancho then went back to his packsaddle, having
evoked a laugh from the depths of his master's melancholy and given Don Diego fresh cause for astonishment.

*Don Quixote then inquires how many children the
Knight of the Green-Colored Greatcoat has, and the
latter begins speaking of his eighteen-year-old son, a
student at Salamanca, who, it seems, is more interested
in poetry than in scholastic pursuits, a circumstance that
rather worries his father. The Knight advises that the
youth be permitted to follow his bent, since he is not
under the necessity of making a living. (Cervantes
takes this opportunity to express his views on poetry,
by putting them into the mouth of his protagonist.)*

"Poetry in my opinion, my dear sir," Don Quixote
went on, "is a young and tender maid of surpassing
beauty, who has many other damsels (that is to say, the
other disciplines) whose duty it is to bedeck, embellish,
and adorn her. She may call upon all of them for service,
and all of them in turn depend upon her nod. She is not
one to be rudely handled, nor dragged through the
streets, nor exposed at street corners, in the market

place, or in the private nooks of palaces. She is fashioned through an alchemy of such power that he who knows how to make use of it will be able to convert her into the purest gold of inestimable price. Possessing her, he must keep her within bounds and not permit her to run wild in bawdy satires or soulless sonnets. She is not to be put up for sale in any manner, unless it be in the form of heroic poems, pity-inspiring tragedies, or pleasing and ingenious comedies. Let mountebanks keep hands off her, and the ignorant mob as well, which is incapable of recognizing or appreciating the treasures that are locked within her. And do not think, sir, that I apply that term 'mob' solely to plebeians and those of low estate; for anyone who is ignorant, whether he be lord or prince, may, and should, be included in the vulgar herd.

"But," Don Quixote continued, "he who possesses the gift of poetry and who makes the use of it that I have indicated, shall become famous and his name shall be honored among all the civilized nations of the world. You have stated, sir, that your son does not greatly care for poetry written in our Spanish tongue, and in that I am inclined to think he is somewhat mistaken. My reason for saying so is this: the great Homer did not write in Latin, for the reason that he was a Greek, and Vergil did not write in Greek since he was a Latin. In a word, all the poets of antiquity wrote in the language which they had imbibed with their mother's milk and did not go searching after foreign ones to express their loftiest conceptions. This being so, it would be well if the same custom were to be adopted by all nations, the German poet being no longer looked down upon because he writes in German, nor the Castilian or the Basque for employing his native speech.

"As for your son, I fancy, sir, that his quarrel is not so much with Spanish poetry as with those poets who have no other tongue or discipline at their command such as would help to awaken their natural gift; and yet, here, too, he may be wrong. There is an opinion, and a true one, to the effect that 'the poet is born,' [3] that is to say, it is as a poet that he comes forth from his mother's womb, and with the propensity that has been bestowed upon him by Heaven, without study or artifice, he produces those compositions that attest the truth of the line: '*Est deus in nobis*,' etc.[4] I further maintain that the born poet who is aided by art will have a great advantage over the one who by art alone would become a poet, the reason being that art does not go beyond, but merely perfects, nature; and so it is that, by combining nature with art and art with nature, the finished poet is produced.

"In conclusion, then, my dear sir, my advice to you would be to let your son go where his star beckons him; for being a good student as he must be, and having already successfully mounted the first step on the stairway of learning, which is that of languages, he will be able to continue of his own accord to the very peak of humane letters, an accomplishment that is altogether becoming in a gentleman, one that adorns, honors, and distinguishes him as much as the miter does the bishop or his flowing robe the learned jurisconsult. Your Grace well may reprove your son, should he compose satires that reflect upon the honor of other persons; in that case, punish him and tear them up. But should he compose discourses in the manner of Horace, in which he reprehends vice in general as that poet so elegantly does, then praise him by all means; for it is permitted the poet to write verses in which he inveighs against envy and the other vices as well, and to lash out at the vicious without, however, designating any particular individual. On the other hand, there are poets who for the sake of uttering something malicious would run the risk of being banished to the shores of Pontus.[5]

"If the poet be chaste where his own manners are concerned, he will likewise be modest in his verses, for the pen is the tongue of the mind, and whatever thoughts are engendered there are bound to appear in his writings. When kings and princes behold the marvelous art of poetry as practiced by prudent, virtuous, and serious-minded subjects of their realm, they honor, esteem, and reward those persons and crown them with the leaves of the tree that is never struck by lightning[6] —as if to show that those who are crowned and adorned with such wreaths are not to be assailed by anyone."

The gentleman in the green-colored greatcoat was vastly astonished by this speech of Don Quixote's and was rapidly altering the opinion he had previously held, to the effect that his companion was but a crackbrain. In the middle of the long discourse, which was not greatly to his liking, Sancho had left the highway to go seek a little milk from some shepherds who were draining the udders of their ewes near by. Extremely well pleased with the knight's sound sense and excellent reasoning, the gentleman was about to resume the conversation when, raising his head, Don Quixote caught sight of a cart flying royal flags that was coming toward them down the road and, thinking it must be a fresh adventure, began calling to Sancho in a loud voice to bring him his helmet. Whereupon Sancho hastily left the shepherds and spurred his gray until he was once more alongside his master, who was now about to encounter a dreadful and bewildering ordeal.

CHAPTER XVII. *Wherein Don Quixote's unimaginable courage reaches its highest point, together with the adventure of the lions and its happy ending.*

THE history relates that, when Don Quixote called to Sancho to bring his helmet, the squire was busy buying some curds from the shepherds and, flustered by his master's great haste, did not know what to do with them or how to carry them. Having already paid for the curds, he did not care to lose them, and so he decided to put them into the headpiece, and, acting upon this happy inspiration, he returned to see what was wanted of him.

"Give me that helmet," said the knight; "for either I know little about adventures or here is one where I am going to need my armor."

Upon hearing this, the gentleman in the green-colored greatcoat looked around in all directions but could see nothing except the cart that was approaching them, decked out with two or three flags which indicated that the vehicle in question must be conveying his Majesty's property. He remarked as much to Don Quixote, but the latter paid no attention, for he was always convinced that whatever happened to him meant adventures and more adventures.

"Forewarned is forearmed," [1] he said. "I lose nothing by being prepared, knowing as I do that I have enemies both visible and invisible and cannot tell when or where or in what form they will attack me."

Turning to Sancho, he asked for his helmet again, and as there was no time to shake out the curds, the squire had to hand it to him as it was. Don Quixote took it and, without noticing what was in it, hastily clapped it on his head; and forthwith, as a result of the pressure on the curds, the whey began running down all over his face and beard, at which he was very much startled.

"What is this, Sancho?" he cried. "I think my head must be softening or my brains melting, or else I am sweating from head to foot. If sweat it be, I assure you it is not from fear, though I can well believe that the adventure which now awaits me is a terrible one indeed. Give me something with which to wipe my face, if you have anything, for this perspiration is so abundant that it blinds me."

Sancho said nothing but gave him a cloth and at the same time gave thanks to God that his master had not discovered what the trouble was. Don Quixote wiped his face and then took off his helmet to see what it was that made his head feel so cool. Catching sight of that watery white mass, he lifted it to his nose and smelled it.

"By the life of my lady Dulcinea del Toboso!" he exclaimed. "Those are curds that you have put there, you treacherous, brazen, ill-mannered squire!"

To this Sancho replied, very calmly and with a straight face, "If they are curds, give them to me, your Grace, so that I can eat them. But no, let the devil eat them, for he must be the one who did it. Do you think I would be so bold as to soil your Grace's helmet? Upon my word, master, by the understanding that God has given me, I, too, must have enchanters who are persecuting me as your Grace's creature and one of his members, and they are the ones who put that filthy mess there to make you lose your patience and your temper and cause you to whack my ribs as you are in the habit of doing. Well, this time, I must say, they have missed the mark; for I trust my master's good sense to tell him that I have neither curds nor milk nor anything of the kind, and if

I did have, I'd put it in my stomach and not in that helmet."

"That may very well be," said Don Quixote.

Don Diego was observing all this and was more astonished than ever, especially when, after he had wiped his head, face, beard, and helmet, Don Quixote once more donned the piece of armor and, settling himself in the stirrups, proceeded to adjust his sword and fix his lance.

"Come what may, here I stand, ready to take on Satan himself in person!" shouted the knight.

The cart with the flags had come up to them by this time, accompanied only by a driver riding one of the mules and a man seated up in front.

"Where are you going, brothers?" Don Quixote called out as he placed himself in the path of the cart. "What conveyance is this, what do you carry in it, and what is the meaning of those flags?"

"The cart is mine," replied the driver, "and in it are two fierce lions in cages which the governor of Oran is sending to court as a present for his Majesty.[2] The flags are those of our lord the King, as a sign that his property goes here."

"And are the lions large?" inquired Don Quixote.

It was the man sitting at the door of the cage who answered him. "The largest," he said, "that ever were sent from Africa to Spain. I am the lionkeeper and I have brought back others, but never any like these. They are male and female. The male is in this first cage, the female in the one behind. They are hungry right now, for they have had nothing to eat today; and so we'd be obliged if your Grace would get out of the way, for we must hasten on to the place where we are to feed them."

"Lion whelps against me?" said Don Quixote with a

slight smile. "Lion whelps against me? And at such an hour? Then, by God, those gentlemen who sent them shall see whether I am the man to be frightened by lions. Get down, my good fellow, and since you are the lion-keeper, open the cages and turn those beasts out for me; and in the middle of this plain I will teach them who Don Quixote de la Mancha is, notwithstanding and in spite of the enchanters who are responsible for their being here."

"So," said the gentleman to himself as he heard this, "our worthy knight has revealed himself. It must indeed be true that the curds have softened his skull and mellowed his brains."

At this point Sancho approached him. "For God's sake, sir," he said, "do something to keep my master from fighting those lions. For if he does, they're going to tear us all to bits."

"Is your master, then, so insane," the gentleman asked, "that you fear and believe he means to tackle those fierce animals?"

"It is not that he is insane," replied Sancho, "but, rather, foolhardy."

"Very well," said the gentleman, "I will put a stop to it." And going up to Don Quixote, who was still urging the lionkeeper to open the cages, he said, "Sir Knight, knights-errant should undertake only those adventures that afford some hope of a successful outcome, not those that are utterly hopeless to begin with; for valor when it turns to temerity has in it more of madness than of bravery. Moreover, these lions have no thought of attacking your Grace but are a present to his Majesty, and it would not be well to detain them or interfere with their journey."

"My dear sir," answered Don Quixote, "you had best go mind your tame partridge and that bold ferret

of yours and let each one attend to his own business.
This is my affair, and I know whether these gentlemen,
the lions, have come to attack me or not." He then
turned to the lionkeeper. "I swear, Sir Rascal, if you do
not open those cages at once, I'll pin you to the cart
with this lance!"

Perceiving how determined the armed phantom was,
the driver now spoke up. "Good sir," he said, "will your
Grace please be so kind as to let me unhitch the mules
and take them to a safe place before you turn those
lions loose? For if they kill them for me, I am ruined for
life, since the mules and cart are all the property I
own."

"O man of little faith!" said Don Quixote. "Get down
and unhitch your mules if you like, but you will soon
see that it was quite unnecessary and that you might
have spared yourself the trouble."

The driver did so, in great haste, as the lionkeeper
began shouting, "I want you all to witness that I am
being compelled against my will to open the cages
and turn the lions out, and I further warn this gentleman that he will be responsible for all the harm and
damage the beasts may do, plus my wages and my
fees. You other gentlemen take cover before I open the
doors; I am sure they will not do any harm to me."

Once more Don Diego sought to persuade his companion not to commit such an act of madness, as it was
tempting God to undertake anything so foolish as that;
but Don Quixote's only answer was that he knew what
he was doing. And when the gentleman in green insisted that he was sure the knight was laboring under a
delusion and ought to consider the matter well, the
latter cut him short.

"Well, then, sir," he said, "if your Grace does not
care to be a spectator at what you believe is going to

turn out to be a tragedy, all you have to do is to spur your flea-bitten mare and seek safety."

Hearing this, Sancho with tears in his eyes again begged him to give up the undertaking, in comparison with which the adventure of the wind-mills and the dreadful one at the fulling mills—indeed, all the exploits his master had ever in the course of his life undertaken—were but bread and cakes.

"Look, sir," Sancho went on, "there is no enchantment here nor anything of the sort. Through the bars and chinks of that cage I have seen a real lion's claw, and judging by the size of it, the lion that it belongs to is bigger than a mountain."

"Fear, at any rate," said Don Quixote, "will make him look bigger to you than half the world. Retire, Sancho, and leave me, and if I die here, you know our ancient pact: you are to repair to Dulcinea—I say no more."

To this he added other remarks that took away any hope they had that he might not go through with his insane plan. The gentleman in the green-colored greatcoat was of a mind to resist him but saw that he was no match for the knight in the matter of arms. Then, too, it did not seem to him the part of wisdom to fight it out with a madman; for Don Quixote now impressed him as being quite mad in every way. Accordingly, while the knight was repeating his threats to the lion-keeper, Don Diego spurred his mare, Sancho his gray, and the driver his mules, all of them seeking to put as great a distance as possible between themselves and the cart before the lions broke loose.

Sancho already was bewailing his master's death, which he was convinced was bound to come from the lions' claws, and at the same time he cursed his fate and called it an unlucky hour in which he had taken

it into his head to serve such a one. But despite his tears
and lamentations, he did not leave off thrashing his
gray in an effort to leave the cart behind them.
When the lionkeeper saw that those who had fled were
a good distance away, he once more entreated and
warned Don Quixote as he had warned and entreated
him before, but the answer he received was that he
might save his breath as it would do him no good and
he had best hurry and obey. In the space of time that
it took the keeper to open the first cage, Don Quixote
considered the question as to whether it would be well
to give battle on foot or on horseback. He finally decided that he would do better on foot, as he feared that
Rocinante would become frightened at sight of the lions;
and so, leaping down from his horse, he fixed his lance,
braced his buckler, and drew his sword, and then advanced with marvelous daring and great resoluteness
until he stood directly in front of the cart, meanwhile
commending himself to God with all his heart and then
to his lady Dulcinea.

Upon reaching this point, the reader should know,
the author of our veracious history indulges in the following exclamatory passage:

"O great-souled Don Quixote de la Mancha, thou
whose courage is beyond all praise, mirror wherein all
the valiant of the world may behold themselves, a new
and second Don Manuel de León,[3] once the glory and
the honor of Spanish knighthood! With what words
shall I relate thy terrifying exploit, how render it credible to the ages that are to come? What eulogies do not
belong to thee of right, even though they consist of
hyperbole piled upon hyperbole? On foot and singlehanded, intrepid and with greathearted valor, armed but
with a sword, and not one of the keen-edged Little
Dog make,[4] and with a shield that was not of gleaming

and polished steel, thou didst stand and wait for the two fiercest lions that ever the African forests bred! Thy deeds shall be thy praise, O valorous Manchegan; I leave them to speak for thee, since words fail me with which to extol them."

Here the author leaves off his exclamations and resumes the thread of the story.

Seeing Don Quixote posed there before him and perceiving that, unless he wished to incur the bold knight's indignation there was nothing for him to do but release the male lion, the keeper now opened the first cage, and it could be seen at once how extraordinarily big and horribly ugly the beast was. The first thing the recumbent animal did was to turn round, put out a claw, and stretch himself all over. Then he opened his mouth and yawned very slowly, after which he put out a tongue that was nearly two palms in length and with it licked the dust out of his eyes and washed his face. Having done this, he stuck his head outside the cage and gazed about him in all directions. His eyes were now like live coals and his appearance and demeanor were such as to strike terror in temerity itself. But Don Quixote merely stared at him attentively, waiting for him to descend from the cart so that they could come to grips, for the knight was determined to hack the brute to pieces, such was the extent of his unheard-of madness.

The lion, however, proved to be courteous rather than arrogant and was in no mood for childish bravado. After having gazed first in one direction and then in another, as has been said, he turned his back and presented his hind parts to Don Quixote and then very calmly and peaceably lay down and stretched himself out once more in his cage. At this, Don Quixote ordered the keeper to stir him up with a stick in order to irritate him and drive him out.

"That I will not do," the keeper replied, "for if I stir him, I will be the first one he will tear to bits. Be satisfied with what you have already accomplished, Sir Knight, which leaves nothing more to be said on the score of valor, and do not go tempting your fortune a second time. The door was open and the lion could have gone out if he had chosen; since he has not done so up to now, that means he will stay where he is all day long. Your Grace's stoutheartedness has been well established; for no brave fighter, as I see it, is obliged to do more than challenge his enemy and wait for him in the field; his adversary, if he does not come, is the one who is disgraced and the one who awaits him gains the crown of victory."

"That is the truth," said Don Quixote. "Shut the door, my friend, and bear me witness as best you can with regard to what you have seen me do here. I would have you certify: that you opened the door for the lion, that I waited for him and he did not come out, that I continued to wait and still he stayed there, and finally went back and lay down. I am under no further obligation. Away with enchantments, and God uphold the right, the truth, and true chivalry! So close the door, as I have told you, while I signal to the fugitives in order that they who were not present may hear of this exploit from your lips."

The keeper did as he was commanded, and Don Quixote, taking the cloth with which he had dried his face after the rain of curds, fastened it to the point of his lance and began summoning the runaways, who, all in a body with the gentleman in green bringing up the rear, were still fleeing and turning around to look back at every step. Sancho was the first to see the white cloth.

"May they slay me," he said, "if my master hasn't

conquered those fierce beasts, for he's calling to us."

They all stopped and made sure that the one who was doing the signaling was indeed Don Quixote, and then, losing some of their fear, they little by little made their way back to a point where they could distinctly hear what the knight was saying. At last they returned to the cart, and as they drew near Don Quixote spoke to the driver.

"You may come back, brother, hitch your mules, and continue your journey. And you, Sancho, may give each of them two gold crowns to recompense them for the delay they have suffered on my account."

"That I will, right enough," said Sancho. "But what has become of the lions? Are they dead or alive?"

The keeper thereupon, in leisurely fashion and in full detail, proceeded to tell them how the encounter had ended, taking pains to stress to the best of his ability the valor displayed by Don Quixote, at sight of whom the lion had been so cowed that he was unwilling to leave his cage, though the door had been left open quite a while. The fellow went on to state that the knight had wanted him to stir the lion up and force him out, but had finally been convinced that this would be tempting God and so, much to his displeasure and against his will, had permitted the door to be closed.

"What do you think of that, Sancho?" asked Don Quixote. "Are there any spells that can withstand true gallantry? The enchanters may take my luck away, but to deprive me of my strength and courage is an impossibility."

Sancho then bestowed the crowns, the driver hitched his mules, and the lionkeeper kissed Don Quixote's hands for the favor received, promising that, when he reached the court, he would relate this brave exploit to the king himself.

"In that case," replied Don Quixote, "if his Majesty by any chance should inquire who it was that performed it, you are to say that it was the Knight of the Lions; for that is the name by which I wish to be known from now on, thus changing, exchanging, altering, and converting the one I have previously borne, that of Knight of the Mournful Countenance; in which respect I am but following the old custom of knights-errant, who changed their names whenever they liked or found it convenient to do so."

The rest of the chapter is taken up with another harangue of Don Quixote's, addressed to the Gentleman in the Green-colored Greatcoat. Don Diego de Miranda then extends to the knight an invitation to accompany him to his home for a period of rest, an invitation which Don Quixote accepts. They reach there about two in the afternoon.

Chapter xviii *tells "what happened to Don Quixote in the castle or house of the Knight of the Green-colored Greatcoat." He is received most cordially by Don Diego de Miranda's wife and son, and the latter marvels at the strange admixture of sense and nonsense their guest talks. The student-poet and the visitor become involved in a discussion of knight-errantry, and the young man reads some of his verses, which Don Quixote praises highly. When the time comes to take the road again, Sancho is loath to leave, for he has been enjoying good food and drink all the while and hates to go back to "the hunger of forest and desert and the short rations of his ill-stocked saddlebag"—he is careful to see that the bag is well stuffed with provisions.*

The author next introduces another of those extended pastoral episodes which he seems unable to resist.

This one takes up three chapters and part of a fourth (Chapters xix-xxii) *and is concerned with the wedding of a rich peasant, Camacho by name. Don Quixote learns of the event when he encounters a party of travelers who invite him to accompany them to the festivities. The wedding is to be an elaborate one in an open meadow, with dances and other entertainment; and it is expected to be exciting as well, for Basilio, Camacho's despairing rival for the hand of the fair Quiteria, is likely to make a scene.*

Quiteria and Basilio have been sweethearts since childhood, but her father is forcing her into the present marriage because of Camacho's wealth. When he hears this, Don Quixote delivers a short but eloquent sermon on matrimony to which Sancho contributes his own peasant wisdom in the form of proverbs and shrewd sayings (Chapter xix).

Two students in the company get into an argument over swordsmanship and stage a fencing match, with Don Quixote as the referee. Then they go on and reach the village where preparations for the wedding are under way.

Chapter xx *contains a description of the wedding dances and of the good time Sancho has gorging himself at the wineskins and stew-pots—he now favors Camacho, who has provided all this, where before he had taken the side of true love. There is more good dialogue between the knight and his irrepressible squire.*

It is in Chapter xxi *that the drama occurs, when Basilio interrupts the wedding ceremony. After heaping reproaches on Quiteria, he plants his rapier in the ground and—as it appears to every one present— throws himself upon it. As he lies there seemingly transfixed and in a pool of blood, he implores the girl to* give him her hand in marriage before he dies, declaring that he will not confess himself until she has done so. Don Quixote thereupon takes a hand by asserting that this request is a reasonable one, and he begs Camacho to consent. The original bridegroom finally yields, and the service is no sooner performed than Basilio leaps nimbly to his feet as the bystanders cry, "Miracle!"

"No miracle, but a trick," he tells them; they then discover that the blade has passed not through his flesh but through a carefully concealed hollow iron tube filled with blood. The result is a threatened battle between Camacho's followers and the friends of Basilio as both sides line up for the fray; but Don Quixote, mounted on Rocinante and with his buckler braced on his arm, espouses the lovers' cause and compels them all to give way. The knight then accepts an invitation to go to Basilio's village and continue the celebration there, a turn of events that greatly disgusts Sancho, who is distressed at having to leave the "fleshpots of Egypt" for the uncertain fare of a poor man's board.

Showered with attentions by the newly wedded pair, Don Quixote indulges in yet another homily on marriage (Chapter XXII), addressed to the bridegroom, with Sancho chiming in as usual (in this case he has something to say about his own relations with Teresa). After they have spent three days there, adventure beckons once more and the knight asks that he be provided with a guide who will conduct him to the famous Cave of Montesinos. This request is fulfilled by one of the party, who sends for his cousin, a "humanist" and writer of books, to play the cicerone.

The cousin proves to be one of those asinine indi-

viduals with a smattering of learning that Renaissance writers are fond of describing. On the way he tells of the works he has produced or is engaged upon, and there is some amusing banter on Sancho's part.

FROM CHAPTER XXII: *Wherein is related the great adventure of the Cave of Montesinos in the heart of La Mancha, which the valiant Don Quixote brought to a triumphant conclusion.*

WITH this and other pleasing talk they spent the day, and when night came found lodgings in a little village which, as the cousin informed Don Quixote, was not more than a couple of leagues from the Cave of Montesinos; and their guide took occasion to remind the knight that if he was resolved to make the descent, he would have to find ropes with which to lower himself into the depths. To this Don Quixote's answer was that even if it was as deep as Hell, he proposed to see the bottom of it; and so they bought nearly a hundred fathoms of rope, and the following day, at two o'clock in the afternoon, they reached the cave, the mouth of which is broad and spacious, but clogged with boxthorn, wild fig trees, shrubs, and brambles, so dense and tangled an undergrowth as wholly to cover over and conceal the entrance. All three of them then dismounted, and Sancho and the cousin bound Don Quixote very stoutly with the ropes.

"Look well what you do, master," said Sancho as they were girdling him. "Don't go burying yourself alive or get yourself caught so you will hang there like a bottle that has been let down into the well to cool. If you ask me, I would say it is none of your Grace's affair to be prying into this cave, which must be worse than a dungeon."

"Keep on trying and keep still," Don Quixote admonished him. "It is just such an undertaking as this, Sancho, that is reserved for me." [1]

The guide then addressed him. "Señor Don Quixote," he said, "I beg your Grace to view thoroughly and inspect with a hundred eyes what you find down there; who knows, maybe it will be something that I can put in my book on *Transformations*."

"Leave the tambourine," Sancho advised him, "to the one who knows how to play it." [2]

By this time they had finished tying Don Quixote, passing the rope over his doublet, not over his battle harness.

"It was careless of us," said the knight, "not to have provided ourselves with a cattle bell to attach to the rope at my side so that you might be able to tell from the sound of it whether I was still descending and still alive. However, there is nothing for it now. I am in God's hands and may He be my guide."

He knelt and prayed to Heaven in a low voice, imploring God to aid him and grant him success in this adventure, which impressed him as being a rare and dangerous one. Then he raised his voice:

"O lady who dost inspire my every deed and action, O most illustrious and peerless Dulcinea del Toboso! If it be possible for the prayers and entreaties of this thy fortunate lover to reach thine ears, I do beseech thee to hear them. What I ask of thee is nothing other than thy favor and protection, of which I so greatly stand in need at this moment. I am now about to sink, to hurl and plunge myself into the abyss that yawns before me here, simply in order that the world may know that there is nothing, however impossible it may seem, that I will not undertake and accomplish, provided only I have thy favor."

Having said this, he went up to the chasm[3] and perceived that if he was to make a descent he would first have to clear an entrance by force of arm or by hacking away the underbrush; and accordingly, taking his sword, he began cutting and felling the brambles at the mouth of the cave, the noise of which caused a very great number of crows and jackdaws to fly out. There were so many of these birds and such was their velocity that they knocked Don Quixote down, and had he been as much of a believer in augury as he was a good Catholic Christian, he would have taken this as an ill omen and would have declined to bury himself in such a place as that. Finally, he arose and, seeing that no more crows or other night birds were emerging, such as the bats that flew out with the crows, he allowed himself to be lowered into the depths of the horrendous cavern, with Sancho and the cousin letting out the rope as the squire bestowed his benediction and crossed himself an endless number of times.

"May God be your guide," exclaimed Sancho, "and the Rock of France,[4] along with the Trinity of Gaeta,[5] O flower, cream, and skimming of knights-errant! There you go, daredevil of the earth,[6] heart of steel, arms of brass! Once more, may God be your guide and bring you back safe, sound, and without a scratch to the light of this world which you are leaving to bury yourself in that darkness that you go to seek!"

The cousin, meanwhile, was offering up practically the same prayers. Don Quixote then went on down, calling for them to give him rope and more rope, and they let it out for him little by little. By the time they could no longer hear his voice, which came out of the cave as through a pipe, they had let him have the entire hundred fathoms, all the rope there was, and were of a mind to pull him up again. They decided, however, to wait for half an hour, and then they once more began hauling in the line, with no effort whatever, for they could feel no weight on the other end, which led them to think that Don Quixote must have remained behind. Believing this to be the case, Sancho began weeping bitterly and started pulling with all his might in order to learn the truth of the matter; but when they had come to a little more than eighty fathoms, as it seemed to them, they once more felt a tug, which made them very happy indeed. Finally, at ten fathoms, they could see Don Quixote quite distinctly, and as he caught sight of him, Sancho cried out, "Welcome, master, we are glad to see you again. We thought you had stayed down there to found a family."

But Don Quixote said not a word in reply, and when they had him all the way up they saw that his eyes were closed and that, to all appearances, he was sound asleep. They laid him on the ground and untied him, but even this did not wake him. It was not until they had turned him over first on one side and then on the other and had given him a thorough shaking and mauling that, after a considerable length of time, he at last regained consciousness, stretching himself as if he had been roused from a profound slumber and gazing about him with a bewildered look.

"God forgive you, friends," he said, "you have taken me away from the most delightful existence mortal ever knew and the pleasantest sight human eyes ever rested upon. Now truly do I begin to understand how it is that all the pleasures of this life pass away like a shadow or a dream or wither like the flower of the field.[7] O unfortunate Montesinos! O sorely wounded Durandarte! O unhappy Belerma! O tearful Guadiana! [8] And you, hapless daughters of Ruidera,[9] who in your waters display the tears your eyes once wept!"

The cousin and Sancho listened attentively to Don Quixote's words, which appeared to have been uttered in great pain, as though drawn from his entrails. They thereupon begged him to tell them the meaning of it all and what it was he had seen in that Hell he had visited.

"Hell do you call it?" said Don Quixote. "Do not call it that, for it does not deserve the name, as you shall see."

He then asked them to give him something to eat, as he was exceedingly hungry; and so they spread the cousin's sackcloth upon the green grass and laid out what fare the saddlebags could afford, and, sitting down together like the three good friends and companions that they were, they proceeded to make a meal of it, combining lunch and supper. When the sackcloth had been removed, Don Quixote de la Mancha spoke.

"Let no one arise," he said, "but both of you listen most attentively to what I have to say."

CHAPTER XXIII. *Of the amazing things which the incomparable Don Quixote told of having seen in the deep Cave of Montesinos, an adventure the grandeur and impossible nature of which have caused it to be regarded as apocryphal.*

IT WAS around four in the afternoon when the subdued light and tempered rays of the sun, which was now covered over with clouds, afforded Don Quixote an opportunity to tell his two illustrious listeners, without undue heat or weariness, what it was he had seen in the Cave of Montesinos. He began in the following manner:

"At a depth corresponding to the height of twelve or fourteen men, on the right-hand side of this dungeon, there is a concave recess capable of containing a large cart with its mules. A small light filters into it through distant chinks or crevices in the surface of the earth; and I caught sight of this nook just at a time when I was feeling tired and vexed at finding myself dangling from a rope in that manner as I descended into those dark regions without any certain knowledge as to where I was going. And so I decided to enter the recess and rest a little. I called to you, asking you not to give out any more rope until I told you to do so, but you must not have heard me. Accordingly, I gathered it in as you sent it to me and, making a coil or pile of it, I seated myself upon it, meanwhile thinking what I should have to do in order to let myself all the way down to the bottom, as I now had no one to hold me up.

"As I sat there lost in thought and deeply perplexed, suddenly and without my doing anything to bring it about a profound sleep fell upon me; and then, all unexpectedly and not knowing how it happened, I awoke and found myself in the midst of the most beautiful, pleasant, and delightful meadow that nature could create or the most fertile imagination could conceive. Opening my eyes, I rubbed them and discovered that I was not sleeping but really awake. Nevertheless, I felt my head and bosom to make sure it was I who was there and not some empty and deceptive phantom. And my sense of touch and feeling and the coherence of my thoughts were sufficient to assure me that I was the same then and there that I am here and now.

"It was at that moment that my eyes fell upon a sumptuous royal palace or castle, the walls and battlements of which appeared to be built of clear, transparent crystal. The two wings of the main gate were suddenly thrown open, and there emerged and came toward me a venerable old man clad in a hooded cloak of mulberry-colored stuff that swept the ground. Around his head and his bosom was a collegiate green satin sash, and on his head a black Milanese bonnet. His beard was snow-white and fell below his waist, and he carried no arms whatever, nothing but a rosary which he held in his hand, a string on which the beads were larger than fair-sized walnuts, every tenth one being as big as an ordinary ostrich egg. His bearing, his stride, the gravity of his demeanor, and his stately presence, each in itself and all of them together, filled me with wonder and astonishment. Upon reaching my side, the first thing he did was to give me a close embrace.

" 'It is a long time,' he said, 'O valiant knight, Don Quixote de la Mancha, that we in these enchanted solitudes have been waiting for a sight of you, that you might go back and inform the world of what lies locked and concealed in the depths of this cave which you have entered, the so-called Cave of Montesinos, an exploit solely reserved for your invincible heart and stupendous courage. Come with me, most illustrious sir, and I will show you the hidden marvels of this transparent castle of which I am the governor and perpetual guardian; for I am Montesinos himself, after whom the cave is named.'

"No sooner had he informed me that he was Montesinos than I asked him if the story was true that was told in the world above, to the effect that with a small dagger he had cut out the heart of his great friend Durandarte and had borne it to the lady Belerma as his friend at the point of death had requested him to do.

He replied that it was all true except the part about the dagger, for it was not a dagger, nor was it small, but a burnished poniard sharper than an awl."

"It must have been such a poniard," said Sancho at this point, "as that of Ramón de Hoces of Seville." [1]

"I cannot say as to that," replied Don Quixote, "for Ramón de Hoces lived only yesterday and the battle of Roncesvalles, where this unfortunate affair occurred, was many years ago; and, in any case, it does not alter in any way the truth and substance of the tale."

"That is right," said the cousin. "Continue, Señor Don Quixote, for I am listening to your Grace with the greatest of pleasure."

"And mine in relating the story is no less," Don Quixote assured him. "And so, as I am saying, the venerable Montesinos took me into the crystal palace, where, in a low room that was made entirely of alabaster and very cool, I beheld a tomb fashioned out of marble with masterly craftsmanship, and upon it lay a knight stretched at full length. He was not a bronze knight, nor one of marble or of jasper, as you see on other tombs; he was of actual flesh and bone. His right hand, which seemed to me somewhat hairy and sinewy, a sign that its owner had been possessed of great strength—his right hand lay upon his heart; and before I could ask any questions, Montesinos, seeing how amazed I was, went on to explain.

"'This,' he said, 'is my friend Durandarte, flower and mirror of the brave and enamored knights of his age. Merlin, that French enchanter,[2] who they say was the devil's own son, holds him here under a spell as he does me and many other knights and ladies. How or why he did it to us, no one knows; but time will tell, and it is my belief that the time is not far off. What astonishes me is the fact that it is as certain that Duran-

darte died in my arms as it is that it is now day; and
there is likewise no doubt that after his death I took out
his heart with my own hands. It weighed all of two
pounds; for according to the naturalists he who has a
large heart is endowed with greater valor than he who
has a small one.[3] And if it is true, then, that this knight
really died, how is it that he still sighs and laments from
time to time as though he were alive?'

"As Montesinos said this, the wretched Durandarte
cried out in a loud voice:

> 'O my cousin Montesinos!
> the last request I made of thee
> was that when I should be lying
> cold in death, thou wouldst favor me
> by bearing this my captive heart
> to fair Belerma where'er she be
> and ripping it from out my bosom
> with knife or dagger, set it free.'[4]

"Hearing these words, the venerable Montesinos knelt
before the unfortunate knight and addressed him with
tears in his eyes. 'Long since, O dearest cousin, Señor
Durandarte, I did what you requested of me on that
bitter day when we lost you. I took out your heart as
well as I could, without leaving the smallest particle of
it in your breast. I cleaned it with a lace handkerchief
and set out for France with it, having first laid you in
the bosom of the earth with enough tears to wash my
hands of the blood that stained them after they had
been in your entrails. What is more, beloved cousin, at
the first village I came to after leaving Roncesvalles I
put a little salt upon your heart so that it would not
have an unpleasant odor but would remain, if not fresh,

at least well preserved when I came to present it to the lady Belerma.

" 'That lady, like you and me and Guadiana your squire and the duenna Ruidera and her seven daughters and two nieces and many others among your friends and acquaintances, has been held here many a year through Merlin's magic art; and although more than five hundred years have passed, not a one of us has died. The only ones that are missing are Ruidera, her daughters and her nieces, for Merlin would seem to have taken pity on their tears and has transformed them into an equal number of lakes which today, in the world of the living and the province of La Mancha, are known as the Lakes of Ruidera.[5] Seven of them belong to the King of Spain, and the two nieces to the knights of a very holy order called the Order of St. John.[6]

" 'As for Guadiana, your squire, weeping for your sad fate, he was transformed into a river of the same name.[7] When he came to the surface and beheld the sun of that other heaven, he was so grieved at thought of leaving you that he plunged down into the bowels of the earth once more; but inasmuch as he must needs yield to his natural current, he rises again from time to time where men and the sun may see him. The said lakes supply him with their waters, and with these and many others that reach him he enters Portugal with great pomp. But, for all of that, wherever he goes he is still sad and melancholy and does not pride himself upon breeding dainty fish of the kind that are sought after, but only coarse ones lacking in flavor, quite different from those of the Tagus with its golden sands.

" 'All this, O cousin, I have told you many times; and since you do not answer me, I am led to think that you do not believe me, or it may be you do not hear, all of

which pains me, God only knows how much. But now I
have some news to give you which, if it does not assuage
your grief, will not add to it in any way. Know that
here in your presence—you have but to open your eyes
and you will see him—is that great knight of whom the
wise Merlin prophesied so many things, I mean the
famous Don Quixote de la Mancha, who once again
and to better advantage than in past ages has undertaken
to revive in this present age the long-forgotten profession of knight-errantry. It may be that, thanks to his
favor and mediation, we shall be disenchanted; for great
exploits are reserved for great men.' [8]

" 'And even if it be not so,' replied the wretched
Durandarte in a low, faint voice, 'and even if it be not
so, O cousin, I say to you: patience, and shuffle.' [9] And,
turning on his side, he relapsed into his accustomed
silence without uttering another word.

"At that moment a great outcry was heard, accompanied by the sound of weeping, profound sighs, and
anguished sobs; and I turned my head and saw, through
the crystal walls, a procession of exceedingly lovely
damsels passing through another chamber. There were
two rows of them, and they were all clad in mourning
with white turbans on their heads after the Turkish
fashion. At the end of the procession came a lady, as
was to be seen from her dignified appearance, who wore
a flowing white veil so long that it touched the ground.
Her turban was twice as large as the largest of the
others, her eyebrows were so close together that they
met, her nose was somewhat flat and her mouth wide,
but her lips were red; her teeth, when she displayed
them, were seen to be few and uneven but white as
peeled almonds. In her hands she carried a fine piece
of cloth, and wrapped in it, so far as could be made out,
was a mummified heart, all dried and withered.

"Montesinos informed me that all these people in the procession were the attendants of Durandarte and Belerma who had been enchanted along with their master and mistress, and that the last one, with the heart in her hands, was the lady Belerma herself, who with her damsels was accustomed to parade like this four days a week, singing, or rather weeping, dirges over the heart and body of his unfortunate cousin. He added that in case she impressed me as being somewhat ugly, or at any rate not as beautiful as report would have it, this was due to the bad nights and worse days that she spent as an enchanted being, as I could see for myself from the circles under her eyes and her sickly hue.

" 'And do not think,' continued Montesinos, 'that her sallowness and those circles are due to an affliction that is common to women at a certain period of the month, for it has been many months and even years since she has had that experience. It is, rather, the grief that she feels in her heart for that other heart she holds in her hands, which but serves to bring back to memory and revive the misfortune that befell her ill-starred lover. If it were not for that, even the great Dulcinea del Toboso, so famous in these parts and throughout the world, would scarcely equal her in beauty, grace, and dashing manner.'

" 'Hold there, Señor Don Montesinos!' said I at this point. 'Your Grace should tell your story in the proper way for, as you know, all comparisons are odious. There is no reason for comparing anybody with anybody. The peerless Dulcinea del Toboso is who she is and has been, and let the matter rest there.'

" 'Señor Don Quixote,' he replied to me, 'forgive me, your Grace. I confess that I was wrong in saying that Señora Dulcinea could scarcely equal Señora Belerma; for by some means or other I have learned that your

Grace is her knight, and that is enough to make me bite my tongue out before comparing her with anything but Heaven itself.'

"And so the great Montesinos having given me this satisfaction, my heart recovered from the shock it had received when I heard my lady mentioned in the same breath with his."

"But," said Sancho, "I still can't help wondering why your Grace didn't jump on the old fellow and kick his bones to a pulp and pull his beard until there wasn't a hair left in it."

"No, friend Sancho," replied Don Quixote, "it would not have been right for me to do that, for we are all of us obliged to respect the aged, even though they be knights, and especially when they are under a magic spell. But I can tell you that we came off even in all the other questions and answers that passed between us."

The cousin now put in a word. "I do not understand, Señor Don Quixote," he said, "how your Grace in the short time you were down there could have seen so many things and done so much talking."

"How long has it been since I went down?" asked Don Quixote.

"A little more than an hour," Sancho told him.

"That cannot be," said the knight, "for night fell and day dawned, and it was day and night three times altogether; so that, according to my count, it was three whole days that I spent in those remote regions that are hidden from our sight."

"My master," averred Sancho, "must be speaking the truth; for since all the things that happened to him came about through magic, who knows? what seemed to us an hour may have been three days and nights for him."

"That is right," said Don Quixote.

"And did your Grace eat in all that time?" the cousin inquired.

"Not a mouthful," replied Don Quixote, "nor did I feel the least bit hungry."

"Then, those that are enchanted do not eat?" the student persisted.

"They neither eat nor are they subject to the major excretions," was Don Quixote's answer, "although it is believed that their nails, beard, and hair continue to grow."

"And do they sleep by any chance?" asked Sancho.

"No, certainly not," said Don Quixote, "or, at least, during the three days I was with them, none of them shut an eye, and the same was true of me."

"The proverb, 'Tell me what company you keep and I'll tell you what you are,' fits in here," observed Sancho. "Seeing your Grace has been keeping company with the bewitched, who fast and stay awake, it is small wonder if you didn't sleep either while you were with them. But forgive me, master, if I tell you that God—I was about to say the devil—may take me if I believe a word of your Grace's story."

"How is that?" asked the cousin. "Do you mean to say that Señor Don Quixote is lying? Why, even if he wished to, he had no opportunity to imagine and invent such a lot of falsehoods."

"I do not think that my master is lying," said Sancho.

"Well, then, what do you think?" Don Quixote wanted to know.

"I think," replied Sancho, "that Merlin or those enchanters that laid a spell on the whole crew you say you saw and talked with down there have put into your noddle or your memory all this rigmarole that you've been telling us, and all that remains to be told."

"Such a thing could be," said Don Quixote, "but it is
not so in this case; for I have simply told you what I saw
with my own eyes and felt with my own hands. Montesinos showed me countless other marvelous things
which I will relate to you in due time and at leisure
in the course of our journey, for this is not the place to
speak of them. But what will you say when I tell you
he pointed out to me three peasant lasses who were
gamboling and disporting themselves like goats in those
lovely meadows; and no sooner did I see them than I
recognized one of them as being the peerless Dulcinea
del Toboso and the other two as the same girls who had
come with her and with whom we spoke upon the El
Toboso road.

"I asked Montesinos if he knew them and he replied
that he did not, but that he thought they must be some
highborn ladies with a spell upon them. He added that
they had arrived but a few days ago, which to me was
not surprising in view of the fact that many other ladies
of the present time as well as of past ages were to be
found there in various strange and enchanted shapes,
among whom he said he recognized Queen Guinevere
and her duenna Quintañona, she who poured the wine[10]
for Lancelot 'when from Britain he came.'"

As he heard his master say this, Sancho Panza thought
he would lose his mind or die of laughing. Knowing
as he did the truth respecting Dulcinea's supposed enchantment, since he himself had been the enchanter
and the concoctor of the evidence, he now was convinced beyond a doubt that the knight was out of his
senses and wholly mad.

"It was an evil hour, my dear master," he said, "a
worse season, and a sad day when your Grace went
down into the other world, and an unlucky moment
when you met that Señor Montesinos, who has sent

you back to us like this. You would have been better off
if you had stayed up here, with all your wits about you
as God gave them to you, speaking in proverbs and giving advice at every step of the way, in place of telling us
the most foolish stories that could be imagined."

"Knowing you as I do, Sancho," said Don Quixote,
"I take no account of your words."

"Nor I of your Grace's," was the reply, "even though
you beat me or kill me for those I have already spoken
or those that I mean to speak, unless you correct and
mend your own. But tell me, seeing that we are now
at peace: how or by what sign did you recognize the
lady who is our mistress? Did you speak to her, and if
so, what did you say and what did she answer you?"

"I recognized her," said Don Quixote, "by the fact
that she wore the same clothes that she did when you
first made me acquainted with her. I spoke to her,
but she did not answer a word; she merely turned her
back on me and fled so swiftly that a bolt from a crossbow would not have overtaken her. I was for following
her and should have done so had not Montesinos advised me not to waste my strength as it would be in
vain; and, moreover, the hour had come for me to leave
the cavern. He further assured me that, in the course of
time, he would let me know how he and Belerma and
Durandarte and all the others who were there had been
disenchanted. What gave me the most pain, however,
of all the things that I saw and observed, was this. Even
as Montesinos was speaking, one of the damsels who
accompanied the hapless Dulcinea came up to me from
one side, without my having noticed her, and, her eyes
brimming with tears, addressed me in a low and troubled voice.

" 'My lady Dulcinea del Toboso,' she said, 'kisses
your Grace's hand and implores your Grace to do her

the favor of informing her how you are; and being in great want, she also begs your Grace in all earnestness to be so good as to lend her, upon this new dimity petticoat that I am wearing, half a dozen reales or whatever your Grace may have upon you, and she gives you her word that she will pay them back just as soon as she can.'

"I was astonished to receive such a message as this, and, turning to Señor Montesinos, I asked him, 'Is it possible, sir, for the highborn who have been enchanted to suffer want?' To which he made the following reply:

" 'Believe me, your Grace, Señor Don Quixote de la Mancha, this thing that is called want is to be found everywhere; it extends to and reaches all persons and does not even spare the enchanted; and since the lady Dulcinea del Toboso has sent you a request for those six reales and has offered you good security, there is nothing to be done, as I see it, but to give them to her, for she must undoubtedly be hard pressed.'

" 'Security I will not take,' I told him, 'nor can I give her what she asks, for I have only four reales on me.'

"With this, I handed the coins to the damsel—they were the ones that you let me have the other day to bestow as alms upon the poor that I might meet with along the road.

" 'Tell your lady, my dear,' I said, 'that her sufferings weigh upon my heart, and that I only wish I were a Fugger[11] that I might cure them. And you may inform her, further, that there can be no such thing as health for me so long as I am deprived of the pleasure of seeing her and enjoying her discreet conversation. Tell her, also, that I most earnestly beg her Grace to permit herself to be seen and addressed by her captive servant and world-weary knight, and that when she least expects it she will hear that I have taken an oath and made a vow similar to that of the Marquis of Mantua, who swore to avenge his nephew, Baldwin, that time he found him expiring in the heart of the mountains, his vow being not to eat bread off a cloth, along with other trifling stipulations which he added, until vengeance had been had. For I mean to take no rest but to roam the seven parts of the world more faithfully than did the prince Dom Pedro of Portugal [12] until I shall have freed her from this spell.'

"'All this and more you owe my lady,' was the damsel's answer; and, taking the four reales, in place of dropping a curtsy she cut a caper, leaping more than two yards into the air."

"Holy God!" cried Sancho as Don Quixote reached this point of his story. "Can it be that there are in this world enchanters of such power that they have changed my master's good sense into such madness as this? O master, master! in God's name, think what you are doing, look to your Grace's honor, and do not go believing all this nonsense that has turned your head and left you short of wit."

"It is because you love me, Sancho, that you talk that way," said Don Quixote. "Since you are not experienced in worldly matters, everything that is a little difficult seems to you impossible; but, as I said before, I will tell you more later on of what I saw down there, and you shall hear things that will compel you to believe that what I have already told you is the truth and admits of neither question nor reply."

Following the adventure of Montesinos, Don Quixote and Sancho, accompanied by their guide, make for the nearest inn. Along the road they are passed by a man riding on a mule. The animal is laden down with lances and halberds, and the rider is beating it in order

*to make it go faster. This arouses Don Quixote's curi-
osity, which, however, the man declines to satisfy,
merely remarking, "I intend to put up tonight at the
inn . . . and if you happen to be going the same way
you will find me there, where I will tell you marvels."
He then rides on at top speed before the knight can
question him further.*

*Shortly afterward they overtake a youth who is
traveling on foot and who proves to be a former court
page on his way to enlist in the army. He and Don
Quixote have a conversation concerning the sorry way
in which pages are treated. As the knight sees it, the
lot of a soldier is a much happier one, and he proceeds
to set forth his views on the subject, which may be taken
as Cervantes' own.*

From Chapter XXIV: *Wherein are related trifling
matters. . . .*

"BUT for all that," said Don Quixote, "you are to be
congratulated on having left the court with so
worthy an object in view; for there is nothing on earth
more honorable or useful than, first of all, to serve God,
and, after that, one's king and rightful lord. This is especially true of the profession of arms, by which more
honor if not more wealth is to be attained than by following that of letters, as I have said many times. Granting it is true that letters have founded more great houses
than have arms, nevertheless, arms have somewhat of an
advantage over letters, being accompanied by a certain
splendor with which nothing else can compare. Be sure
that you remember what I am about to say to you now,
as it will be of great profit and comfort to you under
hardship: do not let your mind dwell upon the adversi-

ties that may befall you, for the worst of them is death, and if it be a good death, the best fate of all is to die.

"When they asked Julius Caesar, that valiant Roman emperor, what the best death was, he replied: that which comes unexpectedly, suddenly, without having been foreseen; and although he spoke as a pagan who did not know the true God, yet from the point of view of human feeling he was right. Supposing that they kill you in the first skirmish or encounter, or that you are struck down by a cannon ball, blown up by a mine, what does it matter? You die, and that is the end of it. According to Terence, the soldier who dies in battle is more to be admired than the one who lives and seeks safety in flight, and the good soldier achieves fame through obedience to his captain and others in command.[1]

"Remember, my son, that to a soldier the smell of gunpowder is more pleasing than that of civet, and if old age comes upon you while you are still engaged in that honorable calling, even though you be full of wounds and maimed and crippled, at least it will not find you bereft of honor of a kind that poverty cannot diminish. What is more, provisions are now being made for giving aid and relief to old and disabled soldiers; for it is not right to treat them after the manner of certain persons who, when their aged blacks can be of no further use to them, turn the poor creatures out of the house under pretense of freeing them, only to make them the slaves of hunger from which death alone can liberate them. For the present, I do not care to say anything more to you, except that you should get up on the crupper of my steed and accompany me to the inn where you will sup with me; and tomorrow you shall go your way and may God speed you in accordance with the worthiness of your intentions."

The page did not accept the invitation to mount behind Don Quixote, but he did consent to have supper with him; all of which led Sancho to indulge in a few reflections.

"God help you, what a master!" he thought to himself. "Is it possible that a man who can say as many wise things as you have just said could have told the nonsensical and impossible tale that you did of the Cave of Montesinos? Well, well, we shall see."

They had reached the inn by now, just as night was falling, and Sancho was pleased to see that his master took it for a real inn this time and not for a castle as was his wont. As soon as they entered, Don Quixote inquired of the landlord if the man with the lances and halberds was there and was informed that the fellow was in the stable looking after his mule. The cousin and Sancho therefore proceeded to follow his example, seeing to it that Rocinante had the best stall and manger in the place.

Don Quixote cannot rest until he has solved the mystery of the lances and halberds carried by the man on the mule. He goes out to the stable and persuades the stranger to tell his story. It is a weird one, having to do with two village aldermen one of whom had an ass which had strayed into the wood and become lost. The owner of the beast and his friend go to search for it; they separate, and by way of a call each resorts to an exceedingly lifelike imitation of a donkey's braying. Their efforts are so realistic that they succeed in attracting each other time and again, but not the ass, which is eventually found devoured by wolves. Meanwhile each has discovered that the other is a virtuoso at braying, and the owner of the ass feels that this newly discovered talent of his more than makes up for the loss he has suffered.

The fame of the two aldermen's skill soon spreads to the neighboring hamlets, whose inhabitants begin making sport of the matter by braying derisively whenever they meet anyone from the village where the champions live. The joke has been carried so far as to lead to open hostilities on more than one occasion; and the man now informs Don Quixote that on the morrow the "brayers," as they have been dubbed, mean to give open battle to the residents of a certain town who have been among the leaders of the persecution; it is for this purpose that he is bringing the lances and halberds.

At this moment an individual clad as a wandering mountebank and with a patch over one eye enters the inn and asks for a lodging. The innkeeper welcomes him warmly and, addressing him as "Master Pedro," inquires, "Where are the ape and the show?" The reply being that "They are near at hand," the landlord says, "Bring on the show; for there are those in the inn tonight that will pay to see it and watch the ape's clever tricks." In answer to a question from Don Quixote, the innkeeper goes on to explain that Master Pedro is a puppet master who has been going about the countryside giving a performance based upon the old tale of Melisendra (Melisenda), Charlemagne's daughter, and Don Gaiferos (King Gayfer of Bordeaux, one of the emperor's chieftains), the story being a familiar item in the Spanish ballad collections.

Master Pedro also carries with him a "divining ape," which, when a question is put to it, is supposed to whisper the answer in the showman's ear. Don Quixote and the others are dumfounded when, as a result of the ape's "divinations," its owner runs up and falls at

*the knight's feet, calling him and Sancho by their names
and uttering a speech couched in the highflown language of chivalry.*

Suspecting that the puppet master is in league with
the devil, Don Quixote, at Sancho's suggestion, resolves
to try the ape on another question: were his adventures
in the Cave of Montesinos true or false? He receives an
evasive answer, to the effect that they were "in part false
and in part credible," and then is told that the ape's
"power" is gone until "next Friday." The puppet show
begins, with Master Pedro manipulating the figures
while a young lad who travels with him acts as interpreter (Chapter xxv).

As Don Quixote watches the performance and listens
to the boy's commentary, which he interrupts from time
to time, he grows more and more excited, for it is all
very real to him. Finally, as a cavalcade of Moors sets
out in pursuit of the "Christian lovers," he can stand it
no longer and, leaping to his feet, he draws his sword
and slashes the stage and puppets to bits. The audience
is thrown into confusion, Master Perdo bewails the loss
of his stock in trade, and the ape flees in terror.

When the knight has at last been brought to see that
the figures were no more than puppets, he is duly re-
pentant and blames it all on the wicked "enchanters";
he offers to reimburse Master Pedro 'in good Castilian
currency." With Sancho and the innkeeper acting as
arbiters and with some little haggling the damages are
settled, and early the next morning the company breaks
up. Don Quixote for once is able to pay, and does pay
handsomely, for his lodging, and he and Sancho go their
way alone (Chapter xxvi).

It is then revealed (Chapter xxvii) who Master Pedro
really is—none other than Ginés de Pasamonte, the
galley slave who, freed by Don Quixote, later stole

Sancho's ass. Fearful of being caught, Ginés had crossed over into other territory, put a patch over one eye to avoid recognition, and taken to the trade of puppet master, "for he was exceedingly skillful at this and at the art of juggling as well." He had purchased the ape of some freed Christians coming from Barbary and had taught it to jump on his shoulder when he made a sign and pretend to whisper in his ear. The moment he entered the inn he had, of course, recognized Don Quixote and Sancho, and it had been easy to astonish them.

As he sallies forth once more, the knight resolves that, before continuing on to Saragossa, to attend the tournament there, he will have a look at the banks of the Ebro River. On the third day, as he ascends a hill, he hears a "great din of drums, trumpets, and musket fire"; and when he reaches the top he discovers an army drawn up on the plain below. It is the men from the "braying town" who have come forth to give battle to their enemies. Needless to say, he cannot resist taking part in this; he rides up to the front and makes a long speech.

His point is that no individual can insult an entire community, and so "there is no excuse for seeking to avenge such an insult since it really is not one." He then goes on to set forth the four conditions under which "prudent men and well-ordered states may take up arms." These are, in general, the conditions laid down by St. Thomas Aquinas; and Don Quixote adds the Christian admonition to "love your enemies," which means that "there can be no just vengeance."

Listening to all this, Sancho is convinced that his master is a "tologian." He too undertakes to reason with the "brayers" and boasts of his own skill at the art. By way of proof he gives a lusty bray, only to be felled by the staff of a man from the "braying town" who thinks that

Sancho is making fun of them. Don Quixote, lance in
hand, promptly attacks the man who dealt the blow, but
the others intervene and he finds himself under a rain of
stones, which, together with the threatening muskets
and crossbows, causes him to turn Rocinante's head and
gallop away as fast as he can.

Sancho, having recovered his senses, is lifted to his
donkey's back and permitted to follow his master. At a
safe distance Don Quixote pauses to wait for his squire.

CHAPTER XXVIII. Of things that, Benengeli says,
the reader will come to know if he reads attentively.

WHEN the brave man flees, it means that treachery has been uncovered, and it is the part of the
wise to save themselves for better occasions.

This truth was brought out in the case of Don Quixote, who, having aroused the fury of the townspeople
and the ill will and indignation of the squadron, showed
his heels and, without thought of Sancho or the danger
in which he was leaving him, put as much distance
between himself and the enemy as he deemed necessary
in order to assure his own safety. Sancho followed, slung
across his ass in the manner that has been described.
He finally came up, in full possession of his wits by
this time, and as he did so he slid from the gray's back to
Rocinante's feet, all battered and bruised and in a sor-
rowful plight. Don Quixote then dismounted to examine
his squire's wounds and, finding him sound from head
to foot, addressed him angrily enough.

"An evil hour it was, Sancho," he said, "when you
learned how to bray! Where did you ever hear that it
was a good thing to mention the rope in the house of
the hanged man? What counterpoint can braying music

have except that of cudgels? You may give thanks to God, Sancho, that they made the sign of the cross on you just now with a club and not with a cutlass."

"I'm in no condition to answer," replied Sancho, "for it seems to me that I'm talking through my shoulders. Let's mount and get away from here. I'll not bray any more, but I can't help remarking that knights-errant appear to run away and leave their faithful squires in the hands of the enemy to be pounded like privet or like wheat in the hopper."

"He who retires," said Don Quixote, "does not flee. I would have you know, Sancho, that valor not based upon prudence can only be termed temerity, and the triumphs of the foolhardy are to be attributed to good luck rather than to courage. I admit that I retired, but not that I fled; and in this I have merely followed the example of many brave men who have saved themselves for a more propitious time. The histories are full of such instances, but as it would do you no good to refer you to them, I shall spare myself the trouble for the present."

Sancho by now was once more on his gray's back, having been helped up by Don Quixote, who then mounted Rocinante; and, riding slowly along, they made for a grove that was visible about a quarter of a league away. Every so often Sancho would heave a deep sigh or moan as if in pain, and when his master asked him what the cause of it was, he replied that he ached all over, from the base of his spine to the nape of his neck, and it was nearly driving him crazy.

"The reason for that," remarked Don Quixote, "is undoubtedly the fact that the club they used was a long one and caught you all the way down your back where those aching parts are located; and if it had gone any farther down, you would ache still more."

"By God," exclaimed Sancho, "your Grace has taken a great load off my mind and made everything as clear as can be! Body of me! Is the cause of my pain such a mystery that it is necessary to explain to me that I ache wherever the club reached me? If it was my ankles hurting me, there might be some sense in trying to find out what caused it, but to tell me that I'm sore because they beat me is not much in the way of a discovery. On my word, master of mine, the misfortune of another hangs by a hair,[1] and I am every day discovering how little I have to hope for from keeping company with your Grace. This time you have let them club me. Another time, or a hundred times more, it will be the old story of the blanketings and other foolish pranks all over again; and if up to now I've had it only across the shoulders, I'll be getting it later straight in the eyes.

"I'd do a lot better," he went on, "if I wasn't a numb-skull who will never do anything well as long as he lives —I'd do a lot better, I say, by going home to my wife and young ones, to support and bring them up on whatever God may see fit to give me, instead of trailing after your Grace along roads that lead nowhere and highways and byways that don't deserve the name, with little to drink and less to eat. And as for sleeping! Pace off seven feet of earth, brother squire, and if you want any more than that, take another seven; the dish is in your hands,[2] help yourself; so stretch out to your heart's content, and welcome. I'd like to see the one who started this knight-errantry business burned to ashes, or at least the first man who was willing to be a squire to such fools as all the knights-errant of times past must have been. As to those of the present day, I say nothing, for since your Grace is one of them, I must respect them; and what's more, your Grace knows a little more than the devil when it comes to talking and thinking."

"I would like to lay a good wager with you, Sancho," said Don Quixote, "that since you have been running on like this with no one to stop you, you don't feel an ache in your entire body. Talk on, my son; say anything that comes to your mind or to the tip of your tongue; for if it will relieve your pain, I will gladly put up with the annoyance which your impudence causes me. If you are so anxious to go home to your wife and children, God forbid that I should stop you. You have my money; reckon up how long it has been since we left our village this third time[3] and what your wages should be each month, and then pay yourself out of hand."

"When I worked for Tomé Carrasco,"[4] replied Sancho, "father of the bachelor Sansón Carrasco, your Grace's acquaintance, I earned two ducats a month and my board; but with your Grace, I can't say what it should be, for your Grace knows that the squire to a knight-errant does more work than a farmer's helper. The work in the fields may be hard, but at the worst, when night comes we have our *olla* and a bed to sleep in—and that's something I haven't had since I've been serving your Grace, except for the brief time we spent at Don Diego de Miranda's house, and the feast I had on the skimmings that I took from Camacho's pots, and the bed and what I had to drink at Basilio's. All the rest of the time I've slept on the hard earth, under the open sky, in what they call the inclemencies of the weather. I've kept myself alive on scraps of cheese and crusts of bread; and as for drinking, it has been water from the brooks or springs in the bypaths that we traveled."

"I admit," said Don Quixote, "that everything you say, Sancho, is the truth. How much more do you think I should give you than what you had from Tomé Carrasco?"

"As I see it," said Sancho, "if your Grace would give

me a couple of reales more each month, I could consider myself well paid. That is to say, so far as my wages go, for the work I've done. But seeing that you gave me your word and solemn promise to make me the governor of an island, it would only be fair for your Grace to add another six reales, making thirty altogether."

"Very well," Don Quixote agreed, "it is now twenty-five days since we left our village; so reckon it up, Sancho, on the basis of the wage you think you ought to have, and see how much it is I owe you; and then, as I have said, you can pay yourself by your own hand."

"O body of me!" cried Sancho, "your Grace is very wrong in this reckoning; for so far as the island is concerned, we have to count from the day your Grace promised it to me down to the present hour."

"Well," said Don Quixote, "and how long has it been since I made you the promise?"

"If I'm not mistaken," replied Sancho, "it must be more than twenty years and three days, more or less."

At this Don Quixote slapped his forehead with his hand and burst into a hearty laugh.

"Why," he said, "with my wanderings in the Sierra and all the rest barely two months have gone by. And are you trying to tell me, Sancho, that it was twenty years ago I promised you that island? I am convinced now that you would take all the money I have as your wages; and if such is the case and that is what you want, I hereby give it to you; it is yours from now on, and much good may it do you. In order to be rid of so faithless a squire, I shall be content to remain a pauper, without a penny to my name. But tell me, you perverter of the laws of chivalry and the rules that govern squires, where have you ever heard of a squire who made such terms with his lord: 'You must give me so much a month for serving you?' Plunge, O rogue, scoundrel, monster—

plunge, I say, into the *mare magnum* of their histories; and if you find one single squire who ever said or thought of saying such a thing as you have just said, I would have you nail it to my forehead and in addition give me four resounding slaps in the face.

"Turn, then, the reins, or better, the halter of your ass, and go back to your home; for you are not going one step farther with me. O bread ungratefully received! O promises ill bestowed! O man who has more of the beast in him than of the human! So you are leaving me now, are you, just when I was about to elevate you to a position in life where, no matter what your wife might say, people would address you as your Lordship? So you are leaving me just when I had firmly resolved to make you governor of the best island in the world? In short, as you have said before, honey is not for the ass's mouth.[5] An ass you are and an ass you will be to your dying day, for I think that day will come before you ever realize that you are a stupid beast."

Sancho stared hard at Don Quixote as the knight heaped these insults upon him and was so smitten with remorse that the tears came to his eyes.

"Master," he said in a weak and sorrowing voice, "I will grant you that all I lack is a tail and I would be an ass; and if your Grace wants to put one on me, I'll look upon it as well placed and will serve you as a beast of burden all the days of my life that are left me. Forgive me, your Grace; have mercy on my foolishness. Remember that I know little, and if I talk much, that is due to weakness rather than to malice. But he who sins and mends his ways, commends himself to God."[6]

"I should have been surprised, Sancho," said his master, "if in the course of your speech you had not rung in some proverb. Very well, I forgive you, on condition that you do mend your ways and that from now on you do not think so much of your own interests. Rather, you should take heart, be of good cheer, pluck up courage, and trust me to fulfill my promises. Fulfillment may be late in coming, but that does not mean that it is impossible."

Sancho assured him that he would do so, contriving somehow to draw strength from weakness. By this time they had reached the grove, and Don Quixote now sat down at the foot of an elm and Sancho at the foot of a beech (for trees of this sort and others like them always have feet but no hands). Sancho spent an uncomfortable night, his aches returning with the evening dew. Don Quixote as always was deep in reveries; but, in spite of everything, the two of them had some sleep and at sunup resumed their journey toward the banks of the famous Ebro, where they had an experience that is related in the chapter to follow.

After traveling for a couple of days (though commentators have pointed out it should have taken them ten or fifteen), Don Quixote and Sancho reach the banks of the Ebro with its "clear and abundant, gently flowing waters" (Chapter xxix). *As they ride along they catch sight of an empty boat lying in the water, moored to the foot of a tree. It is without oars or rigging of any kind, and to the knight it appears to be inviting him to enter it and go to the aid of some highborn personage in distress, "for that is the way it is in the books of chivalry, in the stories where enchanters figure and speak." Sancho endeavors to dissuade him, but in vain.*

And so they embark, Sancho being deeply grieved at having to leave Rocinante and the ass "to the tender mercies of the enchanters." They drift slowly downstream, and Don Quixote delivers a pedantic and most amusing lecture on the subject of latitude, longitude,

*cosmography, and so on, to Sancho's complete obfusca-
tion. Then they perceive some big watermills, moored
in the middle of the stream for the purpose of grinding
corn, which for Don Quixote at once become a "city,
castle, or fortress where they must be holding some
knight in captivity, or some sorely wronged queen, infanta, or princess, to rescue whom I am being brought
here."*

*Again Sancho's pleadings are of no avail. He may
point out that these are nothing but watermills; the answer he receives is that this is but the appearance given
them by the enchanters who have transformed them. In
the meantime they have drifted so close that they are
in danger of being sucked in by the millwheels. The
millers, equipped with poles, come running to push
the small boat aside and prevent a disaster; but inasmuch as their faces and garments are covered with flour,
Don Quixote takes them to be monsters who are trying
to frighten him. With his customary challenge straight
out of the old romances, he draws his sword and prepares to attack them.*

*The millers, fortunately, are able to prevent the boat
from being sucked in, but not without upsetting it and
throwing its occupants into the water. Don Quixote
happens to be a good swimmer but is dragged down
by the weight of his armor, and the "monsters" have to
dive in and save the pair. No sooner have they reached
the shore than the fisherman who owns the boat appears and, seeing what has been done to his craft, falls
upon Sancho and strips him, demanding at the same
time that Don Quixote make good the loss.*

*This the knight readily agrees to do on condition that
the millers release those whom they are "holding
in durance in that castle." They seek to reason with
him, and he finally gives up the "adventure," being*

convinced that "two powerful enchanters must have clashed," and "this world is nothing but schemes and plots, all working at cross-purposes. I can do no more," he concludes despairingly.

With an address to the "imprisoned" ones whom he has been unable to free, he settles for the boat, after which he and Sancho return to Rocinante and the ass. This marks the end of the adventure of the enchanted bark.

With the Duke and Duchess

(CHAPTERS XXX-XLI)

On the day following the episode that has just been related, as Don Quixote and Sancho emerge from a wood at sunset, they see a group of people at the far end of a meadow, and upon drawing closer they perceive it is a hawking party. Seated upon a richly caparisoned white palfrey is a lady clad in green with a hawk on her wrist, and the knight correctly assumes that she is some great personage and dispatches Sancho to pay his respects.

The squire rides up on his gray, dismounts, kneels before the lady, and makes a speech that is an excellent imitation of his master's highflown manner. The lady replies in the same style, saying that she and her husband the duke will be glad to receive the Knight of the Mournful Countenance at their country home not far from there; for she has read The Ingenious Gentleman, Don Quixote de la Mancha *and knows all about Dulcinea del Toboso, and Sancho himself, as well as the hero of the story.*

Don Quixote is delighted with this response and he draws himself erect in the saddle, settles himself in the stirrups, adjusts his visor, and spurs Rocinante forward. Meanwhile the duchess has informed her husband of what has happened, and they decide to treat their guest as a true knight-errant and humor all his whims. Things do not go so well at the start, however. As Sancho is descending from his gray so that he may hold his master's stirrup, he catches his foot in one of the ropes of the packsaddle and is left hanging with his face and bosom on the ground. Failing to notice that his squire is not there to assist him, Don Quixote throws himself off with a lurch, bringing the saddle with him as he tumbles to earth.

Having been helped to his feet, the knight limps along as best he can and is about to kneel before the noble pair when the duke dismounts and advances to meet and embrace him. There follows an exchange of courtly speeches, with Sancho putting in his word and spouting proverbs as he always does. The duchess is charmed by his drollery and peasant wit, and they all set out for the duke's castle in high spirits (Chapter xxx).

Sancho especially is elated as he thinks of the good living he is going to have. The duke has gone ahead to instruct the servants as to the manner in which they are to treat the guests, and when the rest of the party arrives there is a great show of welcome to "the flower and cream of knight-errantry." Don Quixote is quite astonished at this: it is the first time he believes himself to be a true knight-errant and not a fanciful one, for here everything is happening just as in his storybooks.

There follows a bit of comedy between Sancho Panza and "a dignified duenna," one of the ladies that wait upon the duchess, who is highly insulted when Sancho asks her to go out and see that his gray is properly fed.

The duenna as an institution was a favorite butt of humor in those days, much as the mother-in-law is to-day, and throughout these chapters dealing with Don Quixote's stay at the ducal castle a good deal of fun is had at Doña Rodríguez' expense.

In the presence of his hosts the knight tries to put a stop to his squire's endless prattle, and when he is alone with Sancho he gives him a lecture on manners. Then Don Quixote goes down to the great hall to dine in state with the duke and duchess and "a solemn-faced ecclesiastic, one of those who rule over noble households." Sancho is amazed when he sees the respect that is shown his master and, despite his recent promise to keep a bridle on his tongue, cannot refrain from making comments and narrating an anecdote that proves extremely embarrassing to Don Quixote but which greatly amuses the ducal pair.

The clerical gentleman, meanwhile, becomes more and more out of sorts with all the talk of knights-errant and giants and enchanted Dulcineas, and he ends by sternly reproving the duke and duchess for encouraging such nonsense (Chapter xxxi). Infuriated at this and "trembling from head to foot like a man with an overdose of mercury," Don Quixote rises from his place at the table and delivers an eloquent reply in defense of chivalry, and Sancho comes to his support with a stock of proverbs.

"Long life to him [Don Quixote]," Sancho concludes, "and long life to me, and may he never lack empires to rule and may I always have islands to govern." At this point the duke interrupts: "I hereby confer upon you the government of an island that I happen to possess, and of no small importance." Don Quixote tells Sancho to get down on his knees and kiss the duke's feet for the favor granted him, and Sancho does so; whereupon the cleric *leaves the room in high dudgeon, declaring, "I feel like saying that your Excellency [the duke] is as much of a crackbrain as these sinners."*

The duke apologizes for the chaplain's conduct, an apology Don Quixote accepts in another long speech filled with his own brand of reasoning. After dinner four damsels carry in a silver basin and proceed to wash Don Quixote's beard, in the course of which operation they cover his entire face with lather in a way to give him a most comical appearance. It is a jest of their own invention, and their master and mistress do not know whether to be angry or amused. The two guests are astonished at such a ceremony, and to spare the knight's feelings the duke has the girls give him the same treatment they have accorded Don Quixote.

The talk comes back to the profession of arms and the calling of knight-errantry, and a discussion follows on the subject of Dulcinea del Toboso—as to whether or not there is a Dulcinea. (Here there is a passage that may be regarded as the keynote to Don Quixote's "madness" and the meaning of the tale.)

FROM CHAPTER XXXII: *Concerning . . . incidents, some serious and some amusing.*

THE duchess then requested her guest, since he appeared to have so good a memory, to describe for her the features of the beautiful Dulcinea del Toboso, who, if what fame had trumpeted abroad concerning her loveliness was true, must surely be the fairest creature in the world and even in all La Mancha. Upon hearing this, Don Quixote heaved a sigh.

"If," he said, "I could but take my heart out and lay it before your Highness's eyes, upon a plate here on this table, I should be able to spare my tongue the trouble of telling what is scarcely to be conceived; for in my heart your Excellency would see her fully portrayed. After all, why should I undertake to describe and depict, point by point and feature by feature, the beauty of the peerless Dulcinea? That is a task that should be laid upon other shoulders than mine, being one worthy of the brushes of Parrhasius, Timanthes, and Apelles and of the chisel of Lysippus;[1] artists such as they should preserve that beauty in pictures, in marble, and in bronze, and a Ciceronian and Demosthene[2] eloquence are called for to eulogize it."

"What does Demosthene mean, Señor Don Quixote?" asked the duchess. "That is a word I never heard in all my life."

"Demosthene eloquence," Don Quixote explained, "is equivalent to saying the eloquence of Demosthenes, just as Ciceronian means of Cicero, for they were the two greatest orators in the world."

"That is right," said the duke. "Your mind must have been wandering," he added, speaking to the duchess, "or you would not have asked such a question. But, for all of that, it would give us a very great pleasure if Señor Don Quixote would portray her for us; for I am sure that, even though it be the merest outline or sketch, she will emerge in such a manner as to arouse envy in the fairest of ladies."

"I should most certainly do so," said Don Quixote, "if it were not that the misfortune that befell her a short while ago, of a kind to be wept over rather than described, had blurred my mental image of her. For I must inform your Highness that, some days past, when I went to kiss her hand and to receive her blessing, her approval, and her permission for this third sally of mine, I found her quite a different being from the one I sought. I found her under a magic spell, converted from a princess into a peasant girl, from a beautiful creature into an ugly one, from an angel into a devil, from a fragrant-scented being into a foul-smelling wench, from a fine-garbed, dignified lady into a rustic clown, leaping in the air—in short, from Dulcinea del Toboso into a Sayago[3] country woman."

"God save us!" cried the duke in a loud voice at this juncture. "Who is it could have done such a wrong to the world? Who could have deprived it of that beauty that rendered it joyful, that grace that charmed it, and that modesty that so redounded to its credit?"

"Who?" Don Quixote repeated. "Who could it have been except some malign enchanter of the many envious ones who persecute me? That cursed race of beings was born into the world to darken it, to frustrate the achievements of the virtuous and exalt those of the wicked. These enchanters have persecuted, are persecuting, and will continue to persecute me until they shall have sunk me and my high deeds of chivalry into the deep pit of oblivion. They seek to harm and wound me where they know I am most vulnerable, for to take away his lady from a knight-errant is to rob him of the eyes with which he sees, the sun that lights him, and the sustenance that is his life. I have said many times before and I will say it again, that the knight-errant without a lady is like the tree without leaves, a building without a foundation, or a shadow without the body that casts it."

"There is no more to be said on the subject," observed the duchess; "but, nevertheless, if we are to believe the tale about Señor Don Quixote that was recently published in these parts and that won the praise of all—we are to gather from this tale, if I remember rightly, that your Grace has never seen the lady Dulcinea, that there is, in fact, no such lady in existence, or, rather, that she is a purely fanciful one, created in your Grace's own mind, whom you have endowed with all the charms and perfections that you chose to give her."

"That," replied Don Quixote, "is a long story. God knows whether or not there is a Dulcinea in this world or if she is a fanciful creation. This is not one of those cases where you can prove a thing conclusively. I have not begotten or given birth to my lady, although I contemplate her as she needs must be,[4] seeing that she is a damsel who possesses all those qualities that may render her famous in all parts of the world, such as: a flawless beauty; dignity without haughtiness; a tenderness that is never immodest; a graciousness due to courtesy and a courtesy that comes from good breeding; and, finally, a highborn lineage, for beauty is more resplendent and more nearly perfect in those of lofty extraction than in creatures of a humbler origin."

"True enough," said the duke, "but if Señor Don Quixote will permit me, after having read the story of his exploits I am compelled to remind him that it is stated there that, granted there is a Dulcinea in or out of El Toboso, and granted that she is as supremely beautiful as your Grace has depicted her, she still cannot compare in the matter of ancestry with the Orianas, the Alastrajareas, the Madásimas,[5] or others of that sort with whose names the histories that your Grace knows so well are filled."

"As to that," Don Quixote answered, "I can say only that Dulcinea is the daughter of her works,[6] that virtues shed luster upon the blood-stream, and that a person of low degree who is possessed of them is more to be esteemed than the vicious one who has risen to high station. Moreover, Dulcinea has qualities that well may bring her to a crown and scepter; for a woman who is at once beautiful and virtuous may by her merits come to work miracles, and has locked within her, potentially if not actually, a higher fortune than the one she knows."

"I must remark," said the duchess, "that in everything your Grace tells us you proceed with leaden foot and plummet in hand, as the saying is. As for myself, I shall continue to believe and shall see to it that all in my household do the same—even my lord the duke if necessary—that there is a Dulcinea now living in El Toboso, and that she is beautiful and highborn, a lady worthy of being served by such a knight as Señor Don Quixote, which is the highest praise I can bestow upon her. But, for all of that, there is still some small doubt in my mind, and here I hold a grudge against Sancho Panza; for the story that I have mentioned states that when Sancho brought the lady Dulcinea a message from your Grace, he found her winnowing a bag of wheat, and red wheat at that, a circumstance that leads me to question her exalted lineage."

"My lady," replied Don Quixote, "your Highness should know that all or most of the things that happen to me are beyond the common experience of other knights-errant, being brought about either through the inscrutable will of the fates or through the malice of some envious enchanter. For it is a known fact that all or most of the famous knights-errant either had a special gift that was proof against enchantment or else had flesh that was impenetrable so that they could not be wounded. There was, for example, Orlando, one of the Twelve Peers of France,[7] of whom it is related that he could be wounded only in the sole of his left foot, and with no other weapon whatever than a large pin; and so when Bernardo del Carpio slew him at Roncesvalles,[8] upon perceiving that he could not reach him with his sword, he was compelled to lift him from the ground and strangle him, thus recalling the manner in which Hercules disposed of Antaeus, the ferocious giant who, they say, was Earth's own son.

"By this," he went on, "I mean to imply that I may possibly possess some gift of this sort. Not the gift of invulnerability, however, since experience has frequently taught me that my flesh is tender and by no means impenetrable; nor am I proof against enchantment, having, before now, found myself thrust into a cage, a thing which all the world combined could never have accomplished except through the power of magic. But inasmuch as I succeeded in freeing myself from that spell, I am of the opinion that no one will henceforth be able to hurt me. Accordingly, those enchanters, seeing they can no longer lay their evil hands upon my person, are avenging themselves upon the object that I most love and would deprive me of life by mistreating Dulcinea, in whom I have my being.

"What I think is that when my squire brought her my message, those same enchanters transformed her into a country wench and set her at so low a task as is that of winnowing wheat. But I have already said that the wheat in question was not red, nor was it wheat, but oriental pearls; and, in proof of this, I may inform your Highnesses that when I came to El Toboso not long ago, I was able to find Dulcinea's palace; and the very next day Sancho, my squire, beheld her in her proper form, which is the most beautiful of any on earth, while to me she appeared as a coarse and ugly peasant girl and very rude in her speech, though she herself is the soul of propriety. And seeing that I am not enchanted and, it stands to reason, cannot be, she must be the one who has suffered this injury and has been thus altered, changed, and transformed. That is to say, my enemies through her have had their revenge on me, and it is on account of her that I live amid ceaseless tears until I shall once more have beheld her in her pristine state.

"All this," continued Don Quixote, "I have told you in order that no one may believe what Sancho says about Dulcinea's winnowing or sifting grain; for if they altered her in my sight, it is no wonder if they transformed her for him. Dulcinea is illustrious and wellborn and comes from one of those noble lines such as are to be met with in El Toboso,[9] where they are numerous, ancient, and respected; and, without a doubt, much of the credit for the esteem in which these houses are held must go to her, on account of whom her town will be as famous and renowned as Troy was on account of Helen or Spain by reason of Cava,[10] and with an even better title to fame.

"On the other hand, I would have your Highnesses know that Sancho Panza is one of the drollest squires that ever served a knight-errant. He is so sharp in his simple-mindedness that one may derive no little amusement from trying to determine whether he is in reality simple or sharp-witted. He has in him a certain malicious streak that seems to indicate he is a rogue, and from his blundering you would take him for a dunce. He doubts everything and believes everything, and just as I think he is about to tumble headlong, owing to some stupidity, he will come up with some witticism or other that sends him skyward in my estimation. The short of the matter is, I would not exchange him for another squire even though they threw in a city to boot.

"And so I am in some doubt as to whether it would be a good thing to entrust him with that governorship that your Highness has done him the favor of bestowing on him; although it is true that I discern in him a certain aptitude for governing, and with a little brushing-up of his wits he might make out as well with any government whatsoever as a king with his taxes.[11] Especially since we know from long experience that neither much ability nor much learning is necessary in order to be a governor; for there are a hundred hereabouts who are barely able to read and who yet acquit themselves of their task like so many gerfalcons.[12] The main thing is for them to be possessed of good intentions and a desire to do the right thing always, for they will never lack those who can advise and direct them in what they have to do, just as those who are knights and not scholars pass judgment with the aid of an assessor. My advice to him would be to take no bribe and surrender no right,[13] and there are a few other little points I have in mind that I can bring up when the time comes and that will be useful to Sancho and of benefit to the island he is to govern."

At this point Sancho bursts into the room, followed by a number of scullions carrying a trough filled with dirty dishwater. They insist upon washing his beard in this dubious liquid, and he is very angry. The duke and duchess are amused, but Don Quixote warns the servants to leave his squire alone, Sancho threatens to use his fists on his tormentors, and the mistress of the house finally controls her laughter and orders the scullions to desist. Sancho is grateful for this, and she invites him to spend the siesta hour with her while his master is taking his afternoon nap. (The author has forgotten that, inasmuch as it was sunset when Don Quixote encountered the hunting party, it must now be night and not midday.)

CHAPTER XXXIII. *Of the delightful conversation which the duchess and her waiting women had with Sancho Panza, worth reading and worth noting.*

THE history goes on to relate that Sancho did not take his siesta but, by way of keeping his word, came in to see the duchess almost before he had done eating. As she was very fond of listening to him, she insisted on his sitting down beside her on a low chair. Merely out of good breeding, Sancho declined at first, but the duchess made matters right by telling him that he should sit as a governor and talk as a squire, since in either capacity he deserved nothing less than the seat of Cid Ruy Díaz,[1] the Campeador himself. Shrugging his shoulders, Sancho obeyed and sat down, and all the damsels and duennas then gathered around him and, preserving a deep silence, waited to hear what he might have to say. It was the duchess, however, who was the first to speak.

"Now that we are alone," she said, "with no one to hear us, I should like the Señor Governor to resolve certain doubts that I have, growing out of the story of the great Don Quixote that has already been printed. For one thing, inasmuch as the worthy Sancho never saw Dulcinea, I mean the lady Dulcinea del Toboso, and never brought her Don Quixote's letter, which was left in the memorandum book on the Sierra Morena, how did he dare make up the answer and that tale about her winnowing wheat, a hoax and a falsehood so detrimental to the reputation of the peerless Dulcinea, and so unbecoming to the character of a good and faithful squire?"

Sancho listened to these words without making any reply whatsoever. Instead, he rose from his chair and, with his back bent and a finger on his lips, went all around the room lifting the draperies. Having done this, he came back and sat down again. It was only then that he broke his silence.

"My lady," he began, "now that I have seen that there are no eavesdroppers but only the bystanders to hear what is said, I will answer your question and any other that you may wish to ask me. In the first place, I must tell you that I look upon my master Don Quixote as stark mad, even though at times he says things that to me and all those who listen to him seem so wise and directed in such a straight rut that Satan himself could not do any better. But, for all of that, there is not the slightest doubt in my mind that he's cracked. Well, then, having this in my noddle, I can venture to make him believe things that don't make head nor tail, like that business of the answer to his letter, and that other that only happened six or eight days ago and so is not in the story yet, by which I mean, the enchantment of my lady, Doña Dulcinea; for though I gave him to understand that she was under a spell, there's no more truth in it than over the hills of Ubeda." [2]

The duchess then asked him to tell her about the hoax having to do with the enchantment, and he narrated the incident just as it had happened, at which his audience was not a little amused. The duchess then resumed the conversation.

"As a result of what the worthy Sancho has told me," she said, "there arises a question in my mind, a certain whispering in my ear which says: if Don Quixote is crazy, weak-minded, crackbrained, and Sancho his squire knows it and still continues to serve him and to cling to the empty promises his master has made him, he must undoubtedly be the more foolish and the more insane of the two; and if this is the case, my lady the Duchess, as I am sure it is, you are bound to be reproached for having given him an island to govern; for if he cannot govern himself, how can he govern others?"

"By God, lady," said Sancho, "you've spoken straight to the point; but go ahead, your Highness, and say whatever you like, as plain as you like, for I know it to be the truth. I know that if I had good sense I'd have left my master long ago. But this is my luck, my misfortune, and I can't help following him. We're from the same village, I've eaten his bread, I like him very much, he's generous to me,[3] he gave me his ass-colts, and, above all, I'm loyal; and so it's impossible for anything to separate us except the pick and spade.[4] And if your Highness doesn't want to give me that island that you promised me, well, I didn't have it when God made me, and it may be that your not giving it to me will be all the better for my conscience.

"I may be a fool," he went on, "but I know what is meant by the saying, 'To her harm the ant grew wings.' It may be that Sancho the squire will go to Heaven sooner than Sancho the governor. They make as good bread here as in France, and at night all cats are gray. He is hard up who hasn't broken his fast by two in the afternoon, and there's no stomach that's bigger than another by the breadth of your palm, and you can fill it with straw or hay, as the saying goes. The little birds of the field have God for their provider, and four yards of Cuenca frieze keep you warmer than four of Segovia broadcloth.[5] Once we have left this world and gone down under the earth, the prince travels by as narrow a path as the day laborer, and the pope's body takes up no more feet of earth than does the sacristan's, even though one is higher than the other; for, when we go to the grave, we all make ourselves as small as we can, or they do it for us whether we like it or not, and then it's good night all.

"And so I will say once again that if your Ladyship doesn't care to give me that island because I'm a fool, then like a wise man I'll not let it worry me. I've heard it said that behind the cross stands the devil, and all is not gold that glitters. The peasant Wamba[6] was taken from behind the oxen, the plows, and the yokes to be king of Spain, and Rodrigo was taken from among his brocades, pastimes, and riches to be devoured by serpents, if the old ballads do not lie."

"Of course they do not lie!" exclaimed the duenna Doña Rodríguez, who was one of the listeners. "Why, there is a ballad that tells how they put King Rodrigo while he was still alive into a tomb full of toads, snakes, and lizards, and two days later he cried out from inside the tomb in a low, pain-stricken voice:

'They are eating me now, they are eating me now,
There where I most have sinned.' [7]

And according to that, this gentleman is quite right in saying he would rather be a peasant than a king if he is to be eaten by reptiles in the end."

The duchess could not help laughing at the simplicity of her duenna, nor could she get over her astonishment as she listened to Sancho and his proverbs. She now addressed herself to him.

"The worthy Sancho well knows," she said, "that once a knight makes a promise he strives to fulfill it though it cost him his life. The duke, my lord and husband, though not of the errant variety, is nonetheless a knight, and he accordingly will keep his word with regard to that island he promised despite the envy and malice of others. Let

Sancho be of good courage, for when he least expects it
he will find himself on some island throne, in the seat of
authority, and he will then take over the government,
that he may exchange it for another of triple brocade.[8]
The charge that I would lay upon him is this: that he
look well to the manner in which he governs his vassals,
in view of the fact that they all are loyal and wellborn."

"As to this business of governing them well," said
Sancho, "there's no need of charging me to do that, for I
am by nature kindhearted and charitable toward the
poor. You don't steal the bread from one who kneads
and bakes,[9] and, faith, they'd better not throw false dice
with me. I'm an old dog and know all about *tus, tus*.[10]
I can get the dust out of my eyes when the time comes,
and there are no specks in front of them, either. I know
where the shoe pinches me. I say this by way of letting
you know that the good will find in me a support and
a refuge and the bad will not get a foothold. As I see
it, in this matter of governments, everything depends on
the kind of start you make; and it may be that after
I've been governor for a couple of weeks, I'll have my
hand in and will be better at the job than at work in the
fields, which I was brought up to do."

"You are right, Sancho," the duchess assured him,
"for no one is born educated, and bishops are made out
of men, not out of stones. But to return to the subject
of which we were speaking a short while ago, the lady
Dulcinea's enchantment. I hold it to be certain and thoroughly established that Sancho's idea of hoaxing his
master and making him think that the peasant girl was
Dulcinea, and of leading him to believe that if he did
not recognize her it must be because she was under a
magic spell—I maintain that all this was indeed the invention of one of those enchanters that persecute Don
Quixote; for, in all seriousness, I know from good au-

thority that the country maid who leaped upon the she-ass was Dulcinea del Toboso, and that the worthy Sancho, thinking he is the deceiver, is in reality the deceived.

"There is no more reason to doubt the truth of this than there is to doubt anything simply because we have not seen it with our own eyes. I would inform Señor Sancho Panza that we also have enchanters here, friendly ones, who tell us what goes on in the world, plainly and simply, without any plotting or scheming; and, believe me, Sancho, that sportive lass was and is Dulcinea del Toboso, who is as much enchanted as the mother that bore her,[11] and when we are least expecting it we shall behold her in her proper form, and then Sancho will be freed of the misapprehension under which he is laboring."

"That may all very well be," said Sancho Panza, "and now I am ready to believe what my master told me he saw in the Cave of Montesinos. He says that when he saw the lady Dulcinea del Toboso there, she was wearing the same clothes that I told him I had seen her wearing when I enchanted her for my own pleasure. But it must be just the other way around, as you say, my lady; for it is not to be, and cannot be, supposed that one who is no brighter than I am should have been able to concoct so clever a trick in a moment's time, nor do I think my master is so mad that my weak and feeble persuasion could bring him to believe a thing that is so beyond the bounds of reason. But your Ladyship must not on this account look upon me as a mischief-maker, since a stupid fellow like me cannot be expected to see through the evil designs of those wicked enchanters. I made all that up simply in order to escape a scolding from my master, Señor Don Quixote, and not with any intention of harming him, and if it has come out just the opposite way from what I intended, God's in his Heaven and He judges our hearts."

"That is true," said the duchess, "but tell me, Sancho, what is all this about the Cave of Montesinos? I should like to hear it."

Sancho then related the adventure point by point as it has been set down here.

"From this episode," remarked the duchess when he had finished, "one may infer that, since the great Don Quixote says he saw down there the same peasant girl that Sancho encountered on the El Toboso road, she must undoubtedly be Dulcinea, and that means that there are some very clever and meddlesome enchanters at work around here."

"That is what I say," replied Sancho Panza, "and if my lady Dulcinea del Toboso is enchanted, so much the worse for her; I'm not going to pick a quarrel with my master's enemies, who must be many and wicked. The truth is that the one I saw was a peasant lass and that was what I took her to be and set her down for; and if Dulcinea it was, that is not to be held against me, nor should I take the consequences. But they have to be after me at every step with Sancho said this and Sancho did that, Sancho here and Sancho there—just as if Sancho was nobody at all, instead of being that same Sancho Panza that is now going about the world in books, according to what Sansón Carrasco told me, and he at least is a bachelor of Salamanca, and people like him can't lie, unless the fancy happens to take them or they find it very convenient to do so. There's no reason for anybody's falling out with me, for I have a fine reputation, and I've heard my master say that a good name is worth more than great riches; so, stick me into this governorship and you'll see marvels. He who has been a good squire will make a good governor."

"All that the worthy Sancho has just said," remarked the duchess, "is out of Cato's maxims[12] or, at the least, drawn from the very entrails of Miguel Verino himself, who *florentibus occidit annis*.[13] In short, speaking after his own manner, under a bad cloak you commonly find a good drinker." [14]

"Well, to tell you the truth, lady," replied Sancho, "I never in my life have drunk from malice, though it well may be that I have from thirst, for there's nothing of the hypocrite in me. I drink when I feel like it, and even when I don't feel like it, if they offer it to me, so as not to appear strait-laced or ill bred. If a friend drinks to your health, you'd have to have a heart of marble, wouldn't you, not to raise your glass with his? But though I put on my shoes I never get them dirty.[15] And, anyhow, the squires of knights-errant commonly drink water, for they are always going through forests, woods, and meadows, and over mountains and cliffs, without finding a paltry drop of wine, though they'd be willing to give one of their eyes for it."

"I believe all that," the duchess answered him, "but, for now, let Sancho go and take his rest and later we will talk of all these things at greater length and will make arrangements to stick Sancho into that governorship, as he himself would put it, as soon as possible."

Sancho once more kissed the duchess's hand and begged her to do him the favor of seeing that his gray was well cared for, as it was the light of his eye.

"What gray is that?" inquired the duchess.

"That ass of mine," replied Sancho. "So that I won't have to mention him by that name, I'm in the habit of calling him 'the gray.' When I first came into the castle, I asked this lady duenna to look after him, and she was as angry about it as if I had said she was old or ugly, though it ought to be more fitting and proper for duennas to feed the beasts in the stable than to pose in halls of state. There was a certain gentleman in my village—Heaven help me, how he had it in for those ladies!"

"He must have been some clown or other," said Doña Rodríguez. "If he had been a gentleman and well-born, he would have placed them in his estimation higher than the horns of the moon."

"Come now," said the duchess, "that will do for the present. Be quiet, Doña Rodríguez, and let Señor Panza rest easy and leave the care of his gray to me. Seeing that the ass is his precious jewel, I will put it on the apple of my eye."

"He will do well enough in the stable," said Sancho, "since neither he nor I is worthy of being on the apple of your Highness's eye for a single moment, and I would as soon stab myself as consent to it; for although my master says that in the matter of courtesies it is better to lose by a card too many than a card too few,[16] when it comes to beastly and asinine civilities, we must be careful to steer a middle course."

"Take him along with you to your government, Sancho," said the duchess. "There you'll be able to feast him as much as you like, and you can even pension him off so that he will not have to work any more."

"Do not think, my lady the Duchess," replied Sancho, "that there would be anything so strange in that. I have seen more than one ass go up to a government, and so it would be nothing new if I took mine with me."

The duchess was more delighted than ever with Sancho's amusing conversation, and, having packed him off to bed, she went to tell the duke of what had happened. Between the two of them they arranged to play a famous joke upon Don Quixote, in true knightly style; and, in fact, they carried out a number of jests of that sort which are the best adventures to be met with in this great history.

A week later the duke and duchess stage a boar hunt in which Don Quixote and Sancho participate (Chapter xxxiv). Both the knight and his squire are offered hunting suits; the former declines the gift on the ground that he must soon resume the arduous life of a man of arms and does not wish to be encumbered with luggage, but Sancho is glad to accept, meaning to sell the garment at the first opportunity.

With the duke and other huntsmen Don Quixote bravely goes forth to meet the fierce animal, while Sancho, thoroughly frightened, climbs a tree for safety. But he falls from the bough on which he has perched and is caught on a snag below and left hanging in the air until he is rescued. He has torn a rent in his pretty green suit, which leaves him very disconsolate.

At nightfall there begins an elaborate hoax which the duke and duchess have planned. It is one of the numerous and tasteless practical jokes that they play upon the pair in the course of the knight's sojourn with them. Of a sudden it seems as if the entire wood were on fire, and the sound of trumpets, drums, and other martial instruments is heard, along with frightening battle cries. A postilion rides dressed as a demon and announces that he has come in search of Don Quixote de la Mancha, for whom he has a message from Montesinos. The message is to the effect that Montesinos will soon arrive, bringing with him Dulcinea del Toboso, in order to show her lover what must be done to disenchant her.

Sancho is alarmed, but Don Quixote is firm in his resolve to wait and see what comes of it all. There is a great "tempest of sound," as of many ox-carts rumbling in the distance, and four battles appear to be going on *simultaneously, on all sides of them. They can hear the musket fire, the thunder of artillery, and the shouts of the combatants. Sancho falls in a faint and has to be revived. A number of carts then draw near and pass, each of them bearing a figure to represent some personage out of the romances of chivalry. Then a soothing melody is heard.*

A huge triumphal chariot now approaches, drawn by six gray mules with white linen trappings and preceded by a white-clad penitent with a lighted wax taper in his hand. Standing on top and along the sides of the chariot are twelve other penitents, also dressed in snow-white and bearing tapers. Seated upon an elevated throne is a nymph wearing numerous gold-spangled cloth-of-silver veils, and beside her is a figure in a long robe with a black veil over its head.

The cart pauses opposite Don Quixote, the music ceases, and the black-veiled figure rises, parts its robe, removes its veil, and reveals a death's-head, which startles the knight and fills Sancho with terror. Introducing himself as the ghost of Merlin the enchanter, Death thereupon makes a long speech, addressed to the knight, in the form of a metrical composition of forty-seven lines. The conclusion is one that is not to Sancho's liking:

*"O Don Quixote, wise as thou art brave,
 La Mancha's splendor and of Spain the star!
 To thee I say that if the peerless maid,
 Dulcinea del Toboso, is to be restored
 to the state that once was hers, it needs must be
 that thy squire Sancho on his bared behind,
 those sturdy buttocks, must consent to take
 three thousand lashes and three hundred more,
 and well laid on, that they may sting and smart;*

for those that are the authors of her woe
have thus resolved, and that is why I've come.
This, gentles, is the word I bring to you."

FROM CHAPTER XXXV: *Wherein is continued the*
information that Don Quixote received concerning
Dulcinea's disenchantment, with other astonishing
incidents.

"FOR Heaven's sake!" cried Sancho, "I'd just as soon
give myself three stabs as three thousand lashes.
To the devil with that kind of disenchanting! I don't
see what my backside has to do with it. By God, if
Señor Merlin hasn't found any other way of taking the
spell off the lady Dulcinea del Toboso, she can go to
her grave that way!"

"What!" exclaimed Don Quixote. "I myself will take
you, Don Clown stuffed with garlic, and bind you to a
tree, naked as when your mother bore you, and I will
give you not three thousand three hundred but six
thousand six hundred, and so well laid on that you
will not be rid of them though you rub yourself as
many times as you have been sentenced to have lashes.
And say not a word in reply or I will snatch your heart
out."

"No," said Merlin when he heard this, "it cannot
be that way; for the lashes that the worthy Sancho is
to receive must be inflicted of his own free will and
not by force. It may be done at any time he chooses,
there is no time limit set; but should he wish to spare
himself half the pain of this flogging, he may do so by
permitting the strokes to be given by the hand of another, even though it be a somewhat weighty hand."

"Neither the hand of another nor my own hand nor

weighty nor weighable," replied Sancho. "No one is going to lay a hand on me. Am I, by any chance, the one that bore the lady Dulcinea del Toboso that my backside should pay for the sins of her eyes? My master, yes, seeing that he's a part of her—for he is always calling her 'my life, my soul,' his 'sustenance and support' —he may, and ought, to flog himself on her account and do everything that is necessary to disenchant her, but as for me, *abernuncio!*" [1]

No sooner had Sancho finished saying this than the silver-clad nymph who accompanied Merlin's ghost stood up and, casting aside her thin veil, disclosed what seemed to all of them a most beautiful face. With a masculine assurance and a voice that was not precisely feminine, she then began speaking directly to Sancho Panza.

"O wretched squire," she cried, "soul of a pitcher,[2] heart of a cork tree, with entrails of flint and pebbles! If, brazen thief, they ordered you to hurl yourself down from a tall tower to the earth below; if they asked you, enemy of the human race, to swallow a dozen toads, two lizards, and three snakes; if they wished you to slay your wife and young ones with a deadly, keen-bladed scimitar—if any of these things were required of you, it would be no wonder if you were squeamish and loath to comply with such commands. But to make so much of three thousand three hundred lashes, when every charity schoolboy, poor lad, receives as many every month, is enough to amaze and confound the bowels of compassion in all those who hear of such a thing or who may come to know of it in the course of time.

"O miserable, hardhearted animal!" she went on, "turn those red-owl's eyes of yours—turn them, I say, upon mine, which have been compared to gleaming stars, and you will behold the tears flowing in rivulets,

making furrows, tracks, and bypaths in the fair fields of
my cheeks. Does it not move you, O crafty, ill-inten-
tioned monster, that the flower of my youth (for I am
still in my teens, being a little under twenty) should
thus be consumed and wither away beneath the rude
bark of a country wench? If I do not appear in such a
shape at this moment, that is owing to the special favor
which Señor Merlin, here present, has done me, with
the sole thought that my beauty might soften your heart.
For the tears of a lovely woman in affliction have power
to turn stony cliffs into cotton and tigers into ewe lambs.
Lay on, then, lay on, O untamed beast! Flay that coarse
hide of yours; rouse that energy that you possess but that
inclines you only to eat and eat again; and set at liberty
my own smooth flesh, my loving disposition, my beautiful face. If for my sake you will not relent or come to
reason, do so for that poor knight at your side—I mean,
your master. I can see his heart right now, it is stuck
in his throat not ten fingers from his lips and only awaits
your yielding or unyielding reply to leap forth from his
mouth or go back to his stomach."

At this point, Don Quixote felt his throat and turned
to the duke. "By God, sir," he said, "Dulcinea has
spoken the truth. My heart *is* stuck in my throat, like a
crossbow nut."

"What do you say to that, Sancho?" asked the
duchess.

"I say, my lady," he answered her, "just what I have
said: so far as lashes are concerned, *abernuncio!*"

"*Abrenuncio,* you mean to say, Sancho," the duke
corrected him.

"Let me alone, your Highness," replied the squire.
"I'm in no humor for fine points just now and can't be
bothered by a letter more or less. Those lashes that they
are to give me or that I have to give myself have got

me so upset that I don't know what I'm saying or doing. But what I'd like the lady to tell me—my lady Dulcinea del Toboso—is where she learned that way of asking for a favor. She comes to ask me to lay my flesh open, and she calls me a soul of a pitcher and an untamed beast and a string of other foul names that the devil himself wouldn't stand for. Am I made of brass, do you think? What difference is it to me whether she's disenchanted or not? Does she come bringing me a hamper of fine linen, shirts, handkerchiefs, socks—even if I don't wear 'em—in order to soften me? No, nothing but abuse heaped upon abuse, although she knows that old saying in these parts, 'An ass laden with gold goes lightly up the mountain,' and, 'Gifts break rocks,' and, 'Pray to God and ply the hammer,' [3] and, 'One "take" is better than two "I'll give you's." '

"And now," continued Sancho, "my master, who ought to stroke my neck and pet me until I turn to wool and carded cotton, says that if he gets hold of me he'll tie me naked to a tree and give me double the number of lashes. You kindhearted people ought to bear in mind that it's not merely a squire but a governor that you're asking to have flogged, just as if it was 'Have a drink with your cherries.' [4] Let them learn, plague take it! Let them learn, I say, how to ask for something in the right way and show they had some bringing-up. They should know that there is a time for everything,[5] and people are not always in a good humor. Here I am, feeling so bad I'm fit to burst at seeing my green coat torn, and they come around asking me to flog myself of my own free will, when I feel as much like doing that as I do like becoming an Indian chief." [6]

"Well, the fact is, friend Sancho," said the duke, "that unless you become softer than a ripe fig, you are not going to have that governorship. It would be a fine thing for me to send to my islanders a cruel governor, with bowels of stone, who would not yield to the tears of damsels in distress or the entreaties of ancient, wise, and powerful enchanters and magicians. The short of it is, Sancho, either you whip yourself, let them whip you, or give up all idea of being governor."

"Sir," replied Sancho, "can't they give me a couple of days to think it over and decide what is best for me to do?"

"By no manner of means," said Merlin. "This matter must be settled here, on the instant, and on this very spot: either Dulcinea goes back to the Cave of Montesinos and her former peasant-girl state, or else she will be conveyed as she is to the Elysian fields, there to wait until the requisite number of lash strokes has been administered."

"Come, good Sancho," said the duchess, "pluck up your courage and show a proper appreciation of your master Don Quixote's bread that you have eaten; for we are all obligated to serve him and gratify his wishes, by reason of his generous nature and high deeds of chivalry. And so, my son, consent to this flogging, let the devil go to the devil, and leave fear to little minds; for, as you well know, a stout heart breaks bad luck."

To this Sancho replied with the following foolish question, addressed to Merlin. "Señor Merlin, will your Grace tell me this: after the devil came running up here to hand my master a message from Señor Montesinos, requesting him to wait here as he, Montesinos, was coming to arrange for Señora Dulcinea del Toboso's disenchantment, what happened, anyway? Up to now we've seen nothing of Montesinos or any of his likes."

To which Merlin's answer was, "The devil, friend Sancho, is an ignorant wretch and a great scoundrel. I sent him to your master with a message, not from Montesinos, but from me; for Montesinos is still in his cave, expecting, or better, waiting for, his disenchantment, for there is still the tail to be skinned. If he owes you anything or you have any business with him, I'll fetch him for you and set him down wherever you say; but for the present the thing to do is for you to consent to this penance, which, I can assure you, will be very good for your soul as well as your body: for your soul on account of the charitable impulse that leads you to submit to it; and for your body because, as I happen to know, you are of a sanguine disposition and a little blood-letting will do you no harm."

"There are a lot of doctors in this world," remarked Sancho. "Even the enchanters are doctors now. But since you all urge me to do it, though I can't see it myself, I am willing to give myself those three thousand three hundred lashes, on condition that I can lay them on whenever I feel like it, without any limit on the days or the time. I'll try to get out of debt as soon as possible, however, so that the world may enjoy the beauty of my lady, Doña Dulcinea del Toboso; for it appears that, contrary to what I thought, she really is beautiful after all. Another condition must be that I am not to be obliged to draw blood with that penance, and if some of the strokes happen to be fly-swatters, they are to be counted just the same. And here's another item: if I should make a miscount, Señor Merlin, who knows everything, is to keep track of them and tell me if I'm giving myself too few or too many."

"It will not be necessary for me to stop you from giving yourself too many," said Merlin, "for when you have reached the proper number, the lady Dulcinea will be immediately disenchanted, and she will be so grateful that she will come to seek out the worthy Sancho and thank and reward him for his good work. So you do not need to worry about too many or too few, since Heaven will not permit me to cheat anyone out of so much as a hair of his head."

"Well, then," said Sancho, "it's in God's hands. I accept my hard luck—I mean, I consent to the penance with the conditions that have been laid down."

No sooner had he said this than the clarions struck up once more, accompanied by a great firing of muskets, and Don Quixote threw his arms about Sancho's neck, giving him a thousand kisses on the forehead and on the cheeks. The duke and duchess and all the bystanders showed that they were very pleased, and as the cart got under way once more the beauteous Dulcinea bowed to the ducal pair and dropped a low curtsy to Sancho.

With this, the merry-smiling dawn hastened her coming, the little flowers in the fields lifted their heads, and the liquid crystal of the brooks, murmuring over their white and gray pebbles, went to pay tribute to the waiting rivers. The earth was joyous, the sky unclouded, the air limpid, the light serene, and each of these things in itself and all of them together showed that the day which was treading on the skirts of morning was to be bright and clear. Satisfied with the results of the chase and with having carried out their intention so cleverly and successfully, the duke and duchess now returned to their castle with the object of following up the jest which had thus been begun, as there was no serious occupation that gave them greater pleasure than this.

CHAPTER XXXVI. *Wherein is related the weird and never-before-imagined adventure of the Distressed Duenna, otherwise known as the Countess Trifaldi, together with a letter that Sancho Panza wrote to his wife, Teresa Panza.*

THE duke had a major-domo who was of a very jovial and playful disposition, and he it was who had impersonated Merlin and made all the arrangements for the adventure that has just been described; he had also composed the verses and had seen to having a page take the part of Dulcinea. And so he now, with the assistance of his lord and lady, proceeded to contrive an episode of the strangest and drollest sort that could be imagined.

The duchess inquired of Sancho the next day if he had as yet begun his penitential task which had to be performed in order to obtain Dulcinea's disenchantment, and he replied in the affirmative, saying that the night before he had given himself five lashes. When she wished to know what he had given them with, he informed her that he had made use of his hand.

"That," she said, "is slapping rather than flogging yourself, and it is my belief that the wise Merlin will not be satisfied with such soft measures. It will be necessary for the worthy Sancho to make himself a scourge with prickles or employ a cat-o'-nine-tales—something that can be felt—for learning enters with blood,[1] and the liberty of so great a lady as is Dulcinea is not to be granted for so small a price. Mark you, Sancho, works of charity that are performed lukewarmly and half-heartedly are of no merit but are, indeed, worthless."[2]

"If your Ladyship," replied Sancho, "will give me

some proper kind of strap or scourge, I will lay on with it, so long as it doesn't hurt too much; for I would have you know that, though I am a countryman, my flesh is more like cotton than it is like matweed, and it would not be a good thing for me to ruin myself for another's gain."

"So be it," said the duchess. "I will give you tomorrow a scourge that will suit you nicely, one that will accommodate itself to your tender flesh like a sister."

"Lady of my soul," Sancho said to her at this point, "I would have your Highness know that I have a letter written to my wife, Teresa Panza, giving her an account of everything that has happened since I left her. I have it here in my bosom; all it lacks is an address. I would have your learned Highness read it, for it seems to me to be in true governor style, I mean, the way governors ought to write."

"And who composed it for you?" inquired the duchess.

"I composed it myself, sinner that I am," replied Sancho.

"And did you write it out yourself?"

"That I did not, for I can neither read nor write, though I can sign my name."

"Let us have a look at it," said the duchess. "I am certain that it shows the quantity and quality of your wit."

Sancho drew out an unsealed letter and handed it to her. It read as follows:

SANCHO PANZA'S LETTER
TO TERESA PANZA, HIS WIFE

Though they gave me many good lashes, I went mounted like a fine gentleman;[3] if I have got a good government, it is costing me a good flogging. You will not understand this for the present, my Teresa, but later you will hear all about it. I want you to know, Teresa, that I have made up my mind you are to go in a coach; that is how you ought to go, for any other way of traveling is but creeping on all fours. You are a governor's wife now; see that no one treads on your heels! [4] I am sending you here a green hunting suit that my lady the duchess gave me; you can alter it so that it will make a petticoat and bodice for our daughter.

Don Quixote, my master, according to what I hear in these parts, is a madman with good sense, and a crackbrain who amuses people, and I don't lag behind him. We have been in the cave of Montesinos, and Merlin the magician has laid hold of me for the disenchantment of Dulcinea del Toboso, who down our way is known as Aldonza Lorenzo. With three thousand three hundred lashes minus five that I have to give myself, she will be as much disenchanted as the mother that bore her. Do not say anything about this to anyone; for if you show your privates to other people, some will say they are white and others will make them out to be black.

In a few days from now I will be setting out for my government, where I go with a great desire to make money, which they tell me is the case with all new governors. I will see how things are and will let you know whether you are to come and be with me or not. The gray is well and sends you his warm regards. I don't mean to part with him even though they take me away to be Grand Turk. My lady the duchess kisses your hand a thousand times, so you must return it with two thousand; for, as my master says, there is nothing that costs less or comes cheaper than good manners. God has not seen fit to provide me with another valise containing eight hundred crowns as He did some time ago, but don't let that worry you, Teresa mine, for the bell-ringer's in a safe place,[5] and so far as the government is concerned, it will all come out in the wash. The only thing is, I am told that after I once try it I'll be eating my hands off for it,[6] and if that is the case, it will not come so cheap after all, though, to be sure, the maimed and the crippled have their benefice in the alms that they beg. And so, one way or another, you are going to be a rich woman and a lucky one. God give you luck the best way He can and keep me to serve you. From this castle, the twentieth of July 1614.

Your husband, the governor,
SANCHO PANZA.

"In a couple of respects," said the duchess, when she had finished reading the letter, "the worthy governor goes a little astray. In the first place, he states that this governorship was bestowed upon him in return for the strokes that he is to give himself, when he knows very well—and he cannot deny it—that my lord the duke had promised it to him before that flogging was ever thought of. And in the second place, he shows himself to be too covetous; I would not have him be a gold-seeker,[7] for avarice bursts the bag,[8] and where there is an avaricious governor there is ungoverned justice."

"I don't mean it that way," said Sancho, "but if your Highness thinks that the letter is not what it should be, there is nothing to do but tear it up and write another, which may be an even worse one if it's left to my gumption."

"No, no," protested the duchess, "this one is very good, and I wish the duke to see it."

Following the conversation between Sancho and the duchess, they all retire to a garden where they are to dine. Here begins the episode of the "Distressed Duenna," which continues for several chapters and which the author describes as "long-drawn-out" ("dilatada").

Again there is martial music, and once more Sancho is frightened and takes refuge at the duchess's side as four black-clad figures appear. One of them advances and kneels before the duke. Drawing his veil aside, the newcomer introduces himself as "Trifaldín of the White Beard, squire to the Countess Trifaldi, otherwise known as the "Distressed Duenna," from whom, he says, he brings a message. The countess, he says, wishes to know if Don Quixote de la Mancha is in the castle, for she has journeyed on foot all the way from the distant kingdom of Candaya in order to lay her woes before him.

The duke has the Countess Trifaldi shown in and, turning to Don Quixote, congratulates him on the way in which the fame of his exploits has spread. The knight is duly flattered and makes another of his speeches in praise of the calling that he has chosen.

Chapter XXXVII *is given over to a brief but spirited bit of dialogue between Sancho Panza and the duchess's duenna, Doña Rodríguez, with the duchess acting as moderator. Sancho is suspicious of the affair and asserts his conviction that nothing good can come of anything in which duennas are involved, adding that "no matter what their station or walk in life, they are busybodies and nuisances." This provokes Doña Rodríguez, who launches an attack on squires. The dispute is finally interrupted by the sound of fife and drums, announcing the arrival of the Distressed Duenna.*

This personage and a dozen of her companions, all clad in widow's weeds and with black veils over their

faces, file into the garden (Chapter XXXVIII). *The Count-*
ess Trifaldi brings up the rear, with her squire, Trifaldín
of the White Beard, leading her by the hand. All those
present rise, and the ducal pair and the knight step for-
ward to receive the visitors. The duke conducts the
countess to a seat beside the duchess, and then at last
the Distressed One speaks. She states that, before telling
her story, she would like to know if Don Quixote and
Sancho Panza are there.

At this Don Quixote rises and offers to aid her in any
way he can. She throws herself at his feet and addresses
first him and then Sancho in the exaggerated language
of chivalry, after which she proceeds with her story
(which takes up the balance of the chapter and the
whole of the following one, Chapter XXXIX).

It seems that as duenna to the Infanta of Candaya,
Antonomasia, she had been the go-between in arranging
the marriage of the princess to a commoner. As a result,
the infanta's mother, the queen, had died of grief in
three days' time. When they went to bury her, Malam-
bruno the enchanter, her first cousin, had appeared over
the grave, mounted on a wooden horse, and had
promptly changed the princess into a she-ape and her
husband into a crocodile; after which he had put up an
inscription to the effect that the two lovers were not to
regain their former shape until "the valiant Manchegan
shall come to meet me in singlehanded encounter, since
it is for his great valor alone that the fates have reserved
this unheard-of adventure."

By way of further revenge, Malambruno, through his
magic art, had caused the countenances of all the palace
duennas to be covered with long, flowing beards—and
the Distressed One and her companions raise their veils
to prove the truth of her words. As she finishes her story
the speaker swoons away. As soon as she has recovered

(Chapter xl*), Don Quixote promises to right the wrong
that has been done her, if she will tell him what to do.*

*In reply to this question the Distressed Duenna ex-
plains that Candaya is some five thousand leagues distant by land, but that Malambruno had promised her
that, whenever fate should provide her with a knight to
defend her cause, he would send a certain wooden horse,
said to have been created by Merlin and famous in the
tales of chivalry, to transport her champion. This horse,
named Clavileño the Swift travels through the air,
guided by a peg in its forehead. It is supposed to be ridden by two persons: a knight in the saddle and his
squire on the crupper.*

*No sooner does he hear this than Sancho violently
protests, declaring that under no circumstances will he
mount such a steed. The duchess, however, insists that
he must, and Don Quixote remarks that "he will do as
I bid him." The Distressed One is fervent in the expression of her gratitude.*

CHAPTER XLI. *Of the coming of Clavileño, with
the conclusion of this long-drawn-out adventure.*

NIGHT came on, and with it the appointed moment
at which the famous steed, Claviieño, was to arrive.
Don Quixote was uneasy over the animal's delay in
making an appearance; for it seemed to him that, if
Malambruno was slow in sending the mount, it must
mean either that the adventure was reserved for some
other knight, or that the enchanter did not dare come
forth to engage in single combat. These thoughts were
running through his mind, when, lo and behold! four
wild men clad in green ivy[1] entered the garden, bearing
upon their shoulders a great wooden horse. Having

deposited it upon the ground, one of the savages addressed the company.

"Let him who has the courage," he said, "mount this contrivance."

"I am not going to mount," said Sancho, "for I have not the courage, nor am I a knight."

"And let his squire, if he has one," the wild man went on, "seat himself upon the crupper, putting his trust in the valiant Malambruno, for he need fear no other sword or wile of any sort. There is nothing to do but give a twist to this peg on the horse's neck[2] and he will carry them through the air to where Malambruno waits. But lest the great altitude should cause them dizziness, they must cover their eyes until they hear him neigh, which will be the sign that they have reached the end of their journey."

Saying this, they gracefully retired the way they had come, leaving Clavileño behind them. The moment she caught sight of the horse, the Distressed One turned to Don Quixote and, on the verge of tears, said to him, "O valiant knight, the promises of Malambruno are to be depended upon, the steed is here, our beards are growing; and each one of us, by every hair in those same beards, herewith beseeches you to shave and shear us, to accomplish which you have but to mount this horse, along with your squire, and make a happy beginning of your new journey."

"That I will do, Señora Countess Trifaldi," said Don Quixote, "and with right good will. I will not even lose time by looking for a cushion or putting on my spurs, so great is my desire to see you, my lady, and all the other duennas clean-shaven as you should be."

"That I will not do," declared Sancho, "good will or ill will, it makes no difference. If this shaving business can be accomplished only by my getting up on the

crupper, my master can very well look for another
squire to go with him, and these ladies can find some
other way of making their faces smooth again. I am no
wizard to go flying through the air like that. What will
my islanders say when they hear that their governor is
going out for a stroll on the winds? And there's something else: seeing that it is three thousand odd leagues
from here to Candaya, if the horse should tire or the
giant become vexed, it would take us half a dozen years
to get back again, and there won't be isle or islander in
the world that will know who I am. It's a common saying that there's danger in delay, and when they offer
you a heifer, run with the halter. Begging the pardon
of these ladies' beards, St. Peter is very well off in
Rome.[3] By which I mean to say, I'm very well off in this
house where everyone treats me so well, and whose
master, I hope, is going to be so good as to make me
a governor."

"Friend Sancho," said the duke, "the island that I
promised you is not a movable one, nor is it likely to fly
away; it has roots so deeply sunken in the bowels of
the earth that it is not to be torn up or so much as
budged by a few stout pulls. What is more, you know as
well as I do that there is no office of any importance
that is not obtained through some sort of bribe, great
or small; and what I ask in exchange for this governorship is that you accompany your master, Don Quixote,
so that he may be able to bring this memorable adventure to a conclusion. And whether you come back
mounted on Clavileño, with all the speed that is to be
expected of him, or whether contrary fortune brings you
back as a pilgrim, on foot, going from inn to inn, whenever you do return you will find your island where you
left it and your islanders with the same desire of having
you for their governor that they always had, nor will I

have changed my mind on the subject. And so, Señor
Sancho, do not doubt the truth of what I tell you, for
that would be to do me a grievous wrong when I am so
eager to be of service to you."

"Sir," replied Sancho, "you need say no more. I am
but a poor squire and do not know how to return such
courtesy in the proper way. Let my master mount, then,
cover my eyes, pray God for my soul, and tell me if,
when we are away up there on high, it is all right for
me to call upon Our Lord and ask the angels to protect
me."

"You may pray to God or anyone you like, Sancho,"
said Trifaldi; "for although Malambruno is an enchanter,
he is a Christian and very sagacious and circumspect in
the practice of his art, taking care not to meddle with
other people's concerns."

"Well, then," said Sancho, "God help me, and the
Holy Trinity of Gaeta!" [4]

"Since the memorable adventure of the fulling mills,"
observed Don Quixote, "I have never seen Sancho so
frightened as he is now; and if I were as much given to
omens as others are, his pusillanimity would shake my
own courage a bit. However— Come here, Sancho; with
the permission of these ladies and gentlemen I should
like to have a couple of words with you."

With this, he led the squire to one side, among some
of the garden trees, and there, taking both of his hands,
spoke to him as follows:

"You are aware, brother Sancho, of the long journey
that awaits us. God knows when we shall return or how
much leisure it will allow us; and so I wish you would
retire to your room as if you were seeking something
that is needed for the road, and there in a twinkling pay
something on account toward those three thousand
three hundred lashes that you are supposed to give

yourself, even if it be no more than five hundred for the present. It will be just so many of them out of the way, and a thing well begun is half done."

"By God," exclaimed Sancho, "your Grace must be out of your mind! As the saying has it, you see me pregnant and you want me a virgin. Here, I'm supposed to go seated on a bare board and you'd have me skin my backside before I start! No, no, your Grace is all wrong. Let us go now and see to shaving those duennas, and when we come back, I give you my word, I'll make such haste to fulfill my obligation that your Grace will be more than satisfied. That is all I have to say."

"Well, my good Sancho," replied Don Quixote, "I shall console myself with that promise; and I believe you will keep it, too, for while you may be a simpleton, you are really a trusty fellow."

"I'm not rusty," said Sancho, "only sunburned;[5] but even if I was a little of each, I'd still keep my word."

With this, they came back to mount Clavileño; and as they did so Don Quixote said, "Cover your eyes, Sancho, and take your place; for he who is sending us to such far lands cannot be doing it merely to deceive us, inasmuch as there would be little glory for him in thus tricking those who had put their trust in him. And even though everything should go contrary to what I expect, the honor of having undertaken such an exploit is such as no malice could dim."

"Let us go, sir," Sancho answered him, "for the beards and tears of these ladies are more than my heart can bear, and I shall not eat a bite that agrees with me until I have seen them smooth-faced as they were before. Mount, then, your Grace, but be sure to blindfold yourself. If I am to ride the crupper, it is plain that the one in the saddle must be the first to mount."

"That is true enough," Don Quixote agreed. And,

taking a handkerchief from his pocket, he asked the Distressed One to cover his eyes very carefully; but no sooner had this been done than he uncovered them.

"If I remember rightly," he said, "I have read something in Vergil about that Trojan Palladium,[6] which was a wooden horse that the Greeks offered to the goddess Pallas, and which, being pregnant with armed knights, was later the ruination of Troy. For this reason, I think it would be a good thing to see what Clavileño has in his belly."

"There is no need of that," said the Distressed One. "I will vouch for him. I know that Malambruno is in no wise treacherous or malicious; and, accordingly, Señor Don Quixote, your Grace may mount without any hesitancy whatsoever, and may it be on my head if anything happens to you."

The knight felt that anything he might say regarding his safety would but cast doubt upon his valor; and so, without any further argument, he mounted Clavileño. Trying the peg, he discovered that it turned very easily; and as he sat there, with no stirrups and his legs hanging down, he looked like nothing so much as a figure in some Roman triumph, painted or woven upon a Flemish tapestry. Against his will and little by little, Sancho climbed up and made himself as comfortable as he could on the crupper, which he found to be quite hard; whereupon he asked the duke if it would not be possible to provide him with a pillow or cushion, even though they had to take one from the couch of my lady the duchess or from some page's bed; for the flanks of this horse seemed to him more like marble than they did like wood.

At this point Trifaldi spoke up, saying that Clavileño would not endure any kind of trappings and that the best thing for the squire to do was to sit sideways so that he would not feel the hardness so much. Sancho did as she advised, and, bidding them farewell, he let his eyes be bandaged. He promptly removed the cloth, however, and, gazing tenderly and tearfully at all those in the garden, begged them to aid him in his present trouble with plenty of Hail Marys and Our Fathers, so that God might provide someone to do the same for them when they should find themselves in such straits.

"Thief," exclaimed Don Quixote, "are you by any chance on the gallows or at death's door that you resort to such entreaties? Are you not, soulless and cowardly creature, in the very spot that the beauteous Magalona occupied and from which she descended, not to her grave, but to become queen of France,[7] unless the histories lie? And I here at your side, am I not on a par with the brave Pierres, who sat in this same saddle where I now sit? Cover your eyes, you spiritless animal, cover them I say, and do not give voice to your fears, at least not in my presence."

"Let them go ahead and blindfold me," said Sancho; "but since you won't allow me to commend myself or be commended to God, is it any wonder if I'm afraid we may be going to some region[8] of devils who will make off with us to Peralvillo?"[9]

When their eyes had been covered and Don Quixote had settled himself to his satisfaction, the knight tried the peg, and no sooner had he laid hands upon it than the duennas and all the others there present began calling out to them, "God guide you, valiant knight! God be with you, intrepid squire! Now, now, you are going through the air, swifter than a dart! Already those below are gazing up at you in astonishment! Try not to sway so much, brave Sancho; see to it that you do not fall, for your fall would be worse than that of the rash youth who sought to drive the chariot of his father, the Sun!"

Sancho, meanwhile, was clinging tightly to his master, with his arms about him. "Señor," he asked, "what do they mean by saying that we are riding so high when their voices can reach us just as plainly as if they were right alongside us?"

"Think nothing of that, Sancho," said the knight, "for such flights as these are out of the ordinary course of events, and at a distance of a thousand leagues you can still see and hear anything you like. And do not squeeze me so much or you will throw me off. There is really no reason for you to be disturbed or frightened, for I can swear that in all the days of my life I never had an easier-going mount. It is as if we never stirred from one spot. Banish all fear, my friend, for the truth is, everything is going as it should and we have the wind to our poop."

"So we do," replied Sancho. "On this side it's as strong as if they were blowing on me with a thousand pairs of bellows."

This was the truth, for a number of large bellows were producing the breeze in question. The whole adventure had been so thoroughly planned by the duke and duchess and their major-domo that not a single essential detail was lacking to make it perfect.

"Without any doubt, Sancho," remarked Don Quixote as he felt the puff, "we must have reached the second aerial region, where the snow and hail are produced; it is in the third region that the thunder and lightning are engendered, and if we keep on ascending at this rate, we shall soon be in the region of fire. I do not know how to control the peg to keep us from mounting so high that the flames will scorch us."

Even as he said this they felt a warmth upon their

faces, which came from pieces of tow, easy to ignite and to extinguish, suspended from the end of a reed held at some distance from them.

"May they slay me," said Sancho, "if we're not already in that fiery place, or somewhere very near it, for a good part of my beard is singed already. I've a mind, master, to take a peep and see where we are."

"Don't do that," Don Quixote advised him. "Remember that true story they tell about the licentiate Torralba,[10] whom the devils carried through the air upon a reed, with his eyes shut; in twelve hours' time he arrived in Rome and dismounted at Torre di Nona,[11] which is a street in that city, where he witnessed the rioting, the assault, and the death of Bourbon;[12] and by the next morning he was back in Madrid to give an account of all he had seen. He himself stated that as he was sailing through the air the devil ordered him to open his eyes, which he did, only to discover he was so near the body of the moon that, as it seemed to him, he could put out his hand and take hold of it, and he did not dare look down at the earth or it would have made him dizzy.

"And so, Sancho," the knight concluded, "there is no good reason why we should uncover our eyes, since he who has us in charge will take care of us. It may be that we are merely gaining altitude in order to swoop down upon the kingdom of Candaya as the saker or the falcon does upon the heron, that he may be able to seize the bird no matter how high it may soar. And although it seems to us that it has not been a half hour since we left the garden, believe me, we must have gone a very long way."

"I do not know as to that," said Sancho. "All I can say is that if that Señora Magallanes[13] or Magalona found any pleasure in riding this crupper, she couldn't have had very tender flesh."

The entire conversation of the two brave horsemen was heard by the duke and duchess, who were extremely amused by it; and, wishing to put a finishing touch to this extraordinary and well-planned adventure, they now set fire to Clavileño's tail with some bits of tow, whereupon the horse, which was filled with detonating rockets, at once blew up with a loud noise, hurling Don Quixote and Sancho Panza to the ground half scorched.

By this time the entire band of bearded ladies, La Trifaldi and all the others, had disappeared from the garden, and those that remained lay stretched out on the ground as if unconscious. The knight and his squire rose, rather the worse for wear, and, glancing about them in all directions, were very much astonished to find themselves back in the same garden from which they had started, with all those people prostrate on the earth. And their wonder grew as, at one side of the garden, they caught sight of a long lance that had been thrust into the ground, with a smooth white parchment hanging from it by two silken cords. Upon the parchment, written in large gilt letters, was the following inscription:

The renowned knight, Don Quixote de la Mancha, merely by undertaking it, has finished and concluded the adventure of the Countess Trifaldi, otherwise known as the Distressed Duenna. Malambruno is satisfied in every way,[14] *the faces of the duennas are once more smooth and clean, King Clavijo and Queen Antonomasia have been restored to their former state, and as soon as the squirely flogging shall have been completed, the white dove shall be free of the annoying gerfalcons that persecute it and shall return to the arms of its beloved mate. For it is so ordered by Merlin the Sage, proto-enchanter of enchanters.*

Having read the inscription, Don Quixote understood

clearly that it had reference to the disenchantment of Dulcinea; and, giving thanks to Heaven with all his heart that he had been able to achieve so great a deed at so little peril, thus restoring to the venerable but no longer visible duennas their former countenances, he went over to where the duke and duchess lay, still in a state of unconsciousness.

"Ah, my worthy lord," he said, taking the duke's hand, "be of good cheer—be of good cheer, for it is all over now! The adventure is finished and no harm done, as the inscription on that post yonder plainly shows."

Little by little, like one coming out of a deep slumber, the duke recovered his senses, and the same was true of the duchess and all the others there in the garden who had fallen to the ground; and they all gave such evidence of wonder and astonishment as almost to convince anyone who saw them that the thing they pretended so cleverly by way of jest had actually happened to them. The duke read the inscription with half-closed eyes and then threw open his arms to embrace Don Quixote, assuring him that he was the best knight ever seen in any age.

Sancho in the meantime was gazing about in search of the Distressed One, for he wished to see what she looked like without her beard and whether or not she was as beautiful as her gallant exterior appeared to indicate; but they told him that as soon as Clavileño had dropped to the earth in flames, the entire band of duennas, and Trifaldi with them, had disappeared, but that they were already clean-shaven, without a sign of hair on their faces. The duchess then inquired of him how he had made out on the long journey.

"Señora," replied Sancho, "as we were flying through the region of fire, or so my master told me, I wanted to uncover my eyes a little, but when I asked him if I might do so, he would not let me. However, I have a little bit of curiosity in my make-up and always want to know anything that is forbidden me; and so, very quietly and without anyone's seeing me, I lifted the handkerchief ever so little, close to my nose, and looked down at the earth. It seemed as if the whole earth was no bigger than a grain of mustard and the people walking about on it were a little larger than hazelnuts. You can see from that how high up we must have been."

"Friend Sancho," said the duchess, "you had better mind what you are saying. From what you tell me, you did not see the earth at all, but only the people on it; for if the earth itself was like a grain of mustard and each person on it like a hazelnut, then, obviously, one man would have covered the entire earth."

"That is true," Sancho admitted, "but I had a peep at it from one side and saw it all."

"Look here, Sancho," said the duchess, "with a side peep like that you don't see the whole of anything you are looking at."

"I don't know anything about that way of looking at things," the squire answered her, "but I do think your Ladyship ought to bear in mind that we were flying by enchantment, and it was by enchantment that I was able to see the whole earth and all the people on it, no matter which way I looked. And if your Highness doesn't believe me, neither will you believe me when I tell you that, having uncovered my face all the way to the eyebrows, I found myself so close to the sky that there was not a palm-and-a-half's distance between it and me; and a mighty big place it is, my lady, I can tell you that! Then we went through the region where the seven little she-goats[15] are, and, seeing that as a lad I had been a goatherd in my country, the minute I laid eyes on them I felt like getting down and playing with them a bit, and if I hadn't done so I think I would have burst. And so, what do I do? Without saying anything to my master or anybody else, I slip down off Clavileño as quietly as you please and for three-quarters of an hour I have a good time with those goats, which are like gillyflowers, and all the time Clavileño doesn't stir from the spot."

"And while the worthy Sancho was playing with the goats," said the duke, "how did Señor Don Quixote amuse himself?"

It was the knight himself who answered this question. "Since all these things," he said, "all these happenings, are outside the natural order, it is not surprising that Sancho should say what he does. As for myself, I can only state that I looked neither upward nor downward, nor did I behold either the sky or the earth or the sea or the sandy shore. It is true, I was aware that I was passing through the aerial region and was close upon the region of fire; but that we went any farther than that I cannot believe; and inasmuch as the fiery region lies between the heaven where the moon is and the outmost portion of the aerial one, we could not have come to the heaven where the seven young she-goats are, of which Sancho speaks, without being burned, and since we were not burned, either Sancho is lying or Sancho is dreaming."

"I am neither lying nor dreaming," replied Sancho. "If you don't believe me, ask me to describe those goats for you, and you will see whether I'm telling the truth or not."

"Do describe them for us, Sancho," said the duchess.

"Two of them are green, two are flesh-colored, two are blue, and one is a mixture."

"That," said the duke, "is a new kind of goat. Here in our earthly region we do not have such shades—I mean, goats of such hues."

"Naturally," said Sancho, "there is a difference between heavenly goats and earthly ones."

"Tell me, Sancho," continued the duke, "did you see any he-goat among them?"

"No, sir," was the answer, "and I've heard tell that none ever passed the horns of the moon."

They did not care to question him any further regarding his journey, for they perceived that he was in a mood to go rambling all over the heavens, giving them news of everything that went on there without ever having stirred from the garden. In brief, this was the end of the adventure of the Distressed Duenna, one that provided amusement for the duke and duchess all the rest of their lives. As for Sancho, he had something to talk about for ages, if he lived so long.

Don Quixote now came up to him, to whisper in his ear. "Sancho," he said, "if you want us to believe what you saw in Heaven, then you must believe me when I tell you what I saw in the Cave of Montesinos. I need say no more."

Sancho's Government

(CHAPTERS XLII-LV)

CHAPTER XLII. *Of the advice which Don Quixote gave Sancho Panza before the latter set out to govern his island, with other well-considered matters.*

THE duke and duchess were so well pleased with the successful and amusing outcome of the adventure of the Distressed One that they made up their minds to continue with the jest, seeing what a suitable subject they had when it came to accepting the imaginary for the real. Accordingly, having instructed their servants and vassals as to how to behave toward Sancho in the governorship of his promised island, they informed the squire the next day (which was the one following Clavileño's flight) that he was to make ready to go and assume his gubernatorial duties, as his islanders were waiting for him as for the showers of May. Sancho made a low bow.

"Ever since I dropped down from Heaven," he said, "ever since I looked at the earth from up there and saw how little it is, I am not as anxious to be a governor as I was once upon a time. What greatness is there in ruling over a grain of mustard, or imperial dignity and power in governing half a dozen human beings the size of hazelnuts? For there did not seem to me to be any more than that. If your Lordship would be pleased to give me a little bit of Heaven, even if it was no more than half a league, I'd rather have it than the biggest island in the world."

"See here, friend Sancho," replied the duke, "I cannot give anyone a bit of Heaven, even if it were a piece no bigger than your fingernail. It is reserved for God alone to grant such grace and favors as that. What I can give, I do give you; and that is an island, perfect in every respect, tight and well proportioned and exceedingly fertile, where, if you know how to make use of your opportunities, you may contrive to gain Heaven's riches along with those of earth."

"Very well, then," said Sancho, "let the island come, and I'll do my best to be such a governor that, in spite of all the rascals, I'll go straight to Heaven. It's not out of greed that I want to quit my humble station or better myself; it is because I wish to see what it's like to be a governor."

"Once you try it, Sancho," the duke warned him, "you will be eating your hands off for it, so sweet a thing it is to give orders and be obeyed. You may be sure that when your master gets to be an emperor—as he undoubtedly will, the way things are going for him now—no one will be able to take that office away from him without a struggle, and he will be sick at heart over all the time he lost in not being one."

"Sir," said Sancho, "in my opinion, it is a good thing to be the one to give the orders, if only to a herd of cattle."

"Let them bury me with you, Sancho," said the duke, "if you do not know everything, and I only hope you will be such a governor as your wit seems to promise. But let us leave the matter there. Remember, it is tomorrow that you go to assume the governorship of your island, and this afternoon they will fit you out with the proper apparel and all the other things needed for your departure."

"Let them clothe me any way they like," replied the squire, "for however I go dressed, I'll still be Sancho Panza."

"That is true enough," agreed the duke, "but clothes must be suited to one's rank or dignity. It would not be well, for example, for a jurisconsult to wear the garb of a soldier, or a soldier that of a priest. You, Sancho, will go clad partly as a man of learning and partly as a captain, for in the island that I am bestowing on you arms and letters are equally necessary."

"I don't know much about letters," said Sancho; "in fact, I don't even know my ABC's; but to be a good governor, it's enough for me to be able to remember the

Christus.[1] As to arms, I'll handle those that they give me till I drop, and God help me from then on."

"With so good a memory as that," observed the duke. "Sancho cannot go wrong."

At this point Don Quixote came up and, upon hearing that Sancho was to leave so soon for his government, with the duke's permission, took him by the hand and led him to his room, with the intention of advising him as to how he was to conduct himself in office. Having entered the room and closed the door, he almost forced Sancho to sit down beside him, and then, very calmly, he began speaking as follows:

"Sancho, my friend, I thank Heaven with all my heart that good Fortune should have come your way before I have met with her. I had counted upon my luck to enable me to pay you for your services, but here am I at the beginning of my adventures while you, ahead of time and contrary to all reasonable expectation, are seeing your desires fulfilled. Some there be that count upon bribery, importunity, begging, early rising, entreaties, and pertinacity, and still do not attain what they seek; and then some other will come along and, without knowing the why or wherefore of it all, will find himself in the place and office that so many covet. Here it is that the common saying fits in well, to the effect that there is good luck and bad luck in all the strivings of men. You to my mind are beyond any doubt a blockhead, you neither rise with the sun nor keep nightly vigil, you are not industrious, and yet, as a result of the mere breath of knight-errantry that has been breathed upon you, you find yourself without more ado the governor of an island, as if it were nothing at all.

"I say all this, Sancho, in order that you may not attribute to your own merits the favor you have received. Rather, you should give thanks to Heaven for its beneficence, and, after that, to the great profession of knight-errantry for the potentialities inherent in it. Having, then, disposed your heart to believe what I have said to you, be attentive, my son, to this your Cato,[2] who would counsel you and be the guiding star that leads you to a safe harbor as you set forth upon the storm-tossed sea[3] that is now about to engulf you; for office and high trusts are nothing other than a deep abyss of trouble and confusion.

"First of all, my son, you are to fear God; for therein lies wisdom,[4] and, being wise, you cannot go astray in anything. And in the second place, you are to bear in mind who you are and seek to know yourself, which is the most difficult knowledge to acquire that can be imagined. Knowing yourself, you will not be puffed up, like the frog that sought to make himself as big as the ox.[5] Do this, and the memory of the fact that you once herded pigs in your own country will come to serve as the ugly feet to the tail [6] of your folly."

"That is true," said Sancho, "but it was when I was a lad. Afterward, as a young fellow, it was geese, not pigs, that I guarded. But I can't see what all this has to do with the case. Not all those that govern come from the race of kings."

"You are right," replied Don Quixote, "and for that very reason those who are not of noble origin should be suave and mild in fulfilling the grave duties of their office. In this way they will be able to free themselves of that malicious gossiping to which no station in life is immune. Look to humility for your lineage, Sancho, and do not be ashamed to say that you come of peasant stock, for when it is seen that you do not blush for it, no one will try to make you do so. Pride yourself more on being a good man and humble than on being a haughty

sinner. The number of persons of lowly birth who have
gone up to the highest pontifical and imperial posts is
beyond counting; by way of proving the truth of this,
I could give you so many examples that it would tire
you to listen to them.

"Remember, Sancho, that if you employ virtue as your
means and pride yourself on virtuous deeds, you will
have no cause to envy the means possessed by princes
and noble lords; for blood is inherited but virtue is
acquired,[7] and virtue by itself alone has a worth that
blood does not have. This being the case, as indeed it is,
if perchance one of your relatives should come to your
island to visit you, do not neglect or offend him, but
rather receive, welcome, and entertain him. By so doing,
you will be pleasing Heaven, which does not like anyone to despise what it hath wrought, and at the same
time you will be acting in accordance with the laws of
your own better nature.

"Should you bring your wife to be with you—and it
is not well for those in government to be long without
their womenfolk—teach and instruct her and smooth
down her native roughness; for all that a wise governor
may acquire, a foolish and boorish wife may well
squander and lose for him. In case you become a widower (a thing that may happen), by virtue of your
office look for a better consort. Do not take one to serve
you merely as a hook and fishing rod or as a friar's hood [8]
for the receiving of alms; for, of a truth I tell you, all
that the judge's wife receives her husband will have to
account for on Judgment Day, when he will have to
make in death a fourfold payment for things that in life
meant nothing to him.

"Never be guided by arbitrary law, which finds favor
only with the ignorant who plume themselves on their
cleverness. Let the tears of the poor find more compas-

sion in you, but not more justice, than the testimony of
the rich. Seek to uncover the truth amid the promises
and gifts of the man of wealth as amid the sobs and
pleadings of the poverty-stricken. When it is a question
of equity, do not bring all the rigor of the law to bear
upon the delinquent, for the fame of the stern judge is
no greater than that of the merciful one. If the rod of
justice is to be bent, let it not be by the weight of a
gift but by that of mercy. When you come to judge
the case of someone who is your enemy, put aside all
thought of the wrong he has done you and think only of
the truth. Let not passion blind you where another's
rights are concerned, for the mistakes you make will be
irremediable, or only to be remedied at the expense of
your good name and fortune.

"If some beautiful woman come to you seeking justice,
take your eyes from her tears, listen not to her moans,
but consider slowly and deliberately the substance of
her petition, unless you would have your reason drowned
in her weeping and your integrity swept away by her
sighs. Abuse not by words the one upon whom punishment must be inflicted; for the pain of the punishment
itself is enough without the addition of insults. When a
guilty man comes under your jurisdiction, remember
that he is but a wretched creature, subject to the inclinations of our depraved human nature, and insofar as you
may be able to do so without wrong to the other side,
show yourself clement and merciful; for while the attributes of God are all equal, that of mercy shines brighter
in our eyes than does that of justice.

"If you observe these rules and precepts, Sancho,
your days will be long, your fame will be eternal, rewards will be heaped upon you, indescribable happiness
shall be yours, you will be able to marry off your children as you like, your children and your grandchildren

will have titles to their names, you will live in peace with all men, and in your last days death will come to you amid a ripe and tranquil old age, and the gentle, loving hands of your great-grandchildren will tenderly close your eyes.

"What I have said to you thus far has been in the nature of instructions for the adornment of your soul. Listen now to those that will serve you where your body is concerned."

CHAPTER XLIII. *Of the further advice which Don Quixote gave to Sancho Panza.*

WHO, upon listening to the foregoing speech of Don Quixote's, would not have taken him for a very wise person, one whose wisdom was exceeded only by his integrity? It has frequently been remarked in the course of this great history that it was only when he came to touch upon the subject of chivalry that the knight talked nonsense and that when any other topic was under discussion he showed himself to be possessed of a clear-seeing, unfettered mind, the result being that his deeds were all the time contradicting his own best judgment and his judgment his deeds. And so, in the course of these further instructions that he gave Sancho, marked by a lively play of fancy, he carried to a high pitch both his good sense and his folly.

Sancho listened to it all most attentively, seeking to commit to memory the counsels thus given him, as if to preserve them for future use that he might make a success of his governorship.

"As to your own person, Sancho, and the mode of ruling your household," Don Quixote continued, "the first thing to bear in mind is that you must be neat.

appearing. Remember to trim your nails, and do not let them grow as some do who in their ignorance have been led to believe that long fingernails make the hands look beautiful, just as if that growth, that excrescence, that they neglect to cut were really a nail and not rather the claw of a lizard-catching kestrel. This, I may tell you, is a filthy and unnatural abuse. Another thing, Sancho: do not go with your girdle loosened and your garments slack; for slovenly attire is the sign of a disorderly mind, unless such carelessness is deliberate, as is believed to have been the case with Julius Caesar.[1]

"Be sure to ascertain very carefully just what the revenues of your office are, and, if they suffice for the purpose, provide your servants with respectable and serviceable, rather than showy and brilliant, liveries. And what is more, divide the liveries between your servants and the poor; by which I mean to say: if you have three pages to clothe, see that you clothe three of the poor also, and in that way you will have pages both in Heaven and on earth. This is a new mode of bestowing liveries and one that is beyond the conception of the vainglorious.

"Eat neither garlic[2] nor onions that your breath may not betray your rustic origin. Walk slowly and speak with deliberation, but not in such a manner as to give the impression that you are listening to yourself; for all affectation is bad.[3] Eat sparingly during the day and have a light supper;[4] for it is in the workshop of the stomach that the health of the entire body is forged. Be temperate in your drinking, remembering that he who imbibes too much wine keeps neither secret nor promise. And take care, Sancho, not to roll your food from one cheek to the other or to eruct in front of anyone."

"I don't know what you mean by *eruct*," said the squire.

"To *eruct,* Sancho, is the same as to belch,[5] which is one of the most unpleasant words in our Castilian tongue, although an expressive one. For this reason, those that are careful of their choice of language, in place of 'belch' and 'belchings,' say 'eruct' and 'eructations.' If someone fails to understand these terms, it makes little difference; in the course of time they will come to be readily understood and thus the language will be enriched, for it is determined by popular usage." [6]

"In truth, sir," said Sancho, "that is one bit of advice that I mean to remember: not to belch; for I do it very often."

"Eruct, Sancho, not belch," Don Quixote corrected him.

"Eruct I will say from now on," replied Sancho; "I give you my word, I won't forget."

"Also, Sancho, you must not introduce such a host of proverbs into your conversation; for although proverbs are concise maxims, you very often drag them in by the hair of the head, with the result that they sound more like nonsense than wisdom."

"That is something only God can remedy," said Sancho; "for I know more old sayings than would fill a book, and when I start to speak they all come rushing into my mouth at once, fighting with one another to get out, and so, what happens is, my tongue throws out the first ones it gets hold of, whether or not they are to the point. But I'll remember after this to use the ones that are suited to the dignity of my office; for in the house where there is plenty, supper is soon on the table,[7] and he who binds does not wrangle, and the bell-ringer's in a safe place, and keeping and giving call for brains."

"That's it, Sancho!" cried Don Quixote. "Go on threading and stringing and coupling your proverbs, there is no one to stop you! 'My mother whips me and I keep right on.'[8] I have just done telling you that you should avoid proverbs, and here in a moment you have let go with a whole litany of them that, so far as what we are talking about is concerned, are over the hills of Ubeda. Mind you, Sancho, I do not say that a proverb aptly brought in is not all right, but when you overload your speech with them and string them together helter-skelter, it makes your conversation dull and vulgar.

"But to continue: When you mount your horse, do not throw the weight of your body against the back of the saddle nor ride with your legs held stiffly, straight out in front of you or away from the horse's belly; and, on the other hand, do not sit so limply that it will seem as if you were astride your gray. The way they ride makes gentlemen of some and grooms of others.

"Observe moderation in the matter of sleep, for he who is not up with the sun does not make the most of the day. Bear in mind, Sancho, that diligence is the mother of good fortune, and sloth, its contrary, never yet achieved anything worth while.

"There is one more piece of advice which I should like to give you, and—although it does not have to do with the care of your person—I wish you would be sure to remember it, as I think it will be no less useful to you than the counsels I have already imparted to you. It is this: that you never become involved in a discussion of family trees, at least not when it is a matter of comparing one with another; for, of necessity, one of the two will have to be better than the other, and you will be hated by those whose lineage you have disparaged, while those whose ancestry you have exalted will in no wise reward you.

"As for your dress, you should wear full-length hose, a long jacket, and a cloak that is a little longer still; and by all means eschew Grecian wide-breeches, for they are becoming neither to gentlemen nor to governors.

"For the present, that is all that I think of, Sancho, in the way of advice. As time goes on and the occasion arises, I will send you further instructions if you will take care to keep me informed of the state of your affairs."

"Sir," replied Sancho, "I can see very plainly that all the things your Grace has said to me are good, holy, and profitable, but of what use are they going to be if I do not remember a single one of them? True, what you told me about not letting my nails grow and about marrying again if I have a chance will not slip out of my noddle; but as for all that other mess of hash, I don't remember, nor will I remember, any more of it than I do of last year's clouds. And so you will have to put it down in writing for me. While I may not be able to read or write, I will give it to my confessor so that he can run over it with me and hammer it into my head whenever necessary."

"Ah, sinner that I am!" exclaimed Don Quixote. "How bad it looks for governors not to be able to read and write! For I would have you know, Sancho, that when a man cannot read or is left-handed, it points to one of two things: either he comes of exceedingly mean parentage, or else he himself is of so wayward a disposition that good companionship and good training are wasted upon him. That is a grave shortcoming on your part, and for that reason I would have you at least learn to sign your name."

"I can sign my name well enough," said Sancho. "When I was steward of the confraternity in my village I learned to make certain letters such as they use in marking bundles and which, so they told me, spelled out my name. And, anyway, I can always pretend that my right hand is crippled and have someone else sign for me; for there's a remedy for everything except death, and, seeing that I'm in command and hold the rod, I can do anything I like. 'He whose father is a judge—' [9] you know. And I'll be a governor, which is higher than a judge; so come on and see! Let them make fun of me and slander me; let them come for wool and go back shorn. For whom God loves, his house knows it,[10] and the silly sayings of the rich pass for maxims in this world. Being a governor, I'll be rich, and I mean to be generous at the same time; and that way no one will find any fault with me. Only make yourself some honey and the flies will come to suck you, as much as you have so much are you worth, as my grandmother used to say, and there's no way of getting even with a man of means."

"May God curse you, Sancho!" cried Don Quixote at this point. "May sixty thousand devils carry you off, and your proverbs with you! For an hour now you have been stringing them, and every one is a torture to me. I can assure you that these sayings of yours will one day bring you to the gallows; on account of them your vassals will take the government away from you, or else there will be conspiracies among them. Tell me, where do you find them all, you ignorant lout, or how do you manage to apply them? If I utter one and apply it properly, I have to sweat and labor as if I were digging a ditch."

"In God's name, master," replied Sancho, "you are complaining over very little. Why should you be vexed if I make use of my own property, seeing that I have no other—no other wealth except sayings and more sayings? Here are four that have just popped into my head, as pat to the purpose as could be, or like pears in a basket; but I'm not going to repeat them, for to keep silence well is called *Sancho*." [11]

"That Sancho is not you," said Don Quixote, "for not only do you not know how to keep silent, but you are a mischievous prattler in the bargain. Nevertheless, I am curious to know what the four sayings are that you have just remembered and that fit in so aptly here; for I have been ransacking my own memory—and it is a good one —and none of the sort have occurred to me."

"What better could you ask for," said Sancho, "than these: 'Never put your thumbs between two of your back grinders'; and 'To "Get out of my house" and "What do you want with my wife?" there is no answer'; and 'Whether the pitcher hits the stone or the stone the pitcher, it will be bad for the pitcher,' all of which fit to a hair? Let no one fall out with his governor or with the one who is in command or he will be sorry for it in the end, like him who puts his thumb between his grinders, whether they be back teeth or not, so long as they are grinders that's all that matters. And to whatever the governor may say there's no answer to be made, any more than there is to 'Get out of my house' or 'What do you want with my wife?' As for the stone and the pitcher, a blind man could see that. And so it is that he who sees the mote in another's eye should see the beam in his own,[12] that it may not be said of him, 'The dead woman was frightened at the one with her throat cut';[13] for your Grace is well aware that the fool knows more in his own house than the wise man in the house of another."

"That is not true, Sancho," said Don Quixote, "for the fool knows nothing, in his own house or in the house of another, for the reason that upon a foundation of folly no edifice of wisdom can be reared. But let us leave the matter there. If you make a bad governor, the fault will be yours and mine will be the shame, but I find consolation in the thought that I have done my duty in thus earnestly advising you, with all the wisdom at my command; in this way am I released from my obligation and my promise. May God guide you, Sancho, and govern you in your government, and may He deliver me from the fear I have that you are going to turn the whole island upside down, a thing that I might prevent by revealing to the duke what you are, telling him that your fat little person is nothing other than a bag stuffed with proverbs and mischief."

"Sir," replied Sancho, "if your Grace is of the opinion that I am not fitted for this governorship, I give it up here and now; for I am more concerned for the black-of-the-nail of my soul than for my entire body. As plain Sancho, I can make out just as well on bread and onions as I can as governor on partridges and capons. When it comes to that, all are equal when they are asleep, the great and the small, the poor and the rich; and if your Grace will stop to think, you will remember that you alone were the one who put me up to being a governor, for I know no more about governing islands than a buzzard does, and if I thought for a minute that in order to be a governor the devil would have to carry me off, then I would rather go to Heaven as Sancho than go to Hell as a governor."

"So help me God, Sancho," said Don Quixote, "if only by reason of these last words that you have spoken, I hold you fit to be the governor of a thousand islands. You have by nature a good disposition without which no knowledge is worth anything. Commend yourself to God, then, and try not to lose sight of your main purpose; by which I mean, that you should make it your unswerving aim to do the right thing in all matters that come up for your judgment, for Heaven always favors

good intentions. And now, let us go to dinner, for I
think our hosts are waiting for us."

CHAPTER XLIV. *How Sancho Panza was taken
away to be governor, and the strange adventure that
befell Don Quixote in the castle.*

THEY say that in the original version of the history
it is stated that the interpreter did not translate
the present chapter as Cid Hamete had written it,[1]
owing to a kind of grudge that the Moor had against
himself for having undertaken a story so dry and
limited in scope as is this one of Don Quixote. For it
seemed to him he was always having to speak of the
knight and of Sancho, without being able to indulge in
digressions of a more serious and entertaining nature.
He remarked that to go on like this, pen in hand, with
his mind fixed upon a single subject and having to
speak through the mouths of a few persons only, was
for him an intolerable and unprofitable drudgery.

By way of relieving the monotony, in the first part of
the work he had employed the artifice of introducing
a few *novelas,* such as the *Story of the One Who Was
Too Curious for His Own Good* and *The Captive's Story,*
tales that, so to speak, had nothing to do with the narrative proper, the other portions being concerned with
things that had happened to Don Quixote himself, such
as could not be omitted. He also felt, he tells us, that
many readers, carried away by the interest attaching to
the knight's exploits, would be inclined to pass over
these novelettes either hastily or with boredom, thereby
failing to note the fine craftsmanship they exhibited,
which, however, would be plainly evident when they
should be published by themselves instead of appearing

as mere adjuncts to Don Quixote's madness and Sancho's foolishness.

Accordingly, in this second part it was not his intention to insert any more tales of that kind, whether separate or interwoven with the narrative as a whole, but rather only a few episodes that resembled them, arising naturally out of the course of events; and even with these he meant to be sparing, employing as few words as possible in the telling. He goes on to say that, while thus confining himself closely within the narrow limits of the plot, he wishes it understood that he has sufficient ability and intelligence to take the entire universe for his theme if he so desired and he asks that his labors be not looked down upon, but that he be given credit not for what he writes, but for what he has refrained from writing.

He then goes on with the story by saying that, on the afternoon of the day on which he had given the oral advice to Sancho,[2] Don Quixote presented him with a written copy of what he had said to him, that the squire might look for someone to read it to him. Scarcely had he done so when Sancho lost the document and it found its way into the hands of the duke, who communicated its contents to the duchess, whereupon they both marveled once again at the knight's folly and good sense. And with the object of carrying on the jest, they sent Sancho that same afternoon, with a large retinue, to the place that for him was to be his island.[3]

Now, it happened that the one who was in charge of Sancho and his train was a major-domo of the duke's, a fellow with a keen sense of humor who was at the same time very discreet (for there can be no humor where there is not discretion). He it was who had played the part of the Countess Trifaldi so amusingly, as has been related, and so was well suited for his present role. In addition, he had been thoroughly instructed by his lord and lady as to how he was to behave toward the squire, and as a result everything went off marvelously well.

The moment Sancho laid eyes upon the major-domo, he had a vision of La Trifaldi. "Sir," he said, turning to his master, "may the devil take me right here and now, as a righteous man and a believer,[4] if your Grace is not going to have to admit that the face on that steward is the Distressed One's very own."

Don Quixote gazed at the man attentively. "There is no reason why the devil should take you, Sancho," he replied, "either as a righteous man or as a believer— I don't know what you mean by that—for, while the Distressed One's face is that of the major-domo, the major-domo's countenance is not that of the Distressed One, for if such were the case it would imply too great a contradiction. However, this is not the time for going into all that, as it would involve us in an endless labyrinth. Believe me, friend, we must pray Our Lord most earnestly to deliver us from the wiles of wizards and enchanters."

"It is no joke, master," said Sancho, "for a while ago I heard him speak, and it was like La Trifaldi's voice sounding in my ears. Very well, I'll keep silent; but from now on I intend to be on my guard to see if I can discover any other sign that will tell me whether I am right or wrong in what I suspect."

"That you should do, Sancho," agreed Don Quixote, "and you must keep me advised of all that you discover in regard to this matter and of everything that happens to you in connection with your government."

Finally Sancho and his train set out. He was dressed like a man of the law, and over all wore a tawny-hued, wide-flaring greatcoat of watered camlet, with a cap of the same material.[5] He was mounted upon a mule, his saddle being of the high-backed short-stirrup variety,[6] and behind him, by order of the duke, came the gray, decked out in brilliant[7] silken trappings and such ornaments as are suited to an ass. Sancho every now and then would turn his head to look back at the beast, being so glad of the animal's company that he would not have changed places with the emperor of Germany.

Upon taking his leave of the duke and duchess, he kissed their hands and received the blessing which his master bestowed upon him. Don Quixote was in tears, and he himself was blubbering.

And now, gentle reader, let the worthy Sancho go in peace and good luck go with him. You may expect two bushels[8] of laughter when you hear how he deported himself in office. Meanwhile, listen to what happened to his master that same night, and if it does not make you laugh, it will at least cause you to part your lips in an apelike grin; for Don Quixote's adventures are to be greeted either with astonishment or with mirth.

The balance of the chapter is devoted to the beginning of another "long-drawn-out" episode between Don Quixote and one of the duchess's women-in-waiting, Altisidora by name. When the lady of the house offers to have the knight attended in his chamber by four of her fairest damsels, he declines on the ground of chastity and loyalty to Dulcinea. Going to his room, he finds to his dismay that he has ripped one of his hose and as a result will be compelled to wear a pair of traveling boots that Sancho has left behind. Then from beneath his window come the strains of a lovesick song. It is Altisidora who, in accordance with a preconceived plan, is serenading him. He slams his window shut and goes to bed very out of sorts.

CHAPTER XLV. *Of how the great Sancho took possession of his island and of the way in which he began to govern.*

O PERPETUAL discoverer of the antipodes, great taper of the world, eye of the heavens, sweet shaker of the water-coolers,[1] Thymbraeus[2] here, Phoebus there, archer in one place, in another a physician, father of poetry, inventor of music, thou who dost ever rise and, though appearing to do so, dost never set! [3] 'Tis thee, O Sun, by whose aid man doth beget man,[4] 'tis thee whom I beseech to favor and enlighten my darkened intellect that I may be able to give an absolutely exact account of the government of the great Sancho Panza; for without thee I feel lukewarm, fainthearted, and confused.

To continue, then: Sancho with all his train arrived at a village of around a thousand inhabitants, one of the best in the duke's domains.[5] They informed him that it was called Barataria Island, either because the real name of the village was Baratario, or by reason of the *barato*[6] which had led to the government being bestowed upon him. As they reached the town, which had a wall around it, the officers of the municipality came out to meet them, the bells rang, and all the townspeople evidenced their satisfaction. With much pomp they conducted him to the cathedral to give thanks to God, and then, with a few mock ceremonies, they handed over to him the keys of the city, acknowledging him to be the island's perpetual governor.

The new governor's apparel, his beard, and his little fat figure astonished all those who were not in on the joke, and even those who were, and they were many.

Finally, upon leaving the church, they took him to the judge's chair and seated him in it, and the duke's major-domo then addressed him.

"Sir Governor," he said, "it is an ancient and obligatory custom in this famous island for the one who comes to take possession of it to answer a question that is put to him, one that shall be somewhat difficult and intricate, so that from his answer the people may be able to form an idea of their ruler's intelligence and judge for themselves as to whether they should hail his coming with joy or look upon it with sorrow."

All the time the major-domo was saying this, Sancho was gazing steadily at some large letters inscribed upon the wall facing him, and inasmuch as he did not know how to read, he asked what they were.

"Sir," was the reply, "that inscription is a notation of the day upon which your Lordship took possession of this island. It reads: 'On this day—such and such a day of such and such a year—Don Sancho Panza took over the government of this island and many years may he enjoy it.' "

"And who is it that they call 'Don Sancho Panza'?" asked Sancho.

"Your Lordship," the major-domo answered, "for no other Panza has set foot here except the one who is seated in that chair."

"Well, then, brother," said Sancho, "I will let you know that there has never been any 'Don' in my family. Plain Sancho Panza they call me, and Sancho was my father's name before me, and my grandfather's before him; they all were Panzas, without any 'Dons' or 'Doñas' tacked on.[7] In this island, I imagine, there must be more 'Dons' than there are stones. But enough of that; God knows what I mean. It may be, if my government lasts

four days, I'll weed them all out; for there are so many
of them they must be as troublesome as gnats. Go ahead
with your question, Señor Major-domo, and I'll reply the
best way I can, whether the people are sorry or not."

At this moment there came into the court two men,
one dressed like a peasant, the other like a tailor, for
this latter held in his hands a pair of shears.

"Sir Governor," said the tailor, "I and this peasant
have come before your Grace to have you settle a
difference between us. Yesterday this good man entered
my shop—for, begging the pardon of those present,[8]
I am a licensed tailor, God be praised—and, putting a
piece of cloth in my hands, he asked me, 'Señor, is there
enough here to make me a cap?' Feeling the cloth, I
told him there was. He must have supposed—as I supposed, and I supposed right—that I undoubtedly meant
to make away with a part of the material, being led to
think so by his own maliciousness and the bad opinion
that people have of tailors. He then asked me to look
and see if there would be enough for two. Guessing
what was in his mind, I said yes; whereupon he, per-
sisting in his damnable first intention, went on adding
cap after cap, with me saying, yes, yes, until we were up
to five caps in all. Just a while ago he came to call for
them and I gave them to him, but he doesn't want to
pay me for my labor but insists I should pay *him* or give
him back his cloth."

"Is all this true, brother?" inquired Sancho.

"Yes, sir," replied the man, "but will your Grace
please have him show the five caps he made for me?"

"I'll be glad to," said the tailor. And, with this, he at
once brought his hand out from under his cloak, displaying the five caps upon his four fingers and thumb.
"There they are, and I swear by God and my conscience

there's not a scrap of cloth left; I am willing to submit my work to the inspectors of the trade."

All those present had a laugh over the number of caps and the novel character of this lawsuit. As for Sancho, he considered the matter for a while and then said, "It appears to me that in this case there is no need of lengthy arguments; all that is called for is the judgment of an honest man. And so my decision is that the tailor shall lose his work and the peasant his cloth, and the caps shall go to the prisoners in the jail,[9] and let us hear no more about it."

If the decision in the case of the cattle-driver's purse[10] had aroused the admiration of the bystanders, this one provoked them to laughter; but the governor's orders were nonetheless carried out. Two old men were the next to present themselves before him, one of whom carried a reed by way of staff. It was the one without a staff who was the first to speak.

"My lord," he began, "some days ago I lent this good man ten gold crowns by way of service duly rendered,[11] on condition that he should repay me upon demand. A long time went by without my demanding payment, for the reason that I did not wish to cause him an even greater hardship than that which he was suffering when he sought the loan. However, when I saw that he was making no effort to pay me, I asked him for the money, not once but many times, and he not only failed to reimburse me, he even refused to do so, saying I had never let him take the ten crowns in question. I have no witnesses of the loan, and naturally there are none of the payment since no payment was made. Accordingly, I would have your Grace put him under oath, and if he swears that he did pay me, then I will cancel the debt here and before God."[12]

"What do you say to that, old man with the staff?"
Sancho asked.

"My lord," replied the old man, "I admit that he lent
them to me; but your Grace may lower that rod,[13] for,
seeing that he has had me put under oath, I will also
swear that I paid him back, really and truly."

The governor lowered the rod that he held, and in the
meanwhile the old man who had spoken handed his staff
over to the other one while he took the oath, as if he
found it in his way. Then, placing his hand upon the
cross of the rod, he once more affirmed that it was true
that he had borrowed the ten crowns that were being
demanded of him but that he had paid them back into
the other's hand, the only thing being that the other old
man did not appear to realize it but was all the time
asking for his money. In view of this, the great governor
then asked the creditor what he had to say in reply to
his adversary's statement; whereupon the old fellow who
now held the staff replied that his debtor must undoubtedly be speaking the truth, as he knew him to be
a worthy man and a good Christian. The one who had
lent the crowns added that he must surely have forgotten how and when they had been repaid and that
from that time forth he would never ask his adversary
for anything.

The debtor thereupon took back his staff and, with
bowed head, left the court. When he saw the defendant
leaving in this manner, without saying another word,
and when he perceived how resigned the plaintiff was,
Sancho dropped his chin to his bosom and, placing the
forefinger of his right hand in turn upon his eyebrows
and his nose, remained lost in thought for a short while.
Then he raised his head and ordered them to call back
the old man with the staff who had already left.

They did so, and as soon as Sancho saw him, he said, "Good man, give me that staff. I have need of it."

"Gladly," replied the old man. "Here it is, my lord." And he placed it in the governor's hand.

Sancho took it and handed it to the other old man, remarking, "Go in peace, for you are now repaid."

"Repaid, my lord? And is this reed worth ten gold crowns?"

"Yes," said the governor, "it is; or if it is not, then I am the biggest blockhead in the world. We will see right now whether or not I have it in me to govern an entire kingdom."

With this, he ordered that the reed be broken and laid open there in the sight of all, and in the heart of it they found the ten gold crowns. They were all greatly astonished at this, looking upon their governor as another Solomon. When they inquired of him how he knew that the crowns were there, he replied that it had come to him when he saw the old man hand the staff to his adversary while he was taking an oath to the effect that he had really and truly paid his creditor, and then, when he was through, had heard him ask for it back again. From which it was to be deduced that, even when those who governed were simpletons, God sometimes guided them in their judgments. Moreover, he had heard the curate of his village tell of another case like this one,[14] and if it was a question of not forgetting what he had need to remember, there was not another memory like his own in all the island.

The short of the matter is, one old man went off crestfallen, the other with his money in hand, while those present continued to marvel at the thing. As for him whose duty it was to record Sancho's words, deeds, and movements, he could not make up his mind as to whether he should take the new governor for a fool or set him down as a wise man.

When this case had been concluded, there came into the court a woman holding on tightly to a man who was dressed like a rich drover.[15]

"Justice, Señor Governor! Justice!" she cried, "and if I don't find it on earth, I'll go look for it in Heaven! Beloved Governor, this evil man caught me in the middle of a field and made use of my body as if it had been some filthy rag. Ah, poor me! he has taken from me that which I had guarded more than twenty-three years, defending it alike against Moors and Christians, foreigners and native-born. I was always hard as corkwood, keeping myself as pure as a salamander in the flames or wool among the brambles, and now this fine fellow comes along and handles me with clean hands!"

"It remains to be seen," said Sancho, "whether this gallant has clean hands or not." And, turning to the man, he ordered him to reply to the complaint which the woman had made against him.

The defendant was in a state of confusion. "Good sirs," he answered, "I am but a poor dealer in hogs. This morning I left the village to sell—begging your pardon —four pigs, and what with taxes and cheating they took away from me practically all that they came to. As I was returning home, I fell in with this good dame, and the devil, who likes to jumble everything, saw to it that we were yoked together. I paid her quite enough, but she, dissatisfied, laid hold of me and would not let me go until she had dragged me here. She says that I forced her, but she lies by the oath that I am taking or am ready to take. And that is the whole truth, every particle of it."

The governor asked the man if he had any silver coins

with him, and the drover replied that he had some twenty ducats in a purse that was hidden in his bosom. Sancho then directed him to take the purse out and hand it over to the plaintiff, which the drover did, trembling all the while. The woman took it and, with many curtsies to all present, offered a prayer to God for the life and health of the Señor Governor who thus looked after damsels and orphans in distress. With this, she left the court, grasping the purse with both hands, but not until she first had looked to see if the coins in it were of silver. No sooner was she gone than Sancho turned to the drover, who, with eyes and heart following the purse, was on the verge of tears.

"My good man," he said, "go after that woman, take the purse away from her whether she is willing to give it up or not, and come back here with it."

He was not talking to a fool or a deaf man, for the drover was off at once like a streak of lightning, to carry out the order that had been given him. The bystanders, meanwhile, waited eagerly to see what the outcome of this case would be. Within a short while the pair returned, engaged in more of a struggle than before; she had her petticoat up with the purse in the lap of it while he strove to take it from her. This was not possible, however, so stoutly did she defend herself.

"Justice!" she was crying, "God's justice and the world's justice, too! Behold, Señor Governor, how bold and shameless this ruffian is. In the center of the town and middle of the street he tried to take away from me the purse which your Grace had ordered him to give me!"

"And did he take it?" asked the governor.

"Take it?" replied the woman. "I'd give up my life sooner than I would the purse. A fine young thing I'd be! They'll have to throw other cats in my beard! Ham-

mers and pincers, mallets and chisels, would not be
enough to get it out of my clutches, nor even a lion's
claws. They'd take the soul from out of my body before
they'd do that!"

"She's right," said the man. "I give up. I admit I
haven't the strength to take it away from her." And he
let go his hold.

Sancho then addressed the woman. "Let us have a
look at that purse, my respectable and valiant one," he
said. She gave it to him and he then handed it back to
the man, saying, as he did so, to the one who had been
forced and who had not been forced, "Sister, if you had
shown the same or even half the courage and valor in
defending your body that you have in protecting the
purse, the might of Hercules would not have been
sufficient to overcome you. Be on your way, in God's
name, and bad luck to you, and do not show yourself
again in this entire island or for six leagues around,
under pain of two hundred lashes. Go, then, I say, you
shameless, cheating hussy! Be off with you!"

Frightened by this, the woman left with her head
down, very much disgruntled.

"My good man," said Sancho to the defendant, "return to your village with your money and may God go
with you; and hereafter, if you do not want to lose your
purse, see to it that you do not take it into your head to
yoke with anyone."

Mumbling his thanks, the man departed, and the spec-
tators once again expressed their astonishment at the
wise decisions made by their new governor. All of which
the chronicler duly noted down, to be forwarded to the
duke who was eagerly awaiting his report. And here, let
us leave the worthy Sancho; for his master, greatly excited by Altisidora's music, urgently claims our attention.

In Chapter xlvi the author returns to Don Quixote and Altisidora's wooing of him. The next morning, going down a corridor, Don Quixote encounters the lovelorn maid, who promptly faints at the sight of him —at least she appears to faint. Don Quixote asks that a lute be placed in his chamber the next evening in order that he may "console" her with a bit of song; and upon retiring he finds a guitar, which he employs as an accompaniment to a ballad he has composed in the course of the day. It is a lengthy composition, and as he renders it all the household listen.

In the middle of his song a rope is let down from a balcony directly above his window. To it are attached more than a hundred bells, and the din is further increased when those who are standing above empty a bag full of cats with bells attached to their tails. Some of the felines dart through the window of Don Quixote's room and put out the candles as he, quaking with fear in the belief that they are enchanters, draws his sword and starts slashing at them. One of the cats leaps at him and seizes his nose with its claws and teeth, causing him to cry out with pain, whereupon the duke and duchess take a hand.

They enter the chamber with lighted tapers, and the duke finally succeeds in freeing Don Quixote from the beast. Altisidora herself bandages the wounds which the knight has received in the unequal combat, while he voices his displeasure at not having been permitted to finish the battle with "that scoundrelly enchanter." The maid, meanwhile, reproaches him for his heartlessness, and the ducal pair, a little worried over the outcome of the jest, take their departure. As a consequence of his "bell-and-cat fright" their guest is confined to his bed for the next five days.

CHAPTER XLVII. *Wherein is continued the account of how Sancho Panza deported himself in his government.*

THE history goes on to relate how they conducted Sancho from the court to a sumptuous palace, where, in a great hall, a royal and truly magnificent board was spread. He entered to the sound of flageolets, and four pages came forward to present him with water that he might wash his hands, which he did in a most dignified manner. As the music ceased, he took the seat at the head of the table, that being the only one there was, since no other place had been laid. An individual with a whalebone wand in his hand, who later turned out to be a physician, then stationed himself at Sancho's side, after which they lifted up a fine white cloth, revealing an assortment of fruit and many other edibles of various sorts.

One who appeared to be a student said grace as a page put a lace bib under the governor's chin and another who performed the functions of a butler set a dish of fruit in front of him. No sooner had he taken a bite, however, than the personage at his side touched the plate with the wand and it was instantly removed. The butler thereupon presented a dish containing other food, but before Sancho had had a chance to taste it— indeed, before it had so much as come within his reach —the wand had been laid upon it and a page had withdrawn it as swiftly as the other attendant had borne away the fruit. Astonished at this, the governor looked around at all the others present and demanded to know if this meal was supposed to be eaten by sleight of hand.[1]

"Señor Governor," replied the man with the wand, "one may eat here only in accordance with the usage and custom in other islands where there are governors. I, sir, am a physician and am paid to serve the rulers of this particular island. I am far more attentive to their health than I am to my own, and study night and day to become acquainted with my patient's constitution in order to be able to cure him when he falls sick. My chief duty is to be present at his dinners and suppers and permit him to eat only what is good for him while depriving him of anything that may do harm or injury to his stomach.[2] Thus I had them remove that dish of fruit for the reason that it contained too much moisture, and I had them do the same with the other dish because it was too hot and filled with spices that tend to increase the thirst. For he who drinks much slays and consumes that radical moisture wherein life consists."[3]

"Well, then," said Sancho, "that dish of roast partridges over there, which appears to be very properly seasoned, surely will not hurt me."

"Ah," was the physician's answer, "so long as I live my lord the governor shall not partake of those."

"And why not?" asked Sancho.

"For the reason that our master, Hippocrates, lodestar and luminary of the science of medicine, in one of his aphorisms has stated: '*Omnis saturatio mala, perdicis autem pessima,*' which is to say, 'All surfeit is bad, but a surfeit of partridges is the worst of all.' "[4]

"If that be true," said Sancho, "will the Señor Doctor kindly see what dishes there are on this table that will do me the most good and the least harm and then let me eat them without any more tapping; for by the life of the governor, and may God let me enjoy it, I'm dying of hunger, and in spite of the Señor Doctor and all that

he may say, to deny me food is to take my life and not
to prolong it."

"Your Grace is right, my Lord Governor," replied the
physician. "And so, I may tell you that in my opinion
you should not eat of those stewed rabbits, for it is a
furry kind of food. And that veal—if it were not roasted
and pickled, you might try it, but as it is, there can be
no question of your doing so."

"Take that big dish," said Sancho, "that I see smoking
down there—it looks to me like an olla-podrida;[5] and,
considering all the different things that go to make it up,
I can't fail to hit upon something that will be tasty and
at the same time good for me."

"*Absit*," declared the doctor. "Let us put far from us
any such evil thought as that. There is nothing in the
world that affords less nourishment than an olla-podrida.
Save them for canons, university rectors, or peasant wed-
dings. Its presence is out of place on the tables of governors, where all should be delicacy and refinement. The
reason for this is that always, everywhere and by everybody, simple medicines are more esteemed than are the
compounded ones, since in the case of the former it is
impossible to make a mistake whereas with the others
one may readily do so by altering the proportion of the
ingredients. In my opinion, what my Lord Governor
should eat at the present time is a hundred wafers[6] and
a few thin slices of quince marmalade, which will be
good for the stomach and an aid to digestion."

Upon hearing this, Sancho leaned back in his chair
and, staring hard at the doctor, asked him what his
name was and where he had studied.

"I, my Lord Governor, am Doctor Pedro Recio de
Agüero, native of the village of Tirteafuera,[7] which is
on the right-hand side going from Caracuel to Almodóvar

del Campo, and I hold the degree of doctor from the University of Osuna." [8]

Sancho was greatly incensed by now. "Very well, let the Señor Doctor Pedro Recio de Mal-Agüero,[9] graduate of Osuna and native of Tirteafuera, a village which is on the right-hand side as we come from Caracuel to Almodóvar del Campo—let him get out of here at once; for, if he does not, I swear by the sun that I will take a club and by making use of it, starting with him, will see to it that there is not a doctor left in this whole island, or, at any rate, none of those that I look upon as being ignorant. As for the wise, prudent, and learned ones, I will honor them as divine beings.[10] And so I say once more, let Pedro Recio be gone or I will take this chair in which I am sitting and break it over his head; and if I am called into court for it, I will clear myself by saying that I did God a service by slaying a bad physician and a public executioner. Either give me something to eat or take back your government; a trade that does not feed the one who practices it is not worth two beans."

The doctor was terrified when he saw how wrathful the governor was and would have made a Tirteafuera of that room[11] if at that moment the sound of a post horn had not been heard in the street. Going over to the window, the butler turned and said, "A courier from the duke, my lord; he must bring some message of importance." The courier entered, covered with sweat and very much agitated, and, drawing a paper from his bosom, he handed it to the major-domo, who read aloud the superscription, which ran as follows:

TO DON SANCHO PANZA, GOVERNOR OF THE ISLAND OF BARATARIA, TO BE DELIVERED INTO HIS HANDS OR THOSE OF HIS SECRETARY

"Who here is my secretary?" inquired Sancho when he heard this.

"I, my lord," one of those present spoke up, "for I know how to read and write and I am a Biscayan." [3]

"With what you have just added," remarked Sancho, "you could well be secretary to the emperor himself. Open that paper and see what it says."

The newly fledged [13] secretary did so and, having perused the contents of the letter, announced that the matter was one to be discussed in private. Sancho thereupon ordered them to clear the hall, and when the doctor and all the others with the exception of the major-domo and the butler had gone, the secretary proceeded to read the communication:

It has come to my knowledge, Señor Don Sancho Panza, that certain enemies of mine and of the island are planning to launch a furious assault upon it one of these nights, and it will accordingly be necessary for you to keep a watch and be on the alert in order not to be taken unawares. I have further learned through trustworthy scouts that four persons have entered your village in disguise with the object of taking your life, for the reason that they fear your great ability. Keep your eyes open, observe closely all who come up to speak to you, and eat nothing that is offered you. I will send aid to you if I see that you are in trouble. Meanwhile, in all instances, you are to do the thing that is to be expected of your good judgment.

From this village, the 16th of August, at four o'clock in the morning. Your friend,

THE DUKE.

Sancho was astonished, and so, apparently, were the others. "The thing to be done now," said the governor.

"and it must be done at once, is to throw Doctor Recio into jail; for if anybody is out to kill me, he must be the one, and he means to do it by slow starvation, which is the worst kind of death." [14]

"Moreover," said the butler, "it is my opinion that your Grace should not eat any of the food that is on this table, for it was a donation from some nuns, and, as the saying goes, behind the cross lurks the devil." [15]

"I do not deny it," replied Sancho, "and so for the present give me a slice of bread and three or four pounds of grapes; there can be no poison in that. The truth of the matter is, I cannot go on without eating. If we are to be ready for those battles that threaten us, we must be well nourished; for it is the tripes that carry the heart and not the other way around.[16] As for you, my secretary, reply to my lord, the duke, and tell him that I will carry out his orders exactly as he gives them. And say to my lady the duchess that I kiss her hands and beg her to send a special messenger with the letter and bundle for my wife, Teresa Panza, as that will be a great favor to me, and I will do all in my power to serve her in any way that I can. While you are about it, you may also put in a kiss of the hands for my master, Don Quixote de la Mancha, that he may see that I am grateful for his bread which I have eaten. As a good secretary and a good Biscayan, you may add whatever you like and is most to the point. And now take away this cloth and give me something to eat and I'll be ready for all the spies, murderers, and enchanters that may descend on me or on this island of mine."

A page now came in. "There is a farmer outside who would like a word with your Lordship on a matter of business. He says it is very important."

"It is strange about these people who come to see me on business," said Sancho. "Is it possible they are so

foolish as not to see that this is no time for things of that
sort? We governors, we judges, are we not flesh-and-
blood beings? Are we not to be allowed the time that
is necessary for taking a little rest—unless they would
have us made of blocks of marble? By God and upon my
conscience, if this government of mine holds out (and
I have a feeling that it won't), I'll have more than one
of these fellows who come on business hauled up short.
For the present, show this good man in, but make sure
first that he is not one of those spies or killers that are
after me."

"No, sir," replied the page, "I do not think he is; for
he appears to be a simple soul,[17] and either I miss my
guess or he's as good as good bread." [18]

"There is nothing to be afraid of," added the major-
domo, "for we are all here."

"Butler," said Sancho, "would it be possible, now
that Doctor Recio is no longer with us, for me to eat
something with a little body and substance to it, even if
it is only a slice of bread and an onion?"

"Tonight at supper," the butler informed him, "your
Lordship will be fully compensated for what was lacking
at dinner."

"God grant it may be so," was Sancho's answer.

At this point the farmer appeared. He made a very
favorable impression; for it could be seen from a thousand leagues away that he was a worthy man and a good
soul.

"Who is the governor here?" was the first thing he
asked.

"Who would it be," said the secretary, "if not the one
who occupies that seat?"

"Then, I humble myself in his presence," said the
man; and, dropping to his knees, he sought to kiss the
governor's hand, but Sancho would not permit it. In-

stead, he bade him rise and state what he wanted. The
petitioner did so.

"Sir," he began, "I am a farmer, a native of Miguelturra, a village two leagues distant from Ciudad Real."

"I see we have another Tirteafuera," observed Sancho.
"Say what you have to say, brother; for I will say to you
that I know Miguelturra very well, as it is not very far
from my town."

"Well, then, sir," continued the farmer, "this is the
case that I would lay before you. By the grace of God
I was married, in the peace and with the blessing of the
Holy Roman Catholic Church. I have two sons who are
students. The younger is studying to be a bachelor and
the older one to be a licentiate. I am a widower. My
wife died, or, more properly speaking, a stupid doctor
killed her by giving her a purge when she was pregnant.
If it had pleased God to let the child be born and it had
been a boy, I would have had him study to be a doctor
so that he would not be jealous of his brothers, the
licentiate and the bachelor."

"And in the same way," put in Sancho, "if your wife
had not died or been killed, you would not now be a
widower?"

"No, sir, of course not," replied the farmer.

"Well," said Sancho, "we are coming along; but
hurry, brother, for it is nearer bedtime than business
time."

"I will inform you," the farmer went on, "that this son
of mine who is studying to be a bachelor has fallen in
love with a lass in the same town by the name of Clara
Perlerina, daughter of Andrés Perlerino, another farmer
and a very rich one. That name, I may tell you, is not
one that has been handed down for generations, but is
due to the fact that all the members of this family are

paralytics, and by way of improving on it they call them Perlerines.[19]

"If the truth be told, this lass is like an oriental pearl or a flower of the field only when you look at her from the right-hand side; from the left-hand, not so much so, for on that side one eye is missing which she lost when she had the smallpox. The pockmarks on her face are many and large, but those who are fond of her will assert that those are not scars at all but graves where the hearts of her lovers lie buried. She is so neat that, in order not to dirty her face, she carries her nose turned up, as they say, so that it looks as if it were running away from her mouth. But, with all this, she is very good-looking. Her mouth is wide, and if it were not that ten or a dozen front teeth and grinders are missing, she might pass as one of the comeliest of maidens.

"Of her lips I shall say nothing, for they are so thin and delicate that, if it were the custom to use lips for such a purpose, one might wind them in a skein. Their color is different from that which is commonly seen, and the effect is marvelous: they are speckled with blue, green, and an eggplant hue— But pardon me, Sir Governor, for painting in such detail one who, when all is said, is destined to be my daughter. I love her and to me she is not bad-looking." [20]

"Do all the painting you like," said Sancho. "I'm enjoying it, and if I had only had my dinner, I wouldn't ask for a better dessert than this portrait of yours."

"That," replied the farmer, "is something which I have yet to serve,[21] but we will get to it in due time. I can only assure you, sir, that if I could but paint for you her tall figure and her bodily charms, you would find cause for astonishment; but this cannot be, for the reason that she is so bent and stooped that her knees touch her mouth, yet it is plain to be seen that if she could draw herself erect her head would scrape the roof. She would long since have given her hand to my bachelor son if she had been able to stretch it out, but it happens to be shrunken; nevertheless, you can tell from her broad, furrowed nails how elegant and shapely it is."

"That will do, brother," said Sancho. "You may consider that you have painted her from head to foot. What is it you want now? Come to the point without all this beating around the bush and all these odds and ends that you are tagging on to the story."

"What I desire, sir," the farmer went on, "is for your Grace to give me a letter of recommendation to her father, asking him to be so good as to let this marriage take place. We are not badly matched in the matter of worldly fortune or gifts of nature; for, to tell you the truth, Sir Governor, my son is bewitched, and there is not a day that the evil spirits do not torment him three or four times. Once he fell into the fire, and as a result his face is as shriveled as a bit of parchment. His eyes, too, are somewhat watery. But he has the disposition of an angel, and if it wasn't for his always flaying and punching himself with his fist, he'd be a saint."

"Is there anything else you would like, my good man?" Sancho inquired.

"There is," replied the farmer, "though I hesitate to mention it. But come, come, in any case I cannot let it go on rotting in my bosom. Sir, I would have your Grace give me from three to six hundred ducats to help make up my bachelor son's dowry, by which I mean, to help him set up housekeeping; for, after all, they must live by themselves, without being subjected to the meddling of their families."

"Think it over well," said Sancho, "and see if there is anything else. Don't be bashful but speak right out."

"No, I am quite sure there isn't."

No sooner did the man say this than the governor rose to his feet and picked up the chair in which he had been sitting.

"I swear, Don Country Bumpkin!" he cried, "if you don't get out of my sight at once, you unmannerly lout, and go hide yourself somewhere, I'll take this chair and lay your head wide open! Son of a whore, rascal, devil's painter! Is this any time to come asking me for six hundred ducats? Where would I get them, you stinking cur? And if I did have them, why should I give them to a crafty dunce like you? What is Miguelturra or the whole Perlerines family to me? Away with you, or by the life of the duke, my lord, I'll do what I said! I don't think you are from Miguelturra at all; you are some scoundrel that He has sent here to tempt me! Tell me, you wretch: I've not had the government a day and a half yet, and where do you expect me to lay hand on six hundred ducats?"

The butler motioned to the farmer to leave the room, which he did, hanging his head, for the fellow was obviously afraid that the governor would carry out his angry threat. (The rogue knew how to play his part very well.) But let us leave Sancho with his anger, and peace to them all, while we return to Don Quixote, who, when we last saw him, had his face treated and bandaged as a result of the cat wounds, from which he was not cured in a week's time. Meanwhile, during that week, something happened to him one day which Cid Hamete promises to relate with that truth and exactitude that mark every detail, however small, of this great history.

In Chapter XLVIII *we are back in the ducal castle again. One night about a week after Don Quixote's ex-*

*perience with the cats, as he is lying in bed thinking
of his troubles and with his face done up in bandages, he is startled and alarmed by an apparition that
stealthily enters his room. It is that of a "dignified
duenna" covered from head to foot by a long white
veil, wearing a pair of spectacles, and carrying a candle
in one hand while she shades it with the other to keep
the light out of her eyes. When the duenna looks up
and catches sight of Don Quixote she too beholds
what she takes to be a phantom; for he is wrapped in a
yellow satin coverlet, has a nightcap on his head, and
the glimpse that is afforded her of his face and mustaches through his bandages is a terror-inspiring sight.
Each, in short, is thoroughly frightened of the other.*

*The visitor is so scared that she drops her candle,
leaving the room in darkness. She turns to make for the
door but trips over her skirt and falls to the floor with a
loud thud. Don Quixote then "conjures" her to tell him
who she is, whereupon she reveals her identity. She is
Doña Rodríguez, the duchess's maid of honor, who has
come to ask him to redress a grievous wrong that has
been done her. He at first thinks she is there as a "go-
between," and he sternly warns her that he is chastely
loyal to "the peerless beauty of my lady Dulcinea del
Toboso" and cannot consider "any kind of amorous
dalliance." If she has anything other than that to ask of
him, he tells her, she may go light her candle and return
and they will discuss the matter.*

*When she comes back, and after each has demanded
and received an assurance that no improper advances
will be made, Don Quixote climbs into bed again and
Doña Rodríguez seats herself in a chair some distance
away and proceeds to tell her story.*

*The daughter of well-to-do parents who had lost their
fortune, she had been placed in her youth as a seam-*

stress with a lady of rank in Madrid, where one of the squires of the household fell in love with her. Their mistress had them duly married by the Church, but later she had unjustly dismissed the squire and it was grief over this that brought on his death. As a widow with an infant daughter to care for, the young seamstress was in dire straits until the duchess took her on as a maid. The daughter, by this time a little over sixteen, had grown up extremely beautiful and accomplished, only to be seduced by the son of a rich farmer under a false promise of marriage.

The duke was aware of all this but turned a deaf ear to the mother's complaints, for the reason that the farmer in question was in the habit of lending him money. What Doña Rodríguez now asks of Don Quixote is that he see that justice is done. She goes on to praise her daughter to the skies while telling tales out of school concerning the physical defects of Altisidora and the duchess as well.

Just as the duenna is concluding her story the door is suddenly thrown open with a loud bang. Doña Rodríguez is so startled that she drops the candle again and the room is plunged in darkness. She feels a pair of hands closing about her throat, and at the same time her petticoats are lifted and someone gives her a sound spanking with a slipper. The knight, terrified, lies perfectly still, fearing that his turn will come next; which proves to be the case, for the "silent executioners" —not a word is said all the while—strip the sheet and coverlet from his bed and for the space of half an hour give him a thorough drubbing and pinching.

CHAPTER XLIX. *Of what happened to Sancho Panza as he made the rounds of his island.*

WE LEFT the great governor angry and out of sorts with the roguish farmer-painter, who, put up to it by the major-domo and the major-domo in turn by the duke, had been making sport of him. Sancho, nonetheless, though he may have been but a simpleton, a stupid boor, contrived to hold his own against them all. He now addressed himself to those present, including Doctor Recio, who had returned to the room as soon as the business of the duke's confidential letter was out of the way.

"By this time," he said, "I see plainly that judges and governors ought to be made of brass so that they might not have to listen to those who come to petition them and who insist that they be heard and their business disposed of, no matter what the time or season. And if the poor judge does not hear them and attend to their requests, either because he is unable to do so or because it is not the time set aside for audiences, then they at once begin to curse and slander him, gnawing at his bones and even assailing his family tree. O silly petitioner, foolish petitioner, do not be in such haste as that, but wait for the proper occasion and opportunity. Come neither at mealtime nor at bedtime, for judges are of flesh and blood and must satisfy the needs of nature. All except me, that is to say; for thanks to the Señor Doctor Pedro Recio Tirteafuera, who stands before me here, I cannot satisfy my natural need of eating. He would have me die of hunger, and to this form of death he gives the name of life—may God give him and all his stripe that kind of life, say I, and the same goes for all bad doctors, while the good one merits palms and laurels."

All those who were acquainted with Sancho Panza were astonished at hearing him use such elegant language and did not know to what to attribute it unless it was that offices carrying grave responsibilities sharpened the wits of some men while in the case of others the effect was merely stupefying. Doctor Pedro Recio Agüero of Tirteafuera finally promised that the governor should have his supper that night even though it might be in violation of all the aphorisms of Hippocrates, and with this Sancho was content. He waited eagerly for night and the supper hour to come, and although it seemed to him that time was standing still, the hour so longed for arrived at last. They then served him a dish of beef and onions with a few boiled calves' feet that were rather stale. He fell to, however, more heartily than if they had set before him francolins from Milan, Roman pheasants, veal of Sorrento, partridges from Moron, or geese from Lavajos.

"See here, Señor Doctor," he said in the course of the meal, "from now on you needn't bother to give me dainty dishes or anything special as it would only unhinge my stomach, which is used to goat's meat, beef, bacon, hung beef, turnips, and onions. If I am given other victuals of the kind they serve in palaces, my stomach will turn squeamish and I'll sometimes be sick. What the butler may do is this: he may serve me what are known as ollas-podridas (for the more rotten they are, the better they smell).[1] He may put whatever he likes into them, so long as it is something good to eat, and I will thank him for it, and pay him for it, too, someday. But don't let anyone try to play any jokes on me, for either we are or we are not, and so let us all live together and eat our food in peace and good fellowship.

When God sends the dawn, it is daylight for all. I mean to govern this island without giving up a right or taking a bribe.[2] Let everyone keep his eyes open and look out for the arrow.[3] For I would have you know that the devil's in Cantillana,[4] and if they give me cause for it, they're going to see marvels. Make yourself into honey and the flies will eat you!" [5]

"Señor Governor," replied the butler, "there is certainly much truth in what you have said, and I promise you in the name of all the inhabitants of this island that they will serve your Grace faithfully, willingly, and affectionately; for the mild way in which you have begun to govern affords them no excuse for doing or thinking anything that would be a disservice to your Grace."

"That I can believe," said Sancho, "since they would be fools to think or do anything of the sort. Once more I say to you: see to feeding me and my gray; that is the important thing and most to the point. When the time comes, we will make the rounds. It is my intention to rid this island of all kinds of trash, of all good-for-nothing loafers and vagabonds; for I would have you know, my friends, that the lazy and idle are to a state what drones are to a hive, which eat the honey that the worker bees have made. I propose to aid the farmer, to preserve the privileges of gentlemen, to reward the virtuous, and, above all, to respect religion and to honor those in holy orders.[6] What do you think of that, my friends? Is there something in what I say or not?"

"There is so much in what your Grace says," the major-domo assured him, "that I am indeed astonished to hear a man wholly unlettered, as I believe your Grace to be, uttering so many wise maxims and observations, all of which is quite contrary to what was expected of your Grace's intelligence by those who sent us and by

us who came here with you. Each day new things are
seen in this world, jests are turned into earnest and the
jesters are mocked."

That night they set out to make the rounds, Sancho
striding along with his staff of office in hand, accompanied by the major-domo, the secretary, the butler,
a chronicler, and a number of bailiffs and notaries.
They have gone but a short distance when they come
upon a couple of swordsmen engaged in a duel. Upon
questioning the men the "governor" learns that they
have just left a gambling house. One has won a large
sum of money. The other is one of those gentlemen who
"look on to see whether the play is fair or foul and to
support those who are actually losers and thus prevent
brawls"—in modern American parlance, a professional
"kibitzer."

It was the custom for the lucky ones to give these
onlookers something out of their winnings, and in the
present case the bystander feels that he has not been
paid enough, hence his resort to the sword. To this
the other gentleman replies that he feels he has been
sufficiently generous, inasmuch as those who expect
gratuities from players ought to take what is offered
them when they know the gains are not ill gotten; it is
only sharpers that have to pay a heavier tribute, and
the fact that he has given so little is proof that the game
was honest.

Sancho's decision in the matter is that the winner
must pay the other man a hundred reales and must
disburse an additional thirty "for the poor prisoners."
As for the complainant, he is to take the money and
leave the island at once, under sentence of banishment
for ten years. In conclusion, the "governor" remarks,
"Either I am not good for much . . . or I will do

*away with these gambling houses, for it seems to me
that much harm comes from them."*

One of the notaries speaks up to say that Sancho will
not be able to do away with this particular house, since
it is kept by "a very important personage"; and in any
event, it is those of the lower class that do the most
harm and where the most flagrant abuses are to be
found. "I can see," replies Sancho, "that there is much
to be said as to that."

A constable now comes up, holding by the arm *a*
youth whom he has caught in the act of running away
from the law. Sancho interrogates the young fellow and
receives mocking answers in reply. He ends by sentenc-
ing him to sleep in jail; but when the jester points out
that, while they may jail him, no one can make him
sleep, the "governor" relents and sends him home with
a warning "not to make light of those in authority or you
may fall in with someone who will bring the joke down
on your skull."

A little later two other constables appear with a man
in custody, who, they assert, is in reality a woman in
masculine attire. Inspection proves that this is the case;
and those who are supposed to be tricking Sancho are
as much surprised as he, for the encounter has not been
prearranged. When asked to tell who she is and where
she was going in such a costume, the girl states that she
is the daughter of a wealthy widower and hitherto has
been kept shut away from the world. Wishing to see
what was outside the walls of her father's house, she
had persuaded her brother to dress her in one of his
suits and take her to see the town.

He had accompanied her dressed as a girl; when they
saw the night watch approaching, he had run away and
urged her to do the same, but she had been overtaken
by one of the officers. The brother now is brought up,

*and Sancho, forgiving them on the ground of extreme
youth, has them escorted to their home. In the meantime, the butler has fallen in love with the girl, while
Sancho has thoughts of marrying the young man to
his daughter Sanchica.*

CHAPTER L. *Wherein is set forth who the enchanters
and executioners were who spanked the duenna and
pinched and scratched Don Quixote, together with
what happened to the page who carried the letter
to Teresa Panza,*[1] *Sancho Panza's wife.*

CID HAMETE, that most painstaking investigator
of the minute details of this true history, tells us
that as Doña Rodríguez left her own apartment to go
to Don Quixote's, another matron who was her room-
mate observed her movements; and inasmuch as all
duennas are eager to know, hear, and smell out things,
this one proceeded to follow her so quietly that the
worthy Rodríguez was unaware of the fact. As soon
as the second duenna saw the first one enter the guest's
chamber, true to the tattling character of her kind she at
once hastened to inform my lady the duchess that Doña
Rodríguez and the knight were closeted together, and
the duchess in turn told the duke, begging his permission to go with Altisidora and find out what it was her
serving woman wanted of Don Quixote.

The duke gave his consent, and the two women then
tiptoed along very cautiously to the door of the knight's
room and took up a position near by where they could
hear all that was said. As the duchess listened to Doña
Rodríguez making public property of her mistress's ail-
ments,[2] she was unable to bear it, and Altisidora felt the
same way about it, and so, filled with rage and thirsting

for vengeance, they burst into the chamber, where they spanked the duenna and punished Don Quixote in the manner that has already been described; for insults offered to the beauty and pretensions of women invariably arouse in them a mighty wrath and kindle a passion for revenge. The duchess gave an account of the affair to the duke, who was very much amused by it; and then by way of continuing the jest and having still further sport with the knight, she summoned the page who had impersonated Dulcinea in the little comedy having to do with that lady's disenchantment—a matter which Sancho had entirely forgotten, being so busy with his government. The page was now dispatched to Teresa Panza, Sancho's wife, with her husband's letter and another which the duchess had written, and with a large string of valuable coral beads as a present.

The history goes on to say that the page was very keen-witted and anxious to be of service to his lord and lady, and that he set out right willingly for Sancho's village. Just before entering it he saw a number of women washing clothes in a brook,³ and, going up to them, he inquired if they could tell him whether or not a woman by the name of Teresa Panza lived there, wife of one Sancho Panza, squire to a knight known as Don Quixote de la Mancha. In response to this question, a young lass stood up.

"Teresa Panza is my mother," she said, "the Sancho you speak of is my father, and that knight is our master."

"Come, then, young lady," said the page, "and take me to your mother; for I bring a letter and a present from your father."

"That I will gladly do, my good sir," replied the girl, who appeared to be around fourteen years of age. Leaving the clothes that she was washing with one of her companions and without putting anything on her head or feet, for she was barelegged and her hair was hanging down, she leaped in front of the page's mount and said, "Come with me, your Grace. Our house is on the edge of the village and my mother is there, very much worried because she has had no news of my father for a long time."

"Well," said the page, "I am bringing her some, and such good news that she may well thank God for it."

With the girl leaping, running, and skipping, they reached the village, but before going into the house she called from the doorway, "Come out, Mother Teresa, come out, come out; here is a gentleman with letters and other things from my father."

At these words Teresa Panza appeared, spinning a bundle of flax. She was clad in a gray skirt so short that it seemed they had "cut it to her shame," [4] with a bodice of the same color and a chemise. She was not so very old, although she was obviously past forty; but she was strong of body, robust and vigorous, with a nutbrown complexion.

"What is it, daughter? Who is this gentleman?" she asked as she saw the page on horseback.

"A servant of my lady Doña Teresa Panza," replied the page. With this, he dismounted and went to kneel before Teresa with great humility. "Give me your hands, my lady Doña Teresa," he said, "as the lawful wedded wife of Señor Don Sancho Panza, rightful governor of the island of Barataria."

"Ah, my good sir," she said, "be off with you. Don't do that; for I am no palace lady but a poor peasant woman, daughter of a clodhopper and wife of a squire-errant and not of any governor."

"Your Grace," the page insisted, "is the most worthy wife of an archworthy governor, as proof of which I hand your Grace this letter and this present." And he forthwith took out of his pocket a string of coral beads with golden clasps.

"This letter," he said, placing the beads about her neck, "is from my Lord Governor and the other one and the necklace are from my lady the duchess, who has sent me to you."

Teresa was quite overcome by it all, and her daughter as well. "May they slay me," said the lass, "if our master Don Quixote is not at the bottom of this; he must have given father that government or earldom that he promised him so many times."

"That is right," said the page. "Thanks to Señor Don Quixote, Señor Sancho is now governor of the island of Barataria, as you will see from this letter."

"Read it for me, noble sir," said Teresa, "for although I know how to spin, I cannot read a mite."

"Nor I," added Sanchica; "but wait here a moment and I will go call someone who will read it for us, even though it be the curate himself or the bachelor, Sansón Carrasco. They will be very glad to come and hear news of my father."

"There is no need to call anyone," said the page. "I may not know how to spin, but I can read, and I will tell you what it says." He proceeded to do so, reading Sancho's letter in its entirety, which, since it has already been given in these pages, need not be set down here again. Then he took out the other one, from the duchess, the contents of which were as follows:

Friend Teresa: Your husband Sancho's sterling qualities, his upright character, and his ability have made me feel impelled to ask my own husband, the duke, to give him an island out of the many in my lord's possession. I have received word that he, Sancho, is governing like a gerfalcon, a thing which

I am very glad to hear, and my lord, the duke, also. I thank Heaven most heartily that I made no mistake in choosing him for such a post; for I would have my lady Teresa know that it is extremely hard to find a good governor in this world, but God grant that I do as well as Sancho is doing now.

I send you herewith, my dear, a string of coral beads with gold clasps, and could only wish that they were oriental pearls. However, he who gives you a bone would not see you dead.[5] The time will come when we shall meet and become acquainted, but God only knows what is to be. Remember me to Sanchica, your daughter, and tell her for me that she should hold herself in readiness, for I mean to make a good match for her when she least expects it.

They tell me that in your village you have some large acorns. Send me a couple of dozen or so of them and I shall prize them greatly as coming from you. Write me at length, telling me of your health and how you are doing; and if you stand in need of anything, you have but to open your mouth and you shall have your wish.[6]

From this place. Your loving friend,

THE DUCHESS.

"Ah!" exclaimed Teresa when she had heard the letter, "and what a kind lady it is, how plain and humble! Let me be buried with such ladies as that and not with the *hidalgas* you find in this town, who think that because they are ladies the wind should not touch them, who when they go to church put on as many airs as if they were queens, and who think that they are disgraced if they so much as look at a country-woman. You can see how goodhearted she is. For all that she's a duchess, she calls me her friend and treats me like an equal—and may I see her equal to the tallest belfry in La Mancha!

"As for the acorns, my good sir, I will send her lady-ship a peck of them, and such big ones that people well may come to see them as a show and wonder at them. And now, for the present, Sanchica, entertain this gentleman, look after his horse, get some eggs from the stable, slice plenty of bacon, and give him a meal fit for a prince;[7] for the good news he brings and the good face on him deserve the best there is. In the meanwhile, I'll run out and tell the neighbor women about our good luck, and the father curate and Master Nicholas the barber, for they always have been such good friends of your father's."

"I will do as you say, mother," said Sanchica, "but you must give me half of that string of beads; for I don't think my lady the duchess would have been so stupid as to send them all to you."

"They are all for you, daughter," replied Teresa, "but let me wear them around my neck for a few days, for it seems as if they really gladdened my heart."

"You will be glad, too," said the page, "when you see the bundle that is in this portmanteau; for it contains a suit of the finest cloth, which the governor wore only one day to the hunt and which he now sends to Señora Sanchica."

"May he live a thousand years," said Sanchica, "and the one who brings it no less, and even two thousand if needs be."

Teresa then left the house with the letters and with the beads about her neck, strumming upon the former with her fingers as if they had been a tambourine. Falling in by chance with the curate and Sansón Carrasco, she began doing a dance as she cried, "Faith, and we are no poor relations now! We've got a little government! Let the finest lady there is meddle with me and I'll set her down as an upstart!"

"What's all this, Teresa Panza? Why are you acting like mad, and what papers are those you have there?"

"Those are letters from duchesses and governors, if you call that madness, and these beads that I have about my neck are of finest coral, with Ave Marias and Pater Nosters of beaten gold, and I am a governor's wife!"

"God help us, Teresa, but we don't understand you. We can't make out what you are talking about."

"There, see for yourselves," she said, and handed them the letters.

The curate read them aloud as Sansón Carrasco listened, and the two of them then gazed at each other as if dumfounded. The bachelor asked who had brought the letters, and she replied by saying that they should come home with her and meet the messenger, a young man fine as gold [8] who had brought her another present worth even more than this one. The curate took the beads from her neck and looked at them again and again, and, having made sure that they were really valuable, he was more astonished than ever.

"By the habit that I wear," he declared, "I do not know what to say or think about these letters and presents. On the one hand, I can perceive by touching them the fineness of these coral beads, and, on the other hand, I read here that a duchess is sending to ask for two dozen acorns."

"Make sense out of that for me if you can," said Carrasco. "But come along, let's go see the one who brought this letter; he may be able to throw some light upon the mystery."

They did so, and Teresa returned with them. They

found the page sifting a little barley for his horse and Sanchica cutting a slice of bacon to be fried with the eggs for the page's dinner. Both of them were pleased by the young man's bearing and fine apparel, and after a courteous exchange of greetings Sansón requested him to give them what news he had of Don Quixote, and of Sancho Panza as well. He added that they had read the letters from Sancho and my lady the duchess but were still puzzled, being unable to make out what was meant by Sancho's government, especially the reference to an island, seeing that all or most of the islands in the Mediterranean belonged to his Majesty.

"As to Señor Sancho Panza's being a governor," replied the page, "there can be no doubt. As to whether his government consists of an island or not, is no concern of mine. It is sufficient to state that it is a town of more than a thousand inhabitants. With regard to the acorns, I may say that my lady the duchess is so modest and unassuming that she not only would ask a peasant woman for such a gift as that, but has even been known to send to a neighbor of hers to ask for the loan of a comb. For I would have your Worships know that the ladies of Aragon, however highborn they may be, are not so haughty and punctilious as are those of Castile, and are in the habit of treating people with greater informality."

In the midst of their conversation Sanchica came out, her skirt filled with eggs.

"Tell me, sir," she asked of the page, "does my father by any chance wear trunk-hose since he became a governor?"

"I never noticed, but I imagine so."

"Oh, my God! What a sight it must be, my father in tights! Isn't it strange, ever since I was born I have wanted to see him dressed like that?"

"As things are going now," replied the page, "you will see it if you live long enough. By God, if his government lasts him two more months, he'll be going about in a traveler's hood." [9]

It was plain to the curate and the bachelor that the page was speaking in jest, but the fine quality of the beads and of the hunting suit that Sancho had sent (Teresa had already shown them the garment) seemed to contradict this impression. Meanwhile, they had a good laugh over the wish that Sanchica had expressed, and they laughed still more as Teresa went on to say, "Señor Curate, I wish you would find out if there is anyone going to Madrid or Toledo who could buy me a hoop skirt, the best there is and in the latest fashion; for I certainly mean to be as much of an honor as I can to my husband in his government, that I do, and if I get my pride up I intend to go to court and set up a coach like all the other ladies, for she who is the wife of a governor may very well keep one."

"And why shouldn't you, mother!" cried Sanchica. "Would to God it was today instead of tomorrow, even though they said, when they saw me seated in the coach with my mother, 'Just look at that little nobody, that garlic-eater's daughter, how she rides around at her ease as if she were a female pope!' But let them tramp in the mud and let me go in my carriage, with my feet off the ground. Bad luck[10] to all the gossips in the world. So long as I go warm, let the people laugh! [11] Am I right, mother?"

"Indeed you are, my daughter," replied Teresa. "My good Sancho prophesied all this luck and even better, and you'll see, my child, I'll not stop until I've become a countess. For luck is all in the way you begin; as I've heard your father say many times—and he's the father of proverbs as well—when they offer you a heifer, run with the halter, and when they offer you a government, take it; when they give you an earldom, grab it, and when they say *tus, tus* to you with some nice present, snap at it. It would be just as if you were to go on sleeping and not answer when fortune and good luck stand knocking at the door of your house!"

"And what do I care," added Sanchica, "if somebody or other says, when they see me holding my head up like a fine lady, 'The dog saw himself in hempen breeches,' [12] and so forth?"

Listening to this, the curate was led to remark, "I cannot help believing that every member of the Panza family was born with a bagful of proverbs inside him; I never saw one that did not spill them at all hours and on every occasion."

"That is the truth," said the page, "for the Lord Governor Sancho goes around quoting them at every turn, and even though they may not be to the point, they are very amusing, and my lady the duchess and the duke praise them highly."

"Then, my dear sir," said the bachelor, "you still maintain, do you, that all this about Sancho's government is the truth, and that there really is a duchess in this world who sends him presents and writes to him? As for us, we have handled the presents and read the letters, but still are not convinced and are inclined to think, rather, that this is something that has to do with our fellow townsman Don Quixote. He believes that everything is done by enchantment; and I might say that I should like to touch and feel your Grace to see if you are a ghostly ambassador or a flesh-and-blood being."

"Gentlemen," replied the page, "with regard to myself I only know that I am a real messenger and that

Señor Sancho Panza is indeed a governor; I know that my lord and lady, the duke and duchess, are in a position to give, and have given him this government, and I have heard that the same Sancho Panza is deporting himself in it most valiantly. As to whether or not there is any enchantment in it, that is something for your Worships to argue. I swear by my parents, who are still living and whom I dearly love, that this is all I know about it."

"It may very well be," said the bachelor, "but *dubitat Augustinus.*" [13]

"Let him doubt who will," said the page. "The truth is as I have told it to you, and truth always rises above a lie as oil above water. *Operibus credite, et non verbis;*[14] let one of you come with me, and he shall see with his own eyes what he will not believe with his ears."

"I am the one who should make that journey," said Sanchica. "Take me with you, sir, on the crupper of your hack; I'll be very glad to go see my father."

"Governors' daughters," replied the page, "do not travel the highways alone, but only when escorted by carriages and litters and a large number of servants."

"In God's name," said Sanchica, "I can go just as well mounted on a she-ass as in a coach! What a dainty creature you must think I am!"

"Be quiet, girl," said Teresa, "you don't know what you are saying. This gentleman is quite right. Different times, different manners.[15] When my husband was Sancho, I was Sancha; and now that he's a governor, I am Señora—I don't know if there is anything in what I am saying or not."

"Señora Teresa is saying more than she realizes," remarked the page; "but give me something to eat and let me be on my way, for I intend to return this evening."

"Your Grace," said the curate, "will partake of my frugal fare;[16] for Señora Teresa is more willing than able when it comes to serving such a guest as you."

The page at first declined, but finally had to yield for the sake of his own well-being; and the curate then gladly bore him off in order that he might question him at length regarding Don Quixote and his exploits. The bachelor offered to write the replies for Teresa to the letters she had received, but she would not have him meddling in her affairs, since she looked upon him as being something of a practical joker. Instead, she gave a cake and a couple of eggs to a young acolyte, who copied out two epistles for her, one addressed to her husband and the other to the duchess, which she herself had composed and which are not the worst to be met with in this great history, as will be seen further on.

CHAPTER LI. *Of the course of Sancho Panza's government, with other entertaining matters of a similar nature.*

DAY dawned following the night on which the governor had made his rounds. That night had been a sleepless one for the butler, his mind being occupied with the beautiful face and general attractiveness of the disguised maiden. As for the major-domo, he had spent the remaining hours until daylight in writing to his lord and lady, giving them an account of all that Sancho had done and said, for he was equally astonished by the governor's actions and by his speech, finding in both an admixture of wisdom and simple-mindedness.

The lord governor finally arose and, on orders of Doctor Pedro Recio, made a breakfast on a bit of pre-

serves and four draughts of cold water, though he would
rather have had a slice of bread and a cluster of grapes.
However, seeing there was no help for it, he made
the best of things, with sorrowing heart and a weary
stomach, Pedro Recio having given him to understand
that a light diet of dainty food was the one best
suited to individuals in positions of command and in
offices entailing grave responsibility where one had need
not so much of bodily strength as of mental faculties.
As a result of this sophistry, Sancho suffered hunger
to such an extent that in his heart he was led to curse
the government and the one who had bestowed it upon
him.

Nevertheless, in spite of his hunger and fortified only
by the preserves he had eaten, he undertook to sit in
judgment that day; and the first matter that came before
him was a problem[1] propounded by a foreigner in the
presence of the major-domo and the other attendants.

"My lord," he began, "there was a large river that
separated two districts of one and the same seignorial
domain—and let your Grace pay attention, for the
matter is an important one and somewhat difficult of
solution. To continue then: Over this river there was a
bridge, and at one end of it stood a gallows with what
resembled a court of justice, where four judges commonly sat to see to the enforcement of a law decreed by
the lord of the river, of the bridge, and of the seignory.
That law was the following: 'Anyone who crosses this
river shall first take oath as to whither he is bound and
why. If he swears to the truth, he shall be permitted to
pass; but if he tells a falsehood, he shall die without
hope of pardon on the gallows that has been set up
there.' Once this law and the rigorous conditions it laid
down had been promulgated, there were many who told
the truth and whom the judges permitted to pass freely

enough. And then it happened that one day, when they came to administer the oath to a certain man, he swore and affirmed that his destination was to die upon the gallows which they had erected and that he had no other purpose in view.

"The judges held a consultation. 'If,' they said, 'we let this man pass, without hindrance, then he has perjured himself and according to the law should be put to death; but he swore that he came to die upon that scaffold, and if we hang him that will have been the truth, and in accordance with the same law he should go free.' And now, my Lord Governor, we should like to have your Grace's opinion as to what the judges should do with the man; for up to now they have been very doubtful and perplexed, and, having heard of your Grace's keen understanding and great intellect, they have sent me to beseech your Grace on their behalf to tell them what you think regarding this intricate and puzzling question."

"Certainly," said Sancho, "those judges who sent you to me might have spared themselves the trouble, for I am a fellow who has in him more of the dull than of the sharp; but, nevertheless, let me hear the case once more and it may be that I'll hit upon something."

The one who had propounded the question then repeated it over and over again.

"It seems to me," said Sancho at last, "that I can settle the matter very shortly. This man swore that he was going to die upon the gallows, and if he does, he swore to the truth and the law says he should be freed and permitted to cross the bridge; but if they do not hang him, he swore falsely and according to the same law ought to be hanged."

"My Lord Governor has stated it correctly," said the messenger; "so far as a complete understanding of the case is concerned, there is no room for any further doubt or questioning."

"Well, then," said Sancho, "my opinion is this: that part of the man that swore to the truth should be permitted to pass and that part of him that lied should be hanged, and thus the letter of the law will be carried out."

"But, my Lord Governor," replied the one who had put the question, "it would be necessary to divide the man into two halves, the lying half and the truthful half, and if he were so divided it would kill him and the law would in no wise be fulfilled, whereas it is essential that its express provisions be carried out."

"See here, my good sir," said Sancho, "either I am a blockhead or this man you speak of deserves to die as much as he deserves to live and cross the bridge; for if the truth saves him, the lie equally condemns him. And this being the case, as indeed it is, it is my opinion that you should go back and tell those gentlemen who sent you to me that, since there is as much reason for acquitting as for condemning him, they ought to let him go free, as it is always more praiseworthy to do good than to do harm. I would give you this decision over my signature if I knew how to sign my name;[2] and in saying what I do I am not speaking on my own account but am remembering one of the many pieces of advice which my master Don Quixote gave me the night before I came here to be governor of this island. When justice was in doubt, he said, I was to lean to the side of mercy; and I thank God that I happened to recollect it just now, for it fits this case as if made for it."

"So it does," agreed the major-domo, "and it is my belief that Lycurgus himself, who gave laws to the Lacedaemonians, could not have handed down a better decision than that which our great Panza has rendered

us. Court is now over for this morning," he added, "and
I will give orders that my Lord Governor be served a
meal that is very much to his taste."

"That is all I ask," said Sancho, "that you be fair
with me. See to it that I eat, and then let it rain cases
and problems and I'll make quick work of them." [3]

The major-domo kept his word, it being against his
conscience to starve to death so wise a governor as this;
and, in any event, he expected to have done with him
that night by playing the final joke upon him in accordance with the instructions of his lord and lady. Accordingly, after Sancho had eaten for once in violation of
all the rules and aphorisms of the Doctor Tirteafuera, as
soon as the cloth had been removed a messenger entered
with a letter from Don Quixote addressed to the governor. Sancho ordered the secretary to cast an eye over
it and, if it contained nothing that should be kept secret,
to read it aloud.

The secretary obeyed. "It may very well be read
aloud," he said after he had glanced at it, "for what
Señor Don Quixote has here written to your Grace
deserves to be engraved in letters of gold. You shall
hear for yourself:

LETTER OF DON QUIXOTE DE LA MANCHA TO
SANCHO PANZA, GOVERNOR OF THE ISLAND
OF BARATARIA

Whereas, friend Sancho, I had expected to hear
news of your indolence and follies, I hear, instead, of
the wisdom you have displayed, and for this I give
special thanks to Heaven, which raises the poor up
from the dunghill [4] and makes wise men out of fools.
They tell me that you govern like a man, but that as
a man you are as humble as any beast of the field. In

this connection, I would have you note, Sancho, that it very often behooves those in positions of authority to resist the natural humility of their hearts, and it is indeed necessary for them to do so; for the attire of one who is in a post of grave responsibility should be comformable to his station and not limited by his own humble tastes. Dress well; a stick properly clothed no longer has the appearance of a stick.[5] By this I do not mean that you should deck yourself out with trinkets and showy raiment, or that, being a judge, you should dress like a soldier; rather, the garb should be suited to the office, provided always that it is neat and well made.

In order to win the good will of the people that you govern, there are two things, among others, that you must do: one is to act in a wellbred manner toward every one (this I have told you before); and the other is to see that there is an abundance of food, since nothing weighs more heavily upon the hearts of the poor than hunger and want.

Do not issue many decrees, and when you do, see to it that they are good ones and, above all, that they are observed and fulfilled, for decrees that are not observed are as none at all but, rather, convey the impression that the prince who had the wisdom and authority requisite for issuing them has not had the power to enforce them, and laws that merely hold a threat without being put into execution are like the log that was king of the frogs:[6] at first he frightened them, but in time they came to despise him and mounted upon him.

Be a father to virtue and a stepfather to vice. Be not always strict nor always lenient but observe a middle course between these two extremes, for therein lies wisdom. Visit the prisons, slaughter houses, and public squares, for the presence of the governor in such places is a matter of great importance: it comforts the prisoners, who hope to be speedily released; it is a bugbear to the butchers, who for once give fair weight; and it terrifies the market women for the same reason. Do not show yourself, even though perchance you may be (and I do not think you are) either covetous, a woman-chaser, or a glutton; for when the people and those with whom you have to deal come to know your weakness, they will train their batteries upon you at that point until they have brought you down to the depths of perdition.

Go over time and again, consider and reconsider, the advice and instructions that I gave you in writing before you set out from here for your government; if you follow these counsels you will find in them a ready aid in those labors and difficulties that governors encounter at every turn. Write to your lord and lady by way of showing them that you are grateful; for ingratitude is the daughter of pride and one of the greatest of known sins, and the person who is ungrateful to his benefactors shows clearly that he would be ungrateful to God as well, who has conferred and continues to confer so many blessings upon him.

My lady the duchess sent a special messenger with your suit and another present to your wife, Teresa Panza, and we are expecting an answer at any moment. I have been a trifle indisposed as the result of a certain scratching that was of no great benefit to my nose, but it was in reality nothing at all. If there are enchanters who mistreat me, there are also those that defend me. Let me know as to whether the major-domo who is with you had anything to do with the business of La Trifaldi as you suspected. Keep me informed of everything that happens to you, since the distance is so short and, moreover, I am thinking of giving up very soon this idle life that I lead here, as I was not born for it. I have been asked to undertake a certain business that may bring me into disfavor with my lord and lady; but although this gives me no little concern, it really means nothing to me, for, when all is said and done, I must fulfill the duties of my profession rather than think of their pleasure, in accordance with the saying, *"Amicus Plato, sed magis amica veritas."* [7] If I quote Latin to you, it is because I assume that since becoming a governor you will have learned it. I commend you to God, and may He keep you from becoming an object of pity to anyone.

Your friend,

DON QUIXOTE DE LA MANCHA.

Sancho listened to the letter very attentively, and it was praised by all who heard it for the wisdom it contained. The governor then rose from the table and, summoning his secretary, shut himself up in his room, for he wished to answer his master Don Quixote without delay. He instructed the secretary to write down what was dictated to him, without adding anything to it or leaving out anything, and the following is the letter that he composed:

I have been so very busy that I have not had time to scratch my head or even trim my nails, which is the reason why I wear them so long, God help me. I tell you this, my dear master, so that your Grace may not be surprised that I have not let you know sooner how well or ill I am making out in this government, where I am suffering more hunger than the two of us did when we roamed the forests and desert places together.

My lord the duke wrote to me the other day, advising me that certain spies had come to my island to assassinate me, but up to now the only one I have discovered is a doctor in this town who is hired to kill all the governors that come here. He is Doctor Pedro Recio, a native of Tirteafuera, and from his name your Grace may judge as to whether or not I have reason to fear dying at his hands. This doctor that I am telling you about says that he himself does not cure diseases when they come but aims to prevent them from coming, and the medicine that he gives you is diet and more diet until he has you down to your bare bones—just as if leanness wasn't worse than fever. The short of it is, he is starving me to death and I'm dying of disappointment; for when I came here as governor, I expected to have my meals hot and my drinks cool and to sleep in comfort between sheets of Holland linen, on feather beds, and instead I find that I have to do penance like a hermit. I do not like it at all, and in the end I imagine the devil will take me.

So far, I have not laid hands on any dues or accepted any bribes,[8] and I do not know what to think of it; for they tell me that the governors who come to this island usually have plenty of money which has been given them or lent them by the people of the town, and I understand that this is the custom not only here but with governors in general.

Last night, in making the rounds, I fell in with a very pretty girl dressed like a boy, in the company of her brother who was in woman's clothes. My butler has fallen in love with the lass and has his mind set on having her for his wife, or so he says, and I have picked the lad for my son-in-law. Today we are going to take the matter up with the father of the pair, who is a certain Diego de la Llana, an old Christian and as fine a gentleman as anyone could wish.

I am in the habit of visiting the market places as your Grace recommends, and yesterday I came upon a huckstress selling hazelnuts and found that she had mixed with a fanega of fresh ones an equal measure of empty, rotten nuts, I confiscated them all for the charity school children, who know well enough how to tell one kind from the other, and sentenced her to stay away from the market place for a couple of weeks. My action was heartily approved; for I may tell your Grace that there is no one in this town with a worse reputation than these market women;[9] they are all said to be bold and shameless creatures without a conscience, and I can well believe it from what I have seen of them in other places.

I am very glad to hear that my lady the duchess has written to my wife, Teresa Panza, and has sent her the present, and I will try to show my gratitude at the proper time. I would have your Grace kiss her hands for me and tell her that she has not thrown me into any sack with a hole in it, as she will see from the outcome. I hope your Grace will not have any quarrel with my lord and lady, for if you fall out with them, it is plain to be seen that it will do me harm. And it would be contrary to the advice you yourself have given me for you to be ungrateful to those who have shown you so many favors and have treated you so royally in their castle.

That business of the scratching I do not understand, but I imagine it must be the work of those wicked enchanters that are always tormenting your

Grace, and I'll hear all about it when we meet again. I'd like to send your Grace some present or other, but I don't know what it would be unless it was some of those very curious clyster pipes to be worked with bladders that they make in this island. However, if my office holds out, I'll try to send you something, one way or another. If my wife, Teresa Panza, should write to me, please pay the postage and send the letter on to me, as I am very anxious to hear how my wife and young ones are doing at home. And so, may God free your Grace from those evil-minded enchanters and see me through with my government, safe and sound—though this I am inclined to doubt, for I think I'll rather leave it and my life behind me at one and the same time, the way Doctor Pedro Recio is treating me.

> Your Grace's servant,
> SANCHO PANZA, THE GOVERNOR.

The secretary sealed the letter and dispatched it by courier at once; and then the practical jokers put their heads together and began planning how they would dispatch Sancho from his governorship. That afternoon was spent by him in drawing up a number of ordinances for the proper administration of what he took to be his island. He decreed that there were to be no peddlers of provisions in the state, and that wine might be imported from any region whatever so long as its place of origin was declared in order that a price might be put upon it according to its reputation for quality and the esteem in which it was held, while anyone who watered wine or put a false name on it was to pay for it with his life. He reduced the cost of all shoes and stockings, but especially of shoes, as it seemed to him that the prices being charged for them were exorbitant. He put a tax on servants' wages, which were out of all proportion to the service rendered.[10] He prescribed an extremely heavy fine for those who sang lewd and lascivious songs, either by night or by day, and ordained that no blind man[11] should go about singing verses having to do with miracles unless he could produce trustworthy evidence that the miracles had actually occurred; for it was his opinion that most of the events that formed the burden of their lays were trumped up, to the detriment of the truly miraculous ones.

He created and appointed a bailiff for the poor, not for the purpose of harassing them but to make an investigation of their real status, since many a thief or drunkard of sound body goes about as a make-believe cripple or displaying false sores. In brief, he ordered things so wisely that to this day his decrees are preserved in that town, under the title of *The Constitutions of the Great Governor, Sancho Panza.*

Meanwhile Don Quixote is beginning to tire of life in the castle, feeling that it is contrary to the order of chivalry that he professes. He is anxious, moreover, to set out for Saragossa, to compete in the tournament there. But just as he is about to ask his hosts for permission to leave, the duenna Doña Rodríguez implores his aid in compelling the youth who has betrayed her daughter to marry the girl. The knight at once issues a challenge, and the duke himself undertakes to arrange the details of the encounter. They are seated at table as all this occurs

From Chapter LII: *[The Correspondence of Teresa Panza.]*

AT THIS point, by way of adding the finishing touch to the meal and bringing it to a pleasant close, lo and behold, that same page who had carried the letters and presents to Teresa Panza, wife of Sancho Panza, the governor, now entered the room. The duke and duchess were very glad to see him, being anxious to hear what had happened to him in the course of his journey; but in response to a question from them he replied that he could not make his report in the presence of so many people or in a few words, and so he suggested that they leave it for another time, when they would be alone, and in the meanwhile amuse themselves by listening to the letters that he had brought back with him. With this, he took out the two letters and handed them to the duchess. One of them bore the superscription: "Letter for My Lady the Duchess So-and-So, of I Don't Know Where," while the other was directed "To My Husband, Sancho Panza, Governor of the Island of Barataria, and May God Prosper Him Longer Than He Does Me."

The duchess's bread would not bake, as the saying goes, until she had read the one that was addressed to her. She opened it and glanced at its contents, and then, seeing that it was proper to do so, she read it aloud for the duke and the others to hear:

TERESA PANZA'S LETTER TO THE DUCHESS

The letter that your Highness wrote me, my lady, gave me great pleasure and was very welcome indeed.

The string of coral beads is very fine, and I can say
the same of my husband's hunting suit. This whole
village is happy to know that you have made my husband, Sancho, a governor, although nobody believes
it, especially the curate, and Master Nicholas the
barber, and Sansón Carrasco the bachelor; but that
makes no difference to me, for so long as it is true,
and I am sure that it is, they may all say what they
like—to tell the truth, I would not have believed it
myself if it had not been for the beads and the suit.
In this town everybody thinks my husband is a numb-
skull, fit only for governing a flock of goats, and cannot imagine what other kind of government he would
be good for. May the Lord's will be done, and may
God direct him in the right path for the best interests
of his children.

I, my dear lady, with your Grace's permission, have
made up my mind to take advantage of this fine day[1]
by coming to court where I may stretch out in a
coach and cause a thousand who are already jealous
of me to burst their eyeballs. And so I beg your
Excellency to order my husband to send me a little
money, and let it be quite a little, for expenses are
heavy at court, with a loaf of bread costing a real
and meat thirty maravedis a pound,[2] which is really
frightful. If he does not want me to come, have him
let me know at once, for my feet are itching to be off.
My women friends and neighbors tell me that if I
and my daughter cut a figure and make a fine show
at court, my husband will come to be better known
on account of me than I will be on account of him.
For, of course, there will be many who will ask, 'Who
are those ladies in that coach yonder?' And one of my
servants will answer, 'The wife and daughter of San-

cho Panza, governor of the island of Barataria.' And that way, people will learn who Sancho is, I'll be well thought of, and to Rome for everything.[3]

I am sorry as sorry can be that this year they have gathered no acorns here, but for all of that I am sending your Highness about half a peck; I myself went to the woods to gather them, one by one, but I couldn't find any that were bigger than these—I only wish they were as big as ostrich eggs.

Don't forget to write to me, your Mightiness,[4] and I will be sure to answer, letting you know how I am and whatever news there is in this village, where I remain, praying Our Lord to keep your Highness and not be unmindful of me. My daughter Sancha and my son[5] kiss your Grace's hands.

She who would rather see your Ladyship than write to you,

Your servant,

TERESA PANZA.

They were all very much pleased with this letter, especially the ducal pair; and the duchess then asked Don Quixote if he thought it would be right to open the one addressed to the governor, as she fancied it must be a very good one. The knight replied that she might do so if it gave her pleasure, and they found that it read as follows:

TERESA PANZA'S LETTER TO SANCHO PANZA, HER HUSBAND

I received your letter, my dear Sancho, and I swear as a Catholic Christian that I was within two fingers' breadth of going mad with joy. Listen, brother, when I heard you were a governor, I was so happy I thought I would drop dead; for you know what they say: that sudden joy can kill you just as well as a great sorrow. As for your daughter, Sanchica, she let her water go from pure delight. There before me was the suit that you sent me and the beads from my lady the duchess, for my neck, and there in my hand were the letters with the messenger standing beside me; and yet, in spite of all that, I fancied that what I saw and touched must be a dream, since who would ever think that a goatherd would come to be governor of islands?

But you know, my dear, what my mother used to say: that you had to live a long time to see a lot. I tell you this because I expect to see more if I live longer. I don't mean to stop until I see you a farmer of revenues or tax collector; for while the devil carries off those that abuse such offices, still they always hold and handle money. My lady the duchess will tell you how anxious I am to come to court; think it over and let me know how you feel about it. I will try to be an honor to you by going in a coach.

The curate, the barber, the bachelor, and even the sacristan cannot believe that you are a governor and say it is all some kind of humbug or enchantment like everything that concerns your master, Don Quixote; and Sansón says they are coming to look for you as they mean to get that government out of your head and the madness out of Don Quixote's noddle, but I only laugh and look at my string of beads and go on planning the dress that I am going to make for our daughter out of your suit. I sent some acorns to my lady the duchess and wish they had been of gold. Send me a few strings of pearls if they have any in that island.

The news of this village is that Berrueca has married off her daughter to a good-for-nothing painter who came here looking for anything that offered. The council gave him an order to paint his Majesty's arms over the door of the town hall. His price was two ducats, which they paid him in advance; he worked for a week and at the end of that time had done nothing, saying that he could not bring himself to paint trifling things of that sort. He paid them back the money but got himself a wife by passing himself off as a good workman. The truth is, he has now laid down the brush and taken up the spade and goes to the field like a gentleman.

Pedro de Lobo's son has taken orders and the tonsure, with the intention of becoming a priest. Minguilla, Mingo Silvato's granddaughter, found it out and is suing him for promise to marry her, and the evil tongues will have it that she is pregnant by him, although he stoutly denies it.

There are no olives this year, nor is there a drop of vinegar to be had in all the town. A company of soldiers passed this way, taking with them three village girls; I would rather not tell you who they are, for it may be they will come back and will not fail to find those who will marry them with all their faults, for better or for worse. Sanchica is making bone-lace[6] and earns eight maravedis[7] a day, clear, which she puts into a money box toward household furnishings; but now that you are a governor, you will give her a dowry without her having to work. The fountain in the public square dried up and lightning struck the pillory (it would suit me if that was where it always hit).

I am waiting for an answer to this letter that I may know what you think about my coming to court. And so, may God give you a longer life than He does me,

or at least as long a one since I would not want to
leave you without me in this world.

Your wife,

TERESA PANZA.

These letters were praised, laughed over, relished and
admired; and then, as if to put the seal on everything, the
courier arrived with the one that Sancho had written to
Don Quixote. This also was read aloud and led them
to doubt that the squire was as simple-minded as they
had taken him to be. The duchess then retired that
she might hear from the page what had happened in
Sancho's village. He gave her a full account, leaving
out no slightest detail, and delivered to her the acorns
together with a cheese which Teresa assured him was
very good, being better than those of Tronchón.[8] The
duchess received it with great pleasure; and we shall
leave her there as we go on to relate how the rule of
the great Sancho Panza, flower and mirror of all island
governors, came to an end.

CHAPTER LIII. *Of the troublous end and conclusion of Sancho Panza's government.*

TO IMAGINE that things in this life are always to
remain as they are is to indulge in an idle dream.
It would appear, rather, that everything moves in a
circle, that is to say, around and around:[1] spring follows
summer, summer the harvest season, harvest autumn,
autumn winter, and winter spring;[2] and thus does time
continue to turn like a never-ceasing wheel. Human life
alone hastens onward to its end, swifter than time's self
and without hope of renewal, unless it be in that other

life that has no bounds. So sayeth Cid Hamete, the Mohammedan philosopher; for many who have lacked the light of faith, being guided solely by the illumination that nature affords them, have yet attained to a comprehension of the swiftness and instability of this present existence and the eternal duration of the one we hope for. Our author, however, is here thinking of the speed with which Sancho's government was overthrown and brought to a close, and, so to speak, sent up in smoke and shadow.

On the night of the seventh day after assuming his governorship Sancho was lying in bed, sated not with bread or with wine but with sitting in judgment, giving opinions, enacting statutes, and issuing decrees. In spite of his hunger, sleep was beginning to close his eyelids when of a sudden he heard a great noise of bells and shouting as if the whole island were sinking. He sat up in bed and strained his ears to see if he could make out what the cause of such an uproar could be, but in vain, for the sound of countless drums and trumpets was now added to the din and he was more bewildered than ever and was filled with fear and trembling. Getting to his feet, he put on a pair of slippers on account of the dampness of the floor but did not stop for a dressing gown or anything of the sort. As he dashed out the door of his room, he saw coming toward him down the corridor more than a score of persons carrying lighted torches and unsheathed swords.

"To arms! To arms, Lord Governor!" they cried. "An enemy host has invaded the island and we are lost unless your wit and valor can save us." And, keeping up the furious din all the while, they came to where Sancho stood, dazed and terrified by what he saw and heard.

"Arm at once, your Lordship," one of them said to

him, "unless you choose to be lost, and the whole island with you."

"What have I to do with arming?" replied Sancho. "Or what do I know about fighting? [3] Better leave such things as that to my master Don Quixote, who will settle everything in the blink of an eye and save us all. Sinner that I am, God help me, I understand nothing about these squabbles."

"Ah! my Lord Governor," said another, "what kind of faintheartedness is this? Arm, your Grace; we bring you arms, both offensive and defensive. Arm, and go out into the public square; be our leader and our captain as is your duty, seeing that you are the governor."

"Arm me, then, for Heaven's sake," said Sancho.

They at once produced two large shields which they had brought with them and put them on him over his shirt, one in front and the other behind, permitting him to don no other garment. Through holes that they had made for the purpose they drew his arms and then proceeded to bind him very firmly with pieces of rope in such a manner as to leave him walled in and boarded up straight as a spindle so that he could not bend his knees or stir a single step. They then handed him a lance, on which he leaned to keep from falling, and when they had him in this condition they bade him lead them on and inspire them all with courage, assuring him that he was their north pole, their lantern, and their morning star who would bring this business to a successful conclusion.

"And how am I going to lead on, unlucky creature that I am," said Sancho, "when these boards that cut into my flesh are bound so tight I can't even move my kneecaps? What you are going to have to do is, pick me up in your arms and set me down, crosswise or on my feet, in some passageway, and I'll guarantee to hold it either with this lance or with my body."

"Come, my Lord Governor," said one of them, "it is fear rather than the boards that keeps you from moving. Have done with it and bestir yourself, for it is late and the enemy's numbers are increasing, the shouting grows louder, and the danger is pressing."

As a result of these exhortations and reproaches the poor governor did his best to move, whereupon he fell down to the floor with such a thud that they thought surely he must have broken himself to pieces. He lay there like a tortoise in its shell, or a side of bacon between two troughs, or a boat lying bottom upward on the beach; nor did the jokers feel any compassion for him as they saw him in that plight, but extinguishing their torches they began shouting louder than ever, renewing the cry "To arms! To arms!" with great vigor as they trampled over poor Sancho, slashing so furiously at the shields that covered him that, if he had not drawn his head in, the luckless governor would have been in a very bad way indeed. As it was, huddled into that narrow space, he sweat and sweat again as he prayed God with all his heart to deliver him from this peril. Some stumbled over him, others fell upon him, and one of them stood upon him for a good while, as if he had been in a watchtower issuing orders to an army.

"Over this way, our men!" he cried in a stentorian voice. "Here's where the enemy is charging in full force! Hold that breach! Close that gate! Block those ladders! [4] Bring on the pitch and resin and the boiling oil! Barricade the streets with feather beds!" In brief, he shouted most ardently for every variety of engine, implement, or contrivance that is used in war and in defending a city against an assault.

As he heard and suffered all this, Sancho, thoroughly

mauled and trampled, said to himself, "Oh, if it would only please the Lord to let them go ahead and take this island and let me die or else free me from this torment!" Heaven granted his prayer, and when he least expected it there came a cry, "Victory! Victory! The enemy is beaten and is falling back! Ho, my Lord Governor, rise! Come and rejoice with us and divide the spoils won by the might of that invincible arm."

"Lift me up," said the sorely battered Sancho in a sickly voice. And when they had helped him to his feet, he went on, "The enemy that I have conquered you can nail to my forehead. I don't want to divide any spoils. All I ask is that some friend of mine, if I have any, give me a drink of wine, for I am parched; and let him wipe the sweat from me, as I am dripping wet."

They wiped him off and brought him some wine, unbound the shields, and seated him upon the bed, and then he promptly fainted away as a result of all the fear and excitement and the harsh treatment he had undergone. Those who had perpetrated the joke were now sorry that they had carried it so far and they were relieved when Sancho came to himself again. He asked what time it was and was informed that it was already daylight; and then, without saying another word, he started dressing himself amid a profound silence as they all watched and waited to see why he should be in such a hurry to put his clothes on. At length, when he was fully clad, he little by little (for he was too stiff and sore to walk fast) made his way out to the stable, followed by all those present; and there he went up to the gray, embraced it, and gave it a kiss on the forehead, not without tears in his eyes.

"Come, comrade and friend," he said, "partner in all my troubles and hardships. When I was with you, I had no other care than that of mending your harness and feeding that little carcass of yours. Those for me were the happy hours, days, and years; but since leaving you and mounting the towers of ambition and pride, a thousand troubles, a thousand torments, and four thousand worries have entered my soul."

Even as he said this he was adjusting the packsaddle, without a word from any of the bystanders. He then with great pain and difficulty climbed up onto the gray's back and, addressing the major-domo, the secretary, the butler, Doctor Pedro Recio, and all the others, he spoke as follows:

"Clear the way, gentlemen, and let me go back to my old freedom. Let me go look for my past life so that I may be resurrected from this present death. I was not born to be a governor or to defend islands and cities from enemies that would attack them. I know more about plowing and digging and pruning vines than I do about laws or the protection of islands and kingdoms. St. Peter is well enough off in Rome;[5] by which I mean that each one should follow the trade to which he was born. In my hand a sickle is better than a governor's scepter. I'd rather have my fill of *gazpacho*[6] than have to put up with a miserable, meddling doctor who kills me with hunger. I'd rather stretch out in the shade of an oak in summer and in winter wrap myself in a double sheepskin jacket and enjoy my freedom than go to bed between sheets of Holland linen and dress myself in sables and be no freer than a governor is.

"And so, your Worships, God be with you. Tell my lord the duke that naked was I born and naked I find myself, and so I neither win nor lose. By this I mean that I came into this government without a penny and I leave it without one, which is just the opposite of what generally happens with the governors of other islands. Fall back, then, and let me pass; I must get myself poulticed, for I think that all my ribs are smashed, thanks to the enemies that trampled me last night."

"You must not do that, my Lord Governor," said Doctor Recio. "I will give your Grace a potion that will soon make you as sound and vigorous as ever; and as for your meals, I promise your Grace to do better, by permitting you to eat abundantly of anything you desire."

"You speak too late," said Sancho. "I'd as soon turn Turk as stay here. These jokes won't do a second time. By God, I would no more keep this government or take another, even though they handed it to me between two platters, than I would fly to Heaven without wings. I come of Panza stock, and they are a stubborn lot; if they say odds, then odds it must be even though it may be evens, and this in spite of all the world. In this stable I leave behind me the ant's wings[7] that lifted me in the air so that the swifts and other birds might eat me; let's come back to earth and walk with our feet once more, and if they're not shod in pinked Cordovan leather, they'll not lack coarse hempen sandals. Every ewe to her mate, and let no one stretch his leg beyond the sheet.[8] And so, once again, let me pass, for it is growing late."

To this the major-domo replied, "My Lord Governor, we will gladly permit your Grace to leave, even though it grieves us very much to lose you, as your wit and Christian conduct have endeared you to us. But it is a well-known fact that every governor, before he departs from the place where he has been governing, must first render an accounting, and your Grace should do the same for the ten days[9] that you have been in office, and then you may go and the peace of God go with you."

"No one," said Sancho, "can demand that of me, unless it is someone that my lord the duke has appointed, and I am on my way now to see the duke and will give him an exact account. And, in any case, seeing that I leave here naked, there is no other proof needed to show that I have governed like an angel."

"By God, if the great Sancho isn't right!" exclaimed Doctor Recio. "I am of the opinion that we should let him go, for the duke will be delighted to see him."

They all agreed to this and allowed Sancho to depart, having first offered to provide him with company and anything that he needed in the way of comfort or conveniences for the journey. He replied that all he wanted was a little barley for his gray and half a cheese and half a loaf of bread for himself, adding that since the distance was so short there was no necessity for him to carry any more or better provisions than that. They all embraced him then, and he, weeping, embraced them all in turn after which he rode away, leaving them filled with admiration at the words he had spoken and at the firmness and wisdom of his resolve.

On his way back from his "island" to the duke's castle, Sancho falls in with a company of alms-begging pilgrims and is recognized by one of them, who turns out to be a neighbor, Ricote by name, a Moorish shopkeeper of the village. Ricote and his wife and daughter have been forced to flee from Spain as a result of the royal decrees banishing all those of Moorish extraction from the realm. Upon his friend's bidding, Sancho shares the pilgrims' lunch and wine flask and Ricote proceeds to tell his story.

The gist of it is that he has come back to get a gold hoard which he has left buried outside the village, and he urges Sancho to come with him and help him retrieve it, offering him as an inducement two hundred pounds, but the disillusioned "governor" will have none of it. Sancho tells Ricote of his "island" and the Moor is incredulous. Ricote then goes on to relate the manner in which his family had taken their departure (the husband and father had gone on before to seek a dwelling place for them in Germany), and he stresses the love that Pedro Gregorio, a wealthy Christian youth, has for the daughter (Chapter LIV).

As a result of having spent so much time with Ricote, Sancho fails to reach the duke's castle by nightfall and in the darkness he and his gray tumble into a deep pit. His cries for help go unanswered, but the next morning they chance to be heard by Don Quixote, who is out for a gallop on Rocinante in preparation for the combat that is to come. The knight returns to the castle and informs the duke and duchess of his squire's plight, and with the aid of rope and tackle Sancho is rescued.

The account of his government that Sancho gives the duke is a high point of the story and shows how his character has developed as a result of this mock taste of power, how he has grown in wisdom, and how he and his master have grown into each other.

FROM CHAPTER LV: *Of the things that happened to Sancho. . . .*

SEEING Sancho emerge in such a manner, a student remarked, "That is the way all bad governors ought to leave their governments: like this sinner who comes forth from the depths of the abyss, dead of hunger, pale-faced, and, I'll wager, without a penny to his name."

Sancho overheard him and replied, "It was eight or ten days ago, brother backbiter, that I came to govern the island which they had given me, and not for one hour of that time did I have my fill of bread; the doctors persecuted me and enemies broke my bones and I had no chance to take bribes or collect my dues; and this being so, as indeed it is, I can't see that I deserve to come out in this fashion; but man proposes and God disposes, and different times different manners; let no one say 'I won't drink of this water,' [1] for where you think there is bacon there are no pegs; God knows what I mean and I say no more, though I could if I wanted to."

"Do not be angry at what you hear, Sancho, and do not let it trouble you," said Don Quixote, "for if you do, there will be no end of it. See that your conscience is clear and let them say what they like, since to endeavor to bind the tongues of slanderers is like trying to put doors to the open country. If a governor leaves his office a rich man, they say that he has been a thief; and if he comes out a poor man, they brand him as worthless and a fool."

"Well, this time," replied Sancho, "they'll surely have to set me down as a fool rather than a thief."

Conversing in this manner and surrounded by a crowd of small boys and other people, they reached the castle, where the duke and duchess were waiting for them. Sancho, however, was unwilling to go up and meet the duke until he first had stabled his gray, which, as he remarked, had spent a very bad night. When this had been attended to, he mounted the stairs and knelt before my lord and lady.

"Because," he said, "it was your Highnesses' pleasure and not on account of any merits of my own, I went to govern your island of Barataria. I was naked when I entered upon my government and naked I find myself now, and so I neither lose nor gain. As to whether I governed well or ill, I had witnesses who will say what they will. I answered questions, solved problems, and decided cases at law, and all the while I was dying of hunger to please Doctor Pedro Recio, native of Tirteafuera, doctor to the island and its governor. Enemies fell upon us by night and we were very hard pressed, but the islanders say that it was due to the might of my arm that they came out of it free and victorious, and may God give them health to the extent that they are telling the truth.

"The short of it is that during this time I had a chance to try out the burdens and responsibilities of governing and I find that, by my reckoning, my shoulders cannot bear the weight; it is no load for these ribs of mine, and these are no arrows for my quiver. And so, before the government threw me over, I decided to throw over the government; and yesterday morning I left the island as I found it, with the same streets, houses, and roofs that it had when I came. I asked no one for a loan nor did I try to make any money out of my office; and although I had it in mind to make a few laws, I made none,[2] since I was afraid they would not be kept and then it would be all the same whether I made them or not.

"I left the island, as I have said, with only my gray for company. I fell into a pit but kept on going until, this morning, by the light of the sun, I saw an outlet. It was not so easy to get out of it though, and if Heaven had not sent my master Don Quixote to me, I'd have been there until the end of the world. And so, my lord and lady, the Duke and Duchess, your governor, Sancho Panza, who stands before you here, in the ten days, no more, that he has held the governorship, has come to learn that he would not give anything whatever to rule, not alone an island, but the entire world. Now that I've made this clear, I kiss your Highnesses' feet; and like the small lads who say 'Leap and let me have it,'[3] I give a leap out of my government and pass over to the service of my master Don Quixote; for with him, even though I eat my bread with fear and trembling, at least I get my fill, and in that case it's all the same to me whether it be of carrots or of partridges."

With this, Sancho brought his long speech to a close. Don Quixote had feared that his squire would utter all kinds of nonsense, and when he heard him finish as sensibly as this he gave thanks to Heaven from the bottom of his heart. The duke then embraced Sancho, expressing his regret that the governor had quitted his post so soon and adding that he would provide him with another, there on his estate, that carried with it less responsibility and would prove more profitable. The duchess did the same and gave orders that he be looked after, as he appeared to be suffering from the bruises he had received.

The Last Adventures

(CHAPTERS LVI-LXXIV)

Chapter LVI *is devoted to a description of the encounter between Don Quixote and the young man who is supposed to be the betrayer of Doña Rodríguez' daughter but who in reality is one of the duke's lackeys, named Tosilos, who has been put up to play the part. The understanding is that if Don Quixote wins, his opponent is to marry the young woman. Tosilos has been given orders by the duke to see to it that the knight is not slain; moreover, as soon as he lays eyes upon the lady whose honor is at stake, he falls in love with her and makes up his mind to yield without resistance. The duke is angry at this, but Don Quixote explains it all as the effect of enchantment. The duke has the youth confined for a week or two, under pretense of seeing if he will return to his former shape.*

In Chapter LVII Don Quixote and Sancho at last take leave of their hosts, the parting ceremony being interrupted by the "woebegone" Altisidora, with a lament the theme of which is the knight's hardheartedness in matters of love. In the course of her song she accuses Don Quixote of stealing three kerchiefs and a pair of garters from her, which he with great dignity denies, though Sancho confesses to having the kerchiefs, while the garters are found to be on Altisidora's legs.

After leaving the castle (Chapter LVIII), the knight and his squire ride along until they catch sight of a group of workmen eating their lunch in a meadow beside a number of objects covered with white sheets. The objects in question prove to be images of various saints, designed for use in an altarpiece, and this affords Don Quixote an opportunity to deliver a lecture on the respective virtues of St. George, St. Martin, and San Diego the Moor-slayer. Sancho changes the subject by referring to Altisidora, expressing astonishment that she should have fallen in love with one so utterly lacking in physical charms as his master, a remark that leads Don Quixote to give a brief exposition on the "two kinds of beauty": that of the body and that of the soul.

As they ride on, they find themselves entangled in some nets of green cord strung between the trees. The knight is about to burst through them when two young women dressed as shepherdesses appear before him. They explain that a number of persons from a nearby village have come to the spot to set up "a new pastoral Arcadia" and have already erected some field tents in a wood along the edge of a brook. They invite him to join them, and he accepts. The beaters then begin starting the game, for the nets have been set up to catch *birds. After that, they spread a feast at which the knight is an honored guest and indulges in his customary flowery speech-making.*

He announces that he intends to stand for two whole days in the middle of the Saragossa highway and challenge all comers, forcing them to admit that these ladies disguised as shepherd lasses are the most beautiful and courteous of any in the world. They do their best to dissuade him, but to no avail. As a consequence, when he tries to halt a number of men on horseback who are taking a drove of cattle to market, both he and Sancho and their mounts are knocked down and trampled by the herd. Don Quixote is so shamefaced over this that he does not even turn to say farewell to the Arcadians and rides away in a dejected mood.

That evening they stop at an inn (Chapter LIX), where, as he is having a supper in his room, Don Quixote hears two guests on the other side of the partition discussing a book that purports to be a sequel to Part I of the knight's adventures. (This is, of course, the work by Avellaneda.) When a remark is made to the effect that the book depicts Don Quixote as no longer in love with Dulcinea del Toboso, he can restrain himself no longer, bursts into the other room, and reveals his identity. There follows a conversation in which all present, including Sancho, take part, in belaboring the Avellaneda volume. Don Quixote refuses to read it, characterizing it as "lewd and obscene"; and since the author of the sequel has his hero going to Saragossa to take part in a tournament, the real Knight of La Mancha declares that he will go to Barcelona instead.

They set out for that city the next morning (Chapter LX) and for a week meet with no adventures. One night, as they are resting in a dense grove, Don Quixote falls to thinking of how lax Sancho is about inflicting upon *himself the lashes that are to disenchant Dulcinea, and he resolves to take the matter in hand by administering them himself with Rocinante's reins; but as he goes to undo Sancho's breeches the squire awakens and they have a tussle. Sancho downs his master and will not let him up until he promises to forget about the flogging.*

Shortly afterward they discover round about them the bodies of a number of outlaws or highwaymen that have been strung up to the boughs; and as morning dawns they find themselves surrounded by more than forty living bandits, who proceed to search the saddlebags and Sancho's valise, taking everything they find (Sancho's crowns escape, however, as he carries them in his girdle). Then the leader or captain of the band appears on the scene. He orders his men to desist at once, and they obey. The captain introduces himself as Roque Guinart, the famous Catalan bandit chief. When Don Quixote begins talking about knight-erranty, Roque, who has heard of his exploits, recognizes him immediately and assures him he need have no fear.

At this moment a handsomely attired horseman comes riding up furiously. The rider, who is armed with a fowling piece and a brace of pistols, turns out to be a a greatly agitated young woman who, upon hearing her betrothed was to wed another, has, in a fit of jealousy, shot and gravely wounded him. She has come to Roque to implore him to help her escape to France. He suggests that they first go see if the wounded man is dead; Don Quixote, meanwhile, proffers his aid as a knight. After commanding his men to return the property taken from Sancho and the gray, the captain gallops to the spot where the shooting occurred, accompanied by the young woman. There they discover that her lover is dying, and as she kneels beside him he reveals to her that it was all a tragic mistake. She is grief-stricken and, declining Roque's escort, rides off to enter a convent.

Upon returning to the wood, the captain finds Don Quixote mounted on Rocinante and engaged in making a speech to the bandits with the object of inducing them to give up their mode of life. Roque then makes an appraisal of the loot in the form of money, jewels, and clothing which his men have brought in and divides it equably among them, leading Sancho to observe that "justice is so good a thing that even robbers find it necessary." A sentinel having reported that travelers are approaching along the highway, the chieftain orders that they be brought into his presence.

In the meanwhile he and Don Quixote have a conversation regarding the life of a bandit. Roque states that the motive in his case is a desire for vengeance, and he adds that the objects of his vengeance have "come to be linked together in such a manner that I have taken upon myself not merely my own wrongs but those of others as well"; he ends by expressing the hope that he will find moral salvation in the end. Don Quixote thereupon preaches a short sermon on the subject of repentance and urges Roque to accompany him and learn to be a knight-errant. Roque laughs at the suggestion.

By this time the men have returned with a numerous company of travelers, including two infantry captains, the wife of the president of the vicarial court of Naples and her train, and two pilgrims journeying on foot. After ascertaining the amount of money they have among them, Roque "borrows" a comparatively small sum from the officers and the lady, bestows ten crowns on the pilgrims and ten on Sancho, and lets the captives go their way. They are exceedingly grateful to him, but one of his men objects to such generosity, only to have his skull laid open with a stroke of Roque's sword.

The bandit leader goes off to one side and writes *a*

letter to a friend of his in Barcelona, announcing his intention of setting Don Quixote down on the beach of that city four days from then. The knight will be clad in full armor and accompanied by Sancho on his gray, which should afford the townspeople no end of merriment. The letter is dispatched by one of Roque's followers disguised as a peasant.

This plan is carried out (Chapter LXI). Don Quixote and Sancho are left on the beach during the night of St. John's Eve. As the sun comes up, they have their first view of the sea, and almost immediately a group of liveried horsemen ride out to meet them with "cheers, cries, and Moorish war whoops." One of the gentlemen delivers a speech in the true style of chivalry, and Don Quixote replies; after this they all close in about the knight, and he makes a triumphal entry into the town as a huge crowd looks on. Some of the urchins insert bunches of furze under the tails of Rocinante and the ass, causing the animals to leap and rear and toss their riders to the ground. But the knight and his squire mount again and, accompanied still by music and cheers, are escorted to the home of the wealthy gentleman who is to be their host.

Don Antonio Moreno entertains his guest with all the honors due a knight-errant (Chapter LXII), and Don Quixote is greatly flattered, while Sancho's witticisms keep the entire household amused. Don Antonio and the knight go for a ride through the town; and without his knowing it, a placard is pinned on Don Quixote's back, proclaiming who he is. Once again there is an applauding multitude, and when one of the crowd expresses disapproval of such an exhibition, Don Antonio sends him about his business. "Señor Don Quixote is quite sane, and we who are with him are not fools."

That evening there is a ball, and two mischievous

*ladies insist on dancing with Don Quixote until they
wear him out completely and he is compelled to sit
down in the middle of the ballroom floor. Sancho has to
carry him off to bed.*

*The next day Don Antonio shows his guest a mysteri-
ous "talking head," which is supposed to answer questions that are put to it. It is, of course, a trick device. Don
Quixote is taken in by it, but Sancho has his doubts.*

FROM CHAPTER LXII: *Which deals with . . .
things that cannot be left untold.*

IN THE meantime, Don Quixote wished to go out for
a quiet stroll, for he feared that if he went on horseback the small boys would follow him, and so, accompanied only by Sancho and a couple of servants that
Don Antonio had furnished him, he set out with this
object in view.

As he was going down a certain street he glanced up
and saw a sign in large letters over a doorway, reading:
"BOOKS PRINTED HERE." This pleased him very much, as
he had never seen a printing shop up to that time and
had a desire to find out what it was like.[1] Going inside
with all his retinue, he saw them drawing proofs here,
correcting them there, setting type in one place and
making revisions in another—in short, he beheld everything that goes to make up a large establishment of this
sort. Going up to one of the cases, he inquired what was
being done there, the workmen explained things for him,
and, wondering at what he had observed, he passed on.
He put the same question to another printer, and the
man replied, "Sir, this gentleman here"—and he pointed
to an impressive individual with a rather grave look on
his face—"has translated a Tuscan book into our Cas-

tilian tongue, and I am now engaged in setting the type for it."

"What is the title of the book?" asked Don Quixote.

It was the author[2] who answered. "Sir," he said, "this work in Tuscan is called *Le Bagatelle*." [3]

"And what does *Le Bagatelle* mean in Castilian?"

"*Le Bagatelle*," replied the author, "is equivalent to *los juguetes* in Spanish; and although the title is a humble-sounding one, this book contains much meat and substance."

"I," said Don Quixote, "am somewhat acquainted with Tuscan and pride myself on being able to recite certain stanzas of Ariosto.[4] But tell me, my dear sir, and I ask this not to test your Grace's ability but merely out of curiosity, in the course of your labors have you come upon such a word as *pignatta?*" [5]

"Yes, many times," was the answer.

"And how does your Grace render it into Castilian?"

"How should I render it except by *olla?*" [6]

"Body of me!" exclaimed Don Quixote, "how far advanced your Grace is in the Italian language! I will lay you a good wager that you translate *piace* as *place*, *più* as *más*, *su* as *arriba*, and *giù* as *abajo*." [7]

"I do indeed," said the author, "for those are the proper equivalents."

"And I would venture to take an oath," Don Quixote went on, "that your Grace is not known to the world at large, which always is chary of rewarding men of exceptional ability and works deserving of praise. How many talents have been lost in that way, how many geniuses have been tossed into the corner, how much of real worth has gone unappreciated! But, for all of that, it appears to me that translating from one language into another, unless it be from one of those two queenly tongues, Greek and Latin, is like gazing at a Flemish tapestry with the wrong side out:[8] even though the figures are visible, they are full of threads that obscure the view and are not bright and smooth as when seen from the other side. Moreover, translating from easy languages does not call for either wit or eloquence, any more than does the mere transcription or copying of a document.

"By this," the knight continued, "I do not mean to imply that the task of translating is not a laudable occupation, for a man might employ his time less worthily and with less profit to himself. I make an exception here of those two famous translators: Doctor Cristóbal de Figueroa in his *Pastor Fido* and Don Juan de Jáuregui in his *Aminta*,[9] where happily one may doubt as to which is the translation and which the original. But, your Grace, I should like to know, is this book being printed at your own expense or have you already disposed of the rights to some bookseller?"

"I pay for the printing," said the author, "and I expect to clear at least a thousand ducats[10] on this first edition of two thousand copies, which at two reales apiece ought to sell in no time at all."

"That," said Don Quixote, "is a fine bit of calculation on your Grace's part, but it is plain to be seen that you are not familiar with the ins and outs of the printers and the way in which they all work together.[11] I can promise you that when you find yourself weighted down with two thousand copies,[12] you will be astonished how your body will ache all over, especially if the book happens to be a little out of the ordinary and does not make spicy reading."

"But what would your Grace have me do? Give it to a bookseller who will pay me three maravedis for the rights and think that he is doing me a favor? I do not have books printed to win fame in this world, for I am already well known through my works; it is money that I seek, for without it a fine reputation is not worth a cent."

"Well, good luck and God help you," said Don Quixote; and with this he moved on to another case, where he perceived that they were correcting the proofs of a book entitled *Light of the Soul*.[13]

"These," he said, "are the books that ought to be printed, even though there are many of the sort, for many are the sinners these days, and an infinite number of lights are required for all those that are in darkness."

Going up to another case, he saw that here, too, they were correcting a book, and when he asked the title he was told that it was the *Second Part of the Ingenious Gentleman, Don Quixote de la Mancha,* composed by a certain native of Tordesillas.[14]

"I have heard of this work," he said, "and, in all truth and upon my conscience, I think it ought to be burned to ashes as a piece of impertinence; but Martinmas will come for it as it does for every pig.[15] Fictional tales are better and more enjoyable the nearer they approach the truth or the semblance of the truth, and as for true stories, the best are those that are most true."

Saying this, he stalked out of the printing shop with signs of considerable displeasure.

In the afternoon of the same day (Chapter LXIII) *Don Quixote and Sancho are taken by their host to visit the galleys lying in the harbor. The commander of the fleet, who is called the general, is a friend of Don Antonio's and does the honors in gallant style. Sancho, however, at once meets with a disconcerting experience when, as a prearranged jest, he is seized by members of the crew and sent flying from one lusty pair of arms to another until he has made the entire circuit of the boat and is set down in the poop once more, bruised and breathless, sweating all over, and unable to imagine what has happened to him.*

The knight and squire are vastly astonished by what they see (Sancho even thinks that the oars are the boat's feet) and are not a little frightened by all the noise and clatter as the craft gets under way. Within a short while word comes that a corsair brigantine from Algiers has been sighted, and the fleet prepares to give chase. The brigantine makes an effort to escape but is speedily overtaken and captured. Meanwhile two drunken Turks on the fleeing vessel have discharged their muskets and killed two Spanish soldiers, which leads the general to swear that he will not leave a man of them alive.

Returning to the beach with his prize, the general anchors close to shore in order that the viceroy may come aboard. At the same time he orders the yardarm let down in order that the captain and the rest of the prisoners, about thirty-six in all, may be hanged. The captain is an extremely handsome, gallant-looking youth who appears to be less than twenty years of age. When questioned as to his identity, he astonishes them all by replying that he is a Christian woman. The girl disguised as a ship's captain then offers to tell her life story, and they consent to listen.

It appears that she is a Moorish maiden who has been converted to the Catholic faith. Her affections have been won by Don Gaspar Gregorio, son and heir of the lord of a neighboring village. When the royal decree banishing the Moors from the realm was proclaimed, her father went at once to look for some place of refuge in a foreign land, leaving behind him a buried hoard of gold and precious stones. Obeying his instructions not to touch this treasure, she accompanied her relatives to Barbary and settled in Algiers. Don Gregorio went with

*her, having formed the habit of mingling with the
Moors.*

*Hearing of her wealth and beauty, the king of the
country summoned her, and she begged his permission
to return for the money and jewels by way of ransom for
herself and the others. But the king learned that she was
accompanied by a handsome youth (Don Gregorio), and
his lascivious passions were at once aroused—"for among
those barbarous Turks a handsome boy or youth is more
highly esteemed than the most beautiful of women."
Fearing for her lover's safety, she disguised him as a
Moorish woman and in that garb conducted him before
the ruler, who promptly announced his intention of
keeping the "girl" as a present for the Grand Seignior
and ordered that "she" be taken to a house where the
leading Moorish ladies resided.*

*In accordance with the king's arrangements, the one
now dressed as a captain had set out in a brigantine for
Spain, in the company of a Spanish renegade and with
a crew of Moors and Turks. It was understood that she
and the renegade were to be landed in Christian attire
as soon as they touched Spanish soil; but the Turks had
proved treacherous, had insisted on skirting the coast to
see if they could capture some prize, and as a result they
had all been captured by the general and his galleys.*

*With this the "captain" concludes her story, express-
ing as she does so a fear for Don Gregorio, whose life is
in danger. All she asks for herself is that she be permitted to die like a Christian woman. They are deeply
moved by her tale, and the viceroy himself undoes the
rope that binds her. In the meantime an aged pilgrim
who has come aboard with the viceroy's train runs forward and throws himself at the girl's feet, addressing her
as "Ana Felix, my unhappy daughter!" This is none*

other than Ricote, the Moor whom Sancho had en-
countered on the day he left his government, who has
returned from Germany in pilgrim's guise to recover his
treasure and search for his daughter. Now that he has
found her, he begs the general for mercy.

Sancho speaks up to vouch for the truth of what
Ricote is saying, and the general relents: "Your tears
have prevented me from carrying out my oath." Even
the two Turks are pardoned on the viceroy's urging,
since "their actions savored more of madness than of
defiance." They then begin laying plans for Don Gre-
gorio's rescue, and Don Antonio Moreno takes the
Morisco maid and her father home with him, the viceroy
charging him to show them all the hospitality in his
power.

Distrustful of the plan that has been formed to send
the renegade back to Algiers in a small craft manned
by Christian rowers, Don Quixote (Chapter LXIV)
insists that he himself should do the rescuing, let them
but set him down on the coast of Barbary with his arms
and steed. They succeed in talking him out of this.

FROM CHAPTER LXIV: *Which treats of the adven-*
ture that caused Don Quixote the most sorrow of all
those that have thus far befallen him.

AND then, one morning, as Don Quixote went for a
ride along the beach, clad in full armor—for, as
he was fond of saying, that was his only ornament, his
only rest the fight,[1] and, accordingly, he was never without it for a moment—he saw approaching him a horseman similarly arrayed from head to foot and with a
brightly shining moon blazoned upon his shield.

As soon as he had come within earshot the stranger

cried out to Don Quixote in a loud voice, "O illustrious knight, the never to be sufficiently praised Don Quixote de la Mancha, I am the Knight of the White Moon, whose incomparable exploits you will perhaps recall. I come to contend with you and try the might of my arm, with the purpose of having you acknowledge and confess that my lady, whoever she may be, is beyond comparison more beautiful than your own Dulcinea del Toboso. If you will admit the truth of this fully and freely, you will escape death and I shall be spared the trouble of inflicting it upon you. On the other hand, if you choose to fight and I should overcome you, I ask no other satisfaction than that, laying down your arms and seeking no further adventures, you retire to your own village for the space of a year, during which time you are not to lay hand to sword but are to dwell peacefully and tranquilly, enjoying a beneficial rest that shall redound to the betterment of your worldly fortunes and the salvation of your soul. But if you are the victor, then my head shall be at your disposal, my arms and steed shall be the spoils, and the fame of my exploits shall go to increase your own renown. Consider well which is the better course and let me have your answer at once, for today is all the time I have for the dispatching of this business."

Don Quixote was amazed at the knight's arrogance as well as at the nature of the challenge, but it was with a calm and stern demeanor that he replied to him.

"Knight of the White Moon," he said, "of whose exploits up to now I have never heard, I will venture to take an oath that you have not once laid eyes upon the illustrious Dulcinea; for I am quite certain that if you had beheld her you would not be staking your all upon such an issue, since the sight of her would have convinced you that there never has been, and never can be, any beauty to compare with hers. I do not say that you lie, I simply say that you are mistaken; and so I accept your challenge with the conditions you have laid down, and at once, before this day you have fixed upon shall have ended. The only exception I make is with regard to the fame of your deeds being added to my renown, since I do not know what the character of your exploits has been and am quite content with my own, such as they are. Take, then, whichever side of the field you like, and I will take up my position, and may St. Peter bless what God may give." [2]

Now, as it happened, the Knight of the White Moon was seen by some of the townspeople, who informed the viceroy that he was there, talking to Don Quixote de la Mancha. Believing this to be a new adventure arranged by Don Antonio Moreno or some other gentleman of the place, the viceroy at once hastened down to the beach, accompanied by a large retinue, including Don Antonio, and they arrived just as Don Quixote was wheeling Rocinante to measure off the necessary stretch of field. When the viceroy perceived that they were about to engage in combat, he at once interposed and inquired of them what it was that impelled them thus to do battle all of a sudden.

The Knight of the White Moon replied that it was a matter of beauty and precedence and briefly repeated what he had said to Don Quixote, explaining the terms to which both parties had agreed. The viceroy then went up to Don Antonio and asked him if he knew any such knight as this or if it was some joke that they were playing, but the answer that he received left him more puzzled than ever; for Don Antonio did not know who the knight was, nor could he say as to whether this was a real encounter or not. The viceroy, accordingly, was doubtful about letting them proceed, but inasmuch as he could not bring himself to believe that it was anything more than a jest, he withdrew to one side, saying, "Sir Knights, if there is nothing for it but to confess[3] or die, and if Señor Don Quixote's mind is made up and your Grace, the Knight of the White Moon, is even more firmly resolved, then fall to it in the name of God and may He bestow the victory."

The Knight of the White Moon thanked the viceroy most courteously and in well-chosen words for the permission which had been granted them, and Don Quixote did the same, whereupon the latter, commending himself with all his heart to Heaven and to his lady Dulcinea, as was his custom at the beginning of a fray, fell back a little farther down the field as he saw his adversary doing the same. And then, without blare of trumpet or other warlike instrument to give them the signal for the attack, both at the same instant wheeled their steeds about and returned for the charge. Being mounted upon the swifter horse, the Knight of the White Moon met Don Quixote two-thirds of the way and with such tremendous force that, without touching his opponent with his lance (which, it seemed, he deliberately held aloft) he brought both Rocinante and his rider to the ground in an exceedingly perilous fall. At once the victor leaped down and placed his lance at Don Quixote's visor.

"You are vanquished, O knight! Nay, more, you are dead unless you make confession in accordance with the conditions governing our encounter."

Stunned and battered, Don Quixote did not so much as raise his visor but in a faint, wan voice, as if speaking from the grave, he said, "Dulcinea del Toboso is the most beautiful woman in the world and I the most unhappy knight upon the face of this earth. It is not right that my weakness should serve to defraud the truth.

Drive home your lance, O knight, and take my life since
you already have deprived me of my honor."

"That I most certainly shall not do," said the one of
the White Moon. "Let the fame of my lady Dulcinea
del Toboso's beauty live on undiminished. As for me, I
shall be content if the great Don Quixote will retire to
his village for a year or until such a time as I may
specify, as was agreed upon between us before joining
battle."

The viceroy, Don Antonio, and all the many others
who were present heard this, and they also heard Don
Quixote's response, which was to the effect that, seeing
nothing was asked of him that was prejudicial to Dulcinea, he would fulfill all the other conditions like a true
and punctilious knight. The one of the White Moon
thereupon turned and with a bow to the viceroy rode
back to the city at a mild canter. The viceroy promptly
dispatched Don Antonio to follow him and make every
effort to find out who he was; and, in the meanwhile,
they lifted Don Quixote up and uncovered his face,
which held no sign of color and was bathed in perspiration. Rocinante, however, was in so sorry a state that
he was unable to stir for the present.

Brokenhearted over the turn that events had taken,
Sancho did not know what to say or do. It seemed to
him that all this was something that was happening in a
dream and that everything was the result of magic. He
saw his master surrender, heard him consent not to
take up arms again for a year to come as the light of his
glorious exploits faded into darkness. At the same time
his own hopes, based upon the fresh promises that had
been made him, were whirled away like smoke before
the wind. He feared that Rocinante was maimed for life,
his master's bones permanently dislocated—it would

have been a bit of luck if his madness also had been jolted out of him.[4]

Finally, in a hand litter which the viceroy had them bring, they bore the knight back to town. The viceroy himself then returned, for he was very anxious to ascertain who the Knight of the White Moon was who had left Don Quixote in so lamentable a condition.

Don Antonio Moreno follows the Knight of the White Moon to the inn (Chapter LXV) *and will not give up until he has found out who the stranger is. Don Quixote's conqueror is none other than the bachelor Sansón Carrasco, onetime Knight of the Mirrors, who has finally succeeded in compelling his fellow townsman to give up knight-errantry and return home. Don Antonio reproaches him for having deprived the world of "its most charming madman" but promises not to betray the secret. He doubts that Don Quixote can ever be cured, but the bachelor takes a more optimistic view.*

"Sad and dejected, moody and ill-tempered," Don Quixote goes to bed and stays there for six days. Sancho does his best to console him. The knight insists that, when his period of retirement and seclusion is ended, he will return to his "honorable profession."

At this point Don Antonio enters the room and announces that the renegade and Don Gregorio have landed on the beach. Within a short while they arrive at Don Antonio's house and there is an affecting scene as the lovers are reunited. Plans are then laid to arrange matters with the authorities so that Ricote and his daughter may remain in the country. Two days later Don Quixote and Sancho take their leave. The former is no longer in fighting gear; his armor is loaded on the ass's back.

As they depart from Barcelona (Chapter LXVI), the Knight of the Mournful Countenance turns back to gaze at the spot where he met his downfall, his "Troy" as he terms it. He starts to indulge in a gloomy soliloquy, but Sancho offers him a bit of philosophic advice which cheers him somewhat. Since he does not fancy the prospect of traveling on foot, the squire suggests that they hang the armor up on a tree as a trophy. Don Quixote is at first inclined to fall in with the idea, but on second thought decides it would not be fitting.

On the fifth day of their journey, which happens to be a feast day, the pair encounter a great crowd of merrymakers at the door of an inn. A race is about to be run between a fat man and a lean one, and a dispute has arisen as to how their weights are to be equalized. The fat man, who weighs eleven arrobas, maintains that the lean man, who weighs not more than five, should put six arrobas of iron on his back. As a former governor and judge, Sancho intervenes to settle the argument, declaring that, on the contrary, the fat man ought to prune his flesh down until he weighs the same as the other. The peasants acclaim Sancho for his wise decision and offer to stand drinks at the tavern, but Don Quixote feels that he cannot spare the time.

That night they spend in the fields, where they are approached by a foot courier who at once recognizes them. He turns out to be Tosilos, the duke's lackey, who gives them an account of what happened after they left the castle. He was clubbed for having disobeyed orders, the girl became a nun, and Doña Rodríguez went back to Castile. Tosilos carries a gourd of wine and some Tronchón cheese, which he offers to share with them. Don Quixote declines the invitation but tells Sancho, "Stay with him and drink your fill, and I will ride on very slowly and wait for you to catch up with me."

Sancho and Tosilos have a brief discussion concerning the knight's madness, and the squire then hurries on to overtake his master.

There follows an argument between Don Quixote and Sancho (Chapter LXVII) *as to whether Tosilos is a real lackey or an enchanted figure. The knight is reminded of Altisidora and her professed love for him, and goes on to reproach his squire for having neglected Dulcinea's disenchantment through failing to give himself the necessary lashes.*

Arriving at the place where they had been trampled by the bulls, Don Quixote recalls the shepherds and shepherdesses and their imitation Arcadia. This gives him another idea. He and Sancho will turn shepherd and lead a pastoral life; they will be "the shepherd Quixotiz" and "the shepherd Pancino." Sancho suggests that the bachelor Sansón Carrasco and Master Nicholas the barber—perhaps even the curate—will wish to join them, and there is a discussion as to what names these individuals will bear and what the shepherdesses who are the objects of their passion will be called. Don Quixote goes on to speak of the musical instruments they will employ and the songs they will compose. Sancho begins to have certain doubts and emits a stream of proverbs, which as usual earn him a scolding. They have an unsubstantial supper and Sancho in some disgruntlement falls asleep, thinking of the meals he has had in the houses of Don Diego de Miranda and Don Antonio Moreno and at the wedding of the rich Camacho.

Don Quixote, on the other hand, is unable to sleep (Chapter LXVIII) *and is annoyed by Sancho's slumbers. Rousing him, he insists that the squire "cheerfully lay on three or four hundred lashes of those that you owe toward Dulcinea's disenchantment." Sancho is of a*

*different mind, and they again have an argument on the
subject.* Suddenly they hear "a kind of subdued roar,
a harsh and grating sound," which frightens them both.
It comes from a drove of more than six hundred pigs
that are being taken to market. The sound comes nearer
as the grunting herd rushes on, knocking both master
and man to the ground and passing over them in brutal
fashion. Not only is the knight unseated, but Rocinante
is swept off his feet, the armor and the packsaddle are
thrown to the ground, and everything is confusion.

This incident is in reality symbolic. For the vanquished Don Quixote it is the culminating blow, the
final ignominy, and he accepts it as a just punishment.

Sancho then goes back to sleep ("Go ahead and sleep,
Sancho, since you were born for that purpose. As for
me, I was born to keep vigil"), and Don Quixote, leaning against the trunk of a beech tree, begins singing a
lovelorn air in honor of his Dulcinea.

The next evening, along toward sunset, they encounter a group of horsemen accompanied by a number
of attendants on foot. The riders carry lances and
bucklers and have a warlike appearance. They surround Don Quixote in a threatening manner, at the
same time imposing silence upon him. They then conduct the pair along the road, heaping epithets upon
them but still refusing to permit them to speak, until
finally they arrive at the duke's castle, which the knight
at once recognizes though he is at a loss to explain
the meaning of it all.

Don Quixote and Sancho are picked up bodily and
carried into the courtyard of the castle. (Chapter LXIX).
In the center of the court is a catafalque upon which lies
the body of a beautiful maiden surrounded by wax
tapers in silver candlesticks. At one side is a stage with
chairs, two of which are occupied by personages re-

*sembling kings, for they have crowns on their heads
and scepters in their hands. The captives are deposited
upon a couple of seats down below. The duke and
duchess enter and take their place upon the dais beside
the individuals with the crowns. In the meantime Don
Quixote has discovered that the maiden on the bier is
the beauteous Altisidora.*

*An officer comes up to Sancho and throws over him
a black buckram robe with flames painted on it and
places on his head a miter on which devils are depicted, this being the costume worn by those who
have been condemned by the Inquisition. The sound of
flutes is heard, seemingly from beneath the catafalque,
and a handsome youth appears at the head of the
"corpse" and begins singing to the accompaniment of
a harp. The theme of his song is Altisidora's sad plight
and Don Quixote's cruelty. One of the "kings"—who, it
appears, is Minos, while his fellow judge is Rhadamanthus—interrupts the lament and directs the singer
to tell them at once how Altisidora may be revived.*

*The youth replies that the maid may be restored
to life if all the household attendants give Sancho
twenty-four smacks in the face and a dozen pinches and
half a dozen pinpricks in the back and arms, "for upon
this ceremony Altisidora's salvation is dependent."
Sancho rebels strenuously at this, and Rhadamanthus
threatens him with death if he does not comply. At this
moment a procession of six duennas, all of whom are
wearing spectacles, is seen crossing the courtyard.
Sancho is furious at the idea of permitting them to lay
hands on him, but upon his master's insistence he
finally submits. When it comes to the pinpricks, however, he revolts and, seizing a lighted torch, lays about
him among his tormentors.*

Altisidora then comes to life and there is great ex-

*citement. Don Quixote, especially, is impressed by the
powers his squire has displayed; falling on his knees, he
implores Sancho to bestow a similar favor on Dulcinea
by giving himself the lashes to disenchant her. Sancho
indignantly refuses. As for Altisidora, she thanks him
and promises him a gift of six chemises. At the same
time she reproaches the knight for his heartless cruelty,
which sent her to the other world. All then retire, and
Don Quixote and Sancho are conducted to the rooms
they formerly occupied.*

*Early the next morning (Chapter LXX) Altisidora
visits Don Quixote in his chamber, much to his embar-
rassment. Sancho questions her as to what she has seen
in hell, and she tells of having watched the devils play
a game of tennis, using books for tennis balls. One of
the books was the spurious sequel to Don Quixote,
which was batted to pieces. (From here on Cervantes
to a large degree mars the closing pages of his book
by venting his spleen on Avellaneda.)*

*Then the knight once more explains to the girl that
he cannot return her love, since he "was born to belong
to Dulcinea del Toboso." She becomes very angry and
excited, hurls epithets at him and threatens to scratch
his eyes out. But Sancho laughs at the idea of anyone's
dying of love. The duke and duchess come in and there
is further discussion of Altisidora, with Sancho maintaining that the solution for young ladies is to keep them
busy with their hands. The duchess agrees with this
and promises to see that her waiting woman "is kept
occupied from now on at some kind of needlework." Don
Quixote, meanwhile, has obtained the duke's permission to take his leave.*

CHAPTER LXXI. *Of what befell Don Quixote and his squire Sancho on the way to their village.*

AS THE vanquished and deeply afflicted Don Quixote went his way, he was, on the one hand, overly sad, and, on the other, very happy. His sadness was due to his defeat, while his happiness lay in thinking of the virtue his squire had shown he possessed by resurrecting Altisidora, although it must be admitted he had some difficulty in persuading himself that the lovelorn maiden had really been dead. As for Sancho, he found no cause for rejoicing but was downcast because the damsel had failed to keep her word and give him the chemises.

As he kept going over this in his mind, he turned to his master and said, "Really, sir, I am the most unlucky doctor in all the world. There's many a one that kills the patient he treats, yet insists on being paid even though all he does is write out a prescription for certain medicines which the apothecary—not he—makes up, and in this way he wheedles the sick man out of it. With me, the health of another costs me drops of blood, slaps, pinches, pinpricks, and lashes, and I don't get a penny for it. But I swear, if they bring me any more, they'll have to grease my palm before I cure them; for it is by singing that the abbot gets his dinner, and I can't believe that Heaven has bestowed this power on me in order that I should pass it on to others for nothing."

"You are right, friend Sancho," replied Don Quixote. "It was very wrong of Altisidora not to have given you the chemises she promised you. It is true, the virtue that is in you is *gratis data,* having cost you no effort other than that involved in receiving the torments inflicted on your person; but, nevertheless, I can tell you that, so far as I am concerned, if you want pay for those lashes with which Dulcinea is to be disenchanted, I would gladly compensate you. The only thing is: I am not certain that the cure would be effective if it were paid for, and I would not have the reward interfere with the medicine. But, for all of that, I do not see that there would be any harm in trying; so, think it over, Sancho, and decide upon your price; then administer the flogging and pay yourself off with your own hand, since you are the one who holds my money."

Sancho opened his eyes wide at this offer and pricked up his ears until they stood out a palm's breadth from his head. In his heart he was now quite willing to take a whipping.

"Very well, then, master," he said, "I will hold myself at your Grace's disposition; for I shall be only too glad to gratify your desires so long as I profit by it. If I appear grasping, you must blame it on the love I have for my wife and young ones. Tell me, your Grace, how much is each lash worth to you?"

"Sancho," said Don Quixote, "if I had to pay you in accordance with the great value of the remedy, all the treasure of Venice and the mines of Potosí would not suffice.[1] So, see what you have of mine and put a price on each stroke."

"The strokes," said Sancho, "amount to three thousand three hundred-odd, of which I have already given myself five—that leaves the rest to come. But let the five go for the odd ones; three thousand three hundred at a cuartillo[2] each—and I wouldn't take less if all the world insisted on it—that makes three thousand three hundred cuartillos, or fifteen hundred half-reales, and the three hundred strokes amount to seventy-five reales, which added to the seven hundred and fifty come to eight hundred and twenty-five reales altogether. Deducting these from your Grace's money which I am holding, I'll return home rich and well satisfied even though well flogged; for you don't catch trout[3]—I need say no more."

"O blessed Sancho!" cried Don Quixote, "O kind Sancho! Dulcinea and I will be under obligations to serve you all the days of our life that Heaven may allot us! If she resumes her lost shape—and it is not possible that she should fail to do so—her misfortune will have been her good luck and my downfall a most happy triumph. But tell me, Sancho; when do you propose to begin your discipline? For if you speed it, I will give you an additional hundred reales."

"When?" said Sancho. "Tonight without fail. Let your Grace see to it that we spend the night in the fields, under the open sky, and I will lay my flesh open at the same time."

The night so anxiously awaited by Don Quixote was long in coming; indeed, it seemed to him that the wheels of Apollo's chariot must have broken down and the day was being unduly prolonged, as is always the case with lovers who can never adjust their desires to the course of time. At last they entered a pleasant grove a short distance off the highway, and here, leaving Rocinante's saddle and the ass's packsaddle unused, they stretched themselves out on the green grass and had their supper from Sancho's supply of provisions. Then, having made a powerful and flexible whip out of the donkey's halter, the squire retired for a distance of some twenty paces among a clump of beech trees.

Seeing him set about it so energetically and courageously, his master called after him, "Take care, my friend, that you do not cut yourself to pieces; let there be a space between the lashes and do not be in such haste that your breath will give out by the time you are half done; by which I mean to say, do not lay on so stoutly that life will fail you before you have attained the desired number. And in order that you may not lose by a card too many or too few, I will stand to one side and keep count on my rosary. May Heaven favor you as your good intentions deserve."

"He who is well able to pay doesn't worry about pledges," was Sancho's answer. "I intend to lay them on in such a way that I will feel them and yet not kill myself; for that, I take it, is where the miracle comes in."

Saying this, he stripped to the waist, snatched up the whip, and began, with Don Quixote counting the strokes. He had given himself six or eight lashes when he began to think that the jest was a somewhat heavy one and the price very cheap. Pausing for a moment, he informed his master that he had made a mistake in his estimate and that each stroke ought to be paid for at the rate of half a real and not a cuartillo.

"Continue, friend Sancho," said Don Quixote, "and don't lose courage, for I am doubling your pay."

"In that case," said the squire, "God be with me and let the lashes rain down."

Rascal that he was, however, he stopped laying them on his shoulders and let them fall on the trees instead, uttering such moans every now and then that it seemed as if each one was tearing his heart out. Don Quixote became alarmed at this, fearing that Sancho by his imprudence would do away with himself before the purpose of the thing had been achieved.

"Upon your life, my friend," he called to him, "let the matter rest there, for this impresses me as being a very harsh remedy and we shall have to be patient: Zamora was not won in an hour.[4] Unless I missed my count, you have already given yourself more than a thousand lashes, and that will do for the present; for, to employ a homespun phrase, the ass will bear the load but not the overload." [5]

"No, no, master," Sancho protested, "I will not have it said of me, 'The money paid, the arm broken.' [6] Stand back a little farther, your Grace, and let me give myself a thousand or so more. A couple of flourishes like this and we'll have done with it, and there'll be cloth to spare."

"Well, then," said Don Quixote, "seeing that you are so well disposed, may Heaven help you. Lay on, for I am going away."

Sancho then returned to his task so intrepidly that before long he had stripped the bark off any number of trees, such was the severity with which he whipped himself. As he dealt a tremendous stroke to one of the beeches he raised his voice and cried, "Here shalt thou die, Samson, and all those that are with you!" [7]

At the sound of this agonized wail and the thud of the cruel lash, Don Quixote came running up and snatched from Sancho's hand the twisted halter that served as a whip. "Fate, my dear Sancho," he said, "will not have you lose your life to please me, for you need it to support your wife and children. Let Dulcinea wait for a better occasion. As for me, content with a hope that is soon to be realized, I will bide my time until you have recovered your strength so that this business may be finished to the satisfaction of all concerned."

"Since your Grace will have it so," said Sancho, "so be it. Throw your cloak over my shoulders if you will, for I am all a-sweat and don't want to catch cold—that is a risk that novices run, you know, when they discipline themselves."

Don Quixote did as requested; stripping to his undergarments, he covered Sancho, who slept until the sun awakened him.

They resume their journey. At a village three leagues distant, they stop at a hostelry. This time Don Quixote does not mistake an inn for a castle. They are given a room the walls of which are covered with bits of painted serge. On one of the hangings is depicted the abduction of Helen of Troy from her husband Menelaus and on another the story of Dido and Aeneas. This leads Don Quixote to remark that, had he lived in that time, Troy would not have been burned or Carthage destroyed, as he would have slain Paris and all the misfortunes would have been avoided.

The knight then inquires as to whether or not Sancho is of a mind to flog himself again that night and whether he prefers that it be indoors or out. Sancho replies, 'I'd prefer that it be among trees, for they seem to keep me company and are a wonderful help in bearing the pain." His master suggests that it might be well to wait until they get back to the village, but the squire says he would rather get the business over with while he is in the mood. And once again he starts spouting proverbs.

Don Quixote and Sancho spend the day waiting for night to come so that the latter may complete the task of flogging himself (Chapter LXXII). In the meantime a gentleman who is addressed as Don Alvaro Tarfe arrives at the inn. The knight recalls having come upon this name in leafing through Avellaneda's work and begins questioning the newcomer, who claims to have known Don Quixote personally. The real Don Quixote and Sancho end by convincing the gentleman that he has been deceived, and they persuade him to sign an affidavit to that effect.

That evening, after leaving the inn and parting from Don Alvaro, the knight and squire retire to a grove for the flogging, and again it is the beech trees that suffer. They travel all the next day and night, and Sancho completes his task, which makes Don Quixote very happy. The latter is now expecting to meet his disenchanted Dulcinea at any moment. At last they come to a hill overlooking their village.

As they descend the opposite slope and prepare to enter the town they meet with certain "omens" which convince the knight that he will never lay eyes upon his lady love. Continuing on their way, they encounter the curate and the bachelor Sansón Carrasco, who are out for a stroll, and there is a warm reunion. Then, accompanied by a throng of urchins, they make their way to Don Quixote's house, where the housekeeper and the niece are standing in the doorway. Teresa Panza, dragging her daughter Sanchica by the hand, also comes up to greet her husband. She is greatly disappointed by his appearance, which to her mind is not that of a governor. She is comforted, however, when he tells her he is bringing money with him, and the three of them go home together, leaving Don Quixote in the company of his womenfolk, the curate, and Sansón Carrasco.

Taking his guests to one side, the knight tells them how he was vanquished in combat and compelled to give his word of honor to abandon his chivalrous calling for one year. He goes on to outline his plans for the pastoral life, and while his visitors are dismayed at this new form his madness has assumed, they humor him. The niece and housekeeper overhear the conversa-

tion, and as soon as the curate and the bachelor have left, they descend upon Don Quixote and demand an explanation. He orders them to be quiet and take him to his room, as he is not feeling very well. They put him to bed, give him something to eat, and make him as comfortable as they can.

CHAPTER LXXIV. *Of how Don Quixote fell sick, of the will that he made, and of the manner of his death.*

INASMUCH as nothing that is human is eternal but is ever declining from its beginning to its close, this being especially true of the lives of men, and since Don Quixote was not endowed by Heaven with the privilege of staying the downward course of things, his own end came when he was least expecting it. Whether it was owing to melancholy occasioned by the defeat he had suffered, or was, simply, the will of Heaven which had so ordained it, he was taken with a fever that kept him in bed for a week, during which time his friends, the curate, the bachelor, and the barber, visited him frequently, while Sancho Panza, his faithful squire, never left his bedside.

Believing that the knight's condition was due to sorrow over his downfall and disappointment at not having been able to accomplish the disenchantment and liberation of Dulcinea, Sancho and the others endeavored to cheer him up in every possible way. The bachelor urged him to take heart and get up from bed that he might begin his pastoral life, adding that he himself had already composed an eclogue that would cast in the shade all that Sannazaro[1] had ever written, and had purchased with his own money from a herdsman of

Quintanar two fine dogs to guard the flock, one of them named Barcino and the other Butrón. All this, however, did not serve to relieve Don Quixote's sadness; whereupon his friends called in the doctor, who took his pulse and was not very well satisfied with it. In any case, the physician told them, they should attend to the health of his soul as that of his body was in grave danger.

Don Quixote received this news calmly enough, but not so his housekeeper, niece, and squire, who began weeping bitterly, as if he were already lying dead in front of them. It was the doctor's opinion that melancholy and depression were putting an end to his patient's life. The knight then requested them to leave him alone as he wished to sleep a little, and they complied. He slept for more than six hours at a stretch, as the saying is, and so soundly that the housekeeper and niece thought he would never wake.

At last he did, however, and at once cried out in a loud voice, "Blessed be Almighty God who has given me so many blessings! Truly His mercy is boundless and is not limited or restrained by the sins of men."

The niece listened carefully to what her uncle said, and it seemed to her that he was speaking more rationally than was his wont, at least during his illness.

"Sir," she said to him, "what does your Grace mean? Has something occurred that we know nothing about? What is this talk of mercy and sins?"

"The mercy that I speak of," replied Don Quixote, "is that which God is showing me at this moment—in spite of my sins, as I have said. My mind now is clear, unencumbered by those misty shadows of ignorance that were cast over it by my bitter and continual reading of those hateful books of chivalry. I see through all the nonsense and fraud contained in them, and my only regret is that my disillusionment has come so late, leaving me no time to make any sort of amends by reading those that are the light of the soul. I find myself, niece, at the point of death, and I would die in such a way as not to leave the impression of a life so bad that I shall be remembered as a madman; for even though I have been one, I do not wish to confirm it on my deathbed. And so, my dear, call in my good friends: the curate, the bachelor Sansón Carrasco, and Master Nicholas the barber; for I want to confess my sins and make my last will and testament."

The niece, however, was relieved of this errand, for the three of them came in just then.

"I have good news for you,[2] kind sirs," said Don Quixote the moment he saw them. "I am no longer Don Quixote de la Mancha but Alonso Quijano,[3] whose mode of life won for him the name of 'Good.' I am the enemy of Amadis of Gaul and all his innumerable progeny; for those profane stories dealing with knight-errantry are odious to me, and I realize how foolish I was and the danger I courted in reading them; but I am in my right senses now and I abominate them."

Hearing this, they all three were convinced that some new kind of madness must have laid hold of him.

"Why, Señor Don Quixote!" exclaimed Sansón. "What makes you talk like that, just when we have received news that my lady Dulcinea is disenchanted? And just when we are on the verge of becoming shepherds so that we may spend the rest of our lives in singing like a lot of princes, why does your Grace choose to turn hermit? Say no more, in Heaven's name, but be sensible and forget these idle tales."

"Tales of that kind," said Don Quixote, "have been the truth for me in the past, and to my detriment, but with Heaven's aid I trust to turn them to my profit now that I am dying. For I feel, gentlemen, that death is very near; so, leave all jesting aside and bring me a confessor for my sins and a notary to draw up my will. In such straits as these a man cannot trifle with his soul. Accordingly, while the Señor Curate is hearing my confession, let the notary be summoned."

Amazed at his words, they gazed at one another in some perplexity, yet they could not but believe him. One of the signs that led them to think he was dying was this quick return from madness to sanity and all the additional things he had to say, so well reasoned and well put and so becoming in a Christian that none of them could any longer doubt that he was in full possession of his faculties. Sending the others out of the room, the curate stayed behind to confess him, and before long the bachelor returned with the notary and Sancho Panza, who had been informed of his master's condition, and who, finding the housekeeper and the niece in tears, began weeping with them. When the confession was over, the curate came out.

"It is true enough," he said, "that Alonso Quijano the Good is dying, and it is also true that he is a sane man. It would be well for us to go in now while he makes his will."

At this news the housekeeper, niece, and the good squire Sancho Panza were so overcome with emotion that the tears burst forth from their eyes and their bosoms heaved with sobs; for, as has been stated more than once, whether Don Quixote was plain Alonso Quijano the Good or Don Quixote de la Mancha, he was always of a kindly and pleasant disposition and for this reason was beloved not only by the members of his household but by all who knew him.

The notary had entered along with the others, and as soon as the preamble had been attended to and the dying man had commended his soul to his Maker with all those Christian formalities that are called for in such a case, they came to the matter of bequests, with Don Quixote dictating as follows:

"ITEM. With regard to Sancho Panza, whom, in my madness, I appointed to be my squire, and who has in his possession a certain sum of money belonging to me: inasmuch as there has been a standing account between us, of debits and credits, it is my will that he shall not be asked to give any accounting whatsoever of this sum, but if any be left over after he has had payment for what I owe him, the balance, which will amount to very little, shall be his, and much good may it do him. If when I was mad I was responsible for his being given the governorship of an island, now that I am of sound mind I would present him with a kingdom if it were in my power, for his simplicity of mind and loyal conduct merit no less."

At this point he turned to Sancho. "Forgive me, my friend," he said, "for having caused you to appear as mad as I by leading you to fall into the same error, that of believing that there are still knights-errant in the world."

"Ah, master," cried Sancho through his tears, "don't die, your Grace, but take my advice and go on living for many years to come; for the greatest madness that a man can be guilty of in this life is to die without good reason, without anyone's killing him, slain only by the hands of melancholy. Look you, don't be lazy but get up from this bed and let us go out into the fields clad as shepherds as we agreed to do. Who knows but behind some bush we may come upon the lady Dulcinea, as disenchanted as you could wish. If it is because of worry over your defeat that you are dying, put the blame on me by saying that the reason for your being overthrown was that I had not properly fastened Rocinante's girth.

For the matter of that, your Grace knows from reading your books of chivalry that it is a common thing for certain knights to overthrow others, and he who is vanquished today will be the victor tomorrow."

"That is right," said Sansón, "the worthy Sancho speaks the truth."

"Not so fast, gentlemen," said Don Quixote. "In last year's nests there are no birds this year.[4] I was mad and now I am sane; I was Don Quixote de la Mancha, and now I am, as I have said, Alonso Quijano the Good. May my repentance and the truth I now speak restore to me the place I once held in your esteem. And now, let the notary proceed:

"ITEM. I bequeath my entire estate, without reservation,[5] to my niece Antonia Quijana,[6] here present, after the necessary deductions shall have been made from the most available portion of it to satisfy the bequests that I have stipulated. The first payment shall be to my housekeeper for the wages due her, with twenty ducats over to buy her a dress. And I hereby appoint the Señor Curate and the Señor Bachelor Sansón Carrasco to be my executors.

"ITEM. It is my will that if my niece Antonia Quijana should see fit to marry, it shall be to a man who does not know what books of chivalry are; and if it shall be established that he is acquainted with such books and my niece still insists on marrying him, then she shall lose all that I have bequeathed her and my executors shall apply her portion to works of charity as they may see fit.

"ITEM. I entreat the aforementioned gentlemen, my executors, if by good fortune they should come to know the author who is said to have composed a history now going the rounds under the title of *Second Part of the Exploits of Don Quixote de la Mancha*, to beg his forgiveness in my behalf, as earnestly as they can, since it

was I who unthinkingly led him to set down so many
and such great absurdities as are to be found in it; for I
leave this life with a feeling of remorse at having provided him with the occasion for putting them into writing."

The will ended here, and Don Quixote, stretching
himself at length in the bed, fainted away. They all
were alarmed at this and hastened to aid him. The same
thing happened very frequently in the course of the
three days of life that remained to him after he had
made his will. The household was in a state of excitement, but with it all the niece continued to eat her
meals, the housekeeper had her drink, and Sancho
Panza was in good spirits; for this business of inheriting
property effaces or mitigates the sorrow which the heir
ought to feel and causes him to forget.[7]

Death came at last for Don Quixote, after he had
received all the sacraments[8] and once more, with many
forceful arguments, had expressed his abomination of
books of chivalry. The notary who was present remarked
that in none of those books had he read of any knight-
errant dying in his own bed so peacefully and in so
Christian a manner. And thus, amid the tears and
lamentations of those present, he gave up the ghost; that
is to say, he died. Perceiving that their friend was no
more, the curate asked the notary to be a witness to the
fact that Alonso Quijano the Good, commonly known
as Don Quixote, was truly dead, this being necessary
in order that some author other than Cid Hamete Benengeli might not have the opportunity of falsely resurrecting him and writing endless histories of his exploits.

Such was the end of the Ingenious Gentleman of La
Mancha, whose birthplace Cid Hamete was unwilling
to designate exactly in order that all the towns and vil-

lages of La Mancha might contend among themselves for the right to adopt him and claim him as their own, just as the seven cities of Greece did in the case of Homer. The lamentations of Sancho and those of Don Quixote's niece and his housekeeper, as well as the original epitaphs that were composed for his tomb, will not be recorded here, but mention may be made of the verses by Sansón Carrasco:

> *Here lies a gentleman bold*
> *Who was so very brave*
> *He went to lengths untold,*
> *And on the brink of the grave*
> *Death had on him no hold.*
> *By the world he set small store—*
> *He frightened it to the core—*
> *Yet somehow, by Fate's plan,*
> *Though he'd lived a crazy man,*
> *When he died he was sane once more.*[9]

As for that most wise chronicler, Cid Hamete, he has left us the following address to his pen:[10]

"Here shalt thou remain, hung upon this rack by this brass wire. I know not if thou beest well cut or not, O pen of mine, but here thou shalt live for long ages to come, unless some presumptuous and scoundrelly historians should take thee down to profane thee. But ere they do this thou may'st warn them and say to them as best thou canst:

> *Hands off, o'erweening ones!*
> *Let it by none attempted be;*
> *For this emprise, my lord the King,*
> *Hath been reserved for me.*[11]

"For me alone Don Quixote was born and I for him; it was for him to act, for me to write, and we two are one in spite of that Tordesillesque[12] pretender who had, and may have, the audacity to write with a coarse and ill-trimmed ostrich quill of the deeds of my valiant knight. This is no burden for his shoulders, no subject for his congealed talent; and if perchance thou shouldst come to know him, advise him that he should let Don Quixote's tired and moldering bones rest in their sepulcher and not try to bear him off, contrary to all the laws of death, to Old Castile[13] by raising him from that grave where he really and truly lies stretched out, being quite unable now to sally forth once again on a third expedition. For the two sallies that he did make to the delight and approval of all who heard of them, in foreign countries as well as our own, are sufficient to cast ridicule upon all the ridings forth of knights-errant in times past.

"Doing this, thou shalt fulfill thine obligations as a Christian by giving good counsel to one who wished thee ill, and I shall be the first one to enjoy the fruit of his own writings as fully as he desired, since I have had no other purpose than to arouse the abhorrence of mankind toward those false and nonsensical stories to be met with in the books of chivalry, which, thanks to this tale of the genuine Don Quixote, are already tottering and without a doubt are doomed to fall.[14] *Vale.*"

TWO EXEMPLARY NOVELS

and

"FOOT IN THE STIRRUP": CERVANTES' FAREWELL TO LIFE

TWO EXEMPLARY NOVELS

Prologue

To the Reader

I SHOULD LIKE, if it were possible, dearest reader, to be excused from writing this Prologue—the one I composed for my *Don Quixote* did not turn out so well for me that I should care to follow it here with another. In the present case, a certain friend of mine is to blame, one of the many whom I have acquired in the course of my life, thanks to my disposition rather than to my intellect. He might very well, as the custom is, have made an engraving of me for the frontispiece of this book; for the famous Don Juan de Jáuregui would have provided him with my portrait, and in that way my ambition would have been satisfied, as well as the desire that some have to know what kind of face and figure belong to him who has had the boldness to come out into the market place of the world and exhibit so many stories to the gaze of the peoples. Beneath the portrait my friend might have placed the following inscription:

"This man you see here with the aquiline countenance, the chestnut hair, the smooth, untroubled brow, the bright eyes, the hooked yet well proportioned nose, the silvery beard that less than a score of years ago was golden, the big mustache, the small mouth, the teeth that are scarcely worth mentioning (there are but half a dozen of them altogether, in bad condition and very badly placed, no two of them corresponding to another

705

pair), the body of medium height, neither tall nor short, the high complexion that is fair rather than dark, the slightly stooping shoulders, and the somewhat heavy build—this, I may tell you, is the author of *La Galatea* and *Don Quixote de la Mancha;*[1] he it was who composed the *Journey to Parnassus,* in imitation of Cesare Caporali of Perusa,[2] as well as other works that are straying about in these parts—without the owner's name, likely as not.

"He is commonly called Miguel de Cervantes Saavedra. He was a soldier for many years and a captive for five and a half, an experience that taught him patience in adversity. In the naval battle of Lepanto he lost his left hand [3] as the result of a harquebus shot, a wound which, however unsightly it may appear, he looks upon as beautiful, for the reason that it was received on the most memorable and sublime occasion that past ages have known or those to come may hope to know; for he was fighting beneath the victorious banner of the son of that thunderbolt of war, Charles V of blessed memory."

And if this friend of mine of whom I am complaining had been unable to think of anything else to say of me, I could have made up and secretly given him a couple of dozen tributes to myself such as would have spread my fame abroad and established my reputation as a genius. For it is foolish to believe that such eulogies are scrupulously truthful, since praise and blame never have precise limits. But the short of it is the opportunity was missed, and I have been left in the lurch and without a portrait. Accordingly, I shall have to make use of my own tongue, which, though a stammering one, will not falter when it comes to uttering truths that are understandable even when spoken in dumb show.

And so, kind reader, I will further tell you that you

will by no means be able to make a fricassee out of these *Novels* that I offer you, for they have neither feet nor head nor entrails nor anything that is suited to such a purpose; by which I mean to say that the amorous episodes you will find in some of them are so respectable and restrained, so within the bounds of reason and conformable to Christian conduct, that no one who reads them, either carefully or carelessly, can possibly be moved to evil thoughts. I have given these stories the title of Exemplary; and if you look closely there is not one of them that does not afford a useful example. If it were not that I do not wish to expand upon this subject, I could show you the savory and wholesome fruit that is to be had from each of them separately and from the collection as a whole.

My intention has been to set up in the public square of our country a billiard table where everyone may come to amuse himself without harm to body or soul; for decent and pleasing pastimes are profitable rather than harmful. One is not always in church or engaged in prayer, one is not always occupied with business matters, however important they may be. There is a time for recreation, when the tired mind seeks repose. It is with this object in view that public walks are laid out, water is brought from afar to play in fountains, hills are leveled, and gardens cultivated with such care. There is one thing I will venture to say to you: if I believed that the reading of these *Novels* would in any way arouse an evil thought or desire, I would sooner cut off the hand that wrote them than see them published. At my age one does not trifle with the life to come—I am now sixty-four and a little beyond.[4]

It is to this task that I devote my abilities, in accordance with my natural inclination. What is more, I believe I am the first to have written novels in the Cas-

tilian tongue, since the many that are printed in Spanish have all been translated from foreign languages,
whereas these are my own, neither imitated nor stolen.
My mind conceived them, my pen brought them forth,
and they have grown in the arms of the printing press.
Afterward, if I live long enough, I shall offer you the
Troubles of Persiles, a book that dares to compete with
Heliodorus (if only its boldness does not prove its undoing). But first you shall see, and shortly, the continuation of Don Quixote's exploits and Sancho Panza's
drolleries, and after that, the *Garden Weeks.*

I am promising much in view of the little strength I
have, but who can put a rein on ambition? I would
merely ask you to bear in mind that inasmuch as I have
had the audacity to dedicate these *Novels* to the great
Count of Lemos, there must be some hidden virtue in
them. I say no more, except: God be with you, and may
He give me the patience to bear well the ill that a few
stiff-starched hairsplitters are bound to speak of me.
Vale.

Rinconete and Cortadillo

EDITOR'S NOTE

"Rinconete and Cortadillo" is a tale of the picaresque
and, according to the accounts that have come down to
us, indescribably picturesque city of Seville at the turn
of the seventeenth century. With a large population
representing a hundred or more nationalities and governed by an exceedingly lax and corrupt municipal
administration, the town was filled to overflowing with
thieves, bandits, lawbreakers of every sort. Disorder was
rife. Officers of the law and rogues frequently worked
together, while an "espía doble" lent his services to both
sides. One chronicler, Luis de Peraza, tells us in his
History of the Imperial City of Seville that even small
boys went armed in imitation of their elders, and
thieves' jargon (germanía) was almost a common
speech, one with which Cervantes was obviously well
acquainted. And in the Miscelanea of Luís Zapata, a
work probably written about the end of the sixteenth
century, the following passage will be found:

In Seville there is said to be a brotherhood of thieves,
with a prior and consuls who serve as vendors; it has a
depository for stolen goods and a chest with three keys
in which the loot is kept; from this chest they take
what they need to defray expenses and to bribe those
who are in a position to help them when they are in
trouble. They are very careful to accept only men who
are strong and active and old Christians, their member-
ship being limited to the servants of powerful and high-

placed individuals, agents of the law; and the first oath to which they swear is that, even though they may be drawn and quartered, they will endure it and will not inform on their companions. And so, when something is missing from the home of a respectable citizen and people say that the devil has taken it, the truth of the matter is that it is not the devil but one of these. That they have a brotherhood is certain, and it has lasted longer than the principality of Venice; for although the law has caught a few unfortunate ones, it has never been able to run down the leader of the gang.

With regard to the religious aspect of the community, Rodríguez Marín has this to say:

To be a thief and serve God at one and the same time is something that is very characteristic of the Spanish, and especially the Andalusian, underworld. "Steal the pig and give the feet to God," as the proverb has it, was a practice common everywhere, and rarely was a bandit caught or slain without medals and scapulars being found upon his chest. I myself have heard and copied down some of the prayers that were used by highwaymen sixty years ago in an effort to render themselves invisible against their armed pursuers.

Out of such a setting Cervantes has drawn vivid types. During his residence there he hardly could have failed to absorb all the color and the movement of the place, and with the true novelist's instinct he has put the experience to good use. He has also doubtless embodied much that he learned in prison. Here is the social-realistic—true to life—side of his art; but in the end there is, as always with Cervantes, a larger implication.

The germ of Don Quixote *may be discovered in this*

story. It lies in that contrast, the humorous incongruity, between the world as it is and the world as it ought to be, which constitutes Cervantes' major theme and forms the basis of his finest art. What we have here, in short, is a close-to-life realism, which in itself will doubtless suffice for many but which holds a deeper meaning for those who seek it.

AT THE Molinillo inn, which is situated on the border of the famous plains of Alcudia as one goes from Castile to Andalusia, two lads met by chance one hot summer day. They were around fourteen or fifteen years of age—neither, certainly, was more than sixteen—and both were good-looking enough though very ragged, tattered, and unkempt. Capes they had none, their trousers were of linen, their stockings of flesh. True, they had shoes, but those of the one boy were mere cord sandals that were just about worn out, while the other pair, of the "open work" variety, was minus soles and more nearly resembled fetters than anything else. One wore a green hunting cap, and his companion had on a low-crowned, broad-brimmed hat without a band. Over the latter's shoulder and wound about his chest was a chamois-colored beeswaxed shirt, caught up and stuffed into one sleeve.

The first youth, traveling light and without saddlebags, had what looked like a big lump on his bosom, which later turned out to be one of those Walloon ruffs, starched with grease and so well "embroidered" that it was nothing but a mass of threads. Wrapped up in this garment for safekeeping was a deck of cards, oval in shape, for the reason that, from long usage, the edges had been worn off, and in order that they might last longer they had been trimmed in this fashion. Both lads were sunburned, with long black-bordered nails and hands that were none too clean. One of them carried a short sword and the other a yellow-handled knife of the kind known as a cattle knife.

In the noontide heat, the two of them went out to a portico or lean-to that stood in front of the inn and, sitting down opposite each other, struck up a conversation.

"Sir Gentleman," said the older to the smaller boy, "what is your Grace's country and in what direction are you traveling?"

"Sir Cavalier," replied the one to whom the question had been put, "I do not know the name of my country, nor where I am bound."

"Well," said the older lad, "to be frank about it, you do not appear to be from Heaven, and since this is no place to be taking up your abode, you must be going farther."

"That I am," the younger one answered him. "But it was the truth I told you, for my land is not my land, seeing that all I have in it is a father who does not look upon me as a son and a stepmother who treats me the way one does a stepchild. I go where chance may take me until I find someone who will provide me with what I need to get through this wretched life of mine."

"And does your Grace know any trade?" inquired the big boy.

"None," said the small lad, "except how to run like a hare, leap like a deer, and handle a pair of scissors very neatly."

"All that," the other one assured him, "is very good and useful and a great advantage; for your Grace is bound to find some sacristan who will give you the offering for All Saints if you will cut him some paper flowers for the Tomb that they erect on the altar on Holy Thursday."

"That is not the kind of cutting I do," replied the younger one. "My father, by the grace of Heaven, is a tailor and hose maker, and he taught me to cut leggings, which, as your Grace very well knows, are half-hose with gaiters, properly called spatter-dashes. I cut them so well, really, that I could pass my examination as a master of the craft. The only thing is, my luck is cut so short that my talents go unrecognized."

"All that and more," said the big boy, "happens to the capable. I have always heard it said that the finest talents are the most unappreciated; but your Grace is young and you still have time to mend your luck. If I am not mistaken and my eyes do not deceive me, you have other accomplishments, which you prefer to keep secret."

"That I have," the small boy admitted, "but they are not for the public gaze, as your Grace has very well remarked."

"In that case," said the other lad, "I may tell you that I am one of the most tight-lipped young fellows that you will find for many a mile around here; and in order that your Grace may feel free to unbosom yourself and confide in me, I will first tell you all about my own life, for I think it is not without some hidden purpose that fate has brought us together, and I believe that from now on to our dying day we are going to be true friends.

"I, noble sir," he went on, "am a native of Fuenfrida, a village well known and even famous on account of the distinguished travelers who are constantly passing through it. My name is Pedro del Rincón,[1] and my father is a person of quality, being an agent of the Holy Crusade, that is to say, one who sells papal bulls or indulgences, a *bulero,* or, as people usually say, a *buldero.* I used to accompany him at times, and I learned the trade so well that when it comes to dispensing bulls, I would not take second place to any man no matter how good at it he might be. But one day I came to love the money from the bulls more than the bulls themselves, and having embraced a bag of it, I made off for Madrid, where, with the facilities which that city commonly affords, I gutted the bag in a very short while and left it with more creases than a bridegroom's handkerchief.

"The one who was in charge of the money then came after me, I was arrested, and they showed me little mercy; although, when those gentlemen saw how young I was, they were satisfied with sending me to the whipping post and swatting the flies off my back for a spell, after which I was forbidden to set foot in the capital for a period of four years. But I was patient; I merely shrugged my shoulders and put up with the flogging and the swatting, and was in such a hurry to begin serving my sentence of exile that I did not even have time to get me any sumpter mules. I took what I could of my valuables, those that I thought I was most likely to need, including these cards." (With this, he displayed the deck we have mentioned, which he carried in his Walloon ruff.) "With them I have earned my living by playing twenty-one in all the inns and taverns between here and Madrid. They are, as you can see, worn and filthy, but there is one marvelous thing about them for him who knows how to handle them, and that is the fact that no matter how you cut them, you are bound to turn up an ace.

"If your Grace is at all acquainted with this game, you can see what an advantage a player has who is certain of an ace the first card he cuts, for it will count either one point or eleven, and with the stakes set at twenty-one, his money will stay at home. In addition, I learned from a cook in the household of a certain ambassador a number of tricks at lansquenet and the game known as *andaboba;* so that, if your Grace is able to pass his examination as a cutter of leggings, I could be a master of the science that Vilhan invented.[2] That way, I am sure not to die of hunger; for in any farmhouse to which I come there is someone who is willing to pass the time with a little game, as we are going to find very shortly. Let us spread the net and see if any bird falls into it from among the mule drivers in this inn; by which I mean that the two of us will start playing twenty-one as if we were in earnest, and if anyone wants to make a third, he will be the first to leave his money behind him."

"That suits me," said the other lad. "I thank your Grace very much for giving me an account of your life, and I feel that I must now tell you my own life story, which very briefly is as follows. I was born in the pious village that lies between Salamanca and Medina del Campo. My father is a tailor and taught me his trade; and with my ability, from cutting with shears I went on to cutting purses. I became tired of the cramped life in a small town and the lack of affection my stepmother showed me, and so I left and went to Toledo to practice my calling there. In that city I did wonders; for there was not a reliquary dangling from a hood or a pocket so well hidden that my fingers did not find it out or my scissors clip it, even though it might have been guarded by the eyes of Argus.

"During the four months I spent in Toledo I never once was trapped between doors or caught in the act or chased by constables or turned up by any informer. True enough, there was one week when a spy who worked both with the officers of the law and with us reported my cleverness to the magistrate, who became so enamored of my good qualities that he insisted on seeing me. However, being very humble, I do not like to deal with important personages, and I avoided him by leaving the city in such haste that I too did not have time to provide myself with sumpter mules or small change or a post-chaise or even so much as a cart."

"Never mind about that," said Rincón. "Since we know one another now, there is no need for all these grand airs. Let us make a clean breast of it and admit that we haven't a penny between us or even a pair of shoes."

"So be it," replied Diego Cortado (for that was the younger one's name),[3] "and since our friendship, as you have said, Señor Rincón, is to be lifelong, let us begin with the time-honored ceremonies."

Saying this, Cortado arose, and he and Rincón clasped each other in a warm embrace, then started playing twenty-one with the aforementioned cards, which may have been clean of dust and straw (that is to say, of the king's dues), but not of grease and trickery. After a few hands Diego was able to cut an ace quite as well as his teacher, and when a mule driver came out to the portico for an airing and asked if he could make a third, they agreed readily enough and in less than half an hour had won twelve reales and twenty-two maravedis, which for the muleteer was equivalent to a dozen stabs in the back and twenty-two thousand sorrows. Thinking that, being mere lads, they would not be able to prevent him from doing so, he tried to take the money away from them; but one of the boys drew his short sword and the other his yellow-handled knife and gave him so much trouble that, if his companions had not run out, things undoubtedly would have gone hard with him.

At this point, a group of travelers on horseback happened to come along the road. They were on the way to take their siesta at the Alcalde inn half a league beyond; but seeing the fight between the mule driver and the lads, they hastened to separate them, telling the latter that in case they were bound for Seville, they might join the party.

"That is where we are going," said Rincón, "and we will serve your Lordships and obey your every command."

Without any further hesitation the pair leaped out into the road in front of the mules and took their departure, leaving their victim despoiled of his cash and very angry, while the innkeeper's wife marveled at the good training the rogues had had, for she had been eavesdropping on their conversation. When she told the muleteer that she had heard them say the cards were false ones, he began tearing at his beard and wanted to follow them to the other hostelry in order to get his money back; for, as he said, it was a very great insult, touching upon a point of honor, that two boys should have been able to trick a grown man like him. His companions, however, restrained him, advising him that he should not advertise his lack of cleverness and his gullibility. The short of it is that, while they did not succeed in consoling him, by dint of much talking they prevailed upon him to stay where he was.

In the meantime Cortado and Rincón proved to be such zealous servants that the travelers gave them a lift most of the way, and although they had a number of opportunities to rifle the luggage of their temporary masters they did not do so, since they did not wish to lose so good a chance for making the journey to Seville, a town they very much wished to see. Nevertheless, as they entered the city—which they did at the vesper hour and by the Customhouse Gate in order that the baggage might be inspected and the duty paid—Cortado could not refrain from ripping open the valise or satchel that one of the company, a Frenchman, carried up behind him on the crupper of his mount. With his knife he inflicted so wide and deep a gash that the insides were plainly visible, and he then slyly took out a couple of good shirts, a sun dial, and a small memorandum book.

The lads were none too well pleased at seeing these objects, and assuming that inasmuch as the Frenchman kept the satchel with him it must contain something of greater worth than what they had found in it, they were tempted to make another search but did not do so, thinking that by this time the owner would have removed and put away for safekeeping whatever was left. And so, before the theft had been discovered, they took their leave of those who had been their providers up to now, and the next day they sold the shirts at the old clothes market outside the Arenal Gate, receiving for them the sum of twenty reales.

Having done this, they set out to see the town. They marveled at the size and magnificence of the cathedral and the great throng of people on the river bank; for this was the season for provisioning the fleet, and there were six galleys drawn up along the wharf, the sight of which caused the youths to heave a sigh and fear the day when their misdeeds would take them to the rowing benches for the rest of their lives. They also gazed at the many porters with baskets who were going up and down, and they asked one of them how he liked his job, if there was much work to it, and how much he made. It was a young Asturian whom they questioned, and he replied that it was a very good job on the whole, with no tax to pay, adding that some days he made as much as five or six reales, with which he could eat and drink and have a royal good time, being free to seek whatever employer he liked without having to put up any security, and he was sure, also, of having his dinner whenever he wished, as meals were served at all hours even in the meanest chophouse.

The two friends thought that this did not sound at all bad, and the work was not displeasing to them. Indeed, it seemed to them admirably suited to the practice of their own trade under cover and in safety, for as porters they would find it easy to enter private houses everywhere. They accordingly decided to buy the necessary equipment, seeing there was no examination to be passed, and they asked the Asturian what they should purchase. He told them they needed a couple of small bags, new or at any rate clean, and that each of them should have three palm-fiber baskets, two large ones and a small one, to carry the meat, fish, and fruit—the bags were for the bread.

He then took them where these articles were for sale, and they, with the money they had got for the Frenchman's shirts, bought all the articles in question. Within a couple of hours they had become quite expert at their new trade, as could be seen from the manner in which they handled their baskets and carried their bags; and their mentor thereupon proceeded to inform them where it was they should put in an appearance: mornings at the Meat Market and in San Salvador Square; on fish days at the Fish Market and the Slope; every afternoon at the river; and on Thursdays at the Fair.

This lesson they memorized thoroughly, and early the next morning they took up their stand in the Square. No sooner had they arrived than they were surrounded by other youths engaged in the same occupation, who, seeing the spick-and-span condition of their bags and baskets, judged them to be newcomers. They had to answer innumerable questions and did so very cautiously. Meanwhile, a young student and a soldier had come up, and, observing what clean baskets the novices had, the former summoned Cortado while the latter took Rincón.

"In the name of God, so be it!" both lads cried.[4]

"Sir," said Rincón, "this is a good way to begin, with my first tip coming from your Grace."

"The tip," said the soldier, "will not be a bad one; for I have won a little money and I am in love, and I am giving a banquet today for some of my lady's women friends."

"Very well then, your Grace, go ahead and load me down as much as you like, for I have the will and the strength to carry away this entire market place, and if necessary I'll be glad to help you cook the food as well."

The soldier was pleased with the boy's good manners and told him that if he wished to become a servant he would take him out of such degrading employment; to which Rincón replied that, since this was his first day, he would like to see how good or bad a calling it was, but in case he was not satisfied with it, he promised on his word that he would enter the soldier's service before he would that of a canon. The soldier gave a laugh and loaded the boy well, then pointed out the house where his lady dwelt so that Rincón would know it from then on and he would not have to accompany him when he sent him on an errand. The lad promised to be loyal and well behaved, and the man then gave him three cuartos, and in no time at all Rincón was back at the Square so that he might not miss any chance that offered; for the Asturian had warned him that he must keep a sharp eye out, and had further advised him that, when he was carrying small fish such as dace, sardines, or flounders, he might very well take a few and eat them himself, if only to help defray the expenses of the day; but he reminded him that it should be done with a great deal of caution so that he would not lose his good reputation, which was the most important thing in this business.

Although Rincón had returned as quickly as he could, he found Cortado already back at his post, and his companion now came up and asked how things had gone with him. Rincón opened his hand and displayed the three cuartos, whereupon Cortado brought out from his bosom a purse that once upon a time had been of amber-scented leather and appeared to be rather well filled.

"It was with this," he said, "and a couple of cuartos that his reverence the student paid me off; but take it, Rincón, for fear of what may happen."

He had barely slipped the purse to him when the student came running up in a sweat and frightened to death. Seeing Cortado, he asked if by any chance the boy had seen a purse answering such and such a description and containing fifteen gold crowns, three pieces of two reales each, and a number of cuartos and ochavos, amounting to a certain sum in maravedís. He demanded to know if the porter had taken his money while he, the student, was making his purchases.

Cortado answered with great craftiness and without the slightest sign of agitation. "All that I can tell you about that purse," he said, "is that it surely could not have been lost unless you were careless about where you put it."

"Sinner that I am!" exclaimed the student. "I must have been careless, seeing that they stole it from me."

"That is what I say," Cortado agreed; "but there is a remedy for everything in this world except death, and the first and chief remedy that your Grace should try is patience, remembering that God made us all, and one day follows another, and things come and go. It may be that, in the course of time, the one who took the purse will repent and return it to your Grace nicely perfumed."

"We'll forget about the perfume," said the student.

"And then," Cortado went on, "there are letters of excommunication and interdicts, and there is also such a thing as diligence, which is the mother of good fortune. But to tell you the truth, I shouldn't like to have that purse on me, for if your Grace has any holy orders, I would feel as if I had committed some great incest or sacrilege."

"Sacrilege indeed!" cried the grief-stricken student. "Although I am not a priest but merely a sacristan to a few nuns, the money in that purse was the third part of the revenue from a chaplaincy which a priest who is a friend of mine sent me to collect, and so it is money that is holy and sacred."

"Let him eat it with his bread," said Rincón at this point. "I wouldn't go his security for all he will get from it. There is a day of judgment when everything will come out in the wash, and then we shall see who the scoundrel was who dared to take, steal, and make away with a third of the income from a chapel."

"Tell me, Sir Sacristan, upon your life, how much does the income amount to each year?"

"Income! I'm a son of a whore!" The sacristan was beside himself with anger. "Am I to stand here and discuss the income with you? If you know anything, brothers, tell me; if not, be on your way and Godspeed, for I must go and have the crier announce it."

"That is not a bad idea," said Cortado. "But your Grace must be sure not to forget the description of the purse or the exact amount of money that was in it, for if you are off as much as a penny you will never see it again as long as you live, and that is a prophecy." [5]

"There is nothing to fear on that score," replied the sacristan, "for I remember it all better than I do the sound of the bells I ring. I shall not err by the fraction of a point."

With this, he took from his pocket a lace-bordered handkerchief to wipe the sweat that was dripping from his face as from a still, and no sooner did Cortado lay eyes upon it than he marked it for his own. As the sacristan went away Cortado followed and overtook him on the cathedral stairs, where he called him to one side and began spouting such an interminable rigmarole of nonsense having to do with the theft of the purse and the hope of its recovery that the poor student was quite bewildered as he listened. Unable to understand what the youth was saying, the sacristan had him repeat it two or three times; and thus they stood there, staring each other straight in the eye, with the sacristan hanging on every word and so bewildered that Cortado found the opportunity for which he was waiting and slyly took the handkerchief from its owner's pocket. Then he said good-by, promising to see him again that afternoon. He had his eyes, he said, on another porter, a lad of about the same build, who was something of a thief and whom he suspected of having stolen the purse; he would make it his business to find out within a day or two.

Somewhat consoled by this, the sacristan took his leave, and the boy then joined Rincón, who had been looking on from a distance. Not far away there was another lad with a basket who had witnessed everything that had taken place and who had seen Cortado give the handkerchief to Rincón. He now approached them.

"Tell me, gallant sirs," he said, "are you in the bad books or not?"

"Gallant sir," Rincón answered him, "we do not understand that kind of talk."

"What! You mean to say you are not, gentle Mur-
cians?" [6]

"We are neither from Thebes[7] nor from Murcia,"
said Cortado. "If there is anything else that you want
to know, speak out. If not, go your way, and may God
go with you."

"So you do not understand?" said the young man.
"Very well then, I will feed it to you with a silver spoon.
What I meant to inquire, gentlemen, was whether or
not you are thieves, though I do not know why I should
ask, since I can see that you are. But tell me, how does
it come that you have not yet gone to Señor Monipodio'
customhouse?" [8]

"Why, Sir Gallant," said Rincón, "can it be that
thieves in this country have to pay a duty?"

"If they do not pay," the other lad replied, "they at
least have to register with Señor Monipodio, who is
their father, their teacher, and their protector; and I
accordingly advise you to come with me and render
him obedience, for if you do not do so and dare to commit a theft without his approval, it will cost you dearly."

"I thought," remarked Cortado, "that thieving was a
trade that was free of tax or duty, and that if you paid,
it was in a lump sum with your neck or your shoulders as
security. But since that is the way it is and each land has
its own customs, let us observe those of this country,
which, being the leading one in all the world, must have
the best usages. Accordingly, your Grace may show us
where this gentleman you speak of is to be found, for
I suspect from what I have heard of him that he is a
very influential personage, big-hearted, and a very clever
hand at the business."

"Indeed he is influential, clever, and competent!" was
the youth's rejoinder; "so much so that during the four
years that he has been our leader and our father, not

more than four of us have ended up on the *finibusterrae*, only some thirty have tasted leather, and a mere sixty-two have gone over the road." [9]

"Sir," said Rincón, "the truth is, we come as near to understanding you as we do to flying."

"Let us start walking, and I will explain these terms on the way, together with others that ought to be as familiar to you as the bread in your mouth." He then went on to give them the meaning of various expressions drawn from that form of speech that is known as *germanía*, or thieves' slang. His discourse was not a short one, for they had a long way to go.

"Is your Grace by any chance a thief?" Rincón inquired of their guide.

"Yes," he answered, "that I am, and at the service of God and all good people; although I am not one of the best, seeing that I am still in the first year of my apprenticeship."

"That is something new to me," said Cortado, "to hear that thieves are in this world to serve God and good people."

"Sir," replied the youth, "I do not meddle with tologies;[10] all I know is that everyone in this business may praise God, especially in view of the order that Monipodio keeps among his adopted sons."

"Undoubtedly," observed Rincón, "his rule must be a good and holy one if he is able to make thieves serve God."

"It is so good and holy that I do not know if it could be improved in any way, so far as our trade is concerned. He has commanded that out of what we steal we must give something in the way of alms to buy oil for the lamp that stands before a highly venerated image here in this city; and I must say that this act of piety has had great results, for only recently they gave the *ansia* three times to a *cuatrero* who had done a Murcian on a couple of *roznos,* and though he was weak from quartan fever, he endured it all without singing, as if it were nothing at all, and we who are in the business attributed this to his devoutness, for such strength as he had was not of itself sufficient to enable him to stand the executioner's first *desconcierto.*

"And since I know that you are going to ask me what some of these words mean, I shall cure myself while I am healthy and tell you before you put the question. You may know, then, that a *cuatrero* is a cattle thief; *ansia* is the torture; *roznos* are asses, begging your pardon; and the first *desconcierto* is the turn of the screw that the executioner gives at the start. We do more than that, however: we say our rosary, which is divided according to days of the week, and many of us do not steal on Friday or speak to any woman called Mary on a Saturday."

"All of that sounds marvelous to me," said Cortado; "but tell me, your Grace, do you make any other form of restitution or do any other kind of penance?"

"As for restitution," the youth explained, "there is no use talking about that since it is out of the question on account of the many portions into which the loot is divided, with each of the agents and contracting parties[11] getting his share. For that reason, the one who commits the theft cannot restore anything, and so far as that is concerned, there is no one to urge us to do so. We never go to confession, and if letters of excommunication are issued against us, we never hear of them as we are not in church when they are read, unless it happens to be a feast day and we are attracted there by what is to be had from the great crowd of people."

"And by doing merely this," said Cortado, "you gentlemen think that your life is good and holy, do you?"

"Why, what is there bad about it?" the young man asked. "Isn't it worse to be a heretic or a renegade, to kill your father and mother, or to be a solomite?"

"Your Grace means a sodomite," said Rincón.

"That is what I said."

"It is all bad," said Cortado, "but seeing that our fate would have us enter this brotherhood, let your Grace lead on. I am dying to see this Señor Monipodio, having heard so many fine things about him."

"You will soon have your wish," said the youth, "for there is his house. You gentlemen may wait at the door while I go in to find out if he is free, this being the hour at which he commonly grants an audience."

"Very well," said Rincón.

When they had gone on a little farther the young fellow entered a house that was not very good, indeed it was quite unprepossessing, and the other two waited for him at the door. Soon afterward he came out and called to them, and they entered, their guide telling them to wait a while longer in a small brick-paved court-yard so clean and well scrubbed that it appeared to be covered with the finest carmine. On one side was a three-legged stool and on the other a pitcher with a broken spout on top of which stood a small jug that was in equally bad shape. On the third side was a reed mat and in the middle of it a flower pot, or, as they are called in Seville, a sweet basil jar.

As they waited for Señor Monipodio to come down, the two lads attentively eyed the furnishings of the house, and as he delayed putting in an appearance, Rincón ventured into one of two low rooms that opened upon the patio. In it he saw two fencing foils and a couple of cork shields suspended from the wall by four nails, a large chest without a lid or covering of any sort, and three other reed mats spread out on the ground.

On the wall opposite him was one of those cheap prints of Our Lady, and beneath it was suspended a palm-fiber basket with a white vessel nearby set into the wall, from which Rincón gathered that the basket served as a poor box while the vessel was for holy water, and this turned out to be the truth.

At that moment two youths, each about twenty years old, came in. They were dressed like students and were followed shortly afterward by two porters and a blind man; without saying a word, they all began strolling up and down the courtyard. It was not long before two old men entered, baize-clad and wearing spectacles, which gave them a grave and dignified appearance, as did the rosaries with tinkling beads that they carried in their hands. Behind them came an old woman in a full skirt. She was as silent as the others; she went into the room off the side, took some holy water, and very devoutly knelt before the image. She remained there for some little while; then, having first kissed the ground and lifted her arms and eyes heavenward three times in succession, she arose, tossed some coins into the basket, and came out to join the others in the patio.

In short, before many minutes had elapsed, there were upwards of fourteen persons assembled there, variously clad and from different walks in life. Among the latest arrivals were a couple of swaggering young ruffians with large mustaches, broad-brimmed hats, Walloon ruffs, colored stockings, and large showy garters. Their swords exceeded the length allowed by law, each carried a brace of pistols in place of daggers, and their bucklers were suspended from their girdles. Upon entering, they glanced at Rincón and Cortado out of the corner of their eyes, as if surprised at seeing strangers there, and, going up to them, inquired if they were members of the brotherhood. Rincón replied that they were, and were at the service of their Graces.

Then it was that Señor Monipodio came down, and all of that respectable company were very glad to see him. He appeared to be around forty-five or forty-six years of age, and was a tall man with a dark complexion, close-set brows, and a heavy black beard; his eyes were deep in his head. He had on a shirt without a doublet, and through the opening at his throat could be seen what looked like a forest, so hairy-chested was he. He wore a cloak of baize that fell almost to his feet, which were shod in a pair of old shoes made into slippers. His legs were covered down to the ankles with wide linen breeches, and his hat, with bell-shaped crown and a broad brim, was the kind worn by wandering rogues. From a shoulder belt strapped across his bosom there hung a broadsword resembling those of the "Little Dog" brand.[12] He had short hairy hands and fat fingers with blunted nails. Nothing could be seen of his legs, but his feet were monstrosities, for they were sprawling and covered with bunions. The short of it is, he was the coarsest and most hideous barbarian in all the world. He was accompanied by the one who had brought the two boys there. Their guide, taking them by the hand, now presented them.

"These, Señor Monipodio," he said, "are the good lads I was telling you about. Let your Grace examine them and see whether or not they are worthy of entering our fraternity."

"That I will very gladly do," replied Monipodio.

I have neglected to state that as Monipodio came in all those who were waiting for him immediately dropped him a profound and sweeping curtsy, with the exception of the two ruffians, who merely lifted their hats in a don't-give-a-damn manner (as their kind are in the habit of saying) and then resumed their stroll along one side of the courtyard as he walked up and down the other side. Turning to the newcomers, Monipodio inquired concerning their profession, the country from which they came, and their parentage. It was Rincón who answered him.

"Our profession speaks for itself, seeing that we are here in your Grace's presence. Our country does not seem to me to be of any great importance, nor our parents either, since it is not a question of giving information prior to being received into some respectable order."

"You are quite right about that, my son," said Monipodio. "It is a good idea to conceal the things you speak of; for if luck does not turn out as it should, it is not desirable to have some such entry as this in the books of justice beneath the court clerk's seal: 'So-and-So, son of So-and-So, native of such and such a place, on such and such a day, was hanged or flogged,' or something of that sort, which to say the least does not sound well in the ears of God-fearing folk. And so, I repeat, there is an advantage in concealing your place of origin and your parentage, and even in changing your names, although among ourselves nothing is to be kept secret. For the present, your own names will be enough."

Rincón and Cortado then gave him the information he desired.

"From now on," continued Monipodio, "it is my will that you, Rincón, should be known as Rinconete, and you, Cortado, as Cortadillo, these being names that are very well suited to your age and the rules of our order. In accordance with those rules, however, it is also necessary for us to know the parents' names, for it is our custom every year to have certain masses said for the souls of deceased relatives and for our benefactors. We set apart a certain portion of the swag to pay the fee of the officiating priest; and it is said that these masses, thus duly sung and paid for, are of great benefit to such poor souls, by way of shipwreck.[13]

"Under the heading of our benefactors we include the one who defends us in court; the constable who tips us off; the executioner who shows us mercy; and the person who, when one of our number is fleeing through the street and the crowd in full cry behind him is crying 'Stop thief! Stop thief!' intervenes to stem the torrent of pursuers by saying, 'Let the poor fellow go, he's had enough bad luck, let him go, and let his sin be his punishment!' Then there are those feminine benefactors who with their sweat aid us in prison and in the galleys alike. There are the fathers and mothers who brought us into the world; and there is the court clerk who, if things go as they should, sees to it that there is no crime that is not a misdemeanor and no misdemeanor that gets much punishment. Our brotherhood observes the adversery of each one of these every year with all the pomposity and solemnitude in our power."

"Surely," said Rinconete (who had now been confirmed with this name), "all that is worthy of the most lofty and profound genius which we have heard that you, Señor Monipodio, possess. Our parents are still living, but if they should pass away, we will at once notify this most blessed and well-protected confraternity in order that their shipwreck or storm,[14] the adversery that your Grace speaks of, may be celebrated with the usual solemnity and pomp, unless you think it could be done better with pomposity and solemnitude as your Grace has just remarked."

"That is the way it shall be done," declared Monipo-

dio, "or there will not be so much as a piece left of me."
And, calling to the guide, he said, "Come here, Ganchuelo.[15] Have the sentries been posted?"

"Yes," replied the guide (whose name was Ganchuelo), "there are three of them on watch, and there
is no reason for us to fear being taken by surprise."

"Coming back, then, to what we were talking about,"
Monipodio went on, "I would like to know, my sons,
what it is you can do, so that I can give you work of the
kind you like and suited to your abilities."

"I," answered Rinconete, "know a little trick or two
with the pasteboards; I can play them from up my
sleeve or under the table; I've a sharp eye for a smudged
card or one that's been scraped; I'm a good hand at
ombre, four-spot, and eight-spot; I don't take second
place to anyone when it comes to shuffling or dealing
from the bottom of the deck. As for light-fingered work,
I'm right at home there, there's no one to equal me as
third man in a confidence game, and I can stack 'em
against the best there are." [16]

"That's all right for a start," said Monipodio, "but it's
all old stuff that any beginner knows, and is only good
when you get a sucker in the small hours of the morning.
But time will tell and we shall see. With this foundation
and half a dozen lessons, I trust to God that I shall be
able to make you a famous workman and possibly even
a master craftsman."

"We will do anything we can to serve your Grace
and the other gentlemen of the confraternity," said
Rinconete.

"And you, Cortadillo, what are your accomplishments?" Monipodio asked.

"I," replied Cortadillo, "know the trick that is called
'put in two and take out five.' [17] I can pick a pocket with
neatness and dispatch."

"Anything else?" Monipodio wanted to know.

"No," said Cortadillo, "I'm very sorry, but there isn't."

"Don't let it worry you, my son," said Monipodio, "for you've reached a safe harbor where you will not drown, and a school where you will learn, before you leave, all that you most need to know. But what about the matter of nerve, my lads, how goes it on that score?"

"How should it go with us," said Rinconete, "except very well? We have nerve enough for any undertaking that our profession calls for."

"That is good," said Monipodio, "but what I want to know is, do you have enough to stand it if they give you the *ansia* half a dozen times and not open your lips or call your mouth your own?"

"We already know what *ansia* means, Señor Monipodio," Cortadillo told him, "and we are ready for anything; for we are not so ignorant as to fail to realize that what the tongue says the throat must pay for. We know that Heaven shows plenty of mercy to the bold man (to give him no other name) who, with life and death depending on what he says, acts as if there were more letters in a *no* than in a *si*."

"That will do," said Monipodio at this point. "There is no need of your saying anything more. I may tell you that this one conversation that I have had with you has convinced, obliged, persuaded, and compelled me to give you from now on the rank of senior members, and dispense with the customary one year's apprenticeship."

"I am of the same opinion," declared one of the ruffians. And all those present approved the decision, for they had been listening to everything that was said, and they now asked Monipodio to grant the two lads permission to enjoy all the immunities of the brotherhood, by reason of the good impression the pair had made and their way of talking, which showed that they fully deserved the favor. He replied that he would grant the request by bestowing upon the youths, from now on, the prerogatives mentioned, and at the same time he reminded Rinconete and Cortadillo that they should value all this very highly since it meant they would not have to pay the usual tax of one-half of the first theft they committed or perform any menial functions throughout the whole of the first year; they would not have to carry messages from his agents to any senior brother whether in jail or at the house;[18] they might take their wine straight and eat when and where they liked without asking permission of their leader, and henceforth they would share as fully fledged members in whatever the older ones brought in.

These and other advantages that were offered them the two lads looked upon as a most exceptional favor and they were very polite in expressing their thanks to Señor Monipodio.

At that moment a lad came running up all out of breath. "The constable in charge of vagabonds," he announced, "is coming to this house, but he does not have his men with him."

"Let no one get excited," Monipodio directed. "He is a friend and never comes to do us harm; so calm yourselves, and I will go out and have a word with him."

With this, they all quieted down, for they had been somewhat alarmed. Monipodio, meanwhile, went out the door and stood for some time talking to the constable, then returned and asked, "Who was stationed in San Salvador Square today?"

"I was," said the one who acted as guide.

"Well then," Monipodio demanded, "how does it

come that you did not report an amber purse which someone made away with in that neighborhood, containing fifteen gold crowns, two double reales, and I can't tell you how many cuartos?"

"It is true," admitted the guide, "that such a purse was missing today, but I did not take it, nor do I have any idea who did."

"Don't be playing any tricks with me," Monipodio warned. "That purse must be produced, for the constable who is asking about it is a friend and does us countless good turns every year."

The youth again swore that he knew nothing about it, whereupon Monipodio became so angry that his eyes darted sparks.

"Let no one," he said, "think to jest by breaking the slightest rule of our order, for if he does it will cost him his life. That purse has to be produced. If it is being concealed to avoid payment of the tax, I myself will put up whatever is necessary out of my own pocket, for the constable must by all means be satisfied."

Ganchuelo once more began swearing, with many oaths and curses, that he had not taken the purse nor so much as laid eyes on it; all of which merely added fuel to Monipodio's wrath and caused a stir of excitement among all the others present at seeing their statutes and worthy ordinances thus broken. In view of all this dissension and agitation, Rinconete thought it would be a good thing to calm them down and at the same time please his superior, who was bursting with indignation; and so, having consulted with his friend Cortadillo, and with the latter's consent, he brought out the sacristan's purse.

"Let there be no further question about this matter, gentlemen," he said. "Here is the purse, and in it you will find all that the constable said it contained. My comrade Cortadillo lifted it today, along with a handkerchief which he took from the same person."

Cortadillo then brought out the handkerchief and displayed it. Upon sight of it, Monipodio said, "Cortadillo *the Good*, for such is the name and title by which he is to be known from now on, may keep this kerchief, which may be charged to my account. But as for the purse, it must go back to the constable, who is a relative of the sacristan's. We must comply with the old proverb which says: 'To one who has given you a whole chicken, you can spare a drumstick.' This worthy officer does more for us in a day than we could do for him in a hundred days."

By common consent, those present approved the gentlemanlike conduct of the newcomers and the decision of their superior, who now went out to return the purse to the constable, while Cortadillo was left with a new name, that of *the Good*, just as if he had been Don Alonso Pérez de Guzmán *the Good*, the one who from the walls of Tarifa threw down the knife with which his only child was beheaded.[19]

When Monipodio returned he was accompanied by two girls with painted faces, rouged lips, and bosoms whitened with ceruse. They wore serge half-mantles[20] and were so carefree and shameless in their demeanor that Rinconete and Cortadillo at once recognized them as coming from the brothel, an assumption that was perfectly correct. As soon as they entered they threw open their arms, and one ran up to Chiquiznaque, the other to Maniferro, for these were the names of the two ruffians, Maniferro's being due to the fact that he had an iron hand in place of the one that had been cut off as a punishment for his crimes. The pair embraced the newcomers joyfully and asked if they had brought anything to wet the gullet.[21]

"How could we fail you, my swordsman?" replied the one who was called Gananciosa.[22] "Your runner Silbatillo will be here shortly with a clothesbasket filled with what God has been pleased to give us."

This proved to be the truth, for at that very instant a lad came in bearing a hamper covered with a sheet. They were all very glad to see Silbato, and Monipodio at once ordered them to bring one of the reed mats from the little room off the side and spread it out in the middle of the patio. He then commanded them all to sit down around it in order that they might have a little snack and talk business at the same time. At this point, the old woman who had been praying in front of the image spoke up.

"Monipodio, my son," she said, "I am in no mood for feasting today. For a couple of days now I have had a dizziness in the head that drives me mad, and what's more, I must go finish my devotions before noon and place my candles in front of Our Lady of the Waters and the Holy Crucifix of Saint Augustine, something that I would not fail to do come snow or blizzard. What happened was this. Last night the Renegade and the Centipede brought to my house a washbasket somewhat larger than this one and filled with white linen. I swear to God and upon my soul, the clothes were still wet and covered with suds, which the poor fellows had not had time to remove; and they were sweating so much beneath the weight of the hamper that it was a pity to see the water dripping and pouring from their faces—they were so red that it gave them the appearance of a couple of cherubs.

"They told me that they were on the trail of a cattle

dealer who had just weighed in a flock of lambs at the slaughterhouse, as they wished to get their fingers into a big catskin bag filled with reales that he carried on his person. They did not take the linen out to count it but trusted entirely to my conscience; and may God fulfill my worthy desires and free us all from the clutches of the law, I did not touch the basket, and you will find everything just as it was."

"I believe everything you say, mother," said Monipodio. "Let it stay where it is, and at nightfall I will come and make an inventory of what it contains and will give each one exactly what is coming to him, as I always do."

"Let it be as you have commanded, my son," said the old woman, "and since it is getting late, give me a little swig, if you have one, to comfort this stomach of mine which is feeling very faint."

"Indeed you shall have a drink, mother!" said Escalanta,[23] for that was the name of Gananciosa's companion. She uncovered the basket and brought out a leather flask with nearly two arrobas of wine and a cork vessel that with no trouble at all would hold an azumbre.[24] After filling the vessel, Escalanta gave it to the devout old woman, who took it in both her hands.

"You have poured me a lot, daughter Escalanta," she said, blowing off a little of the foam, "but God will give me strength for everything." And putting her lips to the brim, she drank it all down at a single gulp without pausing for breath. "That's from Guadalcanal," she remarked, "and it has a wee taste of gypsum.[25] May God comfort you, my daughter, who have thus comforted me. The only thing I am afraid of is that it may do me harm, for I have had nothing to eat."

"It won't hurt you, mother," said Monipodio, "for it's over three years old."

"In the Virgin's name, I hope you're right," the old woman answered, and she went on, "Look, my daughters, and see if by any chance you have a spare cuarto to pay for my candles. Being anxious to bring you news of the basket, I came away in such a hurry that I left my purse at home."

"Yes, I have something for you, Señora Pipota," replied Gananciosa (Pipota was the old woman's name).[26] "Here are two cuartos for you, and with one of them I wish you would buy a candle for me and place it in front of Señor Saint Michael; and if you have enough for two, offer the other to Señor Saint Blas, for they are my patron saints. I'd like to have you place one before the image of Señora Saint Lucy also, as I am devoted to her for the sake of the eyes;[27] but I have no more small change, so that will have to wait for another day when I can pay my respects to all of them."

"You will be very wise in doing so, daughter. See to it that you are not miserly; for it is very important to carry your own candles before you die and not wait for your heirs or executors to do it for you."

"Mother Pipota is quite right about that," said Escalanta, putting her hand into her purse. She gave the old woman another cuarto, directing her to place two more candles before whatever saints she thought would be most appreciative and helpful.

"Enjoy yourselves, children," said Pipota as she prepared to leave. "Enjoy yourselves now while there is time, for when old age comes you will weep as I do for all the moments you lost in youth. Remember me to God in your prayers. I go to pray for myself and you, that He may free and preserve us in this dangerous trade of ours, and keep us out of the hands of the law."

With this she went away. When she had left they all sat down around the mat and Gananciosa spread the sheet for a tablecloth. The first thing she brought out of the hamper was a large bunch of radishes and some two dozen oranges and lemons, followed by a large earthenware pot filled with slices of fried codfish. There was also half a Dutch cheese, a jug of fine olives, a platter of shrimp, and a great quantity of crabs, with a thirst-inspirer in the form of capers drowned in peppers, together with three very white loaves of Gandul bread.[28]

There were around fourteen at the meal, and none of them failed to bring out his yellow-handled knife, with the exception of Rinconete, who made use of his short sword. The two baize-clad old men and the one who had served as guide to the boys then began pouring the wine from the cork vessel; but no sooner had they fallen to on the oranges than they were all startled by a loud knocking at the door. Ordering them to be calm, Monipodio went into the low room at the side and took down a shield, then drew his sword, came back to the door, and in a frightful hollow-sounding voice called out, "Who is there?"

"It is I," was the answer from without. "And I, Señor Monipodio, am nobody other than Tagarete.[29] I am on watch this morning, and I have come to tell you that Juliana with the chubby face is headed this way. Her hair is all down and she is crying as if something terrible had happened to her."

At that moment the woman came up, sobbing loudly, and when Monipodio heard her he opened the door and ordered Tagarete to go back to his post and not to make such an uproar the next time he came to report. The man promised to observe this admonition, and Chubby Face then came in. She was a girl of the same kind and profession as the other two. Her hair was streaming, her face was covered with bruises, and upon entering the patio she fell to the ground in a faint.

Ganaciosa and Escalanta ran to assist her, and upon undoing her bosom they found that it was all black and blue as if it had been mangled. They then threw water on her and revived her.

"God's justice and the King's," she cried, "be upon that shameless thief, that cowardly sneak thief, that dirty scoundrel! I've saved him from the gallows more times than he has hairs in his beard. Poor me! Just see for what it is I have squandered the flower of my youth —for a wicked deceiver, an incorrigible villain like him!"

"Take it easy, Chubby Face," said Monipodio. "I am here, and I will see that justice is done you. Tell us how you have been wronged, and before you have finished I will avenge you. Have you had a falling out with your protector? [30] If that is the case, and it is revenge you want, you don't have to open your mouth."

"What a protector!" replied Juliana. "I'd rather be protected in hell than by that lion among lambs and lamb among men. Do you think I'm ever going to eat at the same table or sleep in the same bed with him again? Before I'd do that, I'd see this flesh devoured by jackals. Just look what he's done to me!" And, raising her skirts up to her knees or a little higher, she exhibited her legs, which were all covered with welts. "This is the kind of treatment I get from that ingrate of a Repolido,[31] who owes more to me than he does to the mother that bore him.

"And why do you think he did it? Was it on account of anything I had done? Certainly not. He was gambling and losing, and he sent Cabrillas, his runner, to ask me for thirty reales, and I only sent him twenty-four—may all the hard work and trouble I had in earning them be counted by Heaven against my sins! In repayment for this kindness on my part, thinking that I had more than I did and was holding out on him, he took me this morning and dragged me out into the fields behind the King's Garden, and there, among the olive trees, without even removing the iron buckles, he gave me such a flogging with his belt that he left me for dead. These welts that you see will bear witness to the truth of my story."

She now began screaming again, demanding justice, and again Monipodio and all the young bucks who were present promised that she should have it. Gananciosa took her hand to console her, saying that she herself would gladly give one of her most prized possessions if her own man had treated her the same way.

"For I must tell you, sister Chubby Face," she said, "if you do not know it already, punishment of that sort is a sign of love. When these ruffians beat and kick us, it is then that they most adore us. Come now, own up: after your Repolido had abused you like that, didn't he give you a caress?"

"Did he give me a caress?" said the weeping girl. "He gave me a hundred thousand, and he would have given a finger of his hand as well if I'd have gone with him to his lodgings. I even thought I could see the tears starting from his eyes after he had thrashed me like that."

"There is no doubt of it," said Gananciosa; "and he would weep with pain at seeing what he has done to you; for men like that, in such cases, have no sooner committed a fault than they are sorry for it. You will see, sister: he will come looking for you before we leave here and will ask your forgiveness for everything that has happened. He will be meek as a lamb."

"The truth is," said Monipodio, "that cowardly jailbird had better not set foot inside this door until he has done full penance for his crime. The nerve of him, laying his hands upon this girl's face or body! Why, when it comes to neatness and earnings, she can compete with Gananciosa here, and I can pay her no higher compliment than that!"

"Ay," exclaimed Juliana at this point, "don't be speaking ill of the poor fellow, Señor Monipodio, for however bad he may be, I love him with all my heart. The words that my friend Gananciosa just spoke in his behalf are the breath of life to me. As a matter of fact, I think I'll go look for him right now."

"Not if you take my advice," said Gananciosa, "for it will only make him feel puffed up and more important than ever, and he will treat you as he would a fencer's dummy. Calm yourself, sister, and before long, as I have said, you will see him coming in here full of repentance. If he does not come, we will make up some verses about him that will infuriate him."

"That we will," said Chubby Face, "for I have a thousand and one things to say to him."

"I will be the scribe, if necessary," said Monipodio; "for although I am not a poet by any means, if a man but roll up his sleeves to it he can turn out a couple of thousand couplets in no time at all; and if they are not all they ought to be, I have a barber friend, a great poet, who trims verses at all hours. But let us finish what we have begun by putting away this food, and afterward everything will be all right."

Juliana was content to obey her superior, and they all returned to their *gaudeamus* and within a short while had reached the bottom of the basket and the dregs of the flasks. The old men drank *sine fine,* the young men right heartily, and the ladies said their Kyrie eleisons.[32] The two elders then asked permission to leave, and

Monipodio granted it, charging them to be sure to keep him informed of anything that the community ought to know. They promised to do so and went their way.

Being somewhat curious, Rinconete, after first begging Monipodio's pardon, asked him of what use two such old and dignified graybeards could be to the brotherhood. Monipodio replied that they were what were known in thieves' slang as "hornets," and that their business was to go through the city during the day and spy out houses that might be burglarized at night. They also followed those who drew money from the Bank of India or the Treasury, in order to see where it was taken and what was done with it. Having ascertained this, they tested the thickness of the walls of the house in question and marked the spot for the thieves to drill their *guzpátaros,* or holes, by means of which they effected an entrance. In short, he went on to say, they were quite as useful as any member of the brotherhood, if not more so, and received a fifth of whatever was stolen as a result of their efforts, just as His Majesty gets a fifth of any treasure that is found. They were, moreover, very truthful and upright individuals, God fearing and conscientious; they led model lives and enjoyed a good reputation.

"Some of them," he further explained, "especially the two who were here just now, are so accommodating that they are satisfied with much less than our rules allow them. We have another pair, a couple of porters who serve as furniture movers at times; they know the entrances and exits to all the houses in the city and which dwellings are worth our while and which are not."

"All that is wonderful, if you ask me," said Rinconete, "and I only hope that I can be of some use to this excellent fraternity."

"Heaven," said Monipodio, "always grants worthy

desires." Just then there came another knock at the door, and he went over to see who was there.

"Open up, Señor Monipodio," came a voice in answer to his question, "it is I, Repolido."

"Don't let him in, your Grace!" cried Chubby Face when she heard this. "Don't open the door for that Tarpeian mariner, that tiger of Ocaña!" [33]

Monipodio paid no attention to her, however, and when she saw that Repolido was being admitted, she rose and ran into the room where the shields were, closing the door behind her.

"Get that ugly mug out of my sight!" she screamed from within. "I don't want to see that torturer of innocents, that frightener of tame doves!" [34]

Maniferro and Chiquiznaque held Repolido back, for he was determined to enter the room where Chubby Face was. Seeing that they would not let him go, he called out to her, "Stop it, little spitfire! For Heaven's sake, be quiet if you want to get married!"

"Get married, you rascal!" replied Chubby Face. "Just hear what he's harping on now! You'd like it all right if I'd take you, but I'd sooner marry a skeleton."

"That's enough, you little fool," said Repolido; "it's getting late. And don't let it turn your head to see me come to you so tame and meek, for, by the living God, if my anger mounts to the belfry, the relapse will be worse than the fall; so let's all come down off our high horses and not be giving the devil his dinner."

"I'd give him his supper too," said Chubby Face, "if only I never had to see you again."

"Didn't you hear what I said?" asked Repolido. "By God, Madame Strumpet, I'm losing my temper. I'll be putting them all out by the dozen, even though there's no sale." [35]

"Let there be no rows in my presence," said Monipodio, "Chubby Face will come out not as a result of threats but because of her affection for me, and everything will be fine. When lovers quarrel, their pleasure is all the greater after they've made up. Come on out, Juliana my child, come out little Chubby Face, for my sake, and I will see to it that Repolido begs your forgiveness on his knees."

"Let him do that," said Escalanta, "and we will all be on his side and will insist on Juliana's coming out."

"If you expect me to humiliate myself," said Repolido, "a whole Swiss army couldn't force me to do that; but if it's to please Chubby Face, I may say that I'd not only get down on my knees but would drive a nail straight through my forehead to be of service to her."

Chiquiznaque and Maniferro laughed at this, at which Repolido, who thought they were making sport of him, became very angry. "If anyone," he said, "so much as thinks of laughing at anything that Chubby Face may say against me or I may say against her, I can tell him that he's a liar every time he does so." [36]

Upon hearing this, Chiquiznaque and Maniferro exchanged such a dark look that Monipodio saw there would be trouble unless he took a hand.

"Do not go any further, gentlemen," he warned them. "Let us have no more of these insults; chew them up between your teeth, and so long as they do not reach the girdle,[37] no one will be the worse for it."

"We are quite sure," replied Chiquiznaque, "that such threats were not meant for us; for if we thought they were, the tambourine is in hands that know how to play it."

"We also have a tambourine, Sir Chiquiznaque," was Repolido's retort, "and we too, if necessary, can make the bells ring. I have said that whoever tries to make a joke out of this is a liar, and if anyone thinks otherwise, let him follow me, and with a sword that's shorter by a palm's length I will show him that I mean what I say."

With this, he started to go out the door. Chubby Face was listening, and when she heard how angry he was she came running out. "Stop him!" she cried. "Don't let him go or he'll be up to his old tricks! Can't you see what a temper he's in? Don't you know he's a Judas Macarelo[38] when he gets started? Come back here, you big bully! Come back, light of my eyes!" And laying hold of his cape, she tugged on it. Monipodio came to her assistance and between them they held him back. Chiquiznaque and Maniferro did not know whether to be offended or not and so remained quiet, waiting to see what he would do. Yielding to Chubby Face and Monipodio's entreaties, Repolido now turned. "Friends," he said, "ought not to provoke or make sport of each other, especially when they see that it is not being taken in good part."

"There is no one here," replied Maniferro, "who would want to provoke or make sport of a friend, and seeing that we are all friends, let's shake hands on it."

"Spoken like true friends," declared Monipodio, "and so, shake hands and let that be the end of it."

They did so at once. Escalanta took off one of her clogs and began drumming on it as if it had been a tambourine. Gananciosa snatched up a new palm-leaf broom that happened to be there and by scraping it produced a sound that, while harsh and unpleasing, went well enough with the one that came from the clog.[39] Monipodio broke a plate in two and, taking the pieces between his fingers, began rattling them with great dexterity, thereby providing a counterpoint. Rinconete and Cortadillo were quite astonished by this use to which the broom was put, for it was something they had never seen before.

"So that surprises you, does it?" said Maniferro. "Well it may, for there has never been an instrument invented that is so convenient and ready at hand or so cheap. In fact, I heard a student remark only the other day that neither Negrofeo, who brought Arauz up from hell, nor Marión, who mounted a dolphin and rose from the sea as if he were riding a hired mule, nor that other great musician who built a city that had a hundred gates and an equal number of posterns,[40] ever invented a better one, or one that you can pick up any time and is so easy to learn, since it has no frets, keys, or strings, and you don't have to bother about tuning it. They say it was the idea of a certain gallant of this city who prides himself on being a very Hector where music is concerned."

"That I can well believe," replied Rinconete; "but let's listen to our own musicians, for Gananciosa has just spit on the ground, and that's a sign she's getting ready to sing."

This proved to be the truth, for Monipodio had asked her to render a few popular *seguidillas*.[41] The first to begin, however, was Escalanta, in a small, quavering voice:

"For a red-headed lad of old Seville,
     My heart is all aflame."

She was followed by Gananciosa:

"For a little brown lad I know, any girl
     Would part with her good name."

Monipodio then began rattling his fragments of broken plate in an energetic manner, and he too sang:

"Lovers may quarrel, but when peace is made,
        Their loving pleasure grows."

Chubby Face also could not refrain from expressing her joy, and she took off one of her own clogs and began a dance as an accompaniment to the others:

"Then stop, for it is to your own flesh
        You give these angry blows."

"Enough of that!" cried Repolido. "There's no sense in harping on what's past and done, so take another theme and let bygones be bygones."

The song they had begun might have lasted for some time if it had not been for an urgent knock at the door. When Monipodio went out to see who was there, the sentinel informed him that he had caught sight of the magistrate down at the end of the street and added that the officer was coming that way, preceded by Grizzly and the Hawk, a couple of neutral constables.[42] Upon hearing this, those inside were all greatly alarmed. Chubby Face and Escalanta were so excited that they put on each other's clogs and Gananciosa dropped her broom and Monipodio his improvised clappers. The music ceased, and silence fell on the frightened assemblage. Chiquiznaque was dumb, Repolido was scared, and Maniferro worried. Then everyone quickly disappeared from sight, some in one direction and some in another, and ran up to the roofs and terraces in order to make their escape by way of the other street.

Neither the sudden firing of a harquebus nor a clap

of thunder out of a clear sky ever inspired such terror in a flock of careless pigeons as the unexpected arrival of the officer of the law did in all those good people gathered there. Rinconete and Cortadillo did not know what to do and accordingly remained where they were, waiting to see what the outcome of the squall would be. But the sentinel soon came back to say that the magistrate had gone on past without any sign of suspicion directed at their house.

As this report was being made to Monipodio, a young gentleman came up to the gate, dressed, as the saying goes, like a man about town.[43] Bringing the newcomer into the courtyard, Monipodio ordered Chiquiznaque, Maniferro, Repolido, and all the others to descend. Inasmuch as they had remained in the patio, Rinconete and Cortadillo were able to overhear the conversation that took place between the new arrival and his host. The young gentleman was asking Monipodio why they had made such a botch of the job he had ordered done. Monipodio replied that he did not know what the circumstances were but that the member charged with executing the job was present and would give a good account of himself. At that point Chiquiznaque came down, and his superior thereupon asked him if he had carried out the commission in question, a matter of a knife wound of fourteen stitches.

"Which one was that?" asked Chiquiznaque, "the merchant at the crossroads?"

"That's the one," said the gentleman.

"Well," said Chiquiznaque, "I will tell you what happened. I was waiting at night at the door of his house, and he came home shortly before time for prayers. I went up to him, took one look at his face, and saw that it was so small that a wound of fourteen stitches was out

of the question; and not being able to keep my promise
and follow destructions—"

"*Instructions,* your Grace means to say, not destructions," the gentleman corrected him.

"That was what I meant," said Chiquiznaque. "Well
then, seeing that his face was too small and narrow for
the required number of stitches, and not wishing to
have my trip for nothing, I gave the cut to a lackey of
his, and you can be sure that it was a first-rate one."

"I would rather," said the gentleman, "that you had
given the master one of seven stitches than the servant
one of fourteen. The short of it is, you have not complied with our agreement; but no matter, the thirty
ducats that I left as down payment will be no great loss
to me, and so I kiss your Grace's hands." Saying this,
he took off his hat and turned to go, but Monipodio
seized him by the cloak of varicolored cloth that he
wore and drew him back.

"Just a moment," he said. "We have kept our word
honorably and well, and you are going to have to do the
same. You owe twenty ducats, and you're not leaving
here until you pay or give us the equivalent in security."

"Is that what your Grace calls keeping your word,"
the gentleman demanded, "giving the cut to the servant
instead of the master?"

"How well you get it!" exclaimed Chiquiznaque. "You
don't seem to remember the proverb that says: 'He
who loves Beltrán loves his dog.' " [44]

"But how does that proverb fit here?" said the gentleman.

"Why," Chiquiznaque went on, "isn't it the same
thing as saying: 'He who hates Beltrán hates his dog'?
Beltrán is the merchant and you hate him; his lackey
is his dog; by giving it to the dog you give it to Beltrán,

the debt is wiped out, and we've accomplished our part. So there's nothing to do but settle the account."

"I will back him up in that," added Monipodio. "You took the words right out of my mouth, friend Chiquiznaque. As for you, Sir Gallant, don't be quibbling with your friends and servants but take my advice and pay for the work that's been done. If you would like for us to give the master another one of whatever size his face will hold, you may consider that they are already taking the stitches."

"In that case," replied the gallant, "I will gladly pay the entire cost for both of them."

"Have no doubt about it," Monipodio assured him, "but as you are a good Christian, believe me when I tell you that Chiquiznaque will leave so perfect a scar that people will think the fellow was born with it."

"In view of that assurance and your promise," said the gentleman, "take this chain as security for the twenty ducats I owe and the forty that I will pay you for the cut that is to come. By its weight it is worth a thousand reales, and it may be that it will remain in your hands, for I have an idea I am going to need another job of fourteen stitches before very long."

As he said this he removed from about his neck a chain made up of small links and gave it to Monipodio, who, upon running it through his fingers and weighing it in his hand, saw that it was no product of the alchemist. The leader of the gang was glad to have it and accepted it very politely, for he was extremely well bred. It was arranged that the job should be done that night by Chiquiznaque, and the gentleman then left well satisfied.

Calling all the absent ones down from the roof, Monipodio stood in the center of the group. He took out a memorandum book, which he carried in the hood of his cape, and gave it to Rinconete, as he himself did not know how to read. Upon opening it to the first page Rinconete found the following inscription:

MEMORANDUM OF SLASHES TO BE GIVEN THIS WEEK

" 'First, to the merchant of the crossroads; worth fifty crowns; thirty received on account. Secutor,[45] Chiquiznaque.' "

"That's all, son, I think," said Monipodio; "go on to where it says 'Memorandum of Thrashings.' "

Rinconete turned the page and on the following one found the entry. Beneath it was written: " 'To the alehouse keeper of Alfalfa Square, one dozen heavy blows at a crown each; eight on account. Time limit, six days. Secutor, Maniferro.' "

"You may as well cross that out," said Maniferro. "It will be taken care of tonight."

"Are there any more, son?" asked Monipodio.

"Yes," answered Rinconete, "there is one other that says: 'To the hunchback tailor, known as the Finch, six heavy blows at the request of the lady who left her necklace with him. Secutor, Lop-Eared.' " [46]

"I wonder," Monipodio mused, "why that hasn't been attended to. Lop-Eared must undoubtedly be sick, for it's two days beyond the time limit and it hasn't been carried out yet."

"I ran into him yesterday," said Maniferro, "and he told me that it was the hunchback who was home sick, which is the reason why it wasn't done."

"That I can well believe," said Monipodio, "for I know Lop-Eared to be so good a worker that if there had not been some such reason he would have finished it at once. Are there any more, my lad?"

"No, sir," replied Rinconete.

"Then turn on," Monipodio directed him, "to where it says 'Memorandum of Common Outrages.'"

Rinconete turned the leaves until he came to this inscription:

MEMORANDUM OF COMMON OUTRAGES, NAMELY:
THROWING OF VIALS; SMEARING WITH JUNIPER OIL;
NAILING UP OF SAMBENITOS AND HORNS; PERSONS
TO BE MOCKED IN PUBLIC; CREATING FALSE
ALARMS AND DISTURBANCES; PRETENDED STAB-
BINGS; CIRCULATION OF SLANDERS[47]

"And what does it say below?" asked Monipodio.

"It says," Rinconete continued, "'Smearing with juniper oil at the house of—'"

"Don't mention the house," said Monipodio, "for I know where it is. I am the *tu autem* and the executor in this trifling matter. Four crowns have already been paid against the total of eight."

"That's right," said Rinconete; "it's all written down here, and below it is, 'Nailing up of horns—'"

"Don't read that either," Monipodio again admonished him; "the house and the address do not matter. It is enough to commit the offense without speaking of it in public, for it is a great burden upon the conscience. I would rather nail up a hundred horns and as many sambenitos, providing I was paid for it, than mention the fact a single time even to the mother that bore me."

"The executor in this case," Rinconete informed him, "is Snub-nose."

"That has already been done and paid for," said Monipodio. "Look and see if there is anything else; for if I am not mistaken, there should be an alarm at twenty crowns, one-half down payment and our

whole community as the executor; we have all this
month in which to carry it out, and it shall be done
without fail—it will be one of the biggest things that
has happened in this town in a long while. Give me the
book, lad. I know there's nothing else. Business is a
bit slack just now, but times will change, and it may
be we shall have more to do than we can take care of.
There is not a leaf stirs without God's will, and we cannot force people to avenge themselves, especially seeing
that everyone is now so brave in his own behalf that he
doesn't want to pay for having something done that he
can just as well do with his own hands."

"That is the way it is," said Repolido. "But, look,
Señor Monipodio, let us know what your orders are, for
it is getting late and the heat of the day is coming on
very fast."

"What is to be done," said Monipodio, "is this. You are
all to go to your posts and stay there until Sunday, when
we will meet in this same place and divide everything
that has fallen into our hands, without cheating anyone. Rinconete *the Good* [48] and Cortadillo will have
for their district until the end of the week that part of
the suburbs that lies between the Golden Tower and
the Castle Postern. There they will have no trouble in
working their tricks, for I have seen others that were not
nearly so clever come back every day with more than
twenty reales in small change, not to speak of the silver,
and all this with only one deck and with four cards missing. Ganchuelo," he went on, addressing the youths,
"will show you the lay of the land, and even though you
go as far as San Sebastián and San Telmo, it will not
make much difference, although it is only right that no
one should trespass on another's territory."

The pair kissed his hand in return for the favor he
had done them and promised to fulfil their tasks faith-

fully and well, with all diligence and discretion. Monipodio then took out from the hood of his cloak a folded
sheet of paper containing a list of members and directed
Rinconete to put down his own name and that of Cortadillo; but since they had no ink there, he told them
they might take the paper with them and attend to
the matter in the first apothecary's shop to which they
came. The entry was to read: "Rinconete and Cortadillo,
full members; apprenticeship, none; Rinconete, card-
sharper; Cortadillo, sneak thief." They also were to note
the day, month, and year, but were to say nothing about
their parents or place of origin.

At this point one of the old men known as "hornets"
arrived on the scene. "I have come," he said, "to inform
your Graces that I just now met the young Wolf [49] of
Malaga on the cathedral steps and he asked me to tell
you that he is getting better at the business every day
and that, with a clean deck, he could take the money
from Satan himself. If he hasn't been around to report
and render you obedience as usual, it is because he is
so down and out, but he will be here Sunday without
fail."

"I always did believe," said Monipodio, "that the
Wolf would be outstanding in his line, for he has the
best and cleverest pair of hands for it that anyone could
wish. To be a good worker at a trade, you have to have
good tools with which to practice it as well as the brains
with which to learn it."

"I also," the old man continued, "ran into the Jew in
a lodging house in the calle de Tintores. He was dressed
like a priest and had gone there because he had heard
that a couple of Peruvians were living in the house and
he wished to see if he could get into a game with them,
even though a small one at first, as it might amount to
much more in the end. He also said that he would be

sure to be at the meeting on Sunday and would give an account of himself."

"That Jew," said Monipodio, "is another good hawk and a very clever fellow; but I haven't seen him for days now, and that is not so good. I swear, if he doesn't watch his step, I'll fix him. That thief has no more holy orders than a Turk, and he doesn't know any more Latin than my mother. Anything else new?"

"No," answered the old man, "at least not that I know of."

"Very well then," said Monipodio, "here is a little something for you all." And with this he divided some forty reales among them. "Let no one fail to be here Sunday, and each one will get what's coming to him."

They all thanked him for his kindness, and the young couples embraced once more: Repolido and Chubby Face, Escalanta and Maniferro, and Gananciosa and Chiquiznaque. It was arranged that they should all meet that night at Pipota's house after they had finished the work in hand, and Monipodio remarked that he would also be there to make an inventory of the clothes-basket but that now he had to go and attend to the job of smearing with juniper oil. He embraced Rinconete and Cortadillo and dismissed them with his blessing, charging them that they should never have any permanent lodging or stopping place, as that was best for all concerned. Ganchuelo went with them to show them their post, and took occasion to remind them once again that they should not fail to put in an appearance on Sunday, since he believed that Monipodio intended to give them a lecture on things that had to do with their trade. He then went away, leaving the two lads quite astonished at all they had seen.

Although a mere boy, Rinconete had a naturally keen mind, and having accompanied his father in selling papal bulls, he knew something about the proper use of language. He had to laugh loudly as he thought of some of the words that Monipodio and the rest of that foolish community had employed. In place of *per modum suffragii* Monipodio had said *per modo de naufragio* ("by way of shipwreck"), and in speaking of the loot he had said *estupendo* in place of *estipendio*.[50] Then there was Chubby Face's remark that Repolido was like a "Tarpeian mariner," and a "tiger of Ocaña" (in place of Hyrcania), along with countless other silly things, of the same sort and even worse. (He was especially amused by her hope that the labor she had expended in earning the twenty-four reales would be counted by Heaven against her sins.)

Above all, he marveled at the absolute assurance they all felt of going to Heaven when they died so long as they did not fail in their devotions, and this in spite of all the thefts, murders, and other offenses of which they were guilty in the sight of God. He laughed also, as he thought of the old woman, Pipota, who, leaving the stolen hamper at home, went off to place her wax candles in front of the images; by doing so she doubtless was convinced that she would go to Heaven fully clothed and with her shoes on. He was no less astonished at the obedience and respect they all showed Monipodio, that coarse, unscrupulous barbarian. He recalled what he had read in the latter's memorandum book of the practices in which they were all engaged. And, finally, he was astounded by the careless manner in which justice was administered in that famous city of Seville, with people so pernicious as these and possessed of such unnatural instincts carrying on their pursuits almost openly.

He made up his mind to persuade his companion that they should not continue long in this desperate and evil way of life, one so free and dissolute and marked by such uncertainty. But in spite of it all, being young and inexperienced, he did continue in it for a number of months, and in the course of that time had certain adventures which it would take too long to set down here. Accordingly, we must wait for another occasion to hear the story of his life and the strange things that happened to him, as well as to his teacher Monipodio, along with other events having to do with the members of that infamous academy, all of which should be very edifying and well might serve as an example and a warning to those who read.

Man of Glass

The "El Licenciado Vidriera" (literally, "The Licentiate of Glass" or "The Licentiate Glasscase") is a story concerning which critical opinion has varied somewhat, but most authorities look upon it as one of the best of the Exemplary Novels. Such distinguished scholars as Marcelino Menéndez y Pelayo and Francisco A. de Icaza have believed that here Cervantes is merely using the novel form as an excuse for the stringing together of apothegms—in other words, for saying things that he wanted said; and, in fact, the author does seize the opportunity to express himself forcefully on a number of subjects that are favorites of his: on booksellers (publishers) and their treatment of writers, on actors, dramatists, and the theater, on the state of poetry, and so forth. It would appear much more likely, however, that his real interest lay in the theme of madness— which seems to have been something of an obsession with him, as it was with the mature Shakespeare—and in the bitter ironic twist at the end, with the madman who has regained his sanity being left to starve by a society that previously has supported him and followed him about and that now compels him, in order to live, to embrace the life of a soldier and die on the battle-field.

In a way it is the Don Quixote theme again, though not quite the same, and again the "madness" of the protagonist is questionable. Though in a short story such as *this* there is much less opportunity for the gradual development of character than in a long work like the Don Quixote, even here the licentiate's madness is motivated with a certain realism and credibility, with an avoidance of the miraculous. May we not see in Glasscase a Don Quixote who in place of romances of chivalry has been reading theological tomes and works on moral philosophy? He is the truth teller, the social and moral satirist (for his social satire is motivated always from the moral and religious point of view), who sallies forth to reveal to his fellowmen the lie upon which the existence of nearly everyone is based. The various trades, professions, occupations are in turn subjected to his denuding irony; it is the whole of human society that is under indictment in the sight of Heaven, Plato's heaven of ideals and that of the Christian as well; but in the end it is the idealist himself who is overthrown, just as the Knight of La Mancha was, and once more we are brought face to face with the problem of the world as it is and the world as it ought to be.

Aside from its philosophical implications, the "Man of Glass" is of interest for the autobiographical elements it contains, particularly the reminiscences of Italy (Cervantes, like the hero of the tale, may also have served in Flanders). The young Rodaja's itinerary, the cities he visited, the sights he saw, the wines he drank and the food he ate, may well be a reflection of the author's own experiences. If true, this would confirm the view that Cervantes' acquaintance with Italy was comparatively slight, scarcely going beyond that of a tourist. There will also be found more than one passage that has a light to throw on Cervantes' intellectual and spiritual biography, his attitudes and prejudices, his personal likes and dislikes, his view of his literary contemporaries and of the life that a writer had to lead. When, for instance, we are told that Rodaja carried with him only two volumes, a book containing prayers to Our Lady and a Garcilaso "without notes," are we not perhaps justified in assuming that the author's own pocket library was similarly constituted? It would be in keeping with what we know of Cervantes the devout Catholic and admirer of Garcilaso de la Vega.

On the side of form, this novel presents certain difficulties for the translator which would tempt him to shun the task of rendering it into English. In a number of places the humor is dependent upon word plays, some of which are quite untranslatable while others can only be suggested. But the story impressed this editor as being too good, too important to be omitted, and he has accordingly done his best with it.

A COUPLE of students were riding along the banks of the river Tormes when they came upon a lad sleeping beneath a tree. He was around eleven years of age and dressed like a peasant. Having sent a servant to awaken him, they asked him from where it was he came and what he meant by falling asleep in a lonely spot like that. The lad's answer was that he had forgotten the name of his native province, and was bound for the city of Salamanca to look for a master whom he might serve, but on one condition, that he be permitted to continue his studies. They then inquired if he knew how to read, and he assured them that he not only could read but could also write.

"In that case," said one of the gentlemen, "it is not through any lapse of memory that you have forgotten the name of your birthplace."

"Be that as it may," replied the youth, "no one shall know of it, nor shall they know the name of my parents, until I am in a position to reflect honor on them and it."

"And in what manner do you propose to reflect honor on them?" asked the other gentleman.

"Through the fame that I acquire for my learning," said the boy, "for I have heard it said that out of men bishops are made."

As a result of this reply the two travelers decided to take the lad along with them, and when they arrived at their destination, they allowed him to begin studying; for it is a custom in that university to permit servants to do so.[1] He told them that his name was Tomás Rodaja,[2] which led his masters to infer, by reason of the name and the manner in which he was clad, that he was the son of some poor peasant. Within a few days they had dressed him in a black robe, and in the course of a few weeks he gave evidence of possessing a mind that was quite out of the ordinary. He served his employers so loyally, diligently, and conscientiously that, while in nowise neglecting his books, he gave the impression of being solely concerned with waiting upon them.

And since a good servant is likely to win good treatment from his master, Tomás Rodaja soon became more of a companion to them than anything else. The short of it is that during the eight years he remained with them he became so famous in the university, by reason of his fine intellect and outstanding abilities, that people of all sorts were led to love and esteem him. His principal study was the law, but where he shone most brightly was in the field of literature and the humanities. Fortunately, he had an astonishing memory, and this as well as the keen intelligence he displayed contributed to his reputation.

At length the time came when his masters had finished their own studies and were ready to return to their home, which was in one of the largest cities in

Andalusia. They took Tomás with them, and he stayed there a few days, but it was not long before he felt a great desire to return to his books at Salamanca—a desire that is shared by all those who once have tasted of the pleasant way of life that city affords—and he accordingly asked the gentlemen for permission to leave them. Being courteous and generous-minded, they granted his request and provided for him so well that he was able to live for three whole years on what they gave him.

Expressing his thanks to them, Tomás said good-by and left Malaga, which was the city in which his masters lived; and as he was descending the Zambra slope on the road to Antequera, he fell in with a gentleman on horseback who was gaily clad for the road [3] and was accompanied by two servants, also mounted. Upon joining his new acquaintance, he learned that the latter was going in the same direction, and so they became traveling companions. They spoke of various things, with Tomás revealing his rare qualities of mind while the other gave proof of gallantry and good breeding. The gentleman stated that he was a captain of infantry in the service of His Majesty, and that his ensign was at that moment engaged in recruiting a company in the neighborhood of Salamanca. He went on to praise the life of a soldier, giving a vivid description of the beauty of Naples, the merrymakings of Palermo, the abundance of good things to be found at Milan, the feastings of Lombardy, and the splendid meals to be had in the hostelries. He politely and carefully explained the meaning of such expressions as *"Aconcha, patrón; passa acá, manigoldo; venga la macarela, li polastri e li macarroni."* [4]

He extolled to the sky the freedom that soldiers enjoyed in Italy, but said nothing about the cold of sentry duty, the danger that lay in an attack, the terror of battles, the hunger endured in a siege, the destruction wrought by mines, or other things of that sort, although there are some who look upon these burdensome accompaniments of the military life as constituting its chief characteristic. In short, he talked so long and so well that Tomás Rodaja's judgment began to waver, and the lad came to feel an attraction for this way of life which is always so near to death.

Being extremely well pleased with the boy's good appearance, his qualities of mind, and his manners, Don Diego de Valdivia (for that was the captain's name) invited Tomás, in case he was desirous of seeing Italy, to come along with him and share his mess, adding that, if necessary, he could make the youth his standard bearer, as his ensign was thinking of leaving him shortly. It did not require much urging for Tomás to accept the bid,[5] for he quickly reflected that it would be a very good thing to have a glimpse of Italy and Flanders and various other lands and countries, since long journeys of this sort made men wise. This one at the most would require but three or four years, he was still young, and it would not prevent him from returning to his studies later.

He appeared bent, however, upon having everything to suit his own wishes, and told the captain that he would be glad to accompany him to Italy but that it would have to be on condition that he was not to be compelled to serve under any banner or have his name entered on the regimental rolls, as he wished to come and go as he liked. The captain replied that his being on the rolls would not make any difference as he might have leave whenever he asked for it, and that way might draw the same pay and receive the same treatment as other members of the company.

"But that," said Tomás, "would go against my conscience and against yours as well, *Señor Capitán,* and accordingly I would rather come as a free man than be under any obligations."

"So scrupulous a conscience as yours," remarked Don Diego, "is the sort one would expect to find in a monk rather than a soldier; but have it your way, for we are comrades in any event."

They reached Antequera, and within a few days, by means of long journeys, they overtook the company, which had now been recruited and was ready to set out on the march to Cartagena. It was joined by four other companies, the men being billeted in any villages through which they happened to pass. Tomás now had a chance to observe the overbearing attitude of the commissaries, the bad temper of some of the captains, the graspingness of the quartermasters, the manner in which the paymasters kept their accounts, the resentment of the people in the villages, the traffic in lodgings, the insolence of the recruits, the quarrels with guests at the inn, and the requisitioning of more supplies than were needed. He also perceived that it was almost impossible to avoid falling in with these ways, which impressed him as being neither right nor just.

By this time Tomás was dressed like a popinjay,[6] having laid aside the garb of a student and put on that of "God is Christ," [7] as the saying goes. Of all the books he had previously owned he retained but two, one of them a collection of prayers to Our Lady, and the other a Garcilaso,[8] without notes, both of which he carried in his pockets. They arrived all too soon at Cartagena, for life in the camps afforded a wide variety of experiences and every day there was something new to be seen and enjoyed. The troops then embarked in four galleys bound for Naples, and Tomás had a chance to study the strange life that goes on inside these maritime houses, where most of the time one is eaten alive by bedbugs, devoured by rats, robbed by the galley slaves, annoyed by the crew, and sickened by the roll of the waves. He was frightened by the great storms and tempests, especially two that they encountered in the Gulf of Lions, one of which cast them ashore on the island of Corsica, while the other drove them back to Toulon in France.

At last, gaunt, weary, and soaked to the skin, they arrived at the exceedingly lovely city of Genoa, where they disembarked in the little basin known as the Mandraccio.[9] After having visited a church, the captain and all his comrades repaired to a hostelry where they proceeded to forget past squalls by celebrating their present joy. It was then they came to know the smooth taste of Trebbiano, the full body of Montefiascone, the sharp tang of Asprino, the hearty flavor of those two Greek wines, Candia and Soma, the strength of Five Vineyards, the sweetness and charm of Lady Vernaccia, and the rude bite of Centola, all of which were such lordly vintages that the lowly Romanesco did not care to show its face among them.[10]

After their host had familiarized them with this great variety of wines, he offered to produce before them, not by any sleight of hand or as if painted on a map, but really and truly, such other brands as Madrigal, Coca, Alaejos, and that imperial rather than Royal City,[11] which is the abode of the god of laughter. He gave them their choice of Esquivias, Alanís, Cazalla, Guadalcanal, and Membrilla, not forgetting Ribadavia and Descargamaría.[12] To make a long story short, he named and set before them more wines than Bacchus himself could possible have in all his vaults.

The worthy Tomás also admired the blond hair of the

Genoese lasses and the courteous and lively disposition of the men, as well as the marvelous beauty of the city itself, whose houses, perched high on the cliffs, looked like diamonds set in gold. The next day all the companies that were to go to the Piedmont left the ship. Tomás, however, did not care to make this journey, preferring to go by way of land to Rome and Naples, which he did, his intention being to return by way of the great city of Venice and Loretto to Milan and from there to the Piedmont, where Don Diego de Valdivia said that he would be in case he had not already gone on to Flanders.

Two days later Tomás bade farewell to the captain, and in five days arrived at Florence, having first visited Lucca, a small city but very well constructed, where Spaniards were better regarded and better received than in other parts of Italy. He was greatly pleased with Florence, not only by reason of its charming site, but also because of its cleanliness, its magnificent buildings, its cool-flowing river, and the tranquility of its streets. He remained there four days, then departed for Rome, that queen of cities and mistress of the world. He visited its temples, adored its relics, and marveled at its grandeur. Just as from the claws of a lion one may judge the size and ferocity of the beast, so was his opinion of Rome formed from its marble ruins, the statuary whether whole or mutilated, its crumbling arches and baths, its magnificent porticoes, and huge amphitheaters, the renowned and sacred river that washes its banks to the brim and blesses them with countless relics from the bodies of martyrs that are buried there, its bridges which appear to be admiring one another, and its streets whose very names invest them with a dignity beyond those of all other cities in the world: the Via Appia, the Via Flaminia, the Via Julia, and others of that sort.

He was no less pleased by the manner in which the city was divided by its hills: the Caelian, the Quirinal, and the Vatican, along with the other four whose names show forth the greatness and majesty that is Rome.[13] He likewise remarked the authority that is exerted by the College of Cardinals, as well as the majesty of the Supreme Pontiff and the great variety of peoples and nations that are gathered there. He saw and made note of everything and put everything in its proper place. Having done the stations of the seven churches[14] and confessed himself to a penitentiary father and kissed the foot of His Holiness, being by then laden down with *Agnus Dei's* and beads, he made up his mind to go on to Naples; and inasmuch as it was the dog days, a bad and dangerous time for entering or leaving Rome, and since he had made the journey thus far by land, he decided now to take the boat. If he had marveled at what he saw in Rome, he marveled still more when he reached his destination; for Naples impressed him, as it does all those who have had a sight of it, as being the best city in Europe and even in all the world.

From there he proceeded to Sicily, visiting Palermo, and afterward Messina. The former impressed him by the beauty of its location, the latter by its harbor, while the whole island was a cause for wonderment on account of the great abundance of its products, which has led, and rightly so, to its being called the storehouse of Italy.

After returning to Naples he went on to Rome, and from there to Our Lady of Loretto, in whose holy shrine he was unable to see either walls or partitions, for the reason that they were wholly covered with crutches, shrouds, chains, shackles, manacles, locks of hair, wax figures, paintings, and altarpieces, all of which was a clear indication of the innumerable favors that many had received from the hand of God through the intercession of His Divine Mother, whose most holy image He wished to honor and dignify through a multitude of miracles as a recompense for the devotion represented by those votive offerings that adorned the walls of Her chapel. He also saw the room and chamber that had witnessed the loftiest and most important embassy that all the angels in all the heavens and all the inhabitants of the eternal dwelling places had ever seen or heard.[15]

At Ancona he took ship and went on to Venice, a city that, if Columbus had never been born into this world, would have had no equal; but thanks to Heaven and to the great Hernando Cortés, who conquered the great land of Mexico, Venice the great now has, in a manner of speaking, a worthy rival. These two famous cities have streets that consist wholly of water, the one being the wonder of the Old World, while the other is the marvel of the New.[16] It seemed to him that the riches of Venice were infinite, its government prudent, its site inexpugnable, its abundance a cause for wonderment, its surroundings most pleasant; in short, everything in it was worthy of the fame that it enjoyed throughout the world, a fame that was increased by its famous shipyard, where its galleys and other vessels without number were constructed.

The pleasures and pastimes that our student found here in Venice almost equaled those of Calypso and came near causing him to forget his original intention; but after he had been there for a month, he returned by way of Ferrara, Parma, and Piacenza to Milan, that workshop of Vulcan and envy of the King of France, a city, in brief, of which it is commonly remarked that saying is equivalent to doing,[17] its magnificence being due to the grandeur of its cathedral and the marvelous abundance that is to be found there of all the things that are necessary to human life.

From there he journeyed to Asti, arriving the day before the regiment was to leave. He was very well received by his friend the captain and continued with him to Flanders as his close friend and comrade, in due time reaching Antwerp, a city no less filled with wonders than those he had seen in Italy. He also had a sight of Ghent and Brussels and perceived that the whole country was ready to take up arms and begin the campaign the following summer.

Having seen the things that he desired to see, he then made up his mind to return to Spain and complete his studies at Salamanca; and this at once he proceeded to do, to the very great regret of his comrade, who, when the time for departure came, begged the young man to send back word as to his safe arrival, state of health, and how things were going with him. Promising to do all this, Tomás made his way back to Spain by way of France, but without seeing Paris, which was then up in arms. Upon reaching Salamanca and being warmly welcomed by his friends, he resumed his studies with their assistance until he was graduated as a licentiate in law.

Now as it happened, there came to the city at this time a lady of great worldly experience who was deeply versed in feminine wiles, and at once all the birds of the place came flocking in response to her decoys and enticements, and there was not a single *vademecum*[18] who did not call upon her. Having been told that the lady in question had been in Italy and Flanders, and wishing to see if he knew her, Tomás likewise paid her a visit, and as a result she fell in love with him. He, however, did not reciprocate this feeling, and indeed refused to go to her house unless forcibly taken there by others. Finally she revealed her love to him and offered him what property she had; but inasmuch as he was more concerned with his books than with pastimes of this sort, he did not give her any encouragement whatever.

Seeing herself thus disdained and, as she thought, despised, and realizing that she would not be able to overcome his rocklike determination by any ordinary means, she resolved to employ a method that would be more efficacious and lead to the fulfillment of her desires. And so, upon the advice of a Moorish woman, she put one of those so-called love potions into a Toledan quince[19] and gave it to Tomás, believing that this would force him to care for her, just as if there were in this world herbs, enchantments, or magic words sufficient to sway the free will of any individual. Those who give such potions are rightly called poisoners, for it is really nothing other than poison that they purvey to their victims, as experience has shown upon many and various occasions.

Tomás ate the quince and was at once so violently affected by it that he began to shake from head to foot as if in an epileptic fit. He did not recover for many hours, and when he did, he appeared to be stupefied, and with a thickened tongue was only able to stammer that it was the quince that was responsible for his condition. He told them who the person was who had given it to him, and the law at once took a hand in the case; but when the officers went to look for the guilty party, they found that she, having learned how things had turned out, had taken to cover, and nothing more was heard of her after that.

For six months Tomás was in bed, and in the course of that time he withered away and became, as the saying goes, nothing but skin and bones, while all his senses gave evidence of being deranged. His friends applied every remedy in their power and succeeded in curing the illness of his body but not that of his mind, with the result that he was left a healthy man but afflicted with the strangest kind of madness that had ever been heard of up to that time. The poor fellow imagined that he was wholly made of glass, and consequently, when anyone came near him, he would give a terrible scream, begging and imploring them with the most rational-sounding arguments to keep their distance lest they shatter him, since really and truly he was not like other men but was fashioned of glass from head to foot.

In an effort to cure him of this weird delusion, many paid no attention to his cries and entreaties but came up to him and embraced him, telling him to take a look and he would see that he had not been broken; but the only effect of this was to cause the poor man to throw himself to the ground screaming harder than ever, after which he would lose consciousness for four solid hours. When he came to himself, it was only to beg and plead with them not to do it again. Let them converse with him from afar, he urged, in which case they might ask him anything they liked and he would answer all questions that were put to him as intelligently as anyone could wish, considering that he was a man of glass and not of flesh. The fact was, he asserted, the glass, being a thin and delicate material, enabled the soul to act more promptly and efficiently than could a heavy earthen body.

Some wished to try an experiment to see if he spoke the truth, and they plied him with many difficult questions, to all of which he immediately replied with a display of the keenest intelligence. Even among the learned of the university, including the professors of medicine and philosophy, great astonishment was created upon seeing that an individual so extraordinarily mad as to believe that he was made of glass could still possess so profound an understanding of things that he was able to give the proper answer, and a perspicacious one, on any subject.

Tomás then asked them to furnish him with some kind of sheath for the fragile vase of his body, lest in drawing on a tight-fitting garment he might break himself, and they accordingly provided him with a dark-colored robe and a very wide chemise, in which he clothed himself with the greatest caution, employing a strand of cotton as a girdle; but he would not even consider putting on a pair of shoes. When it came to eating, they had to hand him his food on the end of a stick, in a little straw basket in which they placed whatever fruit was in season. He would have neither meat nor fish and drank only from the fountain or the river by lapping up the water with his hands. When he went out he always walked in the middle of the street, gazing up all the while at the rooftops, for he was afraid that some tile might fall upon him. In summer he slept in the open air, out in the fields, and in winter he went to some tavern and buried himself in straw up to the neck, remarking that this was the only proper bed and the safest one for men of glass. When it thundered he trembled like quicksilver and would run out into the fields and not come back to town until the storm had passed.

His friends kept him shut up much of the time; but when they saw that he was getting no better, they decided to yield to his wishes and let him go about freely. When he made his appearance in the city, all who knew him were astonished and sympathized with him. The small boys surrounded him, but he held them off with his staff and urged them not to come near, saying that, being a man of glass, he was very delicate and brittle and they might readily break him. Young lads, however, are the most mischievous creatures in the world, and despite his screams and entreaties they began throwing stones and other objects at him to see if he really was made of glass as he insisted; but he cried so loudly and made such a fuss that adults came running up to scold the lads and punish them so that they would not do it again. One day when the urchins were annoying him more than usual he turned upon them.

"Listen, you boys," he said, "persistent as flies, filthy as bedbugs, bold as fleas, am I by any chance the Monte Testaccio of Rome[20] that you should be throwing all these tiles and pieces of crockery at me?"

Since they enjoyed hearing his replies and his scoldings, the young ones continued to follow him about, until they came to prefer listening to him to throwing things at him.

He had other experiences as well. As he was walking through the garment district of Salamanca on one occasion, a shopkeeper's wife said to him, "Upon my soul, Señor Licentiate, I am sorry for the trouble you are in, but what can I do, seeing that I cannot weep?"[21] He thereupon turned to her and in measured tones replied, *"Filiae Hierusalem: plorate super vos et super filios vestros."*[22] Hearing this malicious remark, the woman's husband spoke up. "Brother Glasscase,[23] for they tell me that is what they call you, I think you are more of a rogue than a madman."

"It doesn't make a penny's worth of difference," came the reply, "but I can tell you that I am no fool."

Chancing one day to pass the brothel or common inn, he saw many of the inmates standing in the doorway and told them that they were the baggage of Satan's army, lodged in hell's own hostelry. Another time, someone asked him what advice should be given to a friend who was very sad because his wife had gone away with another man. In this case the answer was: "Tell him to give thanks to God for having permitted the other man to carry off his enemy."

"Then he is not to go look for her?"

"Let him not think of it," replied Glasscase, "for if he finds her, what he really will find will be a veritable and perpetual witness to his own dishonor."

"That being so," said the stranger, "what should I do to keep peace with my own wife?"

"Provide her with whatever she needs and allow her to give orders to all those of her household but never to you."

"Señor Glasscase," said a boy, "I'd like to get away from my father, for he is all the time beating me."

"Remember, my child, that the lashes that fathers give their sons are an honor; it is those of the public executioner that are a disgrace."

Standing at the door of a church, he saw a peasant going in, one of those who are forever priding themselves on being old Christians, and behind him came one who was not in such good standing; whereupon, addressing the peasant, the licentiate called out in a loud voice, "Wait, Domingo, until Sabado has passed." [24] He also had his say as to schoolmasters, observing that they were fortunate in that they were always dealing with little angels, and especially so if the cherubs in question did not happen to be little snotnoses. Yet another asked him what he thought of whores, and he replied that the real whores were not the ones so called, but rather neighbor women. [25]

The news of his madness, his replies, and his sayings

had by now spread throughout Castile and had reached the ears of a personage high at court who wished to have him brought there and who charged a friend in Salamanca to send him on. This gentleman, happening to meet the licentiate one day, said to him, "I may tell you, Señor Glasscase, that an important personage at the court wishes to see you and has sent for you." To this the licentiate replied, "Your Grace will please tell that gentleman that I wish to be excused, since I am not adapted to palace life, for I have a sense of shame and am not good at flattery."

Nevertheless, the Salamancan did send him to the court, and by way of transporting him there made use of the following contrivance: they placed him in a straw pannier well balanced with stones on both sides, of the sort that are used for carrying glass, and amidst the straw they placed a few bottles by way of showing that it was glass that was being thus conveyed. Upon reaching Valladolid,[26] they made their entrance by night and removed the licentiate from the basket at the home of the gentleman who had wanted to see him and who now gave him a very pleasant reception, saying, "You are heartily welcome, Señor Glasscase. And what kind of a journey did you have? How is your health?"

"No journey," replied the licentiate, "is a bad one that brings you to your destination, unless it be the one that leads to the gallows. As to my health, I have nothing of which to complain, seeing that my pulse is on good terms with my brain."

The next day, having seen many perches on which were numerous falcons, goshawks, and other birds that are used in fowling, he remarked that falconry was a sport suited to princes and great lords, but that it was to be noted that the expense exceeded the profit that was to be had from it by a ratio of more than two thousand to one. The hunting of hares, he added, was good sport, especially when one made use of borrowed hounds. The gentleman was amused by this display of madness and permitted his guest to go about the city with one man as a bodyguard, to see to it that the boys did not harm him; for he was known to them and to all the court within a week's time, and in each street, at every step he took, and on every corner where he stopped, he had to answer the questions that were put to him. Among those who questioned him was a student, who inquired if he was a poet, since he appeared to have a mind that was apt for anything.

"Up to now," replied the licentiate, "I have been neither so foolish nor so bold."

"I do not understand what you mean by those words, foolish and bold," said the student; and Glasscase then went on to explain, "I have never been so foolish as to be a bad poet nor so bold as to think that I could be a good one."

When another student asked him what opinion he held of poets, he answered by saying that he had a high respect for the science of poetry but none for poets themselves; and when they wished to know what he meant by that, he went on to say that of the infinite number of poets in the world there were so few good ones that they were practically negligible; and thus, since there were no poets to speak of, he could not esteem them, though he admired and reverenced the science of poetry, which contains within itself all the other sciences, makes use of all of them, adorns itself with them, and cleanses them, while bringing to light its own marvelous works that fill the world with profit, delight, and wonderment.

"I am quite aware," he continued, "of the esteem in

which a good poet is to be held, for I remember those
verses of Ovid where he says:

> *Cura ducum fuerunt olim regumque poetae,*
> *premiaque antiqui magna tulere chori,*
> *sanctaque maiestas, et erat venerabile nomen*
> *vatibus, et largae saepe dabantur opes . . .'*

Nor am I oblivious to the great worth of poets, whom
Plato has called the interpreters of the gods, and of
whom Ovid says:

> *'Est Deus in nobis; agitante calescimus illo.'*

And there is that other verse of his:

> *'At sacri vates, et divum cura vocamus.'* [27]

This is said of the good poets, but what of the bad ones,
the poetasters? What is there to say except that they
are the most stupid and arrogant tribe in all the world?

"Did you ever observe one of these latter as he gave
a first reading of a sonnet to a company of people? If
so, you must have noticed the ceremony that he makes
of it as he says, 'I should like your Graces to listen to
a little sonnet that I composed one night. While it is
only a trifle, I think it is rather good.' And with this he
twists his lips, arches his brows, fumbles in his pocket,
and from among countless soiled and half-torn scraps
of paper containing numerous other sonnets, he brings
forth the one that he wishes to recite and finally proceeds to read it in a honeyed, sugary tone of voice. And
if his listeners, either out of malice or out of ignorance,
fail to praise it, he will say, 'Oh, but your Graces surely

failed to hear my sonnet, or else I did not read it properly, and so, I think, it would be well for me to recite it once more; and I hope your Graces will pay greater attention this time, as it is really quite worth your while.' And he will read it once more with fresh gestures and new pauses.

"Then, what a thing it is to hear them when they start criticizing one another! And what shall one say of the thefts that these modern whelps commit upon the grave and ancient mastiffs of their art? What is to be said of those that are always carping at certain illustrious ones of outstanding ability in whom the true light of poetry shines resplendent and who, adopting this pursuit as a relief and relaxation from their many serious occupations, continue to exhibit their lofty conceptions and a truly divine inspiration in spite of the ignorant onlooker who passes judgment upon something of which he knows nothing and abhors that which he does not understand? What of the self-esteem of the one who prides himself upon his own foolishness and would take his place beneath the canopy of fame, or the ignorance that would sit in the seat of the mighty?"

On another occasion they asked him why it was that most poets were poor, and he replied that it was because they chose to be, since they had it in their power to be rich if they only knew how to make use of the wealth that lay in their hands at times—namely, that of their ladies, who were all exceedingly opulent in golden locks, brows of burnished silver, eyes that were green emeralds, teeth of ivory, coral lips, and throats of transparent crystal, while their tears were liquid pearls; and, moreover, the very ground they trod, though it might be hard and sterile earth, at once produced jasmine and roses. Was not the food they ate of purest amber, musk, and civet, and were not all these things the sign and evidence of great wealth? All this and more he had to say of the bad poets, but he always spoke well of the good ones, elevating them above the horns of the moon.

One day, in the San Francisco walk, he came upon some badly painted figures and observed that good painters imitate nature but bad ones vomit it forth.[28] On another occasion, carefully feeling his way for safety's sake, he came up to a bookseller's shop and said to the proprietor, "This trade would please me very much, if it were not for one vice connected with it." When the bookseller asked him what that vice was, he answered, "The tricks that you play when you purchase the rights to a book and the sport that you make of an author if by chance he has it printed at his own cost; for in place of fifteen hundred copies, you go ahead and print three thousand, and while the author thinks that it is his copies that are being sold, it is in reality your own that you are getting rid of."

That same day six criminals who were to be flogged passed through the square, and when the crier called out, "The first one for being a thief—" the licentiate raised his voice and addressed those in front of him, saying, "Take care, brothers, that he doesn't call out the name of one of you." And when the crier came to the word "hindermost," Glasscase remarked, "He must be referring to the bondsman of young lads."[29] One boy thereupon said to him, "Brother Glasscase, they are going to flog a whore," and he answered, "If you had told me it was a pimp they were going to flog I would have understood you to mean that they were going to flog a coach."[30]

Among the other bystanders was a litter bearer, and it was he who put the next question. "How comes it, Sir Licentiate, have you nothing to say of us?"

"No," replied Glasscase, "I have nothing to say, unless it be that each one of you knows more sins than a father confessor, but with this difference: the confessor knows them in order to keep them secret, and you, in order that you may make them public in all the taverns."

One of those lads with mules for hire happened to hear this; for all sorts of people were constantly standing around listening to the licentiate. "Señor Vial," the lad asked, "how does it come that you have had little or nothing to say about us, although we are good people and necessary to the life of the state?" Glasscase had an answer for him. "The honor of the servant," he said, "depends upon that of the master; and so, just look and see whom it is you serve, and you will see how much honor you possess. They are the filthiest trash to be found anywhere on this earth. Once upon a time, before I became a man of glass, I made a journey on a hired mule, and I counted in them one hundred and twenty-one capital defects, inimical to the human race. All you lads have in you something of the pimp, something of the thief, and something of the mountebank. If your masters (for such is the name you give to those you carry upon your mules) chance to be simpletons, you play more tricks on them than this city has known for many years past; if they are foreigners, you rob them; if they are students, you curse them; if they are religious, you blaspheme against them; and if they are soldiers, you tremble from fear.

"You fellows, along with sailors, carters, and pack carriers, lead a life that is all your own and one of a most extraordinary kind. The carter spends his days within the space of a yard and a half, for it cannot be more than that from the yoke of his mules to the front of his cart. Half the time he is singing and the other half he is cursing or yelling 'Get behind there!' when someone tries to pass him. And if by any chance he has to stop to get one of his wheels out of a rut, two good round oaths are of more use to him than three mules.

"Sailors are a fine lot, though unversed in city ways, and they know no other language than that which is used aboard ship. In fair weather they are diligent, but they are lazy in a storm. In a tempest they give many orders and obey few. Their god is their seamen's chest and their grub, and they find amusement in watching the seasick passengers.

"As for the carriers, they have been divorced from sheets and have married packsaddles. They are so industrious and have such an eye for business that they would lose their souls rather than a day's haul. Their music is that of hoofs, their sauce is hunger, their matins consist in speaking their mind, and they go to mass by hearing none."

As he said this, he was standing at the door of an apothecary's shop, and, turning to the proprietor, he observed, "Your Grace has a wholesome occupation, if it were not that it is so bad for your lamps."

"How is it bad for my lamps?" the apothecary wanted to know.

"I say so," replied Glasscase, "for the reason that, whenever you happen to be in need of oil, you supply it from the lamp that is nearest at hand. And there is another thing about this business that is enough to ruin the reputation of the best doctor in the world." When asked what it was, he went on to explain that there were certain apothecaries who, when they did not have on hand what the physician prescribed, would substitute other drugs which they believed to possess the same qualities and healing properties. This was not so, however, and the result was that the prescriptions, badly compounded, had exactly the opposite effect.

Someone then asked him what he thought of doctors, and his reply was, " '*Honora medicum propter necessitatem, etenim creavit eum Altissimus. A Deo enim est omnis medela, et a rege accipiet donationem. Disciplina medici exaltabit caput illius, et in conspectu magnatum collaudabitur. Altissimus de terra creavit medicinam, et vir prudens non abhorrebit illam.*' [31] That is what Ecclesiasticus has to say of medicine and of good doctors, and just the reverse might be said of the bad ones, for there is no class of people more dangerous to the state than they. The judge may pervert or delay justice; the man of law may in his own interest plead an unjust cause; the merchant may drain off our property—in short, all those with whom we must necessarily deal may do us some wrong, but there is none of them other than the doctor who is in a position to deprive us of life itself, without punishment.

"Physicians may and do kill without fear or running away and without unsheathing any other sword than that of a prescription; for there is no means of discovering their crimes, since they at once bury them underground. I recall something that happened when I was a man of flesh and not of glass as I am today. A doctor of the kind I have been speaking of sent a patient of his to another physician for treatment, and three or four days later, upon passing the shop of the apothecary who filled the other doctor's prescriptions, he looked in and inquired if his colleague had prescribed some purge or other. The apothecary replied that, as a matter of fact, he did have such a prescription for a purge, which the patient was to take the following day. The first doctor then asked that it be shown to him, and down at the bottom he saw the words: *Sumat diluculo.*[32] 'That,' he said, 'seems to me a very good remedy. The only thing I am in doubt about is the *diluculo,* as it contains a little too much moisture.'"

By reason of this and other things he had to say concerning all the trades and professions, a crowd always followed him about but did him no injury though he was never left in peace. He would not, however, have been able to ward off the small boys if his bodyguard had not been there to protect him.

Someone asked him what to do in order to avoid envying another, and he replied, "Sleep; for all the time that you are asleep you will be the equal of the one you envy." Another who for a couple of years had been seeking a commission wanted to know what he should do to make things come out right; and the answer this time was, "Mount your horse, and when you see someone bearing such a commission, accompany him until he leaves the city, and you will come out with the thing you desire." [33]

As he stood there in the street a judge went by on his way to a criminal trial, accompanied by two bailiffs and a large crowd of people. "I will wager," said Glasscase upon being informed who it was, "that this judge has vipers in his bosom, pistols in his inkpot, and thunderbolts in his hand to destroy everything that comes within his jurisdiction. I recall once having had a friend in the same position who, in connection with a case that came up before him, imposed so unreasonable a sentence that it exceeded by many carats the guilt of the offenders. When I asked him why he had done this, thereby committing so obvious an injustice, he told me that he expected the case to be appealed and that in this way he was leaving the field open for the gentlemen of the Council to show mercy by moderating this harsh sentence and imposing in its stead one that was proportionate to the crime. I remarked that it would have been better if he had spared them the trouble of doing so, since then he would have been looked upon as a wise and upright magistrate."

In the circle of listeners that constantly surrounded him was an acquaintance of his in the garb of an advocate whom the others addressed as "Señor Licentiate," though Glasscase was aware that the man held no other degree than that of bachelor.[34] "You had better watch out, my friend," he said to him, "or the Redemptionist Friars will pick you up and confiscate that title of yours as strayed or stolen property." [35]

"Come, Señor Glasscase," said his friend, "that is no way to talk; you know very well that I am a man of lofty and profound learning."

"I know," answered Glasscase, "that you are a very Tantalus when it comes to learning, seeing that it is always mounting upward around you, but you never succeed in plumbing its depths."

Having stopped in front of another shop, he saw a tailor standing outside with his hands folded and said to him, "Master Tailor, you are undoubtedly on the road to salvation."

"How do you make that out?"

"How do I make it out?" replied Glasscase. "I make it out from this, that inasmuch as you have nothing to do, you have no occasion for lying. The tailor," he went on, "who does not lie and sew flattery into his garments is out of luck. It is a very strange thing, but among all those who follow this trade you almost never find a workman who will give you a just fit though there are plenty who will give you a sinful one."

With regard to cobblers, he remarked that in their own opinion they never turned out a bad pair of shoes; for if the shoes were too tight and pinched the foot, that was the way they were supposed to be, as men of fashion preferred tight-fitting ones—all you had to do was wear them a couple of hours and they would be as comfortable as sandals; but if on the other hand they were too wide, that was all the better for the gout.

One young fellow with a keen mind, a clerk in the provincial court, pressed the licentiate with many questions and also brought him news of what was happening in the town, for Glasscase was in the habit of discoursing on every subject and responding to all inquiries that were put to him.

"Last night," the youth informed him, "a money-changer[36] who had been condemned to hang died in the jail."

"He did well in dying before the executioner had a chance to sit upon him."

In the San Francisco walk there was a group of Genoese, and as the licentiate went by, one of them called to him, saying, "Come over here, Señor Glasscase, and tell us a story." [37]

"No," was the answer, "I don't care to do so; I'm afraid you will take my million[37] back to Genoa with you."

On another occasion he met the wife of a shopkeeper with a very ugly daughter in front of her who was laden down with pearls and other trinkets. "That is a good idea," he said to the mother, "paving her like that; it makes walking easier for you."

Regarding pastry cooks, he observed that for many years they had been playing at *dobladilla*[38] but without paying the penalty, for they had raised the price of their wares from two to four, from four to eight, and from eight to half a real, at their own good will and pleasure.

He also had no end of fault to find with the puppet

masters, saying that they were a lot of vagabonds who were guilty of indecency in the portrayal of sacred things; the puppets they employed in their shows made a mockery of devotion, and they sometimes stuffed into a bag all or nearly all the personages of the Old and New Testament, and then would sit down upon them to eat and drink in the alehouses and taverns. In short, it was a wonder that perpetual silence was not imposed upon them, or that they were not banished from the realm.[39]

When an actor dressed like a prince went by, Glasscase looked at him and said, "I remember having seen that fellow in the theater; his face was smeared with flour and he was wearing a shepherd's coat turned inside out; but at every step he takes off the stage, you would swear upon your word of honor that he was a gentleman."

"That may very well be," someone reminded him, "for there are many actors who are well born and sons of somebody." [40]

"That is true enough," replied Glasscase, "but what the stage stands least in need of is individuals of gentle birth. Leading men, yes, who are well mannered and know how to talk, that is another matter. For it might be said of actors that they earn their bread by the sweat of their brows, with an unbearable amount of labor, having constantly to memorize long passages, and having to wander from town to town and from one inn to another like gypsies, losing sleep in order to amuse others, since their own well-being lies in pleasing their public. Moreover, in their business, they deceive no one, inasmuch as their merchandise is displayed in the public square, where all may see and judge of it.

"Authors, too, have an incredible amount of work to perform and a heavy burden of care; they have to earn much in order that by the end of the year they may not be so far in debt that they will have to go into bankruptcy; yet for all of that, they are as necessary to the state as are shady groves, public walks and parks, and other things that provide decent recreation."

He went on to cite the opinion of a friend of his to the effect that a servant to an actress was a servant to many ladies at one and the same time: to a queen, a nymph, a goddess, a kitchen wench, a shepherd lass, and many times a page or a lackey as well, since the actress was used to impersonating all these and many other characters.

They asked him who was the happiest man that ever lived, and his reply was, "Nemo, for *Nemo novit patrem; Nemo sine crimine vivit; Nemo sua sorte contentus; Nemo ascendit in coelum.*" [41]

Of fencing experts he remarked that they were masters of a science or art which when they needed it they did not know how to employ, adding that there was something presumptuous in their seeking to reduce to infallible mathematical formulas the angry thoughts and impulses of their adversaries. But his special enmity was reserved for those who dyed their beards. He once saw two men engaged in a quarrel, the one being a Portuguese, the other a Castilian. "By this beard that I have on my face!" the Portuguese exclaimed, laying hold of his beard. It was at that point that Glasscase intervened. "Look here, man," he said, "don't say 'this beard that I *have* on my face'; what you mean is 'this beard that I *dye* on my face.'" [42] Another had a beard that was streaked with many colors, and the licentiate told him that it resembled an egg-colored dung heap. Still another had one that was half black and half white, the result of carelessness in letting the roots grow out.

and he was warned by Glasscase not to be stubborn and get into an argument with anyone, or he was likely to be told that he lied by half a beard.[43]

He had a story to tell of a young woman who was very discreet and intelligent and who, by way of yielding to her parents' wishes, had consented to marry a graybeard. The night before the wedding day the groom went, not down to the river Jordan as the old wives say,[44] but to the bottle of aqua fortis and silver,[45] with which he proceeded to renovate his beard, turning it from snow-white to pitch black. When the hour appointed for the marriage ceremony arrived, the bride, judging the card by its spots,[46] insisted that her parents give her the husband they had promised, as she would have no other. They assured her that the man before her was the same one whom they had introduced as her betrothed. She maintained that he was not and brought witnesses to prove that the bridegroom whom her parents had promised her was white-haired and of grave aspect, and since this one did not answer that description, he must be some other and she was being tricked. Nothing could induce her to change her mind, and so the one with the dyed beard went away and the marriage was called off.

He had the same sort of grudge against duennas, and it was worth hearing what he had to say about the oaths they took and their faithlessness, their shroudlike head-dresses, their prudery and their simperings, and their extraordinary miserliness. He found fault with them for their attacks of stomach weakness, their swooning, their way of talking with more falderals to their speech than they had on their bonnets—in short, their general use-lessness and their affectations.

"How comes it, Señor Licentiate," someone said to him, "I have heard you speak ill of so many professions, but I have yet to hear you say anything about scriveners, although there is so much to be said?"

"I may be made of glass," he replied, "but I am not so fragile as to let myself drift with the current of public opinion, which most of the time is wrong. As I see it, the scriveners provide a grammar for backbiters, and are what the musical scale is to a singer; for just as one can go on to the other sciences only through the gate of grammar, and just as a musician must first hum[47] before he sings, so it is by speaking ill of scriveners, bailiffs, and other agents of the law that slanderers begin to display the malignity of their tongues. If it were not for the scrivener, truth would go through the world under cover, persecuted and mistreated, just as Ecclesiasticus says: *'In manu Dei potestas hominis est, et super faciem scribae imponet honorem.'* [48]

"The scrivener is a public official, and without his aid the judge cannot properly fulfill the duties of his office. Scriveners must be freeborn, neither slaves nor the sons of slaves, of legitimate birth and not bastards, nor should they come of any bad racial stock; they have to swear secrecy and loyalty and promise not to engage in any usurious practices; and neither friendship nor enmity, profit nor gain, should cause them to fail to fulfill their functions with a good and Christian conscience. If this office, then, calls for so many good qualities, why should it be thought that, of the twenty thousand scriveners that there are in Spain, the devil reaps his own special harvest? I do not believe, nor should anyone believe, that this is true; for I may tell you that they are the most necessary class of people that are to be found in well-ordered states, and if they take too many rights, they also commit too many wrongs, and out of these two extremes it is possible to strike a happy medium that causes them to look sharp and watch their step."

As for bailiffs, he declared it was not strange if they had many enemies, since it was their business to arrest you, to remove your property from your house, or hold you under guard while they ate at your expense. But he charged lawyers and solicitors with being negligent and ignorant, comparing them to doctors who, whether or not the patient recovers, collect their fee; these gentlemen of the legal profession did the same regardless of whether they won or lost their case.

Someone asked him which was the best land, and he replied that it was the one that was the most fertile and productive.

"I did not ask you that; what I meant was, which is the better region, Valladolid or Madrid?"

"Madrid for the extremes, Valladolid for the middle."

"I do not understand what you mean," said the one who had asked the question.

"In Madrid, the sky and earth; in Valladolid, the mezzanines." [49]

Hearing one man tell another that as soon as he had come to Valladolid his wife had fallen very ill, as the region [tierra] did not agree with her, Glasscase spoke up and said, "It would have been better for her if she had eaten earth [tierra] in case she is of a jealous disposition." [50]

Speaking of musicians and foot couriers, he implied that neither had much of a future, for the most that the latter could hope for was to become mounted couriers, while the former could look forward only to a place in the royal band. He likewise had something to say of those ladies known as courtesans [cortesanas], remarking that all or most of them were more courteous [corteses] than they were healthy [sanas]. In church one day he saw them bringing in an old man for burial, baptizing an infant, and conferring the bridal veil upon a woman, all at one and the same time, and he observed that religious edifices were battlefields where the old met their end, children conquered, and women triumphed.

When a wasp stung him on the back of the neck he did not dare shake it off for fear of breaking himself, but nonetheless he complained of it, and when asked how it was that he felt the wasp since his body was made of glass, he replied that the insect must be some slanderer, for their tongues and stings were sufficient to destroy bodies of bronze, not to speak of those made of glass.

A very fat friar happened to pass the place where he was standing. "That good father," said one of the listeners, "is so consumptive he can hardly walk." Glass-case was annoyed by this. "Let no one," he admonished them, "forget what the Holy Spirit has said: '*Nolite tangere Christos meos*' ";[51] and then, his anger increasing, he told them to look into the matter and they would find that of the many saints canonized by the church in those parts during the last few years and elevated to the number of the blessed, none had been named Captain So-and-So, or Secretary Don So-and-So to So-and-So, or the Count, Marquis, or Duke of This-or-That, but had been plain Friar Diego, Friar Jacinto, Friar Raimundo, etc. They had all been monks and friars, for religious orders are the orange groves of Heaven and provide the everyday fruit for God's table. He went on to say that the tongues of slanderers were like the eagle's feathers which gnaw and eat away all those of other birds that are placed with them.[52]

Concerning gamblers and gambling-house keepers he had extraordinary things to relate, averring that they were nothing but public cheats who would force the winner to contribute to the kitty, all the while hoping he would lose so that his opponent would obtain the deal and win and the house would get what was coming to it. He lauded the patience of one gambler who, despite the fact that he had been playing all night and losing and was in a hellish temper, nevertheless did not open his mouth but was willing to endure the martyr-dom of a Barabbas, providing only that his opponent did not cut the cards. He also praised the conscientious-ness of the keepers of certain respectable houses who would not think of permitting beneath their roof any games other than ombre and hundred-points, and yet, without any fear of complaints on the part of their customers, managed to come out at the end of the month with a larger kitty than those who permitted other games in which money changed hands in the twinkling of an eye.[53]

The short of the matter is, he said such things that, if it had not been for the screams he gave when anyone touched or drew near him, the garb that he wore, the limitations of his diet and the manner in which he drank, his refusal to sleep anywhere except under the open sky in summer and amid the straw in winter, all of which obvious signs of madness have been set forth above, no one would have believed that he was anything other than one of the sanest individuals in this world. His illness continued for two years or a little longer, and then a monk of the order of St. Jerome, who was particularly skilled in teaching deaf mutes to understand what was said to them and, to a certain de-gree, to talk, and who had also had experience in curing the mad, undertook to treat the Licentiate Glasscase, being moved to do so out of charity; and treat him he did, and cured him, and restored him to his former state of reason, sound judgment, and good sense.

As soon as he saw that his patient was once more a

healthy man, he clad him in scholastic garments and had
him return to the capital, where Glasscase gave as many
proofs of being sane as he formerly had of being mad,
and where he was in a position to resume his profession
and render himself famous by it. The licentiate now
called himself Rueda[54] and not Rodaja, and he had no
sooner entered the city than he was recognized by the
small boys, who, seeing him dressed so differently than
was his wont, did not dare to shout at him or ask him
any questions but merely followed him, saying to one
another, "This cannot be the madman Glasscase, can
it?" "My word, but it is. He is sane again; and yet one
can be a well-dressed madman. Let us ask him something and settle the matter."

The licentiate heard all this and was silent, for he was
more abashed and bewildered now that he had his
senses back than he had been before. The word spread
from the boys to the grownups, and before Rueda had
reached the place where the Councils were held, more
than two hundred persons of every sort were following
him. In the crowd was more than one professor, and
upon reaching the court they all crowded around him;
whereupon, becoming aware of the throng, he raised
his voice and addressed them.

"Gentlemen, I am indeed the Licentiate Glasscase,
but not the one you knew of old; I am now the Licentiate Rueda. Events and misfortunes such as happen in
this world with Heaven's permission had deprived me
of my reason, but God in His mercy has restored it to
me. In view of the things I said to you when I was
mad, you may form an idea of what I shall say and do
now that I am sane. I am a graduate in law at Salamanca, where I studied under the handicap of poverty
yet obtained second honors, from which you may infer
that it was my own abilities rather than any favors

shown me that won me the rank I hold. I have come here to this great sea that is the capital to swim and earn my living, but unless you leave me alone, I shall have come only to drown and meet my death. For the love of God, do not let your following me about become a persecution,[55] else that which I gained as a madman, namely, my livelihood, shall be lost through my having recovered my senses. Those questions that you used to ask of me in the public squares you may now put to me at home. They tell me that I used to answer them very well on the spur of the moment; but you shall see now how much better are the answers that I give when I have thought them over."

They all listened to him, and some of them drifted away. He returned to his lodgings with less of a crowd at his heels, but when he came out the next day, it was the same story all over again. He preached another sermon, but it did no good. It was costing him much, and he was earning nothing by it, and when he saw that he was on the verge of starvation, he made up his mind to leave the capital and return to Flanders, where he thought to avail himself of the strength of his arm, since he could not make use of that of his intellect. Putting his resolution into effect, he exclaimed as he was about to take his departure, "O court, you who more than fulfill the hopes of audacious pretenders and cut short those of the competent, you provide in abundance for shameless mountebanks and let the wise who have a sense of shame die of hunger!"

Saying this, he set off for Flanders, where the immortality that he had begun to win in the domain of letters was achieved by him through force of arms, in the company of his good friend, Captain Valdivia, and even as he died he left behind him the reputation of being a prudent and very brave soldier.

"FOOT IN THE STIRRUP":
Cervantes' Farewell to Life

From *The Troubles of Persiles and Sigismunda*

EDITOR'S NOTE

It seems to the editor that there could be no better way of bringing this volume to a close than by presenting the words that Cervantes wrote as he lay facing life's last grim—and greatest—reality, the coming of death. Aubrey Bell has justly remarked that the Dedication and Prologue to Los Trabajos de Persiles y Sigismunda, *which were composed four days before the author died and after he had received Extreme Unction, constitute "the most pathetic and magnificent farewell in all literature."*

As to the Persiles *itself, little need be said here. Like the* Galatea *a romance of the Arcadian school, it was first published in 1617, the year following Cervantes' death; and it has commonly been assumed in the past, though somewhat incongruously from the literary point of view, that this exceedingly immature—not to say amateurish—work was produced during the same period as the masterly second part of the* Don Quixote.

The evidence adduced by scholars, it is true, appeared to support this theory; but more recently the American Cervantist Professor Mack Singleton of the University of Wisconsin has expressed the well-documented opinion that, on the contrary, this is a youthful

797

effort of which Cervantes was ashamed and which he had tossed aside for long years, only to resurrect it, upon the insistence of his family, as he lay dying, in order to provide them with a little much-needed money.

According to this view, all that the author did, on his deathbed, was to add a Dedication and a Prologue, both of which, it is pointed out, are couched in general terms and have no particular relation to the book in question. Professor Singleton draws attention to the fact that even the incident of the student in the Prologue, which he takes to be fictitious, is a working over of one to be found in the prose dialogue that forms the postscript to Journey to Parnassus. *Yet at the same time he is ready to admit that this Prologue is "a very beautiful piece of writing." (See "The 'Persiles' Mystery," in* Cervantes Across the Centuries, *pp. 256-63.)*

All this, however, has nothing to do with the pleasure and edification to be derived from a reading of the pieces given below. Granting that the Persiles *is unworthy of Cervantes' genius (Mr. Bell, for one, would not agree), it at least has the merit for us of having prompted the creator of Don Quixote and Sancho Panza to afford us one last glimpse of the noble mind and genial spirit that animated his life and work.*

Dedication

TO DON FERNÁNDEZ DE CASTRO,
Count of Lemos, of Andrade, of
Villalba; Marqués of Sarriá,
Gentleman of His Majesty's
Chamber, President of the
Supreme Council of Italy,
Knight-Commander of La Zarza
and the Order of Alcántara.[1]

I COULD WISH that those old verses, so celebrated in their day, which begin with the line "One foot already in the stirrup," [2] were not so well suited as they are to this letter; for I might start it with the same words, by saying: "With one foot already in the stirrup, and with the agony of death upon me, great lord, I write to you."

Yesterday they gave me Extreme Unction, and today I take my pen in hand. The time is short, my pains are increasing, my hopes are diminishing; and yet, with it all, the desire I have to live keeps me alive.[3] I would that might be until I kiss Your Excellency's feet; and it is possible that my happiness at seeing Your Excellency safely back in Spain would have the effect of giving me life. However, if it is decreed that I am to lose it, let Heaven's will be done. I at least would have Your Excellency know the state of my feelings, and know that you have in me a servant so devoted that he would even go beyond death to show his good intentions.

In spite of everything, as though by the gift of prophecy, I share in the joy occasioned by Your Excellency's return, rejoice to see you pointed out, and am doubly glad that my hopes are coming true in the widespread fame that accompanies Your Excellency's good deeds.

I still have in mind certain odds and ends of *The Garden Weeks* and *The Famous Bernardo;*[4] and if by any chance, through a stroke of good fortune on my part which would be nothing short of a miracle, Heaven should let me live, then you shall have a sight of them and, along with them, the conclusion of the *Galatea,* a work of which I know Your Excellency is fond.

Meanwhile, you have my continued good wishes: may God keep Your Excellency as He may see fit. From Madrid, the nineteenth of April, in the year one-thousand-six-hundred-and-sixteen.

Your Excellency's servant,

MIGUEL DE CERVANTES

Prologue

AS IT HAPPENED, dearest reader, a couple of friends and I were coming from the famous village of Esquivias—famous for a thousand reasons, one of them being its illustrious families while another is its most illustrious wines—when I noticed someone behind us spurring on his mount in great haste with the apparent desire of overtaking us, a desire which he clearly manifested by calling out to us to slacken our pace a little. We waited for him, and a sparrow-like student came riding up on a she-ass; for he was all clad in dark gray, with leggings, round-toed shoes, sword and scabbard, and a Walloon ruff with matching tassels—the truth is, there were but two of them left, since the ruff was continually slipping down on one side, and it was all he could do to straighten it again.

"You gentlemen," he remarked as he reached our side, "must be after some office or benefice in the capital, seeing that His Eminence of Toledo and His Majesty are now there. It surely could be nothing less in view of the speed at which you are traveling; for this donkey of mine, I may tell you, has come out the winner in more than one race."

It was one of my companions who answered him. "Señor Miguel de Cervantes' hack," he said, "must bear the blame; he is somewhat long-paced."

No sooner did he hear the name Cervantes than the student slid down from his mount, letting his saddlebag fall on one side, his portmanteau on the other (for he was carrying all this luggage with him). He ran up to me and threw himself upon me and seized me by the left hand.[5]

"Ah, yes!" he cried, "so this is the maimed one who is whole, the wholly famous and brilliant writer, in short, the darling of the Muses!"

Upon hearing all these compliments lavished upon me in so short a space of time, I felt it would be a lack of courtesy not to show my appreciation; and accordingly I put my arm about his neck, which nearly caused him to lose his Walloon ruff altogether.

"That," I said, "is an error into which many of my ill-informed friends have fallen. I, sir, am Cervantes, but not the Muses' darling nor any of the other foolish things you say I am. Your Grace had best catch your donkey and mount him. We have not much farther to go, and we will have a good talk as we ride along."

The student courteously did as suggested and, reining in somewhat, we continued on our way at a leisurely pace. The conversation happening to turn upon my illness, the worthy student promptly deprived me of all hope by saying, "That sickness of yours is dropsy, and all the water in the ocean cannot cure you, no matter how sweetly you drink it. Señor Cervantes, you should take care to restrain your drinking, but do not forget to eat."

"That," I replied, "is what many have told me; but I might as well resign myself not to drink any more at all, just as if I had been born for no other purpose. My life is drawing to a close, and at the rate my pulse is going it will end its career, at the latest, next Sunday, and that will be the end of me. Your Grace has made my acquaintance at a critical moment, and I have not enough time left to show my gratitude for the good will toward me which you have displayed."

At this point we reached the Toledo bridge, and I proceeded to cross it while he rode off to enter the city by the bridge of Segovia. As to what may be said about all this, my reputation will take care of itself: my friends will take pleasure in repeating such things, which give me an even greater pleasure as I listen to them. We turned to embrace each other once more, and then he spurred his donkey, leaving me as ill-disposed as he was ill-mounted on that she-ass of his.

He had afforded me a fine opportunity to write some charming things about him; but all times are not the same. A time will come, perhaps, when I shall knot this broken thread and say what should be said but which I cannot say here. Good-by, thanks; good-by, compliments; good-by, merry friends. I am dying, and my wish is that I may see you all soon again, happy in the life to come.

NOTES

Notes

To DON QUIXOTE

PART ONE

PROLOGUE

1. The opening lines of the Prologue have been taken as evidence that Part I was composed in prison (see the Introduction, p. 2).

2. In its original form this proverb reads *"Al rey mando"*— "I give orders to the king"; compare "An Englishman's house in his castle."

3. "Liberty is not well sold for all the gold there is": from a fable, *"De cane et lupo"* ("The Dog and the Wolf") by the twelfth-century Walther (Gualterus) Anglicus; compare Aesop and La Fontaine.

4. "Pale Death stalks with equal tread the huts of the poor and the palaces of kings": Horace, *Odes,* I, iv, 13-14.

5. "But I say unto you . . .": Matthew 5:44, and Luke 6:27, 35.

6. "For out of the heart . . .": Matthew 15:19 and Mark 7:21.

7. "So long as you are well off, you will have many friends, but let the skies be overcast and you will be alone": Ovid, *Tristia,* I, ix, 5-6; the Cato referred to is Dionysius Cato, author of the *Disticha de Moribus,* a verse treatise on morals and manners widely used as a school text in the Renaissance era; Rabelais and other writers allude to it.

8. The valley of Terebinth is the valley of Elah, mentioned in I Samuel 17:2; in the Vulgate, Elah is rendered as Terebinthus.

9. Cacus is the noted thief of classical mythology; see Ovid's *Fasti,* I, 543 ff., Vergil's *Aeneid,* VIII, 190 ff., and other Latin writers.

10. "The Bishop of Mondoñedo": allusion to the *Epistolae Familiares* (1539-45) of Fray Antonio de Guevara; Ormsby finds this "a touch after Swift's heart."

11. Leon the Hebrew (d. 1520) was the author of the *Dialoghi d'Amore*.

12. The *Amor de Dios* of Cristóbal de Fonseca was published in 1594.

13. On the Campo de Montiel, see Chapter II, notes.

CHAPTER I

1. An attempt has been made to identify Don Quixote's native village as Argamasilla de Alba, in La Mancha, but it is more likely that Cervantes had no particular village in mind.

2. Feliciano de Silva was the author of the *Chronicle of Don Florisel de Niquea*, published in 1532, 1536, and 1551; the passage quoted immediately below is from this work, and the one that follows is from Antonio de Torquemada's *Don Olivante de Laura* (1564).

3. This is a reference to the *History of Don Belianís of Greece* by Jerónimo Fernández (1547).

4. Sigüenza was one of the so-called "minor universities" and a good deal of fun was poked at its graduates.

5. "The Knight of the Flaming Sword" is the protagonist of the ninth book of the *Amadis* series.

6. Rinaldo of Montalbán: one of the principal characters in Boiardo's *Orlando Innamorato*.

7. Galalón (Ganelon) was the traitor of the Charlemagne legend.

8. The *real de vellón* was a coin worth about five cents; the cuarto, or four-maravedi piece, was the eighth part of a real.

9. Gonela was an Italian jester in the service of the Duke of Ferrara (1450-1470).

10. "All skin and bones": a common expression in classic literature, found in Plautus and elsewhere.

11. The name Rocinante is from *"rocín"*—"a hack."

12. *Quixote* (*quijote*) literally means the piece of armor that protects the thigh; Quijada and Quesada were distinguished family names.

CHAPTER II

1. *"Armas blancas"* is properly "blank armor," with no device, but Don Quixote takes it in the sense of "white."

2. The Campo de Montiel was famous as being the scene

of the battle, in 1369, in which Peter the Cruel was defeated by his brother Henry.

3. On Puerto Lápice and the windmills, see Chapters VIII and IX.

4. This inn, according to Ormsby, is said to have been the Venta de Quesada, a few miles north of Manzanares on the Madrid-Seville road; the house itself, burned down about a century ago, has been rebuilt, but the yard at the back with its draw-well and stone watering trough is said to be as it was in Cervantes' time.

5. "Worthies of Castile"—"*sanos de Castilla*"; this appears to be gypsy argot for "thieves in disguise"; "*castellano*" means both "Castilian" and "a castellan."

6. This verse quotation and the one preceding are from an old ballad, "Moriana en un Castillo" possibly dating from the fourteenth century.

7. These lines are a parody on the opening lines of the ballad of Lancelot of the Lake; cf. Chapter XIII.

CHAPTER III

1. The places mentioned by the landlord as the scenes of his youthful adventures are all more or less identifiable. Los Percheles was the name of the site outside Málaga where fish were dried and sold. The Isles of Riarán was a disreputable suburb of the same city. The District of Seville was an open space on the river side of the town, near the Plaza de Toros, where fairs were held. The Olivera of Valencia was a small square in the center of the city. The Rondilla of Granada is said to have been in the Albaycin quarter. The Horse Fountain of Cordova refers to a section on the south side of the town that took its name from a stone horse standing over a fountain. The other expressions are self-explanatory. All these localities are said to have been the haunts of rogues and thieves.

2. This is an old plaza in Toledo.

CHAPTER IV

1. The barber was also the surgeon.

2. "*Haldudo*" means "full-skirted."

3. The sense of "perfumed" is "completely," "to perfection."

4. "By Roque" is an obscure oath.

5. Alcarria was a sparsely populated region in the valley of the Tagus; Estremadura was a province noted for its backwardness.

6. Civet, a favored perfume, was imported in cotton packing.

7. Guadarrama was noted for its spindles.

CHAPTER V

1. According to the old ballads, Carloto (or Charlot), Charlemagne's son, sought to kill Baldwin in order to marry his widow; sorely wounded, Baldwin was found and succored by his uncle, the Marquis of Mantua.

2. The love of the Moor Abindarráez and the beautiful Jarifa (Xarifa) was a favorite theme with Moorish and Christian minstrels and was incorporated by Jorge de Montemayor in the second edition of his celebrated romance, *Diana* (1561).

CHAPTER VI

In this chapter Cervantes gives us a critical survey of the literature of sixteenth-century Spain as represented by the romances of chivalry and the pastoral novels. See the informative and charmingly written article on "Don Quixote's Library," by Esther B. Sylvia, in *More Books, The Bulletin of the Boston Public Library*, April 1940, pp. 135-52. The works mentioned here were all more or less well known.

1. *Exploits of Esplandián:* fifth book of the Amadis of Gaul series, published in 1521.

2. *Amadis of Greece:* work by Feliciano de Silva (1535), ninth book of the Amadis series.

3. *Don Olivante de Laura:* work by Antonio de Torquemada (1564); *The Garden of Flowers* by the same author was translated into English, in 1600, as *The Spanish Mandeville*.

4. *Florismarte of Hircania:* by Lenchor Ortega de Ubeda (1556).

5. *Platir the Knight:* fourth book of the Palmerin series (1533).

6. *The Knight of the Cross*, by an unknown hand, appeared in 1543; a second part, by Pedro de Luxan, was published in 1563.

7. *The Mirror of Chivalry*, one of the most popular of

the Carolingian romances, was published in four parts at Seville (1533-50).

8. Turpin was a monk of Saint-Denis and Bishop of Reims (mentioned by Rabelais); his *Fables* (1527) belong to the Carolingian cycle; in *The Mirror of Chivalry* he is constantly cited for his veracity, and the Italian writers Ariosto, Boiardo, and Pulci speak of him as "Turpin who never lies in any place."

9. Matteo Maria Boiardo was the fifteenth-century author of the *Orlando Innamorato*.

10. "Place him upon my head": a gesture of respect.

11. "The Captain" is an allusion to Ariosto's Spanish translator, Gerónimo Jiménez de Urrea, whose version was published at Antwerp in 1549.

12. Allusion to the *History of the Deeds of Bernardo del Carpio* by Agustín Alonso of Salamanca (Toledo, 1585).

13. Reference to *The Famous Battle of Roncesvalles* by Francisco Garrido de Villena (Valencia, 1555).

14. The *Palmerin de Oliva* (Salamanca, 1511), of uncertain authorship, is the first of the Palmerin cycle. The *Palmerin of England* appeared in 1547, translated into Spanish from the first Portuguese edition (1544?); see W. E. Purser, *Palmerin of England* (London, 1904).

15. On *Don Belianís,* see Chapter I, note 3.

16. This clause provided that when a person overseas was sued or indicted he might have a certain allowance of time in which to put in an appearance.

17. *The History of the Famous Knight, Tirant lo Blanch,* by Johannot Martorell and Johan de Galba, was first published in the Catalan language at Valencia in 1490; a Castilian version appeared at Valladolid in 1511.

18. On Jorge de Montemayor's *Diana*, see Chapter V, note 2. Gil Polo's continuation was published at Valencia in 1564. This was the best of the Spanish pastoral romances; see H. A. Rennert, *The Spanish Pastoral Romances* (Philadelphia: University of Pennsylvania Press, 1912; originally published at Baltimore in 1892 by the Modern Language Association). "The Salamancan" is Alonso Pérez; the exact date of his *Diana* is uncertain. There is a copy of the first edition of Gil Polo's *Diana Enamorada* in the British Museum.

19. *The Ten Books of the Fortunes of Love:* published at Barcelona in 1573.

20. *The Shepherd of Iberia:* by Bernardo de la Vega (Seville, 1591). *The Nymphs and Shepherds of Henares:* by Bernardo González de Bovadilla (Alcalá de Henares, 1587). *The Disenchantments of Jealousy:* by Bartolmé López de Enciso (Madrid, 1586).

21. *Filida's Shepherd:* by Luis Gálvez de Montalvo of Guadalajara (Madrid, 1582).

22. *Treasury of Various Poems:* a work by Pedro de Padilla (Madrid, 1580).

23. López de Maldonado's *Cancionero* (Madrid, 1586).

24. Alonso de Ercilla y Zúñiga's *Araucana* (Madrid, 1569, 1578, 1590), dealing with the struggle between the Spaniards and the Araucanian Indians of colonial Chile, is commonly regarded as a great Latin-American epic; see Arturo Torres-Ríoseco, *The Epic of Latin-American Literature* (London: Oxford University Press, 1942), pp. 15-19. The *Austriada* (Madrid, 1584) has for subject the exploits of John of Austria. *Monserrate,* by the dramatist Virués, gave M. G. Lewis the inspiration for his famous novel *The Monk.*

25. *"The Tears of Angélica":* this is the *Angélica* of Luis Barahona de Soto (Madrid, 1586).

CHAPTER VII

1. *La Carolea,* by Jerónimo Sempere (Valencia, 1560), deals with the victories of the Emperor Charles V. *León of Spain,* by Pedro de la Vezilla Castellanos (Salamanca, 1586), is a poem in twenty-nine cantos, treating the history of the city of León.

2. No work of this title is known; Luis de Avila is the author of a prose commentary on the wars with the German Protestants.

3. Frestón was a magician reputed to be the author of *Belianís of Greece.*

4. Sancho's wife appears under several different names in the course of the story.

CHAPTER VIII

1. "Machuca" means "the Pounder."

2. The Biscayans, or Basques. were supposed to speak broken Spanish, one characteristic of their speech being the use of the second person for the first, a peculiarity which I have represented (as does Motteux) by substituting the objective for the nominative case.

3. There is a play here on the double meaning of *caballero:* "knight" and "gentleman."

4. The usual expression was "carry the cat to water"—"*llevar el gato al agua.*"

5. Agrajes, whom Don Quixote quotes, is a belligerent character in the *Amadis of Gaul;* the expression is one used at the beginning of a fray.

6. Part I of the original four-part division of the first volume of *Don Quixote* ended with this chapter. The device of breaking off the tale between parts is common in the romances of chivalry.

CHAPTER IX

1. "The tongue in question" is Hebrew.

2. Two arrobas would be about fifty pounds, two fanegas a little over three bushels.

3. "Panza y Zancas": "Paunch and Shanks."

CHAPTER X

1. The Holy Brotherhood was a tribunal, dating from the thirteenth century, for dealing with crimes committed on the highway and in the open countryside.

2. "I know nothing about omecils": play on the words "*homecidio*" and "*omecillo*"; the phrase "*no catar omecillo a ninguno*" means not to bear ill will, or a grudge, toward anyone.

3. "Mambrino's helmet": allusion to Boiardo's *Orlando;* it was, however, not Sacripante but another personage, Dardinel, who paid so dearly for the helmet of Mambrino, the Moorish king. Another allusion to the *Orlando* occurs a few paragraphs farther on—"men of arms that came to Albraca to win the fair Angélica."

4. "Sobradisa" is an imaginary realm.

5. "*Terra firma*": in the *Amadis of Gaul,* Firm Island is the promised land for the faithful squires of knights-errant.

CHAPTER XI

1. The foregoing passage is of interest as representing the classical conception of the "Golden Age" that mankind was supposed to have enjoyed once upon a time.

2. The verse form in this ballad is trochaic tetrameter with assonant rhymes in the second and fourth lines, a variety of rhyme which is impossible to imitate in English but which

in Spanish, owing to the stressed vowels in that language, is admirably adapted to singing. The ballad has accordingly been rendered with ordinary rhymes.

CHAPTER XIII

1. "*Quintañona*": Spanish name, meaning a woman with a hundredweight (*quintal*) of years, i.e., a centenarian.

2. These lines are from the ballad that is parodied in Chapter II; the ballad will be found in the *Cancionero de Romances* (Antwerp, n.d.) and in Agustín Durán's *Romancero General* (Madrid, 1849-51), No. 352.

3. The *Felixmarte of Hircania*, referred to as *Florismarte of Hircania*, has been mentioned as one of the books in Don Quixote's library (Chapter VI).

4. These lines are from the *Orlando Furioso*, XXIV, 57.

5. The word "*gachupín*" literally means a Spaniard living in or returned from the colonies.

CHAPTER XV

1. Yanguas was a district in northern Castile.

2. Untranslatable word play on "*feo Blas*" ("ugly Blas") and "Fierabras"; on Fierabras's balm, see Chapter X, p. 129.

3. Another pun that cannot be rendered literally, being a play on "*sin costas*," meaning "without (court) costs," and "*sin costillas*"—"without ribs."

4. "The city of the hundred gates" is ancient Thebes.

CHAPTER XVI

1. The knight did this as he entered the fray.

2. "This starry stable": in the sense of "starlit"; the phrase "*estrellado establo*" has troubled translators; Shelton omits it, Jarvis renders it as "illustrious," and Motteux has "wretched apartment."

3. This work by an unknown hand, bearing the title *The Chronicle of the Noble Knights Tablante de Ricamonte and Jofre, Son of Count Donason*, etc., published at Toledo in 1531; there is a copy in the British Museum; a later version is attributed to one Nuño Garay.

4. Allusion to a character in the *novela* entitled *Story of Enrique de Oliva, King of Jerusalem, Emperor of Constantinople* (Seville, 1498).

5. Reference to a children's tale which is part of the European folklore heritage.

CHAPTER XVII

1. This phrase is from the beginning of one of the old Cid ballads.

2. The coronado was a coin worth about a sixth of a maravedi.

3. The wool carders of Segovia were famous throughout Spain.

4. On the Horse Fountain of Cordova, see the notes to Chapter III.

5. The name given to a low quarter of that city.

1. "Ceca" (literally, "a mint") was the name given to a part of the Mosque of Cordova; a proverbial expression corresponding to our "from pillar to post."

2. Reference to Amadis of Greece.

3. According to Ormsby, "Suero de Quiñones, hero of the *Paso Honroso* at Orbiga in 1434, used to fight against the Moors with his arm bare."

4. The sense of this motto is either "trail my fortune" or "my fortune creeps"; there may be a double meaning. The asparagus plant would suggest the latter interpretation.

5. The present Guadalquivir River.

6. Granada is on the Genil River.

7. Tartessus was an ancient maritime city of Spain.

8. Jerez (Xerez), near Cadiz, is noted for its sherry wines; our word "sherry" is derived from the name.

9. River flowing from the Cantabrian Mountains and emptying into the Douro River below Valladolid.

10. This river of Spain and Portugal, emptying into the Atlantic, flows underground a part of the way.

11. The primary meaning of the word in the original, "*peladilla*," is "sugar almond"; the secondary, "small pebble."

12. In this case the word used, "*almendra*," is literally "an almond."

13. Doctor Andrés Laguna translated Dioscorides, with copious notes, in 1570.

14. The original reads, "I will send to the devil flock and shepherd's crook (*bato y garabato*)."

CHAPTER XIX

1. Sancho means to say Mambrino (see Chapter x); Malandrino ("*malandrín*"—"rascal") is a play on Mambrino.

2. "*Encamisados*": commonly those wearing shirts (*camisas*) over their armor as in a *camisado*, or night attack.

3. There is a word play here on "*derecho*"—"right" or "straight," and "*tuerto*"—"wrong" or "crooked."

4. There is a confused text here in some of the editions; I have followed the first edition. The latter part of the chapter in Ormsby is badly jumbled.

5. In translation, "Moreover if any, persuaded of the devil. . . ."

6. Reference to a ballad of which John Gibson Lockhart has a version; see Sylvanus Griswold Morley's *Spanish Ballads* (New York: Henry Holt, 1911), pp. 118 ff.

7. Literally, "The dead man to the grave, the living to the loaf"—"*Vaya se el muerto a la sepultura y el vivo a la hogaza.*"

CHAPTER XX

1. The original reads: "*Les aguó el contento del agua.*"

2. This proverb recurs a number of times throughout the *Don Quixote*.

3. The Horn is the constellation of Ursa Minor, with a curved shape somewhat like a hunting-horn; in this method of telling the time of night by the stars, the arms were extended in the form of a cross and the hour was indicated by the position of the Horn in relation to the arms.

4. The story that Sancho undertakes to tell is an old one, probably of Oriental origin, found in the Italian collection, *Cento Novelle Antiche;* there are also Latin and Provençal versions.

5. Sancho means Cato Censorino, or Cato the Censor; he believes it to be derived from "*zonzo*"—"blockhead."

6. Compare Swift's *Gulliver's Travels*, Part II, Chapter I: "I was pressed to do more than one thing which another could not do for me."

7. "An old Christian," as distinguished from a Moorish or Jewish convert, or "new Christian."

8. This is literal—"*Todo saldrá en la colada.*"

9. Compare the reference to Firm Island a little farther on; see also Chapter x, note 5.

10. *"More turquesco"*: "Turkish fashion."

11. Tag end of a proverb: "Whether the pitcher hits the stone or the stone the pitcher, it will be bad for the pitcher."

CHAPTER XXI

1. The reading of the first edition, *"pesada burla,"* has been followed here; a later edition has *"pasada"* in place of *"pesada,"* which has led some translations to render the phrase as "the late joke," "the late jest."

2. Allusion to a proverb, "Please God that it be marjoram and not turn out to be caroway."

3. The original has *"malandantes"*—"unfortunate" thoughts, but there is a slight play on *"caballero andante"* —"knight-errant."

4. Earlier translators have "cuts off," in accordance with a later reading, *"corta"*; but the first edition has *"harta,"* an obvious misprint for *"harpa,"* from *"harpar (arpar)"*— "to tear" or "claw."

5. Sancho means Mambrino.

6. *"Mutatio capparum"*: literally, a changing of hoods; reference is seen to a seasonal change of hoods on the part of the cardinals.

7. Speaking of this story, Ormsby remarks: "Cervantes gives here an admirable epitome, and without any extravagant caricature, of a typical romance of chivalry. For every incident there is ample authority in the romances." John Gibson Lockhart, in his notes to the Motteux translation, says: "The reader of romance does not need to be told how faithfully Don Quixote . . . has abridged the main story of many a ponderous folio. The imaginary career of glory which he unfolds before the eyes of Sancho is paralleled almost *ad literatim* in the romance of Sir Degore. . . . The conclusion of Belianís is almost exactly the same sort of adventure."

8. There is some question as to what is meant by the expression *"vengar quinientos sueldos"*; in any event, the gentleman of La Mancha's income was not a large one by modern standards, the sueldo being worth anywhere from one to three cents.

9. In the original, *"Ruin sea quien por ruin se tiene"*; compare the heraldic motto (Order of the Garter): *"Honi soit qui mal y pense."*

10. For the play on *"litado"* and *"dictado"* I have adopted Ormsby's rendering.

11. A reference is seen here to Pedro Tallez Girón, third Duke of Osuna, afterward Viceroy in Sicily and Naples; the duke is described as "a little man but of great fame and fortunes."

CHAPTER XXII

1. Manchegan signifies "of La Mancha."

2. The first edition reads *"tres precisos de gurapas"*; a later edition has *"tres años"*—"three years." There are a number of specimens of rogues' argot in this chapter.

3. Allusion to the ceremony of public flogging and the riding of the offender through the streets.

4. A proverbial expression.

5. Don Quixote may believe in enchanters but not, apparently, in love sorcerers.

6. The first edition has *"no hay diablo"*; later editions have *"sumista"* in the place of *"diablo,"* rendered by Motteux as *"casuist"* and by Ormsby as "accountant."

7. Reference to the famous sixteenth century classic which has been attributed to Diego Hurtado de Mendoza.

8. This proverb properly reads: "Do not go looking for five feet on a cat."

9. At the beginning of the chapter it is stated that the two men on horseback carried muskets.

CHAPTER XXIII

1. For one reason or another this description of the theft of Sancho's ass was omitted from the first edition, and the result has been a good deal of coufusion in the text and on the part of editors, commentators, and translators. Thus, later in the chapter, the author speaks of Sancho as still having his donkey, while farther on he again alludes to the theft. In Part II, Chapter iv, Sancho himself advances an explanation to the effect that "the one who wrote the story must have made a mistake, or else it must be due to carelessness on the part of the printer." "I believe," says Professor Schevill, "that Cervantes, upon completing [the first edition] wished to introduce the incident of the theft and for that reason wrote an [additional] sheet, leaving it with the manuscript, and then forgot the additions and the changes they neces-

sitated. Obviously the printer did not know what to do with the loose leaf and introduced it later, while the text of [the second edition] was on the press." As the text orginally stood, the episode of the galley slaves and the following one (the finding of the valise, the meeting with the goatherd and Cardenio, and so on) occurred on the same day, which was too much action for so short a space of time; that was doubtless why Cervantes desired to insert an interlude.

CHAPTER XXV

1. Poor Rock (Peña Pobre) was so named because those who sojourned there lived in extreme poverty; Clemencín suggests it was Mont St. Michel, but Ormsby believes the Island of Jersey would be a better identification.

2. The sense of the name Beltenebros is "darkly fair."

3. The Hippogriff was the winged horse on which Astolfo went to seek news of Orlando; Frontino was the steed of Brandamante's lover, Ruggiero.

4. This is the first reference to the theft of the ass to be found in the first edition.

5. There is some confusion here, as the lint was kept in the saddlebags which were left in the innkeeper's possession.

6. Sancho means, of course, "redemption."

7. Reference to the lay brothers who acted as servants in schools and monasteries and who wore their hair cut short but without the tonsure.

8. This reading occurs in the first three editions; it represents, perhaps, a mistake on the part of the author.

CHAPTER XXXI

1. A little over three bushels, the fanega being equivalent to 1.6 bushels.

2. A gesture of reverence; compare Chapter VI, notes.

3. The sense is that a good thing (gift) is good in any season; Ormsby cites the Scottish proverb: "A Yule feast may be done at Pasch." Rodríguez Marín points out that sleeves were originally given as presents and hence came to signify a gift.

4. Gypsies were in the habit of putting quicksilver in the ears of a beast for sale, by way of quickening its pace.

5. Compare our saying: "A bird in the hand is worth two in the bush."

6. Sancho misquotes the proverb: "He who has the good and chooses the bad, let him not complain of the bad that comes to him."

7. On this expression, see Chapter IV, notes.

CHAPTER XXXV

1. In connection with the battle of the wineskins, Lockhart draws attention to the well-known story in Apuleius's *The Golden Ass.*

2. There is some question as to the sense of the expression *"ciertos son los toros"*; Ormsby in a note explains it as "expressive probably of popular anxiety on the eve of a bullfight," and renders it, "there's no doubt about the bulls."

3. The cuartillo was the fourth of a real.

4. The cuarto was a coin worth four maravedis.

CHAPTER XLIII

1. Allusion to Diana; see Vergil's *Aeneid*, IV, 511: *"Tria virginis ora Dianae."*

2. That is, Daphne; the allusion is a frequent one in Cervantes; see Schevill's *Ovid and the Renaissance in Spain* (Berkeley: University of California Press, 1913), p. 184; compare Pliny's *Natural History*, IV, 8.

3. The Spanish verb *"cecear"* is untranslatable; it literally means the sort of sound that Andalusians make in pronouncing the sibilant *ce.*

4. Lirgandeo was the tutor and chronicler of the Knight of the Sun; Alquife was the chronicler of the Knight of the Flaming Sword, Amadis of Greece.

5. Urganda is a personage in the *Amadis of Gaul* who in a manner combines the traits of Morgan the Fay, Vivien, and Merlin.

CHAPTER XLIV

1. This is the reading of the first edition; other editions have "Mambrino"; "Malino" may be a malapropism on Sancho's part.

CHAPTER XLV

1. The first three editions have *"sobrebarbero,"* which, it has been suggested, may possibly mean "supernumerary barber"; certain modern editions have *"pobre barbero,"* or "poor barber," the reading that has been adopted here.

2. Allusion to the proverb "Laws go as kings like."

3. Agramante and King Sobrino are personages in Ariosto's *Orlando Furioso* (see Cantos XIV and XXVII).

CHAPTER XLVI

1. The early editions all have *"león manchado"*—"spotted lion"; but later editors have adopted the reading *"manchego"* —"of La Mancha."

2. From *"mentir"*—"to lie."

CHAPTER XLVII

The heading of Chapter XLVII in the original does not properly correspond to the text; Ormsby has "Of the Strange Manner in Which Don Quixote de la Mancha Was Carried Away Enchanted."

1. It was considered an utter disgrace for a knight to ride in such a vehicle.

2. We have previously been told (Chapter XLV) that the officers were three in number.

3. A proverbial expression, equivalent to our "pull in your horns," "pipe down," etc.

CHAPTER XLVIII

1. There was a proverb which ran: "The tailor of El Campillo, who threaded his needle and stitched in vain." *El Sastre del Campillo* was the title of a couple of plays and a *novela* of the period.

2. These plays are by Lupercio Leonardo de Argensola; see Otis Howard Green's *The Life and Works of Lupercio Leonardo de Argensola* (Philadelphia: University of Pennsylvania Press, 1927).

3. The *Ingratitude Avenged* (*La Ingratitud Vengada*) is by Lope de Vega; the *Numantia* (*Numancia*) is Cervantes' own piece; *The Merchant Lover* (*El Mercader Amante*) is the work of Gaspar Aguilar; and *The Fair and Favoring Enemy* (*La Enemiga Favorable*) is from the pen of Francisco Agustín Tárrega.

4. What Cicero said was: *"Comoedia est imitatio vitae, speculum consuetudinis, imago veritatis"*—"Comedy is an imitation of life, a mirror of manners, and an image of the truth"; these words are quoted by Lope de Vega in his *New Art of Making Comedies* (*Arte Nuevo de Hacer Comedias*).

5. The Spanish word here is *"aparencia."*

6. There has been a good deal of discussion as to what Cervantes meant by "foreigners," since the theater of France and Italy at this time was in a state of decadence, while the English did not "scrupulously observe" the rules in question; the author may have been thinking of certain poetic manuals or treatises from abroad that, possibly years before, were commonly discussed by those associated with the playhouse.

7. The allusion is to Lope de Vega; it was this reference that gave offense to the dramatist, though Lope in his *New Art of Making Comedies* gives expression to practically the same cynical views that are here under attack; later, in Cervantes' own dramatic piece, *The Fortunate Procurer* (*El Rufián Dichoso*), he was to revise the opinions set forth in this passage.

8. Professor Schevill characterizes this as a "reactionary doctrine," one which would have rendered impossible the creation of a national and popular theater; he further describes it as a "feeble imitation" of Plato's views as expounded in the seventh book of *The Republic;* Plato was frequently cited by those who favored such a censorship.

9. The Spanish is *"hacer aguas menores o mayores."*

PART TWO

CHAPTER I

1. A popular expression said to derive from the game of chess.

2. This ballad has not been identified.

3. The dobla was a coin worth around ten pesetas; not to be confused with the gold doblón, or doubloon, worth twenty pesetas.

4. According to Ormsby, *"andar estaciones"* means to visit certain churches and offer prayers in order to obtain indulgences.

5. These knights are prominent in the Spanish romances of chivalry or in the pages of Ariosto and Boiardo. The *Cosmography* is a fictitious work; on Turpin see Part I, Chapter VI, note 8.

6. The reading of the first edition, *"no quiero quedar en mi casa,"* has been followed here; some editions have *"me*

quiero," which Ormsby renders, "And so I will stay where I am"; Motteux has, "I do design to stay where I am."

7. The first edition has *"descubrir"*—"discover"; I have adopted Schevill's emendation: *"describir."*

8. On Goliath's height, see I Samuel 17:4.

9. An account of these bones is given in the *Jardín de Flores Raras o Curiosas* of Antonio de Torquemada; they are also mentioned in Haedo's *Topografía de Argel.*

10. References to the Spanish version of Pulci's *Morgante Maggiore,* published at Valencia in 1533 under the title of *Libro del Esforzado Gigante Morgante.*

11. Medoro was famous for his devotion to his master Dardinel; as he knelt beside Dardinel's body he received a wound of which Angélica cured him.

12. This couplet is misquoted from the *Orlando Furioso,* xxx, 16.

13. The Andalusian poet is Luis Barahona de Soto, author of *La Primera Parte de la Angélica;* the Castilian is Lope de Vega, author of *La Hermosura de Angélica.*

14. The text at this point is very confused.

15. As a matter of fact, the famous poet Góngora did write some satiric verses on this theme, and Quevedo touches on the subject in a heroic poem on Orlando's love and madness.

CHAPTER II

1. The original has ". . . *insulas ni insulos";* for "island" Don Quixote always says *"insula,"* which is the form that occurs in the *Amadis;* this highbrow term is too much for the housekeeper and the niece, who are in the habit of saying *"isla."*

2. The *hidalgos* (originally, "sons of somebody") were gentlemen by birth, the *caballeros* by station in life.

3. "Don" today is a universal form of address where Spanish is spoken, but in Cervantes' time its use was restricted.

4. Literally, "two yokes"—*"yugadas,"* the "yoke" being the amount of land a team of oxen could plow in a day.

5. There was a proverb, *"Hidalgo honrado antes roto que remendado"*—"An honored gentleman goes ragged rather than patched."

6. A proverbial expression.

7. A proverbial expression.

8. Eggplant in Spanish is *"berenjena."*

CHAPTER III

1. That is, the garb of the secular clergy; *"Por el hábito de San Pedro!"* was a proverbial exclamation.

2. There was no edition at Antwerp until 1673, and none at Barcelona before 1617; Cervantes may have heard of the edition of Brussels (1607).

3. Don Quixote (Cervantes) here takes up some of the criticisms that were made of Part I.

4. That is, "The day is not yet over," or "Life is yet young."

5. The play in the original is on *"grama-"* and *"-tica."*

6. *"Mezclar berzas con capochos"* was a proverbial expression.

7. Another reference to this personage will be found in Chapter LXXI.

8. Motteux, as usual, has "orthodox" for "Catholic."

9. This saying as it occurs in other Spanish authors is: *"De pajo o de heno mi ventre lleno"*—"With straw or hay I fill my belly."

10. Reference to Alfonso [Tostado Ribera] de Madrigal, Bishop of Avila, who died in 1450; he is said to have left over sixty thousand written pages, but his works have now been completely forgotten.

11. See the *Epistles* of Pliny the Younger, Book III; he attributes the saying to his uncle, Pliny the Elder; it is quoted again in Part II, Chapter LIX.

12. "Worthy Homer sometimes nods"; compare Horace, *Ars Poetica,* 359: *"Indignor quandoque bonus dormitat Homerus."*

13. "The number of fools is infinite"; see the Vulgate, Ecclesiasticus 1:15.

14. An expression meaning to feel the pangs of hunger: ". . . *me pondra en la espina de Santa Lucia."*

15. Literally, "do penance with him"—*"hacer penitencia con él."*

CHAPTER IV

1. See the *Orlando Furioso,* XXVII, 84, and Boiardo's *Orlando Innamorato,* II, 40.

2. Literally, "raise it a good span higher than what it is."

3. The word employed here is *"ripio,"* a mixture of mortar and gravel for filling the spaces between large stones.

4. It was St. George who aided Pedro I of Aragon to defeat the Moors, at the battle of Alcoraz, in 1096; the festival was in celebration of this event.

5. Such oaths as "body of me," "body of the world," etc., are milder forms of swearing by the Sacrament (body of Christ); compare the English " 'od's body."

6. This is the historic battle cry, *"Santiago, y cierra España!"*

7. A proverb: *"Quando viene el bien, metelo en casa."*

8. A proverb.

9. That is to say, in a roadside ditch.

10. Cervantes is, of course, being satirical here, but it is likely that he did not have any particular poets in mind.

11. The *décima* was, properly, a ten-line stanza; the *redondilla* was a four-line stanza, the last line rhyming with the first. Poetic acrostics were very popular in Cervantes' day.

CHAPTER V

1. A proverb.

2. That is to say, it is better to take someone you know, with all his faults.

3. On this, see Matthew 27:17, 21; Mark 15:11; Luke 23:18.

4. Attention has already been called to Molière's use of this scene (*Le Bourgeois Gentilhomme*, Act III); see "Notes on the Spanish Sources of Molière," by Sylvanus Griswold Morley, in *Publications of the Modern Language Association of America*, XIX, 1904, pp. 270-89.

5. An inversion of the proverb "Laws go as kings like"; compare Part I, Chapter XLV.

6. In the original this is a rhyming proverb.

7. The Infanta Uracca was the daughter of Ferdinand I of Castile; upon being left out of her father's will, she threatened to enter upon a life of ill fame.

8. There is a play on *"almohadas"*—"pillow" or "cushion," and the racial name Almohade; the Almohades were Moors who ruled in Africa and over half of Spain from 1130 to 1273.

9. Literally, "I will dress him up fine as a palm branch."

CHAPTER VI

1. It was necessary to see that neither of the combatants had the sun in his eyes.

2. The *sambenito* was the garment worn by those who, having been tried by the Inquisition, had confessed and repented; it was a yellow linen robe painted over with devils and flames, and the condemned were clothed in it as they went to the stake.

3. The "real gentry" has reference to the *hidalgos.*

4. These verses are from an elegy by the well-known poet Garcilaso de la Vega, written on the death of the Duke of Alva's brother, Don Bernardino de Toledo (*Elegía primera,* verses 202-204).

CHAPTER VII

1. A play on the double meaning of *"ventura"*—"good fortune" and a "venture" or "risk."

2. St. Apollonia prayed to the Virgin for relief from the toothache and her prayer was granted.

3. The original has *"No hay más que bachillear"*; the noun *"bachiller"* means either a bachelor of arts or a babbler or loquacious person.

4. *"Hablen cartas y callen barbas";* the sense is that where there is a written agreement, words are unnecessary.

5. A proverb: *"Quien destaja no baraja";* translators before Ormsby rendered this proverb as "He who cuts does not shuffle"; both the verbs *"destajar"* and *"barajar"* have double meanings, the former signifying "to contract to do a job" and "to cut a deck of cards," the latter meaning "to shuffle the cards" and, in old Spanish, "to wrangle."

6. A proverb; compare our saying "A bird in the hand. . . ."

7. In Spanish this is a rhyming proverb.

8. Literally, "you speak pearls."

9. That is, goes to the slaughter.

10. This is the reverse of the "bird in hand" saying.

11. On this, Ormsby remarks that the truth of this "has always been recognized by politicians, diplomatists, and agitators."

12. The original text mentions only the niece as entering at this point—obviously an oversight on the part of the printer.

CHAPTER VIII

1. Reference to Garcilaso's Third Eclogue, verses 53 ff.

2. *"Debe de andar mi honra a coche acá, cinchado . . ."*; the phrase *"a cocha acá, cinchado"* has been much discussed by commentators; it appears to be a call used by swineherds (still in use in La Mancha, according to Fitzmaurice-Kelly), but, as Schevill points out, the meaning is simply that Sancho's honor is being mishandled and dragged in the mud.

3. An allusion is seen to Vicente Espinel's *Satira contra las Damas de Sevilla*.

4. This is the Pantheon, today known not as All Saints' but as the Tempio de Santa Maria della Rotonda.

5. There is a word play in the Spanish, *"cortesísimo Cortés."*

6. Don Quixote here appears to be enumerating the seven mortal sins.

7. *"Julio"* in Spanish means both "July" and "Julius."

8. According to Orsmby, the allusion is to San Diego de Alcalá, canonized in 1588, and San Salvador de Orta, or San Pedro de Alcántara, canonized in 1562.

9. This is literal: *"Sucedió cosas que a cosas llegan."*

CHAPTER IX

1. Beginning of the old ballad of *Conde Claros*.

2. "Left the wood," not "descended from a hill," as in Motteux, where the word *"monte"* is incorrectly rendered; the reference is to the grove of oak trees mentioned at the end of the preceding chapter.

3. This is literal: *"reposaban a pierna tendida."*

4. A proverbial saying.

5. Beginning of a popular ballad of the Carolingian cycle, which John Gibson Lockhart has translated; the quotation is given here in his words.

6. Lockhart also has a version of this ballad ("The Moor Calainos").

CHAPTER X

The sentences contained in the opening paragraph of this chapter are transferred by Ormsby (who follows the Spanish editor Hartzenbusch) to the beginning of Chapter xvii, on the ground that they more properly belong there in connection with the adventure of the lions; however, it has seemed best to follow the first edition.

1. Two well-known proverbs which, in slightly varying form, are to be found in Spanish, Portuguese, and Italian.

2. Sancho misquotes the saying which runs: "Many think there is bacon where there are no pegs" (i.e., pegs in the smokehouse on which to hang the bacon); the proverb occurs a number of times in *Don Quixote*.

3. Lines from a popular ballad; *"Con cartas y mensajeros"* —"With letters and messengers."

4. From a rhyming couplet: "Fall there, O thunderbolt, on Tamayo's house"; the implication is, "not on mine."

5. Meaning, of course, to look for the impossible.

6. Salamanca was full of bachelors of arts; the sense of this expression and of "trying to find Marica in Rávena" is "to look for a needle in a haystack."

7. Compare our sayings, "A man is known by the company he keeps" and "Birds of a feather flock together."

8. Ormsby explains that these are "the lists of bachelors qualified for degrees"; Motteux' rendering is, "As they do professor's chairs so that everybody may know whom they belong to."

9. According to Ormsby, "ordinary brocade had only a triple border."

10. Sancho says *"cananeas"* for *"hacaneas"*; Ormsby's rendering has been adopted here.

11. This is addressed, not to the ass which the girl rides, but to Sancho (Shelton and Jarvis take it as applied to the ass); the expression is a popular one and is cast in the form of a rhyme.

12. An obscure oath.

13. ". . . *en agallas alcornoqueñas"*; Ormsby has "into oak galls"; Motteux, "into gall nuts"; Jarvis, "into cork galls."

14. The *jineta* was a saddle with high pommel and cantle and short stirrups.

CHAPTER XIV

1. Reference to the fine imposed in some confraternities, the wax being for use in churches.

2. According to Covarrubias, this proverbial expression is derived from rabbit-hunting with the crossbow, the sense being "let each hunter look out for his own bolts."

3. This proverb occurs a number of times.

4. The Italians have this proverb: *"Gatto rinchiuso doventa leone."*

5. This is the form employed by a monarch in response to a petition.

6. The knobs or buttons to keep the spurs from going in too far.

7. The text of the first edition is somewhat jumbled here; I have followed such editors as Hartzenbusch, Rodríguez Marín, and Schevill.

CHAPTER XVI

1. Partridges in Andalusia were used as decoys.

2. Orsmby has "first saint in the saddle"; Jarvis and Motteux "first saint on horseback"; a saint, for that matter would have been more likely to ride a donkey than a horse.

3. This saying was a popular one in the Renaissance era; according to Caelius Rhodiganus (1450-1525), "The poet is born, the orator made."

4. Ovid's beautiful line: *"Est deus in nobis; agitante calescimus illo"*—"There is a god in us, he stirs and we grow warm" (*Fasti*, VI, 5); compare the third book of the *De Arte Amandi*.

5. As Ovid was.

6. The laurel tree.

CHAPTER XVII

1. *"Hombre apercebido medio combatido"*; literally, "A man who is prepared has his battle half fought"; the Italian form of the proverb is nearer the English: *"Chi è avvisato è armato."*

2. It has been remarked that lions coming from Oran would have been landed at Cartagena, and so would not have been met by Don Quixote on the road to Saragossa.

3. A knight of the time of Ferdinand and Isabella whose name occurs in ballads relating to the siege of Granada; he is the hero who figures in the incident of the glove in Schiller's poem "Der Handschuh"; compare Leigh Hunt's "The Glove and the Lions" and Browning's "The Glove."

4. The *"perrillo,"* or "little dog," was the trademark of Julián del Rei, famous armorer of Toledo and Saragossa.

CHAPTER XXII

1. Line from an old ballad.

2. A proverbial saying.

3. The word here is *"sima,"* a deep cavern, an abyss, or a chasm; some commentators have believed that this may have been an ancient mine shaft.

4. Sancho means the Virgin of the Rock of France (Peña de Francia); the allusion is to a site between Salamanca and Ciudad Rodrigo where an image of the Virgin was discovered in the fifteenth century; a Dominican monastery was later erected on the spot.

5. Reference to a chapel dedicated to the Holy Trinity on the promontory of Gaeta, to the north of Naples.

6. Ormsby's rendering has been adopted here.

7. Compare Psalms 102:11, 103:15, 109:23, and 144:4; also Ecclesiastes 6:12; as the poet Calderón was to put it: *"La vida es sueño y sueño de sueño"*—"Life is a dream and a dream of a dream."

8. These are characters from the literature of chivalry; the squire Guadiana was supposed to have been transformed into the river of that name.

9. Reference to the lakes near the hamlet of Ruidera, some fifteen miles southeast of Argamasilla, where the waters of the Guadiana rise to flow down into the plains of La Mancha.

CHAPTER XXIII

1. This personage has not been identified.

2. Merlin was Welsh, though the Bretons tried to claim him; Malory in his *Morte d'Arthur* calls him "a devil's son."

3. On this, the Spanish lexicographer Covarrubias has an interesting comment to make (in his *Tesoro de la lengua castellana,* under the word "Corazón"): "Timorous animals have a proportionately larger heart than others, animals such as the hare, the deer, the mouse, and similar ones mentioned by Aristotle, *lib.* 3, *De Partibus Animalium;* and so, when we say by way of praise that a man or animal has a great heart [courage] we do not mean that his heart is great in size but in ardor" (cited by Schevill).

4. Cervantes, writing here from memory, has mingled and altered two old ballads.

5. According to this passage the lakes were ten in

number, but the author has previously spoken of them as seven; according to some there were fifteen, while others say eleven.

6. The two lakes referred to were within the domain of this order.

7. The river of this name flows underground for a part of its course.

8. A proverb.

9. A proverbial saying among card players.

10. In the original there is a play on *"vino"*—"wine" and *"vino"*—"he came"; allusion to a ballad some lines of which are given in Part I, Chapter xiii; on Quintañona, see Part I, Chapter xiii, note 1.

11. Reference to the wealthy family of Bavaria; during the Renaissance the Fuggers of Augsburg were celebrated bankers and financiers.

12. The "seven parts of the world" was a familiar concept of the age. The Infante Pedro was the second son of John I of Portugal and brother of Prince Henry the Navigator; he traveled widely in Europe and the East between 1416 and 1428; an account of his voyages, published at Lisbon in 1554, was popular in Spain.

CHAPTER XXIV

1. It is not known where Cervantes got this, but it is not from Terence.

CHAPTER XXVIII

1. Both the Spaniards and the Portuguese have this proverb.

2. Allusion to pouring broth from the *olla*, or stew-pot.

3. Don Quixote (Cervantes) forgets that Sancho did not accompany him on the first sally.

4. In Part II, Chapter ii, the name of the bachelor's father is given as Bartolomé.

5. This proverb will also be found in Part I, Chapter lii.

6. A rhyming proverb in the original.

CHAPTER XXXII

1. The first three men were famous Greek painters of the fourth and fifth centuries B.C.; Lysippus was a fourth-century B.C. Greek sculptor.

2. Don Quixote uses the form *"demostina"* instead of the more usual *"demosteniana."*

3. Sayago was a district near the Portuguese frontier noted for its uncouth speech and manners.

4. On these sentences, see the Introduction, p. 32.

5. Oriana was the lady of Amadis of Gaul; Alastrajarea, in the chivalric romances, was the wife of the prince Don Falanges of Astra; Queen Madásima was another heroine of the old tales.

6. This proverb, quoted a couple of times in Part I, ran, "Every man is the son of his works."

7. The Twelve Peers of France were legendary figures.

8. On Bernardo del Carpio, see Part I, Chapters I and VI.

9. According to Diego Clemencín, there was no nobility in El Toboso, not even small gentry, the population being made up of Moorish peasants; there has been some futile discussion as to whether or not Dulcinea had a real life prototype.

10. In the ballads, "La Cava" is the name given to Florinda, daughter of Count Julián, who is said to have been seduced by King Rodrigo and "through whom Spain was lost."

11. A proverbial expression.

12. According to Rodríguez Marín, an allusion to the agility of these birds; the phrase puzzled Ormsby.

13. A rhyming proverb: *"No hagas cohecho, / Ni pierdas derecho."*

CHAPTER XXXIII

1. Reference to the famous ivory seat which the Cid won by the capture of Valencia; as the old chronicle (cited by Clemencín) has it: "When the Cid returned to Castile, the king, Don Alfonso, invited him to take a seat beside him, and when the Cid out of modesty refused, His Majesty ordered him to sit upon the ivory chair."

2. Expression used in connection with a speaker who wanders far afield (Covarrubias). Ubeda was a small town in the upper Guadalquivir valley; the region is not particularly hilly, and the origin of the saying is obscure.

3. The original here is *"es agradecido,"* which Clemencín emends to *"soy agradecido"*—"I am grateful," though there appears to be no good reason for the change; Ormsby (edi-

tion of 1885) has "I'm grateful," but the Fitzmaurice-Kelly edition of his translation reads, "he is free-handed"; Motteux, "he is grateful"; Jarvis, "he returns my love."

4. Jarvis's rendering is: ". . . nothing in the world can part us but the sexton's spade and shovel."

5. Segovia was noted for its manufacture of fine cloth.

6. Wamba was a king of the Gothic line in the Iberian peninsula (672-680).

7. The duenna begins to quote another version of the ballad, *"Despues que el rey don Rodrigo,"* that appears in the *cancioneros* (*Cancionero de Romances* of Antwerp, and Durán's *Romancero General,* No. 606).

8. Commentators have seen a confused text here, finding it difficult to make sense out of the conclusion of this sentence, but the idea seems to be that Sancho will constantly improve his lot; both Motteux and Jarvis mistranslate.

9. A rhyming proverb in Spanish; compare our "Don't kill the goose that lays the golden egg."

10. Reference to the propitiatory sounds addressed to a dog ("nice doggy"); the proverb runs: "There's no use saying *'tus, tus'* to an old dog."

11. The duchess is imitating Sancho's way of talking.

12. Allusion to the *Disticha,* a well-known school text, of Dionysius Cato.

13. Miguel Verino was the author of a collection of moral couplets, the *De Puerorum Moribus Disticha,* which was in wide use in European schools; dying young, he was the subject of a Latin epitaph by Politian, which began, *"Michael Verinus florentibus occidit annis"*—"Miguel Verino died in the prime of life." Commentators point out there is nothing surprising in the duchess's being able to quote Latin, as this was by no means an uncommon accomplishment among Spanish ladies of high rank in Cervantes' time.

14. On this, Ormsby observes: "The commonplace explanation is that we should not trust to appearances"; the Portuguese say, "Under a good cloak is a bad man."

15. Sancho means to say that he never gets drunk.

16. The usual form of this proverb was: "As much is lost by a card too many. . . ."

CHAPTER XXXV

1. Sancho says *"abernuncio"* in place of *"abrenuncio,"* an expression meaning "far be it from me" or "fie on

that!" The Latin form of the word is *"abrenuntio,"* from *"abrenuntiare"*—"to renounce," as for example, in Christian writers, "to renounce the devil and all his works."

2. *"Alma de cántaro"*; idiomatic for "fool."

3. A rhyming proverb, the sense being "work and pray"; Ormsby cites a number of sayings corresponding to this one in other European languages.

4. In the sense of something fitting, a suitable accompaniment.

5. Literally, "that all times are not the same."

6. *"Como de volverme cacique"*; Motteux and Jarvis stumble over the expression; *cacique* is literally a West Indian chief.

CHAPTER XXXVI

1. An expression proverbial with schoolmasters of the time.

2. This statement on works of charity was suppressed by the Inquisition in the majority of the editions of *Don Quixote* printed in Spain following the edition of Valencia in 1616.

3. A proverbial expression, deriving apparently from someone who had been whipped through the streets mounted on an ass.

4. This is literal. Ormsby has "Take care that nobody speaks evil of thee behind thy back."

5. The sense is that while the bell-ringer may sound the alarm, he himself is safe in the belfry.

6. Translated "for it," but literally, "after it"; an expression denoting great eagerness or desire.

7. The word in the original is *"orégano,"* which literally means "wild marjoram," but some would here read *"orógano,"* from *"oro"*—"gold," and *"gana"*—"desire"; for purposes of translation "gold-seeker" would seem to be near enough.

8. This proverb occurs a number of times.

CHAPTER XLI

1. This was the traditional garb of "savages" in theatrical performances in Cervantes' time.

2. It has been stated previously that the peg was in

the forehead; Ormsby notes that in the case of the magic horse in the *Arabian Nights* the guiding peg was located in the neck, and he alludes to Chaucer's "Stede of bras"— "Ye moten trill a pin stont in his ere."

3. This proverb (the Portuguese also have it) occurs several times.

4. On the Holy Trinity, see Part II, Chapter xxii, note 5.

5. The word play here is really untranslatable; Don Quixote says, *"eres hombre verídico,"* and Sancho, mistaking *"verídico"* for *"verdecico,"* meaning "greenish," replies, *"No soy verde, sino moreno"*—"I am not green but brown-skinned." For once at least I have adopted a rendering from Motteux; Ormsby has: "Thou art veracious"—"I'm not voracious."

6. Don Quixote has his mythology somewhat confused; according to legend, the Palladium was an image or statue of Pallas that fell from heaven at Troy and during the Trojan war was borne off by Ulysses and Diomedes because the fate of the city depended on its possession.

7. Magalona's husband was King of Naples, not of France.

8. Fitzmaurice-Kelly and others would read *"legión"* here in place of *"región"*; it may be a slip on Sancho's part.

9. Peravillo was the place near Ciudad Real where the Holy Brotherhood executed its prisoners.

10. Torralba was tried by the Inquisition in 1528 on charges of dealing in magic; his trial became famous in song and story.

11. Elsewhere (in his *Persiles y Sigismunda*) Cervantes refers to Torre di Nona as being a prison.

12. Allusion to Charles, Constable of Bourbon under Francis I, who went over to the side of the Emperor Charles V and aided in the defeat of the French monarch at Pavia in 1525; he died two years later in the first assault on Rome by the imperial army. See the account in Benvenuto Cellini's *Autobiography;* for an account of Bourbon's treason, the reader may be referred to my *Marguerite of Navarre.*

13. Magallanes is the name of the great Portuguese navigator known to us as Magellan.

14. ". . . *por contento y satisfecho a toda su voluntad"*: an expression used by notaries, something like "for value received"; Cervantes employs it in a legal document in con-

nection with the sale of two of his comedies, under date of March 5, 1585.

15. That is, the Pleiades.

CHAPTER XLII

1. The Christus was the cross preceding the alphabet in school primers, and "not to know the Christus" was an expression signifying complete ignorance.

2. Once again the reference is to Dionysius Cato and his *Disticha.*

3. Cervantes' phrase here, *"mar proceloso,"* has the flavor of classical Latinity; compare St. Augustine (*De Civitate Dei,* v, 22): *"procellossimum pelagus."*

4. Compare Psalms 111:10 and Proverbs 1:7 and 9:10; fathers customarily employed this maxim in exhorting their sons, either by word of mouth or in writing.

5. In the well-known fable of Aesop and Phaedrus.

6. Reference to the peacock's lordly tail; when it looks down at its feet, the bird is supposed to be ashamed; the image is a popular one with the Spanish mystics.

7. Cervantes here alters an old saying: "Blood is inherited and vice sticks.

8. Begging friars would refuse alms but suggest that donations might be thrown into their hoods. The text literally reads: "or as the 'I don't want any' of your hood."

CHAPTER XLIII

1. See Suetonius's *Life of Julius Caesar,* Chapter 45.

2. The smell of garlic was regarded as the mark of the countryman.

3. *"Toda afectación es mala";* this is the second of the two passages in the *Don Quixote* in which this statement occurs; in the other instance (Part II, Chapter xxvi) it is put into the mouth of Master Pedro, the puppet master.

4. Another version of the proverb runs: "Eat little [for the midday meal], have a little more for supper, sleep at the top of the house, and you will live [long]."

5. In his *Tesoro de la lengua castellana,* published four years before the second part of Don Quixote appeared, Covarrubias lists the words *"regoldar"*—"to belch," and *"regveldo"* (*"regüeldo"*)—"belching," but says nothing against their use, though he condemns the practice for which they stand as "a discourtesy and boorishness, especially

when done in front of persons to whom respect is to be shown."

6. Compare Horace, *Ars Poetica*, 71-72: ". . . *si volet usus, / quem penes arbitrium est et ius et norma loquendi.*"

7. The Portuguese also have this proverb.

8. A proverb.

9. This proverb reads in full: "He whose father is a judge goes to court with assurance."

10. "*A quien Dios quiere bien, la casa le sabe*"; there is some doubt as to the meaning here, whether it is "his house knows it" or "his house is sweet to him."

11. A play on the saying "*Al buen callar llaman santo*"— "To keep silence well is called holy"; "*santo,*" with the old spelling "*sancto,*" is transformed into "*sancho,*" and Sancho Panza proceeds to apply it to himself.

12. Compare Matthew 7:3-4 and Luke 6:41-42.

13. An older version of the proverb has "Death was frightened. . . ."

CHAPTER XLIV

1. On this, Ormsby observes that "The original, bringing a charge of misinterpretation against its translator, is a confusion of ideas that it would not be easy to match."

2. In connection with these counsels it is pointed out that Cervantes is indebted to the *Galateo Español* of Gracián Dantisco, published at Barcelona in 1593; a copy of this work is preserved in the British Museum.

3. Professor Schevill thinks that in this island episode the author may be indebted to a passage in the second part of the *Amadis of Gaul*.

4. The phrase "*en justo y creyente*" has the idiomatic sense of "immediately"; in English, in order to bring out the full flavor and meaning of the expression, it is necessary to give it a double translation.

5. The cap is the *montera;* "watered camlet" ("*chamelote de aguas*"), according to Covarrubias, is camlet whose sheen is reminiscent of sea waves.

6. That is, the *jineta;* this saddle the Spaniards had taken over from the Moors.

7. In Spanish, "*flamantes*": "brilliant" or "brand-new" trappings.

8. Literally, "two fanegas"; the sense here is, of course, figurative.

CHAPTER XLV

1. ". . . *meneo dulce de las cantimploras*"; Covarrubias defines the "*cantimplora*" as "a copper jug with a very long neck for cooling water or wine, by placing or burying the jug in the snow or moving it about in a vat containing snow"; and Pellicer comments: "By the heat of the sun (which the author is here apostrophizing) thirst is excited in summer, which makes it necessary to shake the coolers"; the effect is intended to be farcical.

2. Thymbraeus (meaning: of Thymbra or Thymbre, a city in Troas that contained one of Apollo's temples) came to be an epithet of Apollo.

3. This passage has been seen as a possible caricature of some poem of the day.

4. See Aristotle's *Physics*, II, 1.

5. The attempt to identify Sancho's "island" (Barataria) has been a favorite sport among commentators, many of whom seek for political allusions of one sort or anther; Pellicer would identify it as Alcalá del Ebro, on the peninsula formed by the bend of the Ebro River.

6. In modern Spanish "*barato*" is an adjective meaning "cheap," but in old Spanish it is also a noun signifying "jest"; it has the latter meaning here.

7. Compare Teresa Panza's remarks in Part II, Chapter v; the abuse of the title of Don by those without the worldly means to live up to it was frequently commented upon in Cervantes' day.

8. It was originally the custom to beg pardon when some unclean or vile subject was mentioned; later such expressions came to be interjected without rhyme or reason.

9. Rodríguez Marín believes that Cervantes is alluding sarcastically to the quality of clothing (and food as well) furnished to prisoners.

10. Cervantes apparently had originally put this case first and then had changed the order but neglected to elide the reference earlier in the chapter; Ormsby in his translation rearranges the incidents.

11. Another notary's phrase: "*cor hacerle placer y buena obra.*"

12. This was the procedure known in civil law as "*juramento decisorio*," when one party agreed to abide by what the other swore.

13. The rod of justice held by Sancho; it was lowered in order that the witness might place his hand upon the cross of the rod and take his oath upon it.

14. Commentators are agreed that the episode is taken from the Life of St. Nicholas of Bari as inserted in the *Golden Legend* of Jacobo de Voragine, thirteenth-century archbishop of Genoa.

15. The following anecdote will be found in printed form as early as 1550, in the devotional work of Francisco de Osuna, *Norte de los Estados,* published at Burgos in that year; there are other traces of the story that go back as far as 1531.

CHAPTER XLVII

1. "Sleight of hand": *"como juego de massecoral"*—literally, "like a trick of Master Coral," an expression said to derive from the fact that charlatans and jugglers, stripping off their cloaks and jackets, were in the habit of performing in doublets of the hue of red coral.

2. Cervantes is here caricaturing a custom that existed in Spain—that of having physicians present at the tables of princes to advise what foods should be eaten and to see that royal appetites were restrained.

3. According to Clemencín, "physicians formerly applied this term [radical moisture] to a certain subtle and balsamic humor which, so they believed, conferred vigor and elasticity upon the fibers that make up the bodily texture"; Covarrubias cites Albertus Magnus: *"Humidum est vitae qualitas et potentia."*

4. Doctor Recio is not quoting Hippocrates; there was a prevalent saying to the effect that "All surfeit [indigestion] is bad, but that of bread is the worst of all"—*"Omnis saturatio [indigestio] mala, panis autem pessima"*; the doctor substitutes "partridges" for "bread."

5. An olla-podrida is a highly seasoned dish of meat and vegetables cooked in a bulging, wide-mouthed pot or jar known as an *olla;* the term has been carried over into English.

6. *"Cañutillos de suplicaciones"*; this is the thin, rolled wafer known in modern Spanish as *"barquillo."*

7. Tirteafuera is a village in La Mancha (not an imaginary one as some have supposed) that has disappeared from modern maps; the doctor locates it with a fair

degree of accuracy. The name literally means "Be off with you."

8. This institution has been referred to in Part II, Chapter I. Founded in 1549, it existed until 1820; in its prime it was an important cultural center.

9. The physician's name, "Agüero," means "omen," which accounts for Sancho's play upon it, "Mal-Agüero"—"bad omen."

10. Literally, "I will place them on my head and honor them." For the expression "place them on my head," compare Part I, Chapter VI.

11. That is, would have left the room in a hurry.

12. The Biscayans were prominent in the royal service under Charles V and Philip II; they were noted for their ability and loyalty, and many of them held secretarial posts.

13. Literally, "newborn."

14. *De muerte adminícula y pésima, como es de la hambre*"; "*adminícula*" is a word of Latin derivation which seems out of place in Sancho's mouth and does not make too much sense here; most translators in various languages have rendered it as "slow death" or something of the sort.

15. This proverb has occurred a couple of times before.

16. Elsewhere (Part II, Chapter XXXIV) Sancho says, "It's the tripes that carry the feet, not the feet the tripes."

17. The expression "soul of a pitcher" ("*alma de cántaro*") once more.

18. Compare the French peasant's expression, "*Bon comme le pain*"; for the European peasant in general bread has a significance that is almost sacramental.

19. "*Perelesía*" is paralysis or palsy; "*Perlerinas*" connotes "*perlas*"—"pearls."

20. Rodríguez Marín cites the popular Spanish sayings, "An ugly person whom one loves appears beautiful" and "The black beetle calls its young ones grains of gold."

21. This passage is somewhat obscure.

CHAPTER XLIX

1. "Olla-podrida" literally means a "rotten pot."

2. This expression has previously occurred; see Part II, Chapter XXXII, note 13.

3. See the excerpt from Part II, Chapter XIV, and note 2.

4. The general sense is: there is disorder or a disturbance somewhere.

5. This proverb has occurred in Part II, Chapter XLIII.

6. Rodríguez Marín observes that "we have here an excellent program of government, set forth in only four lines of type"; whether or not one agrees, there can be little doubt that Sancho is voicing Cervantes' own view of government and society.

CHAPTER L

1. In the original it is "Teresa Sancha."

2. The literal reading is "making public the Aranjuez of her issues"; the duenna had told Don Quixote of an issue of blood which the duchess had in each leg; the term for "issue" ("discharge" or "flux") in Spanish is *"fuente"*—literally, "spring" or "fountain"; the fountains of Aranjuez were famous.

3. Ormsby tells us that "Argamasilla is the only village in La Mancha where such a sight could be seen; an arm of the Guadiana flows past it.'

4. Tag line of one of the Cid ballads (*"A Calatrava la Vieja"*); there are allusions in other ballads to this mode of punishment inflicted on light women, and a number of later Spanish writers refer to it.

5. A proverb

6. Literally, ". . . and your mouth will be the measure."

7. Aubrey Bell in his *Cervantes* (pp. 12-13) cites this passage as an instance of what he elsewhere (p. 42) calls "the independence and happy poverty of the peasant."

8. *"Como un pino de oro"*; a *"pino de oro"* was a small ornament or trinket stuck in the hair.

9. The word here is *"papahigo"*; according to Covarrubias, this was a half-mask covering the face and used by travelers as a protection against the air and the cold; Ormsby has: "take the air with a sunshade."

10. Literally, "a bad year and a bad month."

11. A rhyming proverb in Spanish.

12. Another proverb in rhyme that runs: "The dog saw himself in hempen breeches and did not know his companion"; a variant is: "The countryman saw himself . . . and was proud as proud could be." The Italians have a saying to the effect that "A rustic made a nobleman does not know his own relatives."

13. "Augustine doubts it," an expression employed by casuists and by students discussing dogmatic questions.

14. John 10:38: "Though ye believe not me, believe the works."

15. *"Cual el tiempo, tal el tiento"*—"As the time [occasion], so the behavior"; compare the proverb quoted in Part II, Chapter IV: "Manners change when honors come."

16. Literally, "will do penance with me"; compare Part II, Chapter III.

CHAPTER LI

1. These subtleties enjoyed a great vogue in the schools of the day; the first one proposed for Sancho's consideration goes back to the ancient Greek logicians (the story of the King of the Crocodiles, the Epimenides Paradox, etc.); see the discussion by Bertrand Russell and Alfred North Whitehead, *Principia Mathematica*, Vol. I, p. 61; a good deal of investigation has been done by modern mathematical logicians with the object of circumventing all known paradoxes within a completely formalized logical system; Russell's Theory of Logical Types represents one of these attempts.

2. Commentators have called attention to the fact that on two previous occasions (Part II, Chapters XXXVI and XLIII) Sancho has stated that he did know how to sign his name.

3. Motteux has the literal rendering: "I will snuff them away into air—*"yo las despabilaré en el aire"*

4. Compare Psalms 113:7: "He raiseth up the poor out of the dust, and lifteth the needy out of the dunghill."

5. There were a number of forms of this proverb: "Trim a bough and it will look like a young man," etc.

6. See the well-known fable by Phaedrus.

7. This saying is commonly attributed to Aristotle, being a free rendering of a passage in his *Nicomachaean Ethics;* compare, also, Plato's *Phaedo*, XL: "If you would follow my advice, think not of Socrates but of the truth"; a Spanish proverb runs: *"Amigo Pedro, amigo Juan, pero más amiga la verdad"*—"Pedro is a friend, Juan is a friend, but a greater friend is the truth."

8. Variation on the proverb previously quoted: "Take no bribe and surrender no right."

9. Speaking of Cervantes' dire poverty, Aubrey Bell (*Cervantes*, p. 43) observes: "He had suffered . . . from the insults of market-women, whose fierce loquacity covered a falseness in their weights."

10. Compare our modern price-control and wage-fixing.

11. Herrera, Philip III's physician, delivered an address to the throne on the state of mendicity in Madrid, with particular reference to the abuses perpetrated by the blind and those who pretended blindness.

CHAPTER LII

1. Literally, "to take this fine day into my house"; allusion to the proverb "When good luck comes along, open the door and let it in [take it into your house]."

2. This means that the loaf cost about five cents, and meat about ten cents, a pound.

3. "*Y a Roma por todo*": a proverbial expression.

4. "*Vuestra pomposidad*": a farcical expression.

5. It is to be noted that this son does not appear as a character in the story, though he is mentioned a number of times; Professor Schevill thinks it strange that Teresa does not refer to the lad in her letter to his father.

6. A linen lace made with bobbins.

7. "Eight maravedis," a little over three cents.

8. Tronchón is "a small municipality in the province of Teruel, diocese of Saragossa, now forgotten in the guidebooks and travel narratives" (Schevill, translated from the Spanish note).

CHAPTER LIII

1. Compare Shakespeare's *Twelfth Night*, Act V, Scene 1: "And thus the whirling of time brings in his revenges."

2. The text here may not appear to make sense, but it is what Cervantes wrote; needless to say, the passage has occasioned a lively controversy among editors and commentators and a number of emendations have been made; I am inclined to agree with Duffield that the author's intention was probably humorous, a desire to poke fun at the "Mohammedan philosopher," Cid Hamete; accordingly, like Duffield and Ormsby, I have let the passage stand.

3. "About fighting": literally, "about reinforcements"— "*de socorros.*"

4. Scaling ladders.

5. This proverb occurs a number of times.

6. The *gazpacho* is a kind of cold broth made with bread, olive oil, water, vinegar, garlic, onions, etc.

7. Allusion to the proverb "To her harm the ant grew wings."

8. The Portuguese also have this proverb.

9. It was seven days, not ten, according to the statement made earlier in the chapter.

CHAPTER LV

1. The Portuguese add to this: "or eat of this bread."

2. What of Sancho's "Constitutions"? See Chapter LI.

3. A children's game; there is some uncertainty as to how it was played; Rodríguez Marín believes it is the modern game of "four corners" (*"cuatro esquinas"* or *"cuatro cantillos"*).

CHAPTER LXII

1. Schevill draws attention to the fact that the printing shop is an imaginary one and that there were no Barcelona editions of the spurious *Don Quixote* and of the work entitled *Light of the Soul*, referred to later on.

2. Properly, the translator.

3. *"Le Bagatelle"*: that is, *The Trifle;* it is not known whether any Italian work with this title ever existed.

4. Literally, "to sing (*"cantar"*) certain stanzas"; Cervantes' debt to the *Orlando Furioso* should be obvious to any reader of *Don Quixote*. According to Aubrey Bell (*Cervantes,* p. 19), during Cervantes' five-years residence in Italy he had "learned sufficient Italian to read the poems of Ariosto and Tasso in the original," but as Professor Schevill notes, his recollections of the language are marked by a certain nebulousness (*"nebulosidad"*)" and would appear to be auditory rather than visual, as indicated by the manner in which he transliterates and Hispanicizes Italian vocables.

5. *"Pinata"* in the text. A *pignatta* is an earthenware cooking-pot.

6. *Olla* is Spanish for stew-pot.

7. *"Piace (place)"* is "pleases"; *"più (más)"* is "more"; *"su (arriba)"* is "up"; *"giù (abajo)"* is "down."

8. This comparison is not original with Cervantes; it had previously been made use of by Diego de Mendoza, the author of *Lazarillo de Tormes,* and by Luis Zapata in the preface to his translation of Horace's *Ars Poetica,* published in 1591. See Cervantes' observations on the translation of poetry in Part I, Chapter VI.

9. *Pastor Fido* is the work of Battista Guarini (Venice,

1590); the Spanish version by Cristóbal Suárez de Figueroa was first published at Naples in 1602, and in a differing form was printed again at Valencia in 1609. Jáuregui's rendering of Torquato Tasso's *Aminta* was published at Rome in 1607, and a second edition appeared at Seville, after Cervantes' death, in 1618.

10. According to Clemencín, this is bad arithmetic; since a thousand ducats is a sum equivalent to eleven thousand reales, and since the returns on an edition of two thousand at six reales the copy would amount to twelve thousand reales, there would be left only a thousand reales—a very small sum—for the cost of paper, printing, and other expenses.

11. "It is amusing," says Lockhart, "to see, in many passages of his works, how completely Cervantes understood the tricks of the booksellers of his time." The author also touches on the subject in his *novela* "Man of Glass" (*El Licenciado Vidriera*) and in *Persiles and Sigismunda*.

12. One thinks of the American Thoreau carrying home the unsold copies of his first book, *A Week on the Concord and Merrimack Rivers,* and remarking that he now had a library of nine hundred volumes, some seven hundred of which he himself had written!

13. *Light of the Soul* is a work by the Dominican friar Felipe de Meneses, first published at Seville in 1555; there were a number of later editions, but none is known to have been printed at Barcelona; the full title reads: *Light of the Christian Soul against Blindness and Ignorance,* etc.

14. The title-page of Avellaneda's work identifies him as "*natural de la villa de Tordesillas*"; his correct title is *The Ingenious Gentleman, Don Quixote de la Mancha, Which contains his third sally and is the fifth part of his adventures* (Tarragona, 1614); see the English translations by Captain John Stevens (London, 1705) and by William Yardley (London, 1784).

15. It was the custom to kill pigs on St. Martin's day; the proverb ran: "To every pig comes its Martinmas.

CHAPTER LXIV

1. Compare Part I, Chapter II.
2. This is from the marriage ceremony.
3. That is, confess that the other is in the right.

4. Untranslatable pun on the double sense of *"desiocado"* —"dislocated" and "cured of madness" (from *"loco"*— "mad").

CHAPTER LXXI

1. Proverbial expressions denoting fabulous wealth; Potosí, now in western Bolivia, is noted for its silver mines.

2. A cuartillo was one-quarter of a real; Schevill estimates that Sancho's fee would amount to 61.1 gold crowns.

3. The proverb runs: "Trout are not caught with dry breeches.

4. In the original, a rhyming proverb: *"No se ganó Zamora, / En una hora."* This all but impregnable fortress held out for a very long time, and in the course of the siege King Sancho II lost his life. The Portuguese have the saying too; compare our "Rome was not built in a day."

5. A proverb.

6. Another rhyming proverb: *"A dineros pagados, / Brazos quebrados";* that is to say, no more work to be had out of a person after he has been paid for it.

7. According to Rodríguez Marín, the Andalusians have a saying: "Here shall die Samson with all the Philistines!"

CHAPTER LXXIV

1. Jacopo Sannazaro, Neapolitan poet (1485-1530), was the author of the *Arcadia;* see the edition published at Torino in 1888.

2. Literally, "pay me for good news"—*"dadme albricias";* this expression has occurred a number of times before.

3. With regard to Don Quixote's real name, see Part I, Chapter I; there the name is given as Quijana (Quixana).

4. A rhyming proverb: *En los nidos de antaño / No hay pajaros hogaño."*

5. Literally, "from the doors inward (*"a puerta cerrada"),"* an expression still employed in Andalusia and elsewhere.

6. It was a custom among the people, in the case of women, to give a feminine termination to a name with a masculine ending.

7. This thought is expressed in a number of Spanish proverbs and verses, such as: "The weeping of the heir is dissimulated laughter"; "Dead man to the grave, the living to the loaf"; etc. Ormsby finds this a "piece of commonplace cynicism" that is "uncalled for and inconsistent with what

has gone before"; he objects on the same ground to the scolding administered to Avellaneda and to Sansón Carrasco's doggerel.

8. That is, penance, communion, and extreme unction.

9. These lines are a doggerel imitation of the epitaphs composed by village poets; Clemencín and others, as well as Ormsby, have objected to their introduction here.

10. Sannazaro concludes the *Arcadia* with an address to his flute.

11. These lines are from a ballad on the death of Alonso de Aguilar that has been translated by Lockhart.

12. That is, that pretender of Tordesillas.

13. At the close of the spurious *Don Quixote*, Avellaneda tells how the knight, after being released from the madhouse of Toledo, "purchased for himself another and better steed and made a tour of Old Castile, where stupendous and never-before-heard-of adventures befell him."

14. This proved to be true; no new romance of chivalry appeared after *Don Quixote*, and only a few of the old ones were reprinted. The last work in this category was the *Policisne de Beocia*, published at Valladolid in 1602.

To TWO EXEMPLARY NOVELS

PROLOGUE

1. The pen portrait of himself that Cervantes gives us probably provided the basis for the painting of him that has been attributed to the artist Juan de Jáuregui (1583-1641), a canvas supposed to have been executed in the year 1600 and which was later accepted as authentic by the Spanish Royal Academy. It is clear from the author's own words that no portrait existed in 1613, three years before his death.

2. Cesare Caporali of Perusa had published a poem entitled *Viaggio in Parnaso*, in 1582; but Benedetto Croce has pointed out that the two works are quite different, Cervantes' being six times as long as the other.

3. It is not clear whether Cervantes' hand was maimed or

lost. Professor Mack Singleton (*Cervantes Across the Centuries,* pp. 237-38) calls attention to a textual inconsistency. See the Prologue to the *Persiles and Sigismunda,* p. 801.

4. Cervantes was sixty-six years of age in 1613.

RINCONETE AND CORTADILLO

The probable date of composition, according to F. Rodríguez Marín, is 1601-1602; according to James Fitzmaurice-Kelly, 1603-1604. There is in existence a manuscript, based upon a first draft and differing somewhat from the printed text, that was copied out, before 1609, for Cardinal Niño de Guevara by the prebendary of the cathedral of Seville, Francisco Porras de la Cámara (indicating that the princes of the Church were not above such reading as this). I have followed the text of the first edition (1613), correlated with the Madrid edition of 1614, as given in Rudolph Schevill and Adolfo Bonilla y San Martín, *Obras Completas de Miguel Cervantes Saavedra.*

The topography of the story is exact. The Molinillo inn at which the two lads meet was situated on the road from Toledo to Cordova; it was two leagues from Tartanedo and four leagues from Almodóvar del Campo; and the Alcalde inn, as stated, was half a league distant. Alcudia was a valley in the province of Ciudad Real. Fuenfrida (today Fuenfría), where Rinconete was born, was a pass in the Guadarrama Mountains formerly used by the Spanish kings upon their journeyings; it was three leagues from Segovia on the road to Toledo. The "pious village" from which Cortadillo came, between Medina del Campo and Salamanca, was doubtless Mollorido, seat of a bishopric. (I have followed the first-edition reading, *"piadoso lugar,"* and not the one given by subsequent editors, *"en el Pedroso, lugar . . ."*).

The allusions to sites in and about Seville are similarly accurate: the Customhouse Gate (puerta de la Aduana); the Arenal Gate (puerta del Arenal) and the Old Clothes Market (Baratillo) nearby; the Meat Market (Carnicería), the Fish Market (Pescadería), the plaza de San Salvador, the little square known as the Costanilla, or Slope, and the plaza de la Feria, or the Fair; the King's Garden (Huerta del Rey), the Bank of the Indies (Casa de Contratación), the Treasury (Casa de la Moneda), the plaza de la Alfalfa, the Golden Tower (Torre del Oro), the Castle Postern (postigo del Alcázar), San Sebastián field and the chapel of San

Telmo, the calle de Tintores—all these places have been definitely located.

An attempt has even been made to identify Monipodio's house, and a late nineteenth-century scholar, Adolfo de Castro, would place it in the present calle de Troya, formerly the calle de la Cruz, as he finds that the courtyard of this house (No. 4) corresponds with Cervantes' description of the thieves' patio. The shrine of Our Lady of the Waters (Nuestra Señora de las Aguas) was in the church of El Salvador; it is still venerated today, as it had been long before Cervantes wrote. The crucifix of St. Augustine, a fine specimen of fourteenth-century Romanesque sculpture, was then to be found in the church bearing his name, but today it is preserved in the church of San Roque.

1. The word *"rincón"* means "nook" or "corner."

2. Vilhan, or Bilhan, was the legendary inventor of the game of cards.

3. From *"cortar"*—"to cut."

4. Expression used in entering upon a new undertaking.

5. The customary conclusion of a "fortune" as told by a gypsy.

6. That is, thives.

7. In the original there is an untranslatable play on sounds here.

8. The literal meaning of Monipodio is a gang, in the underworld sense.

9. Reference is to hanging, flogging, and the galleys.

10. Theologies.

11. In the Spanish (*"ministros y contrayentes"*) there is a jocular allusion to the marriage ceremony, through a play on the double meaning of *"ministros"*—"ministers" and "agents."

12. Trademark of the fifteenth-century swordmaker, Julián del Rey, a Moorish convert patronized by the King.

13. *"Naufragio"* ("shipwreck") is here a solecism for *"sufragio,"* or "suffrage," in the ecclesiastical sense of an intercessory prayer or petition. For "swag" Monipodio says *"estupendo"* ("stupendous") in place of *"estipendio"* ("stipend"). On this passage, see p. 758 following. Rodríguez Marín finds these word plays unworthy of Cervantes.

14. *"Tormenta"* means "storm" and also "misfortune" or "reverse."

15. The meaning of *"ganchuelo"* is "a little hook."

16. This passage, in sixteenth-century thieves' jargon, has been freely rendered in an effort to give the general sense. A number of the terms are still in doubt.

17. The pickpocket puts in two fingers to ascertain the size of the pocket and what is in it, then all five to remove the contents.

18. The "house" here is the brothel.

19. Don Alonso Pérez de Guzmán el Bueno was governor of the city of Tarifa when it was besieged, in 1293, by Prince Don Juan of Castile, who had revolted against his brother, Sancho IV. Don Alonso's infant son had fallen into the hands of the enemy, and when Don Alonso was called upon to surrender or see his child slain, he detached his dagger from his belt and threw it down from the wall as a sign of defiance. The babe was slaughtered. Cervantes is in error in referring to this son as being Alonso's only one.

20. The *"medio manto"* or *"manto negro doblado"* was the legally required garb of prostitutes.

21. *"Mojar la canal maestra"*—literally, "wet the main canal." Compare our expression "down the main hatch."

22. The sense of the name is "the earner" or "the winner." Silbatillo is a diminutive of *"silbato"*—"a whistle."

23. Escalanta is from *"escalar"*—"to climb" or "to enter surreptitiously."

24. Two arrobas would be eight and a half gallons; an azumbre is a little more than half a gallon—quite a drink for an old lady!

25. The white wine of Guadalcanal (there was also a red wine) was one of the most famous of sixteenth-century vintages.

26. From *"pipa"*—"cask" or "hogshead," in allusion to her drinking capacity.

27. St. Lucy, virgin martyr who had her eyes burned out, is especially venerated by those afflicted with diseases of the eye.

28. The bread of Gandul, renowned in the sixteenth and seventeenth centuries, came from a little village of that name near Seville.

29. The Tagarete was a stream that formed a moat at Seville and there emptied into the Guadalquivir. Its waters are said to have been rather foul-smelling. According to Rodríguez Marín, the implication is that the Tagarete of the story was a *tributary* of Monipodio.

30. *"Respecto"*—euphemism for "pimp"; in argot, the *respecto* was a sword.

31. The sense is, a thief who sells what others have stolen.

32. Proverbial expression meaning to drink nine times.

33. She means a tiger of Hyrcania. The "Tarpeian mariner" is a pun on the first line of an old ballad: *"Mira, Nero, de Tarpeya, / A Roma como se ardía. . . ."* Ocaña is near Madrid.

34. The "tame doves" are servant maids.

35. An expression from the old markets, meaning to smash everything without regard to consequences.

36. Giving of the lie in this fashion was a common means of provocation among bullies; it has nothing to do with anything said by Chiquiznaque or Maniferro.

37. Where the weapons are carried.

38. Solecism for Judas Macabeo (Maccabaeus).

39. The use of the broom as a musical instrument is mentioned by a number of Spanish writers.

40. Negrofeo is Orfeo (Orpheus), Arauz is Euridice, Marión is Arion, while the other reference is to Amphion.

41. The *seguidilla* is a Spanish verse form consisting of a seven-line stanza with a complicated structure commonly based on assonance. The word has come to mean a popular air or dance tune. The lines in the original are in couplets. I have substituted a well-known English form.

42. That is, they worked for neither side, did not molest the "brotherhood."

43. *"De barrio."*

44. "Love me, love my dog."

45. Executor.

46. *"Desmochado."* His ear had probably been cut off as a punishment.

47. The vials, of course, contained offensive or injurious liquids; greasy, foul-smelling juniper oil is still occasionally employed for revenge by Andalusian peasants; the nailing up of the *sambenito*, or flame-colored robe, worn by penitents, when going to the stake, amounted to an accusation of heresy or of being a Jew; the horns, indicating a cuckold, were employed at least as late as 1911 (Rodríguez Marín).

48. It was Cortadillo to whom this title was given.

49. *"Lobillo,"* diminutive of *"lobo"*—"wolf" or, in jargon, "thief."

50. See note 13.

MAN OF GLASS

The date of composition has been given as 1604 or 1605.
If the latter date is correct, it was probably written about the
same time as "The Colloquy of the Dogs." I have followed
Schevill and Bonilla's reproduction of the first-edition text
(1613), disregarding the variants of the so-called Madrid
edition of 1614. In the matter of notes and linguistic interpretation, I have drawn as usual on Rodríguez Marín and on
the special edition of this tale by the modern editor Narciso
Alonso Cortés.

1. As in all his fiction, Cervantes here is a realist in the
manner of detail. Thus there is nothing improbable in
Rodaja's being permitted to enroll at the University of Salamanca while acting as a servant to the two wealthy students.
As Alonso Cortés has pointed out, penniless youths of
scholastic bent frequently maintained themselves in this
fashion.

2. The word *"rodaja"* means "a small wheel."

3. The Spaniards, who wore dark clothes in town, donned
showy garments for travel on the highway.

4. Macaronic Italian of the sort spoken by Spanish soldiers. "Landlord, prepare us a meal; come here, you rascal;
bring on the *maccatella*, the chicken, and the macaroni."
The meaning of *"maccatella"* (*"macarela"*) is uncertain; it
was perhaps a dish composed of pounded meat balls. The
correct Italian forms would be: *"Acconcia, patrone; passa
quà, manigoldo; vengano la maccatella, li pollastri, e li mac-
cheroni."*

5. Expression from the game of cards.

6. The soldiers dressed themselves, at their own expense,
in gay-colored garments calculated to catch the eyes of the
ladies.

7. *"Dios es Cristo":* the term implied swaggering bullies.

8. The famous poet Garcilaso de la Vega (1503?-1536)
who was Cervantes' model.

9. Name given to the southeastern portion of the harbor
of Genoa.

10. These wines are Italian vintages. Trebbiano was a
sweet white wine from the banks of the Trebbia; Montefiascone came from the place of that name in papal territory;
Asprino was a white wine of Capua or Naples; the wine of
Candia (*malvasía*) was made of grapes grown on that is-